Lawyers *in the* Dock

Learning from Attorney Disciplinary Proceedings

Richard L. Abel

UNIVERSITY PRESS

Oxford University Press, Inc., publishes works that further Oxford University's objective of excellence in research, scholarship, and education.

Oxford   New York
Auckland   Cape Town   Dar es Salaam   Hong Kong   Karachi   Kuala Lumpur   Madrid   Melbourne
Mexico City   Nairobi   New Delhi   Shanghai   Taipei   Toronto

With offices in
Argentina   Austria   Brazil   Chile   Czech Republic   France   Greece   Guatemala   Hungary   Italy
Japan   Poland   Portugal   Singapore   South Korea   Switzerland   Thailand   Turkey   Ukraine
Vietnam

Copyright © 2008 by Oxford University Press, Inc.

Published by Oxford University Press, Inc.
198 Madison Avenue, New York, New York 10016

Oxford is a registered trademark of Oxford University Press
Oxford University Press is a registered trademark of Oxford University Press, Inc.

All rights reserved. No part of this publication may be reproduced, stored in a retrieval system, or transmitted, in any form or by any means, electronic, mechanical, photocopying, recording, or otherwise, without the prior permission of Oxford University Press, Inc.

First printing in paperback, 2010
ISBN 9780199772872 (paperback : alk. paper)

Library of Congress Cataloging-in-Publication Data

Abel, Richard L.
  Lawyers in the dock: learning from attorney disciplinary proceedings / Richard L. Abel.
  p. cm.
  Includes bibliographical references and index.
  ISBN 978-0-19-537423-0 (hardback : alk. paper)
  1. Lawyers—New York (State)—New York. 2. Legal ethics—New York (State) I. Title.
  KFN5076.5.A2A73 2008
  174'.309747—dc22
                                                                            2008025009

Printed in the United States of America on acid-free paper

Note to Readers
This publication is designed to provide accurate and authoritative information in regard to the subject matter covered. It is based upon sources believed to be accurate and reliable and is intended to be current as of the time it was written. It is sold with the understanding that the publisher is not engaged in rendering legal, accounting, or other professional services. If legal advice or other expert assistance is required, the services of a competent professional person should be sought. Also, to confirm that the information has not been affected or changed by recent developments, traditional legal research techniques should be used, including checking primary sources where appropriate.

(Based on the Declaration of Principles jointly adopted by a Committee of the American Bar Association and a Committee of Publishers and Associations.)

You may order this or any other Oxford University Press publication by
visiting the Oxford University Press website at www.oup.com

Lawyers *in the* Dock

Contents

Foreword vii

Preface....................................... ix

    1. Trust and Betrayal............................. 1

Part One: Neglect............................... 61
    2. Juggling Too Many Balls 71
    3. Practicing Immigration Law in Filene's Basement...... 105
    4. The Overachiever 193

Part Two: Fees................................. 207
    5. *Bleak House* in America........................ 215
    6. The Perils of Perfectionism 289

Part Three: Excessive Zeal 375
    7. The Purloined Papers.......................... 389

    8. Restoring Trust 491

References.................................... 529

Index... 561

Foreword
by Sandra Day O'Connor

Our legal system is built on the trustworthiness of lawyers. Clients must trust the fidelity of their lawyers. Adversaries must trust the representations of opposing counsel. Courts (and other fora) must trust lawyers to submit truthful evidence, correctly cite the law, and make legitimate arguments.

The vast majority of lawyers diligently strive to deserve this trust. It takes only a few betrayals, however, to seriously damage the reputation of lawyers, both individual and collective. If the legal profession is to prevent breaches of trust, it needs to understand how and why they occur.

The files of disciplinary bodies offer an underutilized window on lawyer deviance. Richard Abel has analyzed disciplinary proceedings against seven New York lawyers to illuminate three of the most common—and troubling—ethical problems: neglecting clients, overcharging them, and displaying excessive zeal. The detailed case narratives and biographies illuminate the situations and motives that sometimes lead lawyers to betray the trust placed in them. Drawing on these insights, the book proposes several practicable reforms that could help restore public faith in the legal profession. It is useful to all of us who hope to maintain high ethical standards for lawyers in today's world.

Preface

I started studying the legal profession in 1973 because UCLA law school, which I had just joined, needed another instructor to meet the new mandate that it require all students to receive instruction in professional responsibility. This was the ABA's response to the Watergate scandal, whose central perpetrators were lawyers, from President Nixon on down. I have taught and written about the profession ever since. Because I approach legal questions from an interdisciplinary perspective, I have focused on social organization: the structure and actions of the profession and its subgroups. As a scholar, I have been able to draw on, and engage with, the extensive literature on the sociology of work and the professions. As a teacher, however, I have remained uncomfortably aware that most of my colleagues and students are more interested in the rules governing the ethical dilemmas individual lawyers confront in their practice—rules that the Multistate Bar Examination tests.

Since I recognize the importance of those questions, this book is my attempt to address them. I wanted to present ethical issues in such a way that readers—law students, practitioners, and the lay public—could see how lawyers come to engage in questionable behavior and how they and we explain it. Only if we gain a better understanding of the etiology of ethical violations can we hope to reduce them. Toward this end, I needed detailed accounts of ethical misconduct. Disciplinary proceedings construct such narratives. In New York, cases that result in public reprimand, suspension, or disbarment are public. The records tend to be extensive. Trials often extend over days, even weeks. They are bifurcated into guilt and penalty phases; in the latter, the convicted lawyer has a strong incentive to offer mitigating evidence. Because lawyers must document their actions, they often submit voluminous exhibits. Because the lawyers' careers are at stake and they are accustomed to litigation, they often file numerous motions, write lengthy briefs, and exhaust their appeals.

In fall 2003, when I was teaching at NYU, I studied six cases decided by the First Departmental Disciplinary Committee of the Supreme Court, Appellate Division. I am grateful to Sarah Jo Hamilton, secretary to the Committee on Character and Fitness, and her staff, for giving me a place to work, helping me select cases, and retrieving the files. A number of UCLA law students assisted my research: Sundari Wind (2004), Michael Campion (2005), Nathanial Bach (2006), and Daniel Cha (2008). The UCLA Law Library was extraordinarily efficient and helpful, as always. I also want to thank three of the lawyers involved in the cases (Joseph F. Muto, Philip A. Byler, and Deyan R. Brashich) who kindly agreed to talk to me about what clearly had been, and remained, a very painful experience, and Mr. Muto and Mr. Byler for contributing responses to their case studies. Walter Bottger (my law school classmate), who was appointed to represent infants in the case involving Mr. Brashich, lent me additional documentation and answered my questions. I learned from the opportunity to present talks on some of these cases in many fora: University of Massachusetts–Amherst, Brooklyn Law School, NYU Law School, Yale Law School, New York Law School, CUNY Law School, the Association of American Law Schools (San Francisco), the Law and Society Association (Vancouver), Radboud University Nijmegen, Rijksuniversiteit Groningen, the Working Group for Comparative Study of Legal Professions (Berder, France), and the University of North Carolina Law Review (which published an earlier version of Muto's case). I also benefited from the support of the UCLA Academic Senate Committee on Research, the UCLA Law School Dean's Fund, and a sabbatical.

Chapter 1

Trust and Betrayal

I. The Imperative of Trust

Many people are compelled to trust lawyers. Clients must trust their fidelity, opposing counsel their truthfulness and adherence to agreements, and courts and administrative agencies their compliance with procedural rules. Betrayals have serious, sometimes catastrophic consequences. The public may lose faith in the capacity of the legal system to produce justice.[1] Adversaries may insist on written agreements or rebuff negotiations.[2] Legal proceedings may become even more formalistic, rigid, slow, and expensive.[3] Because most lawyers are trustworthy most of the time, betrayal is the aberration calling for explanation. Furthermore, it is easier to study breaches of norms than to study conformity.[4] This book uses the

---

[1] Tyler & Degoey (1996).
[2] Lewicki & Bunker (1996).
[3] Tyler (2001) found that trust increases the willingness of people to follow rules.
[4] Garfinkel's "breaching experiments" (1967) illustrate this, as do the numerous legal anthropological studies of "trouble cases," from Llewellyn & Hoebel (1941) onward. Howard Gardner and his colleagues have taken the opposite approach of explicating exemplary behavior. Fischman et al. (2004).

records of disciplinary proceedings against New York City lawyers to understand how and why they betrayed trust.

As social animals, humans cannot live without trust.[5] Indeed, trust is an essential element of primate development. Psychologists have found that monkeys raised without nurturing mothers or mother substitutes are emotionally impaired.[6] Erik Erikson identified trust as the first, essential stage in human development.[7] Many adults who abuse intimates (children and partners) were themselves abused as children. Because Hobbes believed that trust is indispensable to society, he argued that government is necessary to control innate human selfishness.[8] Machiavelli predicated his cynical advice to the Prince on the assumption that *others* would be trusting.[9] Writers depict societies without trust—real or fictional—as dystopias.[10] Some scholars argue that betrayal in one setting diminishes willingness to trust elsewhere.[11]

Trust is created and reinforced through reciprocal interaction between people in ongoing relationships.[12] Its strength tends to vary with the duration of the relationship.[13] Malinowski observed the operation of reciprocity among trading partners in the Trobriand Islands.[14] Later anthropologists have found that traders engage in one-shot transactions with goods that can immediately be evaluated (e.g., rice) but establish ongoing relationships to exchange goods whose quality cannot be assessed ex ante (e.g., crude rubber).[15] (But individual clients can neither evaluate their lawyer's performance nor form ongoing relationships with lawyers.) Homans saw trust as an elementary building block of all societies.[16] Game theory analyzes the conditions encouraging or discouraging cooperation—which rests on trust.[17] Those who cannot trust others must either restrict their social interaction or deploy a variety of protective mechanisms, all of

---

[5] O'Neill (2002) (Reith lectures).
[6] Harlow (1958).
[7] Erikson (1950; 1963: 269).
[8] Hobbes (1994).
[9] Machiavelli (1940). Herzog (2006) has updated this perspective.
[10] E.g., Turnbull (1972) (the Ik of Uganda); Gambetta (1988b) (Sicilian Mafia); Martin Scorsese's film *The Departed* (Boston gangsters).
[11] Williamson (1993) and Putnam (2000) argue it does, Hardin (2001) and Titus (2001) that it does not. Peters & Welch (1980) and Shover et al. (1994) offer empirical evidence it does not.
[12] Polanyi (1944); Macaulay (1963); Blau (1964); Sahlins (1972).
[13] Hardin (2001: 3; 2002: 3).
[14] Malinowski (1926; 1935).
[15] Yamaguchi (2001: 140).
[16] Homans (1958).
[17] E.g., Axelrod (1984); Frank (1988); Dasgupta (1988); King-Casas et al. (2005).

which increase transaction costs.[18] Adam Smith taught us that specialization enhances productivity.[19] But Durkheim added that the division of labor increases the necessity of trust and transforms its content.[20] Luhmann agrees that trust is essential to manage the growing social complexity.[21] The combination of specialized production and generalized consumption, which enormously increases the variety and lowers the cost of goods and services, also creates informational asymmetries between producers and consumers and therefore breeds dependency, with its inevitable agency costs.[22] The professions are an extreme example of this development. Indeed, Barber argues that "trust is ideally the primary mode of control in the relations between professionals and their clients."[23] Law imposes fiduciary duties on many agents acting for principals who lack the time, skill, capacity, or desire to perform the tasks themselves.[24] Employers work hard to secure their employees' trust in order to discourage shirking.[25]

As traditional societies modernize, reciprocity is less able to ensure trustworthiness. This trend affects not only market exchange but also governance.[26] Citizens in representative democracies must trust politicians to promote public, not personal, interests.[27] But the rewards and punishments of an ongoing exchange are not the only explanations for the importance of trustworthiness, which can also reflect the trustee's belief that the entrustor is trusting, the trustee's moral principles or character, and the trustee's cultural dispositions.[28] It is not surprising, therefore, to find strong national variations in trustfulness.[29] Trust is a moral resource, a form of social capital, which *grows* with use rather than being depleted.[30] We speak about "investing" trust in others. But because trust also is a public good[31]—beneficiaries need not contribute to its creation and preservation

---

[18] Limerick & Cunnington (1993: 95–96).
[19] Smith (1976).
[20] Durkheim (1947). Some argue that the importance of trust is increasing, e.g., Tyler & Kramer (1996).
[21] Luhmann (1979: 5, 8, 15).
[22] Friedman (1962); Fama (1980); Ensminger (2001: 186).
[23] Barber (1978; 1983: 131).
[24] Kim Christensen, "He Built a Fortune on a Widow's Funds," Los Angeles Times A1 (1.27.07) (trustee investing trustor's funds for own benefit).
[25] Miller (2001: 320).
[26] Braithwaite & Levi (1998).
[27] Bianco (1994); Garment (1991); Putnam (1993).
[28] Bachrach & Gambetta (2001: 153).
[29] Mackie (2001).
[30] Hirschman (1984: 93); Coleman (1990).
[31] Kramer et al. (1996).

to enjoy its rewards—there may be systematic underinvestment.[32] Those who trust initially tend to persist, sometimes out of moral duty or commitment,[33] whether or not the trusted acts in a trustworthy manner.[34] Indeed, new diagnostic tools reveal that trusting behavior actually changes brain patterns.[35] Because distrusters, by contrast, lack experience in trusting, they tend to be more gullible when they do trust.[36]

People in traditional societies had to trust only intimates or acquaintances, whom they knew well and interacted with repeatedly. The inhabitants of modern societies must trust strangers.[37] As Ross observed a century ago, "wider interdependencies breed new treacheries."[38] Entrustors may rely on group membership,[39] overlapping networks,[40] or shared ascribed characteristics (race, ethnicity, religion).[41] Investment advisers promote their common identity with the investor (e.g., fellow Harvard alums) to encourage trust (which they may then betray).[42] Judgments of trustworthiness tend to be "fast, shallow, and context-sensitive."[43] Soon after Castro seized power in Cuba, unsecured loans proliferated within the Miami émigré community, where members knew each other and exit was virtually impossible.[44] When trustor and trustee share group membership or ascribed characteristics, the trustee's treatment of the trustor powerfully affects trust.[45] Where there is no prior relationship, the entrustor may nevertheless be willing to trust someone whose relationships with *others* may

---

[32] Akerlof (1970); Arrow (1974: 23).
[33] Kramer & Goldman (1995).
[34] Brann & Foddy (1988); Messick et al. (1983).
[35] Henry Fountain, "Study of Social Interactions Starts With a Test of Trust," New York Times A19 (4.1.05).
[36] Yamagishi (2001: 122).
[37] The "take-off" of the English economy in the mid-nineteenth century offered increasing opportunities for betrayal of trust. Robb (1992). For a moral account of trust, see Uslaner (2002). For a sociological explanation, see Powell (1996) and Burt & Knez (1996). For an enforcement perspective, see Doig (2000).
[38] Ross (1977: 37).
[39] Meyerson et al. (1996), but see Stolle (2001). Ponzi schemes often originate within groups, such as Mormon churches in Utah. Ganzini et al. (1990).
[40] Michael Lewis, "Harvard's Expensive New Course: Fraud 101," Bloomberg.com (6.21.04) (investors relying on fellow Harvard alumnus).
[41] Heimer (2001: 60-62); Bachrach & Gambetta (2001: 165-166); Nee & Sanders (2001) (basing trust on these qualities can also limit economic activity to ethnic ghettos).
[42] Lewis, supra.
[43] Messick & Kramer (2001: 98), drawing on case studies of the New York garment industry; Uzzi (1998); and the Minnesota Mycological Society, Fine & Holyfield (1996).
[44] Hardin (2002: 126).
[45] Tyler (2001: 296-297).

be damaged by betrayal.[46] (The fabrication of such relationships enabled the scam in *Six Degrees of Separation*.[47]) The micro-loan program of Bangladeshi Nobel Prize winner Muhammad Yunus is based on the interest of members of the debtor's group in seeing that the loan is repaid so that they in turn can borrow.[48] The third alternative source of trust is an institution that will sanction betrayal (e.g., courts and lawyer discipline).[49]

Willingness to trust increases with the amount of education and status of the corresponding institution; indeed, trust appears to be learned in college.[50] High trustors both raise and lower their estimates of trustworthiness more rapidly than do low trustors, based on experience.[51] Furthermore, high trustors make more accurate estimates of cooperation and defection in a non-iterated prisoner's dilemma exercise with an anonymous partner.[52] The best strategy for the gullible is either to accept social isolation or to restrict themselves to established relationships.[53] Entrustors may be willing to take small initial risks in the hope of attaining large gains later.[54] This, of course, is the premise of the classic big con (discussed below).[55] Hardin argues that, because the short-term loss from misplaced trust typically exceeds that from trust forgone, "it is relatively easier to flip from trust to distrust than to create trust where there has been distrust for very good reasons of the risks at stake."

> Distrust comes easily because it can be built on a limited bit of behavior by the distrusted. Trust, however, requires too rich an understanding of the other's incentives for it to come easily to many people. . . . Instead of taking chances on the relationship, distrustful parties put more effort into securing themselves against its breakdown by use of devices outside the relationship—and this reduces dependency on the partner. Hence distrust is circularly reinforced by the actions it provokes.[56]

---

[46] Heimer (2001) (referral to illegal abortionist); Hardin (2001: 4; 2002: 140).
[47] Guare (1994).
[48] Hardin (2002: 127).
[49] Hardin (2002: 25).
[50] Yamaguchi (2001: 127–128).
[51] Id. 133.
[52] Id. 136.
[53] Yamaguchi (2001: 125).
[54] Hardin (2002: 138).
[55] Leff (1976: chapter 4).
[56] Hardin (2002: 90–91).

Depositors defrauded by the Southland Industrial Banking Corporation "harbored feelings of bitterness and anger even 10 years following the victimization."[57] The relatively powerless have particular reason to distrust the relatively powerful.

> If a much more powerful partner defaults . . . she might be able to exact benefits without reciprocating. Moreover, she might be able to dump partners willy-nilly and replace them with others, while they cannot dump her with such blissful unconcern because there may be few or no others who can play her role.[58]

It is not surprising, therefore, that the largest survey of lawyers found that whites trusted lawyers more than blacks did.[59]

This brief overview reminds us that trust is an essential social lubricant and glue. Yet it is a fragile sentiment, much easier to destroy than create. Trust can come to resemble the surface of a charred, eroding hillside—denuded by the fire of betrayal, in which the rain carves ever deeper gullies. Consider the difficulty at two extremes of social organization—international relations and marriage—of convincing antagonists to take mutual confidence-building steps in order to reverse the downward spiral of suspicion. Trust becomes increasingly hard to produce and preserve as societies grow in size and complexity. Professions—an extreme manifestation of the concomitant division of labor—are especially dependent on trust. Clients turn to lawyers only in extremis[60] and, therefore, very rarely: an average of just twice in a lifetime.[61] Only the ultra-wealthy still have "family solicitors." Because individuals are the prototypical "one-shot" clients,[62] they cannot rely on familiarity in choosing lawyers, who in turn have little stake in cultivating a reputation in order to attract future business. Clients are forced to use unreliable signals of lawyer trustworthiness, such as shared ascribed characteristics. But although people (especially

---

[57] Titus (2001), citing Shover et al. (1994).
[58] Hardin (2002: 100–101).
[59] Curran (1977: 249–252).
[60] Melinkoff (1973); Fried (1976).
[61] Curran (1977: 185, 190) (a third of the population had never seen a lawyer; among those who had, 44% had seen a lawyer only once and 26% just twice).
[62] Galanter (1974).

Americans) love to hate lawyers,[63] society is impoverished if lawyers are not consulted. Lawyers counsel clients to obey the law ex ante and moderate ex post conflict about whether the law has been violated.[64] Lawyers facilitate social, economic, and political interaction. Without them, people turn to protective mechanisms (which increase transaction costs) or, more likely, retreat into social isolation, which expresses and fosters an alienation that corrodes civil society. Subordinated groups use lawyers less and have less faith in the legal system;[65] action and belief mutually reinforce each other. (There is a clear, and telling, analogy with the positions of North and South on the battle between protectionism and free trade.) For all these reasons it is essential to understand how lawyers can regain the trust of their clients.

II. The Lessons of Betrayal
A. How Betrayal Differs from Mistakes and Crimes

Before betrayals of trust can be addressed, they need to be distinguished from two overlapping behaviors: mistake[66] and ordinary crime. When we trust others to act on our behalf, we expect them to do so competently. Although we may be disappointed, even angered, by mistakes, we usually do not feel betrayed, even if the mistake was negligent. A large literature examines the errors of professionals, especially medical doctors, that can have catastrophic consequences.[67] We usually are more interested in anticipating and preventing such mistakes than in punishing them.[68] Indeed, Charles Bosk called his classic study of surgical errors "Forgive and Remember";[69] Atul Gawande characterized his and his colleagues' errors in practicing the "imperfect science" of surgery as "Complications";[70]

---

[63] Galanter (2005). In reviewing this book, I argued that Daumier expressed similar criticisms in nineteenth-century France. Abel (2007).
[64] Sarat & Felstiner (1995).
[65] Curran (1977: 239–254).
[66] Vaughan (1996) thoroughly explored the difficulty of drawing this distinction before concluding that the Challenger disaster was the result of mistake, not misconduct.
[67] E.g., Wachter & Shojania (2004).
[68] E.g., Cooper et al. (1978; 1984); Charles et al. (1985); Rosenthal (1987); Girard & Hickam (1991); Bovbjerg & Petronis (1994); Deckard et al. (1994); Entman et al. (1994); Ely et al. (1995); Lens & van der Wal (1997).
[69] Bosk (1979).
[70] Gawande (2002).

Chapter 1

and a leading study of physician mistakes used the title "To Err Is Human."[71] Whereas substance abuse is punished severely and aggravates ordinary crime, the same abuse mitigates professional misconduct and is treated rather than punished.[72] Most lawyer errors are mundane: missed deadlines, forgotten appearances, lost documents, mathematical miscalculations, flawed factual investigations, poor client communication.[73] Yet incompetence shades into betrayal as it becomes pervasive, prolonged, and incorrigible.[74]

The problem of distinguishing betrayal of trust from ordinary crime resembles the long-standing controversy over the definition of white-collar crime.[75] Insofar as we trust others to obey the law, by our own complying with the law and making ourselves vulnerable to lawbreakers, *all* criminals betray our trust. To protect ourselves from crime, however, we rely less on trust than on police and prisons, locks and gated communities, avoidance and self-defense. We refrain from crime less because we trust others to reciprocate than because we view it as wrong and fear punishment. And when we are criminally victimized—vandalized, burgled, or mugged—we are more likely to feel violated, outraged, or vulnerable than betrayed. (Victimization by intimates is different precisely because it does betray trust.) Although disciplinary bodies disbar lawyers who commit felonies, many of those crimes do not betray the trust invested in the offender qua lawyer.

Betrayal offers unique and dramatic insights into the operation of trust—which is one reason treachery is a favorite literary theme.[76] The following is an unsystematic traversal of the terrain of trust, focusing on the crevasses of betrayal.

B. Parents and Surrogates

Because all infants must learn to trust their parents, children readily transfer that trust to parental substitutes, often establishing a pattern of trusting anyone who is older or who enjoys greater authority or status. The breach

---

[71] Kohn et al. (2000).
[72] Bissell & Jones (1976); Degi et al. (1997); Dubois & Haehnel (1997); Hancock (1997); Fallberg & Borgenhammar (1997); Irvine (1997); Tempelaar (1997).
[73] ABA Standing Committee (1986; 1989; 1996; 2001); Arnold & Kay (1995) (Canada); Davies (1998) (UK); State Bar of California (2001).
[74] Shapiro (1990) poses the "complicated questions ... about how to differentiate between abuse and normal variability in talent, candor, honesty, conscientiousness, selflessness, or fidelity."
[75] David Friedrichs (1996) entitled his text on white-collar crime "Trusted Criminals."
[76] Hardin (2001: 31–32).

of such basic trust is particularly damaging. Catholic priests who sexually abused children and youths under their pastoral care are one of the most egregious examples.[77] These abuses persisted not only because the Church covered them up, often just transferring perpetrators to other parishes, but also because the victims blamed themselves, rightly fearing that their accusations would not be believed. Children's trust can also be betrayed through sexual abuse by teachers[78] (fictionalized in *The History Boys*[79] and *Four Weddings and a Funeral*) and other mentors.[80] Working parents depend on child care providers—and feel betrayed when these people conceal or distort information about their backgrounds or mistreat their charges.[81]

C. Environmental Polluters

Because we must share our planet, we trust others not to damage or destroy common goods, such as land, water, and air. Individuals cannot prevent such damage or, often, even know that it is happening. Global warming is a perfect example. True, we enact laws against environmental harm, backed by regulatory agencies. But because enforcement is always inadequate, often woefully so, we must trust voluntary compliance. Hence we feel betrayed when pollution exposes us to risk, especially when perpetrators conceal the danger or their responsibility. Examples include the release of toxic substances such as dioxin,[82] the U.S. military's exposure of its soldiers (as well as Vietnamese soldiers and civilians) to Agent Orange,[83] Union Carbide's killing and maiming of thousands near its

---

[77] Laurie Goodstein, "Trail of Pain in Church Crisis Leads to Nearly Every Diocese," New York Times § 1 p. 1 (1.12.03); William Lobdell, "From Monk to Sex Plaintiffs' Advocate," Los Angeles Times B1 (1.19.03); "Excerpts From Report on Abuse by Members of the Catholic Clergy," New York Times (2.28.04); William Lobdell, "Vatican Aware of Abuse for Centuries, Study Says," Los Angeles Times B1 (6.20.04); Pam Belluck, "Ex-Priest Convicted in Rape of Boy in Boston," New York Times A14 (2.8.05); Elizabeth Mehren, "Former Priest Found Guilty of Child Rape," Los Angeles Times A10 (2.8.05); Neela Banerjee, "Catholic Group Receives 1,092 New Sex Abuse Reports," New York Times (2.19.05); William Lobdell and Jean Guccione, "Orange Diocese Gives Details on Sex Abuse," Los Angeles Times A1 (5.18.05); Bera (1995); *Boston Globe* (2002); France (2004); McKiernan (2004); Frawley-O'Dea (2007).
[78] Sarah Lyall, "British Boarding School Walls Hid Abuse," New York Times A8 (10.11.04).
[79] Alan Bennett, who wrote the play and film script, acknowledged elsewhere that such abuse was common. Bennett (2006).
[80] Peter Y. Hong, "Scientist in Sexual Abuse Case Hears Recordings in Courtroom," Los Angeles Times B1 (7.18.06).
[81] Lisa Belkin, "Knowing Noreen," New York Times Magazine 39 (1.7.07).
[82] Whiteside (1977).
[83] Schuck (1987).

CHAPTER 1

Bhopal plant,[84] above-ground nuclear testing in Nevada,[85] a mining company's fatal polluting of its workers' homes and the community,[86] Pittston Mining's destruction of several West Virginia towns when its dam burst,[87] and a W.R. Grace subsidiary's dumping of toxic waste near waterways.[88] Employees must also trust employers to make working conditions safe.[89]

D. Manufacturers

Despite the maxim "caveat emptor," buyers usually must trust sellers' representations about the quality and safety of goods and services—and even the buyer's need for them.[90] That is one reason used-car dealers typically rank at the bottom of the prestige hierarchy. The accelerating pace of technological change constantly intensifies this dependence. We trust those who contract to maintain or repair our esoteric but indispensable gadgets to do, and charge, only what is necessary. We feel betrayed when they deliberately misdiagnose, perform unnecessary procedures, or bill for fictitious work or parts.[91] There is nothing new about this. In 1941 two researchers traveling across the United States were cheated by auto mechanics 60 percent of the time;[92] an economist who recently replicated this experiment in Canada was cheated 80 percent of the time.[93] In the 1950s half of a sample of watch repairers cheated their customers;[94] in 1965 automobile warranties and repairs represented the single largest category of complaints to the Federal Trade Commission.[95] In the 1990s regulators and courts found repair fraud in many well-respected national firms: Sears Auto Centers,[96] Pep Boys, Goodyear Auto Centers, Tune-upmasters, Midas Muffler & Brake, Montgomery Ward Auto Express, Econo Lube N' Tune, and Kmart Auto Centers.[97] EZ Lube agreed to a $5 million

---

[84] Weir (1987).
[85] Ball (1986).
[86] Wallace (1988).
[87] Stern (1976); Erikson (1976).
[88] Harr (1995).
[89] Reutter (1987); Guarasci (1987); Caudill (1987); Frank (1987).
[90] Blumberg (1989).
[91] "Another fiddle factor favoring small business crime in the retail and service economy results from the widespread ignorance of customers regarding what they do and don't need, how to satisfy a need, and what to pay." Barlow (1993).
[92] Riis & Patric (1942).
[93] David Leonhardt, "When Trust in an Expert Is Unwise," New York Times C1 (11.7.07).
[94] Strodtbeck & Sussman (1955–1956).
[95] Leonard & Weber (1970).
[96] Callahan (2004: 30-32).
[97] http://www.carinfo.com/repair2.html. Last visited 2/28/07.

settlement in 2008.[98] Appliance repair continues to offer an invitation for fraud.[99]

The first products liability opinion, in 1944, declared that "the consumer no longer has means or skill enough to investigate for himself the soundness of a product . . . and his erstwhile vigilance has been lulled by the steady efforts of manufacturers to build up confidence by advertising and marketing devices such as trade marks."[100] Nowhere is this truer than in the pharmaceutical industry (where the doctrine originated).[101] Medicines promise health but often inflict iatrogenic injury. Drug companies promoted diethylstilbestrol (DES) to prevent miscarriage; it was not only ineffective but also caused adenosis and vaginal adenocarcinoma in users' adult daughters.[102] A.H. Robins aggressively marketed the Dalkon Shield IUD, which caused pain, injury, and reproductive problems.[103] Merck was forced to withdraw the painkiller Vioxx after it was shown to have underreported side effects, including heart attacks.[104] Boston Scientific withdrew its stents after lying about their safety.[105] Guidant recalled its defibrillators after concealing their flaws.[106] Johnson & Johnson ignored warnings about its heartburn drug Propulsid.[107] Apotex has been accused of misrepresenting the side effects of its thalassemia drug L1.[108] Pharmaceutical companies offer a wide range of inducements to

---

[98] David Haldane, "EZ Lube agrees to $5-million settlement," Los Angeles Times B3 (1.3.08).
[99] Parrick Healy, "Appliance Story Owner Jailed in Fraud Case," New York Times B5 (11.11.03).
[100] Escola v. Coca Cola Bottling Co. of Fresno, 24 Cal.2d 453 (1944) (Traynor, J., concurring).
[101] Angell (2005).
[102] Sindell v. Abbott Laboratories, 607 P.2d 924 (Cal. 1980); Hymowitz v. Eli Lilly & Co., 73 N.Y.2d 487 (1989); Apfel & Fisher (1984).
[103] Mintz (1985).
[104] Barry Meier, "Questions Are Seen on Merck's Stand on Vioxx," New York Times A1 (11.24.04); Alex Berenson, "At Vioxx Trial, a Discrepancy Appears to Undercut Merck's Defense," New York Times C1 (7.20.05); Alex Berenson, "In Training Video, Merck Said Vioxx Did Not Increase Risk of Heart Attack," New York Times C4 (7.21.05); David Brown, "Maker of Vioxx Is Accused of Deception," Washington Post A1 (4.16.08).
[105] Barnaby J. Feder, "Boston Scientific to Pay $74 Million to Settle U.S. Stent Case," New York Times C4 (6.25.05).
[106] Barry Meier, "Citing Flaws, Maker Recalls Heart Devices," New York Times A1 (6.18.05); Barry Meier, "Guidant Says Flaw Is Found in More Types of Heart Units," New York Times C1 (6.25.05); Barry Meier, "Guidant Consultant Advised Company to Release Data on Defects," New York Times C3 (3.9.06).
[107] Gardiner Harris and Eric Koli, "Lucrative Drug, Danger Signals and the F.D.A.," New York Times A1 (6.10.05).
[108] Gina Kolata, "In Drama Pitting Scientist vs. Drug Maker, All Are Punished," New York Times F4 (6.14.05); Shuckman (2005).

CHAPTER 1

physicians to prescribe and endorse their drugs,[109] even for off-label use.[110] They have been accused of providing false data to the FDA.[111] Individual pharmacists also betray trust: one diluted the prescriptions he filled, depriving users of any benefit.[112] Even corporate buyers of pharmaceuticals (such as hospitals) are betrayed by pharmacy benefits managers, who accept payments from manufacturers to promote their products.[113]

E. *The Exploding Service Economy*

In postindustrial societies, we are at least as dependent on the specialized expertise of service providers as we are on manufacturers. Because most people value health above all, we depend most profoundly on those who provide medical services. Doctors can betray trust in many ways. The most egregious are those who kill their patients—most notoriously, Mengele and other Nazi doctors,[114] but also health care professionals (including nurses) directed by other motivations, such as "mercy" killings[115] or harvesting organs for transplants.[116] These crimes seem more

---

[109] Melody Petersen, "Doctor Explains Why He Blew the Whistle," New York Times C1 (3.12.03); "Court Papers Suggest Scale of Drug's Use," New York Times C1 (5.30.03); "Big Drug Company May Face Charges for Its Marketing," New York Times A1 (5.31.03); Gardiner Harris, "Pfizer to Pay $530 Million over Promoting Drugs to Doctors," New York Times C1 (5.14.04); Gardiner Harris, "As Doctor Writes Prescription, Drug Company Writes a Check," New York Times § 1 p. 1 (6.27.04); Barry Meier and Stephanie Saul, "Marketing of Vioxx: How Merck Played Game of Catch-Up," New York Times A1 (2.11.05) (over competitor Celebrex); Gardiner Harris, "In Article, Doctors Back Ban on Gifts from Drug Makers," New York Times A11 (1.25.06); "Seducing the Medical Profession," New York Times A24 (2.2.06); Stephanie Saul, "Doctors and Drug Makers: A Move to End Cozy Ties," New York Times C1 (2.12.07); Mary Engel, "Young Doctors See Drug Makers' Freebies as a Bad Habit," Los Angeles Times A1 (2.4.07); Gardiner Harris and Janet Roberts, "Doctors' Ties to Drug Makers Are Put on Close View," New York Times A1 (3.21.07); Gardiner Harris, "F.D.A. Limits Role of Advisers Tied to Industry," New York Times A1 (3.22.07); "Senators to Push for Registry of Drug Makers' Gifts to Doctors," New York Times A16 (6.28.07); Brennan et al. (2006); Topol & Blumenthal (2005).

[110] Callahan (2004: 52–56) (Parke-Davis's Neurontin).

[111] Ford Fessenden, "Studies of Dietary Supplements Come under Growing Scrutiny," New York Times A1 (6.23.03); Carey (1987); Barry Meier, "Narcotic Maker Guilty of Deceit over Marketing," New York Times A1 (5.11.07).

[112] Draper (2003).

[113] Milt Freudenheim, "Medco to Pay $29.3 Million to Settle Complaints of Drug Switching," New York Times C1 (4.27.04).

[114] Lifton (1986).

[115] Neal & Smith (1998); Mendelson (1998); Fairer (1983); Coney (1994); Richard Perez-Penya, David Kocieniewski, and Jason George, "Through Gaps in System, Nurse Left Trail of Grief," New York Times § 1 p. 1 (2.29.04); Smith (2004) (Dr. Harold Shipman in the UK).

[116] Charles Ornstein and Tracy Weber, "Transplant Surgeon Charged with Trying to Hasten Patient's Death," Los Angeles Times A1 (7.31.07); Amelia Gentleman, "Kidney Thefts Shock

heinous than violence by strangers because of the trust patients invest in their doctors. Nurses may abuse their most vulnerable patients: the very young or old, physically disabled, or mentally ill.[117] Medical experimenters may neglect to obtain informed consent, misleading participants about the dangers; the Tuskegee syphilis experiment is the most troubling example (because its subjects were illiterate black sharecroppers).[118] Doctors who abuse substances betray patient trust in their competence.[119]

Like car mechanics, health care providers can perform unnecessary services, for which they bill third-party payers (private insurers or the government).[120] (Gogol's *Dead Souls* served as a precursor.[121]) Patients trust doctors to make treatment choices that are in their best interests, and they feel betrayed when doctors take money from manufacturers of the medical devices they implant[122] or when psychiatrists[123] or oncologists[124] accept payments from the pharmaceutical companies whose

---

India," New York Times A3 (1.30.08) (400–500 by a ring of 4 doctors, 5 nurses, 20 paramedics, 3 private hospitals, 10 pathology clinics, and 5 diagnostic centers, over 9 years).

[117] Raven (2002).

[118] Jones (1993); Deborah Sontag, "Abuses Endangered Veterans in Cancer Drug Experiments," New York Times § 1 p. 1 (2.6.05).

[119] Centrella (1994); Degi et al. (1997); Lens & van der Wal (1997); Dubois & Haehnel (1997); Hancock (1997); Fallberg & Borgenhammar (1997); Irvine (1997); Tempelaar (1997); Rosenthal (1997).

[120] Vaughan (1982); Geis et al. (1985); Tillman & Pontell (1992); Jesilow et al. (1993); Lens & van der Wal (1997); Liederbach (2001); Dix (2002); Clifford J. Levy, "Doctor Admits He Did Needless Surgery on the Mentally Ill," New York Times A27 (5.20.03); Kurt Eichenwald, "Tenet Healthcare Paying $54 Million in Fraud Settlement," New York Times A1 (8.7.03); Kurt Eichenwald, "How One Hospital Benefited on Questionable Operations," New York Times A1 (8.12.03) (coronary bypasses); Christine Hanley, "Clinics Find Surgery Scam Pays," Los Angeles Times B1 (6.20.04); Jonathan D. Glater, "In a Surgery Capital, a Swirl of Fraud Charges," New York Times § 3 p. 1 (7.10.05) (unnecessary surgery, mainly on immigrants); Daniel Yi, "Insurers Denying Claims from Holistic Dentists," Los Angeles Times C1 (6.18.06) (mass extractions); Alex Berenson, "Incentives Limit Any Savings in Treating Cancer," New York Times C1 (6.12.07).

[121] Gogol (1965).

[122] Barry Meier, "Implant Program for Heart Device Was a Sales Spur," New York Times A1 (1.27.05); Reed Abelson, "Whistle-Blower Suit Says Device Maker Generously Rewards Doctors," New York Times C1 (1.24.05); "Possible Conflicts for Doctors Are Seen on Medical Devices," New York Times A1 (9.22.05).

[123] Gardiner Harris, Benedict Carey and Janet Roberts, "Psychiatrists, Children and Drug Industry's Role," New York Times A1 (5.10.07); Gardiner Harris, "Psychiatrists Top List in Drug Maker Gifts," New York Times A14 (6.27.07).

[124] Alex Berenson and Andrew Pollack, "Doctors Reap Millions for Anemia Drugs," New York Times A1 (5.9.07); Alex Berenson, "Cancer Drug Representatives Spelled Out the Way to Profit," New York Times C6 (6.12.07).

CHAPTER 1

drugs they prescribe.[125] Pharmaceutical companies pay for half of all mandatory continuing education for doctors—and predictably push their own products during the courses.[126] Doctors have a conflict when they refer patients to pharmacies and diagnostic or other medical procedures in which they have a financial interest. Doctors who prescribe drugs over the Internet without examining patients,[127] perform illegal cosmetic surgery,[128] or promote dubious anti-aging treatments[129] commit deliberate malpractice motivated by greed.

Doctors[130]—especially psychotherapists[131]—take advantage of the profound power imbalance Freud called transference by indulging in sexual relations with patients. Examples include such prominent figures as Joseph Breuer, Sandor Ferenczi, Wilhelm Reich, Carl Jung, Ernest Jones, and Karen Horney.[132] Before the rise of modern medicine, the clergy enjoyed at least as much authority as doctors do today, if not more, and also betrayed it by engaging in sexual relationships with parishioners,[133] as in the notorious case of Henry Ward Beecher and Elizabeth Tilton[134] and Nathaniel Hawthorne's fictional account of Arthur Dimmesdale and Hester Prynne.[135] Those who claim to mediate between man and God are uniquely well positioned to trade grace for money, in what Arthur Leff calls "the Godcons."[136] When people donate to charities—secular fraternal organizations such as the Shriners,[137] or

---

[125] See generally Campbell et al. (2007); Brody (2007).
[126] Daniel Carlet, "Diagnosis: Conflict of Interest," New York Times A23 (6.13.07).
[127] Ronald D. White, "SLA Pursuer Loses MD License," Los Angeles Times B1 (1.24.03); Lisa Richardson and Charles Ornstein, "Out-of-State Doctors Fined by California," Los Angeles Times B6 (2.12.03); "State Chasing Web Medics Who Prescribe Sight Unseen," Los Angeles Times A1 (2.17.03).
[128] Alex Kuczynski, "Psst: Want to Buy Some Wrinkle Remover?" New York Times § 9 p. 1 (2.16.03).
[129] Duff Wilson, "Aging: Disease or Business Opportunity?" New York Times § 3 p. 1 (4.15.07).
[130] Gartrell et al. (1992); Jorgenson (1995); Cullen (1995); Lens & van der Wal (1997); Hancock (1997); Flagler & Lalm (1997); Wilbers et al. (1992); Dix (2002).
[131] Chesler (1972); Butler & Zelan (1977); Burgess (1981); Gartrell et al. (1986); Gabbard (1989; 1994); Lyn (1995); Lewis (1995); Acker (1995); Benowitz (1995); Rutter (1995); Scott Gold, "Child Psychiatrist Arrested in Molestation Cases," Los Angeles Times B1 (4.6.07).
[132] Schoener et al. (1989); Schoener (1995).
[133] Fortune (1992).
[134] Fox (1999).
[135] Hawthorne (2006).
[136] Leff (1976: 57–61). The Catholic Church's sale of indulgences was a centerpiece of Martin Luther's critiques and a stimulus for the Reformation.
[137] Stephanie Strom, "In Shriner Spending, a Blurry Line of Giving," New York Times A1 (3.19.07) (much of the money Shriners donated to maintain their hospitals goes to members' entertainment).

churches[138]—they expect their funds to be devoted toward philanthropic or religious ends and feel betrayed if money is diverted to private uses by members or ministers. People buy insurance to secure peace of mind (as the law acknowledges by awarding emotional distress damages *only* for breaches of insurance contracts). One of the greatest sources of anxiety is the prospect of poverty in old age (the ancient fear of the poorhouse). Insurers betray the customer's trust when they sell long-term care policies and then renege on their obligations.[139]

In an information age, we depend on others for facts and interpretations that would be too expensive to acquire ourselves or too difficult to understand. Principals trust their broker-agents to be exclusively loyal and are betrayed when those agents serve themselves or others. For 27 years Bernard Berenson, the great Renaissance scholar, authenticated works of art for the leading art dealer Joseph Duveen—who paid him a secret commission after the sale.[140] Students trust their universities to provide disinterested information about educational loans (without which few could attend) and feel betrayed when they learn that some lenders pay the schools to promote their programs.[141] Insurance brokers claim to obtain the best deal for insured parties. But even the most sophisticated purchasers—large corporations buying commercial insurance—have been betrayed by brokers who accept secret commissions from insurers.[142] We

---

[138] Larry Rohter, "Brazil's Top TV Preachers Land in Hot Water in Miami," New York Times A3 (3.19.07) (Estevam and Sonia Hernandes, founders of the Rebirth in Christ Church, arrested with $56,467 in hidden cash).

[139] Charles Duhigg, "Aged, Frail and Denied Care by Their Insurers," New York Times A1 (3.26.07) (Conseco, Bankers Life, Penn Treaty).

[140] Secrest (2004).

[141] Jonathan D. Glater, "Lenders Pay Universities to Influence Loan Choice," New York Times A16 (3.16.07); "Colleges Hiring Lenders to Field Queries on Aid," New York Times A1 (3.29.07); "Millions to Be Repaid After College Loan Inquiry," New York Times A13 (4.3.07); "College Officers Profited by Sale of Lender Stock," New York Times A1 (4.5.07); Jonathan D. Glater and Karen W. Arenson, "Federal Official in Study Loans Held Loan Stock," New York Times A1 (4.6.07).

[142] Joseph B. Treaster, "An Inquiry into Insurance Payments and Conflicts," New York Times C1 (4.28.04); "Some Questions on Fees Insurers Pay to Brokers," New York Times C1 (5.18.04); "Spitzer Insurance Inquiry Expands to Employee Benefits," New York Times C1 (6.12.04); Gretchen Morgenson, "Hat Trick: A 3rd Unit of Marsh under Fire," New York Times § 3 p. 1 (5.2.04); Joseph B. Treaster, "Broker Accused of Rigging Bids for Insurance," New York Times A1 (10.15.04) (Marsh Inc.); "The Latest Financial Services Scandal," New York Times A26 (10.20.04); "A.I.G. Says It Is Target of Midwest Inquiry," New York Times C1 (10.22.04); "Insurance Chief Quits in Inquiry Led by Spitzer," New York Times A1 (10.26.04); "Marsh Pledges to Change the Way It Does Business," New York Times C1 (10.27.04); Thomas S. Mulligan, "Marsh Bars Special Commissions from Insurers," Los Angeles Times C1 (10.27.04); Gretchen Morgenson, "Insurance Broker's Cozy Ties May Prove Hard to Untangle," New York

CHAPTER 1

trust the scientists at the National Institutes of Health to make objective judgments about the efficacy and safety of medical procedures and devices—and feel betrayed when they accept payments from manufacturers.[143] We trust pharmaceutical companies to make full disclosure of the outcomes of clinical trials—and feel betrayed when they conceal negative findings.[144] We trust doctors conducting those trials to be impartial—and feel betrayed when they have an undisclosed investment in the product they are testing[145] or when the pharmaceutical companies influence the results,[146] for instance, by paying doctors substantial honoraria to talk to investors about the prospects of the drugs they are testing.[147] We trust doctors promoting drugs to tell the truth. Pfizer paid Michael Jarvik, the inventor of the artificial heart, to declare, "When diet and exercise aren't enough, adding Lipitor significantly lowers cholesterol." The ad showed Jarvik single-sculling on a lake. But Jarvik is not a cardiologist, is not licensed to practice medicine, and cannot row; a stunt double with a similar receding hairline impersonated him. Jarvik's longtime collaborator

---

Times A1 (10.27.04); Joseph B. Treaster, "Insurance Broker Settles Spitzer Suit for $850 Million," New York Times A1 (2.1.05).

[143] David Willman, "NIH Staff Must Report Payments," Los Angeles Times A15 (5.19.04); "NIH Imposes Ban on All Outside Payments to Its Employees," Los Angeles Times A16 (9.24.04); "The National Institutes of Health: Public Servant or Private Marketer?" Los Angeles Times A1 (12.22.04); "NIH Seeks Outside Inquiry of Scientist," Los Angeles Times A20 (1.28.05); "NIH to Ban Deals with Drug Firms," Los Angeles Times A1 (2.1.05); "NIH Seeks 'Higher Standard,'" Los Angeles Times A12 (2.2.05); Gardiner Harris, "Agency Scientists Divided over Ethics Ban on Consulting," New York Times A18 (2.2.05); David Willman, "NIH Chief Calls for Ethics Summit," Los Angeles Times A1 (2.12.05); Ricardo Alonso-Zaldivar, "NIH Employees Object to New Ethics Rules," Los Angeles Times A14 (2.24.07); Gardiner Harris and Alex Berenson, "10 Voters on Panel Backing Pain Pills Had Industry Ties," New York Times A1 (2.25.05); David Willman, "New Rules Will Cost Dissidents at NIH," Los Angeles Times A16 (3.3.05).

[144] Barry Meier, "Major Medical Journals Will Require Registration of Trials," New York Times C1 (9.9.04); Benedict Carey, "Antidepressant Studies Unpublished," New York Times B1 (1.17.08); Turner et al. (2008).

[145] Reed Abelson, "Financial Ties Are Cited as Issue in Spine Study," New York Times A1 (1.30.08) (as high as $250,000); Gardiner Harris, "Cigarette Company Paid for Lung Cancer Study," New York Times A1 (3.26.08); Barnaby J. Feder, "New Focus of Inquiry Into Bribes: Doctors," New York Times B1 (3.22.08); Gardner Harris and Benedict Carey, "Researchers Fail to Reveal Full Drug Pay," New York Times §1 p. 1 (6.8.08); Psaty and Kronmal (2008).

[146] Krimsky (2004); Bekelman et al. (2003); Schulman (2002); Thompson et al. (2001); Gale (2003); Stelfox et al. (1998); Bero et al. (1992); Rochon et al. (1994); Dana & Loewenstein (2003); Shuckman (2005); Petersen (2008).

[147] Stephanie Saul and Jenny Anderson, "Doctors' Links with Investors Raise Concerns," New York Times A1 (8.16.05); Topol & Blumenthal (2005); cf. Stephanie Saul, "Doctor Accused of Leak to Drug Maker," New York Times C10 (1.31.08) (peer reviewer for New England Journal of Medicine sent manuscript critical of GlaxoSmithKline drug to manufacturer, which in the past had paid him $75,000 in speaking fees).

said, "He's about as much an outdoorsman as Woody Allen."[148] Pfizer canceled the campaign.[149] Even nonprofits that champion the interests of disease sufferers, such as the American Heart Association, fail to disclose that they receive money from the pharmaceutical companies whose drugs they endorse ($2 million from Merck/Schering-Plough for defending Vytorin).[150] Courts trust expert witnesses and feel betrayed when they lie—such as the doctors who falsely claimed that plaintiffs suffered from exposure to asbestos[151] or silicon,[152] and the doctor who falsified a report on the Staten Island ferry pilot whose negligence killed several passengers.[153] Scientists trust their colleagues to adhere to the scientific method (since it would be prohibitively costly to check every experimental result)—and are betrayed when those colleagues falsify data.[154] Several commentators have argued that the university's disinterested pursuit of truth has been distorted by market forces: donations, contract research, and the revolving door between academia and industry.[155] Non-specialists trust experts to collect and evaluate evidence—and feel betrayed when the experts falsify or misinterpret, even if the public has no stake in the knowledge claim. "Piltdown Man" is the locus classicus: unearthed with great fanfare in 1912, only to be exposed 40 years later as a fraud (an orangutan jawbone attached to a modern human skull).

We trust journalists to report accurately. Readers, other journalists, editors, and publishers all feel betrayed when reporters concoct facts, as in the notorious case of *New York Times* reporter Jayson Blair, as well as other, less sensational fabricators: Janet Cooke of the *Washington Post*, Mike Barnicle of the *Boston Globe*, Michael Finkel of the *New York Times Magazine*.[156] We trust reporters and editors to use their professional

---

[148] Stephanie Saul, "Drug Ads Raise Questions for Heart Pioneer," New York Times A1 (2.7.08).
[149] Stephanie Saul, "Pfizer to End Lipitor Ads by Jarvik," New York Times C1 (2.26.08); "Lipitor's Pitchman Gets the Boot," New York Times (2.27.08) (editorial).
[150] Stephanie Saul, "Heart Group Backs Drug Made by Ally," New York Times C1 (1.24.08).
[151] Jonathan D. Glater, "Reading X-Rays in Asbestos Suits Enriched Doctor," New York Times A1 (11.29.05).
[152] Jonathan D. Glater, "The Tort Wars: At a Turning Point," New York Times A1 (10.9.05).
[153] Sewall Chan, "Doctor Admits to Lying About S.I. Ferry Pilot's Medical History," New York Times B2 (6.24.05);
[154] Overbeke (1997); Kenneth Chang, "Researcher Loses Ph.D. over Discredited Papers," New York Times D2 (6.15.04); Matthew L. Wald, "E-Mails Reveal Fraud in Nuclear Site Study," New York Times A9 (4.2.05).
[155] Thompson (1970); Horton (2004); Bok (2003); Shapin (1995).
[156] David D. Kirkpatrick, "A History of Lying Recounted as Fiction," New York Times B1 (2.7.03); "Times Reporter Who Resigned Leaves Long Trail of Deception," New York Times § 1 p. 1 (5.11.03); "Witnesses and Documents Unveil Deceptions in a Reporter's Work," New York

CHAPTER 1

judgment about what is newsworthy—and feel betrayed when the government pays for coverage.[157] Even some bloggers, who present themselves as fiercely independent, accept payment to push products from PayPerPost, ReviewMe, Loud Launch, and SponsoredReviews.com.[158] Equally, we expect news sources to talk without remuneration[159]—and feel betrayed when they are paid, especially when the dirt turns out to be phony.[160] Reporters must earn the trust of their sources by resisting the temptation to extract information deceptively.[161] Advertisers trust newspaper circulation figures in deciding where to buy and what to pay—and feel betrayed when these are inflated.[162] Readers credit authors based on their representations and ostensible identities—and feel betrayed when

Times § 1 p. 22 (5.11.03); "Betrayal of Trust: The Jayson Blair Scandal," Letters to the Editor, New York Times A30 (5.13.03); Stephanie Simon, "Subjects Seem Unfazed by a Reporter's Misdeeds," Los Angeles Times A1 (5.19.03); Jacques Steinberg, "Writer's Work In USA Today Is Called False," New York Times A1 (3.20.04); "Newspaper Editors Move to Tighten Safeguards," New York Times C1 (3.22.04); Stephen Braun, "USA Today Editor Quits under Cloud," Los Angeles Times A1 (4.21.04); Jacques Steinberg, "Editor of USA Today Resigns, Citing Reporter's Fabrications," New York Times A1 (4.21.04); "Panel Says Poor Standards Allowed Deception at USA Today," New York Times A15 (4.23.04); Richard B. Schmitt, "Second USA Today Editor Resigns amid Scandal," Los Angeles Times, A12 (4.23.04); James Rainey, "Newspaper Columnist Resigns After Inquiry," Los Angeles Times A12 (5.13.05); Glass (2003); Blair (2004); Callahan (2004: 83–88); Finkel (2005).

[157] David R. Kirkpatrick, "TV Host Says U.S. Paid Him to Back Policy," New York Times A1 (1.8.05); James Rainey, "Case Shines Harsh Light on 'Pundit Industry,'" Los Angeles Times A14 (1.8.05); Tom Hamburger, Nick Anderson, and T. Christian Miller, "Tax-Funded White House PR Effort Questioned," Los Angeles Times A1 (1.8.05); Stuart Elliott, "A Paid Endorsement Ignites a Debate in the Public Relations Industry," New York Times C2 (1.12.05) (company owned by Armstrong Williams, conservative commentator and columnist, paid $240,000 by Dept of Educ. to promote No Child Left Behind Act; PR company Ketchum, owned by Omnicom Group, paid Graham Williams company); Anne E. Kornblut, "Bush Prohibits Paying of Commentators," New York Times A18 (1.27.05); "Third Journalist Was Paid to Promote Bush Policies," New York Times A13 (1.29.05); "Pentagon Investigating Payment for Articles," New York Times A13 (2.5.05); Timothy L. O'Brien, "Spinning Frenzy: P.R.'s Bad Press," New York Times § 3 p. 1 (2.13.05); Anne E. Kornblut, "Administration Is Warned about Its 'News' Videos," New York Times A11 (2.19.05); "The Muck Stops Here," Los Angeles Times M3 (2.27.05); David Barstow and Robin Stein, "Under Bush, a New Age of Prepackaged TV News," New York Times § 1 p. 1 (3.13.05); "And Now, the Counterfeit News," New York Times A22 (3.16.05); Marion Just and Tom Rosenstiel, "All the News That's Fed," New York Times A27 (3.26.05).

[158] Josh Friedman, "Blogging for Dollars Raises Questions of Online Ethics," Los Angeles Times C1 (3.9.07).

[159] Byron Calame, "Money, a Source and New Questions about a Story," New York Times § 4 p. 12 (3.25.07) (Kurt Eichenwald paid Justin Berry $2,000 for a story about child pornography).

[160] Tom Gorman, "A High-Wire Fall in the Media Circus," Los Angeles Times A12 (5.12.03).

[161] David Carr, "At Sundance, Art and Journalistic Ethics on Trial," New York Times B3 (1.25.07).

[162] Jacques Steinberg, "Belo Moves to Reassure Advertisers After Scandal," New York Times C1 (8.17.04).

these are falsified: Clifford Irving's (un)authorized biography of Howard Hughes;[163] an allegedly true story of a 10-year-old orphan who learned Indian ways from his Cherokee grandparents, which turned out to be a white Southern racist's fiction; an ostensible bildungsroman by an East Los Angeles Chicano homeboy, which was written by a 70-year-old Jewish graduate of Andover and Yale.[164] "Margaret B. Jones" wrote an enthusiastically reviewed "memoir" of growing up as the daughter of a native American parent brought up by an African American foster family in South-Central Los Angeles and delivering drugs for the Bloods gang at 13. But it was pure fiction.[165] Postmodernists were infuriated when Alan Sokal published his hoax, "Transgressing the Boundaries: Towards a Transformative Hermeneutics of Quantum Gravity," in the prestigious journal *Social Text*. Grichka and Igor Bogdanov turned the tables on the "hard" scientists by publishing five meaningless articles in highly reputable peer-reviewed physics journals.[166]

Investors who sensibly seek to diversify their portfolios but cannot investigate all the corporations whose shares they buy necessarily rely on their brokers' advice. But researchers' recommendations are biased by self-interest: secret commissions and undisclosed investments.[167] Henry Blodget, Merrill Lynch's Internet expert, recommended companies for which the securities firm was doing lucrative investment banking business.[168] Brokers sell "shelf space" to mutual funds by placing them on

---

[163] The subject of the film *The Hoax* (2007); see A. O. Scott, "Trust Story of a Fake Story about Hughes (Really)," New York Times B10 (4.6.07).
[164] Abel (1998: 280).
[165] Margaret P. Jones, Love and Consequences (New York: Riverhead Books, 2008). She was Margaret Seltzer, all white, who grew up with her middle class birth family. Motoko Rich, "Gang Memoir, Turning Page, Is Pure Fiction," New York Times A1 (3.4.08). For other recent fakes, see Motoko Rich, "A Family Tree of Literary Fakers," New York Times A17 (3.8.08)
[166] Robin (2004: chapter 7).
[167] Landon Thomas Jr., "Market Makers and Big Board Reach a Deal," New York Times C1 (2.18.04); Landon Thomas Jr. with Gretchen Morgenson, "2 Analysts Likely to Pay $20 Million in Fraud Case," New York Times C1 (4.28.03); Gretchen Morgenson, "In a Wall St. Hierarchy, Short Shrift to Little Guy," New York Times C1 (4.29.03); Stephen Labaton, "10 Wall St. Firms Settle with U.S. in Analyst Inquiry," New York Times A1 (4.29.03); Patrick McGeehan, "A Subject Barely Mentioned at Merrill Meeting," New York Times C4 (4.29.03); Raymond Hernandez, "Finding Fraud on Wall St. May Be a Step to Higher Post," New York Times C4 (4.29.03); Landon Thomas Jr., "UBS Analyst Forced Out for Remark," New York Times C1 (7.3.04); "S.E.C. Orders Mutual Funds to Cease Incentive Pay," New York Times C3 (8.19.04); Gretchen Morgenson, "How to Succeed on Wall Street, Conflict-Free," New York Times § 3 p. 5 (12.19.04); "'The Bonfire of the Vanities,' 2005 Edition," New York Times § 3 p. 1 (11.20.05); "Trust Sued over Backing Retiree Plan," New York Times C1 (4.5.07).
[168] Callahan (2004: 3–8).

recommended lists in exchange for higher commissions.[169] Pension fund consultants have personal interests in the investments they recommend;[170] campaign contributions influence how public pension funds invest their money.[171] Investors rely on market makers to buy securities at current prices and are betrayed when the market makers engage in self-dealing.[172]

Public accountants may betray investors and lenders who rely on their audits, out of an interest in the companies to which they provide services.[173] Accountants were complicit in some of the largest recent financial scandals, most notably Enron, in part because they earned higher profits from consulting than from auditing.[174] Ernst & Young audited a firm with which it had a business relationship.[175] PriceWaterhouseCoopers was sufficiently concerned about the fallout to buy a full-page *New York Times* advertisement captioned "building public trust, a status report," which declared that "those who audit the financial statements of public companies ... must ... have the courage and the integrity to do the right thing" and concluded that "trust must be earned every day."[176]

Management has a duty to maximize shareholder interests. At least since Berle and Means we have known that the separation of ownership from control creates agency problems.[177] Many of the recent financial scandals involved managers pursuing self-interest at the expense of shareholders, lenders, and employees: Columbia Pictures,[178] Cendant, Elan, Royal Ahold, Parmalat, Bank of Credit and Commerce International,

---

[169] Josh Friedman, "State Sues Firm over Mutual Fund Sales," Los Angeles Times A1 (12.21.04).
[170] Lynn O'Shaughnessy, "A 401(k) Picks a Mutual Fund. Who Gets a Perk?" New York Times § 3 p. 5 (2.15.04); Mary Williams Walsh, "Concerns Raised over Consultants to Pension Funds," New York Times § 1 p. 1 (3.21.04); Mary Williams Walsh, "In Louisiana, a Pension Official Blows the Whistle on Adviser Conflicts," New York Times § 1 p. 16 (3.21.04).
[171] Mary Williams Walsh, "Political Money Said to Sway Pension Investments," New York Times A1 (2.10.04).
[172] Landon Thomas Jr., "Market Makers and Big Board Reach a Deal," New York Times C1 (2.18.04); Schlegel (1993).
[173] Hanlon (1994); Williams (2002); Brewster (2003); Toffler (2003).
[174] Jerry Hirsch, "Enron Audit Fee Raises Some Brows," Los Angeles Times A1 (1.23.02); Leslie Wayne, "Seeking Top Berth in Pursuit of Enron," New York Times C6 (1.12.02); Patrick McGeehan, "Masters of the Universe, Leashed (for Now)," New York Times § 3 p. 3 (7.18.04); Smith & Emschwiller (2003); Callahan (2004: 142–152).
[175] Floyd Norris, "Big Auditing Firm Gets 6-Month Ban on New Business," New York Times A1 (4.17.04).
[176] New York Times C3 (6.11.03).
[177] Berle & Means (1932). On management fraud, see Sorensen et al. (1980).
[178] McClintick (1982).

Robert Maxwell, Nick Leeson and Barings Bank, Adelphia,[179] ImClone,[180] RiteAid, Tyco,[181] Global Crossing,[182] Computer Associates,[183] Royal Dutch/Shell,[184] WorldCom,[185] Xerox,[186] Bristol-Myers,[187] Halliburton,[188] Lucent,[189] Commercial Financial Services,[190] even a public corporation such as Fannie Mae,[191] and of course Enron.[192] The use of stock options as remuneration for executives (and directors) not only conceals from shareholders the size of the pay package but also creates temptations for insider trading and market timing.[193] But if the 1990s boom produced more than

---

[179] Roger Lowenstein, "The Company They Kept," New York Times Magazine 26 (2.1.04).

[180] Constance L. Hays, "Former Chief of ImClone Is Given 7-Year Term," New York Times C1 (6.11.03).

[181] Jonathan D. Glater, "Character to Be Major Issue in Tyco Trial," New York Times C1 (5.6.04); Andrew Ross Sorkin, "Ex-Chief and Aide Guilty of Looting Millions at Tyco," New York Times A1 (6.18.05).

[182] Gretchen Morgenson, "Global Crossing Settles for $325 Million," New York Times B1 (3.20.04); Timothy L. O'Brien, "A New Legal Chapter for a 90's Flameout," New York Times § 3 p. 1 (8.15.04).

[183] Alex Berenson, "Guilty Plea Seen in Computer Associates Case," New York Times (9.22.04); Alex Berenson, "Ex-Chief of Computer Associates Is Indicted on Fraud Charges," New York Times A1 (9.23.04); Alex Berenson, "Ex-Executives of Computer Associates Plead Not Guilty," New York Times (9.24.04).

[184] Stephen Labaton and Jeff Gerth, "Oil Giant's Officials Knew of Gaps in Reserves in '02," New York Times A1 (3.9.04); Jeff Gerth and Stephen Labaton, "Shell Withheld Reserves Data to Aid Nigeria," New York Times A1 (3.19.04); Heather Timmons, "Shell Reduces Estimate of Reserves Again," New York Times C1 (3.19.04).

[185] Stephen Labaton, "MCI Agrees to Pay $500 Million to Shareholders in Fraud Case," New York Times A1 (5.20.03); Gretchen Morgenson, "3 Banks Had Early Concern on WorldCom," New York Times A1 (3.17.04).

[186] Floyd Norris, "6 from Xerox to Pay S.E.C. $22 Million," New York Times C1 (6.6.03); Callahan (2004: 140–144).

[187] Eric Dash, "Bristol-Myers Agrees to Settle Accounting Case," New York Times C1 (8.5.04).

[188] Gretchen Morgenson, "Suit Accuses Halliburton of Fraud in Accounting," New York Times C1 (8.6.04).

[189] Ken Belson, "Lucent Fined $25 Million by S.E.C. in Fraud Case," New York Times C1 (5.18.04).

[190] Porter (2004).

[191] Gretchen Morgenson, "Reading Fannie Mae's Scary Cookbook," New York Times § 3 p. 1 (9.26.04).

[192] McLean & Elkind (2003); Swartz & Watkins (2003); Rapoport & Dharan (2004); Landon Thomas Jr., "Deals and Consequences," New York Times § 3 p. 1 (11.20.05); Whelan (2007).

[193] Gretchen Morgenson, "In the Timing of Options, Many, Um, Coincidences," New York Times § 3 p. 1 (12.5.04); Gretchen Morgenson, "Are Options Seducing Directors, Too?" New York Times § 3 p. 1 (12.12.04). (executives more likely to benefit from well-timed option grants if directors also paid with options); "10 Ex-Directors from WorldCom to Pay Millions," New York Times A1 (1.6.05); Jonathan D. Glater, "A Big New Worry for Corporate Directors," New York Times C1 (1.6.05); Kurt Eichenwald, "Ex-Directors at Enron to Chip in on Settlement," New York Times B1 (1.8.05); Anabtawi (2004); Bebchuck et al. (2006a; 2006b).

its share of betrayals,[194] there were plenty of precursors, such as OPM[195] and National Student Marketing.[196]

F. *Tilting the Playing Field*

Competitors who expend effort and resources in the hope of reward and who play by the rules, trusting others to do so, feel betrayed when winners break those rules.[197] Investors' expectations of a level playing field are violated when insiders trade on secret information.[198] Mutual funds favor some investors over others through stale pricing, letting the privileged make late trades and extract unique profits.[199] Courts of law promise equal justice, but judges systematically favor parties who have made campaign contributions.[200] Athletes seek an illegal advantage by using drugs or proscribed equipment (Sammy Sosa's corked bat, Barry Bonds,[201] NASCAR races,[202] the 2007 Tour de France,[203] even modifications of Soap Box Derby entries[204]) or falsifying their ages to compete with younger, less capable rivals.[205] Teams recruit unqualified players—college athletes who fail the academic requirements, for instance.[206] Television contestants get

---

[194] Lowenstein (2004); Mahar (2004).
[195] Gandossy (1985).
[196] SEC v. Nat'l Student Mktg. Corp., 457 F. Supp. 682 (D.D.C. 1978).
[197] Gehring (2003).
[198] Jenny Anderson and Michael J. de la Merced, "13 Are Accused of Trading as Insiders," New York Times C1 (3.2.07).
[199] Kenneth N. Gilpin, "How Scandal Can Help the Fund Industry," New York Times § 3 p. 7 (11.2.03); Stephen Labaton, "Extensive Flaws at Mutual Funds Cited at Hearing," New York Times A1 (11.4.03); Diana B. Henriques, "He's the Go-To Guy for Fund Investigators," New York Times § 3 p. 6 (11.16.03); Mark Hulbert, "It's Bad. But It Isn't Market Timing," New York Times § 3 p. 6 (11.16.03); Josh Friedman, "Franklin to Settle Trading Charges," Los Angeles Times C1 (8.3.04).
[200] Adam Liptak, "Looking Anew at Campaign Cash and Elected Judges," New York Times A14 (1.29.08); Palmer (2008). See also the Los Angeles Times investigation into influence and corruption in the Nevada judiciary: Michael J. Goodman and William C. Rempel, "In Las Vegas, They're Playing with a Stacked Judicial Deck," Los Angeles Times A1 (6.8.06); "For a Vegas Judge and His Friends, One Good Turn Led to Another," Los Angeles Times A1 (6.9.06); "How Some Nevada Judges Stay Under the Radar," Los Angeles Times A1 (6.10.06); Don Woutat, "Three Las Vegas Judges Face High Court Review," Los Angeles Times A4 (6.23.06).
[201] Bill Pennington, "The Commissioner of Baseball Is on Deck," New York Times B10 (5.12.07).
[202] Jim Peltz, "NASCAR Hits Waltrip Hard," Los Angeles Times D1 (2.15.07); Callahan (2004: 73–83, 236).
[203] Doreen Carvajal, "After Scandal, Cycling Struggles for Sponsors," New York Times C5 (5.11.07); Juliet Masur, "When the Wheels Come Off a Sport," New York Times § 4 p. 1 (5.13.07).
[204] Woodley (1982).
[205] Callahan (2004: 69–72) (Danny Almonte in Little League).
[206] Callahan (2004: 234–35).

the questions in advance (Charles Van Doren on *Twenty-One*)[207] or are coached (allegedly by *American Idol* judges).[208] Record companies give disk jockeys "payola" for radio play time.[209] We expect artists and performers to do their own creative work and feel betrayed when an ostensible child prodigy did not paint the pictures she signed,[210] singers lip-synced videos (e.g., Milli Vanilli), or a classical pianist played in an extraordinary range of styles—by stealing from others' recordings.[211] Because educational achievement brings substantial rewards (both money and status), we feel betrayed when students cheat on tests, plagiarize, or pad resumes.[212] Wealthy parents buy their children diagnoses of learning disability to increase the time they are allowed for taking the SAT.[213] High proportions of job applicants falsify their resumes—even for such exalted positions as Bausch & Lomb CEO, Notre Dame football coach, head of the U.S. Olympic Committee, and MIT Dean of Admissions![214] Joseph Ellis, a Mount Holyoke College history professor and Pulitzer Prize–winning author, fabricated a past that included fighting in Vietnam, civil rights activism, even being a high school football star.[215] Celebrity chef Robert Irvine, host of "Dinner Impossible" on the Food Network, falsely claimed a British knighthood, ownership of a castle in Scotland, friendship with Prince Charles, and having cooked for four presidents.[216] Nobel laureate Rigoberta Menchú's best-selling autobiography exaggerated and falsified

---

[207] Fictionalized in the film *Quiz Show*.
[208] Jacques Steinberg, "An Inquiry into Charges by 'Idol' Contestant," New York Times C5 (5.6.05).
[209] Jeff Leeds, "Record Labels Said to Be Next on Spitzer List for Scrutiny," New York Times C1 (10.22.04); Jeff Leeds and Louise Story, "Radio Payoffs Are Described as Sony Settles," New York Times A1 (7.26.05); Jeff Leeds, "EMI Agrees to Fine to Resolve Payola Case," New York Times C3 (6.16.06).
[210] David Carr, "At Sundance, Art and Journalistic Ethics on Trial," New York Times B3 (1.25.07).
[211] Dennis Dutton, "Shoot the Piano Player," New York Times A25 (2.26.07); Alan Riding, "Pianist's Widower Admits Fraud in Recordings Issued as His Wife's," New York Times B3 (2.27.07); "Now, a CD Called 'Plagiarism in B Flat,'" New York Times A20 (3.2.07).
[212] Alan Cooperman, "Air Force Academy Probes Alleged Cheating by Cadets," Washington Post A3 (2.10.07); Erika Hayasaki, "One Poor Test Result: Cheating Teachers," Los Angeles Times A1 (5.21.04); "More Cases of Test Cheats Alleged," Los Angeles Times B1 (6.23.05); "Cheating on Tests," Washington Post A26 (2.15.07); Karen W. Arenson, "South Korea: 900 SAT Scores Canceled," New York Times A1 (3.13.07) (similar scandals in India and China in early 1990s); McCabe (1992; 1999); McCabe & Bowers (1994); McCabe & Trevino (1996; 1997); McCabe et al. (2001); Callahan (2004: 203–219).
[213] Kelman & Lester (1997).
[214] Callahan (2004: 220–22); Tamar Lewin, "M.I.T.'s Admissions Dean Resigns; Ends 28-Year Lie About Degrees," New York Times A1 (4.27.07).
[215] Robin (2004: chapter 3).
[216] Lawrence Van Gelder, "Arts, Briefly: Chef Cooks Up Hoax," New York Times B2 (3.4.08).

CHAPTER 1

what she and her Mayan people had suffered.[217] Readers and other writers (competing for recognition) feel betrayed when scholars like Philip Foner, Morton Smith, Stephen Oates, Stephen Ambrose, Michael Bellesiles, and Doris Kearns Goodwin,[218] as well as journalists,[219] plagiarize or make up data.

Most of us voluntarily (if unhappily) comply with tax laws, even though we know the likelihood of an audit is very low, because we trust others to do so—and feel betrayed when we learn that evasion is widespread and flagrant.[220] Nationwide tax preparation services help individuals file fraudulent returns.[221] "Charitable" scams advise that individuals have no obligation to file tax returns—and pocket $2 million in "donations."[222] Some of the largest and most respected accounting firms created and sold wealthy individuals and companies illegal tax shelters, thereby betraying all of the compliant, who had to pay higher taxes.[223] Jenkens & Gilchrist, recently one of the largest (600 lawyers) and highest-earning law firms (one partner earned $93 million in five years), dissolved after paying the IRS $76 million for devising and selling aggressive tax shelters.[224]

---

[217] Robin (2004: chapter 6).
[218] Sara Rimer, "When Plagiarism's Shadow Falls on Admired Scholars," New York Times A23 (11.24.04) (Laurence Tribe and Charles Ogletree of Harvard Law School); Robin (2004: chapter 1); Karen W. Arenson, "In a Charge of Plagiarism, an Echo of a Father's Case," New York Times C13 (3.14.07) (father, a New Jersey business school professor, accused of plagiarism in a 1982 book; daughter resigned from another New Jersey business school after being accused of plagiarizing her doctoral dissertation); Peter Steinfels, "Was It a Hoax? Debate on a 'Secret' Mark Gospel Resumes," New York Times A12 (3.31.07); Hoffer (2004).
[219] Katharine Q. Seelye, "USA Today Reporter Quits over Lifting Quotations," New York Times C5 (5.6.05).
[220] David Cay Johnston, "Pioneer of Sham Tax Havens Sits Down for Pre-Jail Chat," New York Times C1 (11.18.04); Joseph B. Treaster, "A.I.G. Says It Is Target of Midwest Inquiry," New York Times C1 (10.22.04) (for selling income-smoothing products); "A.I.G. Agrees to Big Payment in U.S. Cases," New York Times (11.25.04); Callahan (2004: 10, 177–179) (IRS estimates annual shortfall at $250–500 billion).
[221] Lynnley Browning, "U.S. Accuses Part of Tax Chain of Fraud," New York Times C3 (4.4.07) (Jackson Hewitt).
[222] David Cay Johnston, "U.S. Sues Man It Accuses of Selling a Tax Scheme," New York Times C3 (4.4.07).
[223] David Cay Johnston, "Ernst & Young to Pay U.S. $15 Million in Tax Case," New York Times C1 (7.3.03); "I.R.S. Takes Aim at Big Shelters and Hopes Message Filters Down," New York Times § 1 p. 1 (7.6.03); Lynnley Browning, "Suit Accuses KPMG and Others of Selling Illegal Tax Shelters," New York Times C1 (8.17.04); Lynnley Browning, "KPMG Wrote New Versions of Shelters Ruled Illegal," New York Times C1 (8.26.04); David Cay Johnston, "Pioneer of Sham Tax Havens Sits Down for Pre-Jail Chat," New York Times C1 (11.18.04); "Auditors: Too Few to Fail," New York Times C1 (6.25.05); Lynnley Browning, "How an Accounting Firm Went from Resistance to Resignation," New York Times § 1 p. 1 (8.28.05).
[224] Lynnley Browning, "Texas Law Firm Will Close and Settle Tax Shelter Case," New York Times C3 (3.30.07).

Other instances of collective action against narrow self-interest vary with participants' trust that others will do their share: military service (draft evasion), jury duty (shirking), voting (turnout), and resource conservation (gas guzzlers and speed limit compliance).

G. *How Betrayal Illuminates Trust*

Peering through the looking glass, from the perspective of betrayal, confirms the indispensability of trust and the personal and social costs of its violation. Many individual clients invest in lawyers the faith that the clients, as children, had to place in their parents and that some then transferred to teachers, priests, and doctors.[225] Justice is essential to our moral environment just as air and water are to physical survival. Lawyers can either protect that commons or selfishly despoil it, overfishing the credulous until only cynics remain. Lawyers construct and operate the collectivities (private corporations, NGOs, and government) that are our society's fundamental constituents. With accelerating technological change, we are all too aware of our utter dependence on products whose safety and quality we cannot evaluate. In a service economy we also are increasingly dependent on providers such as lawyers. Even with the Internet (and partly because of it) we are overwhelmed by an explosion of information, which no individual can digest or comprehend. Because we cannot evaluate the information's accuracy—the way we can kick a car's tires and test-drive it—we demand unalloyed loyalty from those who sell or vouch for the information, as a surrogate for verification (hence the centrality of conflict-of-interest rules). As competition intensifies in every sphere of life (with globalization and the erosion of ascriptive barriers) and extends to new ones (everything is now ranked), trust in the results rests on belief in the fairness of the rules of the game. Compliance with the law ex ante and acceptance of adverse legal judgments ex post both depend on trust that others are law-abiding and that the legal system produces just outcomes.

III. The Sociology of Trust Violation

A. *Confidence Games*

The necessity for trust creates many opportunities for profit, some of them abusive. The myth that the great circus impresario P. T. Barnum boasted

---

[225] Both Jerome Frank (1930) and Harold Berman (1963) have written about law's role as the father.

CHAPTER 1

"there's a sucker born every minute" reveals more than the fact that he never uttered the phrase. Barnum's contemporary, Edgar Allan Poe, maintained that "to diddle" is man's "destiny."[226] Confidence men—celebrated in print[227] and film[228]—offer another perspective on the creation and betrayal of trust. Although David Maurer's classic account of "The Big Con" (on which this paragraph is based) may sound archaic, everyone with an e-mail account is inundated with entreaties (usually couched in fractured English) to help free the "Spanish prisoner" and reap an enormous reward.[229] Although the Internet has made such appeals virtually costless, they would not persist without an endless supply of gullible marks. It is the mark's greed that makes con games possible.[230] The real difficulty, however, is not to convince the mark that *he* will make money (something marks are all too ready to believe) but to explain how the *con man* will.[231] Both swindlers and sellers must prove not only that they *can* benefit the mark/buyer but that they *must* do so.[232] Some grifters may feel compunction over conning the uncomplaining mark, but most "do not admit any pangs of conscience at having swindled a victim."[233] Although confidence games are relatively uncommon and may seem exotic, they closely resemble legitimate businesses: "They only carry to an ultimate and very logical conclusion certain trends which are often inherent in various forms of legitimate business."[234]

One difference between "Swindling and Selling"[235] is that most businesses expect customers to return and therefore must retain their trust, whereas a crucial step in the con is "cooling out the mark."[236] (That is why one-shot sales are more likely to resemble swindles.[237]) Because marks often have made their money by shady means, they tend to be less suspicious of others who engage in subterfuge.[238] Indeed, "scams increase

---

[226] Quoted in Sante (1999: vii).
[227] Melville (1964); Twain (1993) (the Duke and the Dauphin).
[228] *The Lady Eve* (1941); *The Sting* (1973) (based on Maurer); *The Grifters* (1990).
[229] Recipients have been striking back by conning the con men. Thomas Crampton, "A Web Cadre Turns the Tables on African Scam Artists," New York Times C7 (7.2.07).
[230] Maurer (1999: 2). The scheme invented by Charles Ponzi is a classic example. Zuckoff (2005).
[231] Leff (1976: 13).
[232] Id. 130.
[233] Maurer (1999: 121, 208).
[234] Id. 3, 20, 179; cf. Levi (1981).
[235] Leff (1976).
[236] Id. 159.
[237] Caplovitz (1963: chapter 10).
[238] Maurer (1999: 26–27).

the lure by painting themselves as a bit shady and the victim as something of a co-conspirator."[239] Yet con artists also flatter the mark by exaggerating his honesty.[240] Marks' business success deludes them into believing they possess unusually good judgment about finance and people.[241] Those played for the long con let themselves be convinced that "no one will suffer but the rich and dishonest bookmakers."[242] Afterward, many victims are too embarrassed by their gullibility, cupidity, and culpability to tell anyone.[243] A banking fraud victim admitted, "We were gullible. And we were greedy."[244] Victims of trading offenses blame themselves for seeking suspiciously good bargains.[245] Leff observes, "all swindles are at least for some period of time consensual crimes. . . . Until late in the play [the swindled] are not natural allies of the regulators, but are made to see themselves as in league *against* the protective agents of the state."[246] The few who insist on calling down the law may get their money back.[247] Marks so badly want to believe in the bona fides of the deal that they may keep the faith even after the con man has explained the swindle, sometimes demanding to play again.[248] "[O]ne of the surest ways to become a personal fraud victim is to have been a victim."[249]

Con men have their own code of behavior: don't swindle a drunk, help pay for bail or legal representation of others on the con, honor debts to grifters.[250] Con men pay off banks to transfer money and pay off the police, often agreeing not to swindle locals and sometimes obtaining a municipal grifting monopoly.[251] Although the con man is primarily motivated by money, "the constant excitement of playing for high stakes gets into his blood . . . returning to thievery or professional gambling would be to lose professional status."[252] The con man "loves his work and is constantly experimenting to see what new angle he may develop, what

---

[239] Titus (2001).
[240] Maurer (1999: 118).
[241] Id. 104.
[242] Id. 37.
[243] Id. 79. See Goffman (1952).
[244] Titus (2001). Walsh & Schram (1980) draw analogies between the experiences of fraud and rape victims.
[245] Croall (1989).
[246] Leff (1976: 182).
[247] Maurer (1999: 223).
[248] Id. 102, 128–129; Leff (1976: 84–88).
[249] Titus (2001).
[250] Maurer (1999: 121, 151).
[251] Id. 221–224.
[252] Id. 146, 172.

technical point he can improve upon."²⁵³ There is a striking resemblance to the *Masters of the Universe*, which debuted a half century later.²⁵⁴ As an inside trader said, "Something deep inside me forced me to try to catch up to the pack of wheeler-dealers who always raced in front of me. . . . I was addicted to the excitement, the sense of victory."²⁵⁵

B. White-Collar Crime

Edwin Sutherland's presidential address on "The White Collar Criminal," delivered to the American Sociological Society in December 1939, opened a new domain in criminology.²⁵⁶ He defined it as "crime committed by a person of respectability and high social status in the course of his occupation." Others have challenged each element, emphasizing the occupational means rather than the offender's high status.²⁵⁷ Indeed, recent research has revealed that "white-collar criminals are generally much closer in background to average Americans than to those who occupy positions of great power and prestige."²⁵⁸ The research and theory Sutherland stimulated have informed my approach to lawyer misconduct. He argued that

> financial loss from white collar crime, great as it is, is less important than the damage to social relations. White collar criminals violate trust and therefore create distrust, and this lowers social morale and produces social disorganization on a large scale.²⁵⁹

His examination of the 70 largest manufacturing, mining, and mercantile companies uncovered extensive and varied forms of illegality: antitrust violations, price fixing and discrimination, embezzlement, tax evasion, fraudulent bankruptcy, war profiteering, unfair labor practices, betrayals of shareholders by executives, stock market manipulations, securities fraud, insider trading, misleading financial statements, and mixing of corporate and personal funds.²⁶⁰

---

²⁵³ Id. 203.
²⁵⁴ Wolfe (1987).
²⁵⁵ Levine (1991: 390); see also Stone (1990).
²⁵⁶ Geis & Goff (1983: ix). It was published as the lead article in the American Sociological Review the following year. Sutherland (1977).
²⁵⁷ E.g., Quinney (1963; 1964); Hartung (1950).
²⁵⁸ Weisburd et al. (1991: 62).
²⁵⁹ Sutherland (1983: 10).
²⁶⁰ Id. 26 ff.; 39 ff.; 153–154.

Like Maurer (his contemporary), Sutherland emphasized the close resemblance between legal and illegal business practices, quoting Thorstein Veblen:

> The ideal pecuniary man is like the ideal delinquent in his unscrupulous conversion of goods and persons to his own ends, and in a callous disregard of the feelings and wishes of others and of the remoter effects of his actions, but he is unlike him in possessing a keener sense of status and in working more far-sightedly to a remoter end.[261]

Indeed, a decade before Sutherland, Robert Merton had observed that "on the top economic levels, the pressure toward innovation not infrequently erases the distinction between business-like strivings this side of the mores and sharp practices beyond the mores."[262] More than 40 years later, Howard Becker concluded his classic study of "Outsiders" by declaring that "people who engage in acts conventionally thought deviant are not motivated by mysterious, unknowable forces. They do what they do for much the same reasons that justify more ordinary activities."[263] Contemporary criminologists consistently confirmed the similarities between legal and illegal businesses.[264] A study of fraud convictions in a British magistrate's court found that the "practices are often regarded by traders as involving 'normal marketing strategies,' justified on the grounds of competition."[265] Studies of tax evasion emphasize its similarity to legitimate strategies of tax minimization.[266] Business people believe that unethical acts are widespread and that most others would commit them—even if they themselves would not do so.[267] A recent text asks, "Where ... is a line to be drawn between entrepreneurship, commercial innovation, sharp practice and fraud?"[268]

Samuel Insull, on trial for antitrust violations following the collapse of his utilities empire, remarked "that he could not understand why he was being prosecuted since he had done only what all other businessmen were doing." Sutherland generalized this protestation of wounded

---

[261] Veblen (1912: 237).
[262] Merton (1930).
[263] Becker (1973: 192).
[264] Clarke (1990); Passas & Nelken (1993); Slapper & Tombs (1999).
[265] Croall (1989).
[266] McBarnet (1988; 1991); McBarnet & Whelan (1999); Cook (1989).
[267] Baumhart (1961); Silk & Vogel (1971); Madden (1977).
[268] Croall (2001: 94), citing Mars (1982); Ruggiero (1996).

innocence: "the professional thief conceives of himself as a criminal and is so conceived by the general public. . . . The businessman . . . thinks of himself as a respectable citizen and, by and large, is so regarded by the general public."[269] Ordinary crime is a "Who Done It?" There is no question whether "it" is criminal. In white-collar crime, by contrast, the perpetrator's identity usually is clear; the question is whether the conduct is criminal.[270] This ambiguity is what makes white-collar crime interesting.[271] Sutherland noted that "businessmen develop rationalizations which are designed to conceal the fact of crime. Fraud in advertising is rationalized by the statement that every one puffs his wares."[272] Thirty years earlier Edward Ross declared that law "has no claim of its own" on what he called "the criminaloid," who "cannot see why everything may not be 'arranged,' settled out of court."[273]

Writing shortly after Sutherland, Marshall Clinard found that businessmen who consciously violated wartime regulations did "not consider that they ha[d] committed crimes and, therefore, could not possibly be treated as criminals."[274] Pharmaceutical employees who concealed a drug's dangerous side effects did not express "any strong repugnance or even opposition to selling the unsafe drug. Rather, they all seemed to drift into the activity without thinking a great deal about it."[275] Convicted of blatant price fixing in 1961, a Westinghouse executive expostulated, "Illegal? Yes, but not criminal." A Carrier Corp. executive convicted in the same scandal claimed he had been "reasonably in doubt" that price fixing was illegal: "Certainly, we were in a gray area. I think the degree of violation, if you can speak of it that way, is what was in doubt." The convicted president of a smaller company protested, "We did not fix prices. . . . All we did was recover costs." Another "assumed that a criminal action meant damaging someone, we did not do that." Executives felt entitled to suppress competition that was hurting their company. "There was not personal gain in it for me." "If I didn't do it, I felt someone else would."[276] White-collar criminals filter deviant acts "through a sanitizing, ideological prism, which gives

---

[269] Sutherland (1983: 228, 230).
[270] Braithwaite & Geiss (1982).
[271] Aubert (1952); Nelken (2002).
[272] Sutherland (1983: 233); cf. Croall (1988).
[273] Ross (1977: 36).
[274] Clinard (1977: 90).
[275] Carey (1978: 394; 1987).
[276] Geis (1977: 122–124, 126); Sonnenfeld & Lawrence (1978).

them the appearance of not being criminal."[277] An executive convicted of antitrust violations described his behavior as "a way of doing business before we even got into the business. So it was like why do you brush your teeth in the morning."[278] A corrupt city councilor made a similar plea of necessity: "I am by nature a wheeler-dealer. How else can you be a successful politician?" "I did what is business. If I bent the rules, who doesn't?"[279] Employees likewise rationalize stealing from bosses or customers on grounds of their own inadequate compensation.[280] "It's not really hurting anybody—the store can afford it."[281] Sara Willott and her associates have vividly reported the language through which both working-class and upper-middle-class male offenders rationalize their crimes.[282] Even the non-criminal public is more tolerant of theft from large businesses and government than from individuals and small businesses.[283] Disciplined lawyers offer a similar slew of self-righteous rationalizations.

Ross had observed that "within his home town, his ward, his circle" the "criminaloid" is "perhaps a good man. . . . Very likely he keeps his marriage vows, pays his debts, 'mixes' well, stands by his friends, and has a contracted kind of public spirit."[284] Sutherland was equally convinced that personality traits could not explain which businessmen committed white-collar crimes,[285] a view widely shared by other observers.[286] Criminologists agree that "the fact that the behavior is complex, technical, and not readily observable by inexperienced citizens" creates opportunities for white-collar crime.[287] Sutherland's preferred theory of "differential association"[288] has been largely discredited[289] and seems inapplicable to most lawyer deviance. So does Howard Becker's theory of deviant careers, the effect of labeling, and membership in organized deviant groups.[290]

---

[277] Simon & Eitzen (1993: 333).
[278] Benson (1985: 591).
[279] Chibnall & Saunders (1977: 42).
[280] Ditton (1977) (bread sales and deliveries); Mars (1973) (waiters); Mars (1974) (dock workers); Mars & Nicod (1984) (waiters); Chibnall & Saunders (1977: 143) (city councilmen).
[281] Zeitlin (1971: 22).
[282] Willott & Griffin (1999); Willott et al. (2001).
[283] Smigel (1956).
[284] Ross (1977: 30–31).
[285] Sutherland (1977: 47; 1983: 262–263); Cohen et al. (1956).
[286] Bromberg (1965); Selling (1944); Spencer (1965); Blum (1972); Box (1983); Coleman (1985: 196–197); Punch (1996).
[287] Sutherland (1983: 255).
[288] Id. 240.
[289] Clinard (1952: 309–310); Lane (1977: 109); Braithwaite (1985).
[290] Becker (1973).

CHAPTER 1

Lawyers' ethical violations are often unique and unrepeated; for most lawyers, discipline terminates the behavior; and action is generally individual, not collective. Solo practitioners are overrepresented among the disciplined. Indeed, whereas juveniles may gain peer respect by being labeled deviant, sanctioned lawyers lose their significant investment in professional reputation (and suffer economically).

David Matza reformulated Sutherland's concept of differential association as a theory of "drift" in order to understand juvenile delinquency.[291] Both the similarities to and differences from lawyer deviance are telling. Matza criticized prior criminologists for exaggerating the divide between criminals and others.[292] The delinquent "is rather a normal youngster—except that he belongs to what is essentially a different though related culture. Instead of learning our precepts, he learns others."[293] Delinquents "intermittently play both delinquent and conventional roles."[294] Matza saw actors as

> neither compelled nor committed to deeds nor freely choosing them; neither different in any simple or fundamental sense from the law abiding, nor the same; conforming to certain traditions in American life while partially unreceptive to other more conventional traditions.[295]

Delinquents "agree that someone should be apprehended and punished, but it ought to have been someone else.... The delinquent may claim that 'others get away with it.'"[296] (Disciplined lawyers often raise similar objections to "selective prosecution.") Few delinquents engaged in "radical justification," asserting "the righteousness of an act in and of itself." Instead, most "justify their behavior through apology" (precisely the self-abasement that occurs during the penalty phase of the disciplinary process). Some stress the crimes they would never commit: "There is a class of unapproved victims."[297] (Disciplined lawyers often protest that at least they did not dip into client trust accounts.)

---

[291] Matza (1964).
[292] Id. 11.
[293] Id. 18.
[294] Id. 26.
[295] Id. 28.
[296] Id. 41.
[297] Id. 44.

Matza sought to stress the delinquent subculture's "integration into the wider society" rather than "its slight differentiation." One critical integrative mechanism is neutralization, through which "norms may be violated without surrendering allegiance to them."[298] "Criminal law is especially susceptible of neutralization because the conditions of applicability, and thus inapplicability, are explicitly stated." (That is even truer of the ethics of lawyers, whose professional skills involve rule manipulation and evasion.) Neutralization operates through negation of responsibility, a sense of injustice, the transmutation of crime into tort, and the primacy of custom.[299] The delinquent negates responsibility because he "is subject to frequent oscillation between sensing himself as cause—humanism—and seeing himself as effect—fatalism"[300] ("We're disturbed," as the Jets sing to "Officer Krupke" in "West Side Story."[301]) (Lawyers who neglect their clients similarly blame case overload—for which they are responsible.) The juvenile delinquent's sense of injustice often emerges as "a simmering resentment—a setting of antagonism and antipathy—within which the variety of extenuating circumstances may abrogate the moral bind to the law."[302] "[T]he offender *occasionally* sees his offense as prompted by virtue and justifies it" by reference to "the traditional precepts of manliness, celebrating as they do the heroic themes of honor, valor, and loyalty."[303] (Lawyers who champion clients fighting injustice may feel that the role justifies ethical violations on the client's behalf.) The delinquent's justifications "often seem unduly legalistic."[304] (Lawyers facing ethical charges, not surprisingly, take every possible procedural point—including some that do not pass the laugh test.)

"The subculture of delinquency collects examples of inconsistency." "The sense of inconsistency is likely to be heightened when legal agents possess great discretion or when the principles that guide decision are diffusely or mysteriously delineated."[305] (Lawyers may be even more emphatic about inconsistency, because only a tiny fraction of deviant acts are punished, and both charging and sentencing are highly discretionary.) Juvenile

---

[298] Id. 60. See Sykes & Matza (1957).
[299] Matza (1964: 61).
[300] Id. 88.
[301] "We're disturbed, we're disturbed/We're the most disturbed/Like we're psychologic'ly disturbed."
[302] Matza (1964: 101).
[303] Id. 156.
[304] Id. 103.
[305] Id. 111.

delinquents redefine legal violations as "torts—acts that are wrong and, if they lead to personal harm, warrant redress and compensation. But they are not deemed worthy of inclusion in the criminal law."[306] (White-collar criminals in general, and disciplined lawyers in particular, argue that they can wipe the slate clean by restitution.) "With the exception of judges, all of the offices that regularly oversee the conduct of juveniles share a single overriding characteristic. They are all *marginal professions*."[307] (This may be even more salient for lawyers, many of whom see disciplinary system personnel, even its judges, as their professional inferiors.) Matza calls the other main integrative mechanism the "subterranean convergence" between deviant and conventional traditions—what students of white-collar crime saw as the similarity with ordinary business practices.[308] As those writers found,

> The will to repeat old infractions requires nothing very dramatic or forceful. Once the bind of law has been neutralized and the delinquent put in drift, all that seems necessary to provide the will to repeat old infractions is preparation.[309]

For lawyers, too, there is no reason to stop committing ethical transgressions that are both profitable and unsanctioned.

Criminologists have been properly cautious in generalizing about white-collar criminality, in part because the rubric embraces a wide range of divergent behavior (as does lawyers' ethical misconduct).[310] The first large-scale study after Sutherland found that relatively few of the nearly 500 largest manufacturing companies were the target of a disproportionate number of criminal actions brought by 25 federal agencies.[311] Much of this concentration was attributable to recidivism.[312] Although criminologists argue that white-collar crime is more instrumental and less spontaneous or emotional than other crime,[313] an analysis of 17 case studies of misconduct by public sector organizations found a deliberative weighing

---

[306] Id. 87, 169–170, 174.
[307] Id. 144.
[308] Id. 63.
[309] Id. 184.
[310] Weisburd et al. (1991: 39–42).
[311] Clinard & Yeager (1980: 116).
[312] Id. 126–127.
[313] Chambliss (1967); Clinard & Meier (1979: 248); Braithwaite & Geis (1982: 302); Coleman (1987); Downes & Rock (1995).

of costs and benefits in only two.[314] Donald Cressey's embezzlers (discussed below) did not carefully calculate potential gain and risk.[315] Indeed, because they did not consider themselves criminals, they did not anticipate punishment (whereas they were acutely aware of their urgent need for money).[316] Some even seemed to court discovery.[317] Rational choice theory may oversimplify here, as elsewhere.[318]

Greed is a common motive.[319] A study of World War II price regulation violations found they were unrelated to sales, profits, or firm size but did vary with supply shortages.[320] This and other studies reported correlations between violation and attitude toward the regulations.[321] Although smaller companies are overrepresented among prosecutions for minor violations, this may reflect selection bias among administrative agencies and prosecutors rather than the distribution of deviant behavior.[322] (The reasons for the disproportionate number of solo and small firm practitioners in disciplinary proceedings are hotly contested.) Indeed, Clinard and Yeager found that larger corporations were overrepresented among violators.[323] There also is disagreement about whether competition or oligopoly fosters illegality.[324] Violations of the Fair Labor Standards Act and World War II price regulations varied inversely with the business cycle.[325] Financially straitened individuals and firms, not surprisingly, were more likely to commit crimes.[326] (Financial need seems to explain why some lawyers dip into client trust accounts; several of the disciplined lawyers described below profited from their ethical violations, whether or not that was their only motive.)

The more pervasively firms were regulated, the lower the rates of violation.[327] Crime (predictably) varied inversely with the likelihood of

---

[314] Vaughan (1998).
[315] Cressey (1953: 118).
[316] Id. 121.
[317] Id. 124.
[318] E.g., Lemert (1964).
[319] Conklin (1977); Wheeler (1992).
[320] Clinard (1977: 96).
[321] Id. 99; Ball (1977: 186–188).
[322] Nelken (1983); Sutton & Wild (1985); Coleman (1985: 223–224); Croall (1989; 2001: 58–59); Hutter (1988); Cook (1989).
[323] Clinard & Yeager (1980: 119, 130) (but not more per unit size).
[324] Compare Clinard & Yeager (1980: 165–66) with Kugel & Gruenberg (1977: 36, 47).
[325] Lane (1977: 105); see also Geis (1977: 130) (electric industry price fixing).
[326] Katona (1946: 241); Staw & Szawajkowki (1975); Clinard & Yeager (1980: 129); Simpson (1986); but see Nelken (1997).
[327] Lane (1977: 112); see also Weisburd et al. (1991: 89) (banking highly regulated; lower crime rates).

sanction, either formal (legal) or informal (reputational).[328] Pharmacists were more likely to violate prescription rules if they saw themselves as professionals-businessmen rather than simply as professionals.[329] Pharmaceutical company quality-control managers were more likely to cut corners if they reported to sales departments rather than senior executives.[330] (Lawyer deviance is often blamed on the decline of professionalism.[331]) Investigators have discovered significant differences in the kind and quantity of criminality by industry, that is, between the manufacturing of heavy electrical equipment,[332] boxes,[333] and liquor.[334] One of the largest and most systematic studies of white-collar crime found that many of the convicted professionals exhibited other forms of deviance: battering spouses, abusing substances, incurring heavy debt.[335] Indeed, these subjects "evidence[d] prior criminality to a much greater extent than most practitioners and scholars would have expected."[336] (Lawyer deviance is often associated with marital and financial problems, and concomitant substance abuse— but not in any of my cases.) Crime seriousness did not vary significantly with gender and varied only weakly with race, but it did increase with age, which offers

> special opportunities to develop social networks within organizations over long periods of time. Trust that develops between business associates, or those in business and their customers, not only lends credibility to misrepresentations but also facilitates the development of complex offenses.[337]

Hence, crime reflects opportunity rather than inexperience or insufficient socialization. (Disciplined lawyers similarly tend to be older.)

Because white-collar crime is undertheorized and too heterogeneous to permit robust generalization, criminologists repeatedly call for additional case studies of particular crimes[338] or for "industry-by-industry"

---

[328] Braithwaite & Makkai (1991).
[329] Quinney (1977: 192–93).
[330] Braithwaite (1984).
[331] Kronman (1993); Glendon (1994); Linowitz (1994).
[332] Geis (1977).
[333] Sonnenfeld & Lawrence (1978).
[334] Denzin (1977); Braithwaite (1989).
[335] Weisburd et al. (1991: 56–58).
[336] Id. 66.
[337] Weisburd et al. (1991: 83, 91).
[338] Geis & Meier (1977b: 3).

analyses.[339] Thirty years after these self-criticisms, Croall reiterated that "the rich ethnographic accounts of offenders' motivations or subcultures, which have had such an important influence on theories of conventional crime, are not available for white collar crime."[340] Van Hoorebeeck agreed: "Much criminology as we know it does not seem to have a clue about the world out there."[341] One promising strategy is the use of "autobiographical accounts by small business employers and employees who have participated in crime networks."[342] Howard Becker concurred that "there are not enough" studies of deviant behavior.

> An area of deviance of the utmost importance for sociological theorists has hardly been studied at all. This is the area of professional misconduct. . . . For all the wealth of sociological descriptions of professional behavior and culture, we have few if any studies of unethical behavior by professionals.[343]

A decade later, Coleman reaffirmed that "the least researched and least understood of all white-collar crimes are probably crimes in the professions."[344] Becker exhorted criminologists to "study the drama of moral rhetoric and action in which imputations of deviance are made, accepted, rejected, and fought over."[345] Thirty years later, de Haan and Loader also "insist that perpetrators of crime are moral subjects striving reflexively to give meaning to their actions before, during and after the crime."[346] Nelken has urged greater effort "to 'appreciate' the perspective of those engaged in white-collar crime."[347]

Becker attributed the neglect of professionals to the fact that "deviance within organized conventional institutions is often protected by a kind of cover-up. Professional associations handle such matters privately."[348] He commended C. Wright Mills for demonstrating "the variety of methods that can be used to study the powerful and especially the study

---

[339] Coleman (1985: 226).
[340] Croall (2001: 80).
[341] Van Hoorebeeck (1997: 515), quoted in De Haan & Loader (2002).
[342] Barlow (1993).
[343] Becker (1973: 166–167).
[344] Coleman (1985: 112).
[345] Id. 186.
[346] De Haan & Loader (2002: 245).
[347] Nelken (1994; 1997; 2002).
[348] Becker (1973: 168–169).

of those documents that become public . . . by virtue of the workings of governmental agencies."[349] The detailed case records produced by the New York Departmental Disciplinary Committees (which I use in this book) are an invaluable, and largely untapped, data source for remedying such ignorance. Becker also admonished researchers that the people studied "often have trouble recognizing themselves and their activities in the sociological reports written about them. We ought to worry about that more than we do."[350] I hope that the following accounts are recognizable by anyone who has been, or has interacted with, a lawyer.

Some theorists explicitly emphasize the betrayal of trust (as Sutherland did in 1939).[351] A federal prosecutor defined white-collar crime as "illegal acts committed . . . by concealment or guile, to obtain money or property."[352] The necessity for trust arises out of the agency problem, which creates information asymmetries about knowledge and actions the agent conceals from the principal.[353] Principals use several strategies to reduce the risk of betrayal: choosing the agent, shaping the agent's incentive structure, and creating penalties for and insurance against breach. But these are always imperfect. Susan Shapiro observes that "the violation and manipulation of the norms of trust—disclosure, disinterestedness, and role competence—represent the modus operandi of white collar crime." These betrayals include lying, shirking, stealing, self-dealing, selling the privileges of trust to outsiders, and role conflict generally. Shapiro calls for "the marriage of a systematic understanding of the distribution of structural opportunities for trust abuse with an understanding of the conditions under which individual or organizational fiduciaries seize or ignore these illicit opportunities."[354] I have tried to do that in this book.

C. Case Studies of Criminals Betraying Trust

Certain criminal acts seem most closely analogous to lawyers' ethical transgressions. I have drawn on two American studies of embezzlement and two English studies of crime at work.

---

[349] Id. 194, citing Mills (1956).
[350] Id. 191.
[351] Sutherland (1977: 40); Shover & Wright (2001b: 1).
[352] Edelhertz (1970: 3).
[353] Shapiro (1990).
[354] See also Coleman (2001).

1. American Embezzlement

In his classic book *Other People's Money*, Donald Cressey framed "the central problem" of embezzlement as how to explain

> that some persons in positions of financial trust violate that trust, whereas other persons, or even the same person at a different time, in identical or very similar positions do not so violate it.[355]

Based on interviews of convicted embezzlers at one federal and two state prisons, Cressey concluded that

> trusted persons become trust violators when they conceive of themselves as having a financial problem which is non-shareable, are aware that this problem can be secretly resolved by violation of the position of financial trust, and are able to apply to their own conduct in that situation verbalizations which enable them to adjust their concepts of themselves as trusted persons with their conceptions of themselves as users of the entrusted funds or property.[356]

Cressey noted that some embezzlers had become accustomed to deceit in childhood: "If you are adept at deception on a small scale it is so much easier on a large scale."[357] Following Sutherland, however, he rejected explanations "in terms of unusual or abnormal personality traits."[358]

Cressey saw parallels with the behavior of electrical company executives: some embezzlers were trying to save their businesses (typically a bank),[359] and most denied their criminality—"I know I am a criminal only in a technical sense."[360] "This is wrong, but it is not criminal."[361] They distinguished their behavior from real criminality. One said,

> Maybe it was the phony reasoning that I was going to put it back, and maybe it was that I had lawful possession of the

---

[355] Cressey (1953: 12).
[356] Id. 30.
[357] Id. 40.
[358] Id. 143.
[359] Id. 45, 47, 67.
[360] Id. 68.
[361] Id. 103–104.

CHAPTER 1

money I took. *I'd go into the store at night and would never think of taking a coat or suit or anything, because I didn't have lawful possession of that.*[362]

Others concurred: "I've never stolen because that is a thing I never believed in."[363] "We could have sold houses that we didn't own . . . but we never did anything like that."[364] "Some fellows have the intention to embezzle to use the money for a good time," but to "use it for working capital . . . isn't embezzlement."[365] Only the few who became career embezzlers saw themselves as thieves.[366]

Some, nevertheless, acknowledged selfish motives. They sought to compete with others in display or to enjoy a lifestyle they had briefly attained but could not afford to maintain.[367] Like those who committed other crimes at work, embezzlers compared their (inadequate) pay with their bosses' conspicuous consumption.[368] (As Merton[369] noted, Durkheim applied his theory of anomie to crime: "Wealth, exalting the individual, may always arouse the spirit of rebellion, which is the very source of immorality."[370]) Some observers have cautioned that growing inequality—CEOs making 550 times as much as their employees—will produce more white-collar crime.[371] (Income disparity within the legal profession has also increased, although not as dramatically, from 6:1 between the top and bottom quartiles in 1975 to 10:1 in 1995.[372] Several disciplined lawyers expressed resentment at the inflated incomes and social pretensions of large firm practitioners.)

Embezzlers need both the opportunities and skills they find at work: "The manipulations I made were a part of that routine."[373] They had little difficulty rationalizing their actions. Cressey drew his title from Dumas: "What is business? That's easy. It's other people's money,

---

[362] Id. 69.
[363] Id. 101.
[364] Id. 106.
[365] Id. 112.
[366] Id. 114, 133.
[367] Id. 37, 49–57.
[368] Id. 58.
[369] Merton (1930).
[370] Durkheim (1951), quoted by Croall (2001: 91).
[371] Box (1983); Tucker (1989).
[372] Heinz et al. (2005: 161).
[373] Id. 82–84.

of course."[374] Some saw their behavior as indistinguishable from legitimate commerce. One embezzler pronounced, "In the real estate business there is nothing wrong about using deposits before the deal is closed." Another analogized himself to an automobile dealer:

> He uses the finance company's money, the finance company uses the bank's money, and the bank is using John Doe's money, your money, right along. Every day in business a man has to use John Doe's money, the little man's money.[375]

They insisted that everybody does it: "I've been told that 90% of the people do what I did in this respect."[376] Like lawyers who "borrow" from client trust accounts, many embezzlers intended to replace the money and were convinced they could do so.[377] They blamed customers for unreasonably demanding their funds, toppling the pyramid scheme.[378] Like other criminals (both ordinary and white collar), they had their own rules, which allowed them to betray customers but not employers: "I never took any money from the company, it was the people I skinned."[379] As Ross observed, one embezzler protested, "I was a respectable citizen."[380]

Dorothy Zeitz's replication with convicted women embezzlers found many similarities[381] and some significant differences.[382] (Women are underrepresented in white-collar crime generally, by reason of structural position, not socialization or culture.[383]) Her subjects believed that "the use they made of their talent did not differ in any significant way from that displayed by other people in business for themselves."[384] They, too, denied their criminality: "I am not 'a thief at heart' and I would not have embezzled except for the pressure of mounting unpaid bills."[385] Although

---

[374] Id. 96, quoting Alexandre Dumas, *La question d'argent* (1857), Act II.
[375] Id. 111.
[376] Id. 103–104.
[377] Id. 103–104.
[378] Id. 105.
[379] Id. 107.
[380] Id. 110.
[381] Weisburd et al. (1991: 84) found no gender difference in the seriousness of the white collar crimes committed by their sample.
[382] Zeitz (1981); cf. Daly (1989).
[383] Weisburd et al. (1991).
[384] Id. 107.
[385] Id. 44.

CHAPTER 1

basic needs initially drove these women to crime, constantly rising aspirations for material goods prompted further embezzlement.[386] But female embezzlers differed from their male counterparts in seeking to satisfy the needs of *others*: dependent children or other relatives, or husbands or male partners who sponged off of them. Prefiguring Carol Gilligan,[387] Zeitz noted that her informants felt "that any conduct, including trust violation, is justified when it offers the only available solution to problems seriously affecting the welfare or potential loss of a child or husband."[388] And unlike male embezzlers, most women regretted their actions and accepted punishment.

A few women, however, like a few of the men, were professional criminals, whose only regret was being caught.[389] These women protested that they had hurt no one (because their business victims were insured), had stolen less than others, and had been punished more harshly. Like the men, they emphasized the crimes they did *not* commit: "We didn't do anything to physically hurt anybody. They didn't have to give us their money at gunpoint."[390] "My next caper, if there is one, is going to be big time, baby, big time all the way."[391] Like Maurer's grifters, professional women embezzlers blamed their victims: "All of the people I supposedly cheated wanted to get something out of it too." "[N]obody ever 'makes' a sucker out of another person. They have to be a little shady too."

> The whole bunch I dealt with were as larcenous as I. The only difference is, I took all the risks and landed in prison. They ended up "the poor little old victims." Bullshit![392]

Like Maurer's con men, Zeitz's con women took intrinsic satisfaction in their activity: "the excitement and ego-rewarding thrill of the chase, the sense of power derived from the use of their wits or the manipulation of their victims, and the sheer enjoyment of playing a part in a scenario wholly unrelated to the real world in which they lived."[393] But Zeitz also encountered an analytic problem that pervades white-collar

---

[386] Id. 37, 39.
[387] Gilligan (1982).
[388] Zeitz (1981: 63).
[389] Id. 91.
[390] Id. 96.
[391] Id. 92.
[392] Id. 92.
[393] Id. 107.

criminology: those who engaged in behaviors the *law* treated as equivalent differed sharply among themselves. Zeitz identified a number of distinct categories: obsessive protectors, romantic dreamers, victims of pressure or persuasion, greedy opportunists, vindictive self-servers, asocial entrepreneurs, and reluctant offenders. She paraphrased Conklin's[394] study of robbery: "Each type of offender had a different reason for appropriating other people's money or property and a different degree of commitment to crime."[395] As Tolstoy began *Anna Karenina*, "Happy families are all alike; every unhappy family is unhappy in its own way." These differences demonstrate the need for the case studies I offer in this book.

2. English "Fiddling"

Gerald Mars also found that "most of the 'criminals' do not regard what they are doing as remotely blameworthy and secondly, they appear at all respects to be no different from other people."[396] Echoing Poe (in English argot), Mars found "fiddling" to be "entrenched," "woven into the fabric of people's lives," "essential to the operation of many businesses." It was "not the anarchic behaviour of a lawless rabble, but was subject to rule."[397] Drawing on the work of anthropologist Mary Douglas,[398] Mars used the variables of grid (intensity of social structural constraints) and group (strength of the collectivity) to divide jobs into four categories.[399] Among Hawks (weak grid and group, e.g., small business owners or waiters; solo and small firm lawyers fit here), "fiddles and flexibility are part of the way things actually work, and indeed often the reason *why* things work."[400] "[T]ake away the fiddle in a hawk job, and you are likely to alter the mode of the task completely."[401] Society "covertly expects [fiddles] of the hawk."[402] Workers fudge time records (just as lawyers pad hourly bills). Delay (at which lawyers are particularly adept) "becomes a powerful device when linked with poor communication (incomplete information)."[403] Delay may be a means of justifying a higher price: "The time taken to

---

[394] Conklin (1972: 182).
[395] Zeitz (1981: 123).
[396] Mars (1982: 1); for another English perspective on similar phenomena, see Henry (1978).
[397] Mars (1982: 18–19).
[398] Douglas (1970).
[399] Mars (1982: 25–34).
[400] Id. 42.
[401] Id. 65.
[402] Id. 57.
[403] Id. 55.

repair a watch is always vastly longer than it need be in order to obscure the essentially simple nature of most watch repairs."[404] Hawk fiddles are distinguished by "their open-endedness, their moral ambiguity and most important their pragmatism." But envious, competitive, less successful colleagues may expose hawk fiddles by invoking bureaucratic controls, motivated by what Harold Bridger[405] calls "institutionalized envy."[406] This is exactly how many disciplined lawyers portray their "victimization" by competitors.

Workers in donkey jobs (strong grid, weak group, e.g., domestic servants and supermarket cashiers) engage in fiddles against customers and bosses.[407] "At first it was a fantastic strain, but after a few months it became easily managed routine." Superiors may be complicit: "Every now and then one of the managers will come up to you, usually with a packet of tea, and put it close to the till . . . and say 'put that through a couple of hundred times, will you?'" Like other deviants, clerks have their own rules: "You'd never do it to an old person" or parents with young children. These workers "are likely to feel resentment at the constraints that bind them." They fiddle "to gain control," resorting to sabotage if necessary.[408] Employers respond with greater control (increasing the grid), provoking further resentment, which in turn breeds more fiddling.[409] For this reason (among others) "experienced store detectives insist that the stereotype of the deviant sales clerk as 'the new girl who is improperly socialised' just does not square with the facts . . . that their most typical deviants are in fact trusted and experienced middle aged–women employees. But they are also difficult to catch!"[410] (Similarly, the modal disciplined lawyer has practiced for several decades.) "[A]ll donkey job money fiddles have a high risk of detection because . . . they are repetitive. If the [bus] conductor wants to make any sizeable profit from issuing used tickets, he must repeat the fiddle again and again."[411]

Wolfpack jobs (strong grid and group, e.g., garbage collector or longshoreman; large firm lawyers fit here) resist "internal schisms, rivalry and competition" by controlling rank within the group and the allocation

---

[404] Id. 146.
[405] Bridger (1971).
[406] Mars (1982: 58).
[407] Id. 66–69.
[408] Id. 70, citing Taylor & Walton (1971).
[409] Id. 80.
[410] Id. 176.
[411] Id. 85–86.

of people to jobs.[412] The group establishes rules limiting illegality. Wolves embrace a common rationalization: "It's all insured and nobody's heard of an insurance company going broke. In any case, they've made millions out of this port and it's us who do the work."[413] (Large firm lawyers who pad bills offer similar rationalizations.)

Vulture jobs (weak grid, strong group, e.g., salesmen and hotel workers; court appointed criminal defense lawyers might fit here) resemble Maurer's long cons and Leff's sellers (although Mars seems unacquainted with either book).[414] Vulture jobs are especially common in "triadic occupations," which permit "collusion between employers and workers who are able to fiddle customers by short-changing them" and fiddles by employees "who overload and undercharge their friends and relatives."[415] "Trainee fiddlers must pass through a process of education and transformation which will ensure that they do not threaten other workers already in post," an experience well captured by the concept of the moral career.[416] The trainee's

> personal book-keeping is dogged by Sod's Law: his earnings are well below expected levels; his vulnerability to management control is too easily demonstrated. In desperation he looks not just for a way out but for an *explanation*. The fiddle provides it. It says that "unless you substitute a system of justice for the bureaucratic system, its inbuilt unmanageability will defeat you."[417]

"The deviant worker among vultures . . . is not the worker who fiddles but the 'straight' worker who *refuses* to fiddle" or the one who fiddles too much.[418] "[T]he unofficial management attitude to fiddling emerges as 'Do it, but don't tell me how.'"[419] But because these fiddles require active cooperation among some and tacit tolerance by others, there is a constant risk of disclosure. "They do not have the craft mastery and mystery of the watchmaker, the lawyer and the hospital consultant." Reflecting on the

---

[412] Id. 89–103; cf. Lazega (2001).
[413] Id. 106, quoting Mars (1972).
[414] Id. 109.
[415] Id. 149.
[416] Id. 113.
[417] Id. 133–134.
[418] Id. 122.
[419] Id. 134.

CHAPTER 1

quarter-century since he wrote the book, Mars saw information technology shifting jobs down-grid, thereby increasing the number of donkey jobs.[420]

Jason Ditton drew on his experience as a bakery roundsman (bread deliverer and salesman) for his doctoral research, which became his superb book on *Part-Time Crime: An Ethnography of Fiddling and Pilferage*.[421] He sought "to do for the fiddler . . . what Cressey did for the embezzler."[422] Fiddling "is a subculture of legitimate *commerce* itself."[423] "Fiddling was practised by most . . . of the salesmen," who "were successfully able to conceive of it as non-criminal action."[424] Goffman observes that "the neophyte role centres upon over-emphasis of the prescriptive aspects of the final role."[425] New salesmen were quickly and inescapably socialized into fiddling:

> [W]hilst learning the job, the recruit is gradually made aware of the fact that 'mistakes' (responsibility for which he has already agreed to) and thus 'shortages' are inevitable. Once low pay and long hours have become a reality for him, he is considered to be morally and technically ready for a demonstration that both problems may be solved by overcharging customers.[426]

Goffman describes a cycle of "alienation and mortification followed by a new set of beliefs about the world and a new way of conceiving of selves."[427] Ditton describes how the "novice 'latches on' to something."[428] Roundsmen placed the blame for their fiddles on the company, which charged them with shortages: "it's the company what *make* you . . . what you are, because *they're* twisting *us*!"[429] Supervisors rationalize their own role by blaming recruits: "The corruption is there in the mind every time, we don't corrupt people, we try to put them off, or warn them not to

---

[420] Mars (2006: 290).
[421] Ditton (1977).
[422] Id. 15.
[423] Id. 173.
[424] Id. 9.
[425] Id. 26, citing Goffman (1961: 82).
[426] Id. 17.
[427] Goffman (1961: 155).
[428] Ditton (1977: 30).
[429] Id. 41–42.

overdo it."[430] Indeed, supervisors suspect "those who seem over-eager to fiddle, or who do so too early."

The simplest fiddle was overcharging, which "exploits the trustful basis of customer relations specifically built up for that purpose, with the talent and poise of the con-man."[431] Like other deviants, roundsmen set their own limits, refusing to fiddle the disabled.[432] Some customers tacitly cooperated with the fiddle, passing the costs on to *their* customers[433] (as corporations do when they overlook bill padding by their lawyers). "[O]nce he has fiddled, the salesman can never look at the world in quite the same way."[434]

> No amount of careful chaperoning can wholly obliterate the 'moral experience' of fiddle discovery. . . . Typical misalignment—'surprise, shock, chagrin, anxiety, tension, bafflement, self-questioning'[435]—soon fades as a swift succession of practical experiences prompts case-hardening.[436]

The roundsman "develops attachment to the possible profits and to the increased standard of living that they bring."[437] "[S]upervisors become suddenly willing to offer frank and open descriptions of the fiddle."[438] Defection is discouraged by the threat of bad references.[439] "Training is concluded when fiddle occasions . . . are defined as ordinary."[440] "But teaching the men to fiddle *does* carry the seeds of its own destruction" when roundsmen begin to steal from their employers. (Ditton estimates that employee theft, in which most participate, costs employers more than 16 times as much as burglary and robbery cost their victims.[441]) Employers who socialized employees to fiddle customers respond with moral outrage and sanctions when employees fiddle *them*. One roundsman complained,

---

[430] Id. 25.
[431] Id. 18.
[432] Id. 97.
[433] Id. 19.
[434] Id. 20.
[435] Id. 20, citing Strauss (1959: 93).
[436] Ditton (1977: 34).
[437] Id. 41–42.
[438] Id. 36.
[439] Id. 33.
[440] Id. 40.
[441] Id. 86–88.

"They seem to think that taking bread from them is wrong, and fiddling their customers is right."

The roundsman's ability to fiddle depends on two asymmetries in his relationship to the customer: "The customer's high status is coupled with scanty knowledge, and the server's low status is balanced by the considerable extent and scope of his interaction knowledge." This leads servers to develop cynicism, which Goffman calls "subtle aggressiveness."[442] Interactions "may be sincerely read as 'meaning' (by the customer) or just cynically as 'form' (as the server does)."[443] (Hochschild has generalized this performance of emotions.[444]) "To a service performer, interaction is just talk. And any talk will do. When accused of fiddling, for example, Wellbread salesmen claim 'give' em any excuse and they'll believe it.'"[445] (Lawyers concoct similarly factitious excuses for neglecting clients.) But this cynicism conflicts with management demands "that the men be an absurdly *idealistic* audience" for their customers. "Endless 'sincere' smiling is recommended, along with enthusiasm, courtesy, friendliness, cheerfulness, smartness, and neatness."[446]

Just as Zeitz distinguished women embezzlers' motives, so Ditton differentiates roundsmen fiddlers' styles. The "Rogue" possesses "sufficient interactional ingenuousness to be able to deny the deed, smile, and then, deprecatingly, admit it," while subsequently adopting a tone of "injured righteousness," refusing "to believe he could be in the wrong."[447] The "professional" is the "cool, calculating expert," who deliberately creates trust in all his dealings, paying off potential accusers.[448] "Robin Hoods" claim to act in the public interest, euphemizing stealing and reselling as "recycling." One protested: "I never rob anybody unless they've got more money than I have ... some of them, the old girls, I give them a bit back."[449] The "Shark" steals from his mates, incurring ostracism and status degradation.[450] The "Righteous-straight" are "rule devotees," who perform a "'lateral arabesque' (or, pseudo-promotion)"; they are "funneled into a mock heroisation spiral, typically being sent ... grandly named to a depot where

---

[442] Id. 46, citing Goffman (1959: 22).
[443] Id. 48.
[444] Hochschild (1983).
[445] Ditton (1977: 49).
[446] Id. 55, 59; cf. Hochschild (1983).
[447] Id. 123, 126.
[448] Id. 126–127.
[449] Id. 129.
[450] Id. 130–131.

they can do no further organizational damage."[451] Only certain stylistic transformations are possible: professional to shark and righteous-straight to rogue but neither vice-versa.[452]

Ditton offers an extensive analysis of how fiddling roundsmen respond to accusations. He distinguishes between defensive and offensive denial and three levels of admission: qualified, mitigated, and full.[453] Roundsmen employ a range of strategies to frustrate customer complaints: "tactical righteousness," ignoring the accusation and effectively denying the injury, or just talking to prevent "the free running of alarm." "It becomes clear to the cynical roundsman that the actual content of 'talk' isn't too important." Some "plead variations on the 'I don't know what came over me' theme," while offering restitution.[454]

Roundsmen also must account to themselves. Some adopt a "partial honesty" policy, which "allows the salesman righteously to conceive of himself as not all bad."

> I don't do it all the time . . . you've got to have respect for some people, otherwise life would be unbearable . . . you'd be just one big fiddle, that's all your life would consist of . . . it would make me feel evil if I did it too much.[455]

Lofland calls this "conventionalization": "continuing to believe that the general class of deviance in question is wrong and subjectively unavailable, but managing to avoid defining the actual act as an instance of the subjectively unavailable class."[456]

Roundsmen adopt a variety of guilt reduction devices, which closely track Matza's neutralization techniques[457]: "I couldn't help it"; "they've got you by the short and curlies, by the time you realise that you *can't* check everything, it's too late, you've agreed to pay the shortages"; "it's greed, isn't it? Let's face it, everybody will make an extra couple of bob if he can"; "the way they treat you . . . made you feel, 'Oh. All right, if you're going to rob me, I'm going to rob you'"; "If I don't do it, somebody else will"; "It

---

[451] Id. 133–134.
[452] Id. 136.
[453] Id. 153, Table 6.1.
[454] Id. 159–160.
[455] Id. 164–165.
[456] Lofland (1969: 86).
[457] Matza (1969).

Chapter 1

isn't really me, it's only work."[458] They engage in "insulation": "separating reflected knowledge of self as violator from one's 'natural' self . . . the judged act from the self *itself*."

"At Wellbread's a certain amount of self-*camouflage* is provided by the sheer procedural similarity in skills between fiddling and selling."[459]

> [F]iddling is the sort of deviancy which is "likely to be socially invisible when, to the unwary, it seems to be a natural part of some conventional setting." Within the victim population, the "known aboutness" . . . is slight, and its "obtrusiveness" (the extent to which it interferes with the ongoing interaction) imperceptible. . . . [Fiddling resembles] "situational delicts"; infractions where the victim is not only unaware of the date of the offence and the identity of the culprits . . . but also . . . whether any infraction has in fact occurred.[460]

"Adequately to 'ignore' possible accusations, retaliative counter-denunciation is essential."

The bread salesmen developed a host of rationalizations. "They believe, almost to a man, that fiddling is inevitable, widespread, and thus justifiable. One said to me 'Look, in every job, where there's a loophole, there's a fiddle.'" Another concurred: "*Everybody* is doing it, even the shops where you're doing it, they're doing it to somebody else . . . perhaps even just to the tax man, and the government is doing it to another government."[461] Roundsmen see supervisors doing it to the company—and to other roundsmen.[462] They also see themselves as victims: "The milkman charges me a bit extra every week . . . all door to door selling is the same."[463] As Leff emphasized, there is a close family resemblance between swindling and selling, which share "the cynicism that comes naturally with . . . constantly dealing with stupid people." One roundsman said, "the bloke [customer] is a bloody fool if you can get away with it." Like other criminals, roundsmen find it easier to rationalize stealing from companies: "You don't feel so guilty with the big stores . . . you know that

---

[458] Ditton (1977: 165–166).
[459] Id. 167.
[460] Id. 168, citing Goffman (1963: 67; 1971: 133).
[461] Id. 168–169.
[462] As do other workers, see Horning (1970: 57).
[463] Ditton (1977: 169).

they are allowed wastage"; "it's not like taking it from one person ... the corporation wouldn't be hurt ... they just jack the price up and screw the customer."[464] Underenforcement is construed as tolerance: "They know what goes on, and they don't do much about it."[465] Roundsmen justified fiddling by reference to the onerous work and low pay: "I just think of it as subsidising my wages, that's all."[466]

Because fiddling is what Matza calls a "'subterranean' version of the conventional culture of business," public reaction is "subject to faddish oscillation ranging from sympathetic tolerance to outright suppression."[467] (Public and professional reactions to lawyer "ambulance chasing," which is equally embedded in personal injury practice, display similar alternation between tacit condonation and moral crusade.[468]) "Conventional business manages to succeed only by practising one set of values whilst publicly espousing another." "The fiddler, exasperatingly, actually *operates* upon the basis of capitalism's *justifying* philosophy."[469] "[F]iddling at Wellbread's is psychologically supported by extending the excusing conditions of selling—specifically the caveat emptor rider."[470] Guilt is assuaged "by various counter-denunciations (especially 'they deserve it') which are proudly collected in gullibility testimonials, and shared with peers."[471] "[O]ver-insulation of the self denies the theoretical possibility of apprehension and thus ... cannot prepare the self." The "shock of entrapment hits 'self-made' deviants particularly hard. Adult shoplifters, caught in their 'part-time' occupation frequently resort to 'the lies, rationalisations and alibis characteristic of children.'"[472] "For salesmen at Wellbread's the control context of fiddling is *commercial* rather than *legal*."

> [I]f *legal* control may be characterised as having a moral basis, guilt orientation, formally bureaucratic style, 'fine' technical-judicial decision making, and public hearings; then, in contrast, *commercial* social control has a calculative basis, a profit

---

[464] Id. 170. See also Cahn (1955: 199); Smigel & Ross (1970: 7).
[465] Id. 171.
[466] Id. 171.
[467] Id. 173–174, citing Matza (1969: 105).
[468] Reichstein (1965).
[469] Ditton (1977: 175).
[470] Id. 176.
[471] Id. 179; see also Horning (1970: 72).
[472] Id. 181.

orientation, an eclectic ad hoc ness in its decision making procedures, and a particularly 'rough' sense of justice.[473]

"The structural features of the commercial control setting most emphatically do *not* produce the conditions of identity degradation suffered by 'classical' criminals."[474]

D. Framing Questions about Disciplined Lawyers

The literatures on white-collar crime generally—and specifically that on confidence games, embezzlement, and fiddling—helped frame my inquiry into how and why lawyers betray trust. After centuries of seeking to associate deviance with class, race, skull type, or personality, criminologists now agree that deviants, paradoxically, are not different. Of course they differ in being punished. But no distinctive biologies or biographies destined them for punishment. Nor do all of them suffer from Cressey's nonshareable financial problem (or any other common cause). Whatever challenges they may confront are faced by thousands of other lawyers who do not violate ethical rules. Many lawyers experience pangs of greed and urgings of need, but so do all of us. Even the behavior of the disciplined is not all that different from the conduct of other lawyers. Deviance's very ordinariness is what allows it to persist. Many lawyers learned to violate ethical rules by imitating practices that seemed widely accepted, or at least condoned—a social hypocrisy that fosters cynicism. Indeed, many disciplined lawyers make precisely that complaint: everybody does it, I just happened to get caught. Or worse—I was singled out unfairly. Low levels of apprehension and punishment encourage such beliefs. And just as confidence games, swindling, embezzlement, and fiddling resemble legitimate business activity, so too are the differences between ethical and unethical law practice often are subtle. Both boundaries are much murkier than those demarcating ordinary crimes like murder, rape, and theft. Business and law compel competition—to succeed or survive in the market, to outwit adversaries through negotiation or defeat them in court. Both business and law depend on and engender trust, which creates abundant opportunities to transgress.[475] White-collar criminals and legal ethical violators betray one-shot customers, marks, and clients, who can neither rely on nor shape reputation.

---

[473] Id. 181–182.
[474] Id. 183.
[475] Frankel (2006); Frankel & Fagan (2007).

Like the con man's mark and the swindler's bargain hunter, some clients also are tempted by the same greed that drives their lawyers. Although some lawyers, like grifters and professional embezzlers, rationally choose to violate ethical rules in the pursuit of profit, coldly calculating the unlikelihood of punishment, most drift into such conduct unselfconsciously. That is one reason why they are genuinely surprised (and outraged) when they are caught. It is not their routine deviance but the unpredictable crack-down that calls for explanation (typically in terms of conspiracies—by ungrateful clients, envious competitors, and officious bureaucrats). Whereas ordinary criminals are aware, and sometimes proud, of their outlaw status, white-collar criminals and disciplined lawyers vehemently deny their culpability. They point to their high social status and sterling character not just in mitigation of doing wrong but also as proof that they never could have done wrong. They emphasize the rules they did *not* break. Some advance noble motives: embezzling to save the business (and their employees' jobs) or displaying excessive zeal on behalf of a deserving client. Deviants endlessly invent rationalizations: blaming victims (who sometimes cooperate by blaming themselves), insisting that no one was harmed or that the "victims" could afford it, denying personal cupidity or gain, and offering restitution. All these patterns are evident in the cases that follow.

IV. Learning from Lawyer Discipline

The records of disciplinary proceedings offer an underutilized window on lawyer misconduct. Some researchers have used them to do quantitative evaluations of the regulatory process (speed, case attrition, penalty, bias)[476] or demographic analyses of the kinds of cases or lawyers prosecuted.[477] But only two exploit the records for insight into how and why lawyers misbehave.[478] I first realized the pedagogic potential of case histories when I showed my professional responsibility class a video of four Michigan lawyers talking about their experiences of discipline.[479] But though the screen powerfully communicated the lawyers' personalities, case files are

---

[476] E.g., Gilb (1956); Smith (1961); Marks & Cathcart (1974); Steele & Nimmer (1976); Tisher et al. (1977); New South Wales Law Reform Commission (1979); Brockman & McEwen (1990); Guttenberg (1994); Gallagher (1993; 1995); Arnold & Hagan (1995); Sahl (1999); Moliterno (2005).
[477] Carlin (1966); Shuchman (1968); Arthurs (1970); Royal Commission (1979: vol. 2, sec. 9); Arnold & Hagan (1992).
[478] Kelley (2001); Regan (2004).
[479] Dubin (1985).

CHAPTER 1

far richer and more reliable than the accuseds' inevitably imperfect and biased memories; and the written page can convey greater detail and nuance than the brief statements by talking heads. The disciplinary files also were far more extensive than the 3- to 20-page presentence investigation reports and the 1- to 3-page narrative accounts of offenses used in the most extensive recent American study of white-collar crime.[480] Lawyers record and retain almost every communication with clients, adversaries, and courts. Judicial and disciplinary proceedings produce verbatim transcripts. Prosecutors conduct extensive investigation and discovery. Faced with dishonor, even loss of their careers, accused lawyers use every possible tool to avoid conviction. Disciplinary hearings last days, often weeks, producing thousands of pages of testimony and sometimes almost as many pages of exhibits. If the tribunal finds the lawyers guilty, the penalty phase lets them introduce mitigating evidence, which is often very revealing, about autobiography and character.[481]

I chose to study cases in New York and California for two reasons.[482] First, these are by far the largest jurisdictions in the United States, together containing more than 275,000 lawyers, a quarter of the nation's legal profession and more lawyers than any other country.[483] Second, I teach at UCLA and taught at NYU in the fall of 2003 (when I collected these studies). In both jurisdictions, cases that end in public reprimand, suspension, or disbarment become public records. Despite their drawbacks, these files have one overwhelming advantage over alternative research methods: *others* have spent the thousands of hours gathering, ordering, and presenting voluminous information about the actors and events.

But reliance on disciplinary records inevitably introduces biases.[484] Ethical rules stigmatize some misbehavior more than others. Complainants (overwhelmingly clients, but occasionally opposing counsel or judges), prosecutors, and hearing panels impose their own priorities. Critics have repeatedly noted that solo and small firm lawyers are overrepresented and large firm lawyers underrepresented in disciplinary proceedings.[485] Studying New York City lawyers in 1960, Jerome Carlin found that the frequency of ethical violations varied inversely with client status, firm size,

---

[480] Weisburd et al. (1991: 14–15).
[481] Maruna (2000) argues for the importance of the perpetrator's own narrative.
[482] A forthcoming book will present the California cases.
[483] In 2000 New York had 142,487 (13.2%) and California 133,846 (12.4%). Carson (2004: 49, 161).
[484] Levin (1998).
[485] Shuchman (1968).

and quality of law school attended and directly with the instability of clientele, intensity of competition, client exploitability and expendability, and permissiveness of the office climate.[486] About the same time, Joel Handler found similar patterns in a midwestern city of 80,000, even though the bar was not stratified.[487] A study of Australian lawyers 20 years later also found that complaints against lawyers varied inversely with firm size: nearly half targeted solo practitioners, who were little more than a quarter of the profession; only 12 percent targeted 4–9 partner firms, containing 22 percent of lawyers; and just 1 percent named the larger firms, containing 10 percent.[488] In California in 2000–2001, more than two-thirds of investigations and more than three-fourths of prosecutions involved solo practitioners, who were less than a fourth of all lawyers, whereas just 5 percent of investigations and 2 percent of prosecutions involved firms of 11 or more, containing 42 percent of all lawyers.[489]

Six of the seven New York City lawyers I studied effectively practiced alone (if some were nominally associated with others). The one exception—a partner in an elite real estate boutique firm—also engaged in atypical misbehavior. I make no claim, therefore, that my cases are representative of the population of lawyer misconduct. We will need many more case studies before drawing even a tentative map of this terrain. Nor do I believe my cases constitute the most serious misconduct. Certainly scandals implicating large firm lawyers—OPM in the 1970s,[490] the savings and loan collapse of the 1980s,[491] and the financial scams of the 1990s (of which Enron is iconic)[492]—cost many more people much more money. Each of those affairs deserves its own book—as shown by Milton Regan in his excellent case study of a Milbank Tweed partner[493] and Susan Shapiro in her magnificent account of the complexities of conflict of interest (which especially bedevils large firm practice).[494] I hope there will be many more such narratives. But the power of corporations and their lawyers to inflict massive harm should not blind us to the serious injuries caused by

---

[486] Carlin (1966: tables 42, 44, 45, 48, 49, 74, 76, 117, 133).
[487] Handler (1967: chapter 6).
[488] New South Wales Law Reform Commission (1980: 16, 23).
[489] State Bar of California (2001: tables II–III). The Bar concluded that the complainants, not the disciplinary process, were responsible for this disparity.
[490] Gandossy (1985).
[491] Law & Social Inquiry (1998).
[492] Swartz & Watkins (2003); McLean & Elkind (2003).
[493] Regan (2004).
[494] Shapiro (2002).

CHAPTER 1

solo and small firm lawyers. As recently as 2000, after all, 48 percent of all private practitioners worked alone, and another 15 percent practiced in 2–5 lawyer firms; together they constituted nearly two-thirds of the private practicing profession.[495] Furthermore, almost all individual and small business clients use those lawyers.

In order to choose my New York cases, I read more than 200 opinions by the Appellate Division First Department (which regulates lawyers in Manhattan), gradually developing categories of the most common situations. I chose not to pursue several. One of the most common causes of discipline—commingling and misappropriating client trust accounts[496]—also is one of the least interesting. The rules are clear, the conduct unambiguously wrong, and the motives banal (cash flow problems, substance abuse, marital acrimony). Simple technical reforms (greater control by banks, regular or random audits, mandatory liability insurance), already in place in other jurisdictions, could greatly reduce the incidence.[497] Lawyers are disbarred automatically following felony convictions, but many of these crimes have little to do with their professional roles.[498] The same is true of discipline for fraud and nonpayment of civil judgments. Some of the behaviors the profession has outlawed—notably solicitation of personal injury clients—seems to me unobjectionable, even praiseworthy.[499] And some interesting cases were quite rare: sexual harassment, sending anonymous defamatory letters, providing false information to the police.

That left me with three categories: neglect, excessive fees, and overzealous advocacy. The first two are the most common reasons for client complaints. The *ABAJ* recently included them in its "Top 10 Ethics Traps."[500] (Delay also is one of the most frequent complaints of patients about health care systems.[501]) The last, although infrequent, complements

---

[495] Carson (2004: tables 7, 8).
[496] 83% of disbarments in Ontario. Arthurs (1970: 240).
[497] In 2004, 33 states required financial institutions to notify the lawyer disciplinary body of an overdraft on a client trust account; 11 states conducted random audits. Most states have client protection funds, but the ceilings are low. Hazard et al. (2005: 816).
[498] Pinaire et al. (2006).
[499] Abel (1987).
[500] Ward (2007).
[501] British Medical Association (2003). After a 74-year-old woman died of an aneurysm while pleading to see her doctor in a Kaiser Permanente waiting room in 2002, the California legislature directed the Department of Managed Health Care to promulgate rules to remedy this. But although the law required the rules by January 2004, the Department did not release its proposal until 2007. And when HMOs and doctors objected, the Department gave them until

the others in two respects: it is one of the most common sources of *lawyer* dissatisfaction (about discourtesy and loss of gentility in the profession)[502]; and it is the inverse of the others, exhibiting excessive loyalty to clients rather than too little. Within each category I looked for extreme cases, which were more dramatic and, arguably, more revealing of underlying motivation. True, they are less typical. But because a few recidivist lawyers (like other deviants) are responsible for multiple ethical violations,[503] it is especially important to understand their behavior.

That neglect is the single most common complaint by individual clients is confirmed by more than 40 studies, ranging over 75 years and across many American jurisdictions, Canada, the UK, Scotland, Australia, and Denmark.[504] Interviews with disciplinary personnel in 17 American jurisdictions in the early 1970s found that clients complained most frequently about lawyer unresponsiveness.[505] The most comprehensive public opinion survey found that, though most Americans who had used lawyers called them highly attentive, significant proportions rated them poor or fair for promptness (13%), concern (14%), explaining (13%), keeping clients informed (21%), and paying attention (11%).[506] The general public (including those who had not used lawyers) were more critical: 59 percent agreed that lawyers were not prompt about getting things done, 39 percent that "lawyers will take a case ... (even) if they (do not) feel sure they know enough about that area of the law to handle the case well," 33 percent that "lawyers work harder at getting clients than in serving them," and 50 percent that "lawyers are generally not very good at keeping their clients informed

---

October 2008 to suggest their own. Jordan Rau, "Rules for HMOs are in limbo," Los Angeles Times B1 (2.5.08).

[502] Kronman (1993); Glendon (1994); Linowitz (1994).

[503] Of the subjects of complaints in New South Wales, 86% had been the subject of other complaints. New South Wales Law Reform Commission (1980: 22). The same is true of drunk drivers, career criminals, polluters, etc.

[504] Abel (2006: 1495-1498); see also Attorney Grievance Commission of Maryland, 28th Ann. Report: July 1, 2002, through June 30, 2003, Exhibit B (twice as many disciplined for neglect and failure to communicate than for any other violation); Attorney Registration & Disciplinary Commission of the Supreme Court of Illinois, 2002 Ann. Rep., pt. II.D.; Michigan Attorney Discipline Board, 2003 Ann. Rep, app. B; Lawyers' Professional Responsibility Board of Minn., Ann. Rep. 18 (2003) (60/81 open probation files); Disciplinary Commission of the Supreme Court of Indiana, 2002-2003 Ann. Rep., App. D (third of pending grievances); Report of the Official of Chief Disciplinary Counsel, 59 J. Mo. B. 233, 246 (2003) (largest category of grievances); Va. State Bar, Office of Bar Counsel, 2001-2002 Ann. Rep. 1 (most common complaint).

[505] Marks & Cathcart (1974: 210).

[506] Curran (1977: table 5.15).

CHAPTER 1

of progress on their cases."[507] Not surprisingly, neglect also is the single largest cause of malpractice claims.[508] Other common law jurisdictions report similar findings. Nearly a third of English respondents felt that solicitors did not take sufficient interest or do enough (30%) or were too slow (29%), and nearly a sixth (15%) felt solicitors did not communicate with clients or keep them informed of progress.[509] The same was true in Northern Ireland[510] and Scotland.[511] In Australia, delay was the most common complaint to the New South Wales Law Society (29%), followed by negligence (12%) and poor communication (8%).[512]

Although all clients resent lawyers' fees, individual clients do so most strongly. More than half the American public agreed that "lawyers' fees are (not) usually fair to their clients," and more than two-thirds believed that "most lawyers charged more for their services than they are worth."[513] A 1970s study found that fee agreements were rarely reduced to writing.[514] In Denmark, fee disputes were a third of all complaints.[515] Fee disputes were less prominent in Britain[516] and Australia,[517] perhaps because of the widespread availability of legal aid and fee shifting to losing parties. Still, 40% of English respondents thought lawyers were "mainly after your money," and 45% felt "their charges are too high for the work they do."[518] Many dissatisfied clients complain about their fees to disciplinary bodies.[519] Although these refer most such disputes to arbitration, some complaints do implicate ethical rules.

Clients, of course, do not complain about their own lawyers' excessive zeal. Rather, many lawyers feel pressure from clients to facilitate

---

[507] Id. tables 6.2, 6.3, 6.8.
[508] Pfennigstorf (1980: tables 3–4); Gates (1984; 1985–1986); ABA Standing Committee (1986; 1996: tables 3–5).
[509] Royal Commission (1979: vol. 2, table 8.34); see also Justice (1970: 12); Lewis (1996: table 4.26).
[510] Royal Commission (1979: 22.48).
[511] Royal Commission on Legal Services in Scotland (1980: vol. 2, Appendix 4, tables 33–34, 37–38, 41).
[512] New South Wales Law Reform Commission (1980: 12, 13, 57–59).
[513] Curran (1977: table 6.4).
[514] Steele & Nimmer (1976: 852–854).
[515] Blomquist (2000: Appendix 2, table 2).
[516] Royal Commission (1979: vol. 2, table 8.34); Royal Commission on Legal Services in Scotland (1980: tables 35–36).
[517] New South Wales Law Reform Commission (1980: 57–59, 109).
[518] Jenkins & Lewis (1995: table 23).
[519] Second most common complaint to the Illinois State Bar Association, 1928–1948. Steele & Nimmer (1976: table 6); 24% of complaints to Solicitors Complaints Bureau. Lewis (1996: table 4.26).

illegal activity.[520] And 38 percent of Americans believe that "most lawyers would engage in unethical or illegal activities to help a client in an important case."[521]

In the following chapters, I introduce each of these topics, explicating the ethical rules governing lawyer behavior and analyzing how disciplinary bodies have dealt with violations before presenting the case studies.

---

[520] Levin (1994); Levi et al. (2004); Rostain (2006b); Simon (2007).
[521] Curran (1977: table 6.5).

Part One

Neglect

New York forbids a lawyer to "handle a legal matter which the lawyer knows or should know that he or she is not competent to handle," to do so "without preparation adequate in the circumstances," or to "neglect a legal matter entrusted to the lawyer."[522] Although New York forbids a lawyer to fail "intentionally" "to carry out a contract of employment,"[523] it has not adopted several more specific Model Rules requirements: "reasonable diligence and promptness,"[524] keeping the client "reasonably informed" and "promptly comply[ing] with reasonable requests for information,"[525] making "reasonable efforts to expedite litigation,"[526] and making "reasonable efforts" to ensure that supervised lawyers conform to the Rules.[527]

The real problem, however, is not the standard's vagueness but its enforcement. As I mentioned in the first chapter, neglect is the most common ground of malpractice claims. Liability is relatively easy to prove.[528] But clients need to know that counsel have been negligent; lawyers compound laypersons' difficulty in evaluating professional negligence by denying them essential information.[529] And there is little point in suing unless lawyers have malpractice insurance: Oregon is the *only* jurisdiction requiring it. Only four states compel lawyers to tell clients whether they carry minimum insurance; another five mandate disclosure only on the annual registration statement (which few clients know about and fewer consult). Although premiums are relatively low compared to those for

---

[522] DR 6-101, 22 N.Y.C.R.R. § 1200.30. The Model Rules have moved this to 1.1, where it belongs.
[523] DR 7-101, 22 N.Y.C.R.R. § 1200.32.
[524] Model Rule 1.3.
[525] Model Rule 1.4(a)(3) and 1.4(a)(4).
[526] Model Rule 3.2.
[527] Model Rule 5.1.
[528] dePape v. Trinity Health Systems, Inc., 242 F. Supp.2d 585 (N.D. Iowa 2003); Ramos (1994; 1995).
[529] Lerman (1990: 722 n.261) (concealing that lawyer failed to meet deadline).

PART ONE

doctors,[530] large proportions of the bar go bare—especially those lawyers most likely to commit malpractice.

Clients may alleviate the harms of neglect by seeking to reopen adverse decisions on grounds of inadequate assistance of counsel (although this does nothing to deter or punish lawyer misbehavior). In 1984 the U.S. Supreme Court established criteria for criminal defense that satisfied the Sixth Amendment right to counsel.[531] Subsequent studies, however, have found that the decision had little effect: over five years only 4 percent of challenges succeeded, and *none* in 6 of the 12 circuits.[532] Defense counsel conducted no investigation and made no motions in three-fourths of New York City homicide cases and in an even higher proportion of other felonies—and they gave clients as little as 15 seconds to decide whether to accept a plea.[533] Courts are even less sympathetic to such claims in civil cases. Clients generally are bound by their lawyers' actions.[534] Many jurisdictions set aside civil judgments only if lawyers engaged in "positive misconduct."[535]

That leaves clients with only one remedy: a disciplinary complaint. But most disciplinary bodies are reluctant to punish neglect with more than a private admonition.[536] For suspension or disbarment they require egregious misconduct.[537] I read some 40 cases of public discipline by the First Department for neglect between 1999 and 2003. Although many substantive areas were represented, these lawyers tended to practice

---

[530] Recently they were about $4,000, compared to hundreds of thousands for some doctors. Gail Cox, "Malpractice Epidemic Is Receding," Nat'l L.J., Mar. 16, 1998, at A1; John Gibeaut, "Good News, Bad News on Malpractice," ABAJ 100 (Mar. 1997); David Hechler, "Malpractice Policies Going Up," Nat'l L. J., June 3, 2002, at A1.
[531] Strickland v. Washington, 466 U.S. 668 (1984) (death penalty defense).
[532] Georgetown Law Journal (1988).
[533] McConville & Mirsky (1987).
[534] Link v. Wabash R.R. Co., 370 U.S. 626 (1962) (client bound by lawyer's failure to attend pretrial conference); but see Gardner v. United States, 211 F.3d 1305 (D.C. Cir. 2000) (reversing dismissal for lawyer failure to attend motions hearing).
[535] Daley v. County of Butte, 227 Cal. App.2d 380, 38 Cal. Rptr. 693 (1964); Carroll v. Abbott Lab. Inc, 32 Cal.3d 892, 187 Cal. Rptr. 592, 654 P.2d 775 (1982) (misconduct must obliterate attorney-client relationship); but see Panzino v. City of Phoenix, 196 Ariz. 442, 999 P.2d. 198 (2000) (rejecting rule); Community Dental Services v. Tani, 282 F.3d 1164 (9th Cir. 2002) (allowing relief where lawyer's gross negligence resulted in default).
[536] Florida Bar v. Neale, 384 So. 2d 1264 (Fla. 1980); Committee on Legal Ethics v. Mullins, 226 S.E.2d 427 (W.Va. 1976); ABA Informal Op. 1273 (1973); ABA Comm. on Ethics and Prof. Resp., Formal Op. 335 (1974).
[537] Attorney Grievance Comm'n v. Werner, 553 A.2d 722 (Md.) 1989); Office of Disciplinary Counsel v. Henry, 664 S.W.2d 62 (Tenn. 1983); In re Albert, 212 N.W.2d 17 (Mich. 1973); In re Kennedy, 176 S.E.2d 125 (S.C. 1970); Matter of Neal, 20 P.3d 121 (N.M. 2001); see Green (2003).

personal injury,[538] immigration,[539] divorce,[540] real estate,[541] and estates law.[542] Some of these lawyers committed other offenses as well: misappropriation of client escrow accounts,[543] overdrawing of client escrow accounts,[544] failure to return unearned fees,[545] and wrongful payment of their own fees out of the estate.[546]

Lawyers offered a variety of excuses for neglecting clients. One argued that incompetence was to be expected; after all, law practice was not "brain surgery" or "rocket science." He found writing letters to clients burdensome and had no secretary. He accepted too many cases because, as a former legal aid lawyer, he claimed he was "too caring an individual."[547] Another stated that he had expanded his solo practice too rapidly.[548] (Other jurisdictions have consistently held that workload does not excuse neglect.[549]) One blamed his personal injury clients for his own failure to pursue their claims.[550] Another argued that an intransigent insurer was responsible his own failure for 12 years to tell a client he had been unable to settle a personal injury claim.[551] One justified inaction on the grounds that he was a "country lawyer," retained to find an experienced personal injury attorney, and that he had appeared only as a "convenience" to the client.

---

[538] Matter of Lawrence, 748 N.Y.S.2d 749 (1st Dept. 2002); Matter of de la Cruz, 746 N.Y.S.2d 162 (1st Dept. 2002); Matter of Hubbert, 735 N.Y.S.2d 118 (1st Dept. 2002); Matter of LeBow, 727 N.Y.S.2d 88 (1st Dept. 2001); Matter of Mager, 723 N.Y.S.2d 470 (1st Dept. 2001); Matter of Birman, 710 N.Y.S.2d 596 (1st Dept. 2000); Matter of Nwaka, 707 N.Y.S.2d 458 (1st Dept. 2000); Matter of Gould, 686 N.Y.S.2d 759 (1st Dept. 1999) (two prior admonitions).

[539] Matter of Leavitt, 738 N.Y.S.2d 313 (1st Dept. 2002); Matter of Anschell, 731 N.Y.S.2d 145 (1st Dept. 2001); Matter of Gural, 2003 WL 21027651 (N.Y. App. Div. 1st Dept. 2003); Matter of Bechet, 713 N.Y.S.2d 735 (1st Dept. 2000); Matter of Brooks, 708 N.Y.S.2d 22 (1st Dept. 2000).

[540] Matter of Hubbert, 735 N.Y.S.2d 118 (1st Dept. 2002); Matter of Rodriguez, 732 N.Y.S.2d 398 (1st Dept. 2001); Matter of Rosenkrantz, 2003 WL 1995645 (N.Y. App. Div. 1st Dept. 2003); Matter of Frank, 695 N.Y.S.2d 91 (1st Dept. 1999).

[541] Matter of Block, 723 N.Y.S.2d 23 (1st Dept. 2001).

[542] Matter of Mager, 723 N.Y.S.2d 470 (1st Dept. 2001); Matter of Silberstein, 709 N.Y.S.2d 185 (1st Dept. 2000); Matter of Lubin, 694 N.Y.S.2d 357 (1st Dept. 1999); Matter of Hecht, 687 N.Y.S.2d 48 (1st Dept. 1999); Matter of Zucker, 685 N.Y.S.2d 187 (1st Dept. 1999).

[543] Matter of Lawrence, 748 N.Y.S.2d 749 (1st Dept. 2002).

[544] Matter of Rodriguez, 732 N.Y.S.2d 398 (1st Dept. 2001); Matter of Mager, 723 N.Y.S.2d 470 (1st Dept. 2001).

[545] Matter of Anschell, 731 N.Y.S.2d 145 (1st Dept. 2001).

[546] Matter of Silberstein, 709 N.Y.S.2d 185 (1st Dept. 2000).

[547] Matter of Hubbert, 735 N.Y.S.2d 118 (1st Dept. 2002).

[548] Matter of Frank, 695 N.Y.S.2d 91 (1st Dept. 1999).

[549] Matter of Loomos, 90 Wash.2d 98, 579 P.2d 350 (1978); In re Fraser, 83 Wash.2d 884, 523 P.2d 921 (1974).

[550] Matter of Gould, 686 N.Y.S.2d 759 (1st Dept. 1999) (AD found some of these allegations credible).

[551] Matter of Mager, 723 N.Y.S.2d 470 (1st Dept. 2001).

Although he claimed to have the file in storage, he admitted, first, that it was only a few "pieces of paper," and then that it was just a "file jacket."[552] One lawyer conceded his neglect but sought immunity from discipline on the grounds that immigration counseling was not the practice of law.[553] Some fabricated documents to create the illusion of activity.[554] Because neglect tended to be chronic, several lawyers were recidivists.[555] Some moved across jurisdictions to evade punishment.[556] A few fled to their countries of origin.[557] Reenacting the behavior charged, some did not even bother to answer the complaint or defend themselves,[558] although they occasionally sought to justify noncooperation with the DDC.[559] Some accepted suspension on grounds of physical or mental disability.[560]

---

[552] Matter of LeBow, 727 N.Y.S.2d 88 (1st Dept. 2001).

[553] Matter of Bechet, 713 N.Y.S.2d 735 (1st Dept. 2001).

[554] Matter of Block, 723 N.Y.S.2d 23 (1st Dept. 2001) (letter to judge and three proposed orders); Matter of Silberstein, 709 N.Y.S.2d 185 (1st Dept 2000).

[555] Matter of de la Cruz, 746 N.Y.S.2d 162 (1st Dept. 2002) (suspended in 2001 for neglect and abandonment of practice); Matter of Stein, 745 N.Y.S.2d 540 (1st Dept. 2002) (ignored complaints of neglect in 2000); Matter of Stein, 731 N.Y.S.2d 735 (1st Dept. 2001); Matter of Hubbert, 735 N.Y.S.2d 118 (1st Dept. 2002) (ignored complaints of neglect in 2000); Matter of Lenoir, 733 N.Y.S.2d 178 (1st Dept. 2002) (admonished for neglect in 1987 and for neglect and misrepresentation to client in 1995); Matter of LeBow, 727 N.Y.S.2d 88 (1st Dept. 2001) (admonished in 1995 for multiple violations); Matter of Rosenkrantz, 2003 WL 1995645 (N.Y. App. Div. 1st Dept. 2001) (admonished in 1996 for threatening adversary with criminal prosecution); Matter of Silberstein, 709 N.Y.S.2d 185 (1st Dept. 2000) (admonished for advancing fees to self in estate matters in 1989 and 1994); Matter of Reaves, 707 N.Y.S.2d 459 (1st Dept 2000) (suspended in 1998 for failure to cooperate with neglect investigation); Matter of Brooks, 708 N.Y.S.2d 22 (1st Dept. 2000) (two earlier admonitions for neglect and 1998 suspension for failure to cooperate with neglect investigation); Matter of Lubin, 694 N.Y.S.2d 357 (1st Dept. 1999); Matter of Gould, 686 N.Y.S.2d 759 (1st Dept. 1999); Matter of Hecht, 687 N.Y.S.2d 48 (1st Dept. 1999) (admonished for neglect three times between 1993 and 1995); Matter of Zucker, 685 N.Y.S.2d 197 (1st Dept. 1999) (admonished in same matter in 1998).

[556] Matter of Anschell, 731 N.Y.S.2d 145 (1st Dept. 2001) (Washington state to Alberta to NY to Alberta to NY).

[557] Matter of de la Cruz, 746 N.Y.S.2d 162 (1st Dept. 2002) (Philippines); Matter of Gujral, 2003 WL 21027651 (N.Y. App. Div. 1st Dept. 2003) (India); Matter of Saffir, 703 N.Y.S.2d 30 (1st Dept. 2000) (presumed to have fled abroad).

[558] Matter of Muri, 755 N.Y.S.2d 75 (1st Dept. 2003); Matter of Lawrence, 748 N.Y.S.2d 749 (1st Dept. 2002) (not at office listed with OCA; not represented by lawyer whose name he gave); Matter of Stein, 745 N.Y.S.2d 540 (1st Dept. 2002); Matter of Hubbert, 735 N.Y.S.2d 118 (1st Dept. 2002); Matter of Alpert, 733 N.Y.S.2d 5 (1st Dept. 2001); Matter of Mager, 723 N.Y.S.2d 470 (1st Dept. 2001) (blamed nonappearance on court appearances without docket numbers and medical problems without doctors visits); Matter of Birman, 710 N.Y.S.2d 596 (1st Dept. 2000); Matter of Ageloff, 709 N.Y.S.2d 564 (1st Dept. 2000); Matter of Donovan, 706 N.Y.S.2d 103 (1st Dept. 2000) (evaded DDC and then claimed lack of notice in Idaho); Matter of Ghinger, 687 N.Y.S.2d 72 (1st Dept. 1999); Matter of Zucker, 685 N.Y.S.2d 187 (1st Dept. 1999).

[559] Matter of Siegel, 754 N.Y.S.2d 1 (1st Dept. 2002).

[560] Matter of Feuerstein, 711 N.Y.S.2d 12 (1st Dept. 2001); Matter of Hecht, 687 N.Y.S.2d 48 (1st Dept. 1999).

Two of the neglect cases I present below involved lawyers handling large numbers of cases: personal injury in one instance, immigration in the other. To do this, the lawyers needed to generate and dispose of the volume. They relied heavily on non-lawyers for both. This practice implicated other ethical rules. New York prohibits lawyers from engaging in personal or telephone solicitation or paying for referrals from laypersons (who may solicit).[561] It also prohibits lawyers from aiding the unauthorized practice of law or sharing fees with non-lawyers.[562]

American lawyers (even more than their counterparts in other countries) long have aggressively defined, expanded, and defended the boundaries of their monopoly.[563] One of the early, notorious attempts was the prosecution of the author of the book *How to Avoid Probate*.[564] State bars have tried to define the provision of printed legal forms—and, more recently, software—as unauthorized practice of law.[565] Jurisdictions have enjoined a variety of legal acts[566]: the preparation of no-fault divorce papers,[567] estate planning instruments,[568] and living trusts[569]; the creation and transfer of land trusts[570]; the representation of consumer groups and trade associations[571];

---

[561] DR 2-103(a)(1), (b), N.Y.C.R.R. § 1200.8. Bailey v. Morales, 190 F.3d 320 (5th Cir. 1999) (Texas statute regulating ambulance chasing by chiropractors and others violates First Amendment).

[562] DR. 3-101(a), N.Y.C.C.R. § 1200.16; DR 3-102(a), N.Y.C.C.R. § 1200.17.

[563] Rhode (1981); Denckla (1999); Rose (2002).

[564] Matter of New York County Lawyers' Association v. Dacey, 28 A.D.2d 161, rev'd on dissenting opinion in Appellate Division, 21 N.Y.2d 694 (1967); Dacey (1965).

[565] Palmer v. Unauthorized Practice of Law Committee, 438 S.W.2d 374 (Tex. App. 1969) (sale of will forms with instructions UAP); Unauthorized Practice of Law Committee v. Cortez, 692 S.W.2d 47 (Tex. 1985) (advising whether to file form is UAP); Unauthorized Practice of Law Committee v. Parsons Technology, Inc., 1999 WL 47235 (N.D. Texas 1999), vacated and remanded, 179 F.3d 956 (5th Cir. 1999) (Texas legislature amended law after district court held Quicken Family Lawyer software to be UAP); People v. Landlords Prof'l Servs., 215 Cal. App.3d 1599 (1989) (selling kit or filling out form not UAP but advice is); New Jersey State Bar Ass'n v. Divorce Ctr. Of Atlantic County, 194 N.J. Super. 532, 477 A.2d 415 (Ch. Div. 1984) (Ibid.); Fadia v. Unauthorized Practice of Law Comm., 830 S.W.2d 162 (Tex. App. 1992) (will kits UAP); Office of Disciplinary Counsel v. Palmer, 115 Ohio Misc.2d 70, 761 N.E.2d 716 (Bd. Unauth. Prac. 2001) (general advice not UAP); State v. Winder, 42 A.D.2d 1039 (1973) (divorce kits not UAP).

[566] See Selinger (1996).

[567] Florida Bar v. Brumbaugh, 355 So. 2d 1186 (Fla. 1978); Florida Bar v. Furman, 451 So. 2d 808 (Fla. 1984), appeal dismissed, 444 U.S. 1061 (1980). For a critical view, see Rhode (1976).

[568] In re Mid-America Living Trust Associates, Inc. 927 S.W.2d 855 (Mo. 1996).

[569] Florida Bar re Advisory Opinion—Nonlawyer Preparation of Living Trusts, 613 So. 2d 426 (Fla. 1992); Florida Bar v. American Senior Citizens Alliance, 689 So. 2d 255 (Fla. 1997).

[570] Florida Bar v. Hughes, 824 So. 2d 154 (Fla. 2002).

[571] Idaho St. Bar Ass'n v. Idaho Pub. Utilities Comm'n, 637 P.2d 1188 (Idaho 1981); Turkey Point Property Owners' Association, Inc. v. Anderson, 666 A.2d 904 (Md. App. 1995);

Part One

the transfer of real property by non-lawyer escrow agents[572]; the preparation of quit claim deeds to divide real property[573]; and the offering of oral advice.[574] Lawyers have been prosecuted and disciplined for helping laypeople practice law.[575] But some jurisdictions have allowed laypeople to perform limited functions: to use form contracts for house sales,[576] prepare mortgage documents,[577] provide limited advice on completing legal forms,[578] complete and file legal documents,[579] represent employees in labor grievances[580] and before unemployment compensation boards,[581] collect debts,[582] and file bankruptcy petitions.[583] Virginia has gone further than most, letting laypeople represent clients before tribunals, act as claims adjusters and collection agencies, do estate planning and settlement, proffer tax advice, conduct real estate transactions, and represent trade associations before administrative agencies.[584] However, efforts to rationalize and liberalize these rules generally have been unsuccessful.[585] An ABA proposal to let non-lawyers appear before state administrative agencies never made

---

[572] State Bar of Arizona v. Arizona Land Title & Trust Co., 366 P.2d 1 (Ariz. 1961), opinion on rehearing, 371 P.2d 1020 (Ariz. 1962). This was overturned by a constitutional amendment, which passed overwhelmingly. Merton E. Marks, "The Lawyers and the Realtors: Arizona's Experience," 49 ABAJ 129 (1963); Bennion, Van Camp, Hagen & Ruhl v. Kassler Escrow, Inc., 635 P.2d 730 (Wash. 1981) (en banc) (invalidating statute authorizing real estate brokers and title companies to transfer property).

[573] Fifteenth Judicial District Unified Bar Ass'n v. Glasgow, 1999 WL 1128847 (Tenn. App. 1999).

[574] People v. Divorce Associated & Publishing Limited, 407 N.Y.S.2d 142 (1978); Matter of Estate of Margow, 77 N.J. 316 (1978); Florida Bar v. Brower, 402 So. 2d 1171 (Fla. 1981); Oregon State Bar v. Smith, 942 P.2d 793 (Or. App. 1997); Florida Bar v. Schramek, 616 So. 2d 979 (Fla. 1993); Lawline v. American Bar Association, 956 F.2d 1378 (7th Cir. 1992), cert. denied, 510 U.S. 992 (1993) (ABA rules upheld against challenge by lawyers, paralegals and laypeople answering legal questions and referring clients to legal aid and low-fee lawyers).

[575] People v. Macy, 789 P.2d 188 (Colo. 1990) (reviewing living trust forms a lay person will sell); In re Juhnke, 273 Kan. 162 (2002) (employing a disbarred lawyer).

[576] Cultum v. Heritage House Realtors, Inc., 694 P.2d 630 (Wash. 1985); In re Opinion No. 26 of the Comm. On the Unauthorized Practice of Law, 654 A.2d 1344 (N.J. 1995); Countrywide Home Loans, Inc. v. Kentucky Bar Ass'n, 113 S.W.3d 105 (Ky. 2003).

[577] Perkins v. CTX Mortgage Co., 969 P.2d 93 (Wash. 1999).

[578] In re Amendment to Rules Regulating the Florida Bar, 510 So. 2d 596 (Fla. 1987).

[579] Arizona Code of Judicial Administration § 7-208 (certified legal document preparers).

[580] Hunt v. Maricopa County Employees Merit System Commission, 127 Ariz. 259, 619 P.2d 1036 (1980).

[581] Henize v. Giles, 22 Ohio St.3d 213, 490 N.E.2d 585 (1986).

[582] National Revenue Corp. v. Violet, 807 F.2d 285 (1st Cir. 1986) (invalidating Rhode Island law preventing all but RI lawyers from doing debt collection).

[583] Wall Street Journal, August 28, 1991, at B4.

[584] Virginia Supreme Court, Unauthorized Practice Rules and Considerations; Consumer Real Estate Settlement Protection Act, Va. Code §§ 6.1-2.19 et seq.; Real Estate Settlement Agent Registration Act, Virginia Code §§ 6-1-2.30.

[585] Justice (1991); Benedectis (1991); Talamante (1992).

it to the House of Delegates.[586] The ABA abandoned its attempt to draft a uniform definition of the practice of law, and the Department of Justice threatened it with anti-trust prosecution.[587]

Lawyers have attempted to lower the price of their own services by "unbundling": limiting their work by leaving some tasks to pro se clients.[588] But this may expose lawyers to discipline[589] or malpractice liability.[590] They have sought to reduce their costs by delegating to paralegals,[591] but they may be disciplined for allowing non-lawyer employees to do lawyers' work,[592] and they are liable for the quality of the work product.

The First Department has routinely enforced anti-solicitation rules against lawyers who paid for cases.[593] After New Jersey disciplined several lawyers for setting up an RV near the Durham Woods Apartment Complex following a catastrophic gas explosion, New York acted reciprocally.[594] One such case had interesting parallels to the second story I narrate below.[595] Curt Meltzer formed Golden Mountain International Inc. with his long-time paralegal and office manager, Annie Chan-Eng, sharing ownership and profits equally. He facilitated her practice of immigration law—and both of them neglected clients. When two clients demanded their fees back, Meltzer wrote them angry letters and threatened to call

---

[586] ABA Comm'n on Nonlawyer Practice (1994); ABA (1995); Crystal (2001).
[587] "Utah and Arizona Define Practice of Law: ABA Group Opts Not to Set Model Definition," 71 U.S.L.W. 2642 (Apr. 15, 2003).
[588] ABCNY Ethics Committee (1996); ABA Section of Litigation (2003); MacNeal (1997); Hyman & Silver (1998).
[589] Maryland Legal Assistance Network, Informal National Survey of Ethical Opinions Related to "Discrete Task Lawyering" (2003) (unethical to write pleadings, sell divorce forms or advise clients without accepting responsibility as a lawyer); Ricotta v. California, 4 F. Supp. 2d 961 (S.D. Cal. 1998) (ghost-writing pleading is evasion of responsibility).
[590] Nichols v. Keller, 15 Cal.App.4th 1672 (1993) (filing workers compensation claim without advising about third party tort claim could be malpractice "even when retention is expressly limited"); Keef v. Widuch, 747 N.E.2d 992 (Ill. Ct. App. 2001) (Ibid.).
[591] ABA Standing Committee (1991); ABA (1998).
[592] In re Lester, 578 S.E.2d 7 (S.C. 2003) (real estate closings); In re Sledge, 859 So. 2d 6761 (La. 2003) (volume solo practitioner let subordinates use his signature stamp on pleadings, discovery responses, and correspondence); Spencer v. Steinman, 179 F.R.D. 484 (E.D. Pa. 1998) (failure to supervise paralegal who issued subpoena to nonparty without notice to parties); Mays v. Neal, 938 S.W.2d 830 (Ark. 1997).
[593] Matter of Santalone, 750 N.Y.S.2d 272 (1st Dept. 2002); Matter of Hankin, 745 N.Y.S.2d 169 (1st Dept. 2002); Matter of Setareh, 703 N.Y.S.2d 91 (1st Dept. 2000).
[594] In re Ravich, Koster, Tobin, Oleckna, Reitman & Greenstein, 715 A.2d 216 (N.J. 1998); Matter of Meaden, 697 N.Y.S.2d 285 (1st Dept. 1999).
[595] Matter of Meltzer, 741 N.Y.S.2d 240 (1st Dept. 2002).

the police if they came to his office. The Appellate Division censured him.

In the following three cases, I seek to explain how the lawyers came to neglect their clients, through reference to both structural variables (firm, clientele, and subject matter) and biography (history and character).

Chapter 2

Juggling Too Many Balls

I. Mass Processing Personal Injuries

David Kreitzer grew up in Cambria Heights, Queens, graduated from the University of Louisville in 1969, taught special education for a year, and then worked his way through John Marshall Law School in Chicago (day and evening), graduating in 1974, when he was admitted to the New York bar. He was married, with two daughters (13 and 21) at the time of the 1994 disciplinary hearing. He began his legal career at Shank and Steifman, a commercial practice in Hempstead, leaving after six months to do collections for Senate & Krumholz until 1981 or 1982. He was treated at Sloan Kettering for Hodgkin's disease in 1976. "I continued to work throughout the period of time that I was under treatment—didn't miss a day's work, except for the initial . . . hospitalization," he stated. When his own practice grew large enough he went solo as a personal injury lawyer, starting with a hundred cases. By 1988 he had a thousand active files and was working seven days a week, assisted by a secretary and some part-time help. In 1987 he hired his first associate, Sheldon Liebenstein, a recent graduate. "The majority of cases I was working on them, on a day to day basis. Once in a while I would say to him, you know, this is your file, work on this." Within a year he replaced Liebenstein with Leonard Shube, another recent law graduate. In 1989 Kreitzer went into partnership with Donald Vogelman, who handled only criminal cases. That year doctors found a large tumor in Kreitzer's esophagus. Giving him only six months to live, Sloan Kettering wanted to remove his voice box and move up his stomach. Instead, Kreitzer went to Dr. Dattatreyudu Nori, who was pioneering internal radiation. The treatment was successful. Kreitzer did not think his illness had had any effect on his ability to practice law.

He had two or three associates by 1991, four by 1994. In 1991 or 1992 he hired a file clerk and "encouraged him to go to paralegal school, which he paid for half and I paid for half." When he qualified as a paralegal, Kreitzer hired another file clerk. From 1991 he had two full-time secretaries. In 1992 Kreitzer replaced Shube with Karen Emma, Paul Robinson, and Alan Hodish, all recent graduates, who had their own caseloads. "Prior to that . . . late '80s, maybe to about '90, there was no specific designation . . . no one had 150 files, whatever it was . . . to work on." Associates with problems "usually come to me." As a result of the staff hired between 1990 and 1994, the office "is running much smoother." It handled "nearly 1,200, 1,300 cases" at a time.

On August 3, 1993, Kreitzer was charged with neglect in three cases. He initially denied almost everything, adding subsequently that his actions "did not result in any permanent loss to the clients." During the period of the charges his

> practice was expanding to an extent that beginning in 1989 he was required to employ . . . an associate attorney. He now employees [sic] three full-time and one part-time secretary, three full-time attorneys and one paralegal. Respondent's general reputation and character in both his professional and social circumstances are excellent.

The hearing began on December 1, 1993, and resumed on May 4, 1994.[596] Sarah Jo Hamilton appeared for the Departmental Disciplinary Committee (DDC) and Nicholas C. Cooper for Kreitzer. Irwin Kahn chaired the panel, which included Michael Conforti, Mary C. Daly, and lay member James Milligan.

---

[596] HP 25/93.

Juggling Too Many Balls

Robert Webber suffered severe hand injuries when he was struck by a Long Island Railroad train after drinking at Twins Inn bar on January 25, 1980. He retained Kreitzer, who wrote a claim letter to the railroad on May 29 and served summonses on the railroad and inn on October 21. Kreitzer served a complaint on the railroad on February 14, 1981; but though it was answered on May 9, with a request for a bill of particulars, he did not provide this until February 2, 1983, two years later. And though he learned that Twins Inn Corp. was not the proper defendant, he did not serve the correct defendants, Edgar and John Aaraas, until January 21, 1983. He talked to counsel for the couple between March 1983 and May 1984 but took no further action against them or the railroad until November 1991, when he scheduled depositions. At Webber's request, the deposition was adjourned and never rescheduled, and the case was never calendared.

Webber testified that he was unemployed and took multiple medications: Zoloft for depression, Basapar for anxiety, Proloxin for racing thoughts, and Benedril. He suffered from major depression and was borderline schizo-effective. Just before the accident he had been drinking heavily with Jack Cross, a friend. He left the bar and walked down the train tracks. "[T]he gravel from the railroad grating ended right at the front door to the bar and it was like three or four steps to the tracks without any kind of fence or warning or anything." He also thought he had been "over served at the bar." The train amputated his left thumb, which a doctor replaced with his second to right toe. His father, who was going through a divorce, recommended Kreitzer. "He said he would look into it. He would drive out and take pictures of the site." "[H]e said this would be a tough case . . . but not an impossible case to prove. He said he felt he could win it and that's why he was taking it." Webber then moved to Dallas for 18 months in 1982–1983 but gave Kreitzer his address and work phone. "And I told him that if he scheduled the deposition for the holidays I would be home to be there for it." Then he lived in Fort Lauderdale for 30 months, again informing Kreitzer. "My mother was calling him at this time as well on my behalf trying to find out what was going on with the case." "I told him that airfares were low . . . and that there would be no problem for me to fly home for . . . the deposition, no matter when it was scheduled." He called Kreitzer three or four times. "I called and if it was the springtime, Dave said, well, we'll check back in the fall. If it was the fall he said, check back in winter. He never gave me a month." Webber returned home in 1986 and consulted another firm, Seidman and Seidman, which obtained the file from Kreitzer. "They said that there was evidence such as witness

Chapter 2

testimonies missing from the file. And that the case was basically in their terms, screwed up, and they would not touch it." Kreitzer scheduled the deposition. "I couldn't make it. I called and it was supposed to be rescheduled another day. The day before it was supposed to be rescheduled I called to make sure it was going on . . . his secretary told me that the LIRR backed out of it." Kreitzer never called Webber again. On cross-examination, Kreitzer agreed that there had been no examination before trial (EBT), and Webber had never been deposed, although he was still a client and available in New Jersey.

Cross-examined by Cooper, Webber acknowledged he had been depressed since 13, but stated that

> the accident maximized my depression . . . it gave me something else to be depressed about. It's like people with toes on their hands are freaks, you know. . . . People look at it—oh, what happened to your hand?

Although Webber gave Kreitzer an account of the accident by Jack Cross, the lawyer never interviewed his drinking buddy. About a year ago Webber told Kreitzer he wanted to drop the case.

> I was really despondent because I do suffer from major chronic depression and a sense of hopelessness and I felt after ten years, 11 years, even 12 years, without a deposition, that the case had become so hopeless.

But Kreitzer "said no . . . he thought he could bring it to settlement." Although unsure whether Kreitzer would return phone calls, Webber "never got that sense that he was trying to avoid me." Kreitzer insisted Webber's case was "still viable."

Kreitzer explained that although liability in the Webber case was "very poor," he took such cases if there were substantial injuries. "[P]retty much my philosophy is somewhere down the line we should be able to get some sort of settlement." He could have asked Webber to find another lawyer or moved to withdraw, but he kept "hoping that we'd get a settlement." He admitted to Hearing Panel member Michael Conforti, however, that the case was never calendared. He "really [didn't] have an answer as to why . . . we didn't address the bill of particulars" for two and a half years "other than the fact that maybe it was just too many cases and by myself, you know, at the time." "The plan is to still continue with it. Refile or just to get it to the secretary for a preliminary conference." After Webber contacted Seidman and Seidman, one of those lawyers told Kreitzer "he had told Mr. Webber that he felt that there was no liability on the case. But I still felt that maybe we could turn it into some money. . . . The office practice here is not to give a case up."

Margarita Del Valle slipped and fell in front of a grocery story in early 1983. On March 8 Antonio Loiti Madariaga, a lawyer she had consulted about other matters, referred her to Kreitzer, who handled the case himself. He served a summons on June 27 and received an answer on September 13. On August 2 and 16, 1983, he asked her to sign medical releases, which she did on August 30. Then he did nothing for three years other than serve a bill of particulars on July 23, 1984. Del Valle "heard from him about a year later that he was going to send me a letter to go and see a private doctor. . . . I went and I never find out . . . what was going on." "I guess [my case] fell into a corner because I never heard anything. I was always the one who got in touch with him, or . . . his secretary." She only got through to him twice. He always said "Call me back next month" or "Give me, make it about two months, because I'm working on it." "I'm just waiting for a day in the calendar call to go to court." On May 14, 1987, he filed a note of issue and statement of readiness, which was stricken by consent because there had been no EBT. He did nothing more and had no "specific explanation" why he had waited almost three years after the bill of particulars to file the note of issue. "A general explanation, yes, probably just got caught up with too many cases. I just wasn't, I just didn't address it." He never meant to abandon the case.

On cross-examination Del Valle claimed, "I called him every week, every time I had a chance, I called him, he never was in the office." And he never returned her calls or told her about settlement attempts.

> The only thing I asked Mr. Kreitzer every time I called him was, "How is my case doing, has it been approved?" You know, "What is going on with it?" And he told me, "Well, what it is you should understand that, you know, when—we are trying to get a jury for the trial and that takes time. We have to get a date in the calendar to go to court." That was always the same thing that he told me, so I figured hey, we will wait for the date.

CHAPTER 2

In 1990 or 1991, "I called his office and I didn't get no response. I got very annoyed." A friend recommended another lawyer. "He says, 'Since when is this going on?' I told him a year. [The case actually was seven or eight years old.] He says, 'You know, I don't believe that one of my colleagues is taking so long to do a case.'" Together they called Kreitzer's office. He then wrote to her for the first time but never sent her any court documents. Kreitzer said it was "settled to the satisfaction of the client" by the new lawyer in May 1993.

Carmen Rivera directed traffic for the New York City Department of Transportation. She retained Kreitzer on March 28, 1988, for a car accident three days earlier. He got the doctor's report in June and filed a no-fault claim with her insurer for medical expenses in November but then did nothing until filing the summons and complaint three years later. She telephoned him "maybe three times, four times... a year" from then until complaining to the DDC. Whenever they talked he said: "'Call me back in three months.' He was supposed to get a court date, something like that." He wrote to her in January 1992 that it would be settled in 60 to 90 days, but "after the three months there was no settlement, so then I went to another lawyer." However, she stuck with Kreitzer, who sent her a similar letter in June 1992. When he learned in March 1993 that the defendant was uninsured, he applied for additional payment from Rivera's uninsured motorist coverage but did nothing more. His answer to the disciplinary complaint claimed the case was "the subject of active settlement negotiations and should be concluded soon." It settled for the uninsured motorist coverage limit a week before the disciplinary hearing (something he could have done six years earlier). He explained that he had handled it alone until the last year or so. "In 1990 I was sick and out of the office for a period of time... but I can't say specifically that was the reason why."

The DDC filed six more neglect charges in February 1995. Kreitzer's answer admitted many of the factual allegations but said the charges were untimely, duplicative (because they constituted a single act of neglect), and "precluded based upon principles of fundamental fairness and due process." Hearings were held on May 17 and June 28, 1995.[597]

Evans Veguilla retained Kreitzer on June 10, 1984, to sue New York City for injuries he suffered as a police officer when he fell out of the window at his precinct. The two had met in 1978 when Veguilla worked for Gimbel's, where Kreitzer was house counsel. Kreitzer served the notice

---

[597] Only Kahn and Conforti participated.

of claim on September 5 and the summons and complaint on August 30 and September 26, 1985. But although the City sought a bill of particulars three weeks later, he did not provide it for nearly five years and did nothing further until the EBT, scheduled for October 21, 1991 and adjourned to January 31, 1992, was finally conducted in December 1992. The case was settled on February 1, 1994.

Veguilla also retained Kreitzer on May 3, 1985, to bring a medical malpractice claim against Long Island College Hospital for treatment of a gunshot wound. Kreitzer wrote the hospital on May 7 and December 13, requesting Veguilla's medical records, and on March 27, 1986, seeking to negotiate with the hospital's insurance carrier. He served the summons on October 6, 1987, and the complaint on November 19. Veguilla had received a three-quarters disability pension in July 1986 and moved back to Puerto Rico at the end of that year. After

> almost a year I began to contact Mr. Kreitzer to see what the status was with regards to the lawsuit . . . and several long years past [sic] and every year I would contact him monthly, at least twice, three times a month, either by phone or by letter. And he would just tell me that, you know, it's pending. I'm working on it. . . . Several times I had made visits to New York on other business and I would visit him in his office to find out what was going on. He would give me the same response. At times during the Christmas holidays he would visit Puerto Rico and I would visit him at the hotel. He would then give me the same response. . . . I used to call him up at times, maybe even four times a month, five times a month. What's going on, babe? Why haven't you said what you were going to do last month? He would tell me, I'm working on it, I'm working on it. I told him, Dave, I'm going to miss a chance to get some type of reconstructive surgery because I had two operations then on the . . . injury and it didn't work out. . . . His idea was . . . that the longer I show that I'm unable to work, the better it was for me.

The hospital demanded a bill of particulars on December 10, 1987. Kreitzer waited until June 6, 1990, to ask Veguilla for the necessary information. Veguilla faxed it within a week, adding "Why wasn't this done back in December, 1988? I hope it doesn't *delay this matter longer* than necessary.

After all, an answer was requested *in 20 days*!!"[598] Kreitzer did not submit the bill of particulars until September 13, 1991, nearly four months after the demand and did nothing further until requesting a preliminary conference on August 19, 1993. Following the January 1994 conference and the April EBT, the case was settled on August 18, after Veguilla complained to the DDC.

Kreitzer offered his 1990 illness to explain the five-year delay in providing the bill of particulars, "but I think this one I did discuss with Mr. Veguilla not to push the case because he was alleging a long term disability." However, Veguilla said his income had fallen from almost $40,000 to $25,000. "I told [Kreitzer] I couldn't afford any further therapy or any type of reconstructive surgery. So I wanted these cases . . . handled as quickly as possible."

> The Long Island College Hospital case went the same route as the case against the City. It was a prolonged thing. I never heard anything definitely, concrete. I never saw anything. I requested it . . . numerous times. . . . I even told him this in letters, that I had spent a small fortune trying to contact him. . . . I always spoke to him, he always was good enough to answer the phone. But his reply was always the same. It's pending. . . . I used to get things two or three years later that he had told, promised me that he would do years before. You know, certain documents from the courts and requesting information which he had commented to me years before he . . . had never filed.

Kreitzer confirmed this: "I would say, Ritchie, it was still pending and there hasn't been an offer." Veguilla claimed to have sent Kreitzer more than 240 letters but had not kept copies. Kreitzer was "sure" his phone bills would show that Veguilla did not telephone two or three times a month. Veguilla was unhappy with the $75,000 and $30,000 settlements in the two cases—too little for reconstructive surgery—which he accepted only "after what [Kreitzer] told me."

Leonard Levit emigrated from Russia in 1979. On December 1, 1984, he retained Kreitzer to sue Flatbush General Hospital for the January 5 wrongful death of his mother, Sheyna, who had been admitted for a heart

---

[598] Staff Exhibit 62.

problem but died of a urinary infection. Levit's ex-wife, a urologist, suspected malpractice. Whenever Levit spoke with Kreitzer "he always told that the case in progress. And that it will take time. . . . He told me call me maybe in three months." The hospital answered Kreitzer's July 16, 1985, complaint on September 3, seeking a bill of particulars. On December 20 it also interpleaded Dr. Engracio G. Villanueva, Jr., who answered and demanded a bill of particulars on March 20, 1986. On March 3 the hospital moved to preclude for failure to provide discovery. The court issued an order on consent for discovery within 60 days. Kreitzer served the bill of particulars on Flatbush on May 16 but did not comply with discovery by Villanueva, who moved to dismiss on that ground on January 15, 1987, and for an order of preclusion on July 27. At the discovery conference on September 15, 1988, Kreitzer was ordered to provide medical authorizations for discovery within 30 days but failed to do so. Compliance conferences were scheduled for January and May 1989; Flatbush wrote to Kreitzer on June 29 requesting compliance. When Kreitzer sent authorizations for release of medical records only to Flatbush, Villanueva moved to dismiss in July, and Flatbush joined the motion on September 5. Although Kreitzer served his answer on opposing counsel, he failed to file it in court. He offered a copy of the receipt from United Lawyers Service dated October 31: "Filed opposition affirmation with J. Levin." But Kreitzer conceded "it never somehow got submitted to the court." The court dismissed the case on March 8, 1990, and denied Kreitzer's motion to vacate on April 30. Asked if he had ever contemplated taking action against United Lawyers, Kreitzer replied "I may have at that time, just for a little while . . . but I don't . . . think—I may have."

Kreitzer told the DDC, "The motion [to vacate] was denied based upon there not being . . . an affidavit . . . from a physician." He claimed that in July 1990 (four months after the case was dismissed) he had written a doctor, who declined to opine. He also claimed to have written Levit on April 30: "Please contact my office at your earliest convenience to schedule an appointment herein to go over this matter." But Kreitzer did not persist in either factual contention.

After Levit remarried in 1992 "my second wife told me it takes probably . . . too long. It was about . . . eight year by that time." He called Kreitzer, who "told me O.K. you can make an appointment and I will explain you what's . . . the status of your case." Levit went to Kreitzer's office on May 11. The lawyer did not say there were "problems, absolutely not. He make me believe that the case in progress." "I thought it takes long time in cases like that." "What I understood... [was] that a court request[ed the] . . . name and address of the physician that took care my mother before she was admitted to the hospital. And . . . this paper was not . . . given to the court and that's why case was dismissed."

> I came together with my wife. And he told me that he had invite me because he . . . want to just show me that . . . your case in progress, it's not like I don't do nothing. And meantime, here, let in other room and brought a thick package with papers from—you see? This is your case. And so I told, so what's going to be next step? He told me so far hospital didn't offer me any settlement. And so I told him what going to be next then? He told me I'm not a doctor, so first I have to evaluated this, spoke with . . . professionals to evaluate your case. And I told him how long it will take. And he told me call me in few weeks or a month. . . . So, after that time me and my wife contact him again by telephone and he told us he didn't found yet a doctor. And then I call him again and he told, I found a doctor but he wants something, [$]2,600, and he's crazy. O.K.? So he continue search for a doctor. And eventually, each time when he told that you will come, you can see from my correspondence over there, each time nothing happened. So we sent him one of those letters state, can you explain what is the status of the case, if there is any time limitation on this case, because so many years.

On cross-examination Kreitzer conceded,

> I don't think I . . . told him the case was actually dismissed. . . . I told him that we needed a doctor in order to make a motion to vacate. . . . I may have not told him specifically what the motion was. . . . I showed him I had a very, I had a thick file at the time. And he said, yeah, I see you're . . . working on it. I said "but I have a problem. I have to get an expert." I must have said it to him two or three times. . . . I told Mr. Levit that I had some problems with the case and that I had to get an expert.

But Kreitzer never said the case had been dismissed. "I felt it would have been very hard for him to understand what had taken place with the court and everything like that." "I had difficulty getting . . . we've never been able to get an expert to confirm that there was liability on the case." Asked by Conforti what he had done before April 1990 to obtain an expert, Kreitzer said "I didn't speak to anyone other than Mr. Levit's [ex-]wife at the time . . . who was a doctor in Russia. And I think she was taking her boards in New York." But he never proposed that she submit the affidavit. Asked if one was required, Kreitzer replied "I'm not sure if . . . you were at that time or not."

He wrote Levit again on October 10, 1992:

> Since I saw you in May I have not been able to arrange for a specialist to review the medical records of your mother as I indicated I hoped to do. I was on trial in the Supreme Court Nassau County during the past few weeks of September and hope to schedule an appointment with a doctor within the next two months or so. As soon as the appointment is scheduled I will advise you accordingly.

He approached two other doctors on January 18, 1993 but could not explain the three-year delay. The liability problem was

> that the care of Mr. Levit's mother during that period of time when she was at Flatbush General, there was no deviation . . . she was a sick woman and that there was nothing that was done affirmatively, whether by an act of [sic] omission, which ultimately caused her death.

After Levit complained to the DDC, it sent him a copy of Kreitzer's file in February 1994.

> And then when we look through this paper, we found out that there is no case. Case was closed years ago. I think in 1991 . . . we couldn't understand why . . . this story that he is going to evaluate . . . I was also surprised that he . . . dropped this case because he couldn't produce paper like who is my mother's physician, in time to the court.

Kreitzer insisted, "[T]he status is it's still in the office . . . it still technically has been dismissed, though." Asked by Kahn how long ago, he said "it's been a

CHAPTER 2

couple of years, actually—three years." But Conforti retorted that it had been dismissed five years earlier and that Kreitzer had had no contact with Levit since 1992.

Shirley Elizabeth Gibson was stopped at a red light on September 17, 1986, when a NYC Transit Authority bus hit her; while she was waiting to make a police report, a car driven by Ernest Jordan hit her again. After being referred to Kreitzer by the Staten Island firm of Chelli and Bush, she gave him all the information. "Some things I had to supply two times," she said." He served a summons on the City on December 15, 1987, and a verified complaint on February 9, 1988. The NYCTA answered on February 29, requesting a bill of particulars. Kreitzer took three years to respond because he "didn't get to it." He was hospitalized "from around March or April [1990] through the summer." He finally provided it on October 26, 1990, but did nothing more. On August 20, 1991, the NYCTA moved for discovery of medical records or preclusion. On November 12 the court ordered compliance within 30 days, but Kreitzer did nothing. Although he knew that cars driven by Ernest Jordan and Margaret Wright were involved in the accident and told Gibson he would sue both, he failed to sue Jordan within the statute of limitations and did not tell his client. On November 18, 1989, he sued Wright, who answered and demanded a bill of particulars on January 20, 1990. On March 18, 1991, Wright demanded discovery and moved to dismiss on October 2 for failure to comply. On October 25 Kreitzer served an amended bill of particulars. Although the motion to dismiss was denied on November 26, Kreitzer was sanctioned $300 for delay.

For the first two and a half years after her accident Gibson heard from Kreitzer "quite often . . . and whenever I called he was readily available." "[T]he last correspondence was in '89 [January 6], and after that I didn't hear from Mr. Kreitzer at all unless I sent him a registered letter or called. He never returned any of my calls." She talked instead to his associates, Karen Emma and Leonard Shube. (Kreitzer confirmed they had handled the case between 1991 and 1993.) When she asked why subsequent communications omitted Ernest Jordan, who had been named in the original complaint, "they accused me of being nasty because I hung up several times." She kept asking about Jordan. "[A]t least [once] a month for over a year, every month I was [sic] called. I sent registered letter to him several times. They completely act as if he [Jordan] never existed." Asked by Cooper why he never told Gibson he had missed the statute of limitations, Kreitzer replied, "She never asked me specifically—me personally. . . . There's no question, it could have jeopardized the case to a certain extent."

She was notified of the EBT monthly for a year, but each was postponed, the last in February 1992. "At some time I know that I mentioned I was going to go to the Bar if I didn't have any satisfaction. You know, the accident happened in 1986." In July 1993 Kreitzer answered Wright's summary judgment motion, which was denied on October 4. Although Wright made a settlement offer on March 9, 1994, Kreitzer did not inform Gibson until September 19, when she was in California. Listening to her daughter read it, Gibson thought $4,000 was too low and told her daughter to rip it up; she never spoke to Kreitzer about it. The accident exacerbated an earlier injury. "My turning has been greatly incapacitated, turning my head back and forth. I have constant spasm."

Kreitzer confirmed that after sending Gibson the settlement offer he never heard from her and was unsure he had sent a reminder. He explained that she "had a very weak case as far as her injuries . . . there was no fractures, no lacerations resulting in disfigurement . . . the medical documentation, because she was very difficult as far as cooperating—one report we had . . . showed treatment of, I believe, less than 90 days." The $4,000 offer "was more value than the case [had] to begin with."

> I didn't prepare the lawsuit. I had a—office manager working at the time who was doing a lot of the pleadings, and she omitted the Jordan vehicle when she prepared the . . . second summons and complaint. . . . The only way Jordan could be brought into the case was if they were third party by . . . one of the other parties involved in the lawsuit. . . .
>
> Conforti: What was your practice with regard to reviewing pleadings that went out of the office?
>
> Kreitzer: I allowed that Laura Schmidt [the office manager] to pretty much do the pleadings at that time. And I would sign the . . . affirmation.
>
> Conforti: Where did she go to law school?
>
> Kreitzer: She didn't go to law school.
>
> Conforti: . . . She was not an attorney?

Chapter 2

> Kreitzer: No . . . as to an automobile accident case I would let her do it. She would be doing that on her own, yeah, an automobile and probably a slip and fall. But other than that, we would have drafted the complaint ourself. . . . And actually, there came a time when . . . I was aware that Jordan really should have been a party and I asked [Schmidt] about it. . . . She'd only picked up on a page in the police report.

After an attorney referred Hector de la Hoz on December 6, 1985, Kreitzer wrote Cosmopolitan Associates (the tortfeasor) and its insurance company but then misplaced the file on December 29, 1986, and did nothing further for nearly five years, when he prepared a summons and complaint against Cosmopolitan and Eugene Katz and Sidney Eisikoff, which he served on February 13, 1992. The court granted Cosmopolitan's November 20 motion to dismiss because the statute of limitations had expired. Kreitzer made no further effort to sue the others, explaining that the "case got misplaced for a period of time. We didn't locate it until after the statute had actually run." Six years after the accident, "we commenced the suit anyway" because several members of Cosmopolitan Associates had moved without filing change of address forms "and it was my belief that there might be considered to be a waiver on the issue." The motion to reopen was denied, and although he filed a notice of appeal on October 5, 1993 "nothing has been done further." Based on subsequent research, he concluded, "I don't think . . . we're going to be able to win on appeal."

Carolyn Severa was in a car accident in September 1987 while pregnant. Her son Matthew was born on November 14, 1987, with moderate to severe cerebral palsy—non-verbal and confined to a wheelchair. She had been admitted for delivery to Nassau Hospital in Portchester but then sent by ambulance to the SUNY Stony Brook hospital. "[T]here wasn't oxygen on the drive over." Her husband sued for divorce soon after the birth, and she asked Kreitzer to represent her in that action in February 1988. "While I was there I was explaining what was going on at the hospital and at that point we started, you know, proceedings against the hospital also." On February 10, 1988, Kreitzer filed a claim against the state, which answered demanding a bill of particulars on April 25. Conferences were held on June 22 and December 20, and depositions were scheduled for February 1 and 10, 1989. But no depositions were taken, and at a February 28 conference, Kreitzer agreed to discontinue the claim because the hospital records showed no causal connection between its treatment and the child's injuries.

> Cooper: Did you have the client's consent to discontinuance . . . ?
>
> Kreitzer: I didn't speak to the client before the discontinuance. I told her after . . .
>
> Cooper: . . . Did you consider it to be still an active case or not? . . .
>
> Kreitzer: It was dormant really. We weren't doing anything.
>
> Cooper: Was any effort made to secure a medical expert?
>
> Kreitzer: . . . Once we got the hospital records—they were very voluminous . . . we had somebody look at it.
>
> Cooper: So you felt that . . . it was appropriate to rely on . . . that single opinion?
>
> Kreitzer: That's right.

Kreitzer told Conforti he could not remember the expert's name or specialty or whether he wrote a report.

Severa testified:

> I called periodically, like every six months, my mother even called for me because we didn't hear anything. But then I really wasn't too concerned by that because he did say it would take about seven years to get to court. So I just assumed everything was rolling along beautifully.

After her husband moved back in "we just kind of let [the divorce] go." But in 1991 she told Kreitzer to revive the divorce and asked about the tort claim. "And he said everything is going beautiful and fine, and there's no problems."

> Cooper: Did you ever ask Mr. Kreitzer or anyone in his office at any time, whether there was a medical expert available to testify in your case?

Chapter 2

> Severa: . . . I didn't think I needed to. I didn't know any of the procedures on it. Mr. Kreitzer was handling everything.

Growing concerned in 1993, however, she consulted Bruce Seger, who took over the case.

> I was lead [sic] to believe that none of the papers were filed that should have been. . . . Mr. Seger did tell me that I was advised . . . from Mr. Kreitzer that, he told me verbally that he was putting a stop to the case years prior—which never happened.

When Seger called Kreitzer about another of Severa's cases and asked about the Stony Brook lawsuit, Kreitzer said he had discontinued it. Seger sent a substitution of attorney form, but the matrimonial and personal injury files were "just lumped up" and "we couldn't locate the file." Kreitzer had his "paralegal come in . . . on a weekend, went through all the files. Could not locate it. I told [Seger] we would gladly give him the file if we could locate it."

> I said to him, give us a little bit more time, I think we're going to locate it . . . and then he in fact wrote me I think a letter . . . saying that the client was going to go to the Disciplinary Committee. And I said to him, hey, we're looking for this file . . . and we never located it.

Kreitzer agreed he "may not have signed [the substitution of attorney form] because I had no file," reluctantly admitting to Conforti that he was still attorney of record. He could not remember writing Severa that her case had been dropped.

> Hamilton: Since the case was discontinued, who was to commence proceedings again if such were desired? . . .
>
> Kreitzer: It would have been up to Ms. Severa . . .
>
> Hamilton: And you made that clear to her?
>
> Kreitzer: I told her we had discontinued the case based upon the expert stating that there was no causal relationship . . .

Hamilton: Did she ask you, can't we get someone else? . . .

Kreitzer: I don't recall.

The DDC filed five more neglect charges on November 20, 1995. Kreitzer answered on December 11. John Tartaglia's 15-year-old daughter was bitten by a dog on April 20, 1985. On August 5, 1986, he retained Kreitzer, who served a summons on Peter de Gaetano, Jr., on November 17, 1986. But though the defendant did not answer, Kreitzer failed to seek a default judgment. Instead, more than five years later he served another summons on de Gaetano and Josephine Rossi, who answered, demanding a bill of particulars, which Kreitzer did not provide for more than two years. He characterized the second complaint as an "exercise of his independent professional judgment." He served a note of issue on May 5, attended a preliminary conference on June 5, and had the girl examined before trial on September 29. In support of his sworn answer to Tartaglia's disciplinary complaint, Kreitzer gave the DDC letters he claimed to have sent the defendants on March 11, 1987, and June 2, 1988.[599] But both referred to the lawsuit commenced November 26, 1991 (years after the letter were purported to have been written). Hamilton accused Kreitzer of "an effort to mislead the Committee." But Cooper maintained there was "nothing in this record that will indicate that they were quote-unquote, false and fraudulent . . . so our position is that this was an obvious error. Mr. Kreitzer is not aware of how this came to be." Cooper speculated it might have been "done by a secretary through a computer subsequently." Claiming not to have noticed the anomaly until the DDC drew it to his attention, Kreitzer denied he had "knowingly submitted same to the Committee with an intent to deceive" but was "at a loss to explain these obvious mistakes" He also was "not aware of why it took so long but that it was an infant's case in any event and there was no tolling [sic—he means running] of the statute or prejudice to the client." His only explanation for the five-year delay between the first and second summons and complaint was that "actually '90 I guess I was out for some periods of time with my illness. . . . There were three or four hospitalizations . . . at least a week each time. And then there was some other periods that I was out. I had bed rest after the hospitalizations."

---

[599] Staff Exhibits 69 and 70.

Chapter 2

Donna Richardson and her minor daughter Danielle were injured in a fire in their apartment on August 1, 1983. Donna retained Kreitzer to sue her landlord. After writing a claim letter on August 18, he did nothing for nearly three years, when he filed a summons; he did not serve the complaint until after the landlord moved to dismiss, a year later. The landlord answered and demanded a bill of particulars, which Kreitzer failed to provide for three years, despite two further requests. He had no explanation for the delay. He also disregarded all discovery demands. On October 15, 1991, the defendant made a motion to vacate the note of issue, which was granted on November 17, with $100 costs. The landlord moved to dismiss for the third time in 1992 for failure to provide discovery; Kreitzer complied just before the return date. On June 4, 1993, the landlord's insurer offered Danielle $7,500 and Donna $2,500. Kreitzer took a year to convey the offer, providing Donna with a release for her claim and promising to prepare an infant compromise order for Danielle. Donna sent Kreitzer the signed release in October. Although Kreitzer forwarded it on November 17, the insurer failed to deliver the settlement check; Kreitzer did not investigate until Donna complained to the DDC the following year. He took two more years to prepare the infant compromise order. Cooper explained that Kreitzer "was severely ill in the '89, '90 period and we would argue that this contributed to what was possibly a delay but not a delay that would rise to the level of neglect." Kreitzer postponed submitting the compromise order for Danielle because "she had a preexisting condition which required medical proof that said condition was not exacerbated by this accident." His office "did not realize that no check had been issued until being notified of the complaint herein."

Henry Johnson retained Kreitzer on September 5, 1985, for an August 22 auto accident. He took three years to serve a summons on Jack Grunes, who answered and demanded a bill of particulars the following year. Kreitzer took a year to serve this and two more to notice the defendant's deposition and schedule his own client's, but the latter was delayed seven times, finally on occurring on September 11, 1994. Kreitzer requested a preliminary conference on July 1 and served a note of issue on February 10, 1995. The Supreme Court transferred the case to civil court, where Kreitzer purchased another note of issue on June 20. Cooper explained that Kreitzer had asked Johnson's physician, Dr. Clyde Weisbart, for a medical report "more than 20 or 25" times. "His hands are basically tied in his prosecution of this case by the fact that he was unable to secure medical information." But he conceded he could have subpoenaed the doctor or obtained an order to produce the records.

Charle Stroman retained Kreitzer on June 20, 1989, for injuries she and her minor daughter incurred in a June 16 car accident. More than two years later he served the summons and complaint on Aston Burke, who answered and demanded a bill of particulars on May 5, 1992. Kreitzer sent Burke's insurer the medical information and got a settlement offer; Charle was paid in July. But Kreitzer failed to prepare the infant compromise order for two more years. Charle finally signed the supporting affidavit in January 1995, and the matter was calendared in March.

On May 20, 1991, attorney Antonio Loiti Madariaga referred Anna Perez's April 30 slip-and-fall to Kreitzer, who took two and a half years to file the summons against Filipp Dituri. He corrected the defendants' names and accident location four months later, explaining that we "inverted numbers, probably somewhere." Although he wrote the defendants later that year about their failure to answer, he did not move for a default. Cooper explained "there was no record ever filed of a defect in the sidewalk [i.e., the legally necessary prior notice]. So that there was really no cause of action in this case."

Kreitzer blamed any problems in these cases on his associates. The Tartaglia matter was handled by associates from 1992. If "'neglect' occurred during that period, Respondent had no knowledge thereof nor authorized any acts of neglect by said associates." The Richardson case "was assigned to associate counsel . . . from about 1992 on. So for the period . . . any allegations with regard to mishandling it were at a time when it was under the control of . . . the associate," first Paul Robinson and then Robert Greenstein. Cooper said Strohman was "a case where the original matter was being handled by an associate," but Kreitzer testified he had managed it through the 1992 settlement; an associate (Seth Greenberg) took over in 1994 or 1995. Kreitzer said associates had handled Perez.

In January 1996 the DDC added failure adequately to supervise an employee to each count. The hearing resumed on May 8.

> Cooper: The real issue here is . . . what was the appropriate degree of supervision that Mr. Kreitzer was to practice over his own associates. Now he can't be there looking over their shoulder every day . . . it's a pretty small office where basically in pretty close confines and people are expected to come forward

CHAPTER 2

if there's problems. And he will inquire from time-to-time whether there are problems...

Conforti: Under your argument an attorney who hires ten associates and then exercises absolutely no supervision over them can't be held responsible if they neglect...

Cooper: O.K., we're not talking about civil liability.... There's been no expert testimony here as to what standard is expected within the profession in the negligence field in these situations. So what I'm saying is that he believed that he was conducting a reasonable degree of supervision. And the fact that mistakes occur not withstanding that degree does not ipso facto lead to the conclusion that he's guilty of professional misconduct.

The Hearing Panel found neglect in Webber, Del Valle, Rivera, Veguilla, Gibson, de la Hoz, Richardson, Strohman, and Perez, but not Tartaglia or Johnson. It found misrepresentation in Levit but not Gibson or Tartaglia: "anyone reading the letters would see them for what they are, obvious mistakes rather than shrewd or diabolical attempts to play fast and loose with the Committee."

II. Penalty

The Panel proceeded directly to mitigation. The respondent presented Dr. Nori, who had been chief of service at Sloan Kettering and was now at Cornell Medical Center. Although Kreitzer had told the panel "he did not think that his illness affected his ability to practice law," Nori called such "denial" "not an uncommon answer from a patient who . . . went into remission from cancer." Since being treated by Nori in 1990, Kreitzer had "helped several dozens of patients who are in the last phases of life—some of them practically he forced them to come and see me." Each year Nori brought together his successful cases to give "a good feeling to . . . the patients undergoing treatment." Kreitzer "was number one in that program, participating actively, giving his time" and was "a key member of the video giving his life story." Kreitzer had two courses of chemotherapy over three to four months at the end of 1989, followed by four to five weeks of radiation; recovery could take two months.

Cooper proposed a six-month suspension in light of Kreitzer's cancer, "which I think Dr. Nori has indicated, although Mr. Kreitzer may not be able to acknowledge, definitely affected his ability to conduct his practice in a manner in which possibly it should have been conducted." As his caseload expanded from 150 to 1,000 "he did the best he could to cope with and keep up with that." The DDC sought three years. Although cancer treatment may have affected Kreitzer's ability over a few months, his neglect "lasted years and years, preceding and going up and passed [sic] the bout with esophageal cancer." Kreitzer had received four prior admonitions (one each in 1989 and 1990, two in 1991), one with respect to Richardson. After the first charges were filed, the DDC continued to receive neglect complaints. "This is not the case where the Respondent, saying 'oh boy, I'm in trouble. I've got a complaint of three neglects' . . . really made a move to clean up his act." Cooper responded that the charges only involved "several matters." "But we don't have 1,000 clients lining up here saying, you know, gee, David Kreitzer is really not so great anymore."

On July 12, 1996, the Hearing Panel found neglect by Kreitzer's associates. "Respondent simply would assign these matters to associates without any supervision or review at all." The same was true of office staff. His "inability to attend to even the mundane and routine requirements of a law practice which specializes in personal injury litigation" was graphically illustrated by his failure to complete two infant compromise orders. "Given the special duty owned [sic] to infants, who are not in any position to protect themselves, we find such laxity inexcusable." It recommended a year's suspension, which Kreitzer accepted.

But the Appellate Division suspended him for three.[600] It agreed that Kreitzer's neglect of the two minors most clearly exemplified his "insensitivities to the needs of his clients." His "lackadaisical approach" caused actual prejudice in two instances (de la Hoz and Gibson). His attempt to blame associates and nonlegal employees was "unavailing." He was guilty of "intentionally misrepresenting to his client Levit that the case was progressing, *two years after* it had been dismissed."

Two months after Kreitzer was suspended, his firm paid Chicago Insurance Company (CIC) $63,467 for an unlimited extended reporting period endorsement of his malpractice policy. In November 1997, eight months after learning of the suspension from the successor firm of

---

[600] Matter of David M. Kreitzer, 229 A.D.2d 188, 653 N.Y.S.2d 572 (1st Dept 1997).

CHAPTER 2

Pariser & Vogelman, CIC rescinded the policy and sought a declaratory judgment of its invalidity. CIC alleged that when Kreitzer & Vogelman applied for insurance in 1994 it failed to state whether Kreitzer had been the subject of any disciplinary action in the previous four years. When he had sought to renew the policy in 1996, he had failed to disclose any new claims. The federal court denied both parties' summary judgment in January 2000[601] and their renewed motions in August 2002.[602] The judge ruled for CIC in June 2003.[603] Kreitzer claimed he did not answer whether he had "been the subject of . . . disciplinary action" because he did not know whether this included the then pending investigation. "While clever, Kreitzer's explanation lacked credibility . . . ." The following year Kreitzer again "failed to disclose in the Application the disciplinary proceedings and approximately 30 claims." In April 2004 the Appellate Division ruled that one of the disciplinary complainants, Lindenman, did not have to prove he would be able to collect the personal injury judgment in a case where Kreitzer had committed neglect in order to pursue a malpractice claim against Kreitzer.[604]

III. The Ten Percenter Scheme

While Kreitzer was suspended, the DDC sought an order on March 3, 2000, that he be further disciplined for a criminal conviction. He and 44 others had been indicted on June 23, 1995, for multiple counts of commercial bribery and fraud.[605] The investigation began in 1991, when attorney Jay B. Itkowitz reported that a middleman, John Prins, had asked for payment to expedite settlement of an insurance claim. Manhattan District Attorney Robert Morgenthau announced the investigation in 1994. The scheme involved bribes totaling $500,000 to eight middlemen and $300,000

---

[601] Chicago Insurance Co. v. Kreitzer & Vogelman, 1/12/2000 N.Y.L.J. 1 (col. 4), 1/12/2000 N.Y.L.J. 36 (col. 2).
[602] Chicago Insurance Co. v. Kreitzer & Vogelman, 8/2/2002 N.Y. L.J. 26 (col. 1).
[603] Chicago Insurance Co. v. Kreitzer & Vogelman, 6/12/2003 N.Y.L.J. 27 (col. 6).
[604] Lindenman v. Kreitzer, 4/9/2004 N.Y.L.J. 1 (col. 3); 4/12/2004 N.Y.L.J. 18 (col. 1); 7 A.D.3d 30, 775 N.Y.S.2d 4 (1st Dept. 2004).
[605] Josh Rogers, "Indictment of 21 Lawyers and Others New Jolt for Downtown Legal Circles," Downtown Express, Sep. 26, 1995; "Manhattan Grand Jury Indicts 47 Lawyers and Adjusters," 2–16 Mealey's Litig. Rep. Ins. Fraud 9 (1995); Matthew Goldstein, "23 Lawyers Arrested in Insurance Scheme; Inflating of Settlements in Tort Cases Charged," 9.22.95 N.Y.L.J. 1 (col. 3); Rita Henley Jensen, "28 Lawyers Snared in Alleged Scam," 81-Nov A.B.A.J. 28. Another lawyer was suspended for two years for his participation. Matter of Seth Rotter, 241 A.D.2d 81, 670 N.Y.S.2d 445 (1st Dept. 1998).

to 16 adjusters to expedite and perhaps inflate $19 million in insurance payments to the clients of 21 lawyers. In May 1997 the trial judge denied a motion to dismiss, calling it "sophistry" to argue that the payments were analogous to tipping a *maître d'* for a better table.[606] Six months later the judge denied the remaining technical motions and declared the indictment ready for trial.[607] Kreitzer pleaded guilty on December 3, 1999, to one count of second degree commercial bribery (a misdemeanor), receiving a one-year conditional discharge and a $1,000 fine.

On July 14, 2000, he entered a prehearing stipulation.[608] The DDC hearing occurred on July 27. On November 7, 2000, Referee Laurie Zeligson found that in 1990 or 1991 Kreitzer had asked Joel Cohen (an attorney) to negotiate with insurance adjusters for better settlement offers through what was known as the "ten percenter scheme," in which the middleman split with the adjuster a kickback of 10 percent of the settlement. Kreitzer agreed to pay Cohen to deal with AIG adjuster Salvatore Caccavale, giving Cohen about $5,000 in cash to handle Lorraine Murray's claim, which ultimately settled for $90,000. Cohen "expedited" another half dozen cases for Kreitzer, who made similar arrangements with Edward Quigley, Chris Galfinopolis, and John Timoney. Even after being subpoenaed during the DA's investigation, Kreitzer agreed to pay Cohen to expedite another case "because Cohen told him that he would not be making any payments to adjusters in connection with his work." Kreitzer admitted to "expediting" 13 cases. He "knew what he did was wrong, he took full responsibility for his actions and stated that his actions brought embarrassment to himself, his family and the bar."

> In hindsight, my head was in the ground. It was an improper thing to do. But at the time, other attorneys [were] doing it, I did not believe—and since there wasn't any nexus between myself and the potential insurance representative, that there was anything wrong—other than maybe some ethical violations. But in hindsight, I—I stand here saying I acknowledge it was wrong.

He again "offered evidence relating to his work with certain cancer organizations following his two bouts with cancer" and sought a six-month suspension beginning with the expiration of his present one (which had

---

[606] Matthew Goldstein, "Bribery Charges Against Attorneys Survive," 5/7/97 N.Y.L.J. 1 (col. 3).
[607] People v. Joseph Reynolds, 12/2/97 N.Y.L.J. 27 (col. 1).
[608] RP 16/00.

CHAPTER 2

been extended pending the outcome of this proceeding). He distinguished other cases on the ground that he had already been suspended for three years for "unrelated acts of neglect." The DDC said Kreitzer's justification "that it was a common practice" undermined his claim of remorse.

In a post-hearing brief Kreitzer asserted that the Committee had not "substantiated any evidence to show Respondent had knowledge of payment being made to third parties with the exception of the Murray case." But his prehearing stipulation stated,

> There were a total of thirteen (13) separate instances where Respondent agreed to pay and subsequently paid a "middleman" to expedite a pending matter with an insurance company where it was Respondent's understanding that the "middleman" would pay a portion of the money he received from Respondent to the insurance company adjuster.

The referee felt Kreitzer was "not fit to practice law" and would have recommended disbarment but accepted the DDC proposal of a five-year suspension.

The Hearing Panel agreed to five years but shared "the Referee's conclusion that 'Respondent is not fit to practice law' and her view that the record would support a recommendation that Respondent be disbarred."[609] Before the Appellate Division Kreitzer then claimed to have admitted paying middlemen in only nine instances and again requested a six-month suspension. But the Appellate Division disbarred him.[610]

A month later Kreitzer moved to reargue. "With the exception of the single act Respondent pled guilty to there was no testimony given by Respondent or any evidence submitted that monies given by the Respondent to the 'middlemen' were actually paid by the 'middlemen' to employees of Insurance Companies." "The 'middlemen' were not at the Insurance companies." "There were attorneys as well as other individuals who were 'middlemen.'" "Settling a case by an attorney, Joel Cohen, for another attorney, David M. Kreitzer, where there was no money paid to an employee of an Insurance Company, was not an act of wrongdoing." He offered in mitigation "that I have twice been striken [sic] with cancer.

---

[609] HP16/00: John L. Warden (chair), Charles L. Brieant III, Justice E. Driscoll III, Patricia Handal, and Henrietta Lyle.
[610] Matter of Kreitzer, 281 A.D.2d 35, 722 N.Y.S.2d 505 (1st Dept 2001).

First with Hodgkins Disease and later with Upper Esophageal cancer. Each time I was treated with massive doses of radiation and chemotherapy." He had "participated in assisting cancer patients" and "recently completed a book on cancer survival which is presently being circulated to major cancer institutions in hopes of helping others." He appended the 112-page double-spaced manuscript. "I apologize to this Court and did to the referee for my conduct."

The DDC objected that Kreitzer continued to claim "he was unaware that the fees he was paying to the 'middlemen' were to be used for the purpose of bribing the insurance company adjusters." Kreitzer replied he never denied "understanding" that the money he gave to a "middleman" was given with the "understanding" that it was to be given to an insurance adjuster. But for the court to find that it happened without "proof of it actually occurring" was "tantamount to conviction of a crime without the predicate of the actual crime being committed." "Notwithstanding my understanding [that] the monies given to the 'middleman' was [sic] to be given to the insurance adjusters, there was never and still is no evidence... of money being paid by a 'middleman' to an insurance adjuster." The Appellate Division denied his motion for reargument.[611]

Kreitzer repeated the same arguments in his motion for leave to appeal to the Court of Appeal, appending a transcript of the Referee's hearing. One of the middlemen

> had this apparatus that he was working on doing, possibly. But I don't think anything was actually—and I may have actually told him on a couple of cases to try and settle it for me under that... apparatus that he, you know, saying he had this agency that he was—but I don't—but he did not settle, as far as I recall, anything for me during that period of time. But I did discuss a couple of cases with him.... We were going down to the hearing once and... I think we gave him the medicals on something. But... it didn't pan out, for whatever reason.

After Kreitzer received the DA's subpoena, Joel Cohen

> called me up and specifically—since at that point we had an idea what this was all about, said that—because I knew his

---

[611] Matter of Kreitzer, 287 A.D.2d 356, 732 N.Y.S.2d 855 (1st Dept. 2001).

negotiation skills, he was hurting for, you know, for money. And he said, look, I'm just going to call up. I'll try and settle the case for you. . . . I paid him some—some money. I don't recall the amount. . . . I knew he was hurting for money and—but I also knew that he made this representation to me. You know, like I had heard him before on the phone, so I knew he was saying that—Joel was honorable in that sense, so I believed him 100 percent.

The Court of Appeal denied leave to appeal.[612]

IV. Betraying Clients and Adversaries

As a plaintiff's personal injury lawyer, Kreitzer had a predictable MO: accept every case with significant damages, serve a complaint, and wait for the check. He took Webber's case because he had lost his thumb, even though liability was "very poor" (Webber had fallen down drunk on perfectly visible railroad tracks and lain there on a January night as the train approached). As he stated, "[P]retty much my philosophy is somewhere down the line we should be able to get some sort of settlement. . . ." Declaring that "the office practice here is not to give a case up," Kreitzer sought to transmute neglect into persistence and loyalty to clients. For lawyers with enough cases to produce an adequate cash flow, speed is irrelevant. Their goal is less to maximize recovery than to minimize cost, and doing nothing is costless. They take action only when compelled (by statutes of limitation or motions to dismiss). Defendants naturally are happy to delay: they preserve capital (on which they earn interest) and drive desperate plaintiffs to settle for less. And defense counsel paid by the hour are at least indifferent to delay and may even profit from it. But the consequences for personal injury victims can be disastrous. Of the thirteen complainants, seven recovered nothing; one of the six recoveries was by substituted counsel; another successful client failed to recover from a second defendant. That is a very high ratio of losses for a personal injury lawyer (if these are representative of his caseload), one that can be sustained only by mass processing. The nine victims who did recover (some cases had more than one) waited 3 to 14 years (a mean of 8.6, a median of 10; see table).

---

[612] Matter of Kreitzer, 97 N.Y.2d 609, 765 N.E.2d 301, 739 N.Y.S.2d 98 (January 15, 2002).

Yet Kreitzer had no shortage of clients: he boasted of having 1,200–1,300 live cases. Four of the thirteen complainants had been referred by other lawyers (two by the same one), whose qualms about the quality of representation must have been allayed by the referral fee and the prospect of reciprocal referrals. Enough defendants and insurers settled to generate a cash flow sufficient to pay the salaries of three associates, a file clerk, and more than three secretaries. Kreitzer was so wedded to this approach—and perhaps incapable of recognizing that he was doing anything wrong—that he simply disregarded complaints. Before these charges were filed in August 1993, he had been admonished four times for neglecting and mishandling legal matters: in 1988, 1990, and twice in 1991. While the initial charges were pending, further charges were filed in February and again in November 1995. Cooper (his lawyer) made light of the complaints: they concerned only "several matters"; "we don't have 1,000 clients lining up here saying, you know, gee, David Kreitzer is really not so great anymore." But most clients had no standard by which to judge his behavior and lacked the resources or knowledge to complain. Even a dissatisfied client often had to be urged to complain by another. And enough clients must have received *some* settlement to make Kreitzer's contingent fee operation profitable. Even some of these complainants found him accessible and reassuring, demonstrating that a good "bedside manner" can hide extreme misconduct. But at least one client successfully sued for malpractice when his complaint was dismissed for failure to serve a bill of particulars.[613] Even more incredibly, Kreitzer persisted in the "ten percenter scheme" after being subpoenaed by the District Attorney.

Forced by the caseload he generated to delegate much of the work, he employed inexperienced associates, paralegals, and even office managers to practice law (presumably to maximize his own profit).[614] The inevitable consequence was numerous errors, many serious. Kreitzer served the wrong defendant; his office manager omitted a critical defendant from the complaint. One complaint had the wrong address for both the defendant and the accident. Kreitzer filed a notice of issue before an EBT. He failed to secure clients' medical authorizations for discovery. He failed to file an answer to a motion to dismiss in one case and to move for a default

---

[613] Lindenman v. Kreitzer, 7 A.D.3d 30, 775 N.Y.S.2d 4 (1st Dept. 2004) (lawsuit against successor firm that bought Kreitzer's firm after he was suspended).

[614] Two associates were no longer members of the New York Bar in 2007. The law schools and bar admission dates of the others were as follows: St. Johns 1989; New York Law School 1992; Boston University 1993; New York Law School 1994; and Brooklyn Law School 1995.

Chapter 2

Chronology of Kreitzer's Neglect Cases

Client	Accident date	Complaint served	Request for bill of particulars	Months before bill provided	Outcome	Reason	Years from accident to recovery
Webber	1.25.80	2.14.81	5.9.81	21	None	Incorrect defendant	
Del Valle	Early 1983	6.27.83		10	Substituted counsel settled 5.93	Inaction	10
Rivera	3.25.88	3.24.91			Settled after 4.93 under uninsured motorist policy		5
Veguilla (1)	6.10.84	8.30.85	10.18.85	56	Settled 2.1.94		10
Veguilla (2)	Before 5.3.85	11.19.87	12.10.87	45	Settled 8.18.94		10
Levit	1.5.84	7.16.85	9.3.85	8	Dismissed 3.8.90	Failure to file answer in court	

Gibson	9.17.86	2.9.88	2.29.88	32	One defendant settled 3.9.94; other dismissed	Statute of limitations	8
De La Hoz	Before 12.6.85	11.18.89 2.13.92	1.20.90	21	Dismissed	File lost; statute of limitations	
Severa	11.14.87	2.10.88	4.25.88	Never?	Discontinued without client consent	File lost	
Tartaglia	4.20.85	11.17.86 11.26.91	2.20.92	25	None at time of hearing		
Richardson	8.1.83	8.7.87	9.13.87	37	Settled 10.94; 1997	Failure to prepare infant compromise	11
Johnson	8.22.85	8.10.88	8.25.89	12	None	Failure to get a medical expert	14
Stroman	6.16.89	8.7.91			Settled 7.92 and 3.95	Failure to prepare infant compromise	3
Perez	4.30.91	12.27.93 4.21.94			None		6

CHAPTER 2

judgment in another (instead refiling the latter complaint years later). He failed to observe that there had been no prior notice of a sidewalk defect (essential in slip-and-fall cases). He failed to obtain an expert in a medical malpractice case (consulting only the client's Russian ex-wife, not yet qualified to practice in the United States); he did not know that a doctor's affidavit of merit was necessary. He abandoned another medical malpractice case on the basis of a single expert's opinion without consulting the client. In both instances, he deliberately concealed this from the clients as long as he could, once brandishing as evidence of work a file that may have been from another case. He claimed (and may even have believed) he could reopen a dismissed case three years later without showing cause. He missed statutes of limitations in two cases. He repeatedly disregarded discovery requests until just before cases were to be dismissed. He lost the files in two cases. He failed to prepare infant compromise orders in three. He disregarded or overrode client dissatisfaction with settlement amounts. He took five years to get one client what she could have obtained herself under her uninsured motorist policy. And all this concerned just 1 percent of his 1,300 clients. There is every reason to believe that many of the thousands of other clients he represented during these years suffered similar losses and delays but did not complain to the DDC.

Kreitzer offered a range of explanations. The first was caseload: "Maybe it was just too many cases and by myself, you know, at the time"; "probably just got caught up with too many cases." Cooper said his client "did the best he could to cope with and keep up with" the enlarged caseload. But of course that was no excuse: Kreitzer chose to accept those cases, presumably motivated by money. This problem was aggravated by his illness. But Kreitzer was vague about exactly when he had been in hospital or recuperating at home and maintained he "did not think that his illness affected his ability to practice law." He then sought to neutralize this by having his oncologist testify that cancer patients often are in denial about their disability. But if Kreitzer was unable to serve his clients, he was obligated to find another lawyer to do so. As a cancer patient, would he have accepted similar mistreatment from a doctor who explained that he had too many patients or was sick himself? Kreitzer blamed the judicial backlog; but *he* was responsible for much of the pretrial delay and rarely seems to have tried cases.[615] He claimed some delays were strategic. He

---

[615] We have known for half a century that the personal injury bar is divided into the majority of lawyers who settle most of their cases and a few trial specialists. Carlin (1962); Seron (1996); Parikh (2001).

urged "Mr. Veguilla not to push the case because he was alleging a long term disability." But surely 10 years is far longer than necessary, and Veguilla clearly needed the money for reconstructive surgery *then* to have any chance of rehabilitation. Furthermore, delay cannot help rebut a defendant's allegation that injuries are attributable to a preexisting condition. Kreitzer claimed ignorance: he "did not realize that no check had been issued [to Danielle Richardson] until being notified of the complaint herein." But it was his responsibility to monitor this. He blamed others: the process server for failing to file his answer to the motion to dismiss in Levit (but Kreitzer never considered suing); the treating physician for failing to provide a medical report (but he never subpoenaed the doctor). He deceived one client because "it would have been very hard for him to understand what had taken place with the court and everything like that." Well, yes, Levit would have had a hard time understanding why Kreitzer negligently let the case be dismissed—indeed, why he took it in the first place if there was no liability. Kreitzer did not tell Gibson her case against Jordan had been dismissed because "she never asked me specifically—me personally." But why should a client have to ask her lawyer if her claim had been dismissed? When she did ask why a crucial defendant had been omitted, the firm "accused me of being nasty." In a masterpiece of understatement, Kreitzer admitted this "could have jeopardized the case to a certain extent."

Some excuses were not even excuses. His lawyer argued that Kreitzer was guilty of "mistakes," not "professional misconduct." "There's been no expert testimony here as to what standard is expected within the profession in the negligence field in these situations." Kreitzer took three years to respond to the request for a bill of particulars about Gibson because he "didn't get to it." Others do not pass the laugh test: the letters he claimed to have written Tartaglia in 1987 and 1988 referred to the 1991 lawsuit "by mistake." They were "done by a secretary through a computer subsequently." (Exactly: and backdated to mislead the DDC.) His failure to prepare infant compromises in two cases was acceptable because "there was no tolling [sic—he meant there *was* tolling] of the statute" of limitations and no "prejudice to the client" (other than having to wait *another* three years—a total of fourteen in one case, six in the other). His neglect not only denied his needy clients money but also created the real risk that meritorious claims would be dismissed. When all else failed, he blamed his employees. He had "no knowledge thereof nor authorized any acts of neglect"; "any allegations with regard to mishandling it were at a time

CHAPTER 2

when it was under the control of . . . the associate"; "again, this is a case where the original matter was being handled by an associate." Cooper emphasized this. Kreitzer "can't be looking over [employees'] shoulder[s] every day"; "people are expected to come forward if there's problems." Kreitzer

> believed that he was conducting a reasonable degree of supervision. And the fact that mistakes occur does not ipso facto lead to the conclusion that he's guilty of professional misconduct.

But he *was* responsible for supervising subordinates, especially when he hired inexperienced associates to save money or had his office manager draft pleadings.

His explanations for participating in the "ten percenter scheme" were just as incriminating. "[A]t the time, other attorneys [were] doing it."[616] "I did not believe . . . that there was anything wrong—other than maybe some ethical violations." Precisely! Perhaps this is why he persisted even *after* receiving the DA's subpoena. Kreitzer protested that some of the bribe offers failed to produce settlements, but this did not make *his* conduct less guilty. He was not dealing directly with the adjuster, and there was no evidence they actually got the money. He had paid Joel Cohen for "his negotiation skills" and because Cohen "was hurting, you know, for money." "Joel was honorable in that sense, so I believed him 100 percent." Then why plead guilty to second degree commercial bribery? Kreitzer further compounded this by concealing his disciplinary complaints when applying for retroactive malpractice liability insurance in anticipation of those clients' lawsuits.

I can only speculate why Kreitzer behaved this way. He exemplified the American ideal of upward mobility. Coming from a working-class section of Queens,[617] he attended a low-ranked college (University of Louisville), worked his way through a low-ranked night law school (John Marshall), started as an associate doing collections, went solo in six years, and six years after that was employing eight or nine people to

---

[616] Three years later, another six lawyers were indicted for a similar scheme; they included an unsuccessful candidate for Nassau County District Attorney and a former president of the Staten Island Trial Lawyers Association. Thomas J. Lueck, "6 Lawyers Charged in Personal Injury Scheme," New York Times (June 4, 1998).
[617] Cambria Heights. See Petroski (2003).

manage over a thousand cases. By the time of the 1993 hearing, his law office was on Madison Avenue. He survived Hodgkin's Disease (before he was 30) and esophageal cancer (possibly caused by the earlier treatment) 13 years later, and passionately shared his story with other cancer patients, both in person and by writing a hundred-page manuscript. He worked seven days a week. One of his two daughters was of college age. With more than a thousand cases he must have been making a lot of money, even if he lost more than half the time.[618] But he may have been illiquid. He had a high overhead: more than eight employees and an expensive office. Cash flow in personal injury practice is highly erratic. His participation in the "ten percenter scheme" may have been a way of liquidating claims quickly (at the expense of clients). During his second bout with cancer, his medical expenses must have been high and his earnings lower. Other lawyers in such circumstances dip into client trust accounts. Kreitzer just ran faster. In so doing, however, he inevitably dropped many balls—to his clients' serious detriment.

---

[618] A 1988 article names the lawyer for the "Millionaire Circle Club" of lottery winners as David Kreitzer. Michael Winerip, "Our Towns: Where the Rich Find Comfort In Each Other," New York Times (March 1, 1988).

Chapter 3

Practicing Immigration Law in Filene's Basement

Joseph F. Muto was admitted in the Fourth Department of New York in January 1987. He was employed for two months by a Syracuse real estate firm and for ten months as an assistant district attorney in Cortland County, practiced alone in Syracuse for eighteen months, and then was an assistant district attorney in Rensselaer County for another four before resigning from the bar in October 1990. He was reinstated a year later but suspended in December 1994 and not reinstated until December 1996. In November 1997, at the age of 43, he moved to New York City. Responding to a *New York Law Journal* advertisement, he began doing immigration cases for David Rodkin.[619] In April 1998 he and Karen Gowren Jaffe[620] left Rodkin to open individual practices in space rented from Michael Lee in Chinatown.[621] On February 27, 2001, Muto was charged with neglecting

---

[619] A 1984 Cardozo Law School graduate.
[620] A 1982 Cardozo Law School graduate.
[621] As a result of changes in immigration law, asylum grants increased from 5,131 in FY 1996 to 9,170 in FY 2000 (Mottino, 2000: 14). Chinese applications increased from 6,930 in 1996 to

CHAPTER 3

clients, assisting the unauthorized practice of law, mismanaging his escrow account, and failing to report his address.[622]

At the outset of the disciplinary proceeding, Muto asked for a minute to collect himself. "I just want to get something together here. I'm like nervous as hell." Appearing for the Departmental Disciplinary Committee, Sherry K. Cohen said five clients would testify that they had initially consulted "non-lawyer agents who perform legal services and basically hire [Muto] with little or no involvement of the aliens." He had "no written lease, there's no record of rental payments, there's no record of weekly salary payments" to Michael Lee (whom Muto identified as his landlord and translator) or Lee's wife, Cathy Chen (whom Muto called his paralegal). A "person who is a real lawyer, who has a real bona fide practice, not dependent on third parties, has an office, has an address, had a telephone number." Four clients "never met Mr. Muto." He "can't remember" his clients "because he has over 500 pending matters with the INS right at this moment."[623] "He has no notes of any meetings with these clients. He has no receipts of accepting payment from these clients. He has no calendar entries of meeting with these clients," who could not contact him. His failure to report his current address to the Office of Court Administrator (OCA) showed his "underlying disrespect for his responsibilities as a lawyer." Four judges had complained about him missing hearings. These were "not typical neglect cases. Here, because of the language barriers of the clients and their vulnerability as illegal aliens, they're completely dependent upon third parties." Muto's fees were extraordinarily low; but "$150 to do . . . an individual hearing that doesn't get done . . . is an excessive fee."

Muto began by displaying photographs of his law office. "There's a contention that it's not a bona fide law office. Your Honor will note, my name is on the front of the building." This hearing was "a search for the truth, much like a fox hunt searching for the fox being the truth."

15,502 in 2000. U.S. Department of Justice (2001: F2-F3). This demand created unusual opportunities for lawyers like Rodkin, Muto, and Jaffe.

[622] The referee was John R. Horan, a partner in Fox, Horan & Camerini. Unless otherwise noted, all material is taken from the 1211-page hearing transcript (RP 06/01).

[623] "At Federal Plaza, there are low-cost, high-volume private lawyers who are generally considered to be low-end in terms of degree of attention they can devote to any individual case." Eight "represented from twenty-three to seventy-six cases in a single month," which would amount to 276–912 a year. Over 80% of their clients were Chinese. Mottino (2000: 21, 28–31). One such lawyer was imprisoned "for defrauding the INS and misleading thousands of clients." Mirta Ojito, "Lawyer's Fall Rends Immigrants' Lives," New York Times B1 (October 23, 1998) (Sheldon Walker).

> It's a lot like paint by numbers. . . . It's a painting of a fox hunt.
> . . . We can't leave large blotches of this uncovered and say that's a fox hunt in pastoral England, if you don't see a fox and you don't see trees and you don't see horses.

His Internet search of the phrase "disbarred/suspended attorneys" revealed that the "common thread in every one of these cases" was "dishonest." He stated, "I'm not a dishonest attorney. . . . I may be a little bit disorganized. . . . But we don't disbar or suspend people for being a little bit disorganized here and there." "[I]f every lawyer is held to a standard of perfection, there's going to be no more lawyers."

> I provide quality legal services, Your Honor, at an affordable price for poor people who've been gauged [sic] and used by smugglers. . . . I give 150 percent of my effort and my time. I go in on Sundays very often . . . I work 'til 7:30 or eight at night. . . . I handle a lot of cases. And virtually every one of my clients is overjoyed and happy with my services. There's no greater feeling than seeing a man's case being granted and having him shake my hand and saying she-she, thank you in Chinese—bowing to me and just grabbing my hand. It's heartening to take a walk through Chinatown as I did with my daughter a couple of weeks ago on a Sunday afternoon, and going into a store and having someone come up to me and shake my hand and saying thank you, Muto. Thank you, thank you, lawyer. . . . I had no success in Syracuse. . . . I came here to start a new life. . . . I empathize with these people. They came here with nothing. I came here, I had just a few hundred dollars in my pocket. . . . And I worked and worked and worked, and gave myself, mind, body and soul into this community—into being an accepted member of your legal community. To the point now, I own a small coop in Brooklyn Heights. . . . I support a disabled spouse and two children. . . . If I'm suspended or disbarred, it's going to affect my life personally. I'm not going to get another job. . . . Most importantly, I'm the only low budget lawyer in Chinatown. . . . I'm Filene's basement. My office is physically in the basement. . . . [T]hese complaints which . . . high priced lawyers are behind—this isn't about justice. . . . This is Lord and Taylor trying to put

Chapter 3

> Filene's basement out of business. And these agencies, to a certain extent, are behind it. I don't go to the agencies. . . . I have a sign on the side of my building. I have a good reputation in Chinatown. . . . Why should I go do what we call in the profession the Chinatown crawl . . . the agency lawyers walking from agency to agency to agency, trying to find cases.

Cohen could have had him tailed to "see if he does the Chinatown crawl." She claimed agencies sent him clients. "I don't know. I can't say that they do or don't. I say, I strongly suspect they do," but "I didn't know about it." Michael Lee had told him that "a lot of these people that are coming down with their friends are agencies. And I'm like, oh, I really shouldn't be dealing with these people." But "those were a tiny fragment of the cases."

In order to reopen their deportation cases, clients had to complain to the DDC about their former lawyers.[624] Successor counsel told them, "Just put it down that this guy . . . cheated you. . . . You give me $3,000, I'll take you for a little more of your money." He blamed his failure to attend hearings on his clients. "You go into any master calendar[625] . . . and I guarantee you, you're going to have three, four, five out of 30 cases where they don't show up."

> I have a high volume practice. . . . I'm like an over eager little puppy dog. The client comes in. I want to help them. . . . I do quality work, quality reopens. Granted they don't follow the regs. But . . . the way it's done in New York, the judges just want you to go right to the chase. . . . I get deeply involved in my cases.

I. Winging It

Cohen's first witness, Jan Allen Reiner, an immigration specialist since 1975, described his practice. A client once "refused to cooperate for preparation for a hearing. And did I appear? I absolutely 100 percent appeared." He never scheduled "more than one individual hearing in one day" or "filed documents late." He charged $3,500–$8,000 for an asylum application and could not "imagine under any circumstance, how a lawyer can present an asylum claim competently . . . for $150 or $200." Many of his clients

---

[624] In re Lozada, 19 I&N DEC 637 (BIA 1998).
[625] Roughly analogous to arraignment.

complained "that they never met with any lawyer. When they appeared at the master calendar, out in the hallway, the agency people brought them up and introduced them, this is your attorney." His immigration bar association was investigating unauthorized practice of law by such agencies. On cross-examination, Reiner insisted he "never had any problems" locating clients or "the experience with people replacing me on cases." Even after 25 years, he could not do cases much faster because "the facts of the cases are individual."

Muto admitted agencies were "rampant." But he asked his clients, "How did you . . . find out about me? And they say a friend told me. . . . Am I supposed to plug these people into lie detectors . . . ?" Asked how he got so many cases, Muto replied, "I have a good reputation in the community. I have a sign on the side of my building."

A. *Chang Kui Lin*

In 1992 Chang Kui Lin[626] paid a snakehead[627] $30,000 to smuggle him by boat into Mexico, then overland to Los Angeles, and finally by plane to New York. In March 1993 he applied through Xing Rong Service Company in Chinatown for a work authorization card (C-8), which was granted and renewed annually. When that agency closed, he switched to the Blue Eagle travel agency, also known as Fuzhou Immigration Service Center, whose business card declared, "Chinese Immigration Service Agency, Mandarin, Cantonese, Fuzhouese and Taiwanese . . . immigration, one year work permission, C-8 card, A-5, change to green card." Blue Eagle's Tiffany Dong (or Tung) notified Chang Kui in 1997 of a hearing on his political asylum application based on China's coercive one-child policy.[628] This was the first he had heard of the application. On November 10 he gave the agency a birth notarial certificate, marriage certificate, household registration book, and his wife's abortion certificate and receipt for payment of a 2,000 RMB fine for her second pregnancy. The agency took him to the INS hearing

---

[626] Both the immigration cases and the disciplinary hearing Americanized the word order of Chinese names, putting the patronym at the end rather than the beginning. They also used inconsistent spellings. Because Chinese patronyms are very widely shared—by several complainants in this case—I will use their given names.

[627] The English translation of the Chinese term for smuggler. On the relationship between snakeheads and immigration lawyers, see Elizabeth Amon, "The Snakehead Lawyers," National Law Journal A8 (July 15, 2002).

[628] The Illegal Immigration Reform and Immigrant Responsibility Act of 1996 authorized 1,000 conditional grants of asylum per year based on China's coercive population control. Pub. L. No. 104-208, div. C, 110 Stat. 3009-546 (1996).

CHAPTER 3

but failed to prepare, and the application was denied. On February 6, 1998, Dong told him to appear at Immigration Court on February 26 for a master calendar. He went to the agency that day, paid $250, and was taken to the courtroom by Eddie Ye. "Then the judge [presumably the bailiff] opened the door and asked me to go in with an attorney whose skin was dark colored." Chang Kui did not know his name, never talked to him, and neither paid him nor signed an appearance notice.

This was Gregory Kuntashian, a Yale College graduate who did anti-poverty work in New Haven for a decade before attending CUNY Law School.

> I came to represent Mr. Lin by having received a request that I do so, through a man named Eddie [Ye], who works for a Blue Eagle agency ... that provides a variety of different services for immigrants: translation of documents, interpretation of language.... They will prepare some forms ... which are part and parcel of the immigration process.... And they do also help these immigrants to obtain legal counsel.... Mr. Ye asked me if I would represent Mr. Lin at a master calendar hearing ... in February of 1998 before Judge Ferris.... [Ye translated and] also served as the go-between ... the money that the client meant for me as my compensation ... was given to the agent, who then gave it to me.

He had not met Chang Kui before the hearing. Muto began cross-examination by telling Kuntashian to "chill out, relax." The Referee instructed Muto to "stick to business," refused to allow questions about "other agency dealings with Eddie Ye," and rebuked Muto for asking if Cohen was going to call Ye.

At the master calendar, Judge Noel Anne Ferris directed Kuntashian to produce Chinese government documents by June 26 and scheduled an individual merits hearing for November 3. After the calendar, however, Ye told Chang Kui "the judge was not good."[629] I had to change my case ... to New Jersey," where Chang Kui was working. He paid the agency $310 for the motion; the receipt listed a New Jersey address. But Chang Kui had never lived there and was unable to obtain documentation of residence from his employer, which Ye requested.

---

[629] At the disciplinary hearing, Muto produced two lists ranking the likelihood that judges would grant asylum petitions; Ferris was near the bottom of both. Respondent Ex. A.

Ye again escorted Chang Kui to the November 3 hearing and "told me this Mr. Muto is my attorney, and asked me to follow him." Chang Kui had never met Muto, did not talk to him, pay him, or sign a notice of appearance, and had not "of [his] own volition . . . ask[ed] Mr. Muto to go to court" for him. Muto admitted he had no "independent recollection of meeting a Mr. Lin. However, as a general policy, I would not do a reopen for someone who I haven't met." "I know he came to our office," or at least "somebody went to 401 Broadway." If Eddie Ye "wants to sit there and, you know, lie and say Blue Eagle sent them to me, I mean that's fine." The Referee refused to admit a conversation he had secretly taped with Ye on March 5, 2001. Muto challenged Cohen to "subpoena Eddie Ye."

> [S]how me where my name appears in the Blue Eagle file. . . . Most likely Blue Eagle sent a client to Karen. Karen told me, Joe, do you want to do a change of venue for this man? And I agreed.

He asked the Referee to subpoena Eddie Ye but admitted that the subpoena he had drafted the previous week was invalid. The Referee replied, "You've had weeks, if not months, to subpoena anybody within the jurisdiction. And I'm not going to do it for you."

Muto denied dealing with any service agencies, including Blue Eagle. "There's a common sense factor, here . . . look how big my practice is. . . . I've no need to deal with these people. . . . I have an office in the heart of Chinatown," unlike Claude Maratea[630] and Greg Kuntashian.[631] He and Karen Jaffe

> advertised that practice using her name. Karen Gowren, literally means high and mighty in Chinese.[632] . . . It was very effective. . . . Now Karen's name . . . is on the Blue Eagle file. . . . Eddie Ye may have sent this person to see Karen. . . . Eddie may have been standing next to Gregory and interpreting. I didn't know who Eddie Ye was.

---

[630] In 2007 Maratea, a 1993 Hofstra Law School graduate, was practicing in the mid-town office building where Rodkin had had his office.
[631] By 2007, Kuntashian listed a Chinatown office (2 East Broadway) but was delinquent in his bar membership dues. He paid them on March 8, 2008.
[632] It was Jaffe's idea to use "Gowren," which sounds like Karen and means "high and mighty."

Chapter 3

Muto said "I worked for Karen at the time" but quickly recanted: "I worked with Karen at the time. It just seemed like it was for Karen a few times, which is probably the reason we didn't stay together." She refused to testify.

> Muto: She doesn't want to be cross examined and risk having charges filed against her.
>
> Referee: What kind of charges?
>
> Muto: Dealing with agencies...
>
> Referee: So she dealt with illegal agencies?
>
> Muto: Apparently...
>
> Cohen: And you shared office space with her and shared legal fees with her and did work for her, and your testimony is that you had no idea it was an agency.
>
> Muto: I didn't know Blue Eagle was behind this case . . . it could be just an agency.
>
> Referee: And meanwhile, you were taking seven or ten a day—
>
> Muto: Not back then, Judge. No.
>
> Referee: Five or four a day. And you're asking me to believe that you were new on the street and people were coming in without references from agencies?

Muto offered to "take a frigging lie detector test—excuse my language" but then changed tack.

> I'm going to cut Ms Cohen a break . . . let's say I got this file directly from Eddie Ye. . . . I took over the file. It became my file, my case. . . . this is the only real case of all of these that really gets me angry, because I did not deal with Blue Eagle and I'm really being made to take the fall for something I didn't do. . . . We can go down to the first precinct and I'll . . . sit and take a lie detector test. . . . I didn't know who Eddie Ye was at the time . . . somebody told me he had a problem with his restaurant. I said give him my name. He came over to my

office and I helped him with his restaurant. And I told him I didn't want any of his cases, because Tiffany Dong, his wife, is . . . convicted of immigration fraud.

On cross-examination he denied having any "clue . . . Karen was working with [agents]. I used to assume that we got our . . . cases from the advertisement she ran in the Chinese newspaper."

Muto had learned immigration law from David Rodkin, who paid him $750 a week and $250 for every successful case.

> Muto: I used to love to sit and listen to him litigate. . . . He's an excellent attorney.
>
> Cohen: Were you aware that these were agency cases?
>
> Muto: He would tell me that they were agency cases. Almost everything except his Bangladesh practice. . . . But . . . at the time I was fresh off the bus from Syracuse. I didn't really know what was going on, and a lot of judges were [would] point it out to me. And that's probably the reason Karen and I set up our own practice.
>
> Cohen: Didn't you tell me that you decided to leave Mr. Rodkin's office because you figured you could make at least $2,000 a week in—
>
> Muto: Well, that's another reason, too. . .

At the November 3 merits hearing, Judge Ferris reprimanded Muto for his October 5 change-of-venue motion.[633]

> Court: Mr. Muto, regulations govern changes of venue. Yours is totally inadequate. Why are you filing motions that are not compliant with the regulations?
>
> Muto: I wasn't aware, Your Honor. . .
>
> Court: Well start reading the regulations in the future, counsel. An affidavit is not sufficient. You have to prove address.[634]

---

[633] Staff Ex. 4.
[634] The EOIR Bar Counsel deplored that "there are many immigration lawyers out there who really don't know the immigration laws." Barnes (2003: 1219).

Chapter 3

She denied the motion and asked for the documents that had been due the previous June but refused to accept them "unless you give me an explanation" for their lateness. When Muto had none, she recessed so he could "think of something to say." He returned and claimed that Chang Kui had "advised me he had trouble procuring the documents from his wife in China." (At the disciplinary hearing, Chang Kui insisted, "All the documents were sent from China in October.") Ferris gave Muto two weeks to explain why he hadn't moved to enlarge the time, "Why you didn't act like a lawyer. That's what lawyers do." Muto promised her "You will have it, Your Honor."

Chang Kui could not see Muto before the next hearing on January 20, 1999, because he lacked Muto's business card and office address. Ye took Chang Kui to court again. The court interpreter told Chang Kui the judge would deport him for having failed to provide documentation by the June 1998 deadline. This was the first he had heard about that, because there had been no translation on November 3. Claude L. Maratea appeared for Muto "of counsel" because (according to Chang Kui) "the judge did not like this Muto to be at the hearing." Judge Ferris observed that service on Muto had failed three times at the address he had given (his home at 179 Degraw Avenue, Brooklyn). "I will note for the record that I saw him earlier. That he muttered something and then went scurrying out of my courtroom. I'm going to require Mr. Muto to be produced on this case." Asked about the motion when he appeared, Muto said, "I have to accept responsibility, Your Honor. I didn't prepare the motion. I wasn't sure exactly how you wanted it. I hadn't done one before." Ferris accused him of having "just ignored it." Muto objected: "It actually slipped through the cracks. I apologize." (At the disciplinary hearing, Muto attributed this admission to the fact that Judge Ferris "was screaming at me and I was very distraught when I was in her court."[635]) "I seem to recall it was a motion—this was originally a motion to change venue."

---

[635] In 2006 Muto told me that Judge Ferris was mentally unstable and unable to control her temper. In 2007 the Second Circuit removed Judge Ferris from a Chinese asylum application, calling her behavior "most troubling." When Ferris asked Jian Zhong Sun why he was crying during the hearing, he said "because I have not seen my daughter after 11 years." When he wept again while describing his wife's forced abortion, Judge Ferris interrupted, complaining of "the respondent's disproportionate behavior in this courtroom." Even the judge's supporters noted that she had reduced to tears not only petitioners but also lawyers, translators, and clerks. Nina Bernstein, "Judge Who Chastised Weeping Asylum Seeker Is Taken Off Case," New York Times B1 (9.20.07).

Court: You have, unfortunately, shown utter disregard for any court directives in this matter. . . . I don't think it's appropriate for you to represent this individual because you're not representing him in a fair manner . . . and then by sending in another lawyer who you knew could not answer any of these questions, because you walked out of my courtroom muttering that you weren't going to appear in this case.

Muto: I was feeling nervous coming in here, Your Honor.

Court: Counsel, frankly, given the quality of your representation, that is the first appropriate response I have heard from you. You should be nervous, because you are not doing right by your clients. And you know that I will not tolerate that.

Muto suggested Chang Kui find another attorney but admitted doing nothing to help him.

Court: Mr. Muto, what is it that you're looking through?

Muto: The evidence packet, Your Honor.

Court: Your client just says he's never given you any evidence. How did you come to get this . . . ? I think it's time for you to be forthcoming and honest.

Judge Ferris gave Muto a week "to file a motion with me as to your law office failures in this matter."

Court: I expect you to set up an appointment immediately with your client at an address. Do you have any business cards with you?

Muto: I kind of ran out of business cards today, Your Honor.

Court: Yes, that's what you tell me every time. . . . And we've had repeated problems with your clients saying they don't know . . . how to find you.

When Ye brought Chang Kui to the January 28 hearing, Ferris asked Muto for the motion "to be filed no later than yesterday."

Muto: I did not do it, Your Honor. I had planned.

CHAPTER 3

> Court: Mr. Muto, I'm requesting the Chief Judge of the United States Immigration Court to sanction you.[636] . . . You came back last week and attempted to send in a different attorney. Having said to my clerk that you could not appear because you knew I would be angry. You were quite right. . . .
>
> Muto: I was going to do the work over the weekend. My mother is in the hospital for surgery. She's very ill. And I have the name of the social worker at the hospital who [can] attest to that to verify what I'm saying. . . .
>
> Court: Well, Mr. Muto, that's not how you do it. Right? You know perfectly well it's not the court's job to call social workers at hospitals.

She adjourned the case to let Muto get organized. When it resumed she demanded that Chang Kui prove his residence, refusing to believe he lived at the restaurant where he worked and rejecting his employer's letter. Calling Muto's representation "less than stellar," she gave him a week to file the motion, stating that otherwise she would "not allow you to be this man's attorney anymore."

> Where I see such blatant ignoring of every deadline and every professional standard that exists in this practice, including the fact that you couldn't even write to The Court and ask for an extension claiming a family emergency, but instead, after I've seen you in the court every day this week, claim that you just didn't get to it, because you didn't do it over the weekend. . . . You find the time to represent your clients or you get out of this practice.

She interrupted an argument between Chang Kui and Muto about responsibility for the missing documents.

> Counsel, I'm not going to get between you and your client. You sort it out. If you can't represent this client, don't do it anymore. . . . I am tired of you, Mr. Muto, because you never meet your deadlines. . . . And you are hurting people and I am not going to be a party to that. Hear me well and hear

---

[636] The IC did not obtain authority to discipline for another 18 months.

me clearly. This record is going to the Appellate Division, Disciplinary Committee in its entirety. And I'm requesting action against you.

Muto filed his motion for consideration of late evidence on February 3, claiming that Chang Kui's wife had been "unable to compile the requisite material until late October of 1998." The bailiff called the case at noon the next day.

> Court: I will note that Mr. Muto has poked his head in my door a couple of times this morning, but he has never stopped and he has never made a form [sic] representation on the record as to why his client is not here.

She denied Chang Kui's asylum application and ordered him deported. When they both appeared at 12:10 PM she reopened the case, acknowledging it was scheduled for the next day, but challenged Muto's claim to have an office at 5 Doyers Street. Muto insisted he had his own room, number 14. "I invite you or anyone to come down and look at it."

> Court: As a matter of fact, I tried to do that, Mr. Muto, and it could not be located in that building, although I did see a mailbox which you share with a Chinese travel agent by the name of Dr. He.
>
> Muto: This is ridiculous. Dr. He has got an office across the hall and down.
>
> Court: You share the phone. . . . You previously told me you didn't know [him]. . . .
>
> Muto: I've met him. . . .
>
> Court: [S]hould someone misplace your business card, if they had it, they would have no way of contacting you because you're unlisted. That is not a professional form of doing practice. . . .
>
> Muto: That's an upstate thing.

She rejected his excuses for the delays in providing documentation, closed the record, and suggested voluntary departure. After consulting Chang

CHAPTER 3

Kui, Muto said his client would accept it. Questioned by Ferris, however, Chang Kui insisted on pursuing his application, hoping to appeal the inevitable denial.

(Muto testified in the disciplinary hearing that he had urged Chang Kui to take voluntary departure because "given his demeanor in court and given the judge's demeanor in court . . . there's probably at least a 50–50, if not greater chance that she would have that man taken into custody. That she would, effectively—I don't want to say a kangaroo court type hearing—but she would conduct a hearing in a very short span of time . . . deny his case, and then order him arrested." Muto had not sought to end the case quickly. Reminded that Reiner had testified that asylum applicants rarely take voluntary departure "because they have several bites of the apple later on," Muto explained that "Judge Ferris was very angry at me. She has a problem with me. . . . I asked other lawyers if they would take the case over, and they overwhelmingly said no. Nobody wanted to deal with Judge Ferris. Especially on a case that I had . . . that's like mixing gasoline and matches." But Chang Kui denied discussing voluntary departure with Muto: "I don't speak English. How do you communicate with me?")

Muto then moved to withdraw as counsel on three grounds. Chang Kui "has not been completely up front with me." Muto had "no clue that this case was on for today." Most important, the judge's threatened grievance "will place me in a position where I would be possibly impeaching my client." A friend "in the Fourth Department ethics committee" had advised that withdrawal was mandatory. Ferris questioned Muto's "good faith" in suddenly making the motion after representing Chang Kui at the hearing for half an hour. She gave him until the next morning to file a written motion to withdraw.

> Court: Don't go anywhere Mr. Muto.
>
> Muto: I'm not, Judge.
>
> Court: Your conduct before The Court is unprofessional. It is continuously unprofessional. . . .
>
> Muto: Your Honor—
>
> Court: Excuse me, Mr. Muto, but—
>
> Muto: Actually, Judge, I thought you were done, Judge—
>
> Court: —if you interrupt me one more time, I will have you removed, so be—

Muto: Actually, Judge, it—

Court: —quiet and wait until it's your turn.

She urged Chang Kui to hire another lawyer and ordered Muto to appear the next day. "No excuses will be accepted by The Court, short of you being in the hospital." She denied his request for a postponement. "You accepted the date of tomorrow a week ago." "You are counsel of record . . . until you are relieved by this court."

The next day Chang Kui told Ferris that Muto "asked me to have" Claude Maratea represent him. Ferris rebuked Muto: "it's inappropriate for you to be hiring him. . . . The Respondent is the one who hires his own lawyer. That's the whole problem with this case. I have no evidence he ever hired you directly."

Although he could not remember introducing Chang Kui to Maratea, Muto testified at the disciplinary hearing:

> As a general rule, if someone is going to cover even a master, I will introduce the lawyer to them. I'll say a few words in Chinese [spoken] . . . point my thumb up. And have somebody—maybe a court interpreter, maybe a paid interpreter of another lawyer, explain to them. . . . And I'll say, good lawyer [repeated in Chinese]. . . . And that's how every other lawyer does it.

Maratea acknowledged having just met Chang Kui (actually, they had met in court on January 20). Ferris reprimanded Muto for making the motion to withdraw late and for failing to follow regulations but granted it, telling him "to leave the room and close the door behind you." Maratea suggested "other attorneys who would be more prepared to handle Chinese cases, who have the interpreters and the facility to do this . . . who are not affiliated with outside agencies, so to speak." Ferris adjourned the case for three weeks.

(At the disciplinary hearing Maratea testified he had graduated from Hofstra Law School in 1991 and specialized in immigration law, renting space from a lawyer in Queens. Muto had asked him to handle Chang Kui's master calendar because of Judge Ferris's hostility. After the hearing Michael Lee "got very angry" at Maratea. "He said, why did you do this? What are you doing?" "[A]gents, immigration representatives would call to ask me to appear on [Muto's] behalf." Whenever he was approached by Muto "my next question would be, is this from your office directly or is it through an agent?" because 50–70 percent of the cases he got from Muto came from agents. Maratea "almost always" met the agent and client "in the lobby . . . the agent would bring the file." "The agent speaks Chinese and I communicate through the agent." He was paid $75–100 in cash, sometimes by Muto, sometimes by the agent. Although "there are a number of private practitioners who don't use agents," agents are "very good for getting clients . . . if you're starting out in law . . . they do the grunt work . . . get the documents, speak to the client." It would be "very unlikely" for "an attorney that has a regular practice in immigration court . . . to take a case from a travel agent without knowing it."

Under cross-examination Muto objected that Maratea "doesn't have an office. He deals exclusively with travel agencies. He has the unmitigated chutzpah to come into this room and accuse me of being an agency lawyer." Muto would complain about Maratea to the DDC. "I feel it bears directly on the fact he has a motive to lie." Maratea admitted accepting cases from Howard Chen, a travel agent, but denied asking "how Howard Chen wanted [him] to proceed with that case." Still, Maratea agreed that "one of [his] problems with Howard Chen is that he's . . . over controlling on his cases." Chen "called me often and he's nerve wracking." Muto asked the DDC "to divulge the existence of any agreements not to prosecute Mr. Kuntashian or Mr. Maratea for any offenses relating to travel agencies or ethical violations in return for testimony." But Cohen insisted "there's no deals."

Muto also blamed others. Chang Kui "was a very difficult client." Judge Ferris "hated me. . . . If you want to listen to the tapes . . . then it will really come across . . . screaming at me at a time when my mother is dying, to do this, do that. . . . I was driving to Syracuse every weekend . . . so I could spend a little more time with my mother—and I didn't think I'd see her again." Other judges gave him continuances. "Judge Ferris, you know, abused her judicial discretion by pushing and pushing and pushing and refusing to allow me off this case." The motion for an extension of time to file documents "was very clearly a motion that I'd never done before."

When Ann Hsiung appeared for Chang Kui on February 26, Ferris said she had closed the record three times and would not reopen it "unless a Lazato [sic] motion is made. . . . This is a case that in all honesty, is very likely to go to the Disciplinary Committee." She gave Hsiung a week to read the file and prove Chang Kui's address: "Your client seems to move more than average, to put it mildly." On March 5 she said Hsiung's motion to file documents late did not conform to *Lozada*. "[T]he actions of prior counsel appear to condone, that the case was being governed not by a lawyer, but by some third party." Hsiung replied that the DDC had just refused to accept another client's grievance until the Immigration Court completed the case. Ferris said the INS and DDC were discussing this and insisted Hsiung file a grievance "so that there would be attribution [sic] against just every day someone coming in and saying, oh, it's the other lawyer's fault." When Hsiung instead offered to help Chang Kui file pro se, Ferris said no one would believe he had done so. But Hsiung had "a problem. I don't want Mr. Muto or the other gentleman [Kuntashian] thinking that I personally filed against them. . . . As much as I don't agree with . . . their practice . . . it's really not my business."

> Court: I think there is a problem, though, with what happens in immigration practice often. We have probably 90 percent of the Chinese appeals go into the board allegedly as pro se. And they are not pro se. They are by non–English speaking people and they are written in English. . . . My guess is that those are all being done by the so-called service agencies who are practicing law without a license.

She scheduled the next hearing for June 20, warning Chang Kui not to "go through any third parties who are not in the employ of your lawyer."

Hsiung testified at the disciplinary hearing that she had practiced immigration law since 1983, with her husband, until he was appointed to the immigration bench.

> I find certain clients will tell me that they went to a service center. And most of them will say they did not know that they were applying for asylum. They were only asking for a work organization [sic—"authorization"] card. . . . And they will say then they will go to the court and they don't have any lawyer. And when they go to the court, the agency will provide them with lawyers. . . . The clients will have no direct contact with these lawyers.

She advised clients seeking to reopen removals on grounds of ineffective assistance of counsel "that most of the judges would require them at least

Chapter 3

to file a complaint with the appropriate Disciplinary Committee." She charged $3,500–5,000 for an asylum application. Her four secretaries all spoke English, Cantonese, and Mandarin; three spoke Fuzhou. She usually saw a client for half an hour before agreeing to take the case, three hours before the master calendar, and for three 2–4 hour meetings before the individual hearing. Although 99 percent of her cases were referred by former clients, "I can't say 100 percent that I didn't take any cases from a travel agency.... But I didn't give anybody, even a chance of taking control of the case."

On cross-examination she said she had 70–80 asylum cases pending and 20–30 reopens. Although Muto claimed "there's nothing that needs to be done" for long periods of time, she always had her secretary "pull my file at least one month before the next hearing, to see what has to be done." When Muto speculated that "somebody from an agency" could impersonate a client seeking a reopen, Hsiung replied that she required an ID before notarizing a client's signature. Muto reflected that "you have a little bit of an advantage over me, being Chinese" and wondered what would happen "if somebody didn't check identification . . . there were so many reopens . . . I wasn't checking IDs." He asked if "you ever have instances where . . . you'll send your clients letters, you'll call them. But you just don't hear from them between the hearings." Hsiung responded,

> It never happened in my office . . . my secretary will call the clients to make sure they will meet me at least one and a half months before the hearing date so I can schedule between then to the hearing date, at least two to three times to meet with them and prepare them for a hearing.

When Muto persisted the Referee interrupted: Ms Hsiung "has very ably described her disciplined method of trying to make sure she's prepared each client for the coming hearing. And I think that's one of the points of this proceeding here."

Chang Kui complained to the DDC about Kuntashian and Muto on April 23.[637] Thomas Cahill, chief attorney, replied May 19, asking if the purpose "is to comply with the requirements of Matter of Lozada." Hsiung filed the complaint with the Immigration Court on June 4. The certified letter to Muto at 5 Doyers Street was returned. When Cahill informed the

---

[637] Staff Ex. 10.

court he would not act until the immigration case ended, Ferris expressed frustration. Although Congress had authorized the Immigration Court to hold lawyers in contempt, it could not proceed in the absence of implementing regulations and lacked authority to discipline. Because state procedures were the only recourse, she was asking the Office of the General Counsel of the Executive Office for Immigration Review (EOIR) to meet with Cahill "to explain the problems and the clear misconception which Mr. Cahill apparently is operating [sic]." Her "private opinion" was that the state should act if Chang Kui's allegations were true. She directed that Muto be notified of the next hearing: "In the year and a half he has been practicing before the Court, he has given at least three different office addresses."

Kuntashian and Maratea participated in the July 14 hearing, but Muto had not signed the certified mail receipt and did not appear. Kuntashian refused to answer questions about the service center but conceded he had never possessed Chang Kui's documents. Eddie Ye testified (under IC subpoena) that he managed the Chinese Immigration Service Office. He claimed he had "just translated some documentations" for Chang Kui but admitted he had kept the documents and translations.

> Ye: Now no longer have . . . it seems that the attorney took it away.
>
> Court: What attorney?
>
> Ye: I don't know. . . .
>
> Court: Sir, is it your habit to give away documents that are nothing to do with you, to other people who you don't know?
>
> Ye: No, no, no. . . . Last time this folder was given to the Attorney Muto.

He insisted Chang Kui had hired both attorneys but admitted neither spoke any Chinese language.

> Ye: Just because I know Mr. Kuntashian and Mr. Muto, just because there were a lot of documentations that need to be translated, there was or is a kind of the work relationship.
>
> Hsiung: . . . How did Mr. Lin hire either one of those attorneys?

CHAPTER 3

> Ye: At the time I don't just remember. . . . He was unable to find attorney and he has to know attorney.
>
> Hsiung: . . . Mr. Lin asked you to hire attorney for him?
>
> Ye: Yes, to refer or introduce one for him.
>
> Hsiung: . . . Who pays Mr. Kuntashian or Mr. Muto's fee . . . ?
>
> Ye: . . . Sometimes they paid the attorney. Sometimes . . . they get the money to me for me to deliver it to the attorneys.

Questioned by the INS lawyer, Ye denied providing services other than translation and photographs but admitted to contacting attorneys and making phone calls. He could not remember if the $1,100 Chang Kui paid was his "translation fee." Ferris issued a subpoena ordering Ye to produce "all business records concerning any payments from Mr. Lin to you."

Ferris also noted for the record that she had just "encountered Mr. Muto in the waiting room" and told him about the hearing. He declined to attend, "relying on papers filed in the Appellate Division, which he has not given us a copy of." He claimed to have filed a copy with the IC the previous day. Later in the hearing, the judge found Muto's reply to Cohen, with a handwritten cover letter to herself dated two days hence, which claimed to have been "filed with the window on the 10th floor yesterday." Muto had written, "I rest on this answer" on the advice of counsel "and waive my personal appearance."[638] The four-page handwritten note maintained he took the case without payment, "as a favor" to Kuntashian.

> I am unaware of any third party involvement in this matter, and this individual was furnished with a business card with my address (in China town) and my name (in Chinese). . . . I did file a proper motion for late filed documents . . . this individual was extremely evasive with the court, and myself regarding his address. . . . The record will show that I provided competent and ethical representation. I did review this individual's claim with him, and explained the removal process to him.

When the hearing resumed on July 27, Judge Ferris said there was no record of those documents having been filed. "They appeared in my mailbox

---
[638] Staff Ex. 11.

about an hour after I spoke with Mr. Muto." On August 9, Ye testified he could find no records, claiming he had given them to Muto. On September 20, Ferris agreed to accept additional evidence. At the individual hearing on February 2, 2000, she reaffirmed her belief that voluntary departure had been proposed without Chang Kui's "knowledge, without his consent, and purely at Mr. Muto's suggestion . . . to try to excuse Mr. Muto's failure to comply with court orders." She made the following findings of fact:

> Mr Lin never hired a lawyer prior to hiring Miss Sung [sic] . . . but hired a service agency who both hired and paid lawyers and that those lawyers did not do the respondent's bidding but acted under the authorization, direction, and at the interest of the service agency only. . . . [Blue Eagle] transported the respondent back and forth from their offices in Chinatown. Their offices were the site of the preparation of all applications. . . . [Muto] did not obey court deadlines to file a motion as to why evidence was late. . . . What is perhaps to the court most shocking in this case was, one, an attempt at the last minute to change venue in this case without any basis . . . to get the case away from Judge Farris [sic], myself, and also the fact that the notes of the attorney, Mr Muto, appear all over the file of Blue Eagle.

At the end of the hearing she granted Chang Kui asylum.

B. *Guo Ping Lin*

Guo Ping Lin was smuggled into the United States with more than 100 others on a Taiwanese fishing boat. During the 50-day trip they had only two meals a day and insufficient water, slept on the bare deck, and were threatened with being thrown overboard if they complained. He was detained when he arrived in Los Angeles on September 18, 1998, released on bond on January 6, 1999, and directed to appear at a master calendar on January 22.[639] But because he had not paid the full $30,000 fee, the smugglers collected him from the detention center and imprisoned him with 15–20 other debtors.

> I was repeatedly beaten up by a smuggler. . . . My family, back in China, was told by telephone of the beatings and convinced

---

[639] Complaint to DDC (May 25, 2000).

> that worse might happen to me if the smuggling fees were not paid immediately. . . .
>
> I begged to be allowed to go to the hearing and promised that I would not tell anyone that I was being held, but the smugglers became furious. I got more beaten up. . . .
>
> Around January 20 [25?], 1999 I was taken by Smuggler . . . and flied to New York where I was held in a basement I later learned was in Flushing, New York. In New York, the beatings continued and both a hammer and the dull side of a chopper were used to hit me, cause injuries and pain. . . . While the beating were actually happening, the snakeheads would call my family in China so that they could hear my scream and be convinced that they had to send the rest of the smuggling fee immediately. The full smuggling fee was paid for me by my family in China in the morning of February 4, 1999 and I was released that day. I was sent to my brother's restaurant in Brooklyn and smugglers requested $1500 from my brother for my board and living expenses during my being held period.

His brother's friend took Guo Ping to a Ms. Chao, at 210–212 Canal Street, who "said I was not able to get an adjournment of the hearing because I already failed to show up . . . and had to reopen a case." His brother helped him pay the $300 fee. He did not sign the notice of appearance or affidavit. He later learned that the reopen was handled by Muto, whom he never met. After Ms. Chao told him it was denied, a friend referred him to a law firm, which asked for his file. Ms. Chao "lied to me and told me she did not have it anymore." "She said you don't have to get this anymore because it's used already." When he finally got the file he saw that the affidavit incorrectly declared he had arrived in the United States on January 6, 1999, (among other errors), and the signature was not his (even the name was wrong). The new lawyer "was afraid of the troubles—not convenient," but his friend took him to another, S. Jean Smith, who spent 2 to 3 hours on each of three or four visits.

Guo Ping complained to the DDC on May 25, 2000. Muto answered on July 10.[640]

---

[640] Staff Ex. 28.

Mr. Lin paid me directly, and I kept him apprised of the status of his case. I also provided him with the toll free number, 800-898-7180, which would enable him to check his case's status. I am unaware of any third party involvement in this matter, but cannot rule out the possibility that a third party may have advised Mr. Lin to come to my office.

At the disciplinary hearing, Muto claimed that "somebody came to my office purporting to be [Guo Ping] in mid February of 1999." Smith got Guo Ping's case reopened on August 21, 2000, and got the venue changed to New York.[641]

C. Yi Chen

When Yi Chen was detained by the INS in Buffalo in July 1998 his uncle, Xiao Guang Lin, "read the newspaper and I found a Chinese, an attorney, Michael [Lee]." Lin obtained a $15,000 bond for Yi's release and a business card for "Michael Lee, Operation Manager, Chinese Service Center, Vincent Smith Bail Bond, 7–8 Chatham Square Ste C1-A." A master calendar was scheduled for June 2, 1999. When Yi moved to New York City, his uncle gave him that card, "and he said that was the attorney's office who had bailed me out." Yi consulted Lee, who told him a change of venue motion would be filed, for which he charged $200. Yi returned to the office in April and May 1999 and was assured by Lee and Cathy Chen that he would be notified of the new hearing date in New York City and did not have to go to Buffalo. He never met Muto or noticed his name on the building. "I only recognized the big characters Wun Fa Building, and the basement." Whenever he telephoned, Cathy Chen just handed the phone to Michael. "If you are a law firm, then you should say law firm." On May 28 Muto mailed a notice of appearance on which Yi Chen's name had been forged (wrongly including the middle name "Teng") and a change of venue motion, which the Buffalo IC denied because it had to be filed 15 days before the hearing.[642] When no one appeared at the hearing, the court ordered Yi deported in absentia and his bail forfeited. Yi testified, "If I was told to go to a hearing in Buffalo, I would have been there." When Michael told him the case was closed "I felt he lied and he had taken the money and had not done anything for it. . . . He said that if I still wanted to open the

---

[641] Staff Ex. 29.
[642] Staff Ex. 22.

CHAPTER 3

case, I would give him 100 money." Instead, Yi consulted Robert F. Belluscio, who helped him file a disciplinary complaint on August 10, 1999, and a successful motion to reopen.[643]

Yi's complaint said his uncle had hired the Chinese Service Center because it "has people who speak the Chinese language, like I do." "I thought that this office could represent me, as they were openly practicing immigration law and as Joseph F. Muto, Esq., is an attorney listed in that office." When Yi contacted the office he "was always told that in a few weeks I should receive a notice for a new hearing date." He called on June 1 "and was told that I did not have to attend the June 2, 1999 hearing."

Muto denied he had ever "shared any office with a 'Chinese Service Center' or a 'Vincent Smith Bail Bond.'" "I, and I alone in this office, practice Immigration Law." "Mr. Chen was apprised of the denial of this motion.... I expressly advised Mr. Chen to plan on appearing in Buffalo." Yi retorted, "Mr. Muto is NOT telling the truth.... I NEVER saw or spoke directly with Mr. Muto or any Caucasian at his office." Michael Lee's card said in Chinese, "Specializing in Criminal, Immigration & Bail release." Muto's said in English, "Specializing in Criminal, Immigration, Bail release and court appearances." They had the same address.

Muto stood by his "answer... and expressly den[ied] any wrongdoing." He insisted that Cathy Chen—his "paralegal secretary"—had told Yi to go to Buffalo. But he did not remember if he had ever met Yi.

> Referee: Do you have any record or office diary that shows that you met him?
>
> Muto: ... Begging His Honor's pardon, what do you mean by an office diary showing I met him?
>
> Referee: Well, do you keep a diary as a lawyer...?
>
> Muto: I have an appointment book, Your Honor. But something like somebody coming in for a change of venue, I wouldn't put it in....
>
> Referee: Well, in this case you had an appointment in Buffalo, which isn't even your home town. Why wouldn't that be in your diary?
>
> Muto: ... Maybe it was—if it was a court appearance....

---

[643] Staff Ex. 16.

Although he claimed in his deposition to have diaries for 1998 and 1999, the earliest he produced began June 28, 1999 (two months after the first DDC complaint).

Muto insisted Yi was "adamant" about "not going to go to Buffalo" despite "a 100 percent chance" he would be deported.

> Muto: I seem to remember, though I can't swear to it, that I told Michael that we could all go to Buffalo, because I know places there—I used to live in Buffalo. . . . In fact, I have family in Buffalo for that matter. . . . How many lawyers are going to say, come on, I'll give you a ride to the court in Buffalo. . . . I'm willing to drive him 400 some odd—almost 500 miles to get to court. And he says no.
>
> Referee: So you're really saying that if a client won't go with you, you're not going to go too for the client. . . .
>
> Muto: Well now I realize I probably should go in any case. . . . But I do know as a general order of practice with the Immigration Bar, if a client advised you that they're not going to appear in a remote jurisdiction, the lawyer does not have to appear on their own. . . .
>
> Referee: That may be your explanation, but I certainly give that testimony no weight whatsoever. . . .
>
> Muto: [I]f there's ever a remote case where you don't want to go . . . I'll go there and get the absentia orders. I mean I apologize.
>
> Cohen: Mr. Muto, isn't it a fact that you didn't even remember whether Mr. Chen was a man or a woman when I questioned you about this in December of '99?
>
> Muto: It may have been the case. . . .
>
> Cohen: [I]f you can't remember whether he's a man or a woman, how could you possibly remember . . . what you advised him?
>
> Muto: Because I know general patterns that I would follow . . . because I have family in Buffalo. And that's like, great, I get to

CHAPTER 3

go to Buffalo and... see a Bison's game, go down to the Anchor Bar and have some wings.

Cathy Chen could not remember telling Yi about his hearing. "Maybe Mr. Muto say—he want him come to the office to talk with him, I think." But Yi "didn't come." Then she could not remember his name, did not talk to him by phone, and could not remember anything about a Buffalo hearing. But she insisted, "I would never tell anybody that he... does not need to go to the court... because if I say that I will take a lot of responsibility." Clients might be misinformed by relatives or friends who spoke Fuzhou, which she did not understand.

D. New Orleans Clients

Xue Jie Chen was smuggled to Surinam in January 1999 and then to St. Thomas (U.S. Virgin Islands) on May 14 for $40,000, which included lawyers "hired to bail us out." While in INS detention in New Orleans, he was visited by "a Chinese man [Michael Lee] and woman" (probably Cathy Chen), neither of whom he knew. "They ask me for my name and my ID number and also introduce a very brief resume... if I'm married." The interview was cursory "because we had more than 30 of us being detained there... we went out in a line in time to see them." He never met, retained, or paid Muto. Nevertheless, Muto filed appearances and bail reduction motions for him and seven other New Orleans detainees (none of whom had retained Muto). Muto appeared telephonically at a June 22 New Orleans hearing at which they were released on lower bonds and a master calendar hearing was scheduled for July 9. Someone arranged for all eight to be collected from detention, taken to the airport, flown to New York, and driven into the city. Xue Jie visited the Chatham Square office on July 6 and made a $100 down payment on the $1,200 fee for his asylum hearing. Cathy Chen "told me I did not have to [go to the hearing] because the case will be transferred to New York."

In the New Orleans Immigration Court on July 9, Judge Zlatow noted at 10:30 A.M. that no one was present, although the case had been called two hours earlier, but Muto was on the phone.[644]

---

[644] Staff Ex. 26.

> Court: Mr. Muto, first of all, in none of these cases do I have any motion from your office that you be allowed to appear telephonically today. . . .
>
> Muto: I would respectfully ask that I be allowed to appear telephonically today, even though I did not file a proper motion.
>
> Court: And can you indicate why you did not file a motion?
>
> Muto: No.

Because the INS did not object, Judge Zlatow proceeded.

> Court: As to the non-appearance of the respondents, Mr. Muto?
>
> Muto: . . . They've relocated since to New York City . . . I would respectfully ask for a short adjournment so that I could file a change of venue motion.
>
> Court: Why aren't the respondents now present?
>
> Muto: They're in New York, Your Honor.
>
> Court: That doesn't tell me why they're not here. . . . Mr. Muto, do you have anything else?
>
> Muto: Yes, Your Honor. I would say the financial hardship for them to get down there would be a valid extenuating circumstance. And I would ask for a new hearing date.
>
> Court: Mr. Muto, your request is denied. . . . I have nothing other than your assertions, which are not in evidence, as to the reasons for the non-appearance of the Respondents. And I have no particular reason to rely upon your statements.

On July 23, Zlatow wrote the EOIR General Counsel's Office, summarizing the above.[645] "This failure . . . unfortunately, has not been an isolated incident regarding Mr. Muto's practices, and he had on prior occasions been cautioned concerning his responsibilities in representing individuals before the Immigration Court. . . . The filing of a motion does not act to relieve the attorney from his obligation to attend the hearing, unless

---

[645] Staff Ex. 39.

Chapter 3

the motion is granted." The DDC sent this to Muto on November 10.[646] He answered on January 23, 2000, repeating his excuse to Zlatow.[647] The venue motions had been denied.

> As my clients advised me that they were unable to travel to New Orleans, I did not believe that I was required to travel to the court to merely pick up absentia orders. At all times I advised my clients of their obligation to travel to New Orleans, and my willingness to go with them. All clients refused to go.

Muto scrawled an undated letter in response to Cohen's inquiry of January 25.[648]

> I spoke to those clients in my office and advised that they would be removed in absentia should they fail to attend. . . . I did conference this matter with the court clerk (New Orleans) and also Cathy Chen. I was advised that, contrary to my prior assertion to you[,] that I did *not* file a motion to change venue, the reason I did not file this motion is because when they were released from INS custody, it was less than fifteen days before their hearing. . . . I did not intend to mislead you, rather this was an honest error on my part.

He believed the clients had paid no more than $100, "but I do not possess any proof of this." He insisted Xue Jie was told "his presence would be required at the hearing"; his "failure to appear was due to his own malfeasance and there was no misconduct by myself or my office."[649]

> Xue Jie testified in the disciplinary proceeding:
>
> Later, I think in October, I made a phone call to inquire . . . about when I was going to show up for my first hearing. Ms. Chen told me that my case was not opened yet. . . . A few days later I called her again and she told me the same thing . . . yet the third time I called her she told me my case was closed. . . .

---

[646] Staff Ex. 39.
[647] Staff Ex. 40.
[648] Staff Ex. 43.
[649] Staff Ex. 25.

> She said, on the 9th, I did not show up in person for a hearing....
> Then she said I had to pay another $220, so that they would
> help me reopen the hearing.... Later I went to their office....
> [Michael] told me that the people who came out with me,
> their cases were also closed. And some of them paid $220 to
> get the case reopened.... I was introduced to a lawyer to ask
> what should I do regarding my situation?... I told that person
> about my trip to the office on July the 6th. That person said
> I should file a complaint against Mr. Muto to see if I can get
> my case reopened.

He did and it was.

On cross-examination Xue Jie said he had arrived in New York on June 28, which Muto pointed out was too late to seek a change of venue for the July 9 hearing. Xue Jie denied that he had "any relative who directly went to hire this Mr. Muto" or that he had discussed with Cathy Chen how to raise the money to attend the New Orleans hearing.

Muto insisted that "under no circumstances is an attorney required to travel 1200 miles to pick up in absentia deportation orders ... this is especially true in my case where I have a flying phobia." When Cohen cited local rules, Muto retorted that he appeared telephonically "so for all practical purposes I appeared." Later he changed tack: "I didn't submit a telephonic because the judge told me I had to appear personally."

> Muto: I've never had a judge besides Judge Zlatow take that position ... where are these people to testify, Ms. Cohen.
>
> Referee: Come on.
>
> Muto: I'm sorry.
>
> Cohen: Well they were your clients.
>
> Muto: Well, why aren't they sitting over there testifying against me?

He had returned Xue Jie's $100. "I don't want that to be an admission of any liability. It's just my attitude is that if these people aren't happy, I'm not happy."

When Muto admitted not having malpractice insurance (exposing him to personal liability for the failure to appear), Cohen wondered why

Chapter 3

he "wouldn't want to memorialize the client's statement" refusing to go to New Orleans "and your advice to that client."

> Muto: Well, I've learned a lot, Ms. Cohen. . . . I never had [a] law practice before I came down here, of any real nature. Your Honor. And I've made a lot of changes and I haven't had anybody in a long time say they don't want to be to [sic] court. . . . But in the future, and in fact now, if someone were to say that they don't want to be in court, I would give them a statement in writing in Chinese and English . . . and I'd ask them that they sign it and date it. . . . I was really almost a rookie at that time, Your Honor. And I'd just lost my mother.

Cohen asked if all eight clients had refused to go to New Orleans.

> Muto: I'm a little bit confused by the question . . . do I remember each one coming in one behind the other saying, I'm not going to New Orleans? I have a vague . . . recollection of Michael saying these clients don't want to go to New Orleans, because I seem to recall saying, maybe we could send Karen to New Orleans.

He insisted "it was Cathy that told [Xue Jie] he had to appear," but then conceded, "I speak to only general office procedure." Cheng said she could not remember the case.

> Sometimes I cannot contact with [clients] because they fly to the other state. They just leave their relative's number in New York City and the relative, they work long time in the restaurant. A lot of case I cannot contact with them. And they—a lot of people, they just share one apartment. Sometimes their relative didn't take the phone and the—the friend or some other people . . . doesn't know their name and say nobody live there. . . . Sometimes we write a letter to mail to their address . . . sometimes we don't . . . some people . . . they don't speak Mandarin well. They never go to school.

Cohen scrutinized Muto's office arrangement. He claimed to pay $300 a week in salary and $500 a month in rent to Lee, who was his "landlord, paralegal, translator, and also day trades."

Cohen: [W]hen I first asked you about Mr. Lee, back in December of '99, you . . . described him as a day trader and someone that was not at all involved in your immigration practice?

Muto: That was a misstatement. . . . I guess I was confused. I know Mr. Lee . . . derives a lot of money from day trading. . . .

Cohen: Didn't you describe Mr. Lee as a millionaire?

Muto: Well I kind of look up to the guy, because he's really . . . brilliant. . . . I know he just bought a beautiful home in Douglaston.

Cohen: I'm curious why he would be willing to work for you for $300 a week as a paralegal?

Muto: We have a very good personal relationship. . . . He does manage the bank accounts.

After having denied that Lee had referred clients, Muto admitted, "I've gotten referrals from everybody, from bartenders to God knows who . . . so I just say he's probably sent a couple of clients towards me." He had "a close personal relationship . . . with Michael and Cathy," who had let him name their daughter Jenifer. Cathy said he paid her $300 a week under the table and Michael about the same because his English was better. When she finished testifying, Muto told her to "give Jenifer a hug for me. Thank you. . . . Do you need anything, Cathy? Are you O.K. to get out? Do you want me to call a car service or anything?" (Asked by Cohen during the penalty phase if he could fire Lee, Muto said, "I sublet from him, so I mean that's kind of a convoluted question." He could fire Chen but they had a "close personal relationship.")

Cohen also explored Muto's workload. He interviewed new clients for "half an hour maybe. Fifteen, 20 minutes to half an hour. Usually I'll ask them for their I-589s." His translators were Dr. He (from whom he sublet an office), a girl whose name he forgot, and a high school student working down the hall. (Muto had previously denied sharing an office and phone with Dr. He or even knowing him.) Muto charged $100 for master calendars. "They're really not that hard. It's basically the same . . . law and you want to fit your facts into the law." He handled 20 matters a day at first but denied ever making $2,000 in a single day, though he

CHAPTER 3

boasted that "my record for one week is like $4,000." He had cut back from 10–12 reopens a day to 7–8. He stated that lawyers who asked $2,000–$3,000 were "overcharging their clients."[650]

> Muto: I've had a lot of these cases granted and I have a stack of them sitting over there . . . all cases that have been reopened with that form.
>
> Referee: It's your testimony, then, that you can, within 30 minutes . . . prepare a motion to reopen, having interviewed a client in a language you don't speak.
>
> Muto: I go over the facts of the case with them and if it fits the law, Your Honor, yes. It's a simple matter of basic law school issues . . . if they tell me . . . I have two children, if I go back to China I'll be sterilized. . . .
>
> Cohen: The only way that you could do ten or 12 motions to reopen in a day, as well as seven or eight master calendars, is simply to have somebody else draft the affidavit and send it over to you for your signature?
>
> Muto: Absolutely untrue. And if his honor would like, the CAT [Convention Against Torture] reopens and the various motions to reopen and affidavits that I used are still on file in my word processor and . . . I'll have that word processor brought down this afternoon.

In November 1999, Muto filed an appearance in New Orleans for Ming Yuan Lu. Judge Zlatow allowed Muto to appear telephonically at the November 30 master calendar. At that hearing, however, the judge ordered him to appear in person on January 11. Muto agreed but instead hired Lawrence McGrath, a local attorney who had never handled an immigration matter. When Muto claimed to have gotten McGrath's name "from an immigration attorney that I got off a web page," McGrath replied, "I'm certainly not on any web page to my knowledge." "I actually gave him a name of an immigration attorney in town," but "Muto called me at least twice, maybe three times, and told me that he could not find anyone to

---

[650] New York lawyers charged $1,500–$2,000 for asylum applications and $2,000 for cancellation of removal. See Mottino (2000: 30).

appear on their behalf and the judge would not continue the matter for him. And . . . I'm a sole practitioner myself, I felt sympathetic for the man."

On January 11, McGrath told Zlatow that Muto had said the hearing would be in February, so Zlatow rescheduled it for February 11, which McGrath accepted on Muto's behalf.[651] Muto submitted documentation on January 28 but then wrote to Zlatow on February 8 requesting another adjournment because he had immigration cases in Atlanta and could not "find coverage." Zlatow denied the request when he received it on February 9 because Muto had not made it 14 days before the hearing (as required by local rules), had accepted the hearing date, and had not submitted a copy of the Atlanta hearing notice. Muto also failed to serve his request on the INS District Counsel's office: "the Court does not act as a delivery agent on behalf of either party."[652] Muto telephoned Zlatow on February 11.[653]

> Court: Your office was telephoned by the court here [two days ago] informing you that your request for postponement was denied . . . yet, you are still not present.
>
> Muto: Yes, Your Honor, I tried to come down but I couldn't get on a plane.
>
> Court: I've heard this story from you before, Mr. Muto.
>
> Muto: (inaudible)
>
> Court: Who else are you speaking to, sir?
>
> Muto: No one, Your Honor. Someone walked by me, and I just acknowledged them as they walked by.
>
> Court: Mr. Muto, as far as I'm concerned, you're not properly before the court. I told you this was going to be in person. . . .
>
> Muto: I know, Your Honor, I tried.
>
> Court: You didn't try, Mr. Muto.
>
> Muto: I tried to get on a plane last night, Your Honor, to get to New Orleans. You can talk to the people at Air Tran—

---

[651] Staff Ex. 48.
[652] Staff Ex. 49.
[653] Staff Ex. 52.

Chapter 3

Court: Yes, I'm going to be calling Air Tran and saying was there a person by the name of Muto who tried to get on a plane.

Muto: I really did try.

Court: I don't know what that means, sir. You had notice of this hearing a month ago. Your letter to the court confirmed the date of this hearing which was back on January 28. . . . So what do you mean you couldn't be here?

Muto: I tried to fly out, Your Honor.

Court: There are other means of transportation, Mr. Muto.

Muto: I didn't have that much time, Your Honor.

Court: From January 28 you didn't have time or from the hearing notice of—

Muto: No, Your Honor.

Court: Excuse me. Or from the hearing notice. . . .

Muto: Yes, Your Honor. Your Honor, I tried to come down last night. I did not have enough time, almost two days, the weather being what it is New York to New Orleans.

Court: Sir, the notice was sent to you on January 11 for this hearing today. I don't know what you mean you didn't have enough time.

Muto: I couldn't take two days, Wednesday and Thursday, out of my schedule, Your Honor. I apologize.

Court: Your apologies are not accepted, sir. . . . This is not the first time, you're aware of that.

When Cohen forwarded Zlatow's complaint about this, Muto scrawled a reply.[654] After the Atlanta hearing scheduled for February 11 was postponed to February 14, he stated,

> I initially planned to attend the Friday hearing in New Orleans, then travel to Atlanta for the Monday hearing. However, on

---

[654] Staff Ex. 44, 45.

Thursday evening when I planned to depart for New Orleans via Air Trans 6:30 pm flight, there was inclement weather in New York. This weather, a heavy rainstorm, continued well into the evening. As such, I was unable to fly to New Orleans for the hearing.

Judge Zlatow proceeded to hear the case without Muto. In the disciplinary proceeding McGrath testified telephonically that though he had never met the clients, "It was my understanding that they were prepared."

Muto: Do you feel that these cases were covered competently?

McGrath: Yes, I thought the issues were . . . brought forth . . . basically by the judge. The judge handled the hearing himself. Neither the federal attorney nor I asked many questions. But he did . . . cover the issues of sterilization policies. . . .

Muto: Were the clients' interests and rights . . . protected by you?

McGrath: Yes, I think they were preserved.

Muto expanded on this.

We have an experienced trial attorney with 25 years of experience. Maybe he never appeared in Immigration Court, but he's an experienced trial attorney. It's—my upstate New York background. My father-in-law, who is now deceased, was an auto mechanic. It's much like he worked for a Ford dealership. The fact that he worked for a Ford dealership, he never saw a Chevy diesel. I had a Chevette diesel. Well, he couldn't touch a diesel engine because he didn't know the mechanics of a diesel. But he knew how to change a transmission in my Chevette.

Muto was very touchy about his flying phobia. When Cohen mentioned his June 22 telephonic appearance before Judge Zlatow on behalf of Xue Jie, Muto broke in, "It's acknowledged I have a fear of flying. To chastise me as she is attempting to do because I didn't go to the New Orleans and meet him . . ." That "would require me to leave at least a day and a half by two days before the court date. Drive 1,200 miles. Go into Judge Zlatow's

CHAPTER 3

courtroom and try and convince." Dr. Diana Ronnell, who was treating Muto's flying phobia, testified that she had seen him 75 times since September 1999, often "at the airport, where you've fully believed that you could get on an airplane." "We've gone so far as sitting on the plane, which is a big—big step. And you always believe, actually, up to the point at which you see that door, that you'll be able to do it." Muto did not tell clients because "you always believe that the next time you will be able to do it. . . . You're really one of my most heavily motivated patients." But asked if Muto was unable to reveal the phobia to his clients, Ronnell replied, "He's certainly able to . . . he can say those words. . . . It's more typical of men not to disclose in a professional setting." In his deposition, Muto admitted to not telling his New Orleans clients "because I know I can get to New Orleans if I have to," either driving "or if I have to fly, I guess I could." He reiterated this in the disciplinary hearing: "I honestly believed I could have flown to New Orleans." He had told Judge Zlatow in July "I had trouble getting there. . . . I don't think I would have said I had a fear of flying." He had not acknowledged the phobia in his deposition because "it's a very difficult thing for me to deal with." "I have a packet of air tickets from times I tried to get on planes." He had "since procured co-counsel . . . who have traveled to Houston, to El Paso and to San Francisco for me" and had himself driven to St. Louis.[655]

E. *Hua Ye*

Hua Ye and his wife Ling (Ying) Li entered the United States illegally in 1993 via Bolivia, each paying smugglers $10,000, and applied for asylum on the grounds that Ling was expecting a second child. They initially went to the Fucho Service Center "because they charge a lower rate." His application was rejected in 1995, but she paid $2,100 to a lawyer recommended by a friend, who met with her "quite a few times," got her asylum, and said her husband could reapply. In June 1999, they went to Sin Rong (Xing Long) Fu Wu Si (Chinese Legal Services) at 63 East Broadway, Suite 201. Ling Li explained,

> The owner of the agency, Lin Li Li had been my classmate in China. . . . The lady employee gave my husband an application form and asked him to write his date of birth and signature on the form. We paid a fee of $350, on the understanding that,

---

[655] MapQuest estimates the round trip at nearly 2,000 miles, requiring more than 30 hours.

depending on how far his case would go, we would later pay the balance. The owner Lin Li Li said she would get to lawyer to deal with my husband's case. I trusted her because I had known her since our schooldays and also because I cannot speak, read, or write English.

On June 25 Muto, who had never met Hua, filed a motion to reopen with a notarized affidavit containing a forged signature. It was denied in February 2000. The judge wrote,

> A delay of almost three years after the law [Illegal Immigration Reform and Immigrant Responsibility Act of 1996] was amended is unreasonable absent a reasonable explanation for such a delay. The affidavit of the respondent in the motion to reopen is completely silent as to the reason for the delay in filing of this motion.

Ling continued,

> We kept waiting and asking for news of the application, but we were never told anything. I never saw my lawyer and do not know who dealt with my husband's case. And, not knowing English, I would not have been able to talk to him. Then, about the beginning of September 2000, we went to the agency and they told us that my husband's case had again been denied. They said they did not know the reason.

When the INS detained Hua in Hartford in September 2000, he retained new counsel, Jose L. DelCastillo, who moved to reopen on the grounds that Muto's "one sentence motion" constituted ineffective assistance of counsel. Four days later, Hua complained to the DDC that "the motion appeared meritless and unsubstantiated" and that he had never met Muto.[656] The INS did not oppose the motion to reopen, which was granted two weeks later.

Answering for Muto, Hal Lieberman dismissed Hua's complaint as "completely lacking in merit."[657]

---

[656] Staff Ex. 31.
[657] Staff Ex. 32.

Chapter 3

As you know, Mr. Muto has a high volume immigration practice. It is often the case—and indeed, has become a federal requirement—to complain to a disciplinary or grievance committee of ineffective assistance of counsel—in order to get a matter reopened before the Immigration Court. Apparently, that is the motivation of the instant complaint. . . . Mr. Muto prepared the subject motion in accordance with a format that he (and other attorneys) practicing before the Immigration Court in New York routinely use. He has had documented success using *exactly* this type of motion in similar cases. . . . While short and concise, the motion was appropriate in the circumstances, and the fact that the Court denied it does not mean it was invalid or constitutes a violation of any rule of ethics or professional responsibility. . . . He specifically discussed the case with the client, advised him to call with any questions, and gave the client a toll free number should he wish to check on the status of his case.

Muto said his motion was "basically a re-skinning of another motion that is done by another lawyer who is highly respected. . . . I even added to it. . . . This is a very well drafted motion. Most judges would have granted it." He acknowledged obtaining it 18 months earlier but insisted he had changed more than the name.

Ling denied knowing that Muto was her husband's lawyer.

Muto: Ma'am are you aware that someone—maybe it wasn't your husband—did come to my office purporting to be your husband. . . .

Ling: I don't know where his office is. How can I be there? . . .

Muto: Someone representing himself to be Hua Ye came to my office and requested a reopen. . . .

Cohen: You've testified that you don't have any recollection of anybody coming into your office whose name was . . . Ye.

Muto: I don't know. I'm saying it's a possibility, but I don't know.

Cohen: Well how do you account for Mr. Ye's statement that he never met you? You're saying he sent in somebody else.

Muto: I had heard people had done that. . . .

Cohen: . . . Can you suggest to the Referee what reason an agency would have to send in someone other than the actual client?

Muto: I don't know what makes these people tick. They're not the most ethical. They're not the most scrupulous, Your Honor. I will say that I charge the cheapest rates in Chinatown.

Referee: Can you answer Ms. Cohen's question?

Muto: I'm trying to, Your Honor. . . . I'm not trying be evasive, Your Honor, please. . . . I'm just very nervous and I'm a little bit confused. . . . I don't even know that they did that. Hua Ye could have been lying for that matter. And not every client is honest. . . . I know I charged $100 for a reopen, which is the lowest rates in Chinatown. And it's very possible some unscrupulous people did take advantage of me during that era.

Referee: Tell me why you charge such low rates?

Muto: Essentially, Your Honor, you know, I grew up—I never made much money in Syracuse, and this will come in on aggravation [sic]—and I feel sorry for people. I feel sorry when somebody comes in and doesn't have a lot of money after they paid $40[,000] or $50,000 to a smuggler. I feel sorry when they tell me, could you do it for a little less? And I'll do it, and I've done a lot of pro bono work for people, Your Honor. . . . These people make $5 an hour under the table in a restaurant. I'm not going to take them to the cleaners to the tune of $2[,000] to $3,000 for a simple motion to reopen. Something that could be done in a relatively short time. And when you come right down to it, for an hour's worth of work, $100 I feel is a fair fee. . . . I'm doing, Your Honor, the best deal for my clients in Chinatown with respect to reopens. I have the best rates in Chinatown. And I was really happy that I was getting a lot of clients. And I think I came across . . . how thrilled I seemed to get when . . . somebody would come in and say they saw my name on the board, on the sign in front of my office, and they came in. Ye was one of those clients. . . .

Referee: Did you say Mr. Ye was someone who came in off the street? . . . Without any reference from anyone else? . . .

Muto: To the best of my knowledge, he was not referred by anyone Your Honor. . . . So I took down his facts, I listened to him. I made my notes. I took his case home and I did this at home. . . . I don't have a specific recollection of him, Your Honor, but you know, I could put it together—a recollection based on what was going on at that time. He came in. I spoke to him, probably for half an hour. I said what happened . . . ? You got your I-589? Let me review your I-589. O.K. What's your wife's status? Good. What's her A-number? . . . I gave him a copy of the 800 number and said . . . have a friend of yours, if you know anybody that speaks English in the restaurant check this . . . you're welcome to come into this office any time you want, and we'll check it for you. . . . After the motion was denied, Your Honor, he would receive a letter from my office—and no, I don't have a copy of it. Again, I apologize. I'm saving a lot more material now. But after the motion was denied—for some reason I used an old form on this . . . that says Doyers Street . . . he would receive the decision with a letter from me, outlining what he had to do to appeal the motion. . . .

Referee: Are you saying that you did this?

Muto: I'm saying, as a matter of course, this would be what I would do. However, I do not have an independent recollection in this case. . . .

Referee: Mr. Ye denies that you did that.

Muto: Your Honor, you know, they don't always tell you the true and correct addresses. . . .

Referee: In your office you did not keep a record that you sent the results of the hearing to Mr. Ye.

Muto: Your Honor, no. . . . I should have documented everything. I've learned a lot.

He did not have Hua's file.

> Cohen: So is it your practice not to keep files for as long as a year and a half?
>
> Muto: No . . . I keep all my files, and I have a huge filing area in the back of my office. . . . I may have just sent—given everything to the client . . . to the law office in Hartford that subsequently represented him. I honestly don't know.

Muto blamed the denial of his motion on the bad luck of getting Judge Videla. "I have EOIR statistics. . . . Judge Videla grants very, very few cases in motions."[658] Asked if he had not known that Videla had decided the original asylum petition and thus would hear the reopen, Muto replied: "most of the times I don't remember it and most of the court clerk's offices, they'll say the file has gone to central records out in Missouri."

F. Hong Ren Lin

In November 1998, Muto filed an appearance for Hong Ren Lin, previously represented in removal proceedings by John F. Finnell.[659] Muto submitted documents to court that month and in July and October 1999.[660] When Hong Ren appeared without Muto at the individual hearing on December 7, Judge Paul A. DeFonzo denied the asylum application.[661] The judge complained to the EOIR on February 10, 2000.

> Mr. Lin advised that although he had encountered Mr. Muto in the hallway earlier that day, that Mr. Muto had advised him that he . . . was very busy that day and would not be able to appear with him for his deportation hearing.

---

[658] The more than 200 IC judges vary greatly in their willingness to grant asylum. A study of decisions between 1994 and 2005 found that eight judges granted only 10%, whereas two granted more than 90%, one of them 98%; 10% of IC judges granted 14%, whereas another 10% granted 66%. Among NYC IC judges deciding Chinese asylum petitions, Judge Jankun granted 5.5%, whereas Judge McManus granted 93.1%. Syracuse University, TRAC, Judges Show Disparities in Denying Asylum (July 31, 2006), available at http://trac.syr.edu. Another study found that the rate of asylum grants to Indian applicants by San Francisco IC judges between 2000 and 2004 varied from 3% to 84%. Schrag et al. (2008).

[659] A 1960 Harvard Law School graduate with an office at 2 Mott Street.

[660] Staff Ex. 56, 57.

[661] Judge Defonzo ranked 88 out of 238 judges in the likelihood of granting asylum: http://trac/syr.edu/immigration/reports/judgereports/141/index.html.

Chapter 3

Muto testified that just before his disciplinary hearing he ran into the judge, who reassured him, "I wouldn't worry about that, Mr. Muto." Asked about the documents filed in his name in 1998 and 1999, Muto said, "I didn't even know what was submitted. I mean it could have been something that was kicking around in my office."

> Muto: I remember the case distinctly. I was approached in the hallway on December 7 by a young Chinese woman who asked me if I would represent her client in his hearing that day. I had never seen this woman before. I did not have any record of having met Mr. Lin, nor did I have any record of having his case. More importantly, I checked the case schedule which was posted on the board adjacent to Judge DeFonzo's court, and observed that attorney John Finnell and not myself was listed as the attorney of record. . . . As a matter of procedure, I check the board every day at 4 p.m. to ascertain whether I am attorney of record for any cases which may have "slipped through the cracks." . . . I may have made an appearance for this individual on an "of counsel" basis, but I have no recollection of having done so. . . . I'm not here to inculpate other lawyers. I mean I know Mr. Fennel [sic] deals extensively with agencies. I hadn't been in touch with this client. He was tough to get a hold of. And woman in the hall says, would you take my case. And she was obviously an agency. I looked at the board. I saw Jack Fennel's [sic] name on here and wanted nothing to do with it. . . . I admit that I should have went [sic] into Judge DeFonzo's courtroom . . . and said, Your Honor, I haven't had any contact with this man. I noticed John Fennel's [sic] name is on the board.
>
> Referee: Do you admit that perhaps you should have communicated with your client, Mr. Lin? . . . He's thinking that he has a lawyer named Muto who he's never seen. . . .
>
> Muto: I offer what I offer in mitigation and I accept responsibility. . . . I apologize to the court. . . . Because a lot of it— I don't know procedure. . . .
>
> Referee: You have no explanation as to why you formed a belief some other lawyer was taking your place, except you're

> looking at a calendar on the day itself. So what preparation were you doing for this matter?
>
> Muto: Your Honor, the man hadn't come into my office. We sent a couple of letters out.

Cohen asked for them.

> Muto: I don't have a specific recollection, but I generally will send out letters when the hearing is close. . . . I'm trying to be honest. I'm not trying to be evasive. Sometimes I maybe don't understand. I'll say one thing where I . . . really was meaning something else. . . . [He withdrew the allegation that Lin had been uncooperative]
>
> Cohen: Have you produced one letter that you've ever sent to any client?
>
> Muto: Regarding what, Ms. Cohen? I'm a little confused.
>
> Cohen: Regarding your representation of these clients. . . .
>
> Muto: I gave you like all my New Orleans files. . . .
>
> Cohen: You gave us files that were not related to the complainants.

G. *Ju Jin Jing*

At the November 19, 1998, master calendar, Muto filed an appearance for Ju Jin Jing, who had been represented in her removal proceeding by David J. Rodkin (Muto's former employer). But no documents had been submitted by the July 13 deadline set by Judge Joanna Miller Bukszpan.[662]

> Court: Counsel, before we begin, I want to note for the record that this is the second master calendar . . . I have had to have . . . where I have had to reschedule all your cases because you just came into court, dropped off your ERYR-28, [and] left. And the court was ready to close for the morning. . . . And I cannot

---

[662] Staff Ex. 64. Judge Bukszpan ranked 52 out of 238 Immigration Court judges in the likelihood of granting asylum: http://trac.syr.edu/immigration/reports/judgereports/137/index.html.

be functioning convenient to your schedule, counsel. . . . It is extraordinarily rude and unprofessional of you. . . . When you come into court, you submit your ERYR-28 and you sit until you are called. . . . Last time it forced your client to come back and forth twice to court. . . . I would note that there is no documentation in the file. And I am—the record is closed. . . .

Muto: You're not taking any documents today, Your Honor?

Court: Do you have documents to give?

Muto: I have a medical. I haven't had the time to put together a cover sheet on it, though.

Court: . . . Counsel, you're telling me that if you could, you might have done something today, but you haven't. And no, the record is closed. . . . Actually, the record has been closed for four months.

Five months later, Muto again submitted late evidence, which the judge refused to admit. The May 28, 1999, individual hearing began with the judge addressing Ju Jin.[663]

Court: Where is your lawyer?

Ju Jin: Which lawyer?

Court: Ma'am, do you have a lawyer?

Ju Jin: Yes, I have one. But he hasn't shown up yet. . . .

Court: O.K., I would note this matter was called for one o'clock. It is now 1:30. . . . Ma'am, I'm putting this over. Your attorney has neglected to contact The Court. . . . So we will go forward next time, ma'am with or without a lawyer. . . .

Ju Jin: I need the attorney. Without an attorney, how do I know?

Court: Ma'am you can have this attorney. You can have another attorney. . . . I can't at this point give you a list of free legal

---

[663] Staff Ex. 64.

services because you have an attorney.... Do you want to go forward today without your attorney? Or do you want another date for you to come with your attorney?

Ju Jin: How do I know about this?

Court: Ma'am I can't make a decision for you....

Ju Jin: I cannot decide right now about this....

Court: Because I'm very concerned, I'm putting this on for Tuesday. I expect you to be here with your lawyer that day.

But on Tuesday, June 8, Saul Schneider[664] appeared "of counsel" for Muto.

Court: Counsel, I am extraordinarily distressed about this matter.... I know that you're just sent in today... [but] that only gets The Court more distressed... on May the 28th... not only was counsel not here, but I know from scuttlebutt, that he was also not in about three other courtrooms... God knows what else he didn't show up for.... If he is overextended, then it is his obligation to see to it that he has coverage... not to just leave three or four judges sitting here looking at the ceiling and all his clients looking at the ceiling and four interpreters called at extreme government expenses.... I'm therefore putting this over again to my next master calendar. And I will do so until Mr. Muto has the courtesy, not to mention the professional responsibility, to come forward... that he had the audacity not to come in again today is amazing to this court—amazing.... And if he repeatedly flaunts [sic] this court, I will take appropriate action.

When Muto appeared two weeks later the judge recounted this history.

Court: I called you in, counsel, because your behavior is unacceptable to this court. And if it persists, I'll have to take appropriate action. Do you understand, counsel?

---

[664] A 1991 Cardozo Law School graduate, with an LL.M. from NYU, who practiced in Coney Island in 2007.

Muto: Yes, Your Honor. It was an honest misunderstanding.

Court: . . . You also didn't appear in three other courtrooms that afternoon, counsel. And you also didn't have the courtesy to come in when I called you in at the last hearing. . . . So it's not an honest misunderstanding. It is professional irresponsibility. And I repeat that if you persist in this, I will have to take appropriate action.

Muto: It will not occur again.

But it did. Although Muto had agreed to an individual hearing on July 12, Andrew Wilson appeared, "sitting in for Joe Muto just to—so that the respondent can have some representation and so that she will understand these proceedings and the future proceedings."[665] He was doing so without consulting Muto, who he believed was out of town. The judge addressed Ju Jin.

Court: Your attorney not only didn't show up, but didn't notify the Court and didn't see that there was any coverage for your case today. . . . I'm going to have to call you back into court with your attorney, because he has to be severely admonished by this Court for his rudeness to The Court. . . . I think she has been getting a very raw deal. . . .

Jason Raphael [INS lawyer]: . . . As long as there's a Court Interpreter here . . . I'd just like to present The Court with one possibility, too, which is that she be told . . . that she has recourse, too. You know, I was just looking through the TA notes and the attorney of record, Muto, has—as the Court is aware—

Court: Been flagrant.

Raphael: Yes, been flagrant . . . this almost rises to the level of . . . that kind of case . . . I would like to tell her just personally that she should . . . She can file a grievance with the . . . proper grievance committee.

---

[665] A 1996 CUNY graduate, who also practiced at 401 Broadway, the building containing Rodkin and Jaffe. Muto said in 2006 that he had died young; his Bar dues were delinquent.

Court: I don't . . . feel that it's . . . appropriate for me to do that.

Muto missed the July 20 hearing as well, but Wilson again appeared for Ju Jin. Muto handwrote a letter to Judge "Buckzspan" [sic], dated July 20 but received July 22, to explain his July 12 absence.

> I had numerous master and bond hearings scheduled for Tuesday, July 13, 1999 in New Orleans. My initial plan was to complete my hearings in your court, then fly to New Orleans on Monday evening. When I found that this was not possible, I arranged for Saul Schneider to cover my calendar. I called your clerk on Monday morning from a rest area. I was driving to New Orleans. . . . I had not had any contact with this client since the last court appearance, and advised your clerk that he [sic] may have retained different counsel. I can furnish you with a copy of my phone bill showing a call to 26 Federal at about 10 am on July 12th. . . . It was my belief that the court and the client would not be neglected in this matter.

Muto responded to Cohen's inquiry in November.[666] He had two master calendars on June 8 "neither of which were with Judge Bukszpan." There could have been no master on June 12, which was a Saturday (a typographical error for June 22, when Bukszpan had scheduled a special master calendar for Muto). He "had to be out of the state" on July 12 (although he had specifically requested that date instead of July 21).

> I attempted to arrange coverage with another attorney, but due to an apparent miscommunication, the case was not covered. I do seem to recall calling the Court to apprise them of the problem and to request an adjournment. Upon my return, my client advised me that he [sic] did not want me to represent him [sic] any longer. . . .

> With respect to the May 29, 1999 appearance, I have reviewed my calendar and note that I had two merits hearings set for that morning, one at 9:00 and one at 10:30. In a situation such as this, I arrange for another attorney to cover my masters.

---

[666] Staff Ex. 60.

> I had two other masters which were covered that morning and do not know why this matter was not covered.... Occasionally a judge will not allow anyone but the attorney of record to appear. This may have been the case here.

Muto handwrote a response to Cohen's request for evidence of these allegations.[667]

> I believe that each of these cases went forward [on May 28], and that I represented each respondent.... It would be my practice to appear at these hearings, but I cannot say with absolute certainty that I did. For example, I may have utilized "of counsel" for one or both.... I believe I had master calendar hearings [on June 8] and asked my co-counsel to cover some of them. This is an accepted practice in Immigration Court.

In the disciplinary hearing, however, he admitted not knowing why he had missed the hearing.

> I'll be honest. I suspect I was sick that day, because I don't miss hearings. That's one thing that, you know, if you asked any judge there, I'm always there. I practically live at 26 Federal Plaza.... I should have my own office there.... It was right around the time my cousin passed away. I suspect it might have something to do with that, or it was because I was ill.

Muto also blamed the events of June 22 (when he *did* appear) on "Sol" [sic] Schneider, who "wasn't a very responsible person," "tends to be disorganized," and "would tend to come in late." "He would come in . . . five minutes after the hearing was supposed to begin. He would miss hearings." Muto had stopped giving him cases.

> The fact he came in late, you know, strutted in without having the opportunity to meet the client—and again, you know I'm open 'til, you know, seven, eight o'clock at night. I don't feel it can [be] blamed on me.

---

[667] Staff Ex. 62.

He challenged Cohen to subpoena Schneider. Then he claimed that he had been at a detaining hearing that day, which took priority. "Ordinarily ... if another attorney takes over a case, is retained, your obligation as attorney ends. You do not have to appear." He was not sure he had told Ju Jin that Schneider would substitute. "I hadn't been doing this that long in '99. It had only been just a little over a year."

H. *Abdul Karim*

Abdul Karim legally entered the Bahamas from Bangladesh and was smuggled into the United States in February 1993. He applied for political asylum by reason of activity in a minority political party and was told to appear for a master calendar on April 28, 1998.[668] He had no lawyer because he had heard they cost $2,000 and "somebody said if I don't have money, maybe the court will appoint the lawyer." In the waiting room, however, other Bangladeshis said "if I go without a lawyer ... the judge will not hear my case and I will be in trouble." Somebody pointed out Muto, who agreed to take his case for $500, "a very good offer for me ... I was very, very happy with it."[669] Muto wrote his home telephone number on a piece of paper (he had no business cards).

> He was very busy on April 28, 1998 and instructed me to sign a green notice of Appearance form with him as my attorney. He then instructed me to appear before Judge Bain without him and inform the court that he was my attorney and to seek an adjournment.

The judge rescheduled the hearing for May 26. On May 8, Karim visited Muto's office at 401 Broadway and paid $250. Muto arrived in response to a secretary's phone call.

> He assured me, don't worry, we'll handle it O.K., and everything will be O.K. There's nothing to worry about. . . . I don't have time today, but we will discuss your case and everything. Just leave your papers now and I will study this. . . . He said he

---

[668] Staff Ex. 67.
[669] "Some respondents at Federal Plaza are solicited by lawyers who congregate in hallways and waiting rooms or respondents, desperate to find help, approach lawyers and retain their services on the spot as they enter the courtroom." Mottino (2000: 20).

> will go to the internet and he will study . . . about the human rights and all these things.

But they had no substantive discussion. Karim tried to call Muto numerous times thereafter.

> On May 24, 1998 I called Mr. Muto at . . . his home number. . . . I left a message but Mr Muto did not return my call. On May 25, 1998 I again called Mr. Muto's home and left a message. He returned my call late in the evening and informed me that he had not forgotten my case and that he would see me in court the next day, May 26, 1998.

Muto had another hearing that day "so he was a little bit rushed." At his hearing, Karim commented,

> I did not fully understand what was said but at the end Mr. Muto told me that I could leave and that he would inform me of the next date we had to appear before Judge Bain. I did hear that my next date was going to be sometime in March or April 1999.

Muto said "call me at home and I will send you . . . the appearance paper." Karim called often, sometimes twice a week, sometimes every two weeks, but Muto responded only once, in September.

> I said I'm very worried, you know, my date is coming. . . . He always said, like to don't worry. . . . Now I don't have time, but I will give you a time. And I ask him, you didn't send me a paper, you know, like appearance paper. . . . He said, I don't have your papers now in front of me. But so far I remember it's April 9th, 1999. . . . As my date was closing by, I keep on calling him, you know. And in March, like I just called him and request, you know, that it's so close, the date is so closing by, if he has no time then he can just give me the papers and then maybe I will talk with somebody else.

When Karim went to court on April 9 and did not find his name posted, he went into a room.

> And then I said my name is Abdul Karim and . . . I thought I was having a hearing today . . . [the clerk] looked in the computer and he said, your date is passed, two days before . . . you better call your lawyer. The case is closed. . . . I thought now . . . I have to . . . leave this country, like they will deport me. . . . All the time, you know, I hear everybody said . . . you appear in your case whatever date. . . . I was so much nervous and I went to the judge's room. . . . There was a hearing in proceedings. And I went in there and they said, do you have a case today. I said no. I don't have it. I want to talk about my case and I have something happen, you know. Then I start crying, you know. So judge call me, O.K., come forward. What happened. Tell me. I said . . . my case was the seventh . . . my lawyer didn't told me. My lawyer told me it was the ninth, and I missed my date and my case is closed.

Judge Bain told him to contact the clerk, who scheduled a hearing the following Monday and promised to notify Muto.[670]

> I tried to reach him, you know, on the phone and leave a message that my case is closed . . . I live in Long Island, in Massapequa, and because it's a long way from Broadway. And then this is not very easy for me, you know, to come here all the time. So that time, you know I decided I have to go to . . . his office . . . I went to his office. I saw two guys inside and Mr. Muto's name was still on the door of his room . . . I told them I am here to see Mr. Muto . . . they said . . . he left this office long time . . . you don't have any phone number? I said I have only his home phone number. They said . . . we don't have any other phone number or any forwarding address. . . . [I left a message on Muto's answering machine saying] I don't care about like money and everything you know. I need my papers. If he can't handle it . . . I will get another lawyer . . . by this time and I didn't hear anything from Mr. Muto or anybody, so I called again to—the court clerk [on June 23] . . . he said you know, we gave you another date, there was another date [June 22].

---

[670] Of the 238 Immigration Court judges, Judge Bain was the *most* likely to grant asylum: http://trac.syr.edu/immigration/reports/judgereports/135/index.html.

> You didn't appear that day also. . . . He said now I don't think we can do anything . . . then I started crying . . . then he said, you know, call me again. . . . He talked with the judge and said . . . get another lawyer and he spelled me, you know, something to tell the lawyer to find [he means "file"] the Lazada [sic] motion.

Karim paid $1,000 to Gene Stith in the law offices of Mahipal Singh, whose August 16 motion to reopen for ineffective assistance of counsel was granted in September.

Muto's handwritten answer to Karim's complaint declared,[671]

> [A]s a rule I will not have a client sign a G-28 (green form), and then not appear in court. . . . I told him expressly when he had to be in Court for his next hearing. . . . I did not . . . fail to return Mr. Karim's calls and at all times I apprised him of the need to appear. I also furnished him with an information number 800-898-7186 which would give him his hearing date and time. . . . I find it highly unlikely the court would not apprise Mr. Karim of his hearing date after he explained his purported problem to the judge. . . . I endeavor to be very dilligent [sic] in returning client calls and addressing their needs. I even provide a home number. While I left the office at 401 Broadway in October 1998, a close friend who is also an immigration attorney retained the office. She regularly forwards messages to me. Additionally, I put in a change of address and received mail sent to me at this address. In any event, Mr. Karim, and all of my clients, are apprised by me of their court dates. I have even taken the initiative to learn how to write times and dates in Chinese to assist my clients. Mr. Karim's failure to attend his court hearings was due to his own negligence and not any neglect on the part of my office.

Muto began cross-examination by

> apologizing to you for not doing a good job . . . I realize there's probably more I should have done on your case . . . to the extent

---

[671] Staff Ex. 68.

> that I may have neglected your case, I'll accept responsibility.
> I apologize to you again. And if you ... have your lawyer drop
> a letter to me, I will refund in full your $250 to you. OK? ... If
> I had it with me today, I would give it to you today.

When the Referee asked for his business address, Muto gave Karim a card, adding "if there's a problem call me at home or call Ms. Cohen." But she declined to "act as a conduit for repayments," and the card listed 5–7 Doyers Street when he was actually at 7–8 Chatham Square.

Muto admitted liability on Karim, except for the alleged failure to submit documents. The Referee accused him of not returning Karim's telephone calls.

> Muto: I did call him back. I did answer his calls. I may not
> have answered every one of his calls. I answered, I would say,
> probably most of his calls. At all times I told Mr. Karim when
> his hearing dates were.
>
> Referee: He had a hearing scheduled for May 26, 1998. Is it
> true that ... prior to that day before, you had not returned his
> calls which he made between May 8th and May 26th? ...
>
> Muto: I don't have an independent recollection ... I'll give
> him the benefit of the doubt. ... I discussed his case with him,
> Your Honor, when I took his case on. ... I had done some
> Bangladesh cases ... about half a dozen.

He insisted that both he and Judge Bain had told Karim his hearing was on April 7. "I would give him the hearing notice that the judge issues." But he admitted not appearing that day himself. He "assume[d]" Karim called after April 9, "and I would assume that I would have called him back. However, I don't have an independent recollection." When Cohen objected that Muto prefaced every statement of fact with "I believe," he replied, "I'm not trying to be evasive ... I just don't want to say something ... and have you think I'm lying when I really just don't remember for sure." It was his practice to give essential documents to successor lawyers, but he had no evidence of having done so.

> Cohen: So is it your position that it's Mr. Karim's own fault for
> not showing up, and not yours?

Chapter 3

> Muto: No . . . I should have stayed in better contact with him . . . I give all my clients the 800 number. . . .
>
> Cohen: . . . You heard [Karim] indicate how important his asylum application was for him? . . . How desperately concerned he was? . . . Can you imagine why he would not show up at hearings if he knew about them?
>
> Muto: I don't know, Ms. Cohen. . . .
>
> Referee: And then when he tried to keep in touch with you, you did not respond.
>
> Muto: I'll take responsibility, Your Honor. I don't remember it, but I'll take responsibility. I'm—I'm very honest when it comes to taking responsibility.

I. *Culpability*

Muto also was charged with violating trust account rules. In March 1999, he opened an account and immediately deposited a check from two clients for $30,000. A month later he wrote and endorsed a check to cash for $29,995. One of the clients claimed to be acting as a real estate agent in a failed transaction, on behalf of an unnamed purchaser who wanted the money back in cash. Muto also was paid in cash. (If the DDC suspected money laundering, they did not pursue the matter.) Muto opened another trust account in January 2000, depositing $23,000 over 10 months and using the money for business expenses. Four checks were returned for insufficient funds. Muto claimed he had authorized Michael Lee to conduct all the transactions and the deposits were fees, not client money. "I didn't know you couldn't write an escrow check to cash. I've asked other attorneys and they've said, well, I don't know . . . not one cent of client money has ever been converted, jeopardized or commingled by me." He blamed the postal service for not delivering his change of address forms to the OCA, which a "former grievance committee prosecutor in Syracuse" would testify "happens all the time."

Cohen's brief summation reprised her opening statement. Muto's claim "that imposters came to his office pretending to be the clients and perhaps that's why the clients don't know who Mr. Muto is, lacks even a scintilla of any support." "He has no files. He has no receipts of payment. He has no diary entry of meetings with these people in his office."

"In deposition testimony, he couldn't recall meeting any of the clients. In some cases he didn't know if they were women or men."

Muto responded, "I've had no problems admitting wrongdoing when I screw up." Because most of his 450 cases required brief, infrequent work "it's not really the huge out of control practice Ms. Cohen perhaps wants you to believe it is."

> Why would I deal with agencies? I get people off the street . . . by word of mouth. I have . . . probably the lowest rates in town. I run a Filene's basement law practice. . . . I could bring in trial scripts and notepads, 70 pages. I just sat them down here and they would stack up to about here of immigration—individual asylum cases that I've done. Over 1,000. . . . I've had over 300 cases granted. . . . I work very diligently in my practice. I prep my clients. . . . I get angry when I see lawyers . . . screaming at their clients to take voluntary departure. . . . I went to friends in Canada, I got Canadian country reports . . . nobody has this. . . . They're very, very pro alien. I don't care if it's 150 pages of copying. I don't charge the client.

A few months earlier Judge Weisel had dispensed with a further hearing, saying, "Good job, Mr. Muto. Sir, I'm granting your application for political asylum."

Muto charged $100 for a reopen compared to the $3,000 other lawyers demanded. "To disbar me, Your Honor, to suspend me would be a grave injustice on the people that need services that I provide the most." He now controlled his caseload by referring matters to Karen Jaffe and Ed Kusha. But "if you have a good reputation, as I do, you're going to get a lot of people."

> I had nothing in Syracuse. I had very little money. I know what it's like that when I tell my children . . . we can't afford this, we can't afford that. I know what it's like to have to hold my children and they cried because they can't go to camp. The pet died because we couldn't take it to the vet. . . . I know what it's like to go somewhere else to start a new life, to be so eager and enthusiastic as I was when I came here, and to want to be accepted by your legal community and accepted by your profession. . . . I know, Judge, I'm just rambling.

CHAPTER 3

> I believe some of [the charges] should be sustained, Your Honor . . . [but] I think it's very clear that in many cases I, as much as these clients, was a victim. People came to me. I didn't check proofs. . . . I was just so angry, just so eager and so happy to do the cases.

Asked if he had any other evidence on liability, Muto said "I would only be calling my wife, Your Honor. She's been—she's kind of a basket case, to be honest with you . . . we lost our little boy like ten years ago and she hasn't been the same." When the Referee told him not to "burden the record with things like that," Muto said, "I'm just basically going to, for lack of a better word, just bring up my past and throw myself at your mercy." In his closing statement on liability, Muto said the DDC "has a full investigative staff . . . an investigator could have sat at 26 Federal—followed me there one day and tied this together."

The Referee sustained all the charges.

II. Putting Neglect in Context

In mitigation, Muto submitted his résumé. He had graduated in the top 7 percent of his University of Bridgeport Law School class (1986). He submitted a 1986 form letter from Joseph Lieberman, then Connecticut Attorney General, thanking him for working as a student intern.[672] He had been admitted to the Pennsylvania Bar in May 1987 (and elsewhere claimed membership in Colorado). He received an MBA from New York Institute of Technology in June 1989 with honors in finance. He volunteered his earlier Bar suspension to show "that I accept responsibility," although Cohen had not mentioned it. He introduced an article about disability and golf carts with respect to his flying phobia. He offered an Internet article documenting "the broad, broad, broad discrepancies in Immigration Court," but the Referee rejected it, commenting, "I'll take notice that all kinds of things happen in Immigration Court." He proffered a successful motion to reopen, but the Referee said Ms. Cohen would not "dispute that occasionally and maybe even more than occasionally, you succeeded." Muto maintained that lawyers who "actually got to know their clients and . . . put in a substantial story on a reopening"

---

[672] Respondent Ex. E.

were "just wasting their time." Judges "don't want to be inundated with 25 page motions. They just want to know why you want the case reopened. That's the way it's done in New York." He brought five such motions but "could not find the decisions. I usually give them to the clients."

Although his wife was waiting in the corridor, Muto declined the Referee's offer to hear her. "All she could testify to is that there was a volume, a huge volume of reopens that I had in early 1999." His mother had died, and "I also lost my cousin."

> Referee: Well, those are sad, but they're not so intimate that they would be derailing, I wouldn't think.
>
> Muto: That's true, Your Honor. That and the fact that there was an enormous, enormous volume of convention against torture.[673]
>
> Referee: . . . But it's your decision to become involved with a volume practice.

Invited to call a practitioner, Muto said Karen Jaffe refused to testify. "Nobody wants to expose themselves to cross examination . . . and be the next target." The Referee responded, "there is some—and it's justified, some apprehension in the community that you practice in, that this business of using agents to connect clients with lawyers is not something that has the approval of the court and the Bar."

Because Muto was too disorganized to make a statement—"I don't know procedure at all"—the Referee asked questions. "I really didn't practice much at all in Syracuse, Your Honor. I was very unsuccessful in Syracuse. Occasional Family Court, matrimonials." He had "always wanted to live in New York" and "had a decent amount of job offers here." He had been suspended for a year in 1994[674] but was not reinstated until November 1997 because he did not apply for two years.[675]

---

[673] New York City completed 1,870 Convention Against Torture cases in FY 2000. U.S. Dept. of Justice (2001: 21).

[674] He was first suspended on December 23, 1994. In the matter of Muto, 210 A.D.2d 1008, 621 N.Y.S.2d 994 (4th Dept 1994) (interim suspension); In the matter of Muto, 218 A.D.2d 328, 636 N.Y.S.2d 703 (4th Dept 1995).

[675] He petitioned for reinstatement on November 1996 and was reinstated on January 27, 1987. In the matter of Muto, 234 A.D.2d 1014, 652 N.Y.S.2d 462 (4th Dept. 1996).

CHAPTER 3

Under cross-examination, he acknowledged having resigned in 1990. At the time, he claimed that he had prepared the resignation letter when contemplating a possible career change (an unsuccessful challenge to State Senator Tarky Lombardi, Jr., that November). His wife admitted tricking him into signing it during a marital dispute. When she told him two days after she mailed it, he unsuccessfully tried to withdraw it.[676]

He moved for reinstatement in 1991, claiming his wife had fraudulently submitted it. She had stated under oath that she printed it out from his computer and put it in a pile of papers he signed without reading. But he admitted to having been depressed and dissatisfied with practice and to having made several inquiries about resigning. The 1994 suspension found that he had accepted $500 to do a bankruptcy case and had used the client's $600 filing fee for personal expenses.[677] Other complaints were pending at the time, and while suspended he received a letter of admonition for having neglected 10 clients. During this period, he had been rejected for jobs doing document review and had worked in a non-legal capacity for Blue Cross. His reinstatement application declared,

> I have repaid all funds owing to Walter and Linda Clemens, whose grievance formed the basis for my suspension. Also, I assisted my other clients in obtaining competent counsel at no additional cost to them. I have learned from my mistakes and will never accept monies from any clients without depositing them into an escrow account. I will never accept a case that I alone cannot successfully complete. And I will be totally honest with all clients regarding their cases.[678]

When he moved to New York City he did "per diem for Joanne Simon" but had "to make a little bit more money" and was attracted by David Rodkin's offer of "a chance to make a lot of money." "He hired me as an associate . . . so it wasn't per diem. And he paid me $750 a week, which was more than I ever made." Rodkin continued to refer cases after Karen and he "jumped out on our own" in April 1998. "I also did per diem for different lawyers."

---

[676] "Today's News," 10/10/1990 N.Y.L.J. 1 (col. 1).
[677] In re Muto, 621 N.Y.S.2d 994 (App. Div. 4th Dept. 1994) (interim suspension); In re Muto, 636 N.Y.S.2d 703 (App. Div. 4th Dept. 1995).
[678] In re Muto, 652 N.Y.S.2d 462 (App. Div. 4th Dept. 1996).

The Referee observed that Chinese applicants "need a go-between of some sort . . . these services provide translators . . . they're clearly providing legal advice in my view. Now other than referrals from attorneys . . . from agencies, how did these Chinese immigrants find lawyers?"

Muto: . . . A lot of them come in off the street and my sign. . . . And I've tried really to legitimize my practice, Judge.

Referee: You know what's worrisome about the way you practice is the volume.

Muto: I'm cutting down, Your Honor.

Referee: . . . Why would you have such a high number of cases?

Muto: . . . I won a lot of cases. I have a very high grant rate and . . . a very good reputation. I'm cutting down on the amount of case I have, Your Honor.

Referee: But the evidence I've heard for seven days now, for all I know, there may be many, many other cases where you have been so overburdened with cases or whatever the problem is, that you neglect them. . . .

Cohen: I think 450 cases are those cases that are just pending in the New York Immigration Court. There would be cases out of town as well.

Muto: Not many. . . .

Referee: But given your problems in general, and your fear of flying . . . why would you take any case that involved some other city? . . .

Muto: . . . I'm really cutting down on my cases.

Referee: . . . You're not answering my question. Why would you take a case that . . . required you to go to New Orleans?

Muto: There's a certain denial factor there, Your Honor. And also, I have other lawyers . . . who are only too happy to do trips to New Orleans for me. . . . And I'm not taking these out-of-town cases unless I know I can get to them. . . . I've really learned. I've really pared back my practice . . . parceling out a lot of cases. . . . I'd like more quality time for myself. . . .

Referee: [Ms Hsiung charges $2,000–$3,500] and even that seems to me . . . on the reasonable side. How can you charge $100 or $200 or $300 for the same thing . . . and then have the motivation to turn to your client enough to really do a good job?

Muto: Judge, I'm very motivated. I don't look at the money . . . I love doing the work . . . I should probably charge more and take less clients. . . . I never look at the dollar sign. . . .

Referee: Well, the evidence I've seen indicates otherwise. Because it looks as though you have so many cases and you want to get 100 bucks and then you put in a form motion, which is skeletal. And you say some judges want it that way. Clearly some judges don't. But you don't make an adjustment. . . . You put in probably $100 worth of work. But a lot of the time it isn't worth it. The client loses.

Muto: . . . I'm going to work harder. I'm going to reduce my case load . . . so I could devote more time on the cases I have, and I'll . . . charge appropriately.

Cohen said she had taken six depositions over the course of a year (December 6, 1999, to November 29, 2000), but "today for the first time, you're making the statement that you have pared down your practice." Muto claimed he now did only three or four reopens a week but could not refrain from boasting, "I did three masters today, and they took five minutes each." He had changed his office practices to prevent others from impersonating clients, demanding IDs, and having handwritten depositions notarized. "I try and stay really on top of cases. . . . And I would like to try and initiate some kind of a, you know, I go over my files a lot more vigorously."

In her closing, Cohen declared that Muto's 1994 "representation as to how he's going to go forward in the handling of his practice was completely not fulfilled."

I don't think Mr. Muto gets it. . . . I don't think he fully understands that the manner in which he conducts his practice is

> a per se violation of basic rudimentary practice. . . . The fact that the practice of immigration law at 26 Federal Plaza may fall below . . . the standard that members of the Bar should adhere to, does not excuse Mr. Muto's conduct. . . . [His earlier suspension] reflects a very cavalier attitude towards his practice. . . . [His defenses] communicate an effort to not take responsibility for his conduct; to blame others; to fashion theories that . . . border on the preposterous; and present them . . . to this tribunal with a straight face. . . . Mr. Muto's statement, for example, I give all of my clients an 800 number which they can call and find out their status. Well first of all, as for the Chinese clients, I don't know how they could make that call. . . . Even in Mr. Karim's case . . . that's not what Mr. Karim went to Mr. Muto for.

She sought disbarment.

Muto denied having a "cavalier and callous attitude towards my clients."

> I'm a very caring, very kind, have a nurturing attitude towards my clients. . . . I never had a real law practice before. Things got totally out of hand. And I realize and I recognize it. Yes, I had cases of neglect in Syracuse, but I didn't know how to do a matrimonial. I took on matrimonial cases up there because I needed the money. I had nothing, Your Honor. We had two foreclosures up there, Your Honor, of homes. . . . That's where the money went, to forestall a foreclosure. . . .
>
> I have two small children. I have two grown children. We have a third child who passed away in 1987. And you know . . . when we brought a malpractice action there were lawyers and judges in the Syracuse community who thought I was slightly better than scum pursuing a doctor who they considered . . . was respected.

The Referee cut off this digression.

> I have a great deal of remorse for what happens to the clients. I respectfully disagree that giving the clients an 800 number was an act of callousness. It was an act of courtesy . . . so they

Chapter 3

> don't have to come into my office. . . . I always tell every client, any time you have a question about your case, you feel free to come down to my office and ask me. . . . And, gee, I love helping those along for freedom. I love my work. I love being a member of your legal community down here, and I love your city. I bought a home here. . . . I . . . respectfully draw the court's attention to Matter of Rodkin, where another immigration lawyer, the same one who hired me, had numerous charges and received no more than a letter of admonition.

Cohen quickly objected that the case was confidential. Muto asked for no more than an admonition "because I'm really doing a good job with the clients. Overall, I'm doing an excellent job." The Referee urged him to put something in writing "other than your statement that you have turned a corner—I'm not sure I know how to believe that."

Muto's written submission argued that termination of his "successful high quality/low cost law practice would work a grave injustice on those clients who rely upon him" and could not pay "fees of $3,000 or more." He gave

> the clients an opportunity to retain an attorney who will be personally involved in their case from start to finish and who takes a strong interest in their asylum claim. This stands in stark contract [sic] to the non-lawyer service agency which, despite charging an affordable fee, takes only a peripheral interest in their "customer's" claim at best.

His 450 cases were "in stark contrast to the lesser caseload of the higher priced attorneys." But "these matters, once filed, do not require any additional work." "Often, aside from writing and assembling documents, there is very little that needs to be done on a particular case during this period." His 25 percent success rate (275 of 1,100 cases litigated to verdict) compared favorably with the 15 percent national average for Chinese cases. "This success rate is even more remarkable when one considers that Respondent does not screen away weaker cases, as several attorneys do [and] rarely suggests that a client accept voluntary departure."

He works

> long hours and has an "open door" policy for his clients. They are always welcome to come to Respondent's office at no additional charge to discuss their case. Respondent also devotes many hours to preparing his clients' asylum applications and preparing his clients for court.

The previous day he had won asylum for Qi Qi Zheng (for which he charged only $1,200), after a two-hour hearing before Judge Sarah Burr, who ranked 84th in granting asylum. His clients "receive the same high quality service they would receive at a high priced law firm for a fraction of the cost." Suspension and disbarment "were never meant to be utilized to rid the profession of well-intentioned, honest, hardworking attorneys whose faults were due to inexperience at the practice of law and who were laboring under personal problems."

His mother had been diagnosed with a terminal illness in September 1998 and had died five months later. When her condition had worsened in December, he had frequently driven to Syracuse. But Judge Ferris applied "a great deal of pressure" on him in the Chang Kui Lin case "at a time when Respondent's mother was in the last weeks of her life." He was "a highly qualified attorney who graduated at the top of his class in law school, having served as associate editor of the Law Review." He "compiled a stellar record as a prosecutor in Cortland County where he was entrusted with felony level cases and appeals less than a year after graduation from law school." He had "continually endeavored to improve his practice to better serve his clients." "Suspension will enrich the non-lawyer agencies who Respondent competes with at the expense of those who can least afford it."

Cohen replied that Muto's "neglect of his clients' interests" was "pervasive and extreme; in most cases he never even met or spoke directly to the clients." "[O]ften without the consent of his clients and at the least [sic] minute" he hired "other attorneys to appear on an 'of counsel' per diem basis." His association with non-lawyer agents who controlled his cases "contributed to the poor quality representation." Prior discipline "had no impact." He displayed "continued lack of candor at the hearing," failed "to accept responsibility for his conduct," tended "to blame his clients," and showed "lack of remorse." He twice invoked "an otherwise confidential Letter of Admonition issued to another immigration attorney for whom Respondent initially worked and with whom Respondent still maintains a professional relationship." Unlike Muto, "the other attorney candidly admitted that he had a business relationship with the non-lawyer agent, who notably was identified by the complainant and the other attorney as Michael Lee."

III. Disposition

The Referee began his report by observing that immigration law "is not visible to practicing lawyers and judges who practice primarily in the courts of general jurisdiction" and "has not been the subject of much scrutiny."[679] Muto's Chinese clients were "especially vulnerable" because they did not speak English (only Fuzhou) and depended on "a series of middlemen": "the 'snakehead' who brings [them] in . . . hands [them] on to the 'agency' which in turn provides a translator, a restaurant or factory job and place to sleep, and a lawyer who will try to obtain legal status for him." "The inescapable conclusion is that the persons in these agencies like Respondent's landlord Mr. Ye [sic] are practicing law and according to the testimony herein, doing it badly." The Referee found "a shocking degree of neglect, whether born of carelessness, unconcern, or some deeper psychological cause." Muto's "cross-examination of his former client Mr. Karim was revealing in its weird combination of insult, irrelevance, and admission of professional malpractice." "The low cost of Respondent's sources [sic—"services"], amply demonstrated, yielded only disastrous consequences for each of the complaining witnesses."

> Although it has been clearly established that Respondent has aided the unauthorized practice of law by his reliance upon non-lawyers to procure clients and to do difficult legal work for him (and to do it incorrectly), it is not this aspect of his professional conduct that argues most compellingly for severe sanctions. It is the record of Respondent's truly shocking disregard for his clients' welfare in what is for them one of the most important undertakings of their lives. It is difficult to imagine a state of mind so negligent, so loosely tied to reality, or, at worst, so cynical, as would not even inform his client of the date of an individual hearing, or as would allow deportation orders to issue by default.

---

[679] September 17, 2001.

Muto's expressions of contrition "come too late to have any real significance." His insistence that "he well serves his clients for fees they can afford has an air of delusion about it. After listening to the complaints here, how can he possibly believe that?" His self-representation "displayed general disorganization and a kind of *ad hoc* scatterbrained approach to the issues raised that one can only conclude is further evidence of how he dealt with former clients." His "explanations for his several defaults varied in plausibility from absurd to unlikely. His inclination to put the blame on his hapless clients for his poor motions papers is offensive to say the least." There was "strong evidence of someone unable to organize a legal practice (or his own defense) and unable to manage the responsibility of representing clients with serious legal problems." The Referee recommended disbarment.

The Hearing Panel agreed.[680] Former clients "who had nothing to gain from his punishment" appeared "despite their own precarious positions." Their testimony "established that Respondent was retained not by clients, but by these agents, and that he aided their unauthorized practice of law." Muto challenged only 2 of the 43 charges. He "simply repeated his denial . . . and speculated that he had been the victim of imposters." He neglected "numerous" clients, who "did not have only an economic stake in the outcome of their matters. They involved personal liberty, and in some cases at least, danger of being returned to a country which had persecuted them." "The record in this matter amply demonstrates that Respondent is unfit to practice law, and is a danger to any client who might retain him." The Panel unanimously recommended disbarment.

In her petition for confirmation, Sherry Cohen repeated the neglect charges. Muto "never met, spoke or had meaningful contact with his clients." He

> aided the unauthorized practice of law through his association with non-lawyer agents in Chinese political asylum cases. In most cases, these non-lawyer agents hired Respondent without the knowledge or consent of the clients. . . . In most of the Chinese asylum cases, Respondent relied on and/or delegated responsibility to non-lawyer agents or poorly supervised so-called employees who provided legal services to his clients.

---

[680] Justin N. Feldman (chair), Christopher E. Chang, Michael J. Rosenberg, Burton N. Lipshie, Sally W. Berg (lay member) (October 2, 2001).

Chapter 3

Muto twice sought extensions to file his petition against confirmation "due to the complex nature of this case and the voluminous record which it produced." "Further evidence of the intricate nature of my case is reflected by the fact that the referee's report contained several factual errors and conflicting statements." But his only example was the generalization that Chinese illegal immigrants are male, when a fifth are female. Muto invoked the Americans with Disabilities Act.

> As the sole means of support for a disabled spouse and two small children, I have proceeded pro se since April 2001.... My difficulties in proceeding pro se were apparent at my hearing, and this fact was noted in the referee's report.

He objected to Guo Ping's sensational testimony about being smuggled into the United States and to Cohen's characterization of Muto as an "enabler." He stated that he had "never in any way facilitated the process." He submitted "a series of successful cases which he litigated over a four-week period, and also four cases which he successfully litigated in a single day." His "problems arose more from inexperience at managing a successful law practice than any malicious intent." The *Lozada* decision "has created a situation whereby an individual with nothing to lose often files a complaint against an attorney with the hope of having their case reopened." In the disciplinary hearing, he had "to walk a fine line between zealously advocating on his own behalf and accepting responsibility for those acts that he is culpable of." He had graduated from law school cum laude in two and a half years, had been an associate editor of the *Law Review*, and had received the *Law Review* "scholarship for outstanding academic achievement and writing skills," as well as having received "his school's award for outstanding legal scholarship" at commencement. He was "fulfilling a life long ambition" by gaining admission to the bar.

Numerous service agencies openly advertised in the Chinese newspaper "soliciting unsuspecting immigrants." They

> choose an attorney for their client. The agency and not the attorney controls the case, and often the agency will switch attorneys without the client's knowledge or consent. The client frequently meets the attorney, who has been hired and paid solely by the agency, only minutes before the hearing that will determine his fate.

The evidence of his own dealings with agencies was "at best spectral." He raised questions of equal protection and selective prosecution because "the DDC is cognizant of extensive involvement other attorneys have with said agencies and even utilized two acknowledged agency attorneys to testify against Respondent at his hearing." Maratea admitted to having worked for Howard Chen. Since his own disciplinary hearing, Muto had "observed Mr. Maratea continuing to accept cases for the Chen service agency." In response to Muto's four complaints to the DDC, Maratea "admitted to dealing with a non-lawyer service agency, and even went so far as to say that he has a contractual relationship with Mr. Chen." But the DDC declined to act. "Despite Mr. Kuntashian's known dealings with [the Blue Eagle] agency . . . no disciplinary action was taken." Even David Rodkin received only a private admonition.

Cohen objected that Muto had failed to serve the Committee in a timely manner, despite having been granted a generous extension. This "disregard of the Court's procedures and courtesies as well as his cavalier approach to the veracity of his representation he made to the Court about Mr. Ginnelly's letter [see below] are consistent with the very misconduct at issue and constitute additional factors in aggravation." she claimed. She rebuked him again for disclosing the confidential complaint against Rodkin. The 10th Judicial District had dismissed Muto's complaints against Maratea.

Muto filed a "reply affirmation" over Cohen's objection. "Despite due dilligence [sic] due to the complexity of this matter Respondent was unable to complete his answer and memorandum of law any sooner." He had waited for the letter from Paul Ginnelly (principal counsel to the 5th District DDC for 21 years), who was on vacation (which was "beyond the control of Respondent"). He had not tried to "mislead" the Court. But the long-awaited letter was not very helpful. Ginnelly had been "quite surprised by [Muto's] candor and forthrightness" in response to the charges leading to his 1994 suspension and "impressed by his honesty in regard to his representation of his clients. . . . It was apparent that Mr. Muto had numerous personal problems that impacted on his professional life."

The Appellate Division found that Muto had "failed to demonstrate any causal connection between his mother's illness and his professional misconduct."[681] His "fear of flying is more aggravating than it is mitigating." He "had accumulated a substantial disciplinary history before any

---

[681] Matter of Muto, 291 A.D.2d 188, 739 N.Y.S.2d 67 (1st Dept 2002).

CHAPTER 3

of the events on which the present charges are based." His "culpability is further aggravated by his lack of candor in these proceedings, and by his lack of genuine remorse and contrition, as evidenced by his continued mantra-like recitation, even in this Court, of the baseless assertion that he rendered 'low cost high quality' representation to his ill-served clients." The court disbarred him. Muto told a reporter, "I feel justice was not done in my case."[682] (He told me in 2006 that he planned to apply for reinstatement at the earliest possible time: 2007 in Pennsylvania, 2009 in New York; he had already taken the District of Columbia bar examination.)

IV. Understanding Neglect

The basic complaint against Joseph Muto was incompetence.[683] He neglected clients by taking far too many cases and then failing to maintain files, submit documents, draft motions, follow procedures, and prepare for hearings—or even attend them. He relied on a faulty memory for the dates of hundreds of deadlines and hearings each year, checking the court calendar at 4 P.M. daily "to ascertain whether I am attorney of record for any cases which may have 'slipped through the cracks.'" He often was, and they often did. He did not know what an office diary was. His appointment book did not record the Buffalo hearing. He could not produce any appointment books before June 23, 1999 (two months after Chang Kui's DDC complaint). Relying on memory, he gave Karim the wrong date for his individual hearing and then missed it himself. He admitted no meeting clients before hearings.

> I did not have any record of having met Mr. [Hong Ren] Lin, nor did I have any record of having his case . . . I may have made an appearance for this individual on an "of counsel" basis, but I have no recollection of having done so. . . . I hadn't been in touch with this client.

---

[682] Anthony M. DeStefano, *Unholy Alliances*, Newsday, Aug. 10, 2002, at A5. Muto spent two years day trading, following the lead of Michael Lee; when the market collapsed, he sought a real estate license but was rejected because of his disbarment.

[683] I draw here on a 75-minute interview with Mr. Muto on September 25, 2006 at his office at the New York State Department of Human Rights, 20 Exchange Place, where he had worked since March.

The meetings he did hold were only 15–30 minutes long. He had Abdul Karim file the appearance because Muto was in another court; and he talked to Karim only briefly the night before the first hearing. Muto lacked a regular interpreter, relying on someone down the hall (whose name he could not remember) and a high school student, and borrowing interpreters from the court or other lawyers. Clients could not reach him: he failed to give them business cards,[684] moved without informing them, was never in his office, and did not return their calls to the only number he provided (his home answering machine). He explained having an unlisted number as "an upstate thing." He failed to inform clients of the outcomes of their cases (much less of the progress). Courts could not serve him because he failed to notify the OCA of address changes and had no office. He ignored hearings in Buffalo and New Orleans, disavowing the duty to represent clients, whether or not *they* appeared, until he was discharged by the court. "[U]nder no circumstances is an attorney required to travel 1200 miles to pick up in absentia deportation orders . . . this is especially true in my case where I have a flying phobia." He agreed to appear in person and then substituted another lawyer. He randomly picked a "per diem" lawyer in New Orleans with no prior immigration experience and gave him the wrong hearing date. He appeared by telephone without prior permission and without producing his clients in court. He could offer no evidence he had ever tried to contact a client because he had no files (the only ones he produced for the DDC were irrelevant). He failed to serve motions on his adversary, expecting the court to do it for him. He asked judges to verify his excuses for nonappearance (his mother's terminal illness, flight delays and cancellations). He filed motions late without seeking extensions. He failed to tender evidence of essential facts (and seemed unaware of the difference between allegations and evidence). He submitted documents after the record was closed. He borrowed other lawyers' forms without updating or adapting them to the case (one reason why his motions were denied). His motion papers were perfunctory. Confronted with documents filed in his name, he admitted: "I didn't even know what was submitted. I mean it could have been something that was kicking around in my office." Although he insisted that he drafted his clients' affidavits, he was unable to speak to them and devoted insufficient time. Factual errors suggest the affidavits were copied from others. Clients' signatures were

---

[684] Partly because they dealt exclusively with the agencies. In 2006 Muto asked for my business card but still did not have one himself.

CHAPTER 3

forged, and their names wrong. Muto relied on subordinates who were either incompetent or indifferent (and may actually have been his bosses). They were certainly patronizing to clients: Cathy Chen complained that clients did not have their own apartments or telephone, often did not speak Mandarin, and "never go to school."[685]

Muto projected his own disorganization onto others (just as he projected the agency taint onto other lawyers). He stopped retaining Saul Schneider for "of counsel" appearances because Schneider "came in late, you know, strutted in without having the opportunity to meet the client," "wasn't a very responsible person," "would tend to come in late," was "disorganized," and would "miss hearings."

Muto's own excuses substantiated the charges. He was "fresh off the bus from Syracuse." He "never had a real law practice before." His "problems arose more from inexperience at managing a successful law practice than any malicious intent." He could not see that these were arguments *against* him practicing alone. (Someone told him he should have begun in government, but of course he had—as a prosecutor. He clearly benefited from the structure of his current non-legal job, boasting to me that he was much more productive than the other investigators.) Muto only dug himself in deeper each time he explained why he had failed to move for an extension of time. He had never done one before. (He had just disregarded deadlines for 12 years? In any case, these motions were hardly complicated.) It slipped through the cracks (like the hearings themselves, even when he checked the court calendar). He could not even remember what he was seeking to excuse (confusing the motions to file documents late and to change venue). Given yet another chance, he also failed to meet this deadline. He offered his mother's illness as an excuse even though the judge had seen him in court every day that week. He was unable to grasp that giving the Immigration Court's 800 number to clients who did not speak English failed to fulfill *his* responsibility to keep them informed of the status of their cases.

As the Referee noted, Muto reenacted his incompetence throughout the disciplinary hearing.[686] He opened by declaring "I'm nervous as

---

[685] Eddie Ye seems to have made the decisions to file Chang Kui Lin's asylum application and change-of-venue motion without consulting the client, just as Muto lied about Lin's delay in obtaining papers from China and about his willingness to accept voluntary departure, and substituted Maratea without consulting Lin.

[686] He represented himself because Hal Lieberman, who drafted the initial answer to the charges, "demanded $25,000."

hell" and repeated this during the trial. "I'm trying to be honest. I'm not trying to be evasive. Sometimes I maybe don't understand. I'll say one thing where I . . . really was meaning something else." He could not stay on point, getting distracted at the outset by his absurd metaphor of painting a fox hunt by the numbers. He used an equally outlandish metaphor (his father-in-law, a Ford-trained mechanic, fixing a Chevy transmission) to argue that McGrath, an experienced trial lawyer, could handle an immigration case without training. (McGrath admitted that "The judge handled the hearing himself. Neither the federal attorney nor I asked many questions.") In mitigation, Muto claimed to "know what it's like to have to hold my children and they cried because they can't go to camp. The pet died because we couldn't take it to the vet." In support of his own invocation of the ADA because his *wife* was a "basket case" he introduced an article on disability and golf carts. But he concluded, "I know, Judge, I'm just rambling." He volunteered his earlier suspension before Cohen mentioned it. He even made his inadequacy a defense: "My difficulties in proceeding pro se were apparent at my hearing, and this fact was noted in the referee's report." But if he couldn't even represent himself, how could he possibly represent hundreds of non-English speaking immigrants, in complex proceedings, with much more at stake?

Muto expected others to do things for him: judges to elicit the evidence necessary to support his immigrant clients' petitions, the Referee to lead him through a coherent story and even draft a subpoena after he had botched the job. He suggested that DDC counsel Sherry Cohen relay Karim's phone messages. Judges required lawyers to submit their forms at the beginning of a master calendar and wait to have their cases called; Muto walked in at the end, expecting judges to wait for him. He viewed it as exculpatory that the *other* seven clients he had abandoned in New Orleans had not complained. (They probably had gone underground after being deported in absentia.) He kept breaching confidentiality by repeatedly citing the private reprimand of his former employer, David Rodkin, even after being chastised. He continued to seek time extensions and then missed them, too. He failed to serve papers on the DDC and misrepresented the contents of documents. He accused the Referee's report of "several factual errors" but substantiated only one irrelevance. He seemed to know he was his own worst enemy, declaring, "this will come in on aggravation" (when he meant mitigation).

He admitted some failings. He was a "little bit" disorganized. Things "slipped through the cracks." Caught in contradictions, he insisted, "I'm

CHAPTER 3

trying to be honest. I'm not trying to be evasive. Sometimes I maybe don't understand. I'll say one thing where I . . . really mean something else." He echoed former DDC general counsel Hal Lieberman in insisting that incompetence was not grounds for discipline, and suspension and disbarment were not appropriate for "well-intentioned, honest, hardworking attorneys whose faults were due to inexperience at the practice of law and who were laboring under personal problems."

More often, however, he displayed delusions of grandeur.[687] He was "a highly qualified attorney who graduated at the top of his class in law school, having served as associate editor of the Law Review."[688] He had received the *Law Review* "scholarship for outstanding academic achievement and writing skills" and "his school's award for outstanding legal scholarship" at commencement. (This just made his subsequent performance less excusable.) He "compiled a stellar record as a prosecutor in Cortland County where he was entrusted with felony level cases and appeals less than a year after graduation from law school."[689] He had "a decent amount of job offers" in New York City. (Actually, he scoured the *New York Law Journal* and took menial per diem work "of counsel.") He provided "quality legal services," "quality work, quality reopens." He operated a "successful high quality/low cost law practice." His clients "receive the same high quality service they would receive at a high priced law firm for a fraction of the cost." "I get deeply into my work," he stated, and provide "competent and ethical representation." "[V]irtually every one of my clients is overjoyed and happy with my services." "I'm really doing a good job with the clients. Overall, I'm doing an excellent job." He always discussed cases with clients. He had learned to write dates and times in Chinese. "I'm a very caring, very kind, have a nurturing attitude towards my clients," he stated. He was "an attorney who will be personally involved in their case from start to finish and who takes a strong interest in their

---

[687] In 2006 he claimed that he had gotten the top grade in New York State on the civil service examination for his present job. He also boasted about his score when he took practice exams for the multistate while preparing to take the District of Columbia bar exam.

[688] The University of "Bridgeport Law School found it hard to compete for students with the University of Connecticut, which charged residents only a third as much. After being bailed out by local banks in 1989, it was bought by the Unification Church in 1992. Katherine Farrish, "Final Exams May be Final Indeed: University of Bridgeport Teeters on the Brink," Hartford Courant A1, December 12, 1991; Constance L. Hays, Bridgeport U. Ponders Its Future," New York Times B7, April 27, 1992.

[689] He constantly showed off his inside knowledge of criminal justice: offering to take a lie detector test, proposing subpoenas, suggested Cohen could have had him tailed, secretly taping a conversation with Eddie Ye.

asylum claims." He "devotes many hours to preparing his clients' asylum applications and preparing his clients for court." (Actually, he met the complaining clients for the first time at the courtroom.) "I endeavor to be very dilligent [sic] in returning client calls and addressing their needs. I even provide a home number." (Actually, he was never at his home number and never returned Karim's many, increasingly frantic, calls.) He had "an 'open door' policy for his clients. They are always welcome to come to Respondent's office at no additional charge to discuss their case." (Actually, he was never there and gave them the 800 number so they would not bother him.) His 25 percent success rate in Chinese asylum claims was higher than the 15 percent national average, which was "even more remarkable when one considers that Respondent does not screen away weaker cases ... [and] rarely suggests that a client accept voluntary departure."[690] (Actually, 36 percent of asylum applications were granted nationwide in fiscal year 2000, 47 percent in New York City.)[691] All these delusions were consistent with his continued acceptance of clients in other cities and constantly renewed faith that he could fly despite repeated failures. (He had a drawer full of wasted airplane tickets.) Indeed, he admitted to "a certain denial factor."

Muto's relationship to "agencies" played a prominent but ambiguous role in the proceedings. Both prosecutor and Referee insisted they were concerned with his involvement only to the extent that it showed neglect.[692] Cohen did not prosecute Kuntashian or Maratea, who admitted to working with agencies. Muto's complaints against Maratea were dismissed. Ann Hsiung—said to be an exemplary practitioner—admitted that some of her clients might have come from agencies. Although Rodkin admitted to working with agencies, he received only a private reprimand.[693] Judge Ferris advised Chang Kui Lin to mention agency involvement in his disciplinary grievance. And both the Referee and the Hearing Panel described Muto's work with agencies. Cohen began her case with Reiner's

---

[690] In 2006 he repeated that he had obtained asylum for 307 of his 1,200 clients.
[691] U.S. Department of Justice (2001: 31–31 tables 15, 16).
[692] The agencies clearly were engaged in unauthorized practice of law: collecting evidence, giving advice, drafting documents, deciding legal strategies, maintaining the file. But that was the responsibility of the District Attorney, although the DDC could have disciplined lawyers for facilitating it. In response to comments by practitioners, the EOIR later made it a disciplinary offense to assist "in the performance of activity that constitutes the unauthorized practice of law." 8 C.F.R. § 1003.102(m) (2005).
[693] Rodkin was subsequently suspended for six months for "fronting" for agencies. The Appellate Division noted that he continued to act as counsel of record for agencies after the AD disbarred Muto. Matter of Rodkin, 21 A.D.3d 111 (1st Dept. 2005).

lengthy testimony, presumably to demonstrate the feasibility of practicing without agencies. But though Reiner and Hsiung might eschew them, agencies were indispensable to lawyers like Muto.[694] Immigrants relied on agencies to speak their Chinese dialect, to prepare and translate documents, to guide them through the immigration bureaucracy, and to hire and manage lawyers. Some agencies may have been implicated in human trafficking. Reiner's professional association (of immigration lawyers) was seeking to eradicate "unauthorized practice" by agencies. Yet the effort to eliminate them—like so much American immigration policy—was profoundly hypocritical.

Muto deeply resented the taint of agency association (either because it exposed him to discipline or because it revived the canard that he was not a real lawyer). He offered photos to prove he had an office, whose shingle attracted clients (although they denied noticing it). He claimed to be above the contemptible "Chinatown crawl," challenged Cohen to have him trailed, and repeatedly offered to take a lie detector test. He could not know whether he had agency cases: "Am I supposed to plug these people into lie detectors?" He distinguished himself from the numerous agencies that openly advertised in the Chinese press, "soliciting unsuspecting immigrants." They

> choose an attorney for their client. The agency and not the attorney controls the case, and often the agency will switch attorneys without the client's knowledge or consent. The client frequently meets the attorney, who has been hired and paid solely by the agency, only minutes before the hearing that will determine his fate.

But in displaying such intimate familiarity, Muto admitted guilty knowledge and highlighted the similarities to his own practice.

Indeed, each effort to emphasize his distance from the agencies just further demonstrated his involvement. He admitted knowing that David Rodkin ran an agency practice but claimed that was why he left—only to be confronted with an earlier statement that he had been tempted by the money Rodkin made as an agency lawyer. (Elsewhere Muto claimed

---

[694] Non-lawyer intermediaries dominate other practice areas. "The broker may be another lawyer, an accountant, a real estate or insurance broker or agent, a building contractor, a doctor, policeman, bondsman, precinct captain, garage mechanic, minister, undertaker, plant personnel director, foreman, etc." Carlin (1962: 135–36).

"I never look at the dollar sign.") He accepted Rodkin's referral of Ju Jin Jing and other cases. He accused Karen Jaffe of accepting the Chang Kui Lin case from Eddie Ye at the Blue Eagle agency—but then Muto let slip that he worked *for* Karen. He tried to cure this by claiming he had split with Karen over agency work; but he called her a close friend, wanted her to testify on his behalf, and relied on her to inform clients of his new address. When Muto moved out of Michael Lee's office, Rodkin moved in.[695] Muto took over the Lin case from Kuntashian, who openly admitted agency work. Muto used Maratea to make "per diem" appearances and tried to substitute him in Chang Kui Lin's case, while accusing Maratea of complicity with agencies.

The evidence of Muto's involvement with agencies was overwhelming. He accepted cases from at least three: Michael Lee,[696] Eddie Ye's Blue Eagle, and Sin Rong [Xing Long] Fu Wu Si (Chinese Legal Services). He could not communicate with his Chinese clients without interpreters, most of whom worked for agencies. The agencies prepared the affidavits, because Muto often did not meet clients before hearings and in any case could not talk to them or read their Chinese documents. He had clients throughout the country—New Orleans, Atlanta, Buffalo, St. Louis, Houston, El Paso, San Francisco—none of whom he could have gotten himself. (As non-lawyers, agencies can solicit.) Blue Eagle kept possession of Chang Kui Lin's file and hired four lawyers—Jaffe, Kuntashian, Muto, and Maratea—none of whom Lin met before the hearings. Muto's cavalier assignment of clients to other lawyers without client consent (both for particular hearings and for permanent substitutions) simply repeated his own experience of being hired by agencies, not clients. Agencies showed their contempt for clients and lawyers by forging client signatures on notices of appearance and affidavits. Maratea's testimony about Michael Lee's outburst strongly suggested that Lee was accustomed to controlling cases and lawyers. Maratea testified that he had appeared in some of Muto's other cases at the behest of agents. Muto admitted to collaborating with

---

[695] In 2007 Both Rodkin and Jaffe (now Jaffe-Nierenberg) had offices at 401 Broadway. But by 2006 Jaffe had been suspended from practice before the Immigration Court and the Bureau of Immigration Appeals, and the Second Circuit had ordered her to be relieved as counsel in all cases. Yuan v. Gonzales, 202 Fed. Appx. 506 (2nd Cir. 2006); Liu v. Gonzales, 193 Fed. Appx. 51 (2nd Cir. 2006). When she continued to appear, the Court repeated its order, finding "that her continued representation of petitioners in this case constitutes a manifest injustice that this Court will not tolerate." Lin v. Mukasey, 2007 WL 3407338 (2nd Cir. 2007).

[696] In 2006 Muto admitted to splitting fees with Lee's agency. But he named other lawyers who had done so, complaining that only he got blamed for it.

CHAPTER 3

Rodkin, Jaffe, Kuntashian, Maratea, and Finnell, all of whom worked with agencies. He admitted to taking Jong Ren Lin's case from an agent. Rodkin called Michael Lee an agent; indeed, Muto and Jaffe left Rodkin to work in Lee's suite (and were followed there by Rodkin himself). Lee's business cards advertised his immigrant service agency and bail bond operation. Although Muto denied knowing this, his own cards were virtually identical (which may explain why he never had any to give judges). He denied sharing an office with the Chinese Service Center or Vincent Smith Bail Bond, but they all had the same address. When Cathy Chen answered the phone she passed clients directly to Lee, never mentioning Muto (with whom they could not converse). Muto vehemently denied any involvement in smuggling—but the uninvited appearance of Lee (and probably Cathy Chen) at the New Orleans INS detention center to interview 30 stranger detainees, sign up Xue Jie Chen and seven others, transport them to New York, and arrange for Muto to represent them strongly suggests otherwise. Muto's story that he just rented space from Lee and paid him for translation services was totally incredible. (Muto also claimed to rent the space from Dr. He and to use him and two others as translators.) If Lee was a day-trading genius and millionaire, why would he have needed Muto's trivial payments? Lee controlled all of Muto's books, even client accounts. The $1,100 Chang Kui Lin paid Cathy Chen could not have been for translation. Muto admitted that clients sometimes paid Lee for his own services, that he could not fire Lee or Chen, and that he had no receipts for transactions with them, most of which were in cash. It all is uncomfortably reminiscent of Uriah Heep's domination of Mr. Wickfield in *David Copperfield* close.[697]

Given his victims' powerlessness, Muto's egregious misconduct probably would have escaped scrutiny but for two things. First, successor counsel helped clients file the DDC complaints necessary to reopen their deportation orders for ineffective assistance of counsel. Second, Muto provoked many judges, who expressed discomfort at deporting potentially meritorious applicants betrayed by their lawyers' incompetence.[698] Judges rarely file grievances.[699] These did so in part because they lacked

---

[697] Dickens (1991).

[698] An Immigration judge must "inform the alien of his or her apparent eligibility to apply for any of the benefits enumerated in this chapter and shall afford the alien an opportunity to make application during the hearing." 8 C.F.R. § 1240.11(a)(2) (2005).

[699] Even prompted by the INS lawyer, Bukszpan still did not think it "appropriate" to inform Ju Jin Jing of her right to complain to the DDC. Judges and lawyers together filed only 3.5% of grievances in Michigan in 1972, and lawyers almost certainly outnumbered judges. Steele & Nimmer (1976: 973 table 9).

the usual contempt power, and the EOIR had no disciplinary procedures.[700] Judge Ferris was incensed that Muto had sought to take the Chang Kui Lin case away from her through a fraudulent venue change (apparently at Michael Lee's direction). (Muto submitted a ranking of judges showing Ferris as very unlikely to grant asylum—seemingly oblivious to the fact that this demonstrated his bad faith.[701]) Judge Zlatow was furious at Muto for abandoning clients. Judge Bukszpan was outraged that Muto ignored filing deadlines. All three of them and Judge DeFonzo were angered that Muto repeatedly missed hearings. Bukszpan complained that Muto had left "three or four judges sitting here looking at the ceiling and all his clients looking at the ceiling and four interpreters called at extreme government expense."[702] IC judges traded horror stories about his behavior. Muto's style further aggravated the situation. He peered into Ferris's courtroom before Chang Kui Lin's hearing, muttered that he was afraid of her, and scurried away. He showed disrespect for judges by expecting Ferris to verify his mother's illness and Zlatow to investigate his attempt to fly to New Orleans and by phoning Zlatow from the corridor of a New York courthouse while chatting with passersby. Bukszpan complained that Muto "flaunts the court" (an apt malapropism), showed "audacity," lacked "courtesy," engaged in "flagrant" "unacceptable" behavior, and displayed "professional irresponsibility."[703] Ferris was sufficiently outraged to take the extraordinary step of searching for Muto's alleged office; investigating the building directory and mailboxes, calling information for his phone number; summoning Kuntashian, Maratea, and Eddie Ye to a hearing; and subpoenaing Ye's files. Although Bukszpan declined to urge Ju Jin Jing to file a grievance, Ferris made that suggestion to Chang Kui Lin, and Judge Bain's clerk made it to Abdul Karim. Zlatow had to conduct the hearing himself because of Muto's absence and McGrath's incompetence.

---

[700] Immigration judges obtained this authority on July 27, 2000, 8 C.F.R. §§ 292 & 1003.102 (2000). Before this, only five immigration lawyers had ever been disciplined, four of them before 1980. Hake (2000).

[701] The Transactional Records Access Clearinghouse reports on the performance of some 200 Immigration Court judges: http://trac.syr.edu/immigration/reports/183. This showed, in fact, that 189 of the 238 Immigration Court judges denied a higher proportion of asylum claims: http://trac.syr.edu/immigration/reports/judgereports/143/index.html.

[702] The approximately 220 Immigration Court judges heard over 220,000 proceedings annually during this period, or more than 1,000 each. New York City's 26 judges heard 19,683 matters in FY 2000. U.S. Dept. of Justice (2001: 4, 5 figure 1, 7, table 1).

[703] In 2006 Muto admitted disappointing Bukszpan. He had deliberately missed the hearing in her court because he had a contingent fee case in another courtroom and needed the money.

Even worse, Bain had to deal with an emotionally distraught Abdul Karim interrupting a hearing and bursting into tears.

Although Muto initially denied the charges, he eventually admitted almost all of them and sought to justify himself. (Like all attorneys facing discipline, he "had to walk a fine line between zealously advocating on his own behalf and accepting responsibility for those acts that he is culpable of.") Having recently arrived in New York, virtually penniless, and having succeeded through hard work, he identified strongly with his immigrant clients. He was "the only low budget lawyer in Chinatown," providing access to legal services at an "affordable price." Altruism, not greed, explained his extraordinary caseload. He even claimed to do pro bono work (which he never described and for which he could not possibly have had time). Suspension or disbarment, he claimed, "would work a grave injustice on those clients who rely upon him." He was just an "over eager little puppy dog" who accepted too many clients out of inexperience and naïveté. He "worked and worked and worked" evenings and weekends: "I practically live at 26 Federal Plaza." But he could not resist boasting about handling up to 10–12 reopens or four individual hearings in a single day and earning $4,000 a week by doing 20 master calendars in a day (performing little more than clerical tasks), which suggested both avarice and client neglect. His attempts to explain such volume just made things worse: "matters, once filed, do not require any additional work"; "often, aside from writing and assembling documents, there is very little that needs to be done." He was either underserving or overcharging clients—or both.

Such braggadocio revealed profound insecurities. By gaining admission to the bar, he was "fulfilling a life long ambition." But the 10 years of practice in Syracuse were an unmitigated disaster. He had resigned, fabricated an explanation for the resignation in order to gain readmission, been suspended for misappropriation and admonished for neglecting multiple clients, done embarrassingly brief stints at three different employers, and twice failed at solo practice. When his baby died soon after birth, his medical malpractice lawsuit provoked resentment, not sympathy. Like millions of others, he sought a fresh start in the Big Apple. He quickly seemed to realize his dream: earning far more than ever before,[704] gaining acceptance by the city's "legal community," even acquiring the ultimate New York status symbol, a co-op (albeit with his dying mother's life insurance). Most

---

[704] The $750 a week Rodkin paid him, an annualized $37,500.

of all, he felt the respect and gratitude of his Chinese clients, who bowed and said "she, she [thank you] lawyer" when he strolled through Chinatown on Sundays with his daughter.[705] He had to believe they were attracted by his reputation, not by Michael Lee's agency: "I think I came across . . . how thrilled I seemed to get when . . . somebody would come in and say they saw my name on the board, on the sign in front of my office, and they came in."

Muto oscillated between claiming to have sacrificed himself for his clients and blaming them (and others) for his troubles. While insisting that "I'm very honest when it comes to taking responsibility," he constantly evaded it. The complaints by "high priced lawyers" were "Lord and Taylor trying to put Filene's basement out of business. And these agencies, to a certain extent, are behind it." (On the contrary, Ann Hsiung was anxious that Muto not think she "personally" filed against him: "It's really not my business." Agencies needed him and shunned publicity.) Former clients were filing grievances just to reopen deportation and removal orders. (His clients did the same against predecessor counsel; the strategy succeeded only if the IC found inadequate representation.) He blamed no-show clients for his own failure to appear at hearings, disavowing any responsibility to produce them or to appear regardless. Chang Kui Lin "hadn't come into my office. We sent a couple of letters out" (but Muto had no copies). He declared it general practice to abandon defaulting clients (factually dubious, and ethically reprehensible). He blamed Judge Ferris's "kangaroo court" for his own misrepresentation that Chang Kui Lin accepted voluntary departure (a mistake Ferris exposed). Muto claimed to have terminated Lin as a client for failing to cooperate or tell the truth. After abandoning Ju Jin Jing, he blamed her for replacing him (when he failed to appear). When clients claimed they had never met Muto or signed appearances or affidavits he advanced the bizarre story that someone was impersonating them and he naively had failed to check IDs. Asked why anyone would do that, he replied, "I don't know what makes these people tick. They're not the most ethical. They're not the most scrupulous." "Hua Ye could have been lying for that matter. And not every client is honest." "[I]t's very possible some unscrupulous people did take advantage of me during that era." When clients complained of not being told the outcome of their applications, he retorted that "they don't always tell you the true and correct addresses." He insisted New York IC judges *wanted*

---

[705] In 2006 he said many people still thank him when he walks through Chinatown.

his brief, inadequate motions, denying them out of general hostility to immigrants or personal antipathy to him.[706] (But he moved to reopen without bothering to determine which judge had originally heard the case, and he gave Ferris ample provocation.) He blamed judges for being unsympathetic about his dying mother and flying phobia—but never told them about either.[707] Judge Zlatow was unreasonable to require him "to leave at least a day and a half by two days before the court date. Drive 1,200 miles."[708] (But why did he file an appearance in New Orleans if he could not get there? At the behest of an agency?) He said Judge Bain must have informed Karim of his hearing date—but that was Muto's responsibility. He blamed Karim for not appearing at two hearings—which Muto missed as well! He blamed the OCA and postal service for losing his change-of-address forms (and insisted Ginnelly would testify it "happens all the time"—but he didn't).[709] He blamed Michael Lee for mismanaging trust accounts, which were his own responsibility, and other attorneys for misinforming him about ethical rules he had an obligation to know.

Mutual recrimination among the lawyers was less surprising. Thieves fall out. When Maratea and Kuntashian testified against him, Muto asked Cohen if they had been promised immunity and then filed complaints against them.[710] He repeatedly breached confidentiality by objecting that David Rodkin, his former boss, had received only a private reprimand. He called Karen Jaffe a "close friend" but then blamed her for taking Lin's case from Blue Eagle, declared he had broken with her because of her agency work, and then seemed resentful that she refused to testify for fear of self-incrimination.[711] He voiced the typical plaint of a child caught with

---

[706] Ferris may have empathized with Lin for being mistreated by Muto, but she did not believe illegal immigrants slept on restaurant floors and found it suspicious that they moved often.

[707] In 2006 he was still struggling with this phobia. He climbed the staircase to his second-floor office while insisting he *could* take the elevator. He would try to fly to a forthcoming business appointment in Dallas but admitted that he probably would end up driving.

[708] MapQuest estimates the trip at 1,300 miles and 20 hours each way.

[709] He repeated this story in 2006.

[710] In 2007 Kuntashian was "delinquent" in paying his bar dues, suggesting that he had stopped practicing.

[711] In 2006 Muto still felt unjustly treated. Karen had been admonished several times and had recently been suspended for 30 days for lying to the Second Circuit (twice excusing missed hearings on grounds of illness when she appeared before an Immigration Judge on the same day two blocks away). The New York Appellate Division issued a reciprocal public censure. In the Matter of Jaffe, 832 N.Y.S.2d 177 (1st Dept. 2007). Karen did matrimonials for a non-lawyer agency, signing her name to their work. But he remained friends with both lawyers, boasting that Rodkin recently paid him $1,000 to write an appellate brief. And Muto seemed jealous that both "make really good money."

his hand in the cookie jar: look what the others did (garbing it in the legalese of equal protection and selective prosecution). He claimed a close personal relationship with Cathy Chen. But she covered her ass, not his.

Like most people, Muto lied badly, often contradicting himself as soon as the lie was challenged. After resigning from the bar, he had his wife perjure herself with an incredible story that she had printed out the resignation letter from his computer and put it in a pile of papers he had signed without reading. He preferred evasion. He repeatedly concocted excuses for not appearing in New Orleans rather than disclose his flying phobia to Judge Zlatow. He told Judge Bukszpan it was "not possible" for him to appear in New York because he had driven to New Orleans but never said why he had done so. When he did lie outright, he constantly contradicted himself. He moved for extension of time in Chang Kui Lin's case; he filed no such motion. He was unaware of agency involvement in that case; he dealt directly with Eddie Ye (whom he claimed to know only as a restaurateur!). He offered to drive Yi Chen to Buffalo for the venue change. (Two days of driving for that?[712] With a man to whom he could not speak? Whose gender he could not remember? For a motion filed out of time?) He filed a change of venue motion in New Orleans; he failed to file it. He told Karim his hearing was on April 7; he did not appear himself. He believed John Finnell was appearing for Hong Ren Lin; he told Lin that day he could not appear. He had called the court to explain why he would not appear for Ju Jin Jing; he did not. He had asked Andrew Wilson to appear for Jing "of counsel"; Wilson acted on his own. Another unnamed "of counsel" lawyer failed to appear for her; Muto could not remember if he had arranged for one. He had missed her hearing to appear in another court; he had no records. He piled excuse on excuse, oblivious to the way each undermined the credibility of the others: he appeared for Ju Jin Jing; he could not because of a detention hearing, which took priority; he hired a lawyer to appear of counsel; he did not know if he had told Jing that Schneider would appear for her; Schneider had taken over the case (he did not); Muto was sick; his cousin had died; he was out of the state; he had telephoned the court (he did not); Jing had fired him; he was driving to New Orleans (he never did). He could not follow the cardinal rule of lying: keep it simple. Like Dr. Seuss's little boy on Mulberry Street, his lies became ever more baroque.[713] Although he did not remember meeting Yi Chen

---

[712] MapQuest estimates the trip at 400 miles and 6.5 hours each way.
[713] Seuss (1937).

and could not speak to him, Muto claimed to have told him to appear in Buffalo and to have offered to drive him there personally and even was eager to do so "because I have family in Buffalo. And that's like, great, I get to go to Buffalo and... see a Bison's game, go down to the Anchor Bar and have some wings."

Muto's lies had little credibility because, lacking records or a reliable memory, he could only invoke general practice. He had "a vague... recollection of Michael saying these clients don't want to go to New Orleans." He insisted "it was Cathy that told [Yi Chen] he had to appear" in Buffalo but then conceded, "I speak to only general office procedure." He must have offered to drive Yi Chen to Buffalo "because I know general patterns that I would follow." (But he could not remember if Yi Chen was a man or a woman.) He claimed to have worked on Hua Ye's case at home but then admitted, "I don't have a specific recollection of him, Your Honor, but you know, I could put it together—a recollection based on what was going on at that time." (Exactly: his "memories" were convenient reconstructions.) Muto was a master of the subjunctive. He claimed that "after the motion was denied, Your Honor, [Hua Ye] would receive a letter from my office... he would receive the decision with a letter from me, outlining what he had to do to appeal the motion." But when challenged, he retreated: "as a matter of course, this would be what I would do. However, I do not have an independent recollection in this case." He claimed that Hong Ren Lin "hadn't come into my office. We sent a couple of letters out." But when Cohen asked for them, Muto backed off: "I don't have a specific recollection, but I generally will send out letters when the hearing is close." He ultimately withdrew the accusation that Lin had been uncooperative. "I would give [Karim] the hearing notice that the judge issues." He "assume[d]" Karim telephoned him after going to court on April 9 and "would assume" he had returned that call; but he had no "independent recollection." When Cohen expressed exasperation with Muto for prefacing every factual statement with "I believe," he acknowledged that he did not want to be caught in a lie.

When all else failed, Muto said he was sorry. He apologized to Yi Chen for not appearing and promised not to do so again (but Chen had fired him). He returned fees to clients, as though that made up for their deportation orders. He apologized to Karim and offered to return the fee—but naturally did not have the money with him. Like the "puppy dog" to which he compared himself, he believed that his love for "your city" and "your legal community" merited forgiveness for his repeated messes. He sought to transmute misconduct into incompetence, "honest error," and then plead for pity on the ground of inadequacy.[714] He was inexperienced. He was ignorant. He accepted divorce cases in Syracuse even though he did not know how to do them because he faced two foreclosures. He was overwhelmed by the challenge of representing himself in the disciplinary proceeding (not a great advertisement for his ability to represent asylum applicants).[715] Like Dogberry in *Much Ado About Nothing*, he urged his masters to "remember that I am an ass . . . forget not that I am an ass."[716] Like the Mad Hatter, he told the court he was a "poor man" (provoking the predictable reaction: you're a very poor lawyer).[717] His wife was a "basket case." He supported her and two children (who were deprived of summer camp) and felt this entitled *him* to invoke the ADA. He had lost his mother (a year or more earlier) and a cousin. He suffered from flying phobia. He began his mitigation, "I'm basically going to . . . just bring up my past and throw myself at your mercy."

Like all of us, Muto was a prisoner of his MO. He accepted work beyond his capacity, did it badly or not at all, apologized, offered his inadequacies as an excuse, and promised to reform. He had "continually endeavored to improve his practice to better serve his clients." But he hadn't improved. As Cohen noted, he had made the same promises to secure readmission following his suspension and admonitions in Syracuse. He had promised Judge Ferris to file the motion for an extension of time. He promised to appear on the date he had chosen. But he did none of these. He was nothing if not consistent.

---

[714] When Cohen confronted him with his lie that he had filed a change-of-venue motion in New Orleans, Muto said he had not done so because it was out of time, an "honest error." It was certainly an error; but his statement to Cohen was a lie.
[715] He did not even manage to subpoena Eddie Ye.
[716] Shakespeare, *Much Ado About Nothing*, Iv.ii.70–71.
[717] When, in the trial for the theft of tarts, the Hatter said for the third time "I'm a poor man, your Majesty," the King interrupted: "You're a *very* poor *speaker*." Carroll (1940: chapter 11).

Chapter 3

Response
Joseph F. Muto

By way of introduction, I am a 1986 honors graduate of the University of Bridgeport School of Law. Bridgeport is, as Professor Abel points out, the predecessor of Quinnipiac University School of Law situated in Hamden Connecticut. I served as Associate Editor of my school's law review, and graduated in the top seven percent of my law school class. Completing my legal studies in only two-and-a-half years, I received my school's outstanding legal scholarship award at commencement. I received several offers of employment from small to mid size New York and Connecticut firms in my third year, but at the time chose to return to Syracuse where I had an elderly parent, whom my spouse cared for while I was in law school. Contrary to the assertion that I "scoured the New York Law Journal seeking per diem work" during this period, I had several bona fide offers of employment. Also, why as a third year law student in Connecticut would I only be interested in per diem work? I did, upon relocating to New York City in the fall of 1997, scour the want ads of the Journal seeking per diem and permanent employment as have many others who relocate to New York. It was here that I saw an ad for an immigration attorney, which I answered and which led me to the practice that is the basis of Professor Abel's article. I do wish to extend my thanks to Professor Abel for affording me this opportunity to tell my side of this story. I do not attempt to justify my actions as an immigration attorney; they were wrong and I accept responsibility for them. I do wish to state that the agency practice which is mentioned in the article is widespread and still very much ongoing in the immigration practice in New York City.

My hearing before the First Department Disciplinary Committee took place in or around June of 2001. A fundamental mistake I made was representing myself. The statement that I was nervous as hell is pretty accurate! Who would not be under the same set of circumstances? I tried to provide quality legal representation for all my clients and deeply regret that I failed in some instances to do so. Much is made of the case of Chang Kui Lin. I do not deny that I did a poor job on this man's case. His prior attorney, Gregory Kuntashian, failed to file documents timely. This necessitated a motion by me for receipt of late filed documents. Still, I clearly was not the only person blameworthy, though I do admit that I did wrong here. I never should have accepted this man's case in the first place as I admittedly had overextended myself. As to Mr. Kuntashian, it is admirable that he spent ten years doing anti-poverty work in New Haven and graduated from Yale. Still, this does not change the facts that he accepted this case from an agency (Blue Eagle) and himself failed to timely file the requisite documents. Nor does it change the fact that he was, and for that matter remains, an attorney who derives much of his work from these non-attorney agencies and currently "fronts" for such an agency in Chinatown. As to my comments regarding working for or with Karen Jaffe, I was never her employee but did accept several cases from her when we shared office space at 401 Broadway in New York City. I do not believe it was unreasonable for me, in light of my mother's terminal illness in Syracuse (located 260 miles from New York City) to request a continuance on this case, which had been afforded by several other judges. With respect to the fact that my name appeared "all over the notes of the Blue Eagle file," this is true. However, so did Mr. Kuntashian's and Ms. Jaffe's names as they had this case prior to my undertaking representation.

Much has been made of my furnishing the 800 number of the immigration court to clients. 800-898-7180 allows an asylum applicant, or anyone for that matter, to ascertain the status of their case by following the prompts. This is a classic example of twisting a good deed against the doer. I never stated or intimated to any client that they should call this number instead of contacting me directly. However, one fear that Chinese refugees had was missing their hearings. Often, clients would ask me: "what if my hearing date is changed" or something to this effect. I attempted to reassure them by telling them that they could have an English speaking friend call this number, which is updated daily, and they would know the date, time and location of their next hearing. There was absolutely no malicious intent on my part in providing this number. I in fact accepted responsibility for a client, Abdul Karim, not showing up at my hearing, and did not attempt to blame anyone else.

With respect to my fear of flying, this is a very real problem, which I have struggled to overcome. However, it is a cognizable disability. The attitude some have that "all you have to do is get on the plane and sit down" displays an ignorant mindset. It was wrong of me to accept cases where I would have to fly to remote courts, and I accept responsibility for this. However, Judge Zlatow was the only judge who would routinely refuse to either allow me sufficient time to travel or to change venue—both actions which would be reasonable accommodations for a disability. I should point out that I traveled by land to both Atlanta and St. Louis for court appearances after being afforded sufficient time by the court.

Chapter 3

Also, several judges changed venue in my cases after I requested them to do so based on my disability. As to my taking the stairs for one floor at my present position, why wait for an elevator for one floor!!!! I respectfully point out that I routinely rode the elevators for immigration court on the twelfth and fourteenth floors of 26 Federal Plaza without incident or panic attacks. It is more the height than enclosure which I have a problem with.

I admit that I got in over my head and should never have attempted a high volume low cost law practice. Also, I never should have represented myself. My self representation is the basis for much of what is stated in the article, and, yes, I was disorganized and more than a bit apprehensive given what was at stake. I wish to point out that at no time, under any interpretation of the law, did I violate confidentiality rules by disclosing what David Rodkin had told me about his letter of admonition. Mr. Rodkin made this statement publicly, to me and several others, with no expectation of privacy or confidentiality. At no time was I his attorney, and at no time did his statement regarding his letter of admonition enjoy a privilege of confidentiality once he publicly divulged it. I should point out that subsequently Mr. Rodkin received a short suspension for, in the words of the Appellate Division, engaging in the same sort of conduct I engaged in. Why would the same conduct by one attorney which warrants disbarment warrant only a short suspension for a second attorney who had actually received a past letter of admonition for this conduct? One factor, which is noteworthy, is that the Immigration Court did not expel (their term for disbarment) me as they did several other practitioners but merely *suspended* me for a term of seven years. This is highly relevant as it is the Immigration Court which observed me on a daily basis and was in the best position to judge me.

As far as delusions of grandeur, I only stated what was factual. I did in fact graduate with honors from law school, and also have an M.B.A. conferred with honors. I did in fact prosecute felony level cases and also drafted appeals as a first-year attorney. Very few lawyers, in their first year of practice, are entrusted with felony cases as I was. My biggest mistake was that I took on more than I could handle in private practice. If I stayed in government service, I likely would have been a very successful attorney. This is not a delusion but rather a reflection of my record as a prosecutor in Cortland, New York. I have accepted that it was wrong of me to attempt to operate a high volume low cost law practice and to deal with non-lawyer agencies. I never earned, as stated, $4,000 a week. I believe my record was $4,000 in one month. I agree with Professor Abel that I did in fact accept work beyond my capacity to my clients' detriment, and for this I am deeply sorry. However, I did not convert or commingle funds in New York. I did accept a single check for $30,000 from a long-time client, who was and to this day remains a highly respected member of the Chinese-American business community. This check was drawn on his account and no other. When he asked for the money back in cash as a deal he was working on fell through, I gave it back to him. I was unaware that you could not return escrow money to its rightful owner in cash. However, any allegations of money laundering or dishonesty are blatantly false. I honestly, at the time, saw no wrong in this and was not aware that it was an ethical violation. This man remained a client of mine after this event, and I freely admitted these facts to the disciplinary committee.

In conclusion, I again thank Professor Abel for affording me this opportunity to make a statement. I apologize again to anyone whom I may have harmed in the course of my representation. I did, however, give my best effort to my clients. Sadly, I got in over my head with a large volume practice. I never should have taken on so many cases, and I never should have represented myself in the disciplinary hearing. Still, I believe that I can be a productive member of the legal profession. Professor Abel mentions that I applied to the District of Columbia Bar, and this is a fact. I passed the multistate bar examination with a 150 and the ethics examination with a 100. The basic components of a good lawyer are present in me, ability and desire. With a monitoring/mentoring program like that in several states, including the District of Columbia, I can provide the quality legal representation that I am capable of rendering. Moving from my current position into the legal department, with its structure, would be ideal. I have learned from my experiences as a New York attorney, and would like to return to the profession that I do love and which I sought so fervently to join.

Chapter 4

The Overachiever

I. Covering Up Mistakes

Lawrence M. Furtzaig grew up in the Canarsie section of Brooklyn before moving to Belle Harbor, Queens, and finally Neponsit, Long Island.[718] His parents separated when he was 14 or 15. When they divorced several years later, his father secretly sold the family business, took all the proceeds to California, and stopped paying child support. "Immediately, we had to sell the house that we lived in in Neponsit, move back to a much more modest house," he explained. Furtzaig worked as a mechanic to put himself through SUNY Buffalo, graduating Phi Beta Kappa. Soon thereafter, a friend introduced him to Warren Estis. On December 1, 1980, Furtzaig started working as a law clerk for Rosenberg & Estis, "a boutique real estate litigation firm, principally landlord-tenant law." He entered New York Law School at night the following fall. "I worked more than just during the day time. Sometimes I returned to the firm after law school." The next year he met and started dating Sherry, secretary to the named partners. They married in 1987; five years later she moved to a different firm. "After about

---

[718] R.P. No. 12/2002. All the facts and quotations are taken from the transcript of the hearing by Referee Marilyn W. Levy (July 31, 2002).

CHAPTER 4

five years of trying to have children, we finally scored big time and hit the jackpot" with triplets in 1996; Sherry quit her job.

Furtzaig became an associate at Rosenberg & Estis immediately after graduating in 1985 and was admitted to the bar in 1986. Becoming a non-equity partner just four years later gave him "a sense of recognition . . . I was succeeding in what I was doing." He began to supervise several associates, participated in "setting policy," and assumed "more billing responsibilities, dealing with clients, with collecting invoices." "Fortunately or unfortunately" he was "a fair haired boy, and I was given most of the more complex cases in the firm to work on." He tried cases lasting a year, "a record in the housing court," and took several to the Court of Appeals.

> My basic billing was somewhere between 2,200 and 2,400 hours per year, but it was a very . . . pressurized place . . . the kind of place where you didn't fail. If you did fail, you just didn't want to deal with Gary [Rosenberg] or Warren [Estis]. . . . It was not a pleasant thing by any stretch of the imagination, which is probably why there was a lot of turnover in the firm . . . [which] gave rise to several other split firms of non-equity partners who just didn't deal with it anymore. . . . Words were few and far between. Consequences were large.

Estis, his direct supervisor, was not

> easy to ask for either input or additional help simply because if . . . it wasn't a case that he was interested in directly, he'd have very little of it and basically leave you to fend for yourself . . . until he had a case that he needed your input on and then he dragged you into his office to deal with his case. . . . Even the associates that I supervise, their plates were more or less full.

He often considered leaving but "viewed Warren as a close friend." When four other associates defected "I suspected that one of the reasons that I wasn't even asked [to join them] . . . was because I was closely aligned with Warren." There was no one else to ask for help. Gary "was in charge of appeals and real estate transactions" and "would defer to Warren." Furtzaig's loyalty ultimately earned him an equity partnership in June 2000.

He was the firm's contact with most of its largest clients. Laurie Anker, an associate he supervised, had been handling the case of Alvin and Jeffrey Gilman (a warring father and son) under Furtzaig's supervision for a year. In 1992,

> shortly before trial [she] basically walked into my office and said, "I can't deal with [Jeffrey] anymore, here's the files. . . . If you make me continue dealing with these people, I'm leaving." . . . [The case concerned] a rent strike, which involved four tenants [in] . . . Greenwich Village, who claimed they were subject to rent stabilization while the owner claimed they weren't.

Recognizing that the tenants were right, Furtzaig negotiated settlements with three; but the fourth, who was insisting that the landlord install a formal kitchen, withheld even the agreed-upon rent arrears, about $18,000. Fearing that remodeling would expose lead paint contamination, Jeffrey Gilman refused to do it (even though that would have secured a settlement, thereby avoiding a judicial declaration that the buildings were rent-stabilized). Furtzaig failed to move to restore two of the cases to the calendar when the tenants failed to pay arrears after the repairs were made, as the settlement required. "Ultimately I lied and I paid the money myself," a total of $60,000, he admitted. Had he brought the problem to Estis "he would just say deal with it."

Thereafter, Furtzaig was untruthful in another 10 to 15 cases. He was handling about 20 cases for Samson Management. One involved a tenant who spent the summer in New York and the rest of the year in Florida, subletting her rent-controlled apartment to a Dr. Bono. When Samson learned this, the tenant surrendered the apartment at the end of the summer. Dr. Bono sued Samson and the tenant for wrongful eviction. Taking over the matter when Laurie Anker left for her honeymoon in the middle of the trial, Furtzaig counterclaimed for ejectment. But he failed to pursue the case. In 1993 he told Samson the court had granted Bono summary judgment. But between October 1999 and January 2001, he made numerous false reports to Samson that

> he had moved for use and occupancy (rent); the judge had ruled in the client's favor and that a hearing on the amount owed would be held on March 1, 2000; he would be in court

on December 22, 2000 on the case; that an Article 78 Application he had brought would be heard January 25, 2001; and that the court agreed to render its decision on Article 78 on February 28, 2001.

He made these misrepresentations "because I should have been doing these things . . . and for whatever reason I didn't." He brought a holdover proceeding for Samson against another tenant (Weiss) but failed to file a post-trial brief. "I lied to the client" that he had moved for use and occupancy rent, a warrant for possession had been issued, eviction was scheduled for January 19, 2001, and a motion to restore the case to the calendar was returnable in two weeks. "I failed to finish the case off, a case that should have been a successful case . . . that I had successfully appealed." "There were so many stories. . . . The specific words and the specific instances are of little consequence to my actual wrongdoing." He "assume[d]" the reason was lack of time.

> After the case was fully tried, the court asked for post-trial memorandum. . . . My adversary kept informing the court that he couldn't get the transcript. . . . The transcripts probably were part of the first appeal in any event. And then I just lost track of it.

David Ohebshalom, an associate at the firm, brought in work for his uncle and aunt, Fred and Nader Ohebshalom, and assigned it to Furtzaig's subordinate, Mark Lawrence. It was "a simple holdover proceeding . . . against a deceased tenant's son [Kamran Hakim] . . . who was claiming entitlement to a rent controlled apartment." "After Mark left the firm I let the matter just languish"; but he repeatedly told the client he was litigating it and the defendant was vigorously resisting. The court ordered the plaintiffs to appear for depositions just before the Memorial Day weekend. Fred Ohebshalom told Furtzaig "he'd absolutely not be able to attend because he was going to the Hamptons for the weekend and he was pretty adamant about it."

> I told him that basically because there was no order of preclusion . . . I probably could get it adjourned. And I wrote my adversary informing him that my clients would be out of town and offering to pay for their cost of the stenographers and

> scheduling the deposition the very next week. I never heard from my adversary again except by motion. The motion was to dismiss.... [Judge Lewis F. Friedman] went apoplectic and ultimately a month later dismissed the case for failure to disclose and sanctioned ... the firm ... $500.

Although Furtzaig did not inform the firm, he and David told Fred.

> I assured him that I would start the case again since the dismissal was without prejudice.... And I never did.... He asked me what was going on with it. I told him I moved for summary judgment.

That was a lie.

Judge Friedman's judgment told a different story.[719] The plaintiffs failed to appear for depositions on December 17, 1996, and February 4, 1997; each time Furtzaig claimed he would file a summary judgment motion before the deposition but failed to do so. These excuses "were based on obvious bad faith." After the plaintiffs missed the next date (February 18), the defendant moved for relief. At oral argument on May 9, the court ordered discovery on May 28–29. The plaintiffs did not object then or when the defendant confirmed the date. But the day before the scheduled deposition Furtzaig called to say the plaintiffs were "out of town" and would not appear; the defendant never agreed to this.

> The excuse is feeble at best and is damning for what counsel does not say. Counsel does not disclose when he told the clients about this court's May 9 order.... Presumably this experienced litigation law firm made its clients aware of the firm dates sufficiently in advance that there should have been no problems.... The court is also troubled by the attitude of counsel who states in his affirmation that "this motion is yet another attempt by defendants' counsel to employ strong arm tactics to obtain a favorable resolution of this action."

---

[719] Fred Ohebshalom and Nader Ohebshalom v. Kamran Hakim, New York Supreme Court (June 24, 1997).

Chapter 4

The court had "no doubt that plaintiffs' counsel's conduct was frivolous." Such behavior was "far too common in Supreme Court, New York County."

Related Companies (RC) was a major national developer, responsible for the AOL Time Warner building on Columbus Circle. Furtzaig had been the principal contact ever since RC came to the firm, "successfully and honestly represent[ing] the client in numerous matters regarding the demolition and assemblage of various sites." After RC consulted him about 10 to 12 Central Park West condominiums, he disposed of all but two units. Because the associate in charge left, and his eventual replacement was inadequate, Furtzaig took over the matter. Henry and Rachel Nasser vacated one apartment in early 1999, owing six months' rent. On March 25, Furtzaig wrote RC that he would sue them but never did. He discontinued the termination and holdover proceeding against Alan Kling, the other tenant, because it had been filed in the wrong name.

> And I should have restarted it, but I never did. . . . And then it was just complete stupidity, complete lack of responsibility, and then I started to lie, lying to Bruce [Beale of RC] about what was done and wasn't done . . . and things just went from bad to worse in terms of my lying and deception with the client.

In order to cover up these misrepresentations he fabricated and sent RC copies of a judgment of confession, a judgment for use and occupancy rent, an Appellate Term Order, and a bond.

> Ultimately, my hope was to do the best by the client and figure out a way to resolve the case. In retrospect, of course, I couldn't hide it. It was stupid. It was absurd to even think that I could.

In November 2000 (just five months after becoming an equity partner), he misrepresented to RC that

> something or other was happening, maybe a warrant was going to be executed, or some such nonsense. And then, of course, had to tell him [Beale] that it wasn't going to happen. And, of course the next thing he did was call Warren. I walked into Warren's office and told him what I had done. . . . At that moment I was severely suicidal. Actually, for several weeks,

> months, actually, even probably more than a couple of years before that I'd been staring at my window considering jumping out on various occasions. At that time . . . we spoke the better half of the morning. He called my wife without me knowing. And . . . she came [from Croton-on-Hudson], she took me home. . . . The next day we discussed fully what I had done on the Related [Companies] matters. . . . The client decided to let him and the firm go forward in attempting to remedy what had happened.

Furtzaig continued to handle the matter "because I was known as the best person in the best position . . . with the best knowledge." When Estis asked if Furtzaig had misrepresented anything else, he denied it. "I thought I could make it better." "I didn't refuse to answer questions, but I wasn't honest . . . [and] when pointedly asked about certain matters I lied." But when Estis learned in March 2001 that Furtzaig had fabricated documents, he fired him.

Estis complained to the DDC on June 29 with mixed feelings. Furtzaig had a "20 year history as an honest, credible and ethical lawyer [who was] respected and trusted [and was] one of the firm[']s top litigators and was recognized by colleagues, clients, firm employees and adversaries for his honesty, incisive intelligence, excellent lawyer skills and hard work." The DDC filed its notice of charges involving five clients and nine matters on May 23, 2002. Furtzaig admitted to all of them.[720] He acknowledged "the seriousness of his misconduct and the challenges facing him" but was "hopeful at the end of the disciplinary process he will be able to salvage his career and begin to rebuild his life." At the time of his misconduct he was "suffering from severe depression, which affected his family life, his personal life and profoundly his professional life." His lawyer, Michael Ross, opened by declaring that his client was not "blaming some other person . . . psychosis . . . some flaw in his personality . . . hard times." Rather, this "young lawyer, 44 years old with triplets . . . when overcome by work . . . instead of asking for help, began in a single case to lie and not do work." This "did not permeate all of the cases that he had."

Asked by DDC attorney Mady J. Edelstein what proportion of his workload the neglected cases comprised, Furtzaig first resorted

---

[720] Answering affidavit (June 18, 2002); see also Referee's Exhibit 1: prehearing stipulation (July 30, 2002).

CHAPTER 4

to sophistry: "in reality the matters engaged in my misconduct comprised virtually zero percent of my time because my principal failing is not doing it." But he quickly insisted they represented 2 to 10 percent of his work and were not the most difficult cases. He put some of the blame on the firm's lack of a "centralized" tickler system. "It was done on a group by group basis with . . . associates and partners within a group reporting to their partner in charge who was reporting to their higher partner." But it was his decision not to put some cases on the calendar. Of course "I wasn't about to bill the client for something I didn't do." He did not always cover up mistakes. "There was one case . . . that was dismissed as a result of lack of communication between myself and the process server . . . and I told the client promptly and I restarted the case."

Furtzaig's only witness was Dr. Neil Cohen, who had qualified as a clinical psychologist in 1984.[721] At their first consultation in November 2000, right after RC had informed Estis about his failure, Furtzaig was acutely depressed, suicidal. "This was a man who was wrecked. He felt like his world had fallen apart . . . like he was an awful person . . . profound guilt . . . was the predominant feature of his . . . mood at that time." At first he acknowledged only the last of the RC matters, denying there were any others. Cohen attributed this to Furtzaig's "general style . . . of pushing uncomfortable, painful events away . . . out of his mind." He was hypersensitive "to shame and to embarrassment." He also resisted a referral to Dr. David Hellerstein for medication. Furtzaig explained:

> We all don't like to believe that we need it. Certainly I hate to believe that I need help. And my wife's mother is a long-term patient-victim, [an] example perhaps of medication, who within the preceding year . . . after long-term treatment had attempted to commit suicide for the second time in her life . . . notwithstanding her medication . . . to the point of zombieism, just completely non-functioning as a human being, which my wife and probably I also ascribe to maybe a combination of both her medications as well as her mental illness.

When Estis learned in March 2001 that there were other incidents, Furtzaig "became overwhelmed, agitated . . . some of the black thoughts returned." Admitting the others "has been a long and painful process." At the insistence

---

[721] Furtzaig also submitted two character affidavits by clients.

of his wife, his therapist (Dr. Cohen), and his lawyer (Michael Ross), he finally agreed to see Dr. Hellerstein in the summer of 2001 and began taking medication. He was working 20 to 25 hours a week for five clients out of a basement office in his home. "I always excelled in a courtroom environment... I've tried cases since then."

Cohen characterized Furtzaig as "withdrawn... inhibited in his verbal expression and avoidant of intense feelings." "His life was subsumed [sic] by his career; work took precedence over a social life and recreational pursuits. His wife would complain that he frequently appeared 'closed off' and uncommunicative." He "has been driven by a sense of relentlessness to be the best that he can be at his career" and is troubled by a "fear of failing." His relationship with Estis "is perhaps the most meaningful relationship that this man has had."

> Rather than asking for help or reassurance from his associates at the firm, he instead began to avoid working on the [Gilman] case.... It would have been more painful to risk disapproval and opprobrium from his colleagues, especially his mentor, Michael [sic] Estis, than to address the problem in an ethically appropriate way. This began a downward spiral, where feelings of shame and embarrassment further eroded his self-confidence.

Therapy consisted of "exposure," getting Furtzaig to realize "he can live through his worst fears." "He has become more capable of enjoying the moment, and has defined himself more as a husband and parent than as an attorney." He also was able to express anger at his father for abandoning the family "for a 'swinging' lifestyle."

Furtzaig was the opposite of the pathological liars

> who are really truly incapable of remorse and who don't have what psychologists call a super ego.... It is paradoxically or ironically because his scruples are so high and because he has been so perfectionistic that he has wanted to create the most favorable impression of himself possible.

Cohen believed that "without a Warren Estis in his life, a person who has that kind of position, whose approval he has to work toward and earn," Furtzaig would be unlikely to repeat his behavior. This "implicit pattern

CHAPTER 4

that he had of looking for a father figure is very clear for him." His improving relationship with his wife should lessen the "need for that kind of significant person." Cohen saw "no sign . . . that he's pushing things away" now. Furtzaig requested a multi-year suspension.

The DDC emphasized that he "forged three court orders and fabricated a bond by 'cutting and past[ing]' a genuine bond, and sent them to his client to perpetuate [sic] his deception."[722] No "internal 'warning bell' stopped" him. Furtzaig had offered no proof of a causal connection between his psychological condition and misconduct. He had "not completed the task of understanding the past so that he will not repeat it." He "gave no real explanation for why he did it or how he would avoid falling into a similar pattern again." He offered no evidence that he had overcome his need for a father figure. Indeed, "it is impossible to imagine the practice of law without some encounter with authority figures (clients, judges, colleagues, opposing counsel), some of whom are not going to be pleased with everything the attorney is advocating or the results achieved." The DDC sought disbarment.

The Referee felt that Furtzaig's "own testimony demonstrates that he has not yet completed the task of understanding the past so that he will not repeat it."[723] But she was persuaded by Dr. Cohen that exposure-based therapy, though "slow and painful . . . does work." "A suspension of five years would leave ample time to explore Respondent's capacity to reshape his self-understanding and capacity to practice law without being a danger to the public."

The Hearing Panel of four lawyers and a layperson heard oral argument on October 29 and recommended disbarment (one lawyer dissenting).[724] This was "a sad case of a lawyer, who, for whatever reason, chose to neglect a small percentage of the matters entrusted to him" and to engage in "deceit and misrepresentation." The "possible causal link between his putative psychological problems and his misconduct appears to us to be tentative at best. He did not consult the psychologist until after he was initially caught" and "continued to conceal" all other misconduct from his partners until it also was involuntarily exposed. Dr. Cohen's testimony about "the pressures faced by Respondent in his practice and his desire to please his senior partner and mentor" was "not convincing." "The practice

---

[722] Staff memo (August 30, 2002).
[723] Report of Referee (September 27, 2002).
[724] Report and Recommendation of Hearing Panel (Casimir C. Patrick, chair; William F. Kuntz II; William A. Gallina, Samuel W. Seymour, and Susan Welsher, November 12, 2002).

of law is challenging and . . . the tens of thousands of lawyers in New York State daily face pressures which are difficult to deal with" but did not behave similarly.

Thomas J. Cahill, DDC chief counsel, urged confirmation of the report and recommendation, stating that "Deliberate acts of deceit are not the result of depression."[725] Furtzaig's claim of psychiatric disorder was inconsistent with his "ability to successfully handle the vast bulk of his legal responsibilities throughout his career at the firm." "It strains credulity to believe that Respondent was laboring under a debilitating disorder only with regard to a tiny portion of his legal work." Even Dr. Cohen conceded that "depression does not cause forgery." Furtzaig "gave no real explanation for why he committed his fraudulent conduct or how he would avoid falling into a similar pattern again."

The Appellate Division agreed with the Referee.[726] Even if it rejected Dr. Cohen's evidence, comparable matters had resulted in five years of suspension. "Most cases where this Court has disbarred attorneys involved misconduct that included conversion of client funds or other aggravating factors." The court was impressed that Furtzaig had spent $60,000 to prevent his neglect from hurting his clients. Other mitigating factors included his "unblemished disciplinary record, his full cooperation, his acceptance of his responsibility for his wrongdoing and his true remorse, and his family situation in that he is the sole breadwinner for his wife and six-year-old triplets." Estis told the *New York Law Journal* that Furtzaig's reaction to pressure was "atypical" and "not an appropriate response."[727] "These are individual issues of Larry." Still, Estis was still "extremely fond" of Furtzaig. "The firm's thoughts are with Larry and his family." Two months later, a trial judge ruled in favor of the firm's action to compel its insurer to defend claims based on Furtzaig's misconduct.[728] "In a firm consisting of numerous attorneys, partners and associates, it is not reasonable to impute one lawyer's knowledge of his own wrongful actions to all."

---

[725] Staff memo of law (November 27, 2002).
[726] In the Matter of Lawrence M. Furtzaig, 305 A.D.2d 7, 762 N.Y.S.2d 335, 2003 N.Y. Slip Op. 13023 (1st Dept. 2003).
[727] Anthony Lin, "Law Partner Gets Five-Year Suspension for Neglecting Cases over a Decade," 5/16/2003 N.Y.L.J. 1 (col. 4).
[728] Anthony Lin, "Judge Finds Knowledge of One Attorney's Malpractice Cannot Be Imputed to the Firm," 7/17/2003 N.Y.L.J. 1 (col. 3).

Chapter 4

II. The Difficulty of Admitting Error

"Happy families are all alike; each unhappy family is unhappy in its own way."[729] Furtzaig's family appeared to live the American dream, moving from a Brooklyn apartment to a Long Island house. But this turned into a nightmare when the teenager's father walked out, stole the family's assets, and abandoned them for a "'swinging' lifestyle" in California. Furtzaig worked his way through a public university and a night law school. Even before entering law school, he gained the trust of Warren Estis, the founding partner of a newly launched and highly ambitious law firm, was hired on graduation, and became a non-equity partner in just four years.[730] He was the firm's "fair haired boy," even marrying the partners' secretary. His relationship with Estis became "the most meaningful . . . that this man has had," overshadowing even marriage and fatherhood.

As a non-equity partner, Furtzaig was squeezed from two directions. Partners were sparing with advice but peremptory when they needed work done. Associates only compounded his responsibilities. He could not delegate to them because they were overworked.[731] Indeed, their chronic discontent and poor prospects for advancement led them to dump work in his lap. Always the slave of duty, Furtzaig responded by billing 2,200 to 2,400 hours, which must have meant working more than 3,000 hours (50 sixty-hour weeks: six 10-hour days or, more likely, seven days a week). Clients were even more difficult: the feuding Gilmans (with whom one associate refused to deal), Fred Ohebshalom magisterially blowing off a deposition to spend Memorial Day weekend in the Hamptons, Related Companies anxious to demolish and remodel buildings. The work itself was very stressful: evicting rent-stabilized tenants and collecting back rent. Furtzaig's personal life had its own pressures: five years of infertility treatment followed by the birth of triplets and loss of his wife's salary. As an abandoned son, he may have felt particular pressure to be a responsible husband and father. Most associates and non-equity partners left; he persevered and was rewarded with a full partnership.

Solo practitioners are notorious for neglecting clients, as illustrated by the previous two chapters. But Rosenberg & Estis was a well-respected firm with an effective calendaring system. By 2006 it had more than

---

[729] The opening sentence of Tolstoy's *Anna Karenina*.
[730] By 2006 the firm was billing $21 million and had many of New York City's major developers and landlords among its clients: http://www.rosenbergestis.com.
[731] In 2006 the firm had 19 partners and 15 associates.

30 lawyers and 70 employees. Furtzaig's failures were not the product of incompetence or poor record keeping. On the contrary, because he had to deceive both the firm and its sophisticated clients, the evasions became ever more elaborate and the lies more baroque. He lied to the Gilmans about their tenants' nonpayment of rent—and made up the $60,000 difference out of his own pocket. He lied to Samson about his own failure to eject both Bono and Weiss. He lied to Ohebshalom about ejecting Hakim and restarting the case, and to the court about filing summary judgment motions and securing the adversary's consent to postpone the deposition. He hid the court's anger and $500 sanction from the firm. He lied to Related Companies about the lawsuits against the Nassers and Kling. In order to perpetrate the last lie, he fabricated five documents, including a court order. But RC quickly discovered that the tenants were not paying rent or surrendering occupancy—as Furtzaig must have known would happen.

Like so many overachievers, Furtzaig could not admit mistakes, even to himself. Having rejected the irresponsible father who abandoned him, found a new father in Estis, who made enormous demands on both himself and his "son," and become a father (of triplets!), Furtzaig could not allow himself to fail. He responded to the painful emotions provoked by his mistakes with repression. He had a sense of "profound guilt" and was hypersensitive "to shame and to embarrassment." As he admitted, "I hate to believe that I need help." The fury he expressed toward his mother-in-law was particularly striking because it was utterly irrelevant to this case that she had twice attempted suicide and had medicated herself "to the point of zombie-ism, just completely non-functioning as a human being." Furtzaig was especially repelled by such self-indulgent weakness because he had "been staring at [his] window considering jumping out on various occasions" for "more than a couple of years." He turned his anger against himself for making common, correctable mistakes, producing profound depression. He could not acknowledge those mistakes, much less forgive himself. He could not tell his therapist, who was professionally committed not to judge. Although he "admitted" all the charges to the DDC, he quickly insisted that the affected cases were a small proportion of his total caseload and that he did not bill for work not done. Most of all, he could not admit error to Estis. And so he compounded the relatively minor, remediable mistakes with cover-ups that could not be forgiven by Estis or the bar.

Part Two

Fees

Lawyers energetically enforced *minimum* fee schedules by disciplining price cutters until 1975, when the U.S. Supreme Court held that doing so violated antitrust law.[732] The profession has been much less enthusiastic about fee regulations favoring clients. Most New York lawyers flouted a Rule of Court requiring them to file retainers and closing statements verifying compliance with the schedule of reasonable contingent fees.[733] New York forbids fees that are "excessive," based on more than a dozen factors.[734] It does not follow the Model Rules requirement that the lawyer communicate the fee to the client, "preferably in writing, before or within a reasonable time after commencing representation."[735] However, it does require that contingent fee agreements be written.[736] (The ABA House of Delegates rejected the proposal by the ABA Ethics 2000 Commission that all fee agreements over $500 be in writing.) New York also requires lawyers to submit fee disputes to arbitration at the client's election.[737]

Because most lawyers bill by the hour, there is a great temptation to "run up the meter": billing up to 2,600 hours annually (50 weeks of 52 billable hours, or six days/week of 8.7 billable hours, which means at least 10-hour working days), doing unnecessary work and billing for time spent thinking or work done by secretaries.[738] A law firm partner pleaded guilty to overbilling a client $550,000 in two years under pressure from a named partner (whom he saw as a "father figure") to increase firm revenue.[739] Several studies have documented that bill padding is pervasive and encouraged, even required, by large firms.[740] One survey found that

---

[732] Abel (1989: 118–119); Goldfarb v. Virginia State Bar, 421 U.S. 773 (1975).
[733] Rosenthal (1974).
[734] DR 2-106(a,b); N.Y.C.R.R. § 1200.11.
[735] Model Rule 1.5(b).
[736] DR 2-106(d).
[737] DR 2-106(e).
[738] ABA Commission on Billable Hours (2002); Phillips (2002) (38 years of experience in Phillips, Nizer, Benjamin, Krim & Ballon); Lerman (1994; 1998); Hopkins (1998); Shepherd & Cloud (1999); Wooley (2005).
[739] In re Cooper, 613 N.Y.S.2d 396 (App. Div. 1994).
[740] Lerman (1990; 1999).

16 percent of lawyers thought at least 25 percent of hours were padded; 23 percent admitted double billing; and 35 percent had billed for recycled work.[741] Although half the respondents to another survey said they only rarely or occasionally billed two clients for the same work, three respondents said they did so frequently, and 12% thought others frequently padded hours.[742] In a third survey, 14 percent double billed, 16 percent billed recycled work, and 60 percent worked in firms with no written billing guidelines.[743] A fourth survey found demonstrable fraud in 5–10 percent of firms and questionable practices in another 25–35 percent.[744]

Courts are reluctant to decide whether fees are "reasonable" or "excessive."[745] The Ninth Circuit upheld a complex agreement resulting in a $1 million contingent fee because it was negotiated by a large corporation.[746] But courts are more protective of individual clients. A court declared grossly excessive a one-third contingent fee of $108,000 charged to a surviving spouse for probating an estate and refused to award *anything* in quantum meruit.[747] A court reduced a fee to quiet title from $65,340 to $6,500 based on time and difficulty.[748] Fee arbitration boards do the same. A District of Columbia lawyer charged $26,000 for defending a simple assault. Finding that most lawyers would spend just six hours on such a case and charge only $2,000, and none would charge more than $7,500 in the unlikely event the case was tried, the board awarded $15,000. (The District Bar Counsel had not disciplined a lawyer for an excessive fee in over a decade.[749])

---

[741] Ross (1997) (106 private practitioners).
[742] Ross (1991) (272 respondents).
[743] Fortney (2000; 2003; 2005).
[744] Marquess (1994).
[745] Chin & Wells (1999).
[746] Brobeck, Phleger & Harrison v. Telex Corp., 602 F.2d 866 (9th Cir. 1979); see also McKenzie Constr., Inc. v. Maynard, 758 F.2d 97 (3d Cir. 1985) (court "should be reluctant to disturb contingent fee arrangements freely entered into by knowledgeable and competent parties"); McKenzie Constr., Inc. v. Maynard, 823 F.2d 43 (3d Cir. 1987) (contingent fee generating $790/hour not unreasonable although lawyer usually billed $60/hour).
[747] White v. McBride, 937 S.W.2d 796 (Tenn. 1996); but see Mullens v. Hansel-Henderson, 65 P.3d 992 (Colo. 2002) (recovery in quantum meruit when contingent fee unenforceable); Starkey, Kelley, Blaney & White v. Estate of Nicolaysen, 796 A.2d 238 (N.J. 2002) (recovery in quantum meruit when contingent fee agreement unenforceable because made 33 months after representation began).
[748] Kirby v. Liska, 351 N.W.2d 421 (Neb. 1984).
[749] Tom Schoenberg, "The $26,000 Simple Assault," Legal Times, Apr. 14, 1997, at 1.

The highest courts in New York and California have upheld legislation capping contingent fees.[750] Courts look more closely at contingent fees in personal injury cases.[751] A court found a two-thirds fee per se unreasonable.[752] Courts are particularly hostile to contingent fees without any contingency, as in life insurance claims, invalidating a one-third fee to collect on a policy,[753] a one-third fee where all the lawyer did was inform the life insurer of the date the decedent had enlisted in the Air Force,[754] and a one-fourth fee where the lawyer simply contacted the insurer and received the check.[755] A court reduced a contingent fee because of the ease of proving both liability and high damages.[756] But another jurisdiction held that the trial court lacked authority to determine the reasonableness of a contingent fee when the client did not object.[757] Class actions create particular problems because of the potential for enormous fees. The Sixth Circuit reduced a proposed 20 percent contingent fee ($33 million) for settling a $165 million heart valve class action to just over 5 percent ($10 million).[758]

Disciplinary committees rarely punish lawyers for excessive fees.[759] Massachusetts did so for the first time in 1996, when a lawyer billed over $50,000 for devoting 227 hours to defending a DUI (perhaps because it was the first criminal case he had ever tried).[760] Behavior must be egregious: charging over $47,000 to draft a standard agreement for child custody and support,[761] billing $5,200 in a routine domestic relations matter even though the lawyer failed to answer discovery requests or perform other work,[762] charging $8,000 to collect $23,000, which had already passed to the client by operation of law.[763] Disciplinary bodies are more

---

[750] Gair v. Peck, 6 N.Y.2d 97 (1959), cert. denied, 361 U.S. 374 (1960); Roa v. Lodi Medical Group, 37 Cal.3d 920 (1985), appeal dismissed, 474 U.S. 990 (1985).
[751] The ABA Ethics 2000 Commission on the Evaluation of the Rules of Professional Conduct proposed to add "degree of risk" to the reasonableness factors but rejected a proposal to add "the relative sophistication of the lawyer and the client."
[752] McCreary v. Joel, 186 So. 2d 4 (Fla. 1966).
[753] Rohan v. Rosenblatt, 25 Conn. L. Rptr. 287, 1999 WL 643501 (1999).
[754] Anderson v. Kenelly, 37 Colo. App. 217, 547 P.2d 260 (Colo. Ct. App. 1975).
[755] Horton v. Butler, 387 So. 2d 1315 (La. Ct. App. 1980).
[756] Rosquist v. Soo line Railroad, 692 F.2d 1107 (7th Cir. 1982).
[757] Gagnon v. Shoblom, 565 N.E.2d 775 (Mass. 1991).
[758] Bowling v. Pfizer, Inc. 922 F. Supp. 1261 (S.D. Ohio 1996), aff'd, 132 F.3d 1147 (6th Cir. 1998).
[759] Lerman (1999) (disbarment for systematic overbilling); but see Beam (2006).
[760] In the Matter of Fordham, 423 Mass. 481, 668 N.E.2d 816 (1996).
[761] In re Dorothy, 605 N.W.2d 493 (S.D. 2000).
[762] People v. Hohertz, 926 P.2d 560 (Colo. 1996).
[763] Florida Bar v. Moriber, 314 So. 2d 145 (Fla. 1975) (per curiam).

Part Two

likely to act if the lawyer also conceals a prior bill in requesting court-awarded fees (as also happened in the first case in this section).[764] They scrutinize contingent fee contracts more closely, especially when the client is unsophisticated[765] and the lawyer has invested few hours.[766] One jurisdiction disbarred a lawyer for charging a contingent fee to recover the proceeds of a life insurance policy, since there was no contingency.[767] Disciplinary bodies punish lawyers who charge for overhead,[768] bill clerical services at lawyers' rates,[769] or falsify expense accounts.[770]

Two other potential threats to the fairness of attorneys' fees are germane to the cases that follow. The first is the conflict between lawyers' interests in maximizing fees and clients' interests in maximizing recoveries. The U.S. Supreme Court has upheld the authority of district courts to approve settlements in which defendants give plaintiffs more in exchange for being relieved from the obligation to pay plaintiffs' attorneys' fees.[771] A court has disciplined a lawyer for billing over $41,000 on an hourly basis when the client, rejecting the lawyer's advice, settled for an amount that produced only a $2,000 contingent fee.[772] A lawyer can be liable in malpractice for failing to present a settlement offer to the client.[773] The second problem arises when a lawyer withdraws money from a client trust account to pay a contested contingent fee.[774] The New York rule is clear:

> Funds belonging in part to a client ... and in part presently or potentially to the lawyer ... shall be kept in such special account, but the portion belonging to the lawyer ... may be withdrawn

---

[764] Bushman v. State Bar of California, 522 P.2d 312 (Cal. 1974).
[765] In re Teichner, 470 N.E.2d 972 (Ill. 1984).
[766] Committee on Legal Ethics of West Virginia State Bar v. Gallaher, 376 S.E.2d 346 (W.Va. 1988) (50% contingent fee cut in half).
[767] Committee on Legal Ethics of West Virginia State Bar v. Tatterson, 352 S.E.2d 107 (W.Va. 1986); but see Lawyer Disciplinary Board v. Morton, 569 S.E.2d 412 (W.Va. 2002) (30% contingent fee to recover medical expenses in car accident not excessive based on time devoted). There is ongoing debate over whether the contingencies of tort litigation justify the fees. Compare Brickman (1995; 1996) and Horowitz (1995) with ABA Formal Opinion 94-389 (1994) and Kritzer (2002).
[768] In re Zaleon, 504 S.E.2d 702 (Ga. 1998); ABA Comm. on Ethics & Prof. Resp., Formal Op. 93-370 (1993); "Skaddenomics," Am. Law., Sept. 1991, at 3; Karen Dillon, "Dumb and Dumber," Am. Law., Oct. 1995, at 5.
[769] In re Green, 11 P.3d 1078 (Colo. 2000).
[770] In re Schneider, 553 A.2d 206 (D.C. 1989).
[771] Evans v. Jeff D., 475 U.S. 717 (1986).
[772] In re Panel File Number 99-5, 607 N.W.2d 429 (Minn. 2000).
[773] Moores v. Greenberg, 834 F.2d 1105 (1st Cir. 1987).
[774] In re Haar, 698 A.2d 412 (D.C.App. 1997).

when due unless the right of the lawyer . . . to receive it is disputed by the client. . . .[775]

In the five years 1999–2003 New York disciplined a number of lawyers for their billing practices. A lawyer who had accepted a court appointment under the Criminal Justice Act then charged his Chinese client $10,000 (although he never claimed his CJA payment from the government).[776] A lawyer overcharged clients $51,000 for air travel during 1999–2001 by buying coach class tickets using a senior discount, upgrading to first class, and having his firm reimburse him for the full first-class fare.[777] Lawyers falsified expenses. One claimed a charitable contribution he never made, the conservation of an office painting for which he never paid, and a personal trip for his wife.[778] Another overbilled for airfare, car rental, and a hotel in Las Vegas, where he stayed with a "female companion" while taking a deposition.[779] Under a contingent fee agreement for a third of the "excess of any offer by [the defendant] before suit is instituted," a lawyer paid herself $410,450 out of the $1.25 million settlement. Although she had been practicing nearly 50 years, she claimed to have believed it was "permissible" to withdraw the disputed funds from the client trust account. Arguing that the defendant had made a settlement offer before trial, the client sued her and won a judgment of $281,493 compensatory damages and $145,396 punitive damages. Publicly censured by the federal court, the lawyer failed to report that to the DDC.[780] A lawyer accepted cash advances of at least $8,500 for handling an estate, which he did not disclose to the Surrogate when seeking a $345,000 fee (and continued to deny to the DDC).[781]

Angelina and Nathan Orrico retained Robert G. Harley of Harley & Brown to pursue a medical malpractice claim. In 1992 a jury awarded them $10.7 million. On April 13, 1993, on Harley's advice, they agreed to settle for $2.3 million and signed the following statement he prepared:

> It has been our understanding that we have been retained as your attorneys on a contingency fee basis of one third of the recovery after the deduction of out of pocket expenses.

---

[775] DR 9-102(b)(4) 22 N.Y.C.R.R. § 1200.46.
[776] Matter of Singer, 752 N.Y.S.2d 655 (1st Dept. 2003).
[777] Matter of Cowen, 748 N.Y.S.2d 747 (1st Dept. 2002).
[778] Matter of Welt, 743 N.Y.S.2d 482 (1st Dept. 2002).
[779] Matter of de la Rosa, 736 N.Y.S.2d 371 (1st Dept. 2002).
[780] Matter of Wertheimer, 730 N.Y.S.2d 496 (1st Dept. 2001).
[781] Matter of Santangelo, 701 N.Y.S.2d 355 (1st Dept. 2000).

> It is our recollection that a written retainer setting forth this arrangement was signed by you at the outset of this case. Unfortunately we cannot find this retainer in our files so it will be necessary for you to sign a new one at this time, since we are required by law to file it with the Court. Because some changes in the laws regarding med mal actions have been enacted in the last few years, a retainer signed today would require us to file papers with the Court . . . asking permission for this fee. Otherwise the law requires us to charge a fee that would be smaller than the one third fee we have agreed upon. We can avoid going back to the Court by your signing a predated retainer agreement that expresses the terms that we have, in fact, been operating under. You agreed to do so and, at the same time as the signing of a copy of this letter, you are signing the retainer.

The retainer was backdated to May 1, 1985, two years before the Orricos retained the firm. Three days later Harley filed an affirmation with the Court that this was the original retainer, which "was not timely filed due to an oversight." He got a fee of $759,943 plus expenses. The statute (effective July 1, 1985) would have entitled him to no more than $377,982.

In January 1994 the Orricos found the original retainer, dated May 20, 1987, which provided for a one-third contingent fee (subject to the statutory sliding scale) but reserved the firm's right to move for leave to seek more. They informed Harley, who refused to return the difference. They sued for it and sought statutory treble damages. The firm then asked the court for its one-third fee but was rebuffed. The Orricos obtained a judgment for the nearly $400,000 difference and treble damages. Harley resisted interim suspension on the ground that he could not be an imminent danger because the events had occurred years earlier. He had not satisfied any of the judgment, explaining that the original fee had gone in part to the referring attorney and in part to his own financially strapped firm, which had been forced into Chapter 7. He was disbarred.[782]

The two cases that follow illustrate the agency problems that arise because lawyers are simultaneously seeking to maximize both their own and their clients' interests, as well as the temptation of lawyers unilaterally to appropriate what they believe is fair compensation for their skills and effort expended.

---

[782] Matter of Harley, 746 N.Y.S.2d 137 (1st Dept. 2001), 744 N.Y.S.2d 171 (1st Dept. 2002).

Chapter 5

Bleak House in America

I. Securing Trust Income for Babette Hecht Rose

A. *Antecedents: Babette's Relationship with her Family and Lawyers*

Lucile M. Stern established a testamentary trust giving her two children, Babette Hecht Rose and Edward "Ed" Stern, lifetime interests in half the income from her shares in Kreisler Manufacturing Corporation (her deceased husband's business). On their deaths their children were to inherit per stirpes. Babette's children were Frederick Tobias "Toby" Hecht (46 in 1997, when the disciplinary process began), Marcia Britt (44), Deborah "Ellie" Hecht (42), and Jeanne Baloo (36). Although Toby had earned a BFA from Tulane, had once been a professional dancer, and had studied philosophy for four years, he now owned a small educational company for businessmen in Atcheson, California, that employed his wife and his sister Jeanne. Marcia had "a very low level, service job" at PacBell.[783] Deborah had a jewelry business (but may have depended financially on the lawyer with whom she lived, Bill Kane).

---

[783] Elsewhere he said she was "a school teacher, not very good in business."

Chapter 5

When funded at Lucile's death in 1978, the trust was worth only $78,000. Toby described Kreisler as "a high risk venture, in an economy that was headed towards [the] Defense Department cutting Pratt and Whitney," Kreisler's only customer. A "devaluation of the stock . . . was likely to happen, and it did." "So from a practical point of view, there was no money. So [Edward] had defeated my grandparents in that sense. . . . anything taken out then of his control became real money." Edward had been President of Kreisler since 1971 and was CEO, CFO, Chairman of the Board, and majority shareholder (because he owned 11% separately), as well as sole trustee. For all those roles he received more than $150,000 a year, plus bonuses and benefits.

In February 1950, after divorcing Hecht (whose name she no longer used), Babette "left Scarsdale with my 11-year-old daughter to go as far away as I could get without getting wet, to California." After exhausting her own small inheritance she was virtually destitute because Edward refused to distribute any funds from the trust during its first ten years. "I opened a flower store for five years, that I doubled it when I sold it in '83. . . ." For the first ten years in California she "didn't see [Edward] very much . . . we just sort of drifted away. . . ."

> I had been left a certain amount of money and that was what I lived on for ten years with my one daughter, who was still home with me. And then I had absolutely nothing and went to Florida to see if I could talk to my brother and see what he could do. It never occurred to me that he wouldn't do anything. And I . . . found out that his wife had died and he had never even told me. . . . He said some very terrible things to me. He told me he didn't really care at all.

Toby confirmed that when he was very little his family stopped seeing Edward's. "It was like one of those mysteries when you were a kid." After Toby's parents divorced, his father and stepmother worked for Edward and "corroborated my mother's story that my uncle was this bad guy." Edward had written Babette letters "about him not caring about her and [how he] didn't care if she died and he wasn't going to give her a penny." "My uncle was nasty and hostile, like bitter, like he was out to get my mother." "He was intransigent, uncooperative, beyond belief."

Rejected by Edward in Florida, Babette fled to a friend in Westport, Connecticut, traveling by bus because she could not afford the train.

"I was living then with my friend Elly because I had no place else to live, and I worked at the drugstore there, too." Elly and her sister introduced Babette to a lawyer, Benjamin M. Cardozo. "I was so grateful that somebody talked to me, and I knew from my friends who were very nice people, that he had to be an elegant, nice man." Then in his early seventies, Cardozo had graduated from NYU Law School and had been admitted to the bar in 1942. His father Sydney was practicing with Sydney's cousin, Michael H. Cardozo.[784] Benjamin started his own practice in that office in 1948, inheriting the firm when Michael died in 1951, and Sydney in 1952.

Babette retained Cardozo in August 1987 to remove Edward as trustee and obtain an intermediate accounting. Cardozo asked for "at least a minimum retainer" of $7,500, but she had no money. "I called four of my very nearest and dearest friends and I had all that money within a half hour." On November 12 she signed an agreement:

> I further agree to pay you a reasonable fee. In the event that you are able to negogiate [sic] a settlement with my brother provided said settlement is outright or the court surcharges him for loss of income and order [sic] him to pay me a fixed amount. In such event I agree to pay you an additional fee of 1/3 of any monies received by me.

Cardozo claimed to have had modest expectations at this stage.

> I never anticipated what happened, that we would be so successful as to get her a large cash settlement. I only anticipated and hoped that the trustee would be removed, or at least . . . pay Babette an income. . . .

She had a similar recollection: "I just wanted to be able to live. I did not have in my head that I was going to be rich or wealthy."

Cardozo took her to the Westchester County Surrogate's Court to see the will:

> I told her that I'd like to check it out further and see whether the law stated . . . a cause of action for removal of her brother

---

[784] Grandfather of the present NYC Corporation Counsel; these Cardozos were distant collateral relatives of the judge.

CHAPTER 5

> as trustee, because I had written to the brother, a letter asking if we couldn't settle it, early on, and he said, no.

Having never handled such a case, Cardozo made the initial mistake of combining the trustee removal and intermediate accounting in a single proceeding. In the summer of 1988 he hired Deyan R. Brashich as trial counsel and agreed to divide the fee equally. Brashich is a large man with a loud voice, a chain-smoker and drinker—"After all, I'm a Serb"—who admits "I rub some people the wrong way. I don't try to get anybody to like me, including judges."[785] The lawyers had met two years earlier when Cardozo represented the executor and proponent of a will and Brashich represented the two apparent heirs, elderly women living in a nursing home.[786] Brashich testified that two weeks before the time expired for other heirs to come forward,

> the ne'er do well child of the deceased showed up and got everything. So I told Ben that wasn't fair, and he agreed. So he waived his fee, I waived my fee. He leaned on the broker who was selling this brownstone on the upper east side, that belonged to the deceased, and we put together a kitty for about $25,000 for the two old ladies. So I thought he was a class act. . . . And when he asked, after this was finished, would I join him in helping another old lady? I said, sure, Ben.

Brashich was not motivated by the money. Cardozo "had a client that needed help. I liked him. . . . There were some very interesting legal issues. And it was . . . fun to be with Ben."

> [H]ere you have a guy, Ed Stern, who has taken a company . . . from the very brink of bankruptcy and has all of a sudden made a multimillion dollar company full of cash—retained earnings. Who also has not been overreaching . . . all he was taking for himself was $160,000 a year salary. . . . On the other hand, here he was destroying his sister. On the third hand, here was a trust that started off with a value of $78,000. And . . .

---

[785] David Lombino, "A Voice for the Defense," Litchfield County Times, November 17, 2003.
[786] In 1985 Brashich dissolved the firm in which he had practiced for nearly two decades after his partner died, which may explain his eagerness to team up with Cardozo. Lombino, supra.

is now $4 million. . . . I thought it was going to be a three month summer fight with a settlement, because this was brother and sister. . . . Ed Stern was going to put Babette on a salary with medical benefits . . . and everybody would go home happily ever after.

Shares had risen from $0.25 when the trust was funded in 1978 to $12.00 when Edward was forced to file an intermediate accounting in 1988. The company had bought back large amounts of stock and declared no dividends.

B. Settling the Trust Dispute

On the order of Westchester County Surrogate Evans V. Brewster, Cardozo and Brashich made a settlement offer: $50,000 for past income to clear up Babette's debts, a guaranteed future income, and $40,000 in lawyers' fees— "And it was summarily rejected and we were told that Ed Stern would not settle at any cost." Indeed, Stern's lawyer, Gary Bashian, "president of the trust and estates commission of the Westchester County Bar Association," fought every step of discovery. The trial lasted six days between Christmas 1988 and New Year's 1989. Brashich and Cardozo incurred substantial expenses: expert witnesses, an accountant, Babette's trip from California, depositions, and transcripts. Cardozo wrote a "monumental" posttrial memorandum. On September 28, 1989, Brewster removed Edward as trustee but denied Babette past income and refused to surcharge Edward. Fearing the new trustee would liquidate the stock, exposing the company to a hostile takeover, Edward appealed and obtained a stay of his removal. When Brashich made three or four motions to vacate the stay, Edward's lawyers moved to cite Brashich, Cardozo, and Babette for contempt. Cardozo complied with Brewster's order to "submit an affidavit of legal services on or before October 2, 1989" but did not mention the retainer provision for a contingent fee since "we didn't think it had any applicability because the Surrogate didn't award any money, but merely removed Mr. Stern as trustee." They requested $162,000 in quantum meruit. There was no hearing, however, and no fee was awarded. Indeed, the Appellate Division stay rendered their fee request "a dead issue."

Brashich worried that the stay might mean the AD would decide for Edward. At the same time, declining defense spending was likely to reduce the stock value. "Ed Stern wanted now to put his position and control of Kreisler at rest by settling with us." "[I]t became important to have to deal with the remaindermen, the four kids on Babette's side," Brashich explained. "That's when I first started speaking with Toby Hecht," a "pretty big hearted guy," whose "main concern was to live up to what his grandparents wished." (Brashich also got to know Babette and Marsha, though not Jeanne or Deborah.) Toby claimed to have learned for the first time in November 1989 that his mother needed money. "I found out that [she] had not been able to fix her teeth. That she was very worried about that. That she was sleeping on the floor. And that she was working for a minimum wage. . . ." Toby shared the concern about Kreisler's future and did not want Babette dependent on Edward. Brashich talked to Toby five to ten times about the proposal; and he or Cardozo called Babette daily, because she was their client. "Ben would call her and say this is what has happened. And then I would call Toby."

Toby sent Cardozo the first offer he got from Frederick Lipman (Kreisler's counsel) and his own response.[787] Cardozo replied to Toby and Jeanne on November 7 that the offer was "totally unacceptable."[788] It would give Babette $371,000 in taxable income; the trust would receive $10/share instead of $15, costing it $600,000; and Lipman would be co-trustee. "It was an outrageous proposal and on Friday last I told Lipman to shove it—you know where." "Broke as she is," Babette would just have to wait out the appeal. "But I am confident ultimately we will win. . . ." "I urge you, in the future not to write or otherwise communicate with Ed Stern's lawyers [as] they do not have your best interests at heart. CALL ME FIRST!!"

At the disciplinary hearing Cardozo explained that the proposal would have allowed Edward "to select a co-trustee" and given him "carte blanche to run [Babette's] trust without further accountability." Furthermore, she would lose the $50,000 guaranteed dividends if her preferred shares were sold. Cardozo's attorney, Sarah D. McShea, developed this.

> McShea: Was it at all part of your thinking in turning down this preferred stock proposal, that your fees would not be—
>
> Cardozo: It didn't enter into it. It wasn't good for my client . . . I had no interest in obtaining a fee . . . where the settlement

---

[787] Lipman was a partner at Blank Rome, one of Philadelphia's largest law firms, which now has nearly 400 lawyers. He hired a local lawyer who had been director of the Estate Planning Council of Westchester.
[788] Respondent's Exhibit C4.

wasn't . . . in the best interest of my client. . . . if I had accepted the proposal and the stock was liquidated, it would have been over $1 million and we would have received a third of that under our retainer agreement.

When DDC Hearing Panel Chair Justin Feldman observed that the stock might not have been liquidated for 20 years, Cardozo retorted: "I'm talking theory."

Lipman wrote Toby again on November 21,[789] complaining that Babette's lawyers "want her to be treated better than any other Kreisler common shareholder, including your uncle."

> Regardless of which attorney is correct, she has no assurance that any new trustee, even if she wins, will give her any income whatsoever, let alone an amount equal to your uncle's offer. The only winner from continued litigation will be the lawyers for all sides. Their legal fees will ultimately consume a major portion of both families' wealth. Her lawyers have already advised me that even if they lose the case, they will seek to recover their legal fees from the Trust. At present, their legal fee demand is $175,000 and the appeal has not yet been briefed or argued. A similar demand may be made by your uncle's lawyers.

Cardozo denied this account, saying this. "I never spoke to Mr. Lipman. He and I didn't see eye-to-eye."

Cardozo wrote the four children again on November 28 after Brashich had sent him Lipman's November 21 proposal.[790] With Babette's authorization, Cardozo told Lipman it was unacceptable. "He said after I told him to shove it—he was withdrawing his offer." Lipman's claim that Stern wanted to be fair was "jejune [sic]—nonsense. His idea of fairness is Stern's best interest not your mother's. . . ." "So far, as our fees as well as theirs, the Surrogate must pass on their reasonableness." He was confident the Appellate Division would affirm Stern's removal as trustee within six to nine months. He asked for a copy of Lipman's proposal and urged: "don't commit yourselves without first clearing with Brashich or myself."

---

[789] Respondent's Exhibit C12.
[790] Respondent's Exhibit C5.

CHAPTER 5

Complaining about Edward's contempt motion, Cardozo asked the four children: "Do you blame *me* for being fighting mad. I would like to see Stern hung up by you know what—it ends in balls."

On January 8, 1990, Lipman proposed creating two trusts, with Cardozo as Babette's trustee and Edward as his own. Cardozo explained that "Babette had wanted to have nothing to do with her brother . . . she didn't want him trustee of her own trust." But when Bashian told Lipman the next day that Edward's trust violated *Weeks v. Frankel*,[791] which prohibited a sole beneficiary from being the trustee, Lipman withdrew the proposal. Brewster would not appoint another trustee for Edward's trust because of "the intent of the will that he be sole trustee and if a co-trustee was appointed it might impinge on Stern's ability to vote the stock and control the company."[792] Bashian suggested that each sibling have a "microscopic" interest in the other's trust, but Edward "rejected it out of hand," as well as any co-trustee, because he "did not want to have anybody except himself in control."

Lipman wrote Brashich on February 16, proposing reciprocal indemnifications (though the ultimate settlement contained only Babette's to Edward). Cardozo, who saw the letter, wrote Lipman on February 23[793] that this was unnecessary if all four children consented to the distribution, or appeared, or were cited and defaulted.

Lipman's third proposal was that Edward declare the gain in the trust's value as income, distribute it as stock (176,519 shares to each), and then repurchase Babette's share. Lipman initially valued the stock at $8, but because Kreisler had repurchased two large blocks just before the litigation at a $2 premium he agreed to $10. A separate agreement would establish a trust funded by half of Babette's share ($881,730), giving her a life interest in the income and making Toby trustee; the remainder would be divided into trusts for the four children. Brashich and Cardozo told Lipman the idea was acceptable. They met with Surrogate Brewster, who was "extremely happy" and asked his senior clerk, Arnold Klein, to work out the details.

---

[791] 197 N.Y. 304 (1910).

[792] Lipman made another proposal to Brashich on February 16: "the parties agree to file with the Surrogates' Court of Westchester County . . . a joint petition or petitions requesting the court alternatively to either (A) create two separate trusts . . . or to (B) reappoint Stern as trustee of the existing single trust. . . ." Confronted with this contradiction in the disciplinary hearing, Brashich explained that Edward's trust would be located in Florida, which allows it.

[793] Staff Exhibit 10.

Cardozo wrote the four children again on March 2,[794] forwarding Lipman's latest proposal. "It is the opinion of both Deyan Brashich and myself that this settlement is in your mother's and your own best interests. We request that you sign a consent to such distribution," thereby dispensing with a Surrogate's hearing. "The $1,765,190.00 to be paid by Kreisler to your Mother will be paid to us, as her attorneys. We will deduct our fee pursuant to a Retainer Agreement with your Mother of one-third (1/3) or approximately $588,397.00, leaving a balance of $1,176,793.00 less out-of-pocket disbursements...." After taxes and Babette's debts of about $25,000, she would get $833,503. "This of course leaves you four children without any inheritance from your Grandmother, unless your Mother wishes to execute a will in your favor...." He therefore recommended that Babette keep $125,000 and put the remaining $730,000 into a new trust, giving her an income of $42,000–50,000, with the children as remaindermen. "Brashich and I think it is a good settlement of this difficult and drawn-out litigation." Even if they won at the Appellate Division and a new trustee were appointed, "it may well be years before a resolution may be had," during which time the share price might drop.

> In the meantime, as you know, your Mother's resources are steadily dwindling and her morale is getting lower and lower. A settlement never makes everybody happy, but a good settlement is better than a possible adverse decision by the Appellate Division. Your Mother and ultimately you will continue to be at Stern's mercy and will receive no income as it is the declared policy of Kreisler ... not to declare dividends.

If the trust were preserved, it would not terminate until the deaths of *both* Edward and Babette, whereas this proposal would let them inherit when Babette died.

Cardozo testified that his purpose was "to persuade the children to go along with the settlement...." Their signatures "would have ... made the issuance of citations to them—they all lived in California—unnecessary ... it would have made the approval by the Surrogate just a formal matter." Fees had "nothing to do with" his recommendation.

---

[794] Respondent's Exhibit C6.

> [I]t wasn't possible, as [Surrogate Albert J. Emanuelli, who succeeded Brewster, later] suggested, to split the trust, in our opinion at that time, because of Matter of Weeks. And that proposal was disbanded some years earlier. So the only viable one was the distribution proposal under article 10 [of Lucile's will]. Now it so happened that by distributing the money out to Babette, our retainer agreement applied. But it was a coincidence and not a reason. We were never motivated by greed. It's not my practice as a petitioner . . . some 56 years now, and I've had a lot of clients and . . . our practice is to do the best for our client, regardless of whether we suffer a loss.

There was no conflict of interest with his client. "It was like a negligence case in which, if you recover $1 million, you get a third." He had rejected earlier proposals—to which the retainer would have applied—because they were not in Babette's interest.

The four children had to accept the proposal to avoid a hearing before Brewster. Toby spoke for all but Deborah. He knew Babette felt she had been betrayed before by another lawyer, Joe Levey, in connection with a different trust. She told Toby "she had searched at great length for an attorney and couldn't find one. And that Mr. Cardozo had accepted the case." But "when she told me that she had made an arrangement with Ben Cardozo, things started to unravel . . . she was scared, uncertain, upset . . . unsure of herself in business, and with Mr. Cardozo." She asked Toby "to explain things to her, to act on her behalf, to watch out for her. And that she was very worried, although she loved Ben to death. . . ." Sometimes her "judgment went in the direction of it was [her] money."

Toby "invited all my sisters to participate fully . . . I never wanted to be . . . head of this thing. I just was the oldest and had the . . . most business acumen and the most experience in this. . . . It's Jewish. . . ." "I made a condition to my mother that I would help, but I would not betray the will of my grandparents," whom he had "loved very much." "[T]his was my grandparent's money." Toby did not want to be "crass"; he was a multimillionaire, who had made "well over $1 million last year." But he was concerned about Marcia: "I didn't see a good future for her."

Toby opposed the "sentimental" $100,000 distribution to Babette, which was "a betrayal to my sisters and I." His mother "was not going to be deprived by not having the 100,000." And he objected to Cardozo that there was no guarantee the second trust would be created. But he did *not* object to the attorneys' fee. Cardozo

> was fighting for my mother like heart and soul . . . he was not representing us. . . . He got like upset. . . . He wouldn't accept my decline [of the proposal] . . . in a mood of, o.k., you know, let's talk about it.

Brashich claimed that the idea ultimately "foundered" on the objections of Deborah (to whom he spoke only once, in 1992). She raised tax implications, guided by Bill Kane, the attorney with whom she lived. But "they were too busy running the Persian Gulf War" and "she wanted to have nothing to do with this settlement at this time." Brashich said Deborah "irritated us because she was drafting counter proposals on her own behalf without speaking to her three siblings and her mother."

Toby also blamed the proposal's failure on Deborah, from whom he kept his distance. She had "gotten rid of my mother as a concern in her life. So any benefit that [Brashich] produced for [Babette] was not my sister Deb's concern. . . . She was not married, had no children, had no plans for children. . . . she wanted the money and to hell with them." His mother sent him a pillow on which she had crocheted "No good deed shall go unpunished." Deborah had "begun to assume" an "adversarial" way of dealing with people "where there is assumed distrust . . . deceit . . . conflict."

> She was always there, always present, like . . . an adversary in this . . . pushing about the surrogate . . . pushing basically adversarial distrustful attitude towards like any attorneys . . . they're all creeps and bad guys. . . . she never had a thing to say specifically about them. . . .
>
> She was angry. She never said why, still has not. She made an announcement that she was done having anything to do with my mother and has not since then. . . . Deborah continued, during that time to get increasingly hostile and adversarial throughout the family.

Toby never understood her objection, which he attributed to Kane.

> I met him at two outings. He was a nasty, angry man . . . both times I met him he argued with me. . . . he was like a weird

guy . . . he looked in her letters when she wrote. I knew her. They weren't her writing . . . I think he was an attorney and he was doing this behind . . . he said he was everything . . . he was a spy. . . .

C. Interlude: Deborah's Relationship with Bill Kane

Deborah had met Kane in 1985 and began living with him in 1987.[795] After graduating from Princeton and Yale Law School he had been a lawyer and entrepreneur, accumulating as much as $4 million. But by 1991 he had lost his job, been unable to find work, fought an expensive lawsuit with a former business partner, and increasingly abused alcohol and cocaine. His delusions of having won the Medal of Honor in Southeast Asia, helped to capture General Noriega, and been paid $1 million to trace a Nazi war criminal in South America now extended to masterminding the U.S. military and espionage activities during the first Gulf War. In October 1991, accompanied by Deborah, he made six sperm deposits in California Cryobank, Inc., in anticipation of suicide. At the end of the month he went to Las Vegas, staying in the Mirage penthouse suite while gambling away $20,000, and killed himself on October 30. Denied a fly-over of jets at his funeral because there was no record of military service, Deborah designed a program with images of jets and the words: "Bill Kane: Father, Visionary, Philosopher, Warrior, Hero, Gentleman, Lover, Genius." She kept his ashes in a Chinese urn in her apartment and his hairs taped to a mirror for possible DNA tests of the sperm. His September 27, 1991, will gave her the sperm. But his two children from a former marriage (which ended when they were four and 1.5 years old) contested the will on December 3, represented by their mother (also a lawyer). In June 1992 Cryobank refused to release the sperm to Deborah, who took the dispute to the media. The parties reached a settlement agreement, but the Kane children withdrew in October 1992. In November they sued Deborah for wrongful death. They alleged that Deborah, aware of his depression, convinced him to deposit the sperm six weeks before his death. A week before dying he wrote her an $80,000 check for the balance of his checking account. She bought him the suicide manual "Final Exit" (which he followed) and a one-way ticket to

---

[795] David Margolick, "15 Vials of Sperm: The Unusual Bequest of an Even More Unusual Man," New York Times, April 29, 1994.

Las Vegas and drove him to the airport. The Kane children won an order for destruction of the sperm in Superior Court on December 9, 1992, but lost on appeal in June 1993.[796] The Supreme Court denied review in September.[797] In April 1994 a probate judge awarded Deborah 3 of the 15 vials. By this time Deborah's unpaid legal bills totaled $150,000. The Kane children immediately appealed. As Deborah grew increasingly anxious about the effect of her age (39) on pregnancy, the parties jousted over immediate enforcement of the order. In August 1995 the appeal court held that the appeal did not stay the order.[798] Deborah failed to conceive by artificial insemination the first two times. Before using the last vial, her gynecologist wanted to know the prospects for obtaining the other 12. The probate judge ruled that the property settlement limited Deborah to three vials. The appeal court declined to rule without resolving the Kane children's claim that their father had been mentally incapable in his final weeks. Although the referee it appointed found in July 1996 that Kane had been mentally incapable as a result of Deborah's undue influence, in November the appeal court gave Deborah the remaining vials.[799]

D. Toby's Resistance and Cardozo's Pressure

Lipman testified before the successor surrogate, Emanuelli, on August 3, 1993, that Deborah called him often—"less than a hundred, but it was a lot"—although she "would not take my calls many times. Or didn't return them." She claimed to have counsel, "Mr. Kane, whom she lived with," but "never let me speak to him." "I got tired of talking to her and I offered to pay $1,000 to any counsel of her choice just so I'd not have to talk to her any more and try to make a deal with somebody who was a bit more rational." Lipman "was a little uncomfortable, frankly, dealing with Toby because he wasn't represented by counsel. I kept on urging him to seek his own counsel." "[W]e didn't see any conflict between the children of Ed Stern or the children of Babette Hecht, and their own born and unborn children that would justify the appointment" of a guardian ad litem.

Toby wrote Cardozo on March 27, apologizing for upsetting him on the phone but reiterating that he and his two sisters rejected the proposal.[800] "[Y]ou do not understand our grandmother's wishes or our

---
[796] Hecht v. Superior Court, 16 Cal.App.4th 836 (2d Dist. 1993).
[797] "Ruling Left Intact in Sperm Bequest," New York Times, September 5, 1993.
[798] Kane v. Superior Court, 37 Cal.App.4th 1577 (2d Dist. 1995).
[799] Hecht v. Superior Court, 50 Cal.App.4th 1289, 59 Cal. Rptr. 222 (2d Dist. 1996).
[800] Respondent's Exhibit C8.

CHAPTER 5

concerns in this matter." These differences could not be resolved by telephone or letter.

> Over the past 3-4 months there have been too many conflicting conversations and representations. I have been confused too many times by what is said to me, what is written, and what is reported by my mother.
>
> *In order to get this matter resolved we request that you set up a time for us to meet with the surrogate in his/her chambers to discuss the situation.*

Toby saw the Surrogate as "somebody to act with authority that my sister [Deborah] would accept . . . I wasn't objecting really much to what [Cardozo] was proposing." He asked Cardozo to arrange the meeting by May 3. "After that date we will speak directly to the surrogate." Toby and Deborah testified they did not know the lawyers had submitted an affidavit of legal services to the Surrogate the previous October.

Toby's letter crossed in the mail with Cardozo's March 28 letter, criticizing the children "for resisting the settlement proposal, [and] accusing them of disloyalty to their mother."[801] He reproached them for objecting that the latest settlement agreement did not adequately protect Babette or them and that his fees "are too large." "You, apparently, don't trust your own mother and forget that I took this case on a contingency" and Babette contributed only a thousand dollars of the initial payment. "You forget that so far we won." If they rejected the settlement and Edward's appeal succeeded, "he will continue to run the company for the benefit of himself and the eight (8) grandchildren to the detriment of your mother since it is the declared policy of Kreisler not to declare any dividends."

> You seem to forget that our fee of one third (1/3) is strictly contingent. If we lose on appeal we get nothing, but neither does your mother, if this case was a negligence case and the verdict of the jury was $1,800.00, we would get one third (1/3) of the recovery. This case is no different we receive a premium for winning—and zilch for losing.

---

[801] Respondent's Exhibit B1.

> In your shoes, I dont' [sic] see how you four children want to take the chance of the AD reversing Surrogate Brewster.

The proposed settlement "nails down an excellent result for both your mother and yourselves despite the size of our fee." The alternative was

> too selfish and unrealistic; nor do I believe your grandmother would want her daughter to suffer. [Babette] was the primary beneficiary of the Trust under Lucile's Will, not you four children; although this is Stern's argument . . . I cannot believe that you four children wish to follow in Stern's footsteps.

He urged them to sign the enclosed papers "consenting to the distribution of one half of the stock to your mother as income." "Your mother, I and Brashich would appreciate your reconsidering your position in this matter particularly because of your mother's fragile financial situation. . . ." "Your mother's financial health, and security, if not your own is in your hands. If you feel it is a sacrifice on the part of each of you, *make it*. It is in your own as well as your mother's best interest."

Cardozo told the Hearing Panel that the four children were concerned about losing their inheritance. "But I felt that they should disregard that . . . the settlement terminated their interest and their mother got the money outright, and trust their mother to look after them."

> [A]t the time I wrote that letter it was my belief that we had a contract between Babette and ourselves to pay a one-third fee of any outright settlement. Otherwise we would obtain nothing. It wasn't until much later on—until I think Matter of Warhol was decided and Matter of Strateki was decided [after Emanuelli's decision], that I realized that contracts between beneficiaries of trusts and executors of trusts can be disregarded by the Surrogate. And that the Surrogate has inherent jurisdiction to review all legal fees.

At the time he believed that if he lost the appeal he would not have been entitled to anything under the retainer or from the Surrogate "because we hadn't benefited the trust in any way." Hearing Panel member John Brigandi picked this up later. Emanuelli "seems to indicate by a plethora of

Chapter 5

legal citations here, that it's accepted authority" that "you do not have to" be successful to claim in quantum meruit.

Brashich "totally disagreed" with Cardozo's claim that they would get nothing if the AD reversed, as well as his earlier letter about a contingent fee, "because from the very beginning, while there was a contingency agreement . . . we never followed it. . . . I had already agreed with Toby in January that our fee would be roughly $225,000 and Ben is talking about a contingency . . . when from the very beginning our fees were to be negotiated . . . or on a quantum meruit basis." "I told Toby to disregard the letter." "I told Ben, why are you writing these letters? Stop it." (Brashich told Emanuelli "I think I saw a draft of [Cardozo's March 28 letter] before it went out." But he denied this before the disciplinary hearing, claiming to have been out of the country at the time.)

Brashich's secretary, Caroline Shannon, testified that after his letter "Toby was calling and screaming. Babette was calling and screaming. Dan [Brashich] was pouring oil on troubled waters saying Ben made a factual error. . . . And basically, he's venting." "After Mr. Brashich had talked to Toby and Babette, and Mr. Cardozo where he kind of yelled at him over the phone, it was like forgotten about." Cardozo "realized after Mr. Brashich spoke with him, yeah, I did make a mistake on some stuff and maybe I shouldn't have taken that tone. You have to understand, this is like he was like the head of the family here and he was castigating his kids kind of thing."

Toby testified that he rarely talked to Cardozo, although he did receive 5 to 10 letters from the lawyer describing the settlement proposal. When he got Cardozo's letter "I had to keep reminding myself that he represented my mother and he was attached to my mother, caring about my mother and fighting for my mother . . . but we didn't always share the same interpretation of what that would be." Brashich "was clear that he didn't always agree or support what Mr. Cardozo had written." Toby had talked to Brashich over a hundred times about "the settlement and the different iterations of what was proposed on both sides. Like he had an obligation to represent proposals and considerations to me." The settlement proposals were "beyond . . . what I can count, we changed it, revisited it . . . put it inside and out, backwards and forwards. We examined all the consequences of whatever decisions that we could possibly make." Toby disapproved a proposal "in which everything would stay in Kreisler stock," leaving Babette "vulnerable," and another for "a big cash settlement to my mother," which would violate his grandparents' will. "I knew my mother didn't understand and I didn't understand myself, what would be the consequences . . . but what short circuited that was that it wasn't what my grandparents said. . . ." His mother "very much did not want anything to do with any connection to Ed Stern. And if she could possibly get out of it—nothing to Mr. Cardozo, she did not want an attorney like Joe Levey administering the trust . . . she wanted me. . . ." He agreed to be trustee for the sake of his mother and sisters because otherwise "number one, my mother is back in the position that she didn't want to be in most, where there is somebody else who doesn't care about her, doing this thing."

Brashich urged Toby "to have [his] financial money manager" check the proposal's valuation of Kreisler stock. Toby claimed that price was $3 to 5 above the market because Deborah's objection "put the control of Kreisler in limbo, and that was pressure on my uncle." "[T]here was a very tight group controlling the company, old friends, long time associates . . . and this would unsettle that and their offering of a premium was . . . to make the transaction happen." "[A]ny time there was a possibility that something needed to happen, [Brashich] urged us either get our own attorney, which we ultimately did, or to speak to experts . . . and I always did. It was a business practice of mine." "Holidays, every time anything came up, every time something needed to be planned for, any time my mother needed to be . . . [Brashich] would talk to [Babette] and my sisters. . . ." When Toby had problems with Deborah, Brashich "shared with me . . . what happens to families, and was the strongest request with Deborah, and my father was in this, too, to not let the litigation disrupt the family." Brashich "volunteered to reduce his fee." This "was consistent with his . . . moral point of view about life." Toby had not asked him to do it. Brashich "didn't say it like he was doing me a favor." Another time "he urged me to verify the situation, check marketplace standards."

On April 2 Cardozo replied to Toby's March 27 letter.[802]

> The Surrogate is not going to meet with you since there are no proceedings before him at this time and his decision removing Stern is now on appeal to the Appellate Division, which precludes a settlement in the Surrogate's Court. The only solution short of a decision by the Appellate Division is agreement by all the parties which I do not see forthcoming unless you

---

[802] Respondent's Exhibit C9.

CHAPTER 5

and your sisters sign the Waiver of Citation and Consent forwarded to you last week in my letter of March 28, 1990.

But he offered to meet with Toby in New York. In fact, the Surrogate *had* met with Cardozo, Brashich, and Edward's New York counsel in February. Brashich later claimed, "I told Ben he was wrong" to write this to Toby. "I said not only would the Surrogate be interested in their position . . . but they would have to be a component part of the settlement which ultimately would be before the Surrogate."

Cardozo testified that his letter

is a real bummer, which I never should have written, and which is incorrect . . . because I told Mr. Hecht that the Surrogate wouldn't meet with him, and this just was plain wrong. . . . it wasn't as Surrogate Emanuelli characterized the letter as an attempt to mislead Mr. Hecht. I had no such intention. . . . this is a bad letter. And I apologize to the panel and to the court for writing it.

Chairman Feldman persisted: "the Surrogate had seen all of you in a conference at Lipman's request" in February, "while the appeal was pending." Cardozo again admitted his error but denied any intention to mislead or deceive the children. "I made a mistake. But lawyers make mistakes all the time." Feldman persisted: "Why did you tell him he couldn't meet with the surrogate." Cardozo could only repeat himself:

I was wrong. What can I tell you? I just didn't think. I wasn't thinking straight. . . . I was trying to be persuasive. . . . I thought it was in the best interest of his mother. And I felt, look, most women look after their children.

Following Feldman's lead, he now claimed he really meant to say "look, you could meet with the Surrogate if you want to, but it's not going to do you any good."

In response to McShea, Toby admitted he had not carried out his threat. "I never wanted to meet with the Surrogate. . . .it wasn't a time for personal indulgence, even when Deborah was making me so angry and I was, you know, red in the face. . . ." He would rather have spoken to the Surrogate than deal with "two difficult people," Deborah and Cardozo.

But he testified before Emanuelli that he had not approached Brewster because it would cost more money and "we'd still needed . . . Deyan and Ben for whatever might happen with Stern and Lipman." After writing the April 2 letter, Cardozo said he "backed off and let Mr. Brashich handle it . . . he and Mr. Lipman seemed to hit it off and he also hit it off with Toby Hecht."

E. Deborah Blocks the Settlement

Deborah wrote Toby, Marcia and Jeanne sometime between Cardozo's April 2 letter and Toby's June 20 reply. She asserted her "special" relationship with Babette (and listed everything she had done for her). But when she was 32, "Mom released me from my total support position in the family." Now "I am not taking care of the situation, you are. Maybe it's from the bottom of your heart, maybe it's from guilt, maybe it's for the money . . . only you know." The trust was "a new/old concept for 'where the money is.' A place where Toby does his homework and Marcia and Jeane [sic] assent." She had to decide: "do I look out for myself or just give it to Mom and her latest sympaticos, her attorneys?" Those lawyers were seeking her signature

> about money from the *corpus* of the Trust—originally intended for the Hecht grandchildren—going to lawyers, charging disproportionate and unwarranted fees—last heard in the neighborhood of $600,000.00—to taxes, possibly . . . and to fund a stock purchase transaction by which the cash-poor business enterprise is going to use its suddenly discovered excess cash to purchase the stock from the estate and place total control and ownership in the hands of Ed and his heirs. . . .
>
> In effect we grandchildren will have turned over assets consisting of over two million dollars . . . to lawyers who have not accomplished a single one of their promises and alleged goals, in return for a modest allowance of uncertain duration for Mom. . . . We are to these gentlemen and perhaps to Mom: the ENEMY. . . . I do not trust either Ben Cardozo or Deyan Brashich to look out for anything beyond their fee. . . . their goal has been to break the trust and to alter the beneficiaries, as well as to reclassify the CAPITAL GAINS to be had from any sale of trust assets from their traditional category of corpus

to income—which is both taxable and subject to a contingency fee . . . which the attorneys apparently do not believe would be awarded by the Surrogate Judge.

The Surrogate had removed Edward because of the conflict between his roles as trustee and Kreisler CEO. "I have been told that these are normal and usual grounds . . . and a legal matter with known procedures and straight forward legal precedent that could just as easily have been accomplished by a junior lawyer for a few thousand dollars at most." The attorneys were unable to persuade the court to order Edward to pay them—"an indication that the court rejected their contentions that Ed damaged the trust"—or have the entire trust (including Edward's portion) pay them—"a reasonable indication that the judge did not find that the activities of our mother's attorneys benefited the trust at all."

> That I should be asked to commit such a suicidal act [by signing the consent] is insulting to my intelligence. That I should be vilified for any hesitation in this regard is an insult to my dignity and, perhaps, a libelous one; that family members should accept such accusations, is an insult to the intelligence of those family members who had the skill, fortitude, clarity of mind and intentfulness to create the fortune left in trust to us, their grandchildren.

She wanted the trust dissolved and the corpus distributed to the beneficiaries, each of whom could sell the stock and then decide how much to give "Mom voluntarily each year in accordance with her needs and ours." "That such a format would also minimize fees to be paid to this ineffectual slice of legal life, does not seem to me a defect, but a blessing." Indeed, "I am surprised that failure to propose it does not constitute legal malpractice in the states of New York and Connecticut." She threatened "to put my decision with the surrogate Court."

Toby had offered to give Babette $1,000/month, to be repaid with 10 percent interest after the matter was resolved. Deborah commented: "after I slept on it . . . it felt odd."

> Where were the three of you when for over fifteen years I saw Mom through every aspect of life? Financially as well as emotionally. It never occurred to me to turn to each of you and

expect or ask you to pay me back. After all, most of the time Toby and Marcia weren't speaking to Mom, and Jeanne was in the throws [sic] of growing up.

She hoped this "shed some light on my decisions" and "will perhaps allow the intrafamilial discussion of this matter to proceed on some grounds other than accusatory name-calling."

Toby wrote Deborah and his sisters on June 20.[803] Deborah's letter was "an *announcement* of her intentions . . . *not* a conversation *with* anyone." She "feels that she has been granted the wisdom and intelligence to know what is best for us all. . . ." She had "managed to hurt, insult, and offend just about all of us. . . ." "[S]he has already cost the family more than $250,000 . . . because of her arrogance, distrust, incompetence, prejudice, and pride." Although not "malicious," she was "an intelligent person who is young, lacks wisdom, doesn't appreciate her own incompetence, is full of pride and doesn't realize the significance and consequences of having been given a loaded gun." "[T]his nonsense must stop." "So, Ellie:[804] I am dissatisfied with your actions and your letter in many ways . . . it was a waste of time to read. You should have addressed it to yourself and put it in your diary." "Who do you think you are?! You are PART of the family. You are not THE family. EVERYONE has done their best. Do you think I was eating bon-bons while you were suffering and toiling 'without reservation.'" "Should I ask you to count your hours and their value at that time in your life? . . . Then shall I ask Marcia, Jeanne, and myself to count how many hours and dollars we have spent and assign their value?"

When his wife Linda and he proposed that the court determine the lawyers' fees, Babette rightly pointed out that "she would bear the immediate consequences. This produced an *ethical dilemma*. . . ." He had offered the $1,000/month "to finance a strategy that might work for everyone's benefit." "We figured that the lawyers saw Mom in such a weak position that they could drive us to 'settling' for what they wanted." "*You agreed.*"

> [W]e thought it could be completed in less than 60 days. The family could have gotten $10/share. Paid the taxes. A family member could have been trustee. We would have had to pay

---

[803] Respondent's Exhibit B4.
[804] The name he called Deborah.

Chapter 5

> the tax but maybe we could have cut the lawyers fee in half. Who knows? We more or less accused the lawyers of being unprincipled and said we would wait them out. Not to our surprise, Deyan Brashich told us he disagreed with Ben's stance and would be willing to negotiate.

But Ellie "set us up by agree[ing] and then kicked us by reneging."

> It means that Linda and I must live close to the financial edge for about 8 months. . . . This does not produce peace in our lives or good will to you. Are we going to welcome you back to the family in the future or accept your promises again? I don't think so.

After Kreisler's latest annual report announced that Edward had spent more than a year's profits defending his interests, the stock dropped $1.50 a share, costing the Hechts $264,000. Edward and Babette would have to go to court again, paying lawyers $250–450/hour. If Babette won, the surrogate would appoint a new trustee, probably one suggested by Brashich.

> If you force the lawyers to get nasty . . . they might do a background check on how you have been living while Mom has been suffering, sleeping on futons, unable to afford a doctor.

The judge might rule in favor of the lawyers: "they all live in the same community, work together, and already know one another." "[Y]our moves have been selfish, incompetent, short sighted, prideful, and petty." "You screwed Linda and I up." "Making promises and reneging usually causes damage. Don't ever do this with us again."

> I say we could have gotten $822,000 for us or $205,000 each if I could have settled with Deyan Brashich and Fred Lippman [sic]. I figure you've got us down to about $494,000 or $123,000 each. Over 15 years at 10% interest the difference is enormous. Are *you* going to make up the difference if your [sic] wrong?

> . . .

> *Dear Everyone Else (Including Ellie),*

> ... I have had it with Ellie. I have had enough of us being her victim, being continually upset by her, putting up with her, and trying to make excuses for her behavior. ... I think it is time to ask her to stay away. Unless you tell me I am wrong in some way here, I am sure she cannot be part of my nuclear family. She is expelled. In addition, if you ask, I say that you are foolish to include her in your lives any further.

Deborah did not share his concerns: "you are not married, have no children, have no career, do not work, and do not have a mortgage." Jeanne was "no longer your teenage baby sister ... she may be more competent than you in many areas. ..." He resented that Deborah "minimize[d] my value or competence and exaggerate[d] [her] own." "Linda and I have been producing an income that is in the top 1% of the country for many years." He accused Deborah of "pride, incompetence, and stupidity." "[T]here is lots of future to go without a family to help you, give you power in the world when you need it, protect you, and rely upon." "You leave upsets that last for days ... the only contribution you have been to the family for the past few years is that you force us to build our character." "[Y]ou need an ultimatum ... either you will speak to everyone with respect, take care not to damage people's futures, and do your best to produce peace of mind with each conversation, or as far as I am concerned you are expelled." He urged her to authorize him to negotiate with Brashich and Lipman. But "if you persist in holding your position, and I hear no arguments from any other members of the family, then you are expelled from our family (the Hechts)." In the disciplinary hearing Toby explained that Deborah "had just written this letter to us, sort of like out of the blue ... and I was angry." He was convinced "that it wasn't written by her" but by Kane. "She's not capable of this." "She was cynical ... she had either forgotten or discounted what had gone on ... it's just a shotgun of assessments and assertions."

Brashich testified that between Cardozo's April 2, 1990, letter and February 1991 "Deborah continued to draft proposed settlement agreements and correspond with Fred Lipman." During this period Brashich talked to Toby and Babette "a minimum of four or five times a week ... we might occasionally on the weekend, have three or four or five conversations." "Mr. Lipman withdrew the offer of settlement and then put it back on the table three or four times, to try and get a settlement from Deborah, and advised us that if a settlement was not forthcoming, with the price of

CHAPTER 5

the stock declining, it would be taken off the table." Because of the decline, the premium had grown from $1.75 to $2.50. John Bartels (Brashich's lawyer in the disciplinary proceeding) explained that Edward was "afraid that the price of the stock would drop and the board of Kreisler wouldn't pay the premium, and they were afraid Deborah was going to leave the fold . . . and therefore they wanted this settled without court approval," which would take too long. Brashich agreed to Lipman's demand that Babette unilaterally indemnify Edward because it was "a deal breaker"; the Kreisler board "wanted to be sure . . . that this thing has been put to bed." The goal (explained in a February 13, 1991, letter) was to prevent other shareholders (including the friend who had referred Babette to Cardozo) from suing Edward.

On December 7 Lipman wrote Deborah that "your mother's attorneys recently advised me that they would be willing to have your 'portion' of the fee set by the court."[805] "Your mother's attorney would like to settle this matter by December 31, 1990. *Therefore, time is of the essence.*" He wrote her again on January 8, 1991.[806]

> I hope that you do cooperate, since you will then have an opportunity to have some input in the settlement and will be able to protect your personal interests. However, if you choose not to do so, the settlement will proceed without you.

He reiterated on January 14 that Brashich "has agreed . . . to have your portion of the legal fees set by the Court. . . ."[807]

Deborah replied on January 21 that "I am only interested in my mother's well being and her financial stability."[808] She complained that "not all" the documents had been sent to her and she had had to spend "quite a sum" to get advice and draft objections. "[B]ecause you have explained that the deal is going through with or without my consent, I abstain from signing it" on the ground that "it is not looking after the interest of the beneficiaries but solely in the interest of the present trustee." Lipman's threat "to the affect [sic] that if I don't sign, the judge will take action contrary to the interest of the beneficiaries" was "inciting."

---

[805] Respondent's Exhibit UUU in the Surrogate's proceeding.
[806] Respondent's Exhibit VVV in the Surrogate's proceeding.
[807] Respondent's Exhibit WWW in the Surrogate's proceeding.
[808] Respondent's Exhibit YYY in the Surrogate's proceeding.

Unfortunately, this is where many laymen get "bum deals"—they don't know what deal is the best and end up depending on the expertise of others—lawyers. I would appreciate being kept abreast during the completion of the liquidation of my grandparents [sic] trust. They meant a lot to me, maybe even more since studying their wills these past years.

II. The Settlement Is Approved and the Lawyers' Fees Paid

In February 1991 the other parties settled, and Edward withdrew his appeal. Babette and all her children except Deborah signed releases terminating the trust and discharging and indemnifying Edward as trustee. Toby testified in the disciplinary hearing that he did not understand indemnification, never saw the entire settlement, and did not remember what papers he signed. On redirect by McShea he conceded that indemnification "was not a major part . . . of the negotiation . . . that I was concerned with at the time . . . I was not asked to indemnify anybody at that time."

On February 6 the trust was destroyed; Babette and Edward each got 175,064 shares (the remaining 11,650 shares, worth $92,000, went to Edward "as partial reimbursement for 'administrative expenses' and taxes"). In addition, Babette received $58,000 outright. She simultaneously sold her shares to Kreisler for $1,750,640, paid by four checks for $437,660 made out to her and a child. She established inter vivos trusts with all the children except Deborah, giving Babette the life income, with the corpus to the children; Toby was trustee of each. Cardozo and Brashich agreed to compromise their claim to a third ($583,547) for $500,000; three of Babette's children contributed $125,000 each. On her lawyers' advice, Babette also agreed to indemnify Edward and Kreisler for any losses "arising from the failure of the parties to seek or obtain judicial approval of the extant agreement."

The next day Lipman wrote Brashich about the fourth check for Deborah.[809] "You have agreed to promptly apply for a court determination as to the proper amount of the legal fees and disbursements which you are entitled to receive. . . ." That check remained in escrow because Deborah continued to protest the "disproportionate," "unwarranted" and "predatory"

---

[809] Respondent's Exhibit DDD in the Surrogate's proceeding.

CHAPTER 5

attorneys fees. She ultimately agreed to the settlement provided the Surrogate determine her share of attorney's fees.

Asked by Emanuelli "Did the Surrogate in your mind have continuing jurisdiction. . . .?" Toby replied: "I did not have knowledge that at the end of all of this, that anything needed to come back to the Surrogate to get approval." But in the disciplinary proceeding he claimed to have known that the Surrogate had to approve the settlement, explaining that Emanuelli's "level of specificity" "guaranteed I had to say no." He had "no reason to know that the Surrogate would review fees . . . the specifics were not my concern." He also denied having relied on Brashich or Cardozo for advice in signing the discharge and release but then said Brashich had told him "that if it went in one direction, the Surrogate would take over everything, and otherwise, the Surrogate would be presented with something that we had agreed upon and then the Surrogate would rule." He did not understand the concept of continuing jurisdiction: "continuing is not a word I recognize here . . . that once you finish you were to come in. No . . . I did not know I was to come in . . . and get approval of these." Phrases like trust busting and successor trustee were "gobbledygook to me . . . I tell you that it's offensive to me that it was conducted this way by Judge Emanuelli. . . . He shut me down once and I kept looking at him and he kept shutting me down." However, Toby told DDC attorney Mady Edelstein

> I thought that the request for fees was appropriate. Actually, more generous than I was expecting. . . . I also thought that the good will that they had shown to be betrayed would not be smart for my mother . . . because nobody can compel anybody else to, you know, put everything they've got into doing something . . . they can withdraw. Now they didn't make no threat about that.

The February 6 agreement was never submitted to Emanuelli for approval. Asked whether the Surrogate had approved the $375,000 fee, Cardozo replied "We didn't think it was necessary because of the retainer agreement." He also testified, however, that Lipman had said

> he intended . . . to submit [the agreement] . . . in order to comply with certain tax rulings. But he insisted that only Stern as trustee have that right to apply to the court. So that even if Mr. Brashich and I on behalf of Babette wanted to try

to obtain approval, we were barred . . . from doing so. Now maybe we made a mistake and should have insisted. But if we had insisted, the settlement, in our opinion, would have gone by the boards.

But Cardozo told Emanuelli that he had understood at the time of the settlement that Stern was *not* going to seek surrogate approval.[810]

Brashich testified that "whether the actual determination that the declaration of . . . the gain as income would have to be approved by the Surrogate . . . I left it to Gary [Bashian] and to Fred [Lipman], because they represented the trustee who was the fiduciary." "It was contemplated at the time of closing that there would be court approval . . . they already had drafted the petition . . . and the only reason why the petition was not filed was because Mr. Stern didn't want to pay Mr. Bashian an extra $10,000" to do so. John Bartels, Brashich's lawyer, read from the settlement agreement: "If Kreisler or Stern decide (in their sole discretion) to obtain court approvals . . . you and Babette Hecht will cooperate in every way in seeking it."

The day the settlement was signed and executed Cardozo and Brashich petitioned the Surrogate for fees based on the retainer agreement entitling them to a third of Deborah's share ($437,660) plus costs, a total of $176,367.76, "or some 40% of the fund." They did not disclose they had already received $375,000. On September 26, Emanuelli (who had now succeeded Brewster) denied their motion for summary judgment and ordered Edward to file an intermediate accounting. Emanuelli appointed Alice O'Rourke Rodd and Walter F. Bottger guardians ad litem to represent grandchildren, living and yet unborn.[811] (Cardozo was surprised because the doctrine of virtual representation allowed Edward and Babette to represent their descendants. "We tried to persuade [Emanuelli] it was unnecessary.")

On November 1 Cardozo and Brashich wrote Emanuelli in anticipation of their November 7 conference.[812] "The motion for Summary judgment we repeat raised no triable issue of fact." Babette "joined in our

---

[810] Staff Exhibit 17.
[811] Complaining about the quality of guardians in Westchester, Emanuelli appointed O'Rourke, who lived in New York City but was the daughter of the Westchester County Executive. When she took a new job inconsistent with her guardianship duties she sought the help of Bottger, a friend of her husband. Interview with Walter Bottger, November 20, 2006.
[812] Guardian's Exhibit 10 in the Surrogate's proceeding.

petition awarding us one third of the $437,600 pursuant to the retainer she signed on November 12, 1987, whereby she agreed to pay us one third of any recovery as well as our request for additional fees on appeal to the Appellate Division." The only dispute was with Deborah over their fee. "The compromise was to settle a nasty and expensive litigation . . . as a result of the settlement, Babette Hecht and her four children benefited." The fee objection "is unreasonable, is unjustified and has no merit. Its reasonableness is insulated from review by the fact that the client Babette approved the requested fee." "Our application is not in *quantum meruit*." They distinguished retainers signed by illiterates. "Babette was not illiterate. She is a college graduate." "The retainer was clear and unambiguous. It was not exorbitant." "If the court had found in favor of the trustee, Cardozo & Cardozo, P.C., would have received nothing."

> It is [Babette's] daughter, Deborah, who now violently objects to such fee when she has no standing to do so, having executed a consent irrevocably consenting to the distribution of 176,064 shares of Kreisler stock as income to her mother and thereby causing the trust to cease to exist under her grandmother's will, which she cannot now disavow despite her denial in her affidavit in opposition.

They opposed Emanuelli's order "requesting the trustee to file an accounting and cite all interested parties including all the children and grandchildren of Babette Hecht as all children of Babette and Edward were cited in the prior accountings and removal proceeding and none appeared."

Deborah and Bottger objected to designating the distribution to Babette as "income," the destruction of the trust, the lawyers' fees, their recommendation that Babette indemnify Edward, the potential tax consequences, and the negative impact on grandchildren of the change in measuring lives in the new trusts. Bottger noted that "increases in trust corpus were designated as principal in the intermediate accounting for the period September, 1976 through October, 1988." He and Deborah alleged that the lawyers had deceived Babette and her children by denominating the distribution as income in order to justify claiming their contingent fee, failed to inform Babette about their prior application for legal fees in quantum meruit, and failed to tell the court they had already received $375,000 in legal fees.

Asked by DDC attorney Edelstein whether he had told Babette between September 1989 and February 1991 that the Surrogate could set her fees, Cardozo said he had not "because the retainer agreement was applicable. Unless we . . . petitioned the court for approval of the settlement. And if we did, then by virtue of doing that, the fee would be built into the settlement so that the court would then approve of it." "I didn't think it was necessary" to tell her. "She had an agreement with me. . . ." But Cardozo told another story in his deposition.

> Q: So that your . . . right to compensation did not and you did not intend it to be solely related to this retainer agreement?
>
> A. No, it didn't. . . . It wouldn't have been fair to me . . . because otherwise . . . I would have been working for nothing. . . . I don't work for nothing. Not with this kind of money involved.

Toby had a different recollection of how the lawyers explained their fees. When settlement was close

> Mr. Brashich announced that it was time to talk about fees. . . . they were knights on white horses to my mother. They took very good care of her. So it was a deep emotional pull on my part, of giving thanks to them, that without them there would have been nothing. . . . I later came to understand there was some legal, like shenanigans, from my point of view that as a businessman I don't like.

On Brashich's advice

> I spoke to a friend of mine who is a general counsel for a division of Pacific Bell. I went to my bank's trust department, interrupted a big lunch they were having . . . and I said that there was this trust. I had a question about attorney's fees . . . I said it was in New York, that it was a one-third contingency fee. Was that market standard appropriate? They said yes, the general counsel said yes.

"Once I was satisfied that we were well below what was market standard in what people were advising me, I didn't feel any more need. . . ." "I was a

CHAPTER 5

customer of that bank . . . so I was taken seriously. . . ." His own money manager and CPA agreed. When he told them Brashich had agreed to reduce his fee "they said that was very generous." Toby told his sisters this, and all three agreed. But on cross-examination he conceded that none of these advisers was a New York lawyer. None of the children was represented by counsel during the fee negotiations. Only after Deborah objected to the settlement did Toby and his two other sisters retain a New York lawyer.[813]

Brashich told Toby "there was another way to calculate this . . . where you check the hours." He "represented that the Surrogate has the right to organize that way." But "my position in the matter was, hello, that was not what was agreed upon at the beginning." "I would have been completely satisfied if they insisted we honor the agreement. . . ." "They had made an agreement in good faith when my mother was in bad shape. I checked. They didn't take advantage of her." "[I]t was my responsibility to listen to these conversations about fee because I was looking out for my mother and she trusted me. And I was looking out for my sisters. . . ." Asked by Hearing Panel member Brigandi if quantum meruit would have justified an award much higher than the one-third fee, Toby said no, "it was somewhat under. Like somewhere between $100[,000] or $200,000" less. Brashich said his hourly rate was $250. "I didn't ask for . . . all sorts of papers and accounting and all that stuff." Nor did he request a reduction.

> What I really recall is being happy to pay them the . . . 500,000. I thought they'd earned it. I was embarrassed at our family's behavior. . . . these were guys that had taken care of us. . . . my sister Deborah had messed it up terribly and they were vulnerable. It was a very unfair, bad moment.

Under cross-examination he reiterated that the lawyers told him that if the contingency fee agreement did not apply they could ask the Surrogate to award fees. But Toby had told the Surrogate he did not "recall any conversation about that." Examined by David Feureisen (Brashich's lawyer), Toby was vague about whether the lawyers' fee would be lower if the trust money were not distributed as income but insisted, "I did understand at the time that I could make maneuvers for the sake of reducing their fee, and I would not do that . . . because that would be unethical to

---

[813] This probably was Gerald K. Geist, of Hashmall Sheer & Bank, whom Brashich hired in the Callahan matter (see below).

me to make that move against the attorneys who made it possible in the first place." He had gotten advice from a "professional" that the structure of the settlement would not affect taxes because "eventually, all the taxes would have to be paid. So there's no meaningful. . . ." He also believed it would have made no difference if the distribution were in stock. But his answers reveal incomprehension of settlement. "This was the first thing that came across to me and I accepted Mr. Cardozo's assessment at this . . . very moment. And I did not return to it."

Brashich testified: "Not only did I tell [Toby] I didn't, wouldn't" represent him in any fee application, but I also "urged him to get independent counsel for himself and for his sisters. . . . And Toby told me that he had spent a great amount of time discussing not only the settlement, but also the fees with independent attorneys." In January 1990, when the third proposal was being discussed, Brashich

> told Toby that we had expended $162,000 worth of time and disbursements . . . there was an appeal. There were motions. And we agreed to a fee of somewhere around $225[,000] and $250,000. Then came that year hiatus, with all of the other attendant work, the numerous conferences, proposals, etc. And we then revisited fees somewhere in January, a year thereafter. And we agreed that a reasonable fee should be somewhere around $500,000, based on time spent, the fact that this was contingent in nature, the amount of money that we had expended, and the amount of money that Kreisler had paid in defense, and Fred Lipman had been paid in defending the action.

He was not seeking to maximize his fee, which "had nothing to do with what the outcome was." He had taken the $375,000 fee without Surrogate approval because "after practicing law for 32 years . . . I thought that once the parties had agreed . . . the fees would be blessed by the Surrogate." In response to Deborah's request that the Surrogate determine fees, Brashich filed a petition in which

> I disclosed that I had received a fee and that it had been agreed upon by the parties. I did not specify the amount of the fee in that particular paragraph of the petition. But if you just see that it's been agreed upon and that I was seeking x, y and z, it was apparent on its face.

Chapter 5

He conceded that the fee claimed from Deborah "was grounded on the contingency fee agreement," and if income had not been distributed to Babette "the contingency fee agreement would not come into play."

In response to Hearing Panel Chair Feldman, Brashich conceded Babette would have to pay tax on the distribution, so her net would be less than $1.7 million. "From the start" he had disagreed with Cardozo about the contingent fee

> because if we had gotten her income of $100 a week, were we going to get $33.33 for the rest of her life? It didn't make any sense. . . . and that was why I always negotiated from the amount of time that we had spent, $40,000 prior to trial, $162,000 at the direction of the surrogate, $225,000 when I thought we had a settlement in January and February of 1990, and finally, $500,000 in 1991.

Brashich rejected the Surrogate's finding that he "knew of the ongoing misrepresentations" about fees. "I corrected Mr. Cardozo, and I told Mr. Hecht . . . that Ben Cardozo was wrong." He offered as evidence Toby's June 20 letter to his sisters "saying that Deyan Brashich has told us that the Surrogate approves the fees." But in response to the Hearing Panel lay member he admitted he never wrote the children "specifically telling them that [he] disagreed with Mr. Cardozo." Asked if he now would do things differently, he replied:

> We had such a narrow, an ever narrowing window of opportunity to settle and not lose the premium—would I, in retrospect, put at risk the settlement evaporating, and insisting on prior approval by the surrogate? In retrospect, I would do two things. I would either take that chance and perhaps put Babette and her children at risk. Or I might tell Ben—Ben, let's get another attorney in here . . . who can efficiently move through the Surrogate's Court morass in White Plains, and get this thing approved overnight.

He attributed Emanuelli's "scathing opinion" to the fact that he might have been "a bit abrasive."

> I thought that Ben and I had done such a great job and all of a sudden we were being questioned as to what a great job we did.

I was always willing to settle. I was never given the parameters as to what fees Ben and I would finally be awarded. But even that wasn't that important. The important thing was that the settlement which Babette and her children had agreed to was being attacked.

He thought Emanuelli had done "the right thing with regard to the trusts." But his fee decision was not "fair. The guardian ad litem . . . got more than Ben and I did. The Objectant who withdrew her objections, her attorneys got a bigger fee than . . . Ben and I did." He never expected Emanuelli's opinion to result in a disciplinary complaint "because I was not the person who had participated solely in the settlement agreement, in the indemnification agreement, in the discharge and releases. . . . these were actions taken by parties represented by attorneys on both sides."

On May 26, 1992, Toby wrote a 14-page single-spaced letter to Deborah at their father's address (since she would not reveal hers), with copies to his wife, mother, father and step-mother, sisters, brother-in-law, and Brashich.[814] *"The overall purpose of this letter is to have you stop taking action that puts the trust in jeopardy, even a little bit. It is not to stop you from disputing the attorney's fees."* "[T]o me you exist as a tornado that sort of appears in my life every once in a while and causes damage for no apparent reason." Deborah was "disputing the quality of the work done by the attorneys so as to justify your complaint about their fees," putting their "public identity, character, reputation, and skills on the line." Her lawyer, Arnold Roseman, "attacked the settlement in his Objections which he promised not to do. His attack has made it possible for Ed Stern to begin action to rescind the settlement." If the stock value dropped from $10 to $5, Edward stood "to gain almost $900,000 if he can rescind the settlement," money he could spend "in legal fees and still break even to win not to mention having the satisfaction of tying Mom's money up for years. . . ." "Also, if the settlement disappears they lose *all* of their fees. They have families as well as us." "So, between their entire fee; their public identity/career; their character, integrity, and dignity; their concern for the rest of the Hechts; and their bias against you, they have plenty of reason to make it worth their while to take strong action against you." Brashich "can go for the throat and win if he needs to." In January 1990 "he proposed $350,000 instead of the $600,000 he was legally due from Mom's

---

[814] Respondent's Exhibit B3.

Chapter 5

agreement.... I asked for a detailed report on his hours and expenses, did my own calculations, asked for my own advisors, and negotiated him down to $300,000." For the next four months Deborah refused to agree, at the end of which Edward reneged. Toby and his wife "began to support Mom which we did for a year with $1000/mo from our savings in which we only had $12,000." "[F]inally, new talks were opened and they offered $8/share. This means that because of your actions the family would lose about $352,000." But in response to Brashich's threats, Edward again agreed to $10/share. Brashich now said "the first fee was no longer sufficient. We ... agreed upon $500,000. You cost the family $200,000 in legal fees." "After Ed Stern reneged: Deyan *could* have sold us out. He could have said that he had done his best.... He could have legally blackmailed us into a new fee agreement in order for him to continue...." Deborah should

> understand that I will be quite a weapon for Deyan Brashich, if he asks me to testify under oath about events that occurred to which I have first hand knowledge.... I think Mr. Roseman will be surprised at what I will say as a witness on Mr. Brashich's behalf about some of the Objections he has filed. If I am your adversary and speak to the judge about how events have unfolded in order to stop Mr. Roseman it could get really nasty.

Roseman was concerned with "being right, proving it, and making you and only you money."

> He also wanted to know why Deyan was so greedy. Wasn't $375,000 enough. I said, "Oh, you mean what you are after is making the total fee the $375,000 we have already paid. Do you then plan on having Ellie reimburse us for her share of the fee from her trust?" A looooonnnnggg silence followed. I got the feeling there was a possibility that this man was setting me up.

Roseman had patronized Toby.

> Does he think, for example, that I have not thought about what Deyan and Mr. Cordozo [sic] might have done to make the settlement income so as to get them a high fee. Does he

> think I did not bring the matter up directly and loudly with Deyan and with my own advisors? Does he think we did not check about the tax situation with many people? Does he think the judge wasn't watching this like a hawk to make sure everybody's interests were taken care of and approving of the direction the lawyers were taking.

"You and Mr. Roseman are being warned to stop fighting the way you are before people take action." "You have not been hit yet. No facts have come out."

> Lipman or the judge may try to rescind the settlement. Deyan will start to make motions and take stronger actions. If I am not satisfied shortly, I will join them with Mom, Jeanne, and Marcia to stop you.... If you quit in the middle after people engage ... or lose, they will go after you for damages. If you quit and lose they (including me) will not listen to your cries of uncle when you give up.... *If you are not competent or don't have the time to understand, stop what you are doing!!! There is no shame in that, only honor, if you have simply been naïve as Dad and Elizabeth believe.*"

He demanded that she stop objecting to the settlement. *"If I do not receive a response by the end of May, at the latest, I will begin to take action against you."*

On July 8, 1992, Deborah filed a stipulation reaffirming her agreement with the January 21, 1991, discharge and release and declaring that the sole purpose of her objections was to maintain "that the settlement was fashioned to fit a claim for fees under an attorney's retainer agreement...."[815] She sought to "make plain to all concerned, especially [her] mother and siblings, the true purpose of [her] actions particularly in light of untrue allegations that have been made to her family."

III. The Surrogate's Review

During the seven-day hearing before Emanuelli in June–August 1993, Brashich represented Cardozo and himself. Brashich offered two justifications

---

[815] Respondent's Exhibit XXX in the Surrogate's proceeding.

for his $171,000 fee claim: first that "the retainer agreement . . . is clear on its face" and Babette "ratified and joined in the petition for the payment of fees," and second "on the basis of quantum meruit."[816] Alice O'Rourke Rodd, appointed by the surrogate to represent Toby, Marcia and Jeanne, objected that Brashich had consistently denied having a quantum meruit claim. She called this a case "about greed and incompetence and deception . . . about how two attorneys destroyed a family trust, and hopefully not a family." Asked by Emanuelli if he ever told Babette she could apply to the surrogate for fees on a time and task basis, Brashich said "the question never came up." Emanuelli wondered why: "You're a lawyer." "You have an obligation . . . to tell your client." Brashich replied that "the arrangement had already been made and the issue never came up." In his deposition, Brashich said "I personally have received no money directly from the clients," insisting that the $375,000 came "through" but not "from" the trust. In other cases, he maintained, he had obtained a fee "from the estate or from the trust, without the surrogate's knowledge"; but he conceded "it would appear in the final accounting," whereas this fee did not. He argued that once the trust had disbursed money, the surrogate had no right to trace it. Although Brashich's deposition called the retainer agreement "clear and unambiguous," he now testified that "I don't understand it."

Babette testified that she had consulted four lawyers, none of whom "would even talk to me," before Elly Ente (who gave her a "bed to sleep in") recommended Cardozo. Brashich offered Toby's testimony that the $375,000 paid by the three children

> was an arm's length transaction, that I had in good faith negotiated originally a much lower fee than the one third, and that the particular agreement was passed upon not by myself, but was passed upon by five or six attorneys in the trust department of the California bank. It was passed upon by a professional estate planner, who handles millions of dollars of estates and hires attorneys on a regular basis with regard to this particular kind of work. That it was passed upon by a certified public accountant.

Emanuelli retorted that "the one that has to pass on it is this court."

---

[816] Transcript of Judicial Settlement of Account and § 2110 proceeding, June 25, 28, and 29, July 1, 2, and 19, and August 3, 1993, before Surrogate Albert J. Emanuelli.

Emanuelli: I want it to be clear: were you ever told that Babette's lawyers could come to court, get approval here of their entire fee on a time and task basis?

. . .

Toby: I did not have knowledge that at the end of all this, that anything needed to come back to the surrogate to get approval.

Ed Stern's deposition revealed that he had paid his lawyers $463,241.46; as "the moving party with the burden of proof," Cardozo and Brashich claimed at least as much. But Emanuelli said "it's really not relevant to me . . . what some other lawyers got paid." At this point in the trial (July 1), Emanuelli declared his duty "to preserve money" and expressed his concern that the $375,000 "is not earning interest." That fee did not come from Babette—"she said I'm destitute"—but "from the corpus of the trust." On July 3 he ordered Brashich and Cardozo to pay it to the guardian, who would hold it in escrow, giving them a deadline of July 12 and threatening sanctions, contempt, and incarceration. Brashich obtained a stay from the Appellate Division; on August 3, after it was lifted, he asked for 15 more days to comply because "there are quite a number of assets [that] are not liquid." Emanuelli said "you've got to do better than that . . . your asking for fifteen days is only compounding my concerns." The lawyers ultimately complied.

Deborah testified that "I had always taken care of my mother in many different ways." When Babette said she was considering retaining Cardozo "she wanted me to speak to him and see if I thought it would be a good idea." But when Deborah tried, he told her to "butt out of your mother's business." She had difficulty explaining why she had never asked the Surrogate's Court to set the lawyers' fees.

The Surrogate decided on December 15, 1994, invalidating the indemnification agreement and rejecting the settlement.[817] He found that

> the significance of the second proposal was readily apparent to Messrs. Braschich [sic] and Cardozo. If Babette were to

---

[817] File No. 1976/2260. This is Exhibit C? in the disciplinary proceeding. Cerisse Anderson, "Surrogate Slices Lawyers' Fee, Rejects Settlement," 12/22/1994 N.Y.L.J. 1 (col. 3). The AD dates Emanuelli's judgment of February 23, 1995.

CHAPTER 5

> receive and sell her share of Kreisler stock, she stood to receive more than one and a quarter million dollars to which they would apply their contingent fee retainer agreement. If the existing trust were merely split as in the first proposal, the retainer agreement would be inoperative and Brashich and Cordozo [sic] would be relegated to having their fees fixed on a quantum meruit basis. The second proposal had the potential of creating a fee of almost $600,000.00 instead of the $162,000.00 fee sought in the affidavit of legal services submitted to the Surrogate.

Cardozo's March 2, 1990, letter presented only the second proposal to Babette's four children. But

> the second proposal, without more, would result in the destruction of the trust and deprive the Hecht children of any inheritance from their grandmother. To alleviate this potential loss of inheritance and to appeal to the children's interests, Benjamin Cardozo proposed that Babette use the bulk of the funds she was to receive to create new trusts in which her children would be remaindermen. This letter was reviewed by Attorney Brashich prior to its being sent.

Emanuelli divided the trust in two. He found that "the fees sought by Attorneys Brashich and Cardozo were disproportionate to the work done and results achieved in the earlier litigation."

> It is apparent, from their correspondence, that the parties contemplated that the share of the fee to be borne by Deborah's remainder interest would be fixed on a quantum meruit basis. Despite the settlement agreement, when the . . . [Surrogate's Court] petition was filed, Brashich and Cardozo unilaterally abandoned any notion that they would be paid as agreed based on the quantity and quality of their work.

They sought $22,706.25 "for work opposing Edward's appeal and for motion practice in the Appellate Division" without explaining "why Deborah's remainder interest should bear all of the legal costs." They also sought $5,060 for the present application.

> It is instructive in considering the chameleon-like actions of Brashich and Cardozo's quest for fees in this estate to follow the role of, and the attorneys' reliance on, their retainer agreement.

Because Brewster had not awarded any income, they abandoned their retainer in their first fee application to him. "New life was breathed into their contingent fee agreement with [sic—"when"] the trust busting settlement proposal surfaced early in 1990." Although the settlement was proposed by Edward's lawyers,

> Brashich and Cardozo immediately seized on this method of settlement since it presented an opportunity to receive one-third of the entire value of the Hecht family's interest in the testamentary trust. To the exclusion of all others, they recommended this proposal to Babette and her children. The contingent fee retainer agreement laid the framework for Babette's attorneys to hit "pay dirt" at the unnecessary expense of their client.

When Babette's children objected and proposed placing the proceeds into irrevocable inter vivos trusts, the contingent fee agreement arguably applied to only the $58,000 going outright to Babette, generating a fee of just $19,140. "Because of this, the negotiated fee of $500,000.00 was sought and the retainer agreement was abandoned again," only to reappear in the present proceedings.

Emanuelli found that Brashich and Cardozo represented Babette "in a competent and professional manner," but their agreement to destroy the trust "can only serve to detract from the quality of the legal services rendered."

> Once the attorneys elected to abandon court approval for destruction of the testamentary trust and their legal fees, they diminished the value of their fees. The manner in which Brashich and Cardozo viewed the trust destruction had the immediate effect of creating a conflict of interest between their client and themselves. . . . the "reasonable fee" to which Brashich and Cardozo now deemed themselves entitled was more than three times their own filed estimates of the value of their services. Moreover, the attorneys admitted that . . .

Babette's receipt of the funds was really not "outright" but only constructive, "passing through" into separate trusts shortly after the closing. This potential windfall caused the attorneys to abandon any semblance of undivided loyalty to their client and to advocate a settlement which, on balance, was of more benefit to themselves and to Stern than to their own client.

They also

> did not inform Babette of the consequences of the alternate split trust-no distribution proposal or that this alternate method would result in no recovery for them under the contingent fee arrangement. They continued to insist that if the retainer agreement did not apply, they would be denied fees altogether. They did not tell Babette or the remaindermen of the court's invitation to submit their fee application on a quantum meruit basis or that they had already filed an affidavit for additional services. They permitted their client to enter into an open-ended and potentially devastating indemnification agreement for the sole benefit of Edward Stern to protect him against the consequences of their failure to secure court approval of the settlement. Indeed, they caused the Hecht family to wrongly believe that the court had no interest in, or jurisdiction over, the proposed settlement. They failed to caution their client concerning the invalidity of the unapproved termination of the testamentary trust. . . . Their intransigence and steadfast refusal to acknowledge their misrepresentation and ethical conflicts contributed heavily toward having to resolve the issues in open court leading to further unnecessary legal fees throughout. Finally, they enjoyed the use of the $375,000 removed from the trust without court approval.

Emanuelli granted the lawyers' petition for a quantum meruit fee, setting it at $165,000, but then deducted $50,000 for "unnecessary legal and expert fees incurred by the guardian." He approved $87,000 for Rodd, $48,000 for Bottger, $8,000 for the guardian's tax expert, and $151,000 for Edward's lawyer.

Babette, Cardozo, and Brashich appealed.[818] Babette and her three children denied being deceived by Cardozo and Brashich. Deborah "did not testify to having been deceived." "Thus, two respected attorneys have been publicly damned by the surrogate...." Babette had stated in an April 6, 1995, affidavit:

> Had it not been for the continued perseverance, high ethical conduct and personal selflessness of Benjamin M. Cardozo and Deyan Ranko Brashich for these many years, I would still be sleeping on a futon, starving in an unfurnished apartment.... The settlement was negotiated by intelligent, highly educated individuals and was agreed upon by all those concerned. All of the individuals sought independent counsel for financial and tax advice.... Having read the surrogate's accusations, I wish to state absolutely that there was no deception practiced upon me or any of my children

Jerry Geist, who represented Toby, Jeanne, and Marcia, said at the trial that his clients would testify "that they sought independent counsel and advise [sic] from past professionals and other sources" and "were not tricked or deceived." The brief argued that the proposal that did not generate a contingent fee was "*shot down by Edward and his New York counsel and not by Cardozo or Brashich.*" Because of *Matter of Weeks*, "the division of the existing trust into two trusts ... was never available ... *even though the surrogate bottomed his finding of deceit on its availability.*"

> In finally reaching the decision not to bring the settlement to the surrogate, Lipman was motivated by the following considerations: the advice of Edward's New York lawyer, Bashian, that it was not necessary ... Deborah's constant wavering which caused Lipman to fear that the settlement might fall apart during a lengthy surrogate's court proceeding ... and; Kreisler's agreement to pay $10 a share for the stock that was then trading at $8 which concerned Lipman that if the stock fell anymore, Kreisler would walk out of the settlement.... in view of the surrogate' [sic] criticism of Brashich and Cardozo,

---

[818] Brief by Edward L. Sadowsky, Millard Midonick, and Eric Proshansky, of Tenzer Greenblatt, filed September 21, 1995.

it must be noted that *it was Brashich and Cardozo that took the initiative which brought the settlement to the attention of Surrogate Emanuelli.*

Emanuelli's fee award was "approximately equal to their fee application to Surrogate Brewster, ignoring the fact that the fee application had been made several years earlier and before the intensive and protracted settlement negotiations." Emanuelli awarded all the lawyers "$409,000, as compared with the $375,000 that had been paid to Brashich and Cardozo pursuant to the settlement agreement." They urged the court to apply retroactively an August 1995 law obviating the need for a guardian or surrogate approval of the settlement. Babette "had no fiduciary duty to obtain the approval of the surrogate and was barred by the settlement agreement from doing so." Many cases hold that the surrogate could only approve or reject the settlement, not modify it. "Since the legal fees were a component of the settlement, he could not modify so much of it relating to those fees." The court could only "send the parties back to the bargaining table."

> It is difficult to avoid the conclusion that the surrogate was motivated in good measure by his finding that Babette's attorneys had deceived her, a conclusion he had reached even before the trial but which is not supported by the trial record. . . . A fee of $375,000 for these attorneys who labored for seven years with no compensation, except for the initial retainer of $7,500, and who produced an excellent result in an extremely complex and difficult matter was not excessive. . . . the services of [Deborah's] attorneys conferred no benefit on the trust and must be disallowed. . . . the guardian ad litem did nothing more than support the sentiments expressed by Surrogate Emanuelli. . . .

Deborah's brief argued that Babette "was not aggrieved by the Surrogate's decree, and thus lacks standing to prosecute the appeal."[819] Of the 350 hours Cardozo claimed to justify his $162,000 fee, "103 hours were 'blank,' containing no description of the task performed." Cardozo's April 2, 1990, letter "was only 'partially' true. In fact, the Surrogate's Court could still have entertained settlement discussions, and an appellate loss

---

[819] Filed February 9, 1996, by Arnold D. Roseman and Lawrence F. Fay, of Kent, Hazzard.

would not have left the lawyers with 'nothing.'" "Mr. Brashich knew that these representations were not 'fair,' but Mr. Hecht did not; the letter persuaded him that there would be no point in seeing the surrogate." Contrary to Geist's representations, none of the children testified "they had not been tricked or deceived." Only Toby testified, "and his testimony established that he had, in fact, been deceived...." Brashich and Cardozo

> seek to excuse their failure to convey the trust-splitting proposal, by attributing it to Gary Bashian's opinion that the proposal would violate *Weeks*; but Bashian's opinion letter was dated January 9, 1990, more than one month before Lipman made the proposal to go to the surrogate with the two alternatives.

Brashich and Cardozo "did not, as their brief contends, 'see to it that the settlement was put before the surrogate for his review.'"

> It was Deborah's answer that first accurately portrayed the terms of the settlement, and pointed out that even the unlawful termination of the trust did not accommodate the one-third contingency fee because Babette never received the stock, or the proceeds of its sale outright.

"Had Brashich and Cardozo conveyed to the Hecht family Lipman's plan to present the surrogate with two alternative settlements... the case would undoubtedly have been settled a year earlier" and their "fee would have been fixed by the surrogate."

The guardian's brief argued that Brashich and Cardozo "knew that the premature termination of a testamentary trust in New York was illegal" and "had already failed to convince Surrogate Brewster that the shares of stock in the corpus of the trust should be considered income."[820]

> Nevertheless, the two attorneys immediately embarked on a program to convince their client and her children... to accept the trust-termination proposal, including their large fees. Convincing Babette of any proposal... was no problem since,

---

[820] Filed January 26, 1996, by Walter Bottger.

CHAPTER 5

> as she testified, "I did everything they ... wanted me to do." So Brashich and Cardozo misled her.

They took "a more aggressive approach" with the children. In two letters in November 1989 they had expressed confidence that Brewster's decision would be upheld on appeal; but after Lipman floated his trust-termination proposal they suddenly expressed doubts about the outcome. Their claim to have brought the settlement to the surrogate's attention was "disingenuous," because they failed to inform him that they had already received $375,000 in fees. "Babette's only conceivable role in this proceeding is to provide cover for Brashich and Cardozo in their continued assault on her trust funds."

> [B]y selling the trust-termination proposal to their client and the remaindermen through fraud and deceit, and then exposing her to huge indemnifications and several years of additional litigation, appellants Brashich and Cardozo can hardly be said to have benefited their client. . . . The two attorneys should be pleased that the surrogate did not see fit to charge them the entire amount of their award, and more.

The Appellate Division affirmed on May 28, 1996, rejecting both Babette's objection to the vacatur of the settlement and her lawyers' objection to their fees.[821] On February 18, 1997, Emanuelli ruled on the guardian's request for an additional $52,686 for the 220 hours devoted to the appeal, to be charged to Cardozo and Brashich.[822] This included successfully resisting their motion to stay the surrogate's decision and successfully objecting to their excising 80 percent of the record, "including all the testimony and documentary evidence" of their "deceptions and illegalities." Emanuelli approved $46,300 for the guardian and castigated

> the naked attempt by Brashich and Cardozo to manipulate the record on appeal by filing a patently defective appendix. The court considers such conduct by these attorneys as symptomatic of the same pattern of deceptive and manipulative practices

---

[821] Matter of Stern, 227 A.D.2d 636, 643 N.Y.S.2d 395 (2d Dep't 1996).
[822] Matter of Stern, 2/18/1997 N.Y.L.J. 33 (col. 4).

that precipitated the underlying litigation and for which they were previously surcharged on appeal.

But though their "duplicitous, self-serving actions" justified holding them personally liable, he declined to do so in light of the need "to preserve trust assets" and his fear "that any such award might only precipitate a further appeal."

IV. The First Disciplinary Proceeding

The DDC charged Cardozo and Brashich with dishonesty, fraud, deceit, or misrepresentation, conduct prejudicial to the administration of justice), and personal conflict of interest.[823] On September 17, 1997, the Appellate Division found that the Surrogate's decision was collateral estoppel on liability and ordered a hearing on sanctions.

Edelstein introduced an unsigned, undated typewritten letter from Babette to Deborah[824] (apparently written between Emanuelli's decision and the Appellate Division's affirmation). Babette denied authorship: she never had a typewriter with this typeface, "and there are words in there that I don't use." But she did "remember saying some of these words" and "did feel that way." Cardozo testified Babette sent it to him. "She wrote it. . . . she forgot she wrote it."

In the letter she took "a dramatic step" to "finish whatever is left of our neurotic, disenchanted relationship." "Please do not refer to me or of me anymore as your 'mom or mother.'" Deborah had "made a mockery of my parenting, my love—me." "I am afraid of you. I see you with no conscience, which in turn makes you dangerous." Although Edward had breached his fiduciary trust "to pursue his own goals, gains, and greed," Babette's trust also had been "greatly depleted" by Deborah "and Bill Kane (who did not hang around to see the results of his evil ways . . .)." Babette would not let herself "be agitated by mad antics." She was "horrified and chagrined by what [Deborah] did to my attorneys."

---

[823] DR 1-102(a)(4), 1-102(a)(8) (no longer in effect), and 5-101(a). The Hearing Panel—Charlotte M. Fischman, chair, John E. Brigandi, Justin Feldman, and Patricia Handal (the lay member)—heard testimony on December 12, 1997, and January 15 and 21 and February 4 and 11, 1998. Mady J. Edelstein appeared for the DDC, Sarah D. McShea for Benjamin Cardozo, and John R. Bartels, Jr., and David Feureisen for Deyan Brashich.

[824] Staff Exhibit C to Staff Exhibit 11.

Chapter 5

> All you got out of your escapade was to make the two of them wrong, me stupid and you righteous. . . . Always remember, they secured your inheritance for you and you screwed them. From my grave, I will remind you daily that every penny you spend is dirty, greedy blood money.
>
> The judge is just a man supported by politicians and usually appointed with his own interests and agenda. He did not have the class to deal with my attorneys. Can you imagine giving those guardian angels $135,000 at your behest. What a classless, political act. You know he "owed" them and this was payback time.
>
> Wherever your grandparents are, I hope they are admonishing you with their displeasure. What did your attorneys do but create havoc and collect a large sum of our money. . . . they were out to ruin the only men who would talk to me. My gentlemen worked hard for you and me and you thought I was used. I wasn't. You were had. . . . The judge juggled the money as he saw fit and many people were hurt—what a joke. You lost again.

She predicted what a bad mother Deborah would be (if she succeeded in conceiving with Kane's frozen sperm) and ended with a "proposal" she was sending to her own attorneys, Deborah's lawyer (Roseman) and father, Edward, and a few others. If it was "not heeded, I will expand the list of recipients and let more know the other side of the poor sad woman who wants her baby." Babette wanted the trust administered in California by Toby and Deborah to sign a document "stating you will NEVER challenge any part of the trust again and you will not be able to cheat us again."

> If this is not forthcoming by the end of the month, I will proceed with plan #2. It will be more effective and embarrassing for you than I think even you would like to consider. You've been playing hardball with me long enough, now it's my turn. . . .
>
> I suggest you show this letter to your therapist, your attorney and your friends. . . . There is no possible reason for you not to accept my proposal except for your own rage, anger and jealousy.

Toby's testimony was equally critical of Emanuelli, who "never addressed the dire situation that my mother was in, that there was no guarantee they were going to get anything from anywhere." "I was like stunned at his disinterest. He did not want to hear from me. He did not want to talk to me." "I believe that I was more misled by Judge Emanuelli than I ever was by these gentlemen. . . . I found him presumptive and assumptive, and never talked to the people concerned." "What I did in front of him was not what I considered a satisfactory testifying. Nor was the guardian ad litem, who was supposed to represent us and act in our interest, in the slightest bit interested." "I'm put off by somebody who holds that position, who never speaks to me. He presumes on my behalf, when I'm an adult, to know what is best for me, without checking with me." (The guardian actually represented Babette's grandchildren, born and unborn.)

Cardozo's lawyer, McShea, called Babette, now 70 and living in San Diego. She testified that both lawyers "were in constant communication with me. . . . Mostly they called me. . . . they told me what was going on. They asked my opinion." But "by that time they had worked so hard for me and had done so well for me, and they knew much better than I did, so that's what I did." She "vaguely" remembered the settlement proposal but could not recall approving it. "The only thing I can think of is I didn't want my brother having anything to do with what I had, after his behavior." But she didn't know if she had told her lawyers to do anything. "It's been a long time and I'm old." Her four children had their own lawyer, which "Mr. Brashich said that they should absolutely have" because Cardozo and he "were representing me." "But I have to tell you that I have a very astute son who is a very fine businessman. And whatever they decided between them, that was not my forte." Asked how she felt about her lawyers, Babette said "Do you think I would have flown 6,000 miles in two days to be here for them if I didn't think that my life would be nothing if they hadn't done what they did?" She did not believe they had failed to inform her of a settlement proposal that would have been better for her but worse for them. "I never ever didn't think that they didn't have my best interest at heart. . . ." She "found them very—for me, very honorable" and felt "very protected" by them. "I've lived alone for 25 years and I didn't have anybody to go home and pat me on the back." She had suffered "betrayal from my daughter, my brother destroying me." "I didn't go to another lawyer . . . because I think they were unjustly chastised." She directed most of her anger at Emanuelli. "I was horrified that he took the trust away . . . it's in a trust

CHAPTER 5

now that if I get sick or something happens, I can't touch it . . . if I get Alzheimer's or if I get some terrible disease, I don't know what happens." She felt that the $500,000 fee was fair and claimed to understand the contingent fee agreement. But asked if she had been shown other fee calculations she said only that "there were always a lot of numbers that everybody was coming up with. But I don't know especially." On cross-examination she conceded that Brashich and Cardozo said the Surrogate's decision

> was very unfair, too. . . . when he took away the trust and did all of that and then also had a Guardian ad litem for grandchildren that he never even knew and she [the guardian] was part of a political system up there . . . that was like very upsetting to a poor little person like me who doesn't know anything.

Charles Edward Ramos, a civil court judge, testified that Brashich "seems to comply with what has to be done."

> What I perceive and what I experienced as a practicing attorney in the Surrogate's Court, Westchester County . . . it's not a level playing field . . . when I would appear in that court as an attorney from Manhattan . . . I felt uncomfortable and unwelcome.

On cross-examination he reiterated: "there is a problem with the upstate counties . . . there is a prejudice or predilection in favor of local counsel. . . ."

Cardozo, who would be 83 in May, told the Hearing Panel he was "not in the active practice of law. I have no pending cases, contested or uncontested." He still did some real estate transactions, wills, estate planning, and investment counseling. "I've never done any serious litigation" and always hired counsel for that. He had tried only one case in the previous 30 years. In 1990 he broke his hip and had it replaced; in 1992 he had heart bypass; he also had cataract surgery on his right eye, which had macular degeneration and no sight, and an inoperable cataract in his left. In August 1997 he had an operation on his other hip. He used hearing aids.

Millard L. Midonick was admitted in 1937 and had been a family court judge from 1962 to 1971 and New York County Surrogate from 1972 to 1982. Now a member of Tenzer Greenblatt, he handled Babette's appeal of Emanuelli's decision; he had not known Cardozo before. Hearing Panel member Feldman had known Midonick for about 50 years. Midonick said he had tried "to persuade the Committee not to bring this case." Three of Babette's children had independent counsel.

> And they didn't regard themselves as deceived. And they still don't. And even . . . Deborah, who was . . . a difficult sibling and daughter who didn't like to pay for what she gained from this representation, she didn't think she was deceived.

"Deceived" was an "unfortunate" word. Emanuelli "could have said that the fees were . . . unreasonable and reduce[d] them. . . . one man's unreasonableness is another man's appropriate fee." "The risks of taking on this client and not getting paid as lawyers were enormous." Feldman would not have taken the case. Cardozo and Brashich

> saw Stern paying himself $150,000 a year as a salary . . . paying no dividends, plowing all the money back into the corporation to make himself more secure, while his sister was starving . . . the only reason she didn't starve actually was that her children were giving her a little money. And she didn't have a bed to sleep on.

The $7,500 retainer "isn't pay . . . for a mess like this. They worked for seven years on this. . . . they had to get lawyers from Philadelphia, from Westchester. . . ." "[A]s everybody in the law practice knows, if you take a terrible risk and things turn out much better than you could have hoped . . . you're entitled to be paid contingency rates." One of the lawyers, who was "perhaps more expert than they were . . . testified that . . . this is the most difficult settlement . . . he'd ever seen in his life . . . and I don't think there was any other way to settle it than the way they did. . . ." "There wasn't any option . . . the people who were calling the shots were the lawyers for Stern." Had Midonick been Surrogate in this case he would have "just said it was an improper fee. Not a wrongful thing . . . not necessary to discipline anybody about . . . I might have given a quarter of a million dollars instead of the half million they wanted to take." "I think I've had more experience than Judge Emanuelli."

McShea called several character witnesses. Edward Hayes was a trusts and estates lawyer who had sublet space to Cardozo for nine years, but his testimony was worthless. Robert W. Mullen, who had a law office

CHAPTER 5

in the same suite, said Cardozo "was loyal to his client and went forward full blast for her and her children. And had to handle a slightly dysfunctional family...." During the more than 30 years Sally Broido had known Cardozo he had handled her divorce, the death of her second husband, and all her finances. He suggested an annual retainer rather than hourly billing "because at that time I was really seeing him sometimes four times a week ... and when he thought I needed it, he would even come to my house just to stop in and see if I was o.k." She had to insist on raising the fee. After reading the Surrogate's decision she changed her opinion of *Emanuelli*, not Cardozo. Since Sylvia G. Cline met Cardozo in 1975 he had represented her in buying and selling apartments and drafting her will. Her opinion of him did not change after reading Emanuelli's decision. "Perhaps an honest mistake was made, but in no way would it have been intentional." "He's a gentleman of the old school." Robinson J. Strong knew Cardozo from birth, was the beneficiary of a trust he had drafted, and had worked for him recently. She testified to the usual character traits.

The DDC submitted the record of Brashich's six admonitions for neglect between 1987 and 1990.

1. Carol A. Harding retained him in June 1987 to compel her husband to make payments under their separation agreement. Brashich entrusted the motion to a student, who failed to serve it; he had it redrawn in September and the same student failed again. Brashich prepared the papers a third time, but Harding obtained new counsel. The DDC found that "at one point in time you confused Ms. Harding's matter with another case you were handling."
2. Brashich took over a lawsuit for Frank M. Puzio in 1984 but did nothing for four-and-a-half years and failed to communicate until Puzio filed a complaint.
3. Brashich accepted Faith Saunders's personal injury action against New York City in 1987. Although both she and the referring attorney told him the matter had been removed from the calendar and would be statutorily dismissed if not restored within a year, he did nothing until the summer of 1989, when the referring attorney asked for the file back.
4. In 1991 Brashich failed to follow the rules for withdrawing from pending litigation on behalf of Judith Squiccimarro or to advise the court or opposing counsel, resulting in a default judgment.

5. Sylvia Brady retained Brashich in 1987 in a personal injury matter. But after filing the summons and complaint and trying to settle it he did nothing until May 1991 and failed to communicate with her. The DDC wrote: "more severe discipline has not been imposed only because of your family difficulties and your attempt to advance Ms. Brady's case since May 1991," warning that it would seriously consider filing formal charges for a repetition.
6. After Maja Milenkovic retained Brashich in July 1990 for a divorce he failed to finalize it for two years, doing nothing between April and October 1991.

Brashich testified that he had been born in Belgrade in 1940. Because his father was in the anti-Nazi resistance, the family suffered during the war; after it they made a hair-raising escape from the communist regime, reaching the United States in 1949. Brashich worked to help pay his way through Trinity School in New York and as a welder and painter to pay for Trinity College in Hartford. He graduated from NYU Law School in 1965 and began practicing with a partner. In 1983 the partner started to decline, losing his sight, his family, and his ability to practice. The firm dissolved on August 1, 1985, leaving Brashich "with all of the debts of the partnership, which I had to pay off."

He represented the Serbian Orthodox Church before the U.S. Supreme Court, which led to pro bono work on "a great number of constitutional issues which had nothing to do with the church." One such client was Nicola Kavaja, convicted of terrorist attacks on Eastern European consulates in the United States. While on bail pending appeal in 1979, Kavaja hijacked a plane at LaGuardia, carrying 30 sticks of dynamite, forcing it to fly to O'Hare, with 130 people on board.[825] At the FBI's request, Brashich negotiated for 10 to 15 hours, convincing Kavaja to accept him as a hostage in lieu of the passengers and flight attendants. They flew to JFK, changed planes, and took off for Africa; but Brashich persuaded Kavaja to divert to Shannon and ultimately surrender. Brashich also had tutored remedial history at Columbia School of General Studies for two to three years and been an adjunct at Pace Law School for seven.

He had an apartment on Fifth Avenue and a house in Washington, Connecticut; all three of his daughters had attended Trinity School and

---

[825] Respondent's Exhibit B5: New York Post, June 21, 1979, p. 1: "Hijacker Gives Up In Ireland."

private colleges. He had divorced and remarried in 1986, the year his oldest daughter, Alexis, 18, was diagnosed with uterine cancer, requiring six months of treatment not covered by insurance. His only sibling, Ned, was the victim of "bureaucratic infighting" in the foreign service. Brashich saved his brother's pension; but this campaign preoccupied him for 9 to 12 months between 1986 and 1989. During those years his 75-year-old widowed mother was hospitalized at least five times, and so was her 96-year-old mother. He drove the 110 miles to their home in New Suffolk, Long Island, "two, three, four times a week sometimes." When his mother was in hospital he sometimes had to put his grandmother in a home for the elderly. "I can't tell you how many times I remember having to pull off the road on exit 67—64, in that rest stop, having to catch 15 hours to 15 minutes of sleep, whether it was during the day or at night."

On Christmas Eve 1988 (just before Surrogate Brewster tried Babette's case) Brashich's mother had a stroke. From then until her death in 1993 "she was totally paralyzed, fed through her stomach . . . in a facility in Port Jefferson." But she was "totally alert." He would read her the Serbian newspapers "and she would comprehend, nod, blink her eyes, grimace." On Sundays he would visit her with either his two older daughters (from his first marriage) or his youngest (from his second), because the two families would not talk to each other. He also cared for his first wife. He had to give up teaching at Pace "even though I enjoyed it." In 1992 or 1993 his middle daughter, Audrey, was diagnosed with Hodgkin's lymphoma during her first semester at Brown. Although she was covered by Brown's health plan, he brought her to Sloan Kettering in New York "notwithstanding the difference in costs and rates." "She dropped out of school. She had been a model. She lost all of her hair." "She became a recluse. . . . Attended support groups, but for that year and a half, she was not functioning." During this period he could not visit his mother. "I sleep walked. I just coped . . . it was just treading water . . . keeping alive—getting the most important things done."

Four of the admonitions between May 1, 1989, and August 11, 1992, "were totally justified." There were problems of service in two matrimonial matters.

> I took the priorities that I had with regard to my family, more importantly than an undefended matrimonial. And I did not respond to the clients. And I was wrong with regard to that. . . .

But whenever any of these problems came up, the first thing I did was put that particular problem on a fast track. And every one of the six matters was taken care of.

He had complied with the last admonition on August 11, 1992, "to limit your practice to cases that you have the time and resources to handle in a prompt and professional manner." He now realized "I should have made a motion to be relieved in at least the hospital case and this particular Brady case." But his many family tragedies did not affect his ability to represent Babette "because this one I paid attention to." His mother died in 1993; the following year his grandmother died, his daughter Audrey recovered, "and things went back to normal." He returned to Yugoslavia for the first time in 1993, bringing medical supplies to Montenegro, which led him to represent many Yugoslav business clients. His practice was "successful and thriving." But he continued doing pro bono work for the Albanian Roman Catholic and Muslim communities in the Bronx.

Brashich offered several character witnesses. Caroline Shannon had been his legal secretary in 1974–1976 and 1988–1994, sharing a room and overhearing most phone conversations. After his mother's stroke Brashich visited her at least one full day a week. "I think he was like, physically . . . dead after seeing her." "[W]hen it came to talking about his mother . . . he would start to cry because it really hurt him and it was really draining on him." Sometimes this "would make him work harder . . . there would be like this frenzy. And sometimes things got neglected. . . . certain things were almost like too close to home for him to deal with." At the height of the Stern trust negotiations Babette called the office one or twice a day and Toby daily. "Mr. Brashich made it clear to Toby that he was not Toby's attorney." Under cross-examination Shannon said:

> I thought Emanuelli was off his rocker, in plain English. . . . [Brashich] did not do anything wrong. Mr. Cardozo did not do anything wrong. And the inferences that . . . I did something wrong . . . I take that really personally. . . . [W]hat he found interesting about the case was . . . here he had a woman with four kids. Why weren't these four kids helping her? They thought their mother was crazy. Her son told me that.

Chapter 5

Edith Blumberg, admitted in 1963, met Brashich in 1969 when she was at Bronx Legal Services and suing Judge Florence M. Kelley to compel personal instead of mail service in family court. He offered to file an amicus brief and also handled a case against the Port Authority for building chapels. "He has been particularly generous with one very difficult case that I have been working on for a number of years," for which he never billed. He had referred cases to her (when she entered private practice) without ever requesting a forwarding fee.

John Walshe had worked for Brashich as a clerk before being admitted in 1977; since then they had collaborated in several cases. Brashich had "a very, very busy practice. He's running in circles. He's keeping a lot of balls in the air.... He's back and forth to Yugoslavia fairly regularly."

Edelstein recommended public censure for Cardozo (who was no longer practicing)[826] and six months suspension for Brashich. McShea requested a private reprimand for Cardozo since "the public interest reasons for imposing a public censure upon him don't really apply," and "he will suffer in a way that other attorneys do not, from a public censure ... because of his name, because of his family tie to one of New York's most prominent jurists...."[827] The case would appear on the front page of the *New York Law Journal*. Bartels spoke of Babette's and Toby's "love" for Brashich. "I don't know who, among us, could look back and say with certainty that either he or she could have handled that situation and these pressures of this settlement with this family, as well even as he did." He was not "motivated primarily by money." His children were very successful. "He paid for all this." He read the newspaper to his paralyzed mother. The $7,500 retainer "didn't pay for anything, and they fought it for seven years" and "got her a fund of $1,750,000." They negotiated a $3 premium (when the stock had dropped to $7) although "Lipman was screaming, this Kreisler board won't go for it." Deborah was "part of a totally dysfunctional family." Even after agreeing to submit the fee to the Surrogate "she flipped and brought the settlement into dispute." "What did Brashich and Cardozo get for seven years work going uphill against a public company, a trustee who was a son of a gun, fully funded, a national law firm? They got $110,000." "I don't think this Panel can look at Brashich or Cardozo and think the hell that they've gone through ... hasn't both taught

---

[826] But he was listed in the FindLaw, West Legal, and Martindale-Hubbell Directories in 2006.
[827] Benjamin N. Cardozo.

them a lesson, and won't be a sear [sic] and a brand on them for the rest of their careers."

The Hearing Panel Report[828] found Emanuelli's decision collateral estoppel for the following:

1. Both lawyers had presented Babette with only the trust destruction proposal, which generated taxable income and their one-third contingent fee, without mentioning the split trust proposal.
2. They failed to disclose that the court could fix legal fees on a quantum meruit basis.
3. They led Babette and her children to believe that unless they accepted the settlement as presented the lawyers would receive no fee.
4. They misrepresented that Surrogate Brewster would not meet with the children.
5. They illegally terminated the trust without court approval.
6. They agreed to illegal indemnification of Edward.
7. Their fee petition failed to disclose that they had already received $375,000 without notice to or approval by the court.

The Panel accepted the staff recommendations on sanctions. The lawyers' "self-interest was no greater than that always 'inherent in contingent fees.'" The respondents brought the settlement to the surrogate's attention. Emanuelli's findings "may have been unduly harsh because of the absence of a history between him and the respondents—who had previously dealt with Surrogate Brewster." The panel considered Cardozo's long unblemished career, disabilities, age, and semi-retirement. It was persuaded by the character witnesses that he was "not motivated by money." Some panel members took into account Brashich's personal tragedies and his role in ending the skyjacking. He had tried to correct Cardozo's errors. The Panel noted the "toll on their professional reputations and personal lives" since Emanuelli's opinion. The respondents "appeared candid in expressing their remorse." "We thus underscore that in the First Department, '[the] belief that [a] lengthy disciplinary proceeding has had a chastening effect upon the Respondent[s]' may be considered in mitigation." But "the already public notoriety of this matter in published judicial

---

[828] June 16, 1998.

CHAPTER 5

proceedings suggests the appropriateness of a public rather than a private sanction."[829]

In response to the DDC memo urging confirmation of the report, McShea said it would be

> unfortunate and sad if Mr. Cardozo, who has had a long distinguished and completely unblemished career, were publicly censured. Since Surrogate Emanuelli's decision, Mr. Cardozo has had to defend himself in appellate and disciplinary proceedings; he has had to forfeit fees which his client willingly paid to him; he has had to retain lawyers to represent him; and he has devoted countless hours that should have been spent with his grandchildren to appearances before courts and hearing panels, explaining his conduct and his intentions in representing his devoted and still-loyal client Babette Rose. Mr. Cardozo is remorseful, chastened and saddened by all this.

Edelstein objected to the respondents' attempt to resist the collateral estoppel effect of Emanuelli's decision. McShea retorted that the Appellate Division *should* reject those findings.

But the Appellate Division basically adopted the report.[830] Public discipline was warranted "in any case involving deliberate deceit of a client arising out of self-interest." It was "abundantly clear" that Cardozo "sought to deceive" Babette and her children "in order to obtain a higher fee." But because "Cardozo committed the overt acts of misrepresentation" and Brashich "simply failed to correct all of Cardozo's misstatements" and offered "extraordinary" mitigating factors, it reduced his penalty to public censure.

V. The Second Disciplinary Proceeding

Within three years, however, another charge was filed against Brashich for his representation of Ljubica Callahan as executrix and administratrix of the estate of her deceased husband, Thomas, in state and federal trials

---

[829] The New York Law Journal reported both of Emanuelli's decisions: cutting the two lawyers' fee request, 12/22/1994 N.Y.L.J. 1, and granting the guardian's fee request, 2/18/1997 N.Y.L.J. 33.
[830] Matter of Brashich, 250 A.D.22 71, 680 N.Y.S.2d 214 (1st Dep't 1998).

concerning the validity of two wills, a foreclosure action, and the sale of estate property. After a long marriage, Thomas Callahan's first wife died in the early 1980s, when he was in his eighties. He hired Ljubica as a housekeeper and then married her. Although she spoke little English, she had a business degree and had managed boutiques in the Majestic Hotel (Belgrade's equivalent of The Plaza). At his death on November 9, 1986, he owned a house on Post Lane, Quogue (Long Island), and (through the Shinnecock Bait & Tackle Co.: SB&T Corp.) a bar, restaurant, and tackle shop on Dune Road, Southampton. His only other asset was a $31,960.91 bank account. Ljubica retained Brashich at the suggestion of Serbian friends. She offered for probate a May 27, 1986, will naming her executrix, but Callahan's relatives challenged it. After a first mistrial, a second jury found on May 18, 1988, that it was procured by undue influence, and her appointment was revoked on August 5. The Appellate Division affirmed on November 6, 1989.[831] After a second jury trial in September and October 1990, another will dated December 15, 1985 (identical to the first but not naming her executrix) was admitted to probate on November 19, 1990, and Ljubica appointed administratrix. On June 30, 1989, the Surrogate also removed Charles Rodgers as preliminary executor because he offered the later will for probate but not the earlier.

Since Ljubica needed cash to support herself and run the shop, Acting Surrogate Snellenburg approved an order on February 5, 1988, allowing her to hypothecate the property to North Fork Bank for a one-year $200,000 loan, $100,000 for her living expenses, $50,000 to fund the estate, and $50,000 to operate the bar. By the time she was removed as executrix six months later she had spent it all. The bank foreclosed, selling the shop in 1990 for $1,430,000 (although it had been optioned for $2 million three years earlier). Brashich represented her in this matter. On October 10, 1990, on Brashich's advice, Ljubica brought a federal civil action against preliminary executor Charles Rodgers for failing to sell the shop for $1,600,000; he answered that a court order prohibited him from selling it for less than $2,550,000; the jury believed his version. Although Brashich took this on contingency, Rodgers claimed $43,000 to defend it.

In July 1993 Ljubica petitioned the Surrogate's Court to settle the accounting. In October 1994 she moved to amend the petition to settle claims against the estate, including Brashich's fees. In July 1997 Surrogate

---

[831] Matter of Callahan, 155 A.D.2d 454, 547 N.Y.S.2d 113 (2d Dept. 1989).

Chapter 5

Gail Prudenti ordered a bench trial of objections to Ljubica's accounting, including Brashich's $270,000 in fees and disbursements. (These objections must have been filed by Callahan's disgruntled relatives, even though they could not benefit, Ljubica being the sole legatee.) In his October 25, 1999, affirmation of services, Brashich requested $250/hour, citing "extensive experience in litigated surrogate court matters . . . Matter of Hecht . . . being of note." (The Appellate Division had affirmed his public reprimand less than a year earlier.) At the disciplinary hearing he testified that

> prior to being retained by Mrs. Callahan, I had at least 50 to 60 reported decisions on various issues, both before state courts and federal courts. I had litigated a number of estate matters, not only in New York, but in Connecticut and in Florida. $250 in 1988 was my normal billing rate.

During a six-day trial before Suffolk County Acting Surrogate Weber in February 2000, Brashich requested approval of the $189,897.45 Ljubica had already paid him as of 1990 and sought additional fees. In fact, she had paid more than $250,000, $200,000 on November 30, 1990 (the date she obtained the mortgage, which had been approved for other purposes). Brashich explained at the disciplinary hearing that after payment of taxes and brokers' fees there was less than $1 million in cash and Ljubica's specific bequest was $1 million.

> After that was done, I met with Mrs. Callahan and we went over the costs and expenses and we agreed to a fee. . . . most of my meetings with Mrs. Callahan were at the end of Long Island.

He claimed that the entire dispute lasted ten years because a 1992 petition for an accounting was not resolved until May 30, 2000.

That day the Surrogate found that Brashich had received $255,343.89 for legal services and expenses and on November 30, 1999, Ljubica had paid an additional $32,668 to the law firm of Hashmall, Sheer, Bank & Geist and $25,000 to the tax accounting firm Berman, Goldstein, Tillman & Co. Brashach had not obtained court approval for any of these. Ljubica totally relied on Brashich's advice because he spoke Serbo-Croatian. He prepared checks and papers for her signature. Of the 939.90 hours he claimed, 539.05 were for the trial that found Ljubica had exercised undue influence and another 39.5 for the unsuccessful appeal; these fees of $144,637 were not allowable against the estate since they did not benefit it. The Surrogate also reduced Brashich's $8,675 fee for a routine mortgage closing and loan application and his fee for the second probate proceeding from $30,250 (for 121 hours) to $10,000. Although Brashich had had Ljubica pay Hashmall $32,000 to act as trial counsel in probate proceeding, Brashich testified "that neither he nor Mr. Hashmall had extensive experience in probate or surrogate's matters. . . ." Brashich told the disciplinary proceeding that he had been the sole attorney of record and the only one who participated, but because "at risk was $2 million," he "decided that in the first aborted trial and the second full trial, that I needed someone to second seat me." There was an issue of

> whether or not the marriage was ever consummated. Mrs. Callahan was at that time in her early sixties. Mr. Callahan was in his late seventies, I believe . . . the litigation was extremely bitter. . . . the Donovan side of Mr. Callahan's family did not accept Mrs. Callahan . . . it was more of a feud than litigation.

The Surrogate disapproved the "unreasonable" $25,000 paid to accountants for preparing the "relatively simple" tax return for an estate with only five assets and no liabilities and reduced Brashich's fee for doing so to $5,000. If he "felt he was not qualified to file the tax returns required in this case, for example, either he should not have initially accepted the task of representation of the Estate at all; or he should have sought a much reduced fee for his services." The Surrogate disallowed $23,000 in billings "which were admittedly excess," since Brashich conceded his timesheets "were not accurate." The Surrogate set Brashich's fee for defending a wrongful death action at $63,000 and disallowed office overhead and travel expenses. The estate was "of only moderate size without any major legal impediments to orderly resolution." (Brashich claimed in the disciplinary hearing that it initially was valued at $3 million.) His billing "was greatly in excess of what would be, in any sense, practical or reasonable given the size and complexity of the Estate." In the end the Surrogate allowed legal fees of $90,500 to Brashich and $32,668 to the Hashmall firm. On July 31, 2000 he ordered Brashich to repay Ljubica $263,856 ($153,405.77 plus $110,451 interest) within 60 days. Brashich neither appealed nor complied.

Chapter 5

On August 27, 2001 the DDC charged Brashich with charging an illegal or excessive fee and conduct adversely reflecting upon fitness to practice.[832] He answered on November 27 that Ljubica was personally liable for fees disallowed against the estate, and the Hashmill firm only second-seated him. Edelstein's reply objected that Brashich "has set off the amount he believes is still owed to him against the Order of the Surrogate's Court." The Appellate Division again ruled that the Surrogate's Court order was collateral estoppel on culpability and ordered a hearing on sanctions, appointing Stephen P. Kramer Referee. The hearing began on April 15, 2002, with Brashich representing himself. Edelstein introduced a seventh prior admonition, overlooked in the previous proceeding, in which Brashich had obtained a 1984 default judgment by falsely representing that he had served a summons and complaint.

Brashich explained why he had not complied with the Surrogate's order.

> After the decision came down, I was contacted by Mrs. Callahan, who requested a meeting with me. One of the portions of Surrogate Weber's decision specifically recognizes . . . that I had the right to look to Mrs. Callahan for fees which had not been authorized as a proper charge to the estate, approximately . . . $144,000. This [November or December 2000 meeting, five months after the Surrogate's decision] was in a restaurant at Riverhead on the circle, very close to the Surrogate's Court. And as Mrs. Callahan and I had lunch, Surrogate Weber walked into the same restaurant and had lunch. Not with us, but at a separate table with separate people. And Mrs. Callahan thought that this was—again, a conspiracy against her that all of a sudden Surrogate Weber should find himself in the same place when the two of us were meeting. . . . Before I met with Mrs. Callahan, I inquired of her whether she was represented by counsel. She was not . . . nor did she ever want to be represented by counsel in the future. . . . I told her my position was that I had earned every penny that I was paid . . . that I had gone above and beyond the call of duty in representing her without an assurance of fees for a period of some three years. I told her that I was very unhappy about . . . what had happened to her . . .

---

[832] DR 2-106(a) and 1-102(a)(7).

> that she had been subject to almost 12 years of incessant litigation . . . that her house had burned down in Quogue. . . .

He agreed to reconsider his $144,000 claim. He later told her that he and co-counsel had just won a $1,850,000 judgment, for which he was owed a contingent fee, and proposed to give her $75,000 (instead of the $263,856 the court had ordered, or even the $123,000 difference between that and the $144,000 he claimed she owed him, though he denied owing interest). He urged her to get an attorney or write this understanding in English or Serbo-Croatian, but she said it was unnecessary.

> I fully stand by my agreement with Mrs. Callahan and I will honor it. I have tried to reach Mrs. Callahan. I do not have the telephone number. I have written to her. She has not called me back. The only thing I had was a post office box number.

During the Surrogate trial she "testified that she was satisfied with the work that I had done for her and that she had paid me the fees which she thought were reasonable." But he conceded to the Referee that he was not sure he felt obligated to pay her the $75,000 if he did not obtain the contingent fee.

Under cross-examination he admitted he had neither paid her anything pursuant to the Surrogate's order nor placed the money in escrow. He had brought no action to determine his obligation in light of his contention that she was personally liable for his fees. He had not contacted the attorney who represented her in the accounting proceeding. He had not declared bankruptcy. He had earned legal fees in 2000 and 2001 but owned no real property. He had no retirement plan or savings. "With the illness of my daughter and the tuition for my other two children, college, practically everything that I earn has gone into them the last three years. The woman with whom I live, with, it's her apartment. I own no stocks, bonds."

The DDC sought a three-year suspension, with reinstatement contingent on full restitution. Brashich "did not simply overbill; he collected a significantly inflated fee and retained it for over ten years." Indeed, he requested additional fees in February 2000, "well *after* Surrogate Emanuelli's decision and *after* he was censured."

> In effect Respondent argues that his failure to return fees to the estate should be excused in whole or in part because there

Chapter 5

> is a partial set-off, since Mrs. Callahan is effectively the estate as sole legatee. Yet Respondent admitted that he looked only to *estate* assets for payment of all of his fees, even though Mrs. Callahan had other resources [an apartment in Belgrade and a house outside].

The Appellate Division had already rejected his set-off argument. Mrs. Callahan relied on Brashich's advice.

> On the one occasion when, as the Surrogate noted, there was evidence that Mrs. Callahan questioned Respondent's decisions (regarding the federal suit against a former Executor), Respondent proceeded against her wishes.... The estate was taxed with payment of the prior Executor's legal fees defending the federal suit.

Brashich expressed no remorse about overbilling or failing to comply with the Surrogate's order.

Brashich sought admonition or censure. Between 1992 and 2000 Callahan, "a business school graduate," had never questioned the fees she paid him. At the accounting trial, represented by different counsel, she testified she "was happy to pay what he asked for." At their November 2000 meeting he had agreed not to seek the $144,000 he claimed she personally owed and to pay $75,000 out of his anticipated contingent fee, which she agreed to accept in lieu of the Surrogate's order. "Callahan has stood by her agreement as has Respondent. Callahan has not sought enforcement of the Decree nor has she testified in these proceedings." As sole beneficiary, she was the estate. "[T]he Surrogate's computation of Respondent's fees is difficult, if not impossible, to track." "[T]he sum to be returned to the Estate, in effect to Callahan, being $153,405.77 offset by Callahan's personal liability of $144,637.50, is $8,768.27."

> Callahan initiated the dialogue to end the 13 years of litigation. In a good faith effort to end Callahan's ordeal, Respondent entered in an oral agreement termination [sic] litigation and forestalling additional litigation. Respondent was personally saddened and offended by the ordeal that Callahan endured... [and] genuinely sorry that his client had to suffer so. An effort to preclude further litigation, when undertaken in good faith

and under these unique circumstances should not be construed [as] willful failure to comply with a Court order. Respondent submits that efforts to reach an amicable settlement should be encouraged and not discouraged. . . . The Respondent explicitly stated that he was unhappy as to "what happened to her" and "very unhappy about the final result." . . . By doing so, the Respondent showed remorse and contrition acknowledging that respond [sic] bore responsibility for the events in question.

Edelstein replied that Brashich "recklessly overcharged and overreached by taking the $144,637.50 fee." By "failing to apply for the Surrogate's permission to take this substantial fee from the estate, Respondent succeeded not only in avoiding giving notice to the court and other interested parties, he bypassed the possibility of direct notice to himself . . . that this fee was improper." "Ms. Callahan was not in a position to properly analyze, consent or approve such large fees and expenses." His "set off argument merely evidences his continuing refusal to acknowledge or comply with the Court's Decree. . . ."

The Referee found Brashich not guilty of any "impropriety" in billing Callahan to defend the 1986 will. He had a "credible" belief that she made the November 1990 payment individually. In cutting the hours for the mortgage closing and loan application from 34.7 to 20, the Surrogate was not finding that Brashich had "acted recklessly or intentionally overreached." That he billed $30,250 in the second trial for his own time and $32,668 for the second chair did not show he had "deliberately over-billed." The Surrogate attributed the $23,000 overbilling to inaccurate time sheets, not deliberate or reckless misconduct. The $25,000 accountants' fee was excessive but not reckless. Failure to make restitution is relevant in cases of theft or conversion, but Brashich "testified that he had at the time of the hearing no assets with which to pay either a judgment," and the Staff offered no contrary evidence to disprove this. The Referee recommended no discipline if Brashich paid Callahan $75,000 and obtained an informed release.

The Hearing Panel agreed that disallowance of fees did not retrospectively make them excessive.[833] The Hashmall firm worked on a

---

[833] August 30, 2002. The panel was John L. Warden (chair), Justin E. Driscoll III, David G. Keyko, and Henrietta Lyle (the lay member).

different matter. Had Brashich anticipated that the Surrogate's decision would have collateral estoppel effect in a disciplinary proceeding he might have appealed it. "[T]he Panel also has some sympathy for Respondent arising from the Dickensian nature of the Surrogate's Court probate proceedings." Because Callahan was the sole beneficiary, the distinction between her and the estate was "purely formal," making court approval of the fee less important. The Surrogate never found Brashich's fee for the two trials excessive, which "fee accounts for all but $9,000 of the principal amount of the judgment entered against Respondent."

But the Panel had some criticisms. "The fees and expenses for tax work were clearly out of line, and . . . Respondent has offered no explanation of these amounts." Even if $144,637.50 was a reasonable fee for the two trials

> a competent lawyer mindful of his professional responsibilities does not charge an estate for work not lawfully billable to it. Respondent's treatment of the judgment entered against him is likewise far too casual for a member of the bar. . . . The 1998 censure should have caused Respondent to be meticulous in his request for allowance of fees and expenses from the Callahan Estate and certainly should have led him to negotiate a settlement with Mrs. Callahan through her counsel in the accounting proceeding. . . .

Brashich had acknowledged that his efforts at settlement were "less than ideal," but Callahan had been out of the country a lot.

At the same time, it was "notable that Mrs. Callahan, who was represented by other counsel for the accounting, has neither sought to execute on the judgment nor advanced any complaint to the Committee. . . . Indeed, she declined to appear at the hearing before the Referee." Brashich told the Panel he was arranging a loan to pay her the $75,000. The complaint came from one of the objectors to will, who had no further interest once it was admitted to probate. The conduct occurred during a period when Brashich suffered "numerous personal tragedies."

> Were the Panel free to examine the merits of the charges and not just the issue of sanctions, it might well have confirmed and adopted the Referee's recommendation. Given the Court's finding of violations of two Disciplinary Rules based on collateral

estoppel, however, the Panel cannot accept the Referee's recommendation of no sanction.

It recommended another public censure.

The staff moved to disaffirm. The Surrogate had found that Mrs. Callahan "was not in a position to question Respondent's charges, and instead acquiesced to Respondent's demands for fees." "Any mitigation theory of set-off or settlement is moot since nothing has been paid." Brashich moved to affirm. "None of the prior lapses of professional responsibility were of a venal, fraudulent or dishonest nature. The prior lapses were the inability to complete representation undertaken in a timely fashion due to the personal tragedies. . . ." He "did not willfully disobey the mandate and order of the Surrogate's Court. The Respondent did not have the means with which to comply. . . ." As of September he had "repaid in full the funds which had been subject of the finding." But then he said he had "not been able to secure a loan so as to consummate the settlement. . . ." He was reluctant to borrow from his one relative but "fully prepared to do so" and sought leave to file a satisfaction of judgment within 60 days of the final disciplinary order. Edelstein replied two days later that having failed to comply with the Surrogate's order for 28 months, Brashich should not be given another 60 days.

The Appellate Division ruled that the "1998 censure should have caused respondent to be meticulous in charging fees against the Callahan estate; it should also have prompted him to work out a settlement with Ms. Callahan regarding the $144,637.50 incorrectly charged to the estate. He did neither of these things."[834] It suspended him for a year from May 1, conditioning reinstatement on a satisfaction of judgment or written settlement.

He delayed filing his affidavit of compliance until June 12, 2003, because in April 2000 he had been appointed lead defense counsel for Momcilo Krajisnik before the International Criminal Tribunal for the former Yugoslavia in The Hague. He had promptly sent notice of the suspension to the tribunal, which withdrew the appointment as lead counsel on May 2 but named him legal consultant to the defense team for 90 days. (The ICTY letter said his failure to inform it of his entire disciplinary record "evidences a lack of candour.") He asked the ICTY how to resolve the conflict, and it directed him to comply with the AD's order. The Appellate

---

[834] Matter of Brashich, 759 N.Y.S.2d 445 (1st Dep't 2003).

CHAPTER 5

Division had granted his motion for modification on June 12. In November 2003 he told a reporter he was on leave of absence from law practice due to "regulatory constraints."[835] But he has not applied for readmission.[836]

VI. The Temptations of Champions

Most individual clients are vulnerable. People rightly fear the law. Even the eminent lawyer and judge Learned Hand acknowledged that "as a litigant, I should dread a lawsuit beyond almost anything short of sickness and death."[837] Consequently, individual clients consult lawyers only under duress: when injured, sued, arrested, divorcing, fired, bankrupt, threatened with eviction or deportation, or bereaved. Babette Stern and Ljubica Callahan were unusually vulnerable. Babette had been used to material comfort, first as the child of wealthy parents and then as a stay-at-home mother raising four children in Scarsdale. Divorce ended this. She suffered real hardship in California, lacking both money and marketable skills, barely supporting herself and her daughter by running a flower shop, sleeping on a futon, foregoing dental care. Her estranged brother harshly rejected her appeal for help. Fleeing from Florida to Connecticut by Greyhound, she took refuge with wealthy friends in Westport and worked in a pharmacy. That her "nearest and dearest" paid all but $1,000 of the $7,500 retainer was further evidence of her abject dependence. Cardozo, an "elegant, nice man," seemed a savior (one in a long line, according to Deborah). He offered the only hope of securing the income of a trust whose corpus had grown from an insignificant $78,000 to more than $3 million in just a decade. Toby believed the lawyers exploited Babette's financial distress to obtain her consent to their proposal.

Like many immigrants, Ljubica had relinquished a middle-class life in Yugoslavia—a university degree in business administration, a shop in Belgrade's premier hotel, an apartment and a house—to become a domestic servant in a country where she spoke little English. Then the land of opportunity fulfilled its promise. She quickly married her employer, who soon died, leaving her an estate worth several million dollars. But her husband's Roman Catholic Irish-American relatives deeply resented what

---

[835] Lombino, supra.
[836] Interview with Deyan Brashich, September 21, 2006. Benjamin Cardozo declined to be interviewed. Letter, August 16, 2006. However, he maintained the same law office and was still a member of the bar.
[837] Hand (1926: 105).

they apparently saw as an Eastern Orthodox Serbian immigrant gold digger. Brashich was *her* savior—another Serbian immigrant, who spoke her language and probably was referred through an émigré network that included his mother and grandmother, who also lived in Eastern Long Island.[838]

The dependence of these clients not only exposed them to overreaching lawyers but also made it difficult for them to recognize or complain about misconduct.[839] Even after Cardozo's misconduct had been exposed, Babette continued to insist that "her" lawyers had behaved like "gentlemen." (Other clients shared this view, calling Cardozo "a gentleman of the old school.") Babette felt "very protected" by these "very honorable" men, who had been "unjustly chastised" by the "classless" actions of a Surrogate pursing "his own interests and agenda" "supported by politicians." (Babette apparently divided the world into "classy" and "classless" people and behavior.)[840] Ljubica even interpreted the Surrogate's presence in the restaurant where she was lunching with Brashich as evidence of a conspiracy. (Both lawyers naturally encouraged what psychologists call transference. Other researchers have described a female divorce client's reaction to the letter her male lawyer had written his adversary: "It kind of let me feel that finally . . . I'd found a knight in shining armor.")[841] Like Babette, Ljubica was passive. She readily accepted Brashich's offer of $75,000 in lieu of the $250,000 refund the Surrogate ordered. (Even the $75,000 was conditional upon Brashich receiving a contingent fee in an unrelated case.) She declined to consult another lawyer. Neither client filed a grievance; the first came from Surrogate Emanuelli (provoked by the strong mutual antagonism between him and Brashich, and to a lesser extent Cardozo, whom Brashich called "irascible" and a "curmudgeon");[842] the second came from Thomas Callahan's angry relatives.

Even Toby was generally uncritical of the lawyers. Brashich had told him the Surrogate could calculate fees on a quantum meruit basis, which

---

[838] Their home in Port Jefferson was not that far from hers in Quogue.
[839] See Felstiner et al. (1981). That may be true of elderly clients of trust and estates lawyers generally. See Serge F. Kovaleski and Colin Moynihan, "Lawyer Charged in Astor Case Has Been a Beneficiary in Clients' Wills," New York Times B1 (12.1.07); "Many Clients of Astor Lawyer Left Him Bequests in Their Wills," New York Times A19 (1.4.08).
[840] Compare the distinction between "U" and "non-U" speech and behavior introduced by Alan S.C. Ross and then popularized by Jessica Mitford in the articles republished in her book (Mitford, 1956).
[841] Sarat & Felstiner (1986).
[842] Interviews with Deyan Brashich and Walter Bottger.

Chapter 5

would be $100,000 to $200,000 less than the contingent fee. But Toby declined to seek the reduction because "that was not what was agreed upon at the beginning." After he and two of his sisters each paid the lawyers $125,000, he urged Deborah to do the same. Like Babette, he displaced his resentment from the lawyers to Emanuelli, who was "presumptive and assumptive" and "did not want to hear from me." But he also feared the lawyers would abandon the family. He warned Deborah (whom he blamed for rejecting the settlement at a time when the lawyers' fees were only $300,000) that Brashich "could have legally blackmailed us into a new fee agreement in order for him to continue." Their offer to reduce their fee from $600,000 to $500,000 was "more generous than I was expecting."

The Hecht case was further complicated by family tensions. Although Toby claimed to be his mother's champion, the children's interests clearly diverged from hers. Indeed, he assailed a proposed $100,000 distribution to her as a "betrayal," declaring that she was "not going to be deprived" without it. All the children saw the corpus as rightfully theirs and did not want it depleted by Babette or the lawyers. They were particularly unhappy with any proposal to destroy the trust, leaving them dependent on their mother to create new ones. Babette had previously been estranged from Toby and Marcia and dependent on Deborah. Now Deborah repudiated any further responsibility, provoking Babette to declare she was no longer the mother of that "poor sad woman who wants her baby" but would be a bad mother. Babette even pronounced her dead parents' curse on their granddaughter, adding her own: "From my grave, I will remind you daily that every penny you spend is dirty, greedy blood money." Toby (speaking for Marcia and Jeanne) was equally estranged from Deborah, whom he, too, expelled from the family. While bragging about being a multimillionaire, who had "been producing an income that is in the top 1% of the country for many years," he complained about giving his mother $1,000 a month for a year, out of "savings in which we only had $12,000," which pushed him "close to the financial edge for about 8 months." (He expected repayment with 10 percent interest.) He resented Deborah's lack of respect and threatened "*to take action*," warning: "it could get really nasty . . . you have not been hit yet. No facts have come out." He would "not listen to your cries of uncle when you give up."

Given these conflicts it was imperative that everyone have independent counsel. Deborah relied on Bill Kane, whom Toby reviled as a "nasty, angry man" with delusions of being a spy. (She hired Arnold Roseman only after Kane's suicide.) Babette exalted her "very astute" son as a "very fine businessman." But though Toby also boasted about his business acumen, he admitted not understanding what was going on. He had gotten "professional" (but erroneous) advice that the settlement's tax implications were irrelevant because "eventually, all the taxes would have to be paid." He claimed the Surrogate was "watching this like a hawk," but the lawyers on both sides were determined to keep it away from him. Toby sought legal advice by interrupting a lunch at his bank's trust department, which produced an assurance by the Pacific Bell general counsel (a friend) that the one-third contingent fee was "market standard appropriate." Later, Toby and his sisters consulted Jerry Geist. (His independence was compromised by the fact that he must have been suggested by Brashich, who hired Geist's firm to second-chair the trial of the Callahan will.) The Surrogate ultimately appointed two guardians for the grandchildren, who sided with Deborah.

In the absence of counsel for the children, the lawyers for Edward and Babette faced a difficult situation. Lipman expressed discomfort at dealing with Toby and was so exasperated by Deborah that he offered to pay any other lawyer $1,000 to talk her. But the real problem was the way Babette's lawyers dealt with her children. Cardozo was fiercely partisan to Babette, accusing the children of disloyalty in his March 1990 letter. But Brashich seemed to play both sides. When Toby sent Lipman's first proposal to his mother's lawyers, Brashich warned against responding, directing Toby to "CALL ME FIRST!!" While advising Toby to get his own lawyer, and Ljubica as well (when he pressed her to compromise his $264,000 debt to her for a contingent $75,000), he continued to deal with both of them directly.

The combination of unusually vulnerable clients and unrepresented parties created three problems: the lawyers' fees; their relationship to the settlement proposals; and the Surrogate's oversight of both. The fee agreement Cardozo had Babette sign was hopelessly ambiguous. It provided for a contingent fee of one third of either an "outright" settlement or a court order that "surcharge[d]" Edward for loss of income. Not only were those conditions unclear, but the agreement also was not actually "contingent," for it also obligated Babette to pay "a reasonable fee" (beyond the $7,500 retainer). Although Cardozo repeatedly analogized this case to a personal injury action, there was no uncertainty about the outcome. The will, which he had read, clearly gave Babette half the trust income. Furthermore, Cardozo acknowledged that he would have claimed a fee even if the parties

CHAPTER 5

could not agree. In October 1989 the lawyers responded to the Surrogate's order that they submit an affidavit of legal services by seeking $162,000 based on their time, not the contingent fee agreement (because they had not yet secured any income for Babette). Although Cardozo told both Babette and her children that "the Surrogate must pass on [the fee's] reasonableness," when the Surrogate's order was stayed pending appeal the lawyers proposed to take a third of Babette's trust (*before* taxes) without reference to their time accounting. Cardozo claimed to be unaware that the Surrogate could order quantum meruit fees even though he had practiced estate law for nearly half a century and had just made a quantum meruit claim in this case. He also told Babette and Toby that the contingent fee agreement would deny him *any* fees if he lost the case, even though that agreement entitled him to a "reasonable fee" and the Surrogate could award fees in quantum meruit. Indeed, he adamantly refused to be limited to a contingent fee: "It wouldn't have been fair to me ... because otherwise ... I would have been working for nothing. ... I don't work for nothing. Not with this kind of money involved." In January 1990 Brashich estimated their fees at $225,000 to 250,000. (It is not clear what they had done in the intervening two months to justify the extra $60,000 to 90,000. Brashich apparently included the pending appeal but could not have known what it would cost.) When the parties settled in February 1991, the lawyers "compromised" their $600,000 claim for $500,000, based on "the fact that this was contingent in nature." (Again they disregarded taxes.) Brashich concurred, although he claimed he had *never* viewed their fee as contingent "because if we had gotten her income of $100 a week, were we going to get $33.33 for the rest of her life?" It was Deborah who undid this deal by refusing to contribute $125,000 and insisting the Surrogate determine her share of the fees. Her resistance seems to be related to her fight with the Kane children over Bill's sperm, the need to pay for that litigation, and her uncertain finances following his suicide.

Brashich was representing Ljubica at the same time. She paid him more than $250,000—$200,000 of it on the day he arranged a mortgage of her deceased husband's property, ostensibly to provide her with living expenses. He seems to have overbilled repeatedly: for this routine mortgage, the probate proceeding, another firm to do work for which he was also billing, an accountant to do simple work Brashich could have done, and hours he did not work. When the Surrogate ordered a $263,000 refund, Brashich convinced his unrepresented Yugoslav immigrant client to accept $75,000, payable if he collected a contingent fee in another case. He did not even pay that for several years.

The lawyers' claim to a contingent fee—approximately twice the value of their *own* estimated hours—depended on whether they had produced income for Babette. Their actions initially seemed disinterested. Their settlement offer before trial—$50,000 to Babette immediately and a modest monthly income—would have produced little or no contingent fee (and they sought only $40,000 for their time). They rejected other offers that would have given them a contingent fee but were not in Babette's best interest. The proposal for a distribution of half the trust (which would generate the contingent fee) came from Lipman. But Cardozo and Brashich promptly recommended it to Babette and the children. Only Deborah's intransigence (probably fueled by Bill Kane) aborted this. And the lawyers never presented Babette or the children with the split trust proposal, which would have precluded the contingent fee. Their invocation of *Matter of Weeks* was unpersuasive, because only Edward wanted to be his own trustee (permissible in Florida), and Babette was happy to have Toby as hers. This solution, which Emanuelli ultimately ordered, could have been adopted four years earlier without wasting huge amounts of money on at least eight lawyers. Emanuelli found that Cardozo and Brashich switched between quantum meruit, negotiated, and contingent fees as circumstances changed, in order to maximize their fee, without presenting the alternatives to their client (who should have been offered independent legal advice). I am persuaded by this interpretation (which became collateral estoppel in the disciplinary proceeding).

Surrogates are intended to guard against precisely those dangers. But the lawyers energetically tried to evade Surrogate review and almost succeeded. They advanced two unselfish reasons for doing so: delay and cost. And resolution of the claims did take years: Babette's six, Ljubica's more than ten. But it was the lawyers, not the judges, who were responsible for much of the delay and all of the cost. And in order to avoid the Surrogate they systematically misled their clients. Cardozo told Toby (and thereby his siblings and mother) that the Surrogate would not see them. Although Cardozo admitted this was false and apologized, he could offer no explanation (beyond the unconvincing post hoc rationalization that he meant they would not convince the Surrogate). The lawyers could not settle on a story: Cardozo maintained that the retainer obviated any need for Surrogate approval, Brashich that the Surrogate would approve whatever fee a party accepted. In both cases Brashich disingenuously claimed he was being paid by his clients, not the trust, although the clients had no source of funds except the trust. And Brashich threatened Toby that the "Surrogate would take over everything" if the parties did not agree. The lawyers tried to blame Stern for concealing the settlement from the Surrogate (claiming, inconsistently, that Stern did not want to pay his lawyers for submitting it and that he was going to submit it for tax reasons). The settlement did give Stern control; but why did Babette's lawyers sign away their client's right to a Surrogate's hearing? And how did they reconcile this with their own petition, filed the very date the settlement was signed, asking the Surrogate to order Deborah to pay them $125,000? Why did their response to Deborah's petition that the Surrogate fix her fee admit that the other three children had paid theirs but conceal that the total was $375,000, based on a compromise of the contingent fee agreement? The lawyers' reason for avoiding the Surrogate's Court became clear when it cut Babette's fee from $500,000 to $115,000 and Ljubica's from $244,000 to $90,000, ordering repayment of interest.

How should we understand the behavior of Cardozo and Brashich? Both seemed genuinely moved by their clients' plights. They had met while protecting another elderly woman before collaborating to represent the obviously desperate Babette; and Brashich championed Ljubica, a fellow immigrant with limited English. Brashich devotedly cared for his mother, from the time of the stroke that deprived her of speech (just before Babette's trial) to her death five years later. He must have been appalled that the Hecht children neglected Babette and that they told his secretary their mother was crazy. As an upwardly mobile immigrant, Brashich also was eager to associate himself with Cardozo—a man Brashich twice called a "class act" and who was a distant relative of New York's most famous lawyer (only the middle initial was changed from N to M). Despite their eight decades of combined joint legal experience—Cardozo had practiced nearly 50 years, Brashich more than 30—both made elementary errors: Cardozo combined the trustee removal and intermediate accounting in a single proceeding and was unfamiliar with *Matter of Weeks*; Brashich lost both the challenge to Ljubica as executor and the action against the preliminary executor.

Both lawyers may have been tempted by clients who suddenly faced the prospect of much more money than they were accustomed to managing, depending on the lawyers to secure it while feeling and expressing profound gratitude. The lawyers responded to that dependence—may even have encouraged it—without reminding their clients that every letter, phone call, visit, motion, conference, and trial was billable. Both may have viewed the inflated fees as their due. Brashich seemed so oblivious to his own wrongdoing that a year after the Appellate Division affirmed a public reprimand for his representation of Babette he cited that case as a basis for charging Ljubica $250/hour. (He told me repeatedly that as a Serb he always fought rather than negotiated.)[843] But Brashich may also have needed money. The seven previous admonitions for neglect (as well as the testimony of his secretary) suggest a lawyer accepting more work than he could handle. Like many lawyers, he may have spent everything he earned; at least he denied having any savings in his own name. As an immigrant who had needed scholarships and part-time work to pay for private school, college and law school, he was determined to buy the best for his three daughters. He supported his divorced wife and their two children (both of whom suffered serious illnesses) and his invalid mother and grandmother and had a new wife and child. He lived in a Fifth Avenue apartment and a northwestern Connecticut country home (both, conveniently, in his wife's name). Cardozo and he had been forced to refund the $375,000 (after paying taxes on it). When the Surrogate ordered him to repay Ljubica $263,856 he pleaded poverty, initially disregarding the order and then offering to "compromise" it for $75,000, just as Cardozo and he had offered to compromise their $600,000 contingent fee for $500,000. When Ljubica agreed, he delayed making that payment for years.

Lawyers invest heavily in their human capital: the opportunity cost of years of income foregone; the out-of-pocket cost of constantly rising tuition. The legal profession artificially inflates the value of that investment by restricting entry into and competition within the market for legal services. Lawyers can only obtain the return on those investments to which they have become accustomed by representing collectivities (which can aggregate the benefit and thus justify the cost) or individuals in the relatively rare situations where the stakes are significant and their resources capitalized: sale of a family home and division of a pension (divorce), threats to life and liberty (criminal defense and deportation), the aggregation of future income and commodification of physical and emotional well-being (personal injury), and the distribution of a lifetime's accumulation (trusts and estates). Because individual clients have so much at stake and are dealing with amounts they have never previously managed, they

---

[843] Interview with Deyan Brashich.

Chapter 5

are easy prey for lawyers. There is virtually no competition to drive down prices. The profession does nothing to protect clients. Surrogates could do so but tend to be reactive and are often captured by local lawyers. (Midonick, a highly respected Manhattan Surrogate for ten years, testified that he would have awarded the lawyers $250,000 from Babette and filed no grievance.) It took alienated relatives (Deborah and Callahan's blood kin) and an unusually proactive Surrogate (Emanuelli) to bring these cases before the disciplinary bodies.

Lawyers' fees in the Hecht-Stern case exceeded $1.3 million—not quite "Bleak House," but depressingly close.

Chapter 6

The Perils of Perfectionism

I. Mixing Business with Friendship

A. *The IRS Knocks*

When architect James Morgan left Cushman & Wakefield[844] in 1983 to start his own business remodeling New York City apartments, an accountant convinced him to invest his $400,000 severance pay in a cattle feeding tax shelter. Nearly ten years later the IRS disallowed the shelter and assessed a $180,000 deficiency. The IRS also wanted to know why Morgan had failed to file returns for 1988–1991. He was "stunned."[845] The IRS agent "was most belligerent in terms of why I hadn't paid." Philip Byler

> may have been the first or second person that I called. And we quickly learned the seemingly incredible coincidence that the deduction that the IRS agent was concerned about was something

---
[844] A global real estate firm. In 2007 it had more than 11,000 employees in 192 offices in 58 countries.
[845] Unless otherwise noted, all quotations come from the DDC hearing transcript.

that Phil knew the law on thoroughly from some work he'd done in Ohio.

The Morgans and the Bylers had been close family friends since meeting at Manhattan's Marble Collegiate Church in the mid-1980s. Their children were the same ages; they vacationed together at Lake George in the summer of 1988. Byler had graduated from Harvard Law School, clerked on the Sixth Circuit, and worked for six years at Cravath and another six at Weil Gotshal. At the time of these events he was of counsel at Layton Brooks & Hecht.[846]

Morgan remembered Byler saying "I think you're on solid ground here . . . I think we can clear this up with a couple of letters to the IRS, because the law is very clear on the subject." Morgan wrote Byler on June 23, 1992:

> I can not tell you how much it means to me to have you assist me with the 1983 tax matter. I know I am in good hands and you will do what is possible, although it is a real mess that I am not proud of. . . . I do not believe any significant tax is owed. . . . Again, it feels to me like a divine gift to have a friend like you in this hour of need and I am very grateful for your help.

Morgan testified:

> We discussed a fee only in the sense that I said to Phil, what would it cost if we had to fight this thing? I mean if a couple of letters don't do the job? And he said well, it could cost as much as $20,000. And I said, well, let's let that be our bench mark then. If we can resolve this thing with the IRS for, for less than $20,000 without litigation, we'll do that. But if . . . they still insist that I owe them $180,000 or something in between, we'll have to litigate it, I suppose.

If they did litigate, Byler's fee would be $20,000. They "didn't really discuss" what Byler would charge for negotiating with the IRS because "we're working . . . on the premise that the law is very clear on this . . . and with a

---

[846] 746 Fifth Avenue, 29th Floor. When Morgan appealed to him in June 1992 he was at Stults, Balber, Horton and Slotnik, 1370 Avenue of the Americas.

few letters we should be able to clear this thing up." He was "sure" Byler knew he had not made any money in the previous three or four years. On cross examination Morgan agreed he "consistently was pleased" he had Byler's assistance "because I would have been totally lost without it, and tried to tell him that." Byler "never led me to believe he expected compensation for his services . . . both of us at the outset thought this could be handled fairly expeditiously."

Byler had a different recollection.

> I had a meeting with him on June 19th. I told him my retainer and then I inquired information from him over the course of the next couple of days as to what the situation was in terms of his tax liability and what his financial situation was. Because . . . I knew from our conversations on a social basis that he was having financial difficulties. And therefore, what I did, and told Mr. Morgan orally, was as follows. . . . I would not require a retainer. He didn't have to put any up front money. . . . Two, if we went to litigation, which we thought was likely, it was not, gee, this was going to go away with a few letters, it was likely that we were going to go into litigation . . . I would charge him a flat fee of $20,000, not based on cost. . . . thirdly, he was going to have to file his four years of back returns. . . . And four, that while we were before the agencies . . . I would not bill him but I would carry his case and we would work out the fee depending on the developments in the case and his financial circumstances. It . . . was in essence an agreement to agree. There was always an obligation. . . . [H]e desperately needed counsel. I could provide that counsel. I did so on special terms. I did not do so on terms that would reflect a market rate. . . . [W]e would work it out . . . based on developments in his career, and in the case.

Because Morgan's remodeling business had been failing (with the contracting housing market), he sought a new start in South Africa soon thereafter. In February 1993 he had the $2,000 security deposit for his former New York apartment sent to Byler in partial payment for legal services. "I considered it a gesture I was making to him because he, he was helping me." "I also had no practical way to cash a check in South Africa."

Chapter 6

On April 21, 1994, Byler faxed Morgan in South Africa.

> Accompanying this letter is a "non-bill bill" detailing the work that I have done to date but *not* indicating that any payment is due now or ever. Given the work that I have done over time and given that you may be approaching a decision as to what to do in the near future, I felt that I should provide you an accounting of my services.
>
> Although your tax case may seem to you a curse, you should count your blessings. You have been fortunate to have a friend handle this matter because I knew that the attached would be considered too cheap in the eyes of New York City practitioners and that I would be viewed as crazy not to demand prompt payment, especially in view of: (a) my legal expertise on the cattle feeding investment at issue and (b) the circumstances that I handled and turned around for you in the summer of 1992 when your IRS matter was in Collections, the IRS had issued a Notice of Intention To Levy, the New York State Department of Taxation and Finance had issued a corresponding tax warrant and a New York agent was sounding like he was about to execute against you (in retrospect, an accurate perception).
>
> I will let your conscience be your guide as to any further payment. I can understand your frustration with New York City attorneys and accountants, but *not* with the attached: it reflects the kind of detailed report that I do, the efficiency with which I work and the lower rates (relative to the New York City market) that I charge full-paying clients for real work. Again, count your blessings.

He calculated $12,787.50 for 46.1 hours (at $277.39/hour) plus $110 for expenses, minus the February 1993 payment of $2,181.67, ending: "Bottom line Total Amount Due $_____."

Morgan felt "it was Phil's way of showing me the amount of work he had done on this case. That it had taken a lot longer than either of us had expected." But he did not pay "because the bill said, detailing work that I've done to date, but not indicating that any payment is due now or ever, which seemed rather clear to me."

Morgan returned to the U.S. on business that June on what he expected would be the last visit for a while. He went to Byler's office on June 8 and learned (then or perhaps earlier) that the IRS had reduced the deficiency to $17,000.

> Phil handed it to me and basically said, I think we can settle it for this amount. And I said, well, that's within the $20,000, let's just go through it so that I can understand exactly how this is calculated, because . . . I don't want this thing to come alive again. . . . And so we started to go through this document and realized neither one of us could make head nor tails of what it was saying and how it was being calculated. . . . And I said to Phil, look, I'm going to be here in the States at least another I think two weeks or something. And so there is some time, could you please call the IRS and get clarity so that we have this thing fully understood and resolved. And please let them know I am here to resolve it. I am here to sign the check.

He was also concerned about the New York State claim and unclear if it could be settled for $3,000, so that the whole was less than $20,000. Indeed, six months earlier New York State had seized a $38,000 account. Because Byler said his last conversation with Michael Sinhoff, the state agent, had not been "very positive," Morgan made the call.

When Morgan phoned from his accountant's office in Florida a week later (June 14), Byler told him:

> You're not going to believe this, but in talking to the IRS about this and trying to get this thing clarified, what they've said is, no, there's some error that's been made here and you might even get a refund. And Phil and I, after this adventure for two years or so, sort of had a good chuckle about that in terms of . . . can you believe this? . . . I don't think either of us took it as . . . a terribly likely prospect.

Although Byler gave no dollar amount, "certainly the suggestion was that it was certainly not going to be a significant refund." Morgan "saw it very much like the rent check. And said . . . well, Phil, if we do get, get a check, keep it." Byler made no response. Morgan reiterated this on cross-examination.

Chapter 6

> I felt very grateful that Phil had taken on this assignment at no fee initially discussed . . . I had tried to reciprocate in some small way by showing him my good faith in telling him to keep the first check. I viewed his non-bill bill as . . . a kind of reciprocal statement of good faith. . . . And it just seemed a kind of continuation of this process of . . . being fair with each other.

The refund was still uncertain. "[M]y sense of the conversation was that this was a bit of a joke." Nevertheless, Byler testified that he told Morgan then (and again on June 20): "if I'm looking at it right, it's going to exceed $10,000."

Back in New York on June 20, Morgan dropped in on Sinhoff and "resolved all outstanding issues. . . . I paid him some outstanding levies or taxes or whatever that were due, of a relatively minor nature on these two companies. But with the assurance that . . . I wasn't going to wake up in ten years and have a new set of problems coming." Then he stopped at Byler's office without an appointment. They had radically different memories of this crucial encounter.

Morgan remembered a brief meeting by the elevators in the firm's reception area. He handed Byler "the envelope . . . in which I had put the copies of the material for Michael Sinhoff at the state . . . and said I had a good meeting. . . ." He asked Byler to

> please send a letter recording that conversation [about the possible refund] to the IRS. Because I've come here now to settle this thing, to write a check, to finish it. I'm now leaving for an indefinite period of time and I don't want anybody to contend that . . . I ran away from this.

Byler had already written that letter and gave Morgan a copy.

> And the third thing I said to him was, I've left a check, a signed check, a blank check and a deposit slip with my accountant in Florida, Bruce Dee. And I've included a signed check and a deposit slip in this envelope for you so that when we get this thing resolved with the IRS, we can settle it . . . you can write the check and if necessary, deposit the funds necessary to cover the check.

The check was intended for the IRS "on the assumption that . . . this was a bit of an unlikely prospect that I was going to get a refund." The deposit slip might be needed because "I didn't have $17,000 in my bank account." The additional funds would come from Dee. "[T]hat was all we said . . . we never sat down and never left the . . . waiting area." He did not say or think that the refund was Byler's. In cross-examination he insisted the meeting lasted 5 to 10 minutes—"probably closer to five." He had arrived at Byler's office at 11. "Phil came out within a few minutes." Morgan was in a rush to pick up a rental car, taking a taxi from 57th and Fifth to reach the garage at 33rd and Third at 11:30.

Byler remembered speaking for 12 to 18 minutes in the conference room where they had met on June 8. Because the IRS "didn't have the numbers right," he advised that Morgan did "not have any obligation with respect to that May 20, 1994 30 day notice of intention to levy." He reiterated what he had said over the phone on June 14: there would be a refund, but the amount was not yet determined and it would take several months to process.

> At that point James Morgan pulled out his checkbook. Took out a check and in my presence on the table, signed his name and flipped it, smiling. And said whatever it is, the refund is yours. He took out a deposit slip and not quite flipped it, but turned it around. I picked them up and put them on the packet of documents, which James Morgan handed me, as we were walking down the hallway to the conference room, and said, O.K.

Although Byler testified first that the signed blank check could not have been intended to pay a deficiency, he later admitted one was possible.

Philip R. Forlenza, a lawyer member of the Hearing Panel, asked if Byler thought Morgan "had sufficient information at the time he gave you that offer, gave you the check, to make a binding agreement with you?"

> Byler: [W]e were dealing with the same level of uncertain knowledge. . . .
>
> Forlenza: I'm asking you whether he, and perhaps even you, had sufficient knowledge about the potential upside.
>
> Byler: . . . I felt yes. . . . It almost really didn't matter. It may sound funny, but it didn't matter because what we were talking

CHAPTER 6

> about was money that was not anticipated at the beginning of the representation at all. . . . what was happening was, he was . . . being relieved of $216,000 of tax liabilities. And the fee was being covered by the government.

He denied any understanding that $20,000 was the maximum fee. The Hearing Panel seemed unpersuaded that Byler had *created* money for Morgan, who only recovered what he had paid the government, plus interest.

> Joan Ellenbogen (chair): It's not a gift.
>
> Frederick D. Wilkinson (lawyer member): It's not created.
>
> Ellenbogen: It's not a prize that he won.

Morgan got a series of faxes from Byler in September that "the IRS still wants the $17,000, which tended to reaffirm that this statement in June was a bit of a . . . fluke."

B. The Fee Dispute

On October 18 Byler received the IRS refund check for $52,917, made out to Morgan, his wife, and Byler. He deposited it in Morgan's account (using the slip Morgan had left), waited three days for it to clear, and then made out Morgan's blank check to himself for the full amount (less $50). He wrote Morgan on October 28 (enclosing a letter to Sinhoff) "reviewing what has been done in the last 1 1/2 years . . . being cautious to record the facts so that the dictates of prudence are satisfied in this crazy world of ours."

> Since June 1992, I have represented you because you came to me with a serious legal problem [which he described at length, with citations]. Fortunately, you had a lawyer-litigator in me who had expertise in the tax issue and who jumped in to try to rescue your cases from federal and state tax collection agents.
>
> Today, after 1 1/2 years of my representation: (i) you owe neither the Internal Revenue Services nor the New York State Department of Taxation and Finance anything; (ii) the NYSDTF will be refunding to you all or almost all of the monies it unlawfully seized from you in October without notice to us;

(iii) your legal fees and expenses will have been effectively covered, per our agreement of June 20, 1994, by the refund issued by the Internal Revenue Service; and (iv) you may have some tax deductions for your legal fees and expenses. . . .

The purposes of this letter are: to review developments in the case in connection with our agreement of June 20, 1994 that I take the refund check, if issued by the Internal Revenue Service and for whatever amount it would be, as full payment for my legal services and reimbursement for my out-of-pocket disbursements; to report my specific actions taken in implementation of our agreement . . . and to discuss the considerations which demonstrate that even in the absence of our agreement of June 20, 1994, the amount of the refund check issued by the IRS represents proper and fair payment of me.

[He reviewed the previous six months.] On June 20, 1994, we again met at my office, at which time we agreed that in payment of my legal services and expenses, I would receive the monies provided by the refund check, whatever that refund check was for; to quote your words: "Whatever it is, is yours." To provide me with the means to implement that agreement, you provided me with a blank deposit slip and a blank check (which you signed). . . .

Our agreement of June 20, 1994 had both upside and downside potential.

The upside potential was fair under the circumstances. I had been representing you since June 1992, and it appeared that I was in the process of delivering an excellent result. . . .

The downside potential . . . was not only very real, but in fact, I thought it was probable . . . it certainly looked as if there would be no refund, and I would be duty bound to settle your case, if I could, with no refund (and, no payment for me). . . . [He recounted the recent financial transactions.]

Although the foregoing steps were taken pursuant to our agreement of June 20, 1994, I think that you should understand that the amount of payment, courtesy the "found money" in the IRS refund, represented a proper payment to me.

> [He recited his achievements.] I did the work, without pressing you for payment while . . . you were getting your career going again, and I achieved the result. . . . If all my time and expenses were fully reported as if you were a company, if there were not the cuts and reductions I made so that an individual of more limited means does not react (as individuals have been known to react) by simply refusing to pay any of the bill, and if my billing rate were set to reflect my level of expertise and experience and my result in this case, the document attached as Exhibit 30 would result. However, the possibility of a refund from the IRS and our agreement of June 20, 1994, rendered moot any need to think about such a document. I have received payment pursuant to our June 20, 1994 agreement. My point is that under the circumstances, ever [he means "even"] in absence of our agreement, the amount was a proper and fair return to me.

Exhibit 30 was a new "bill" for 149.2 hours at $350/hour, which amounted to $52,000. When Byler added disbursements of $3,050 and subtracted the earlier $2,181.67 payment, the total was $52,868.34—*exactly* the refund. He offered no explanation for the fact that the hours for items contained in the earlier bill had increased two to threefold.

Byler testified:

> I did not believe I had an obligation to notify Morgan, because given the agreement I believed I had, that IRS refund in whatever the amount was, had been designated as my compensation. It was not client money in my mind. It was my money. I was finally being paid for two and a half years of legal services that had had a tremendous result.

He admitted in response to Ellenbogen that he had delayed writing for a week to prevent Morgan from stopping payment on the check. At the time he thought there was "a significant risk" Morgan would object. "I was concerned by the fact that he was in South Africa and by the fact that I, I didn't know that without the IRS refund check, I would ever see a penny."

Morgan testified he "had never received such a tome without any preparation." It was "written in the most formal kind of manner . . . totally different in style and tone than anything that happened before."

And the cover letter ended in "a most unusual way." Because he found it "very confusing"

> I quickly drafted the questions that were in my mind and . . . sent a fax to Phil [on October 31], saying, I think essentially, gee, I'm glad it looks like things are getting resolved. But it's a bit confusing to me and here are . . . my questions.

"I was trying to figure out how we got from $12,000 to $52,000 in three months." He did not understand why one IRS check was for $27,000 but the notice spoke of a $25,000 refund. He asked Byler: "Why was your deposit into our account and subsequent deposit into yours in the amount of $52,000?" Byler testified he did not consider this fax "a protest of any kind." "I considered it a questionnaire. It wasn't providing an alternative version of events." DDC Staff Counsel Mady Edelstein asked if Byler understood "from that question that your client was putting in dispute the amount of your fee?"

> Byler: No. . . . [T]here was never any counter offer and there was no communication in this period of time as to what he thought was appropriate. And given the value of my services, I felt that was an extremely unreasonable position to take. They should have . . . said something. . . .
>
> Forlenza: That wasn't the question [Edelstein] asked you.
>
> Byler: O.K., I'm sorry.
>
> Forlenza: Mr. Byler, you're an experienced trial lawyer.
>
> Byler: I know, I just—
>
> Forlenza: Listen to the question. You have four Panel members and counsel here expecting you to listen to questions and answer them. And you know that.
>
> Byler: I apologize.
>
> Forlenza: And it's quite clear from all the comments that the Chair has made on three days, that you're not doing that. That's not acceptable.
>
> Byler: I apologize.

Chapter 6

Forlenza: You understand that, don't you?

Byler: I apologize. I'm, I'm—

Forlenza: I'm not interested in your apology. We—this is a very serious matter. You—

Byler: I understand.

Forlenza: —know that

Byler: Oh, yes. O.K., I will—

Forlenza: Then as an experienced trial lawyer, please listen to the question and answer it so that we can do our job.

Byler: O.K., I've been trying to do so. I actually have been.

Forlenza: Please, please.

Byler: I know.

Byler did not believe Morgan could have felt that a $53,000 refund was a "mistake, justifying further discussion about the fee." But he admitted to Forlenza that had it been $1.49 "I probably would want to talk to him about it. . . . I would be going back to him and say[ing], this isn't fair." Had the refund been $80,000,

> my position would have been to discuss with him what he thought was fair. . . . I don't think it's excessive at $80,000. . . . I can justify a $70[,000] or $80,000 figure in terms of being reasonable, given the result and other factors. But in terms of the agreement, I probably would have made a much larger settlement offer to try to resolve the matter.

Byler faxed back the next day. He had "already addressed or anticipated" Morgan's eight questions. "Nevertheless, in an attempt to avoid any misunderstanding, I shall specifically address each. . . ." He had given Morgan "a prompt report on the implementation of our agreement." He had not done so earlier because the "agreement" did not require it and because "quite frankly, I was not going to run the risk of your not paying me, especially now that you live outside the US." Byler had "*not* unilaterally determined my fee and reconstructed our agreement as I would have liked it. That is *false*." It was Morgan who was trying to do so "with the benefit of hindsight."

> [I]t is becoming standard practice for attorneys to insist upon large pre-payment so that they don't get "stiffed" or short-changed by clients with short, convenient memories. You have been fortunate to have an attorney who did not insist upon such pre-payments....

"[Y]ou were very fortunate to have a lawyer of my caliber step in for you without insisting upon any retainer." Morgan's question "about 'earlier billings'... is at best 'cute.'" The "'non-bill'... reflected massive reductions so that it would come down to a number that you would recognize as the least you should pay. But you did *not* agree to pay it." He had no objection to Morgan showing Byler's earlier letter to his brother, Thomas, a George Washington University law professor and leading authority on legal ethics.[847] Byler's October 28 letter had been "reviewed by my older, old fashioned colleague of the last four years, Louis Lauer, Esq., who fully agrees with it (as does also the woman lawyer [Janet] to whom I am still happily married)." He ended: "You should be thankful," omitting the "regards" with which he had signed previous letters.

Edelstein asked why Byler had consulted Lauer.

> Well, it was a less than optimal situation. On the one hand, it was clearly, in my view, my money I hadn't been paid for it, my work. And this had been designated my compensation. I viewed it as within the realm of reasonable.... On the other hand, I was concerned. We did have a deteriorating relationship. I was handling banking documents I had never handled before in that way....

> Edelstein: So would it be fair to say you felt a little uncomfortable writing yourself a check of this size?

> Byler: Well, uncomfortable in the sense that I had never been given this kind of payment mechanism before.

---

[847] Thomas Morgan was a Reporter for the ALI Restatement of the Law Governing Lawyers from 1986 to 1999, an editor (with Ronald Rotunda) of all nine editions of Problems and Materials on Professional Responsibility, codrafter of revisions to the ABA Model Rules of Professional Conduct, and professional ethics consultant to law firms.

Chapter 6

>Edelstein: So your uncertainty had nothing to do with the amount of money involved . . . ?

>Byler: No. . . . this money doesn't exist but for my work. . . . One of the benefits of an agreement that did put me at risk was, I did have the self enforcing mechanism given me.

Morgan faxed Byler on November 9 that he and his wife Karen considered "you and Janet to be among our closest friends with whom we have shared some of the most important years of our lives including the birth of our four children. I have given you my power of attorney and trusted you as both a member of the bar and a close friend. . . ."

Byler had "set about trying to create a legal justification." "From the odd tone of your letters you now seem to be trying to insult and intimidate us into not going to the trouble of finding out just exactly what has happened and come to a fair and reasonable resolution." He felt "disbelief" and "a complete and total sense of sadness and loss as this is not the Phil Byler we have known." It "would only create further damage to try to answer . . . the personal insults." "There was never any such agreement as you describe. . . . I never suggested such an arrangement and you never asked for it." Had there been an agreement, Byler would have called them on receiving the IRS notice and would "not now be telling the State to send checks to me in South Africa (where I can do nothing with them) and withdraw from the case. Those are the actions of a man who knows he is on the 'take the money and run' route." Byler had begun "to prepare [his] defense and smokescreen of letters and exhibits." "You seem to have temporarily lost your lawyer's focus on 'is this right' and focused instead on, 'can I get away with this.'" Byler was trying to "obscure the facts and intimidate us into accepting your actions as we are now on the other side of the world." Byler "could not have had a concern about payment, only a concern as to whether your claim was proper."

"Our agreement from the beginning was that you would not be billing me if we could avoid litigation." Byler had "never suggested you expected to be paid" for the "non-bill." "[W]e never even discussed it." "At the time I was shocked at all the hours you showed and thought they were excessive given what I had seen and thought was needed, but I know you love to talk and write and assumed you were just trying to show me how hard you were working for me." "As there was no fee discussion" in June, "to suggest this elaborate world of 'upsides' and 'downsides' is just pure fabrication in hindsight on your part." "If you now want to call me and have a reasonable discussion of this all, after you give our money back, that would still be what I would want to do." They had always

> felt it would be right to reach an agreement on what a proper fee would be when the matters were all behind us.... However, that is completely different from having you unilaterally determine the fee you wanted and simply removing that amount from our account.... You will remember that in June you wanted me to pay the IRS about $17,000 and it was my insistence that we get an accurate accounting that brought about the turn around that gives us all the prospect of doing better.... That includes YOU—in spite of your effort now to cast this all as—a great and noble risk, taken by the caring lawyer for the indigent but ungrateful client, who by the quality of his legal skill turned disaster into victory and therefore justly claims all the rewards. Nice story, but it did not quite happen that way.

He urged Byler to consult his wife. "We have known you as a person of integrity but your actions now indicate that even you yourself seem to realize that what has occurred so far here is questionable. Let's reverse course and get this straightened out properly." Morgan was sending the file to his brother to help "us to get a clear and fair picture of the facts." "We don't want to litigate this but will if forced to do so." "You are our friends, surely we can be honest and fair with each other. We do not want to have to try to fight with all the damage that would occur to friendships as well as careers, but we also do not want to be taken advantage of and at this point feel we are. A major violation of trust has occurred." "We will hope we will soon have the funds with which to produce a fair and reasonable resolution. We again thank you for your efforts to bring this about and hope we can get this matter back on a reasonable track before further and even more serious damage is done."

Morgan recollected later that

> I responded somewhat angrily . . . because it was only then that I fully realized that something completely unexpected had occurred . . . it seemed to me that Phil was proceeding on the basis of an imaginary agreement that never existed . . . to move in a . . . direction completely on his own track and . . . had this

CHAPTER 6

> very belligerent angry tone with me. And that made me cross and disappointed. . . . by that time I realized that we'd gotten a refund of $52,000 and that Phil had taken it as his fee and had recast . . . the number of hours he spent on everything. To mysteriously produce a bill that exactly matched . . . that amount and agreement . . . this was all just in my view, total fabrication.

Thomas Morgan also faxed Byler that day.[848] After identifying himself, he said:

> It is not for me to give you legal advice, but I have to say that the informal advice you claim to have gotten from others in support of your action was very bad advice indeed. There is no polite way to describe what you appear to have done; you appear to have converted money belonging to your client to your own use. . . . In short, you appear to have stolen from your client. As I tell my classes, there is no more certain basis for disbarment. . . . your conduct in this matter appears to have been—purely and simply—career-ending behavior.

Thomas quoted the ethical rule, concluding that "Your act of comingling [sic] the funds with your own was naked theft" and directing Byler to "IMMEDIATELY deposit the full amount of the funds . . . into your or your firm's Attorney Trust Account." Thomas concluded by suggesting a way of determining a fair fee.

Byler faxed Thomas the same day.[849] Thomas was demanding action within 24 hours "about a supposed fee dispute that until I received your letter, I did not know I had (and I still don't believe I should have)." Many statements were "absurd." Indeed, it was

> one of the most outlandish and disingenuous letters that I have seen any attorney write. I am *not* impressed by it. In fact, some of your accusations are unethical . . . phony and irresponsibly made . . . an attempt to renegotiate your brother's agreement of June 20, 1994, with me which resulted

---
[848] The Hearing Panel excluded this from evidence.
[849] The Hearing Panel also excluded this reply.

in what was long overdue compensation for a terrific job done for him.

How did Thomas "dare now to cry theft and raise the specter of disbarment. . . ." The "strained claim of conversion" was "groundless," "sheer nonsense." "I could more easily and more justifiably accuse your brother and you of fraud in attempting to take my legal services without a real intention to pay." Thomas "should re-check the ethics of making the charges that you do when your obvious purpose is to renegotiate a legal fee." Despite the "unprofessional" letter, Byler was willing to talk but urged a week's hiatus "because I would kindly suggest to you that you need to take a more sober view of the matter." He offered "one last note" on "friendship." He had handled James's tax troubles "in a way that reflected my friendship for and trust of your brother. As far as I am concerned, I deserve a big 'thank you' for bailing your brother out of a serious legal situation." "Instead, I see your brother trying to walk away from his . . . agreement . . . and serious—but frivolously made—accusations are levelled [sic] against me by you. I consider your letter . . . to be one of the worst betrayals of friendship and trust that I have ever experienced in my life."

Byler testified that Thomas

> was making accusations specifically that I had converted the money, that I had engaged in naked theft. He was threatening disbarment. . . . he had combined the accusation of theft with a demand that I renegotiate my legal fee. And I considered that improper. It put me in a terrible situation. Because this was the letter that created the stinking fish. If I escrow money, I am, as far I'm concerned, acting as if I had stolen the money. And I did not and I dared not take such action, given what he was accusing me of. . . . I always [believed] that there was a problem, if you accuse somebody of a crime and couple it with the demand for a civil settlement. . . . [G]iven that accusation, I felt I did not have the . . . situation where I could satisfy any demand on his part—it wasn't asked. It was demanding . . . he was making an accusation which I dared not satisfy in terms of doing anything.

On November 10 Byler responded to James Morgan's fax of the previous day (with a copy to Thomas).

Chapter 6

> [T]o quote Janet: "it does not fly." All it is, is a series of rationalizations and some false statements to justify an attempt on your part to walk away from our agreement of June 20, 1994—an agreement that we most certainly did have. Why on earth would I do as I have without that agreement?

He rejected James Morgan's "snide summary" and "ill-considered attack" and hoped "that sanity can be restored." Morgan's account "is false, and I think you know it. You may more accurately regret the agreement, but at the time it seemed like a good deal for you." "At the start, I was not going to submit bills to you and did not ask for a retainer because you could not, I thought, afford to pay, and I was not going to press you on billing if we did not go into litigation. . . . I did not, however, agree to represent you *pro bono*." Morgan's "shock" at "excessive" hours in the non-bill bill was

> *crazy*. You can say what you have, and you can say that the world is flat. But saying it does not make it true or sensible or responsible. I feel like making a harsher statement because you should have felt uncomfortable about not treating me right and should have felt gratitude that I was attempting to cut a cheap deal for you.

Byler insisted that they had met in the firm's conference room on June 20.

> The one and only thing that we were discussing was the use by me of the deposit slip and signed blank check to implement our June 20, 1994 agreement. . . . We did *not* discuss any other possible use . . . and there was no other business that we had in mind that would have called for it.

During the June 14 phone conversation about the size of the refund "I told you that I could only guess but it may well be over $10,000." Morgan was "engaging in falsity" in denying the agreement. "If it had worked to the 'downside,' I have no doubt that you would have relied upon our agreement." Thomas's letter, "which is obviously based on a false set of facts and a brother's hasty zeal—is wholly incompatible with 'reasonable discussion.'" "[Y]ou are truly being ungrateful; and you certainly have no complaint. The breach of trust that has occurred is on your part in attempting to walk away from our agreement."

Byler testified that when he got Morgan's November 9 fax

> I considered it my professional responsibility to try to resolve the matter in terms of having him face up to the truth. I did not believe I had a professional responsibility to accept what I considered to be unjustified accusations. He had an obligation to pay me. . . . But he wasn't saying anything in his communications as to, if he wasn't going to live by that agreement, what else he should do. I mean I was dealing in a circumstance where accusations were being made but nothing constructive that I could deal with and work with because I hadn't received anything from him until I had implemented the agreement of June 20, 1994, for a year and three quarters. . . . the attitude I was getting in his correspondence was, well, $2,000 seemed enough. And that was just not acceptable.

He had no obligation to send the refund to Morgan or put it in escrow.

> We're talking about a refund that had been specifically designated as my compensation. It was a refund that existed only by virtue of the fact of my work . . . what we were talking about was my retaining possession of what was fairly my money.

There was no fee dispute.

> I did not have a billing relationship. My right to the money was not contingent upon receipt of any billing reflecting hours and reflecting a billing rate. . . . I'm in a situation where, yes, the client doesn't like it. But . . . I'm being put in an unfair situation . . . all my compensation, 98 percent of it, was tied up in what I had belatedly received as deferred compensation. . . . And that was aggravated on top of that by what I considered to be the unreasonable behavior, A, of James Morgan, in not ever saying to this present day even, what was in his mind appropriate. And B, Thomas Morgan accusing me of stealing the money.

In response to Forlenza he again denied there ever was a fee dispute.

Chapter 6

> [G]iven the fact that I could never get a straight answer as to what I should be paid, I didn't feel it as . . . challenged to my right to be paid so much as they were saying that I should [not] have been paid by the, in the way that I have documented . . . what I thought and believe to this day, is that I think James Morgan regretted the agreement he made. . . . I think he was ungrateful . . . given the value of the work I'd performed, it was unreasonable to say, well, you know, we don't want you to have that by the agreement . . . they're taking an unreasonable posture and they had put the escrow demand only through Thomas and in the context I had stolen money. I was in a bind. I was in a damned if you do, damned if you don't situation. . . . The value of the services were such . . . the [$]55,000 was clearly within reason. You could justify a larger amount and do it by billing, [$]75,000, [$]80,000. . . . I was dealing with a difficult situation because I was dealing with a client who, A, was not saying what he should pay . . . but just . . . arguing, arguing. . . . And B, I had this accusation, this stinking rotten fish accusation that I'd stolen the money, so if I go escrow it, I might be in front of this Committee and the DA on charges that I had stolen escrow monies. . . .
>
> Forlenza: Did you think about the possibility of sending a letter which said I take issue with this . . . without any prejudice, I'm going to put it in escrow.
>
> Byler: . . . I didn't believe in that situation that was a safe option. . . .

When Edelstein asked if the October and November faxes did not show him "that your client did not agree with your recollection of a fee agreement in June of 1994," Byler replied: "Did I know? No."

Thomas responded on November 14, thanking Byler for his legal work and seeking to mollify him but reiterating that checks had to be deposited in a client trust account. "If you do not follow that procedure in your practice you are playing Russian Roulette with your career." He offered to talk.

Byler replied the same day. He acknowledged the "vastly improved tone on your part" but insisted that "the objective circumstances—particularly the deposit slip and signed blank check—clearly establish the existence of that agreement." "My record is spotless; indeed my reputation is—rightly—one of the highest honesty and integrity." Thomas's earlier letter showed him "to be the overly zealous advocate for your brother, who took and still takes his brother's word unquestioningly. . . ." "[Y]ou better understand that I will be talking to you as the one telling the truth."

> I will not be drawn into a situation where you have set yourself up as both judge and your brother's advocate. I understand "the game" you wish to play. . . . you are attempting to renegotiate a legal fee, and I do not believe that in these circumstances you can ethically make the kind of accusations that you have.

There was no "genuine" fee dispute. He did not have to deposit his fee in a trust account "not only because of my clear entitlement to be paid, but also because I was so kind to carry your brother's case for years." James "went too long as it was without paying me." "Friends do not dishonor agreements and do not threaten to sully the career and professional reputation of someone . . . who acted in friendship, to bail them out of serious legal trouble. . . ." Thomas's letters of November 9 and 14 "are shameful when held up to the standard of friendship." "I will not . . . respond to threats. . . ."

On November 23 Thomas faxed Byler "in response to our telephone conversation of Thursday, November 16, in which you offered to pay Jim approximately $5500 in settlement of his fee dispute with you if he would sign a statement that your behavior in this matter was proper." James had rejected it and insisted "you address the merits of the matter as he has tried to do." "A statement that your handling of his refund check was proper would be false." Byler did not "carry" Morgan because no fee had been due. The only "meeting" occurred "in the lobby of your office by the elevators and lasted only long enough to exchange pleasantries and hand you the package."

> [T]here is not a fact in the world to justify your withdrawing $52,866.67 from Jim's checking account and putting it in your own. Your act was the most egregious violation possible of the fiduciary duty you owed to Jim and Karen, and no lawyer does what you did without knowing the sanctions associated with it. . . . Jim will have clear and practical options open to him if he determines there is no way to resolve this matter professionally and amicably, and he has set December 7, when he

will leave South Africa for the United States, as the time by which he must make this determination. Jim's options will include a suit against you asking that, based on your breach of fiduciary duty in converting his funds, a court deny you all fees in the matter and subject you to a statutory treble damage penalty. Such a suit, as well as actions based on other theories, would render both you and each partner of Layton, Brooks & Hecht financially liable for your conduct.

James wrote Philip and Janet Byler on November 28. (Both his and Thomas's previous letters were headed "fee dispute.") Thomas's letter had been written from "a lawyer's point of view." Now James wrote for himself and his wife.

> [O]ur sense of injury was justified. Since I was there, I can know with certainty that we had no agreement, as Phil now suggests. I think you must, at least in your heart of hearts, know this as well. . . . A friendship has now been broken and we can only assume our good name is being called into question and will become permanently damaged if we let your false picture of events stand. This is even more central than the financial issues for us. . . . Our hope is that you will call and we can simply work our [he means "out"] a fair settlement on the phone. . . . Failing this, we would gladly accept some form of fair and impartial arbitration. . . . if these are not possible . . . we will with great sadness, but with clarity of purpose, proceed with the legal options that we have. . . .

James wrote them again the next day after receiving Thomas's analysis of the "non-bill bill."

> At the time I felt the hours were grossly inflated in line with the pompous tone of the cover letter which I felt it best to ignore. I thought it was just a way for you to say—look at what a great job I am doing. . . . What is most shocking now however, is the review of these hours against your latest bill. This is revealing as to your billing style and would seem to call into question your honesty. Apparently the work items remain exactly the same, but now the time has expanded from 46 hours

to over 110, often simply by multiplying the previous number of hours by exactly 3. This would seem to test even your persuasive powers to explain.

From now on he would communicate only by fax rather than telephone "so that we retain an absolutely clear record of our communications."

Byler responded that day (with a copy of his contemporaneous letter to Thomas, below). He did not understand James's "concerns about your reputation. I am the one whose professional integrity has come under an unprecedented assault, partly through your brother's misinformed advocacy for you." The purpose of the non-bill bill "was so that you would come around to reaching an agreement with me on paying me." Byler had "made deep cuts in the recording of hours that I actually spent. (The other alternative, charging a New York paralegal's billing rate, was not something that I wanted on the record.)" He sent it "as a matter for your conscience because I felt you needed to come to terms on this matter and I thought it best . . . if you amicably reached an agreement with me on my payment in good faith." Instead, Jim "ignored the subject until June 1994." He had enclosed a bill in his October 28 letter "to show you what legal services of the kind that you received really cost when fully billed. (My hours in that bill are accurately recorded; you do not do the work I did and achieve the results I have without those kind of hours.)" Had he given James "that full bill in April 1994 and demanded payment, you would have gone 'ballistic' and would of course not agreed to pay a cent."

Byler reiterated this in the hearing.

> I decreased the amount of the non-bill. I didn't increase it in the sense of going from the non-bill to the pro forma bill. The pro forma bill was based on the red book entries. . . .

> Edelstein: . . . what number were you working from to arrive at those reductions in preparation of the non-bill bill?

> Byler: I was trying to eyeball something to come in at $10,000. Because that's what was in my mind. If he's going to pay $17,000 to the I.R.S., O.K., he's doing better financially. At least he ought to be able to pay me $10,000 for the work I did.

> Edelstein: The dollars, the bottom line, so to speak, literally, that's what you were aiming for, not accuracy in the particular . . .

Chapter 6

> Byler: Accuracy in the sense of hours. I was using an artificial billing rate . . . I think it was like 200 some dollars.

He claimed he had been billing at $275 to $300 and was trying to raise that to $350. He did not reduce his rate for Morgan, though he claimed to be charging less than other New York City attorneys.

> Byler: [O]n the non-bill . . . I cut [the hours] in order to get the numbers down, the absolute numbers.
>
> Edelstein: But what did you base that cut on? . . .
>
> Byler: An arbitrary cut in order to get down to a number in the range of $10,000. . . . I just uniformly cut in order to do a computation that resulted in the number. . . . It was stupid. . . . Klutzy.

The October bill represented "a more accurate reflection of time," documented by his "Red-Book entries." He claimed that $350 "was a rate I had charged on a number of matters . . . that was the rate that I wanted to charge in '94 . . . I was not able to charge it all of the time with all of the clients." He had recorded 148.5 hours "which struck me about doing pretty good for the nature of the work." Then he tried to choose "the better rate that would get you to about [$]50[,000], [$]55,000. It came out to be around $350." He admitted, however, that his Red Book entries diverged from the October bill, claiming he had cut days from the April bill and then restored the wrong ones in the October bill. But when a lengthy colloquy suggested he had changed time entries in his Red Book, he denied doing so, explaining that "sloppiness is probably the answer."

> Edelstein: So it's just a coincidence that the crossed out material is replaced with numbers that coincide with the later bill?
>
> Byler: No . . . I did combine some days rather than, you know, fiddle around with it more.

Byler wrote Thomas the same day. He deplored "Jim's rejection of my generous, carefully reasoned offer to resolve this matter amicably." Instead, James "wishes to litigate against the lawyer (me) who bailed him out. . . . Thanks and gratitude would be more in order." Thomas's last letter made "unsupportable assertions and misstate[ed] facts." The $20,000 flat fee for litigation "was *not* based on cost but on a cheap deal that I would do for a friend." "Jim may have been used to the cheap deals that I proposed but never implemented when we were dealing in circumstances of what I thought were his limited financial means and his potential liability . . . you might as well admit that, in time, your brother took advantage of a friend." "I did *not* take the IRS refund check; I implemented the agreement of June 20, 1994 . . . there certainly was *no* breach of fiduciary duty, only long overdue payment." "Jim apparently wants to have the benefit of 2 1/2 years of my successful representation without paying for it. To me, that is fraudulent behavior . . . any lawsuit by Jim in this case would be totally without merit and I feel would constitute an abuse of process." "It is totally unreasonable to expect me to submit to arbitration."

Byler testified:

> I did make a settlement offer. There was never any reciprocal offer. Had they come in and said 30, 35, 40, and we'll argue about the rest, I'll say O.K. to that. Maybe if we escrow that amount—but then we've got to talk about maybe you owe me more because, you know, the agreement is what it is, but you're not going to live by that.

On December 5 he again denounced Morgan's "attempt to renegotiate my legal fee." Morgan's "attempt to deny that agreement is dishonest and has already been destructive." The non-bill was a "non-consideration." He repeated his "generous" offer, concluding: "At this point, what I should receive from you is thanks."

Morgan responded two days later, accusing Byler of not forwarding his mail and seeking to obtain mail being held for him at their church. "[T]o make it absolutely clear that you have no authority to act for us, *Karen and I revoke your power of attorney to act for us in this or any other manner.*"

> After returning our property to us, I hope you will reflect on you [sic] recent actions. Nothing that is good and lasting can be built on a lie, no matter how one may have rationalized it in ones [sic] mind. No matter what you may try to tell to others Phil, the reality you can not escape is that *you* know the truth.

CHAPTER 6

> While I am realistic enough not to expect it given the continuing belligerent tone of your letters, Karen and I will continue to hope and pray that you will come to your senses before we have to proceed with the legal options open to us.

Byler retorted that day (by certified mail, return receipt requested), denying Morgan's charges.

> *The Truth.* The truth is that we made our agreement . . . written and documented. . . . you are the one who has lied, and both you and I—as well as the Almighty—know that you are the one who has lied. You are posturing; that is all.

C. *The Disciplinary Complaint*

Morgan complained to the Departmental Disciplinary Committee the following month. In February Byler wrote Edelstein, objecting to the "dishonest and galling" complaint. In his March 17 and 25 affidavits he called it "a case of false accusation by an ungrateful former client and former friend . . . against a conscientious lawyer." In his deposition a year later he insisted "this has always been . . . an attempt to misuse this forum as a way of renegotiating a fee." It had "been one of the most horrendous experiences I have ever had." Morgan "turns around and tried, in a complaint, to destroy my career and my ability to support my family." The following month he filed a 63-page single-spaced motion to dismiss. In May he wrote DDC chief counsel Hal R. Lieberman to complain about Edelstein's "mistaken and at times jaundiced view" of the matter and raise "due process interests involved." "Even Abraham Lincoln was once accused—falsely—of converting client monies to personal use." Lincoln's "ire knew no bounds."

The DDC admonished Byler on July 15, 1996, for violating his obligations to inform a client of the implications of a fee agreement and to escrow the disputed fee.[850] This would lead to formal disciplinary charges if he failed to return or escrow the funds. Byler responded with an 85-page brief to DDC chairman Haliburton Fales II, complaining about the "unconscionable error."[851] "I cannot state strongly enough how ill-considered

---

[850] DR 2-106(D) and 9-102(B)(4).
[851] Philip A. Byler to Haliburton Fales II (August 5, 1996), "Application for Reconsideration of Letter of Admonition/Demand for Formal Proceedings."

the Letter of Admonition is and how unjust it is to me—a lawyer, with credentials who has an otherwise unblemished record."

> The complainant's pretentious claim that it is brought to stop me from doing to others what I did to James Morgan is both galling and insensible. This false complaint is rather brought to misuse this Committee as a way of obtaining money for James Morgan and of his justifying gross ingratitude.

In response to Byler's sworn testimony, Morgan had "submitted only an intemperate, speculative, unsworn reply." Lieberman's failure to discuss the Letter of Admonition "calls into question" its validity. Edelstein replied that Byler was entitled to either a review by Fales or a formal proceeding but had to choose between them; she reiterated this by phone two days later.

Byler wrote again the following week demanding a formal hearing, "which by rule vacates the ill-considered Letter of Admonition." But he simultaneously argued for reconsideration because the complaint "misstates and mistreats the facts," "fundamentally misapplies" the law, and "results in an unjust outcome."[852] It was "a wholly misconceived document, unbecoming to the Committee." "[T]he due process problems in this proceeding . . . require that my Letter Brief be so considered and that I be given an opportunity to be heard personally; and in any event, out of elementary professional courtesy, the factual and legal analysis presented in my Letter Brief should be given thoughtful consideration given the lawyer I am" (which he described in detail, starting with Harvard Law School). He "DEMAND[ED]" that his letter brief "BE READ AND CAREFULLY REVIEWED BY THE COMMITTEE NOW." Were formal charges "mistakenly filed, it would be a continuation of a process in this case that already has gone astray. . . ." He "DEMAND[ED]" that "ANY FURTHER PROCEEDINGS BE MADE OPEN TO THE PUBLIC" in order to expose "the unscrupulous behavior of the client James Morgan, the misconduct of James Morgan's brother-representative (who violated DR 7-105 in this case) and the handling of this case by Staff Counsel." Three days later he elected to forego reconsideration.[853] On November 22 he was served with charges of failing to maintain intact a client's funds and failing to pay funds

---

[852] Philip A. Byler to Haliburton Fales II (August 12, 1996).
[853] Mady Edelstein to Haliburton Fales (August 15, 1996).

CHAPTER 6

due to a client. He answered on February 6, 1997. The liability phase was heard on April 24, May 29, and July 17, 1997, before Joan Ellenbogen (chair), Robert L. Haig, and Frederick D. Wilkinson (a layperson). Edelstein represented the DDC and Angelo Cometa (of Tenzer Greenblatt) represented Byler.[854]

Cometa sought to portray Morgan as a chronic tax evader, claiming that his company still owed over $140,000 in taxes to the City and State of New York. In cross examination he got Morgan to agree that Byler had done a "terrific job" and Morgan had congratulated him "every time that I talked to him." In his opening statement, Cometa said "no one would ever, even to a best friend, devote so much time at the expense of other clients whom you could be working for, and end up with $2,000 and change."

When sworn in Byler announced this was "the fifth time I put myself under oath in this case." He described Morgan's tax shelter as "very, very aggressive" and started to detail its terms, until Ellenbogen interrupted: "I don't know that it's our role to determine whether or not the hours you claim to have put in are valid hours. That's a fee dispute between client and attorney. . . ." Byler explained why he did not have a retainer letter.

> Because my practice . . . is that I have had oral retentions and I've never had a problem before. . . . this was out of the ordinary course. In the ordinary course, for example, when Kay-Three Communications Corporation retained me on a copyright defense, which I won on summary judgment, not even at trial, I had a conversation with assistant general counsel and he basically said you send my bill . . . and that was it. . . . Never a problem. Every bill paid right away. . . . What I did here was special, given the circumstances that James Morgan was in.

Byler agreed in response to Ellenbogen that he had never said Morgan would owe him nothing if there were no refund. Asked what he would have done had it been $200,000, he conceded "there is an excessiveness issue at some point." When Ellenbogen insisted there was a fee dispute obligating Byler to put the refund in escrow, he replied:

> [T]he demand from his brother was to escrow everything. And that was in a particular context. Namely, he accused me

---

[854] The transcript of the liability phase occupied 714 pages.

of stealing the money. And I was unfortunately put in the position that if I then escrowed the money I agree in effect that I had stole [sic] the money, that . . . it was [an] unreasonable amount that I had been paid. That I agreed in effect that he [Thomas] could determine it. . . . I didn't accept any of that. I felt I had no practical alternative but to stand on my legal position that with an enforceable agreement to be paid that amount . . . that the rights to the monies had been transferred to me and that it was not client's funds but my monies. . . . I don't maintain an escrow account in my regular practice, don't handle other people's money. . . .

He denied there could have been a mutual mistake of fact. When Ellenbogen questioned the "coincidence" that the October bill exactly equaled the refund, Byler said

that was happenstance, using $350 . . . there was no agreement on billing rate . . . but that would be a fair and reasonable rate for mine had I not entered into the special terms. . . . If no refund comes through . . . I go to him and say, we should renegotiate.

When Byler sent the "non-bill bill"

it had been a year and three quarters . . . since I had taken the case and I felt, quite frankly, he had abused the relationship. . . . I'm going on and on and on through all this time . . . and he's still not dealing with things. And it turns out he had money in a bank account that got seized that I didn't know of.

Ellenbogen: But you didn't send him a bill, did you?

Byler: No . . . because . . . we didn't have a billing relationship. . . .

Ellenbogen: What would make him think you wanted money if you never had a discussion with him? . . .

Byler: He did know the work I was doing because he received copies of all if [of] what I was doing in terms of the work. . . . And so the purpose . . . of the non-bill was, and it was kind of klutzy, was to give him a nudge to deal with the subject. . . .

Chapter 6

> I did not send him a bill because the nature of the agreement was, the agreement to agree, that we would have to work out the amount.... something is coming in view and so I put together in the form of a bill what was not a bill... because he had no legal obligation to honor any bill.... our agreement to agree from the start was what I would be paid for the agency work would be dependent upon, in part, on what results in the case would occur....

He sought to explain his April 1994 letter: "I was not having any thought in my mind about suing him because he lives in South Africa. Because I don't like the idea of suing a client."

The hearing resumed on May 29 with a third lawyer member, Philip R. Forlenza. Louis Lauer testified they had lunch together immediately after the June 20 meeting. (Lauer had been of counsel at the time; Byler had followed him to that firm, as he had to their previous firm.)

> I said what is the refund going to be? ... he didn't know.... I then said to him that I was concerned about his agreeing to do this because I was afraid that the amount of the refund ... would be substantially less ... than what he would be entitled to get as a matter of his service to the client and the result he produced, which I thought was extraordinary.... He told me that ... Morgan gave him a deposit slip and a check and told him to put the money, the refund, whatever it is it is, into ... his account, and then use the check to pay him. And that would be it. I didn't know how he could do that.

He later explained he was concerned about its adequacy. When the hearing continued on July 17, the panel refused to admit either a client benefit chart prepared by Cometa (since the reasonableness of the fee was not in issue) or evidence that Morgan had outstanding warrants for $104,000 in tax liabilities.

During closing arguments on November 11 Cometa sought to raise "a due process objection to the proceeding based on the fact that John Horan, who we all know, is privately representing James Morgan in an action against—." But the panel cut him off. That was the first they had heard of it. Forlenza rebuked Cometa: "You've created the problem by bring [sic] to our attention something we didn't know." (This was Morgan's civil suit against Byler for return of the refund. Horan was a member of the DDC Policy Committee. It later emerged that Horan's partner, Anthony Davis, helped Morgan file the original disciplinary complaint. Byler had written Horan an angry letter the previous January: "I should have known better at this point to show trust and rely on an oral agreement in a case involving James Morgan, even with someone representing him. From now on I think we are going to have to follow a procedure of written stipulations to define our agreements." In a later letter (after November 7) Byler accused Horan of "an unreasonable refusal on your part to deal with" interrogatories and notices to admit. He also put Horan "on notice that I do consider it to be ethically improper for you both to represent James Morgan in this civil suit and be a member of the Disciplinary Committee. . . .")

Cometa submitted an 89-page single-spaced post-hearing brief to dismiss the charges, which were "a result of the ill-conceived misfocus of Staff Counsel's approach to the case, leading to mistreatment of the facts and misinterpretations of the CPR lacking case support." He quoted Byler's February 15, 1996, deposition:

> [W]hat this has always been about has been an attempt to misuse this forum as a way of renegotiating a fee . . . it's been one of the most horrendous experiences I have ever had. Because as my record shows, it's unblemished. I have been known as somebody who is highly scrupulous and ethical. . . . clients know me as somebody ethical and responsible. And that's what I am. . . . I represented this guy on special terms. And I saved him from financial disaster. And what does he do? He turns around and tried, in a complaint, to destroy my career and my ability to support my family. I find this so very wrong.

He objected to the "lack of fairness" in excluding his client benefit chart and evidence of Morgan's outstanding tax indebtedness, as well as Ellenbogen's evaluation of the evidence. The brief included Byler's March and May 1995 affidavits, February 1996 deposition, February 1997 answer, and a 35-page appendix of cases.

The Staff reply was only 10 double-spaced pages (with a 19-page legal memorandum). Byler had shown "his disdain for the Panel and its rulings." His

> exaggerations reflect a self-serving interpretation of statements and events that is entirely consistent with his self-interested

CHAPTER 6

interpretation of the alleged fee agreement. It is also consistent with his insistence that despite the spate of angry and explicit demand letters from his client and his brother, there was no fee dispute here.

Byler replied with 28 single-spaced pages.

On August 31, 1998, the panel unanimously sustained one charge of failing to deposit client funds in a trust account and one of failing to deliver them to Morgan. Four days before the October 2 sanctions hearing, Cometa wrote the DDC asking to withdraw as counsel. Byler wrote the same day, "surprised by what is a sudden development." Cometa's letter had "inaccuracies and omissions . . . on which, in fairness, I should be heard." "The integrity of the system is at stake." Byler sought "to prevent a misuse of the ethics forum for private purposes." He wished that Cometa, "when he first addressed you about my case had told you about what I accomplished for complainant." It was "not 'ethics' to twist bizarrely this case." The Code of Professional Responsibility was not about

> penalizing lawyers for providing counsel on special terms . . . [or] for producing excellent results . . . [or] about rewarding client ingratitude . . . that seeks to avoid a compensation agreement with that lawyer and certainly not about rewarding unethical accusations asserted in attempting to renegotiate a fee—a violation of DR 7-105.

Cometa should have "noted that Mr. Lieberman refused to meet me on this case." Byler's briefs "showed the Charges to be trumped up and Staff Counsel's case to be without merit."

> Mr. Horan's representation of complainant concerning the same subject matter of this ethics proceeding—arranged by complainant's attorney-brother—irretrievably casts a cloud of impropriety over any action recommended by the panel and imposed by the Committee, particularly since in the state court action, after a whole year, Mr. Horan has done nothing except to obstruct my discovery and thus can only be reasonably presumed to expect the panel and the Committee to assist him. Furthermore . . . any attempt to insist on an escrow (as in the Admonition) must be considered objectively

> as rendering assistance to a Committee member's private state court litigation.

Byler objected to

> the prejudicially unfair evidentiary rulings, comments and conduct of Ms. Ellenbogen as panel chair (which she did while no longer being a member of the Committee). Ms. Ellenbogen's actions in twisting and distorting facts and in restricting my proof was but a continuing of the bizarre approach taken to the case by complainant's attorney-brother (he was assisting Staff Counsel)....

He had paid about 40 percent of the $100,000 in fees and costs owed to Tenzer Greenblatt, but Cometa and he "have not discussed the bill for the last five or six months." Cometa was withdrawing in part because "this case has been very stressful." It must have been "upsetting to hear a client (me) ask such questions as: How would one file an ethics complaint against a member of the committee?"

He urged the DDC to take a "fresh look" and dismiss the case because "what has happened in this proceeding . . . reflects horribly on the system." Anticipating evidence later offered in mitigation, he concluded:

> I don't believe I have deserved what I have been put through in this proceeding. Too much of it has seemed like reckless character assassination. But I have battled on because for me, there can be no compromise with an abuse of authority aimed at perpetrating a lie. There was a time when Americans believed in Sacred Honor. I still do.

II. The Inability to Admit Error

After a month's postponement, Byler represented himself at the November 3 mitigation hearing.[855] Joseph R. Sahid, a retired partner at Cravath (where

---

[855] Byler told me Cometa quit suddenly just before the mitigation phase because he was fed up with being pressured by the DDC to persuade Byler to apologize.

Chapter 6

Byler had been an associate for six years), was there for "moral support, informal advice and counseling." Because Sahid declined to make a formal appearance, the panel let him stay but not to advise Byler or object to testimony. Byler began by challenging the procedure at the prior liability phase, but Ellenbogen reminded him this was a mitigation hearing. Byler offered the usual character affidavits by Sahid, Irwin H. Warren and Michael K. Stanton (both Weil Gotshal partners), Louis Lauer, and Patrick J. Rohan (dean emeritus of St. John's University and an ethics expert). Byler had practiced for 22 years without a contempt citation or complaint. When Edelstein successfully objected to his claim that he had "not even come close to having any kind of disciplinary problem," Ellenbogen rebuked him for continuing to testify over Edelstein's objection. When Byler talked about a Waldorf-Astoria dinner at which a client received an award "in front of a large audience, 400 people," Ellenbogen interrupted: "But you didn't. . . . Please go on to something else." Byler insisted this client "praised me in that acceptance speech and I think it's fair that a large group of lawyers and people in the media heard me described as a 'knight in shining armor.'" He was married, with two teenage sons, and on the board of directors of the local little league. He also coached basketball "because it is an opportunity to work with and provide a role model for youth." "I have tried to contribute to society in a way which, you know, throughout America is important."

When he described his energetic defense in the liability phase, Ellenbogen said there was no "charge of a failure to cooperate." Byler had resisted the admonition because "I wanted to keep my unblemished record. And I generally felt that the admonition was in error in a number of ways outlined in the lengthy brief, which I have marked and we can put it in the record." But Ellenbogen replied it was not "appropriate to reargue the underlying action."

> Byler: I might note that I did not have any meetings with Staff counsel although one was originally scheduled and I did not have—
>
> Forlenza: Mr. Byler, what's the relevance of all this to mitigation?
>
> Byler: Because I tried to cooperate.
>
> Forlenza: We have agreed that you have. . . . Just move on to the character.

> Byler: I was disappointed.
>
> Forlenza: That's irrelevant.
>
> Byler: When the charges came down . . . I did take the position in the answer that there were no violations.
>
> Ellenbogen: We are past that, sir. . . . We are not relitigating that.
>
> Byler: I'm not testifying as to relitigating. I'm stating the procedural history to show—
>
> Forlenza: Let's move on.
>
> Byler: I have prepared two charts to go through certain points . . . to review with you various factors.
>
> Ellenbogen: No . . .
>
> Byler: My testimony, and the reason why I prepared the chart, was I want to make sure that we have before you I have an unblemished record over 22 years—
>
> Ellenbogen: . . . I'm objecting because that you've said.

But Byler continued to proclaim his wronged innocence. He had "over the course of a long period of time, had to expend a lot of time and money in defending myself." This was a "one-time situation," an "isolated situation."

> Byler: I also presented evidence to the best I could that, if anything, the client, even after compensation was received by me, economically benefited. He had—
>
> Ellenbogen: Now you're going back to the merits of the underlying proceeding.
>
> Byler: . . . I'm offering in the sense that when one considers injury to the client, injury to the public . . . there was not injury, that's all. . . .
>
> Ellenbogen: That's your opinion. . . . It wasn't the complainant's opinion. . . .

Chapter 6

Byler: Well, he did testify that—he did testify—

Forlenza: Wait, wait, let's move on. Restrict yourself to factual testimony . . . not argument.

Byler: I just want to make sure that the factual point is covered.

Forlenza: Mr. Byler, do you understand that this panel is asking you to be brief and to the point? And every time someone makes a comment, do you have to have the last word?

Byler: I don't intend to have the last word.

Forlenza: Well, then, work on it. . . .

Ellenbogen objected when Byler consulted Sahid. Byler said he was only asking about the law, but the panel told him to stick to facts.

Byler: I appreciate that very much because some testimony I might try to give or go into I'll confuse my role as advocate which I dearly love. I think—I mean, there are other items which I have my notes on but I don't think it narrowly relates—

Ellenbogen: To the facts.

Byler: —and I will exercise some prudence here and conclude my testimony. . . .

Edelstein cross-examined him.

Edelstein: Have you to today's date returned any funds to Mr. Morgan?

Byler: There has been no request to do so—it's the subject of state court litigation . . . in which there is counterclaims from me for payment by agreement and payment by quantum meruit. . . .

Edelstein: [asked about the DDC investigation and his deposition] And did there come a time when it became clear to you that the Committee's position was that you should return the funds to Mr. Morgan or place them in escrow? . . .

Byler: No.

On redirect Byler maintained the Staff never asked him to return the money to Morgan.

> Ellenbogen: Did Mr. Morgan ever ask you to return monies?
>
> Byler: No, no, no, it was to escrow.
>
> Forlenza: Ever? He's never asked you to return the money?
>
> Byler: Sitting here, my recollection is no, that was never an issue.
>
> Ellenbogen: What is he suing you for? To return the money.

When Byler denied having had any financial problems in June 1994 concerning mortgage, credit cards, and office expenses, Edelstein introduced his June 3 letter to Dr. Jan Moor-Jankowski (the client honored at the Waldorf-Astoria dinner).

> The last time I wrote you about paying my $22,000 bill was April 22, 1994—six weeks ago. . . . I am out of patience with not being paid. Please make sure that I receive the $12,000 next Wednesday (as you promise) and the remaining $10,000 by June 15th. . . .
>
> I am embarrassed that I cannot pay my new office the rent and expenses due now until next week, after I told them I would pay them by Friday of this week (having relied on what Debra and you told me). I am embarrassed about not being able to pay my house mortgage. I am embarrassed about receiving phone calls from Chemical Bank at home (which Janet takes) about past due amounts on my Mastercard and Privilege Checking accounts. I am embarrassed about not being able to pay for certain summer programs for my boys John and James. And all of what I am embarrassed about is very public. . . .
>
> I cannot go any longer without being paid. . . . I feel a sense of unfairness about the present situation: I took responsibility for and won the *Immuno* case for you; I litigated the *Hartford* case for you without charging fees (which would have been $200,000) and brought in a successful result; I achieved the results in the Family Court litigation for you against May

> Louise two years ago, billed you for efficiently done work at a relatively low rate and carried the bill for two years; I have not billed you for what the legal profession would unquestionably see as billable counselling [sic] in your matrimonial case.

Byler told the panel: "there comes a time when you have to start putting your foot down, and that's all that this was about. . . ." Forlenza asked if Byler had been able to pay his mortgage:

> Byler: I did pay my mortgage.
>
> Forlenza: So that was a misstatement?
>
> Byler: It was not a misstatement in the sense that I was not able to pay from current revenues; in other words, I cashed in some stock in June.

Edelstein then asked if Moor-Jankowski had questioned Byler's ethics.

> Byler: He and I had a falling out.
>
> Edelstein: Did that falling out not relate to accusations by your client that you had overbilled him?
>
> Byler: He made, as to bills that had been paid years ago, such accusations knowing that this proceeding was pending. . . .
>
> Edelstein: Did he not accuse you of being deceptive with him?
>
> Ellenbogen: Yes or no.
>
> Byler: I don't recall the specific word "deceptive." . . . But there were harsh words there.

Edelstein introduced Moor-Jankowski's letter to Byler of October 30, 1997:

> For years I remained devoted to you because of our Immuno victory.
>
> Finally, however, I had to dismiss you as my lawyer and I cannot agree to your proposed "face-to-face calm(ly) talk" because, in my repeated experience, you can no longer control

The Perils of Perfectionism

your temper, nor accept documented facts concerning your overbilling and deception of me.

Byler commented: "I thought what statements he was making at the time were very unfair and were very unfortunate because he did know about this proceeding, and he is in his seventies and, I felt, exercised some poor judgment." Moor-Jankowski had been in ill-health "for years."

Ellenbogen: What's wrong with him?

Byler: He's in his seventies, he's got a heart condition.

Ellenbogen: Seventies, we're all approaching that, please.

Byler: There's a combination of health factors.

Ellenbogen: Does he have Alzheimer's?

Byler: The last time I talked to him, no, but—

Ellenbogen: That's all I was asking because that's what you were intimating. . . . You're assuming Mr. Jankowski's reason for writing the letter [to influence this proceeding] and that is improper testimony.

As redirect ended, the panel prevented Sahid from advising Byler, even outside the hearing room, or addressing them (although he claimed to have more mitigation evidence). Ellenbogen concluded:

At hearings such as this, the respondent has an opportunity to come in with or without witnesses to express either—and I'm not dealing with this case in particular—remorse, reasons for a behavior that's aberrant, why hypothetically money was stolen because they couldn't pay a hospital bill for a dying spouse . . . character witnesses to show that what he has been found to have done wrong was an aberration, that it would never happen again.

The problem you have here is that Mr. Byler does not believe that the findings are correct. . . .

The panel then asked its own questions.

Chapter 6

Haig: Mr. Byler, as you sit there today, are you sorry that you didn't put this money in escrow?

Byler: Am I sorry? With the benefit of hindsight, one might have taken a different course of action.

Ellenbogen: No, not "one," he's asking you a specific question.

Byler: Sorry?

Ellenbogen: The answer is yes or no.

Byler: I'm sorry this whole thing happened and that's one part of it.

Ellenbogen: Can you not answer his question yes or no?

Byler: I know why I didn't, yes, I don't know that I can answer yes or no.

Ellenbogen: Fine, he cannot answer your question.

Byler: I am sorry that the thing happened.

Ellenbogen: Please, I'm talking.

Byler: I know.

Ellenbogen: You know?

Byler: Yes, and I was trying to be responsive.

Ellenbogen: No, I'm talking; that means you stop talking . . .

Haig: [rephrased the question]

Byler: I didn't mean to be obstreperous or difficult. I know why I didn't escrow the money at the time. I felt I had earned it. I felt that I was put in an unfair situation.

Haig: Mr. Byler, with respect to—

Byler: But on the other hand—

Ellenbogen: He's talking

Haig: I asked you if you were sorry that you did not place the money in escrow. . . .

Byler: I'm sorry I didn't find a way to have done so that I thought was safe.... with the benefit of hindsight, I would have perhaps tried to handle it in a way of, while reserving my rights—because honestly I felt I had earned the money and I didn't think it was right—but reserving my rights somehow to have done—I don't know why it didn't happen and I guess all that's gone on, if there was an easier way out of this, you know, I'm sorry that somehow I didn't do that.... In retrospect, yes, I'm sorry that I didn't find a way. It's not as simple as just putting money in escrow.

Forlenza: Why not? You testified you didn't do so because you thought it was an admission of guilt—

Byler: Yeah, basically.

Forlenza: —which I personally found extraordinary. Is that still your position as you look back ... is that still your view—

Byler: That was clear—

Forlenza: I guess you don't want to hear the end of my question.

Byler: No, I do. I was too anxious to go ahead.

Forlenza: Well, with the benefit of hindsight and all that's transpired, is it still your view there were legitimate reasons for not putting this money in escrow until this dispute was dealt with....

Byler: I think the position I held at the time and what was briefed to you would constitute legitimate reasons....

Forlenza: [rephrased the question] Your client had clearly a different view of it than you had articulated and there was a demand that the money be put in escrow. My question is, with the benefit of hindsight, do you think that you could have and should have put the money in escrow under those circumstances? ...

Byler: Yes, subject to the risks that I was concerned with at the time....

Forlenza: Do you still think, in retrospect, there was a legitimate risk that you would be prejudicing your position and making some kind of admission ... ?

CHAPTER 6

Byler: [referred to his earlier testimony]

Forlenza: I'm not asking about page 64—

Byler: I know.

Forlenza: —I'm asking for a simple and straight answer. This is the mitigation stage.

Byler: I understand that.

Forlenza: [repeated his question]

Byler: . . . with the benefit of hindsight, I would still say there was a risk. . . . Part of the problem at the time was, I know, I felt I was being very unfairly attacked by accusations that just should not have been made. . . . I was angry with the Morgan brothers . . . and I did rely on the advice of Lou Lauer . . . it was a difficult situation because I don't handle client funds, I don't have an escrow . . . so it's a foreign matter to me. . . .

Forlenza: There then came a time when the Disciplinary Committee took the same position and you had plenty of time on your own or through expert counsel to determine what was a proper course of action.

Byler: But I've always had the expert counsel saying no, there's not an escrow obligation. . . .

Forlenza: [That was just Lauer.] You didn't obtain or get expert counsel advice from anyone else?

Byler: Not at that time. But I will tell you that one of the first things Mr. Cometa told me was—

Edelstein: Objection.

Ellenbogen: Objection sustained.

Byler: —that the—

Ellenbogen: Did you hear "objection"?

Byler: I did hear the objection.

Ellenbogen: Thank you, and it's sustained.

Forlenza: As practicing counsel, you know that it's improper to keep talking while an objection is pending so you get what you want to get on the record. . . . Was an additional consideration in the summer of 1994 your financial consideration that you've testified to earlier today?

Byler: No. . . .

Forlenza: It's your testimony that that financial situation had no impact whatsoever on—

Byler: The decision—

Forlenza: Did you want to hear the end of my sentence?

Byler: Yes, I'm sorry, I apologize.

Forlenza:—had no impact whatsoever on your decision not to put these funds in escrow as demanded by your client?

Ellenbogen: That requires a yes or no, sir.

Byler: Given the wording of your question, I think it did have an impact.

Forlenza: And what was that impact?

Byler: Well, I think the impact was that if I did not have an obligation to escrow and given the fact that I felt I had independently earned the money, period, or whatever way you want to go at it, quantum meruit, by agreement, I wasn't no doubt inclined to take the step of escrowing the money.

Forlenza: You were not inclined?

Byler: Yes.

Forlenza: Because of the financial situation? . . .

Byler: If I generally felt there was a professional obligation, I would have done so.

At the end of this exchange Byler was allowed to consult with Sahid but not to change his testimony. Although Ellenbogen said the panel would not hear argument then, Byler insisted he had an undisputed right to some fee and no obligation to escrow it.

> [W]here you don't have pinning down an undisputed amount and a disputed amount, but just in this kind of very loose situation where, "Yeah, you're owed compensation," but you don't say what precisely—and that's really not fair to a lawyer—I used a reasonable judgment standard in determining what you would call a disputed portion [$5,500].

Edelstein proposed a two-year suspension, with Byler's reinstatement conditioned on escrowing or returning the funds. Byler sought an admonition: "You simply cannot get to the level of suspension." The staff submitted a 14-page double-spaced memorandum of law on sanctions. Byler's 15-page single-spaced brief argued that *any* penalty would encourage clients to evade contracts. He had had to defend against the charges for four years. He had no obligation to make restitution or to escrow and nothing to be remorseful about. He was prepared to escrow only $10,000 to satisfy the state court judgment.

Edelstein wrote Ellenbogen a year later, with a copy to Byler, asking why the panel had not decided. Byler wrote Ellenbogen two days later.

> [T]his matter is . . . over what complainant admitted was a "superb" representation in which I did a "terrific job" bringing "extraordinary results." Ms. Edelstein . . . does not acknowledge . . . that no written report could properly be written except to dismiss the case. . . . [her] unwise request [for a written report] prompts this letter.
>
> . . . the proper course is for you to refer this matter back to the Committee for its *de novo* review (at which time I will seek the long overdue dismissal of this case on the merits). You are not a member of the Committee and have not been a member for years; there is only one member of the panel who is still a member of the Committee, and under the Rules, one member cannot constitute a quorum. . . . none of the Charges were sustained . . . [and] a series of procedural irregularities afflict the integrity of the process resulting in the denial of a fair trial and denial of due process.

He repeated them at length, concluding with "a failure to have the constitutionally mandated impartial and neutral hearing body" and the denial of his request for a public hearing, which was "reversible error in itself."

He sent copies to DDC chair Dennis McInerney and chief counsel Thomas J. Cahill, with a cover letter reiterating his complaints and asking them to review the case so it "can be properly dismissed." He reiterated everything he had done for Morgan and repeated his legal arguments. "It is time for you to step in, for the sake of the integrity of the disciplinary process in the First Department." McInerney replied on November 10: "Since the matter is sub judice, I see no reason to intervene in that process." Byler retorted two days later that McInerney's letter "appears to contain some mistaken premises, and you appear to have overlooked some important points."

1. You write that the panel has rendered "findings" in this case. That is *not* accurate . . . under the applicable legal standard of the preponderance of the evidence, findings could not properly be entered to sustain any Charges.
2. . . . saying that this matter is *sub judice* does not deal with the passage of time or the serious *prejudicial irregularities* that have occurred. . . .
3. . . . due to the prejudicial irregularities . . . any "decision" of this panel . . . cannot stand. . . .
4. [He repeated those procedural objections.]
5. . . . I know my applications are not pleasant to deal with, but one reason that I am pressing the issue is that I have an obligation to the Bar to fight how the disciplinary process has gone astray.

III. The Persistence of Behavior

Perhaps moved by this, the Panel issued its report the next month.[856] "Although it found Morgan generally more credible" than Byler, who "frequently gave evasive and non-responsive answers and on at least one occasion appeared to change his version of Morgan's statement . . . the evidence surrounding the critical factual disputes is inconclusive." Nevertheless, Byler had an obligation to escrow the disputed refund.

> [N]o reasonably prudent attorney could have concluded that the alleged brief conversations with Morgan constituted an unequivocal and enforceable agreement. . . . There were also

---

[856] Wilkinson had died after participating in the liability decision.

significant open issues not resolved by the purported fee agreement.... There is also the question of whether a reasonably prudent attorney would have concluded that Morgan had authorized Respondent to use the deposit slip and blank signed check to transfer the funds . . . without prior notice to Morgan as to the actual amount of the refund. . . . Notwithstanding the vague nature of the purported fee agreement and the unexpected size of the refund, Respondent stubbornly refused to acknowledge that there was even a basis for a dispute. Moreover, Respondent offered a specious explanation for not putting the funds in escrow.

The Panel criticized Byler's lack of candor about Moor-Jankowski, whose representation he offered "as a mitigating factor despite his knowledge that the relationship had ended with a similar dispute." Byler also had denied his financial difficulties in June 1994, which "suggest a motivation for Respondent's adamant insistence that the purported fee agreement was valid and enforceable and his refusal—despite all that had occurred—to place the funds in escrow." The Panel noted the parallels between the two contemporaneous cases:

> Respondent expended significant effort on behalf of his clients and achieved an excellent result; and both cases ended in a bitter dispute with Respondent complaining that his efforts were underappreciated and the clients complaining that Respondent had engaged in misleading and improper conduct as regards his claimed entitlement to fees.

Byler's "self-righteous position . . . so out of touch with reality" was an aggravating factor. "Throughout the hearing, Respondent gave evasive testimony and persistently ignored rulings and instructions by the Panel Chair to stop testifying after an objection was raised or sustained." It recommended a year's suspension and escrow of the funds until the civil litigation concluded.

> Given Respondent's adamant failure to recognize that there was even a bona fide dispute given the unexpected size of the tax refund, let alone recognize that his conduct was improper, the Panel has concluded that nothing short of a suspension will serve to deter repetitive behavior....

Edelstein petitioned the Appellate Division to confirm the report and recommendation. Byler's answer challenged the Panel's jurisdiction because members' terms had expired and relitigated everything, including the exclusion of the Client Benefit Chart. The same day he filed a cross-motion to complete the record, dismiss the charges, or remand the case to the committee. This case showed "the need for reform of the disciplinary process." The "error-ridden" report, "replete with misstatements and omissions," failed to apply "correct contract rules in analyzing the compensation agreement." The recommended sanction was "grossly disproportionate and unprecedented." The Staff memoranda contained "very bad distortions." The trial committed "numerous errors . . . in evidentiary rulings." Byler also filed a 160-page memorandum of law reiterating everything. He deplored the "unprofessional character assassination of Mr. Byler." "[T]he Preamble to the Code of Professional Responsibility recognizes that a free and democratic society depends upon the Rule of Law. Sad to say, this case betrayed the Rule of Law with its rampant denials of due process of law." The "disciplinary process has gone horribly astray." His February 1995 answer had called the complaint "dishonest." His March 1995 affidavit labeled the complainant "absurd." "Nothing then happened until after John Horan's 1996-1998 term on the Committee commenced."

> [T]he report's reliance on a lack of contrition is out of place where Mr. Byler's position continues to be that there were no violations of the Code of Professional Responsibility and where there were so many laudatory aspects to Mr. Byler's representation. . . . Is Mr. Byler suppose [sic] to be remorseful about declining to place in escrow almost the entirety of his compensation, while complainant fully enjoyed the benefits of years of Mr. Byler's representation, in response to a demand made by complainant's brother that unethically coupled an accusation of theft with a further demand that Mr. Byler negotiate a reasonable fee? . . . The report's statement that Mr. Byler was self-righteousness [sic] and "out of touch with reality" reflects a report that indulges in personal attack on Mr. Byler and betrays the commitment of the CPR to the Rule of Law. . . . the denials of due process in this case make the report's attack on Mr. Byler should be considered intolerable [sic]. . . . The phrase "out of touch" would thus be far more appropriately used to describe the panel that was "out of touch" with the law,

Chapter 6

> due process of law, and the Commitment of the CPR to the Rule of Law. . . . With Mr. Byler having an otherwise blemished [sic] record . . . the report must be viewed as bizarre on this point. . . . in effect, the Committee acts as prosecutor, judge, jury and appellate advocate for the prosecutor. . . . Mix into this flawed system, panel members who are non-accountable former Committee members favorable to Staff Counsel and a Committee member who is counsel to the complainant, and the result is a thoroughly biased system that fails the constitutional requirement of an impartial tribunal.

Edelstein's reply objected to Byler's attempt "to place before this Court voluminous documents, under the rubric of 'supplements' to the record, which were either excluded from evidence at the hearing, or never offered. . . ." All Panel members were on the Committee when first appointed. "[T]he Panel exhibited extraordinary patience and courtesy to respondent," who made no request for an open hearing during the proceedings. "Respondent continues to demonstrate that he is a threat to the public because he is either unwilling or unable to recognize even the possibility of error on his part." Byler's cross-motion asked the Appellate Department to protect him from "retaliatory action" and discipline those "responsible for denials of due process in this case." "He continues to demonstrate his disdain for the Panel's rulings by submitting to this Court documents described on the record and expressly excluded from evidence. . . ." His claim that she had advised Ellenbogen to disregard his requests for review of the admonition and for public proceedings was "nonsense."

Byler wrote the Appellate Division clerk three days later, requesting leave for his "Sur-reply Letter Affirmation" to "Staff Counsel's conclusory, ill-focused Reply Affirmation." He relitigated everything.

> Putting to the side that Mr. Forlenza protested too much (to make a Shakespearean allusion), any self-serving statement by a panel in these circumstances cannot begin to justify blithely ignoring, as Staff Counsel does, all the legal and ethical problems created by what is a conflict of interest. . . . (Fn. Mr. Forlenza's approach to issues during the hearing was too often unjustified in disturbing ways . . . and Mr. Forlenza has misrepresented himself in the recent Martindale-Hubbell

in a number of ways, including that he was the Chairman of the Disciplinary Committee in 1997 and 1998....)

The Appellate Division approved the report and recommendation.[857]

> Suspension is warranted where an attorney has failed to return money that belongs to a client.... Even now, respondent has refused to accept any responsibility for his actions or to deposit the funds in escrow, on the specious grounds that returning the money would be an admission of misconduct that would prejudice his position.

It ordered him to deposit the refund with the court clerk in the civil action within 60 days.

Byler sought leave to appeal to the Court of Appeals and a stay of the above order, in a 107-page double-spaced motion restating everything.

> [T]his case is shown to be the most important disciplinary case that this Court can ever decide, one that can lead to needed reform of the disciplinary process in the First Department so as to restore the Rule of Law and provide beneficial guidance and structure to disciplinary matters throughout the State of New York.... [W]hat happened here is a very badly distorted mistreatment of law and fact that is the result of a process that functioned unconstitutionally and unlawfully to the disgrace of the New York legal system. It will follow that this case cannot be decided based upon what is a fictional misstatement of facts in the First Department's opinion that turns day into night.... Appellate Divisions do not have the discretion simply to ignore, as the First Department has bizarrely done here, the governing precedents of this Court.... [Review] will have the salutary effect of arresting a travesty and a miscarriage of justice....

The Court of Appeals denied his motion in October 2000, his motion for reconsideration in December, his motion for reconsideration of the

---

[857] Matter of Byler, 274 A.D.2d 275, 712 N.Y.S.2d 500 (1st Dep't 2000).

CHAPTER 6

denial of reconsideration on February 13, 2001, yet another motion for reconsideration on February 22, and his request for reargument on March 6.

Byler filed an 84-page affidavit of compliance on March 19, relitigating the entire case. His record was "unblemished" aside from this "six-year old proceeding," which involved "denials of due process of law and has not served the sound enforcement of the CPR." He had to "choose the path of honesty and state that I believe the case has been wrongly decided" in order "to be a catalyst for needed reform of that disciplinary process." He wanted to make a "statement for the record about the ethical misfocus in this case, the violations of constitutional due process and the tolerance of the corrupting conflict of interest afflicting this case. . . ." The Panel report "engaged in distorted personal attack amounting to character assassination, not part of a sound analysis of sanctions. . . ." He was "not evasive but rather confirming with a testy Staff Counsel." The "non-committee panel Chair's rulings, instructions and comments" were "erroneous and unfairly prejudicial to my case. . . ." Had the law been "well served"?

> I don't think so. Ends do not justify the means . . . [which] involved serious due process violations, including delegation of decision-making to private persons not authorized by law to act, toleration of a corrupting conflict of interest at the Departmental Disciplinary Committee, the denial of a requested public hearing, reliance on a biased tribunal lacking legal authority to act, reliance on a trial riddled with error having the nature of a private inquisition, a failure to apply the evidentiary standard with a consequent misstatement of facts. . . . Like in any prosecutor's office, individuals can be prosecuting Staff Counsel too long and act in ways that reflect an excess of prosecutorial zeal.

He deplored "the failure to uphold the due process of law" and "the errors" in the Appellate Division opinion, whose order "did not address the multitude of constitutional and legal errors and defects presented by me. . . ." Two weeks ago the Court of Appeals had denied reargument "without statement of reasons."

Early in the affidavit Byler declared he had complied with the AD order, "notwithstanding my conviction that it is contrary [to] law and unconstitutional in the circumstances of this case." Later, however, he "promised compliance with the ordered deposit with the New York County Clerk, notwithstanding my belief that it is mistaken. . . ."

> Based on the assumption that the ordered deposit is not simply a means to put money in the hands of complainant's counsel, I will comply, as soon as I can do so . . . there has been no prejudice from the money not being placed in escrow earlier. The last complaint that anyone can make about me in this six-year old disciplinary case is delay. In any event, in a fair adjudication in Morgan v. Byler, the monies placed with the New York County Clerk should be returned to me in full as my *quantum meruit* compensation for years of effective legal services in a difficult tax shelter case.

On April 1 Morgan's counsel petitioned the court in the civil action to hold Byler in contempt for failing to escrow the refund. The DDC did the same on May 1. Byler replied on June 12 that he was financially unable to comply. He was unemployed and had virtually no assets. The house was in his wife's name. On August 17 Judge Edward Lehner heard oral argument, denied both petitions, and granted Byler's motion to refer his counterclaim for legal fees to Special Referee Frank Lewis, who heard it on September 6. Byler had an accountant with IRS experience testify that the result was "unusually successful and beneficial." Lewis urged the parties to settle, which they did a week later, with Byler paying Morgan $10,000.

Byler submitted a 21-page petition and 35-page affidavit for reinstatement on September 26. Settlement of the civil claim "effectively renders moot the deposit provision" and DDC contempt motion. In opposition to the latter and in support of a cross-motion to hold it in abeyance pending the outcome of the civil action, he had pointed out "legal defects . . . under the New York Judiciary Law" and his "financial inability to comply . . . because of the effects of a prolonged disciplinary case then 6 1/2 years old." He relitigated the entire case. The Appellate Division had "curtly dismissed" his arguments and "did not specifically address the points stated in my Memorandum of Law." For the first time, however, he appeared to acknowledge a need to change.

> I will do what I reasonably can to avoid misunderstandings and disagreements. I believe that in today's world, a written retention and fee agreement is necessary. I have learned the

Chapter 6

> hard way that sometimes people surprise you in unpleasant ways, and due to the fact that legal services are expensive, client disputes as to bills may not be completely avoidable; so it is best to have a written record. In addition, I have resolved to insure that there is no reasonable way that I ever can be said to be handling client funds. . . . finally, I have always understood that if an escrow obligation is accepted, that the obligations and requirements of the escrow are carefully observed.

But he continued to call the sanction "disproportionate in the first place" and "the panel's purported consideration of aggravating factors" "a distorted personal attack."

Although he had promised to deposit the refund in March, he lost his job at Kalow & Springut soon thereafter and could not do so. He described coaching little league teams and his own athletic activities, as well as the quality of his representation of Morgan.

> Given . . . the record at the *quantum meruit* hearing, I respectfully submit that there should be some amount of disquiet about what has happened in this nearly *seven*-year old disciplinary case. . . . Anyone reading this Court's opinion in the public record would have no idea that as a result of my able and conscientious work and representation of the client, the client was the beneficiary of an extraordinary result which experienced people in the field would not think possible. . . .

He accused the Panel and the court of misunderstanding "the law of contract formation." "[I]t may be reasonably questioned why there was a *seven*-year disciplinary case topped off with a suspension, with all the attendant damage such a prolonged case would and did cause to my professional and personal life. . . ." "I believe there is a need to reform the disciplinary process . . . so that . . . the CPR is given a more principled application."

Edelstein opposed reinstatement. Byler had not complied with the August 2000 order to deposit the refund in court within 60 days. "Petitioner did not apply to this Court for a stay of the deposit order, but made multiple applications for a stay to the Court of Appeals. . . . None were granted. None were based on an alleged inability to pay." The order was not moot but "highly relevant to the present application. . . . Settlement of the civil action does not alter the fact the petitioner utterly failed to comply with the Order from its inception to the day of settlement ... or close to one year." This was "an egregious extension of the underlying unethical conduct." Byler also failed to file a timely affidavit of compliance or explain that failure "in spite of repeated notice to petitioner that it was required. Moreover, the Affidavit of Compliance is an admission of *non-compliance* with the Court's Order to escrow funds, accompanied by a vague and unfulfilled promise to comply."

> More generally, petitioner's application fails to evidence any remorse or recognition that his actions in failing to safeguard his clients' tax refund since 1994, as found by this Court, violated his professional duties. Instead, petitioner repeats his justifications for his actions, attacks the sanction imposed, and argues that the pending settlement of the civil suit vindicates his conduct. Petitioner's thoroughgoing rejection of this Court's fundamental findings, his characterizations of the ethics case as a mere fee dispute, and his unabashed defiance of the Court's Order to escrow the disputed funds, warrant outright denial of the petition.

In his 15-page reply affidavit Byler sought "to bring this excessively delayed *seven*-year old disciplinary case to an end." Edelstein's opposition affirmation was "a deliberate attempt to inflame the Court with assertions that do not withstand calm scrutiny." Her "unreasonableness" was another reason to grant his petition. She "unfairly does not report the non-opposition of the Lawyers' Fund for Client Protection." Her "other hit-and-run attacks on reinstatement are unreasonable." He had not argued financial inability in his Court of Appeals motions because he had a job then. He filed his affidavit of compliance promptly after the Court of Appeals rejected his last motion. "As if driving me for years without end to near financial ruin and causing adverse career consequences is not enough, Ms. Edelstein ... complains that I am not remorseful." She "unreasonably ignores that in this case, there were many laudatory aspects to my representation as to which remorse is out of place."

> Second, the matter of "remorse" is only raised because of what happened at the end of the representation in 1994 ... the truly important point for reinstatement today is that I have placed

CHAPTER 6

> on the record in 2001 my resolve concerning written retention and fee agreements, avoidance of client disputes and respect of escrow obligations. . . . The fact that out of conviction, I moved to appeal in the New York Court of Appeals of this Court's order and opinion cannot be a proper basis upon which to oppose reinstatement. . . . [A]s the original suspension was disproportionate in the first place, it should be ended now. . . . Staff counsel's request for summary denial of reinstatement and perpetuation of this prolonged disciplinary case, which would seal my financial and career ruin, should be viewed as calling into question what has happened in this case. I cannot put the following more diplomatically: with all due respect, Staff Counsel misrepresented this case when it was before this Court on the merits and has been unreasonable to a degree that it has reflected an unjustified, unhealthy personal animosity toward me developed in the course of this unreasonably prolonged seven-year disciplinary case. This petition for reinstatement should be summarily granted by this Court so that, among other things, this plague of a disciplinary case is brought to an overdue end.

The Appellate Division denied Byler's reinstatement motion on October 30. He moved for reconsideration on December 6. Horan (Morgan's counsel in the civil action) filed an affidavit calling the settlement of the cross-claims "a fair and just resolution."

> Although I had always believed Mr. Byler was wrong in retaining the IRS refund, and that the AD's decision was correct in the circumstances, I also believe he demonstrated the value of his services to the Morgans in the civil proceedings . . . and that he has been sufficiently sanctioned and that his continued suspension is unwarranted.

Byler argued that this "strongly suggests that this Court must have overlooked a number of points that counsel my reinstatement." He relitigated the entire case, including the evidence he had submitted in the civil action. In August he had passed the MPRE with "an excellent score of 107; the passing grade currently in New York is 72."

[T]he failure to make the deposit cannot fairly be held against reinstatement because this seven-year-old disciplinary case, by unreasonably dragging on for years on end, created the circumstances that put me in a very poor financial situation in which I was not able to make the deposit. With all due respect, it does not serve the administration of justice and the disciplinary process to have a disciplinary case go on and on for years, grinding down the financial resources of a lawyer, and then when a large financial deposit is ordered by this Court almost six years after the events in question in the case, to hold against the lawyer that he cannot afford the deposit.

Edelstein moved to oppose Byler's motion for reconsideration

because he has offered no new evidence that he fully complied with the Court's Order . . . nor does petitioner establish that he recognizes that he engaged in professional misconduct. . . . petitioner *never* deposited any of the disputed funds into Court pending that resolution as ordered. . . . [he] asserts that this Court's Order was effectively of no value from its inception and therefore his non-compliance is justified *ex post facto*. Reinstatement, which requires full compliance . . . should not be granted on such reasoning. . . . As in the past, petitioner's motion lacks any showing of remorse or recognition that his failure to safeguard his client's tax refund since 1994 violated his professional duties as found by this Court.

Byler's reply repeated the same arguments. His only assets were a "401(k) account that was worth approximately $18,000." His wife was a high school biology teacher. He relitigated the entire case. In response to the inquiry about substance abuse in his initial petition he had said he "played on a Stan Musial League baseball team with and against guys in their early twenties." "I continued my June to October practice of swimming in Long Island Sound." He had responded to the suspension by climbing "Longs Peak, a 14,256 foot mountain in Colorado, with my two sons." But the Appellate Division denied the motion on February 26.

Byler petitioned for reinstatement again on August 6. He wanted to support his wife and two sons (now in college and high school) "in a reasonable manner." He declared once again that in the future he would have

Chapter 6

a written retainer and escrow any disputed money. "If I receive a check payable to the order of a client, I will deliver such check to the client and will not accept it in payment of my fee for professional services rendered to the client." "I meant no disrespect to the Court when I did not comply with its order. . . ." He had been unable to do so "and at the same time pay taxes, medical and dental expenses, home mortgage interest and other expenses. . . ." He had had to liquidate his 401(k) to pay Morgan the $10,000.

> Reflecting on this Court's orders, which I have discussed extensively with my current counsel, it is clear to me that if financial circumstances make it impracticable for me to comply with a court order and at the same time meet compelling familial needs, I should make application to the Court to stay the order, or, alternatively, to modify the order in light of such circumstances and then comply with the Court's decision.

Horan resubmitted his earlier affidavit, adding that Byler "now accepts the court's original findings against him . . . and . . . understandings where he went wrong with the Morgans." Louis Lauer, who represented Byler in this petition, submitted his own affidavit declaring that, as a minister's son, Byler had "barely survived the humiliation of this disciplinary proceeding." In 2000 the Bylers had an adjusted gross income of $86,690.14 and expenses of $42,605.

Byler offered "by way of explanation rather than justification" the fact that while unrepresented by counsel (following Cometa's resignation) "a combination of the following circumstances led me not to comply." He lacked the funds.

> At the same time, I felt confident that the pending civil litigation . . . would result either in a judicial determination that I was entitled to retain all of the [money] . . . or in a settlement that provided that I would retain at least 80%. . . .

He listed his legal ethics and general reading (all highly inspirational). The suspension "has resulted in terrible financial and personal hardship for my family and me and has prevented me from building a law practice during the years when many lawyers have reached a high point in their productivity." He was delinquent in paying credit card bills, had exhausted his line of credit, could not afford to repair an inoperable 20-year-old car, and was behind in payments for his other car. Power had been shut off in his house in June 2001, he had had to defer dental care for a broken tooth, his wife required medication, and his younger son was distracted from his studies. (But his 2001 tax return showed that his AGI had increased to $129,000.)

At an August deposition by Andral N. Bratton, the new staff counsel, Byler boasted that at Weil Gotshal, although formally a senior associate, he was doing "a partner's job." He practiced alone in 1990 and then twice followed Louis Lauer to become of counsel, first at Stilts, Palmer, Cortland & Slotnick through 1994 and then at Layton, Brooks & Hecht. Byler left in 1997 and Lauer soon thereafter. For a while Byler practiced in the same office as Joseph Arsogi (a former Cravath partner) and then became of counsel at Kalov, Springer & Bressler (having worked with Bressler at Weil Gotshal). After being suspended he continued to practice in the Southern District of New York until it reciprocally suspended him on May 18, 2001. But on the advice of two DDC staff counsel (Richard Maltz and Richard Michelle) he still practiced in the Eastern District, which did not reciprocally suspend him.

Nevertheless,

> I don't want anybody to think that I have not suffered, my family has not suffered. Very much to the contrary. . . . We have suffered terribly . . . there is an onus to suspension that . . . makes you undesirable in a certain way . . . it occurred just before my 50th birthday. . . . I may look young and healthy, and I am because . . . I try to stay active and have been active with baseball with my boys and the like.

But the impact had been "devastating." "There have been periodic interruptions of phone service . . . right now I don't have long distance service. . . ." "[I]it is painful when you have to deal month in, month out with calls from creditors, calls from the banks. . . ." His wife was "clinically depressed."

> I'm from Ohio. I grew up the son of a Methodist minister. I met my wife because her parents attended my father's church. I mean, the idea of having anything like this go on is . . . just

> devastating. . . . there's a certain sense of right and wrong, which I think we try to uphold and which we try to communicate to our boys and which in our respective ways, my wife teaches school and I'm involved in community matters in terms of dealing with youth, communicating a sense of right and wrong. . . . And this case is just sickening beyond belief.

For a period "I couldn't get through to [his younger son] because of this." His older son, now at Purdue,

> got on the waiting list for West Point. He had the nominations of both Senator Moynihan and Representative Lazio. It didn't quite come through. I sometimes wonder if, because this case has been going on since he's been in sixth grade. . . . we've been a family under siege . . . the magnitude of which just . . . has been sickening.

Bratton vainly tried to redirect Byler to what *he* had done and away from what had been done *to* him.

> Bratton: . . . what is your own role and responsibility for all this?
>
> Byler: Well, I mean, I, I don't want to sound like I don't understand and appreciate the court's findings. I'm not saying that. . . . I don't know how . . . more dire a picture I could . . . present with respect to this. Now, your next question is—
>
> Bratton: [rephrased the above] . . . Today as sitting here in 2002 do you have a dispute with the findings of the court?
>
> Byler: I don't. [He repeated his commitment to write retainers escrow disputed funds.] I don't want anything that I say in terms of hardship to be taken as somehow I don't, you know, mean what I've said in my affidavit. I do mean that. . . .
>
> Bratton: Why don't you explain on the record . . . why you did not deposit the $52,000 as the court required and have a 20/20 hindsight of what you should have done.
>
> Byler: Well, that's a compound question. . . . Now, if we were in court I might say, objection, Your Honor, a compound, but let me proceed with it. . . . I didn't have the money. . . .

> Bratton: So why didn't you go to the courts and just say, look, I don't have the money, can I have a stay on this?
>
> Byler: Well, I, I did ask the Court of Appeals for a stay, and in retrospect I should have . . . asked the Appellate Division. . . .
>
> Bratton: Yeah, but not on financial hardship.
>
> Byler: I did it in requesting a stay . . . one factor being the jeopardization to an individual. And while I didn't spell it out, what I had in mind was the fact that I wasn't going to be able to comply with this order financially. I put it in more general terms perhaps out of pride. I've argued in front of the New York Court of Appeals. . . . So I didn't get down to the nitty gritty detail that in retrospect should have been provided in the first instance. . . .

He thought the civil case was "a practical way of dealing with the situation." "I never believed he would ever be harmed, ever, I mean, the representation actually was, I'm sad to say, because a wonderful representation in terms of results for a client."

Bratton felt that escrowing the refund was moot, "so it's kind of cleaning up here now." Byler repeated "it was a combination of not having the money to do it and maybe having some pride in not being able to admit to the Appellate Division. . . ."

> Bratton: You now today in 2002 understand why this office opposed your first reinstatement or why the court denied your first reinstatement?
>
> Byler: A compound question. . . .Well, I understand that it had to do with a concern that I was rejecting just everything in the court opinion. . . . [M]aybe that's unfortunate . . . I'm a little frustrated . . . because . . . I testified in the disciplinary trial in 1997 that it only takes one bad experience and you know you should have written retainers. . . . it used not to be the practice of lawyers to have written retainers. . . . On the escrow, again, it's a little frustrating to me because my testimony throughout the proceeding was that I don't handle client funds . . . there wasn't a need for an escrow agreement.

CHAPTER 6

> Bratton: You don't dispute that [the] check that was given you from the IRS was funds . . . incident to your practice of law.
>
> Byler: . . . [I]t may sound funny to you now, but that wasn't what I was thinking. It was not the intent of my taking the check when I received it of doing anything other than acting pursuant to what I thought was an agreement, receiving the check as compensation for work already performed. And because of my practice, that was my mentality. I don't dispute right now, looking at it in hindsight because that's what you asked me to do . . .
>
> Bratton: So you understand the moment Mr. Morgan said, hey, I dispute that, you should have put the money back in his account.
>
> Byler: Yeah, there were some other problems in the case, but . . . I'm not in disagreement with that. [He would hand over any check payable to the client.] And if the client says, no, no, you keep it, which is what happened here, he . . . testified he told me to keep it, and that was the agreement as I understood it, I'll say, no, I cannot, what I'll ask you to do is you put that in your bank account and you write me a specific check for the specific amount because then there's no question here about the fact that I'm receiving the monies from you in consideration for the legal work and professional services I have done for you.

Three days later Bratton told the Appellate Division he did not oppose reinstatement. Inability to pay

> does not excuse petitioner for his failure to comply . . . but it does provide an explanation for his actions . . . in contrast to his previous submissions, petitioner acknowledges where he went astray ethically . . . these proceedings have had a chastening effect on petitioner and . . . he knows he had erred grievously by his prior refusal to acknowledge any culpability.

The Appellate Division reinstated Byler on October 1.

IV. The Cost of Contrition

A written retainer probably would have forestalled these ethical transgressions.[858] Why was none executed here? Byler boasted that his commercial clients, with whom he only had oral agreements, always paid their bills without question. Perhaps. But he had other individual clients, like Moor-Jankowski, who did not. Indeed, Byler's constant anxiety about whether his good friend Morgan would pay suggests the lawyer had been stiffed before. Did both Byler and Morgan feel that a written retainer was incompatible with mutual trust? If so, the case exemplifies the danger of mixing friendship with business. Maybe Byler was deliberately vague about his fee in order to increase Morgan's gratitude. And perhaps Byler initially exaggerated his own pessimism about the outcome in order to demonstrate Morgan's need for his own extraordinary, even unique, legal talents. Morgan may have hoped that gratitude would substitute for payment and was eager, even desperate, to believe that Byler could extricate him from the mess he had made of his tax obligations. Unconfined by writing, desire colored memory on both sides. Morgan remembered being assured that he so clearly was not liable that the problem could be resolved with a few letters, for little or no fee. Byler was equally certain he had told Morgan that persuading the IRS would take much more work, justifying his usual fee, limited only by Morgan's ability to pay.

The ambiguities soon deepened. What did the apartment security deposit represent? A convenience for Morgan, who could not cash U.S. dollar checks in South Africa? But he kept several U.S. accounts and almost certainly had other occasions to transfer funds to South Africa. A spontaneous expression of gratitude (demonstrating that nothing was legally *owed*)? Or a payment on account? If the last, did it express any understanding about the ultimate fee? The April 1994 "non-bill bill" could not have been more opaque. Each remembered a different part of the cover letter. Morgan felt that "not indicating that any payment is due now or ever" was "rather clear." Byler naturally emphasized the phrase: "I will let your conscience be your guide." When the prospect changed from reducing the deficiency to increasing the refund, the parties' expectations about its size again diverged. Morgan remembered Byler being discouraging: any refund would be insubstantial. That is why Morgan repeated his impulsive earlier gesture by telling Byler to keep it. Byler remembered

---

[858] The English Law Society required them of solicitors in 1997. Abel (2003: 363).

CHAPTER 6

saying twice in June that the refund would exceed $10,000 (the amount of the "non-bill bill"). The misunderstanding climaxed in their multiply incompatible accounts of the June 20 meeting: where it occurred, how long it took, and especially what transpired. Were the blank check and deposit slip intended to facilitate payment of a deficiency that exceeded Morgan's bank balance? (Morgan also had given a check and deposit slip to his Florida accountant; the IRS still was claiming a deficiency as late as September.) Or was it intended to let Byler pay himself out of the refund? (But even so, his fee remained unspecified.) Could Byler have transposed Morgan's June 14 statement—"if we do get, get a check, keep it"—to the June 20 meeting (when prospects for the refund and its size had improved)?

In the absence of a retainer, Byler had to construct an "agreement" to justify pocketing the refund. His letter informing Morgan invoked the word at least seven times. But he revealed uncertainty about whether Morgan would acknowledge that argument by declaring that "even in the absence of our agreement" he was owed as much as "proper and fair payment" (both words used twice). Sometimes Byler claimed they had a contingent fee arrangement: "no refund (and no payment for me . . .)." But why, then, did he accept the security deposit as his due, send the "non-bill bill," and account for his hours? Why did he take credit for working "without pressing you for payment" and being "so kind to carry your . . . case for two years"? And why did he sound aggrieved at "finally being paid for two and a half years of legal services"? He was not *entitled* to payment any earlier. Why would he have entertained counteroffers? Why wasn't the fee proportioned to the result? He admitted, inconsistently, that he expected payment simply for lowering the deficiency, would have rejected a fee based on a $1.49 refund, and could have justified $80,000 "given the result and other factors."

Byler had difficulty explaining the two "bills." Both seemed result driven: $10,000 was the most he thought Morgan would pay at the time without balking; $52,866.67 was simply the refund (adjusted for minor credits and debits). Byler insisted the identity between bill and refund was just "happenstance." The hours he claimed for tasks *completed* at the time of the first bill doubled or trebled in the second, and the hourly rate rose from the odd $277.39 (presumably chosen to produce $10,000) to $350 (a level to which he was still aspiring). Byler claimed to have "just uniformly cut," made "an arbitrary cut," "deep cuts in the recording of hours" out of friendship in the first bill; but then he billed the same friend at corporate

350   LAWYERS IN THE DOCK

rates for actual hours worked in the second. If the earlier bill represented "massive reductions," why not tell Morgan at the time?

Byler's rhetorical overkill and lawyerly detail were profoundly counterproductive. Morgan denied *any* obligation to pay absent litigation. The purported agreement was "pure fabrication." He had been shocked by the hours claimed in the non-bill bill but attributed this to Byler's boastfulness. Morgan demanded his money back before discussing a proper fee. Byler responded self-righteously, accusing Morgan of trying to "walk away from our agreement." Byler invoked his own behavior as evidence that he had believed there was an agreement (a self-serving and circular argument). He did not strengthen his case by citing Moor-Jankowski's gratitude for Byler's extraordinary exertions and talents since Moor-Jankowski had written Byler that "you can no longer control your temper, nor accept documented facts concerning your overbilling and deception of me." Did Byler think this would not emerge? Or was he unable to hear client anger?

Byler offered several justifications for pocketing the refund. He knew that individuals resisted bills they considered excessive (perhaps Morgan and Moor-Jankowski were not his only deadbeat clients). He was concerned that Morgan was in South Africa. True, that would make debt collection more difficult. But why doubt that Morgan—a best friend, who had shown such gratitude, and for whom he had won such an extraordinary result—would pay willingly? Byler may have been projecting his own uncertainty about the claim's legitimacy. Anticipating resistance, he deposited the refund, wrote the blank check to himself, and delayed telling Morgan so he could not stop payment. Byler also protested too much (the accusation he made against Forlenza). The $55,000 "was clearly within reason." He could have justified $75,000–80,000. He had a "clear entitlement to be paid." "[T]he attitude I was getting in his correspondence was, well, $2,000 seemed enough. And that was just not acceptable." It "didn't matter" that neither knew the size of the refund when Morgan "agreed" to assign it "because what we were talking about was money that was not anticipated at the beginning of the representation at all . . . the fee was being covered by the government." "[T]his money doesn't exist but for my work." He repeated: the refund "existed only by virtue of the fact of my work." It was "found money," "not client money in my mind. It was my money." He repeated: it was "not client's funds but my monies"; he was "retaining possession of what was fairly my money."

CHAPTER 6

He had not escrowed the refund because there was no fee dispute. Confronted with James Morgan's explicit objection to the fee, Byler dismissed this as not "genuine" because he could not entertain the possibility of being wrong. James Morgan was just trying to evade his obligation; Tom Morgan was playing a "game." Byler rejected escrow as letting the Morgans decide how much he was owed; he insisted on absolute control, which any concession jeopardized.

The specialized knowledge professionals painfully acquire makes others depend on them. For many providers, that is one of the role's greatest intangible rewards, which lawyers share with doctors, nurses, therapists, clergy, teachers, and those who maintain the technology on which we increasingly rely, from cars to computers. Byler seemed to value such dependence strongly, perhaps related to his inveterate boasting (both signs of insecurity). He repeatedly returned to his graduation from Harvard, his Sixth Circuit clerkship, his six years at Cravath and six at Weil Gotshal, where he was doing "a partner's job" (but obviously did not make partner). He took credit for the award conferred on Moor-Jankowski "in front of a large audience, 400 people" at the Waldorf-Astoria. When the Hearing Panel noted that *Byler* had not received it, he replied his client called him a "knight in shining armor." In response to a routine question about substance abuse, Byler could not refrain from bragging about his athletic prowess. He still "played on a Stan Musial League baseball team with and against guys in their early twenties," swam in Long Island Sound from "June to October," and climbed a 14,256 foot mountain with his two sons to deal with the emotional trauma of suspension. In his reinstatement application he could not resist bragging that he had read inspirational books about legal ethics and other subjects and earned "an excellent score of 107" on the MPRE, when 72 was passing. (Morgan attributed Byler's "non-bill bill" to his need to boast.)

Byler proclaimed that Morgan "had a lawyer-litigator in me who had the expertise in the tax issue and who jumped in to try to rescue your cases. . . ." "I saved him from financial disaster," "bailed him out." Morgan was "fortunate" (used three times) and should be "thankful" (three times) and show "gratitude" (at least five times). Byler "did the work," a "terrific job," provided "superb" representation, "achieved" results that were "excellent" (twice), "tremendous," "extraordinary" in light of a "very, very aggressive" tax shelter. He even bragged about the craftsmanship of his bill, which "reflects the kind of detailed report that I do, the efficiency with which I work and the lower rates . . . that I charge . . . for real work."

Morgan should "count your blessings" (used twice; an unlikely client response to a $50,000 bill). Byler's offer to return $5,500 was "generous."

As in many divorces, these best friends quickly became worst enemies. Byler portrayed Morgan as feckless, a chronic tax cheat who still owed the government $140,000. Instead of the "thanks and gratitude" that were "in order," Morgan "turns around and tried . . . to destroy my career and my ability to support my family." (Byler felt a similar "sense of unfairness" at Moor-Jankowski's ingratitude.) Morgan was "not treating me right." Morgan retorted that a "major violation of trust has occurred," which threatened "further and even more serious damage." Comparison of the two bills "would seem to call into question your honesty." Byler dismissed this "snide summary" and "ill-considered attack." It was Morgan who had committed a "breach of trust." "Friends do not dishonor agreements and do not threaten to sully the career and professional reputation" of each other. Morgan's position was "obviously" "false" (four times), "and I think you know it"; it was "wholly incompatible with 'reasonable discussion,'" a "series of rationalizations," which Janet Byler (an impartial observer!) said "does not fly." Morgan was "crazy." "[Y]ou can say that the world is flat," but that did not make it "true or sensible or responsible." Tom Morgan's letter was "one of the worst betrayals of friendship and trust that I have ever experienced." James Morgan replied in kind: his and his wife's "sense of injuries was justified." Their "good name" was "being called into question." If they could not resolve the disagreement he would sue. Byler responded that *his* "professional integrity" had "come under an unprecedented assault." Morgan's behavior was "fraudulent." A lawsuit would be "an abuse of process." Morgan's denial of the agreement was "dishonest," "destructive." Morgan revoked the power of attorney and accused Byler of withholding his mail. Byler's claim to the money was "built on a lie"; "*you* know the truth." He "pray[ed] you will come to your senses." "*The Truth*," Byler retorted, was "written and documented." The "Almighty" knew that Morgan was "the one who has lied" (twice) and was "posturing." A friendship that began in church ended with each of them invoking divine sanction.

Byler's character helps explain his behavior within the disciplinary proceeding as well beforehand. He was always right, and everyone else wrong. He had an "unblemished record" (six times) and was "known as somebody who is highly scrupulous and ethical." The non-bill bill was no more than "stupid" and "klutzy." He claimed the October bill was based on "Red-Book entries," then admitted the two diverged but denied changing

CHAPTER 6

the Red Book, and finally admitted making changes but claimed they were trivial. Byler dismissed Tom Morgan's charge—that he had "stolen from your client" and committed "naked theft"—as "absurd," "one of the most outlandish and disingenuous letters." It was James Morgan who was guilty of fraud for taking legal services without any intention of paying. How "dare" Tom Morgan voice accusations that were "unethical . . . phony and irresponsibly made," "unprofessional," "groundless," "sheer nonsense," just an attempt to "renegotiate" the fee agreement. Escrowing the refund after such charges would admit wrongdoing, the "stinking fish." "I might be in front of this committee and the DA on charges that I had stolen escrow monies." He offered to refund $5,500 but only if Morgan declared Byler's behavior "proper." Byler dismissed the "dishonest and galling" disciplinary complaint as a "false accusation by an ungrateful former client and former friend" and an "attempt to misuse this forum as a way of renegotiating a fee." Morgan was "absurd" and his complaint "dishonest." Any penalty would just encourage clients to evade fee contracts. Byler claimed that Moor-Jankowski's disturbingly similar complaint was opportunistic behavior encouraged by the disciplinary proceeding. Because Horan (who represented Morgan in the civil action) served on the DDC, Morgan's disciplinary complaint was just an attempt to advance "a Committee member's private state court litigation." When Cometa withdrew from representing Byler (for not paying $60,000 in fees—exactly Byler's complaint against both Morgan and Moor-Jankowski), Byler professed surprise and accused Cometa of "inaccuracies and omissions."

When the Hearing Panel stopped Byler from arguing that Morgan had benefited from Byler's behavior, the lawyer insisted "there was not injury." He even denied that Morgan had demanded the refund or the DDC had ordered him to escrow it. The Hearing Panel was incredulous.

Forlenza: He's never asked you to return the money?

Byler: Sitting here, my recollection is no. That was never an issue.

Ellenbogen: What is he suing you for? To return the money.

Byler did not comply with the AD order to escrow the refund because he "felt confident" the civil court would award him 80–100 percent of it. In any case "there has been no prejudice." Even when he finally complied he reaffirmed "my conviction that it is contrary [to] law and unconstitutional."

Perhaps the most telling biographical detail emerged in the second reinstatement petition when Lauer, now representing Byler, revealed that his client was a minister's son, who had met his wife at his father's church. He "barely survived the humiliation of this disciplinary proceeding." Byler elaborated:

> [T]he idea of having anything like this go on is . . . just devastating. . . . [T]here's a certain sense of right and wrong, which I think we try to uphold and which we try to communicate to our boys . . . and I'm involved in community matters in terms of dealing with youth, communicating a sense of right and wrong.

Byler could not admit that one factor powerfully influencing him to pocket the refund and flout the AD order to escrow it was financial distress. Doing so would have place in doubt his ability to support his family. But though he denied having any financial problems in June 1994, Edelstein showed that he was dunning Moor-Jankowski—whom Byler portrayed as a profoundly grateful client—for $22,000 because Byler was "embarrassed" (five times) in a "very public" way at not being able to pay his office rent and expenses, home mortgage, and credit card or to send his sons to summer camp. Having excoriated Morgan for financial irresponsibility, Byler was chagrined to be exposed as also living beyond his means. The same fear of public embarrassment prevented him from telling the courts that his money problems had been aggravated by the disciplinary case "unreasonably dragging on for years on end." Instead of asking the AD for a stay on grounds of financial hardship, he sought review in the Court of Appeals.

> And while I didn't spell it out, what I had in mind was the fact that I wasn't going to be able to comply with this order financially. I put it in more general terms perhaps out of pride. I've argued in front of the New York Court of Appeals. . . . it was a combination of not having the money to do it and maybe having some pride in not being able to admit to the Appellate Division. . . .

Byler clothed his actions in the noblest motives. He had a "professional responsibility" to make Morgan "face up to the truth." He had refused the private admonition because "I wanted to keep my unblemished record." For the same reason he "DEMAND[ED]" a public disciplinary hearing. "I have an obligation to the Bar to fight how the disciplinary process has gone astray." "[T]he integrity of the system is at stake." He contested the charges because he did not "deserve" this "reckless character assassination." "[F]or me, there can be no compromise with an abuse of authority aimed at perpetuating a lie. There was a time when Americans believed in Sacred Honor. I still do." He told the Court of Appeals that his was the "most important disciplinary case that this court can ever decide." It should "restore the Rule of Law and provide beneficial guidance and structure to disciplinary matters throughout the State of New York." The proceedings against him were "unlawful," "unconstitutional," a "disgrace," "travesty," and "miscarriage of justice." Even when applying for reinstatement he had to "choose the path of honesty and state that I believe the case has been wrongly decided." He made a "statement for the record about the ethical misfocus in this case, the violations of constitutional due process and the tolerance of the corrupting conflict of interest" and the "need for real reform of the disciplinary process." He wanted to be a "catalyst for needed reform of that disciplinary process."

Byler insisted that he was the injured party, not Morgan. By not paying on account (something Byler never requested), Morgan "had abused the relationship . . . I'm going on and on and on through all this time . . . and he's still not dealing with things. And it turns out he had money in his bank account that got seized that I didn't know of." Byler had been "put in an unfair situation" by a friend who was holding out on him. Morgan had been "unreasonable" (three times) in not suggesting an appropriate fee. He "was just . . . arguing, arguing." Byler found the disciplinary process a "horrendous experience" (repeated), which had committed "unconscionable error." "[H]ow unjust it is to me—a lawyer, with credentials who has an otherwise unblemished record." He repeatedly "DEMAND[ED]" that the complaint be dismissed. Morgan had tried "to destroy my career and my ability to support my family." Edelstein had taken a "mistaken and at times jaundiced view." "[O]ver the course of a long period of time" Byler "had to expend a lot of time and money in defending myself." Just like Lincoln, he too had been victimized by an unjustified complaint. The suspension "has resulted in terrible financial and personal hardship for my family and me and has prevented me from building a law practice during the years when many lawyers have reached a high point in their productivity." The impact had been "devastating."

He enumerated the economic hardships. "[I]t is painful when you have to deal month in, month out with calls from creditors, calls from banks." "[W]e have suffered terribly." "[T]here is an onus to suspension that . . . makes you undesirable in a certain way." His wife was "clinically depressed," and his son had failed to get a place at West Point. "[T]his case is just sickening beyond belief."

The very strengths that made Byler a successful litigator were fatal flaws in a litigant. His only strategy was total warfare, take no prisoners, scorched earth. One index is the more than 800 pages of papers he filed in the disciplinary proceeding (many single-spaced), including a lengthy motion to dismiss, a lengthy brief to the DDC chair, and *three* motions asking the Court of Appeals to reconsider its denial of leave to appeal (followed by a request for reargument). He kept repeating procedural objections long after they had been rejected: Horan represented Morgan in the civil action while a member of the DDC; only one Hearing Panel member still served on the DDC; none of the charges had been sustained; "findings could not properly be entered to sustain any Charges." A "series of procedural irregularities afflict the integrity of the process." He denounced the "failure to have the constitutionally mandated impartial and neutral hearing body" and decried the "unprofessional character assassination of Mr. Byler." "[T]his case betrayed the Rule of Law." The "disciplinary process has gone horribly astray"; it "functioned unconstitutionally and unlawfully to the disgrace of the New York legal system" and was a "travesty and a miscarriage of justice."

He responded to defeat by launching personal attacks. Rather than appeal, he asked the DDC chair and chief counsel to intervene "for the sake of the integrity of the disciplinary process in the First Department." When the chair declined, Byler accused him of deciding on "some mistaken premises" and having "overlooked some important points." Urging the Hearing Panel to decide after a year's delay, Byler declared: "no written report could properly be written except to dismiss the case." After it reported adversely, he urged remand for a de novo review, in which he planned to move for dismissal. The report was "error-ridden," "replete with misstatements and omissions"; it "indulges in personal attacks on Mr. Byler and betrays the commitment of the Code of Professional Responsibility to the rule of law." The Hearing Panel "was 'out of touch' with the law, due process of law, and . . . the Rule of Law." The DDC "acts as prosecutor, judge, jury and appellate advocate for the prosecutor," a "thoroughly biased system." Staff memoranda contained "very bad distortions." Byler attacked staff counsel's "conclusory, ill-focused Reply." He accused panel member Forlenza of misrepresenting himself in Martindale-Hubbell and taking an approach "too often unjustified in disturbing ways." He accused panel chair Ellenbogen of "twisting and distorting facts." In his petition for reinstatement he accused staff counsel Edelstein of a "deliberate attempt to inflame the Court," "unreasonableness," and other "unreasonable" "hit-and-run attacks." She had "misrepresented this case" and "has been unreasonable to a degree that it has reflected an unjustified, unhealthy personal animosity." This "plague of a disciplinary case" should be "brought to an overdue end." The Appellate Division "must have overlooked a number of points."

He relitigated each issue ad nauseam. Rebuked for doing so, he insisted: "I'm not testifying as to relitigating. I'm stating the procedural history to show—" before being cut off. He protested the exclusion of his client-benefit chart (when the benefit to Morgan was never at issue). He second-guessed Cometa's strategy, clearly preferring to represent himself. But he did so badly.

> Forlenza: Mr. Byler, do you understand that this panel is asking you to be brief and to the point? And every time someone makes a comment, do you have to have the last word?
>
> Byler: I don't intend to have the last word.

QED. When Bratton sympathetically sought to lead him through the necessary act of contrition by asking why he had disregarded the AD order, Byler parried: "Well, that's a compound question. . . . Now, if we were in court I might say, objection, Your Honor, a compound, but let's proceed with it." The Panel told him to stick to facts.

> Byler: I appreciate that very much because some testimony I might try to give or go into I'll confuse my role as advocate which I dearly love. I think—I mean, there are other items which I have my notes on but I don't think it narrowly relates—
>
> Ellenbogen: To the facts.
>
> Byler: —and I will exercise some prudence here and conclude my testimony. . . .

But he rarely took that good advice. He continued talking over staff counsel's objection. After Ellenbogen reprimanded him for interrupting her he did so again, provoking an exasperated exclamation: "I'm talking; that means you stop talking."

Once guilt was established, the disciplinary proceeding became a degradation ceremony.[859] Ellenbogen was explicit: the purpose of the penalty phase was to let the respondent express remorse and explain unethical behavior. But Byler could not bring himself to do so. Edelstein argued in aggravation that Byler continued to show "disdain for the Panel and its rulings," offering a "self-serving interpretation" and denying there had ever been any fee dispute. Ellenbogen agreed: "The problem you have here is that Mr. Byler does not believe that the findings are correct. . . ." Haig virtually told Byler what to say: "Are you sorry that you didn't put this money in escrow?" But Byler could not utter the crucial word—without qualification. "With the benefit of hindsight, *one might* have taken a different course of action" (my emphasis). "One," not he; "might," not should. "I don't know that I can answer yes or no." Why not? Asked if he was "sorry" he replied: "I'm sorry this whole thing happened and that's one part of it." "I am sorry that the thing happened." He could only express regret about an amorphous "thing" that "happened," not something *he* had *done*. His failure to escrow was just "one part."

The incoherence of the following quotation is particularly eloquent in light of Byler's usual lawerly precision; he kept interrupting the Panel—and himself—in his urgency to justify and excuse.

> I felt I had earned it. I felt that I was put in an unfair situation. . . . I'm sorry I didn't find a way to have done so that I thought was safe. . . . with the benefit of hindsight, I would have perhaps tried to handle it in a way of, while reserving my rights—because honestly I felt I had earned the money and I didn't think it was right—but reserving my rights somehow to have done—I don't know what it didn't happen and I guess all that's gone on, if there was an easier way out of this, you know, I'm sorry that somehow I didn't do that. . . . I'm sorry that I didn't find a way. It's not as simple as just putting money in escrow. . . . I think the position I held at the time and what was briefed to you would constitute legitimate reasons. . . . with the benefit of

---

[859] Garfinkel (1956).

> hindsight, I would still say there was a risk. . . . I felt I was being very unfairly attacked by accusations that just should not have been made. . . . I've always had the expert counsel saying no, there's not an escrow obligation.

He had been right: "I had earned it" (repeated) and had "legitimate reasons." "Expert counsel" (his friends) had assured him there was no escrow obligation. *He* was the injured party, who had been "unfairly attacked," "put in an unfair situation," and "didn't think it was right." He had simply sought to be "safe," to "reserve his rights" (twice). It wasn't that "simple." He still thought "there was a risk." He had acted "honestly." Escrow just "didn't happen"; things had "gone on." (Again the impersonal pronouns and passive voice.) *He* wasn't responsible; he didn't even know why ("I don't know what"). He was still only willing to escrow $10,000. Awaiting judgment a year later he continued to maintain that he had conducted "what complainant admitted was a 'superb' representation in which I did a 'terrific job' bringing 'extraordinary results.'"

The Hearing Panel report condemned Byler's "self-righteous position . . . so out of touch with reality." During the hearing he gave "evasive testimony" and "persistently ignored rulings and instructions." It recommended a year's suspension because of his "adamant failure to recognize that there was even a bona fide dispute . . . let alone recognize that his conduct was improper." In the petition to confirm, Edelstein agreed that Byler was "either unwilling or unable to recognize even the possibility of error on his part" and "continues to demonstrate his disdain for the Panel's rulings." His counsel retorted that Byler's "lack of contrition" was irrelevant since he denied any violations and "there were so many laudatory aspects to Mr. Byler's representation." But that just compounded the offense. The Appellate Division affirmed, noting that "even now, respondent has refused to accept any responsibility."

In his first petition for reinstatement Byler made himself promise to reform. He would "do what I reasonably can" (note the qualification). The problem was not him but other people, who "surprise you in unpleasant ways." Future clients might dispute fees because "legal services are expensive" (not because he overcharged). Rather than create an escrow account, he would make sure "there is no reasonable way that I can ever be said to be handling client funds." (Any future accusations would be unreasonable.) He kept bragging about what he had achieved for Morgan. He accused the Hearing Panel of misunderstanding contract law. He shifted blame from himself to the DDC: "there should be some amount of disquiet about what has happened in this nearly *seven*-year old disciplinary case." He stressed the "need to reform the disciplinary process" in order to make it "more principled." Edelstein again opposed reinstatement because Byler had maintained that the AD order was "effectively of no value from its inception." He still did not "establish that he recognizes that he engaged in professional misconduct" and "violated his professional duties." Proving her point, Byler responded that Edelstein "unreasonably ignores that . . . there were many laudatory aspects to my representation as to which remorse is out of place." Remorse "is only raised because of what happened at the end of the representation in 1994." (Only? That is why he was suspended.) The "truly important point" was his "resolve" for the future. He could talk only about what he *would do*, not what he *had done*. There had never been any dispute between him and Moor-Jankowski, or Morgan, or the DDC because he had never done anything wrong. Byler's repeated interruption of the Hearing Panel's questions (even after being reprimanded by them for this) and persistence in testifying over Edelstein's objections further illustrate his inability to hear criticism.

He began the second reinstatement petition on the wrong foot, stressing the financial needs of his family (about whom he bragged). He seemed to realize his error: "I don't want anything that I say in terms of hardship to be taken as somehow I don't, you know, mean what I've said in my affidavit." In support, Horan (*Morgan's* counsel in the civil suit) offered the apology Byler could not make: his adversary "accepts the court's original findings against him" and "understands where he went wrong." Although Bratton (who had replaced Edelstein as staff counsel) tried hard to elicit the necessary words, Byler could not bring himself to speak them.

> Bratton: [W]hat is your own role and responsibility for this?
>
> Byler: . . . I don't know how . . . more dire a picture I could . . . present. . . .

Instead of admitting what *he* should have done, he complained about what had been done *to him* (which presented a "dire picture") and proclaimed what he would do in the future. "As if driving me for years without end to near financial ruin and causing adverse career consequences is not enough, Ms. Edelstein . . . complains that I am not remorseful." Asked by Bratton if

Chapter 6

he understood why staff counsel opposed reinstatement and the court denied, Byler parried:

> A compound question. . . . Well, I understand that it had to do with a concern that I was rejecting just everything in the court opinion. . . . maybe that's unfortunate . . . I'm a little frustrated. . . .

His denial of responsibility "maybe" (again the qualification) was "unfortunate" (a bland impersonal abstraction); and it was *Byler* who was frustrated (the pervasive narcissism). He had promised to use written retainers five years earlier (but could not resist the justification that "it used not to be the practice of lawyers"). The requirement of an escrow account was "frustrating" (again) because he did not handle client funds. (He was the wronged party.) That the refund was client funds "wasn't what I was thinking" in 1994 (as though that excused his actions). His only "intent" was "acting pursuant to what I thought was an agreement." "[B]ecause of my practice, that was my mentality. I don't dispute right now, looking at it in hindsight because that's what you asked me to do." He had been right at the time but "in hindsight" did not dispute (double negative) that he had been wrong "because that's what you asked me to do" (not because it was true). Asked whether he now understood he should have put the money in an escrow account, Byler replied: "Yeah, there were some other problems in the case, but . . . I'm not in disagreement with that." Again he had to start with qualifications and deploy the double negative. In the end it was *Bratton* who uttered the magic words: the "petition acknowledges where he went astray ethically . . . he knows he had erred grievously by his prior refusal to acknowledge any culpability." And with that, Byler was readmitted into the fold.

Byler found it almost impossible to appear contrite because he was unrepentant. He responded to my inquiry with a lengthy letter on August 25, 2006, and graciously let me interview him on September 13. The complaint was "an attempt to misuse the disciplinary process for tawdry private purpose and not for the service of the public interest. . . ." He "still consider[ed it] to have been a miscarriage of justice inflicted by a corrupted disciplinary system needing reform." On May 20, 2004, he had written Grace Moran, "one of the attorneys who have standing in the New York ethics world," urging reform of the disciplinary system. That she never responded was a disappointment but was not a surprise. Back in 2002, she had said to me that my case was an embarrassment that the New York Appellate Division-First Department wanted to go away. With the passage of time, the case must look even worse. . . .

His service to Morgan was "a representation that decent people would have been thrilled to have."

Byler fought reciprocal discipline by the U.S. Tax Court. "I initially thought at the time that the timing . . . was odd," since it occurred after he filed his first reinstatement petition. He "still decided to put in a fulsome submission, which was the right decision." His

> operating assumption became that the New York Disciplinary Committee Counsel on my case and Thomas Morgan had goosed persons in the Tax Court to put me through what I was put through as a way of trying to get a reciprocal discipline ruling from the Tax Court so as to deny reinstatement and continue the New York disciplinary case.

But the Tax Court stayed the case until the First Department reinstated him and just "admonished me to be contrite in the future." He was "dissatisfied with that outcome" but recognized that "the Tax Court was uncomfortable with expressly and publicly finding that there was a denial of due process in the New York proceeding. . . ."

Byler sent me many of the papers he had submitted to the DDC, including the "Client Benefit Chart" it refused to admit, which "showed how my representation bestowed economic benefit on the client and the fee was approximately 20% of that benefit." Morgan was a "jerk" who should have been "hammered by the IRS" because the tax shelter was a fraud. Once James Morgan saw the size of the refund he wanted some of it, running to his older brother Tom for help. Both were bullies.

Byler continued to relitigate many of the issues, boasting: "Yes, I did challenge authority. I felt an ethical obligation to do so." He settled his quantum meruit case not because he deserved less than the entire refund but "because getting the state court case resolved would help my reinstatement." He understood that the settlement "infuriated the Disciplinary Committee counsel on my case." He called it "obvious that there is an actor behind the scenes in Thomas Morgan" and held "a very, very critical view of Thomas Morgan's involvement in the case."

CHAPTER 6

Byler had argued to the Appellate Division that "the Hearing Panel was unlawfully composed and out of touch with the evidentiary record, the law and due process of law." He still thought "they ran a bad trial, cutting me off from proving the fairness of the fee agreement and, in order to disparage me for relying on the fee agreement, misstated, distorted and spun things in a way to give the impression that I did not do very much." "[W]hat kind of perverse viewpoint would account for the Hearing Panel's 'observation' about me"?

> Could it be that they considered me "self-righteous" because they saw that I have moral standards and because they felt the need to engage in character assassination in order to justify what they were doing? Could it be that they wrote that I was "out of touch with reality" because while I was focused on the law and the truth, their "reality" was themselves and their connections in the practice? Ironically, at least two of the four panel members may now be said to be unquestionably out of touch with reality because they are dead. In contrast, I am very much alive.

Byler repeatedly told me the DDC got the facts wrong. Because committee members were busy prominent attorneys, the DDC was run by disciplinary counsel, who had too much power. Edelstein had been a prosecutor too long and was a friend of Ellenbogen (the Panel chair); both worked in a Jewish women's organization. "It's all about relationships." He was the outsider.[860] By contrast Bratton, who walked him through the reinstatement process, was from Indiana; they connected as Midwesterners. A democratic society needed the rule of law. Lawyers had a property right in their credentials and deserved more due process. Instead, the disciplinary process operated by discretion and fiat, like the Star Chamber. The DDC failed to quote the Disciplinary Rules or follow the law scrupulously. He had rejected the admonition offered because the DDC had misstated the facts and demanded that he escrow the disputed money. He refused to do so then or subsequently because the law only required escrow in very specific situations, which did not apply in his case. The DDC needed to

---

[860] Only the Panel chair, Joan Ellenbogen, was Jewish; the other members were Frederick D. Wilkinson, Robert L. Haig, and Philip R. Forlenza. The DDC chairs were Haliburton Fales II and Dennis McInerney; its chief counsel was Thomas Cahill.

read the rule. It had pooh-poohed the technical: "that's not fair to a lawyer." He had a contractual right to the money. Since Morgan asked him to escrow it, not to hand it over, there was no fee dispute. He criticized the DDC for charging him with an unfair fee agreement, preventing him from proving its fairness, and then shifting the grounds of discipline to his failure to escrow the funds. They had dropped the "fitness to practice law" charge, without which no one is ever suspended. At most, he deserved an admonition. (In 2007 Byler and Joseph Sahid had joined the Professional Discipline Committee of the New York State Bar Association. Byler "spoke about the need for more principled decision-making" and Sahid "about the need for more transparency in the system."[861])

Byler concluded his letter with some personal information:

> because the disciplinary case got personal in a way that still rankles and that, to be impolitic, I think showed the character defects on the part of the Disciplinary Committee Hearing Panel members, particularly the deceitful and now dead Chairwoman (who was not a member of the Disciplinary Committee when she sat and acted as a Chairperson).

He had quit the ABA ten years earlier because its ideology "was not to my increasingly conservative taste." He had been "married to the same woman Janet for the last 25 years." They had "raised our sons to have courage and character." Both had gone to Purdue University and joined the military, one the Army, the other the Marines. He proudly described his extensive involvement in managing baseball for a wide variety of amateur teams.

> Forever young, I can still hit decently. In 2003, I won a game in the bottom of the last inning with two outs, with a rifled single into center field that brought in the winning run. In 2005, my batting average was .273. . . . I still play full court basketball . . . and I also regularly run. From 1994 through 1997, I ran three marathons and three half-marathons . . . since 2002, I have run the Long Island Half-Marathon every year.

---

[861] E-mail from Philip A. Byler (9.27.07).

Chapter 6

He was an elder of the Huntington Central Presbyterian Church, "a traditionalist congregation often at odds with the left wingers in effective control at the Long Island Presbytery and more than unhappy with the left wingers at the national level."

His personal life was "a very good one." He listed the cases he had litigated and told me at least twice: "I never stopped being a lawyer." His "career has been damaged and is not what it should be." He would never achieve his ambition to be a federal judge. Although he clearly viewed his present firm as a step down,[862] repeatedly referring to himself as Harvard '76, he wrote that it was "a much appreciated safe, comfortable haven."

> There are plenty of high powered attorneys in New York City being paid large sums of monies, many times more than I am, but whose circumstances at their firms are distinctly unpleasant, and I would not trade their situations for mine. I suppose that the better way of handling career disappointment is to focus on the blessings.

---

[862] He is one of five associates at Nesenoff & Miltenberg. He introduced me to Miltenberg, who is 15 years younger, graduated from Brooklyn Law School, and thought Byler should have been an academic. The other associates are more than 20 years younger than Byler; two graduated from New York Law School and the others from Fordham and Tulane.

REPLY

Philip A. Byler

I have been supplied by Professor Abel with what he called a draft "narrative," but what in fact is a mediocre dishonest professors' tale, told for the purpose of a cover up, about the one and only disciplinary case in my legal career—a legal career that now exceeds three decades.

In considering the one and only disciplinary case in my 30+ year legal career and the dishonest professors' tale purportedly about the case, let's recognize at the outset: (i) who is "Byler," called "Phil" by those who know him and even some who do not; and (ii) what Phil Byler did in representing Jim Morgan.

Phil Byler has legal credentials: Harvard Law '76, law clerk to U.S. Court of Appeals judge, alumnus of Cravath, Swaine & Moore and Weil, Gotshal & Manges. Phil Byler has an active litigation practice, including numerous appellate arguments in recent years before the New York Appellate Divisions for the First and Second Departments. Phil Byler is involved in Bar Association activities: the New York State Bar Association (Professional Discipline and Trial Evidence Committees for which he chairs subcommittees); the New York City Bar Association (International Security Affairs); and the American Bar Association (Trial Evidence for which he chairs a subcommittee). Phil Byler has a good family: a wife of 27 years and two Purdue grad sons, one of whom is a U.S. Army First Lieutenant who earned a Bronze Star and Army "V" Medal for Valor for actions under fire during his 15 months as an infantry platoon leader in Iraq and one who is a U.S. Marines Second Lieutenant. Phil Byler has a community presence: Vice President, Director and Legal Advisor of the largest Williamsport Little League/Senior League baseball association on the East Coast; youth baseball coach for ten years, including Williamsport Tournament teams; player-manager of a Long Island Stan Musial baseball team; and Elder of a traditionalist Presbyterian church that has a heavy emphasis on mission work to youth, the homeless and the handicapped and that has acted within the denomination to oppose divestment in Israel and to support our troops. And, Phil Byler did a hugely successful legal representation for the client who filed that one and only disciplinary case in his career.

That legal representation was performed on non-market special retention terms so that counsel could be provided to a client, Jim Morgan,

CHAPTER 6

who was in financial difficulty (his businesses had failed) and whose problem was that after not filing tax returns for four years, he was in active collection— IRS Notice To Levy and New York State Tax Warrant issued—for over $216,000 with the IRS and New York State resulting from the client's involvement in a cattle feed tax shelter invalidated by the IRS as a business sham and the governing precedent in the Southern District of New York written by Judge Edward Weinfeld in *Dunn v United States*, 468 F.Supp.991 (1979), was against it. After nearly 2½ years of my representation, the case ended, because of the tax adjustment schedule put in place by my representation, with the wiping out of all the tax liabilities and the triggering of a federal tax refund and a state tax refund and with my agreed upon compensation provided by a client proposed assignment of the federal tax refund that I testified was legally enforceable and ethically fair. The client testified that his "hour of need." had been a "terrible" situation, that I had represented him on "special terms," that I had done a "terrific," "superb job," "absolutely" achieving "extraordinary results" and that he had told me to "keep" the IRS refund. (Disc. Tr. 29, 57-60, 64-65, 81, 83; Disc. Tr. Resp. Ex. A.) A highly experienced tax expert testified at a quantum meruit hearing that the tax shelter was "highly risky" and had been invalidated by the IRS on the ground that it was a business sham, that I had "hit a home run and a half," explaining that the client received $269,000 of economic benefit in the elimination of tax liabilities and triggering of tax refunds and that the percentage of fee to economic benefit to the client was 20% and that the Redbook time entries that were the basis of the *pro forma* bill to illustrate to the client the fairness of the fee agreement were what it would take to do the case. (Q.M. Tr. 21-93; Q.M. Byler Exs. 1-5.) Given this valuable legal service so beneficial to a needy client, it may fairly asked how in the world could that legal representation give rise to a nearly eight year disciplinary case such that one could imagine a current day Charles Dickens giving it *Bleak House*- type treatment?

The answer to that question will NOT be found in Professor Abel's dishonest professors' tale. The dishonest professors' tale blames Byler, but I have submitted to Professor Abel a 170-page letter showing, with a paragraph-by-paragraph analysis, that the dishonest professors' tale is false history laced with character assassination, suffering from: glaring omission of material information; misstatements, mischaracterizations and misquotations; imprecise and misleading wording; crediting witness accounts that on a certain subject should not be credited and ignoring other dispositive evidence; and outright false statements. Further, a basic flaw of the dishonest professors' tale is that it all but ignores what the quantum meruit record showed. That record sheds a completely different light on the case and makes what happened and was said at times in the disciplinary trial to appear as rather dumb. My case cannot be rationally evaluated without knowledge of the specifics of the quantum meruit record, yet that is precisely what the dishonest professors' tale sets out to do.

To the question why did the Phil Byler case happen, my heretofore politically incorrect but ever truthful answer is as follows. Because the attorney (me) did not have a billing relationship with the client who was a "friend" in financial difficulty, but rather non-market special terms calling for payment to be worked out based on developments in the case and the client's career and because after years of representation the attorney let down his guard with that client when accepting a client- proposed fee agreement that could be made only because of the attorney's work and results achieved, the client's brother, a prominent law school professor by the name of Thomas Morgan, could cynically and did concoct what may be called a lawyerly lie. A lawyerly lie is born of a prevalent but misconceived notion of lawyer advocacy and is still a lie. Here, the lawyerly lie: (i) did not recognize the client's financial circumstances but pretended there were no financial difficulties; (ii) did not recognize the gravity of the client's legal difficulties but rather insanely characterized them as a problem to be easily solved; (iii) did not recognize the special non-market terms extended due to the financial problems of the client; (iv) did not recognize the work that was done but rather essentially ignored it; (v) did not recognize the results achieved but rather essentially ignored them; and (vi) did not recognize the assignment of the IRS refund monies but rather was either silent about it or, given the alternative universe of the lie, treated it as not to be relied upon. Thomas Morgan's lie would illustrate Hitler's maxim that the larger the lie, the easier it is to be accepted.

That "lawyerly lie" became the basis of a prolonged and ethically misfocused disciplinary case. Among other things, that disciplinary case saw: (i) Thomas Morgan exercising undue influence in the Disciplinary Counsel's Office in promoting what were in fact private purposes; (ii) the representation of Jim Morgan by a Disciplinary Committee member in a New York state court case concerning the same subject matter as the disciplinary case and seeking to obtain the IRS refund monies; (iii) a disgrace of a Star Chamber trial, run by an overtly hostile, predisposed attorney who was not a member of the Disciplinary Committee as supposedly required by the Rules of the Appellate Division-First Department and replete with evidentiary error where among many things evidence of value of work for proof of agreement fairness was excluded, Thomas Morgan's accusatory letters were received as expert testimony without cross-examination (Thomas Morgan did not testify) and prejudicial comments reflecting pre-judgment were made; (iv) a state court suspension, notwithstanding the rejection of the unfitness charge under DR 1-102 of the Professional Code of Professional Responsibility, based on case law where there was unfitness found under DR 1-102 of the Code of Professional Responsibility and based on a sleazy piece of character assassination—that I needed to be deterred from doing what I had done again (never mind I have an otherwise unblemished record and I do not handle client funds in my practice) and I was "self righteous and out of touch with reality"; (v) the U.S. District Court for the Eastern District of New York not imposing reciprocal discipline after a full Order To Show Cause proceeding in which my opposition was that there had been a corrupt denial of due process; (vi) in the state court client litigation, a New York State court trial judge denying use of the disciplinary decision and ordering a *quantum meruit* hearing, at which I presented expert testimony, stipulated facts and documents that established my right to be paid what I had received and leading to a settlement favorable to me; and (vii) the Appellate Division-First Department when ordering reinstatement being diplomatically critical of the delay.

The moral of the story is not to blame Byler; the dishonest professors' tale simply goes in a wrong direction. The dishonest professors' tale thus concerns me not just because it would unproductively defame me, but also because it would not lead to addressing important problems for legal ethics and lawyers' discipline that did exist in the case and that should lead to a continuing reform of disciplinary substantive law and procedures. Ethics cases are fact-sensitive, require due process procedures for accurate fact-finding and need substantive ethics law to become a more developed body of law. In absence of such reform, unwisely exercised prosecutorial authority can lead and did in my case to the kind of abuses in this country that traditionally have been found to be unacceptable in the administration of justice founded on the rule of law. The dishonest professors' tale further concerns me because my demand for a public trial was unconstitutionally ignored at the time, yet the author of the dishonest professors' tale has been granted access by the Disciplinary Committee Counsel's Office in Manhattan to what was once a confidential case file in order to write something that to cover up serious problems in the case and to discredit me for having had the audacious courage and true professionalism to challenge what was then a constitutionally infirm disciplinary process.

Consider:
- (i) The economic benefits of the 2½ year representation to the client in the elimination of over $216,000 in tax liabilities and triggering of over $50,000 of net refunds were despite the obstacles thrown up at the disciplinary trial—manifest even there, where the client had to and did admit to the excellent work and results of my representation. (Disc. Tr. 64-65, 83.)
- (ii) At the quantum meruit hearing, I proved with expert testimony, stipulated facts and documents that a reasonable fee was what I was paid with the IRS refund and rent refund monies ($55,048.34), shown by among other things the work done and in the fee being approximately 20% of the economic benefits to the clients from the representation. (Q.M. Tr. 21-93; Q.M. Byler Exs. 1-5.)
- (iii) There was a fee agreement (Jim Morgan admitted under oath that he told me to "keep" the IRS refund—Disc. Tr. 29), and even if it were determined that I should not have relied upon the fee agreement (a judgment made by the disciplinary Hearing Panel by excluding the consideration of the value of legal services and distorting the formation of agreement), the attorney (me) was acting pursuant to what he thought was a fair and binding fee agreement (Disc. Tr. 176, 456–457) that in fact paid a reasonable fee (Q.M. Tr. 21-93; Q.M. Byler Exs. 1-5).
- (iv) The New York state court litigation brought for Jim Morgan by a member of the Disciplinary Committee was resolved by a $10,000 settlement to that attorney's escrow in September 2001 that effectively left me with a fee of $45,048.34, which was over 80% of the original fee;
- (v) There was never an escrow, yet the attorney for Jim Morgan in the state court action filed an affidavit with the Appellate Division-First Department that the settlement was "a fair and just resolution."
- (vi) It was I who attempted to settle the case at the start and received no counter-offer (Disc. Tr. 395-396) and indeed would be rebuffed concerning settlement until the quantum meruit hearing when

CHAPTER 6

there was no escaping from consideration of proof of the value of my services, and the settlement of the state court action in September 2001 was in an amount, considering the time value of money, equivalent to a settlement offer I had made to Thomas Morgan in November 1994.

(vii) A nearly eight-year disciplinary case was not necessary at all to impress upon one's mind the need for written retainers and careful handling of client funds—in 1997 in my disciplinary trial testimony, I testified it only takes one bad experience (here in 1994) to teach the wisdom of written retainers, and my practice was not and is not to handle client funds. (Disc. Tr. 167-168, 208–211.)

(viii) Reciprocal discipline was not imposed by the U.S. District Court for the Eastern District of New York after a full Order To Show Cause proceeding in which my defense was that there had been a corrupt denial of due process in the New York disciplinary case.

The moral of the story thus must be quite different. My view of the moral is three-fold: (i) that disciplinary procedures can like other legal processes be abused for private purposes; (ii) consideration of the value of my services and the substantive subject matter of my representation was key to resolving the case, not an escrow with blinders put on as to the value of my services; and (iii) that, most importantly, there is a need for continuing legal reform, so that disciplinary cases have due process procedures for accurate fact-finding to decide cases and a more developed substantive body of ethics law to guide prosecutors and attorneys in practice alike. As wasteful and as nearly ruinous was my disciplinary case, in my quiet moments, I have had the sense that in time, the case would be a catalyst for beneficial change. When I was facing the career ending dangers in the disciplinary case, I would recite some lines in Shakespeare's King Henry V: "Gloster, 'tis true that we are in great danger; The greater therefore should our courage be. . . ." (Act IV. Scene 1, lines 1-2.) Now, I recite the lines that follow thereafter: "Thus may we gather honey from the weed, And make a moral of the devil himself" (Act IV, Scene 1, lines 11-12.)

In the end, once the false history of the dishonest professors' tale is exposed for what it is, we are faced with a pathetic irony about the dishonest professors' tale—that it was certain people in the legal ethics establishment who unwisely mixed relationships amongst themselves with the adjudication of a disciplinary case, who could not and still cannot admit error, who persisted and are apparently persisting still in dishonest and destructive behavior and who have been so enslaved to the lie of the case that you must resort, years later, to keeping the lie alive.

One last comment: the dishonest professors' tale must be castigated at the outset for going so far at one point as to make fun of my having a sense of personal honor amidst a seemingly never ending disciplinary case. Derision of that sense of personal honor is really very stupid. To quote a great and honorable American in John McCain in his book *Why Courage Matters* (p. 73): "A sense of honor encompasses all the virtues, justice, loyalty, honesty, compassion, courage." Preserving a sense of personal honor helped see John McCain through dark years as a prisoner of war in North Vietnam. The sick, slick cynicism that is an element in the dishonest professors' tale surfaces in its derision of honor, a derision that should not be allowed to cloud thinking so as to avoid consideration of how my disciplinary case may rightly be called a lie and how disciplinary law and procedures need to be reformed.

Part Three

Excessive Zeal

Perhaps the most difficult balancing act for lawyers[863] is accommodating the obligation to represent a client zealously[864] with the direction not to engage in "illegal conduct that adversely reflects on the lawyer's honesty, trustworthiness or fitness" or involves "dishonesty, fraud, deceit, or misrepresentation," "is prejudicial to the administration of justice," or otherwise "adversely reflects on the lawyer's fitness as a lawyer."[865] One of the most hotly debated questions concerns criminal defense lawyers condoning client perjury.[866] Another problem is how far a lawyer may go in extrajudicial statements without prejudicing the outcome of a case.[867] Stephen Keim, an Australian lawyer representing Dr. Mohamed Haneef, accused in connection with the terrorist bombings in London and Glasgow, was so angry at his client's treatment that he openly leaked the 142-page transcript of the police interrogation. This led to Haneef's complete exoneration but a disciplinary inquiry into the behavior of Keim (who was subsequently named Australian of the Year by *The Australian*, which published the transcript).[868] A number of empirical studies have documented

---

[863] E.g., ABA House of Delegates (1998).
[864] DR 7-101, N.Y.C.R.R. § 1200.32.
[865] DR 1-102, N.Y.C.R.R. § 1200.3. See the Hofstra University Law School conference on "Lawyering at the Edge: Unpopular Clients, Difficult Cases, Zealous Advocates" (10.14–16.07). The student newspaper editorialized against participation by Lynne F. Stewart, convicted of smuggling messages out of prison for a terrorist client. Paul Vitello, "Hofstra Polite as Lawyer Guilty in Terror Case Talks on Ethics," New York Times (10.17.07).
[866] E.g., Freedman (1966; 1975); see also Wydick (1995). The larger debate has been continued: Simon (1993); Luban (1993).
[867] Gentile v. State Bar of Nevada, 501 U.S. 1030 (1991) (Nevada disciplined defense lawyer who won acquittal of client after making inflammatory statements; Supreme Court found rule too vague); Ruggieri v. Johns-Manville Products Corp., 503 F. Supp. 1036 (D.R.I. 1980) (refusing to disqualify lawyer from all asbestos litigation after he spoke about the 1935 "smoking gun" memorandum on television).
[868] Raymond Bonner, "Fighting for Justice, Even at His Own Peril," New York Times A4 (1.26.08).

PART THREE

the pervasiveness of abusive discovery.[869] Lawyers must not "engage in undignified or discourteous conduct which is degrading to a tribunal."[870]

The rules seek to give concrete meaning to these broad exhortations. The lawyer must not "counsel or assist the client in conduct that the lawyer knows to be illegal or fraudulent."[871]

> A lawyer who receives information clearly establishing that . . . the client, in the course of representation, perpetrated a fraud upon a person or tribunal shall promptly call upon the client to rectify the same, and if the client refuses or is unable to do so, the lawyer shall reveal the fraud to the affected person or tribunal, except when the information is protected as a confidence or secret.[872]

The ABA has opined that "a lawyer in a civil case who discovers that her client has lied in responding to discovery requests must take all reasonable steps to rectify the fraud, which may include disclosure to the court." The obligation of candor toward the tribunal explicitly supersedes the obligation of confidentiality.[873] A lawyer "shall not knowingly make false accusations against a judge or other adjudicatory officer."[874]

Courts deal with excessive zeal in a number of ways. The U.S. Supreme Court famously ruled that a convicted criminal was not denied adequate assistance of counsel when his lawyer refused to let him give perjured testimony.[875] Courts have struggled with the defense lawyer's obligation to surrender a murder weapon[876] or disclose its location or that of the client's victims.[877] Although the plaintiff's lawyers won a jury verdict of $300,000 compensatory and $650,000 punitive damages for a racially hostile work environment, the U.S. District Judge drastically cut the fee

---

[869] Connolly et al. (1978); Brazil (1980a; 1980b; 1981); Frenkel et al. (1998); Nelson (1998); Sarat (1998); Suchman (1998); Kakalik et al. (1998); Willging et al. (1998); Mullenix (1998); Garth (1998).
[870] DR 7-106(c)(6), N.Y.C.R.R. §1200.37.
[871] DR 7-102(a)(7), N.Y.C.R.R. § 1200.33.
[872] DR 7-102(b), N.Y.C.R.R. § 1200.33.
[873] ABA Formal Opinion 93-376.
[874] DR 8-102(b), N.Y.C.R.R. § 1200.43.
[875] Nix v. Whiteside, 475 U.S. 157 (1986); see People v. Johnson, 72 Cal.Rptr.2d 805, cert. denied, 525 U.S. 914 (1998).
[876] State v. Olwell, 394 P.2d 681 (Wash. 1964); Commonwealth v. Stenhach, 356 Pa. Super. 5, 514 A.2d 114, appeal denied, 517 Pa. 589, 534 A.2d 769 (1987).
[877] Mellinkoff (1973).

award from the lawyers' "normal" $300/hour to $150 for preparation and even less for trial ($50 for one lawyer and nothing for the other) because of aggressive language and behavior toward opposing counsel. The judge also complained to both federal and state disciplinary bodies.[878] A judge sanctioned a lawyer for submitting documents accusing opposing counsel of racism toward the lawyer and her client in an employment discrimination action.[879] The Eleventh Circuit affirmed a U.S. District Judge's denial of a preliminary injunction on the ground that the moving attorney failed to cite controlling adverse precedent—a case in which the attorney had actually participated.[880] The Third Circuit has approved a dismissal for failure to comply with discovery.[881] The Fifth Circuit sanctioned a lawyer for obscenity during a deposition.[882] A U.S. District Judge ordered the suppression of documents obtained by the plaintiff outside discovery from an anonymous employee of the defendant.[883] But the Ninth Circuit has refused to impose Rule 11 sanctions on a law firm for failing to distinguish between arguments "warranted by existing law" and arguments for the "extension, modification, or reversal of existing law."[884]

Disciplinary bodies have sanctioned lawyers for abusing and threatening opposing counsel, witnesses, and judges,[885] misstating facts in oral argument,[886] paying a witness not to testify,[887] advising a client to testify falsely,[888] remaining silent while a divorce client (with whom the lawyer had a sexual relationship) falsely testified to her whereabouts at a time when she was with the lawyer,[889] using the legal process to harass the lawyer's ex-wife,[890] threatening criminal prosecution and altering documents,[891] concealing the gun and money involved in a bank robbery (even if the

---

[878] Lee v. American Eagle Airlines, Inc., 93 F. Supp.2d 1322 (S.D. Fl. 2000).
[879] Thomas v. Tenneco Packaging Co., 293 F.3d 1306 (11th Cir. 2002).
[880] Jorgenson v. County of Volusia, 846 F.2d 1350 (11th Cir. 1988).
[881] Poulis v. State Farm Fire and Casualty Co., 747 F.2d 863 (3rd Cir. 1984).
[882] Carroll v. The Jacques Admiralty Law Firm, 110 F.3d 290 (5th Cir. 1997).
[883] In re Shell Oil Refinery, 143 F.R.D. 105 (E.D. La. 1992).
[884] Golden Eagle Distrib. Corp. v. Burroughs Corp. 801 F.2d 1531 (9th Cir. 1986), reversing 103 F.R.D. 124 (N.D. Cal. 1984).
[885] Office of Disciplinary Counsel v. Mills, 93 Ohio.St.3d 407, 755 N.E.2d 336 (2001); In re Vincenti, 92 N.J. 591, 458 A.2d 1268 (1983).
[886] In re Kalal, 252 Wis.2d 261, 643 N.W.2d 466 (2002).
[887] People v. Kenelly, 648 P.2d 1065 (Colo. 1982).
[888] Florida Bar v. Simons, 391 So. 2d 684 (Fla. 1980).
[889] Committee on Professional Ethics and Conduct of the Iowa State Bar Ass'n v. Crary, 245 N.W.2d 298 (Ia. 1976).
[890] In re Varakin, 1994 WL 606153 (Cal. Bar Ct. 1994).
[891] In re Barrett, 443 A.2d 678 (N.J. 1982).

PART THREE

purpose was to prevent the defendant from disposing of them),[892] knowingly signing a fraudulent escrow agreement,[893] and misrepresenting the lawyer's identity and other facts in the course of an investigation.[894]

The case that follows deals with a particular tension between vigorous advocacy and the integrity of the legal process: what are the obligations of a lawyer who inadvertently obtains privileged documents belonging to an adversary?[895] In 1992 the ABA opined that

> a lawyer who receives materials that on their face appear to be subject to the attorney-client privilege or otherwise confidential, under circumstances where it is clear they were not intended for the receiving lawyer, should refrain from examining the materials, notify the sending lawyer and abide the instructions....[896]

Two years later the ABA reiterated that advice to a lawyer who had received the communication from an unauthorized whistle blower. In 1995, partly in response to the case discussed below, the ABCNY recommended a similar rule.[897] Because the ABA amended its Model Rules in 2002 to limit the receiving lawyer's obligation to just notifying the sending lawyer,[898] it withdrew the 1992 opinion (but not the 1994).[899] The Restatement is unhelpful: "The attorney-client privilege is waived if the client, the client's lawyer, or another authorized agent of the client voluntarily discloses the communication in a non-privileged communication."[900] But what is voluntarily? Jurisdictions adopt different rules and apply the same rule differently depending on the facts, as the following cases demonstrate. In April 2006 the U.S. Supreme Court amended Federal Rules of Civil Procedure 26 allowing a party who discovers it has inadvertently produced

---

[892] In re Ryder, 263 F. Supp. 360 (E.D. Va.), aff'd, 381 F.2d 713 (4th Cir. 1967).
[893] In re Austern, 524 A.2d 680 (D.C. 1987).
[894] In re Gatti, 8 P.3d 966 (Or. 2000); but see Apple Corps, Ltd. v. International Collectors Society, 15 F. Supp.2d 456 (D.N.J. 1998) (no violation when lawyer used deceptive name and story to see if opposing party had violated consent decree).
[895] Perlman (2005); Heafey (2005).
[896] ABA Formal Ethics Opinion 92-368.
[897] Committee on Professional Responsibility, "Ethical Obligations Arising Out of an Attorney's Receipt of Inadvertently Disclosed Information," 50(6) The Record (1995).
[898] Model Rule 4.4(b).
[899] ABA Formal Ethics Opinion 05-437.
[900] Restatement (Third) of the Law Governing Lawyers § 79.

protected information to notify the other party, who must "promptly return, sequester, or destroy" the material.

In response to a trademark infringement claim by Lois Sportswear, Levi Strauss paralegals spent a single day under the supervision of its deputy general counsel segregating 16,000 out of 30,000 pages for inspection.[901] After inspecting the 16,000, Lois requested production of 3,000. Levi Strauss *subsequently* claimed privilege with respect to 22 documents. The court upheld the claim, finding that Levi's precautions in segregating the 16,000 pages were just barely reasonable and the inclusion of the 22 documents inadvertent.

The defendant's lawyer inadvertently sent the plaintiff's lawyer a seven-page letter clearly labeled "PRIVILEGED AND CONFIDENTIAL," addressed to the defendant's senior vice president and headed with the case caption.[902] The Western District of Michigan ruled that "lawyers are not required to stuff the envelopes and deposit the mail in order to protect the privilege." "[C]ommon sense and a high sensitivity toward ethics and the importance of attorney-client confidentiality and privilege should have immediately caused the plaintiff's attorneys to notify defendant's counsel of his office's mistake." Although the court refused to disqualify plaintiff's lawyer or order sanctions, it ordered all copies of the letter destroyed and prohibited its use in the case.

Potter, counsel for American Express, responded to a discovery request by Federal Expressing a package of documents to Milakovic, counsel for Accu-Weather.[903] Having discovered the same day that it contained privileged material, Potter telephoned Milakovic's office the next morning and told his secretary it should not be opened, following up with a fax. A day later Milakovic told Potter by phone that he was researching the privilege claim. But five days later Potter received a letter stating that the package had been opened. The following day Potter accused Milakovic of unethical conduct. The Southern District of New York agreed, based on the 1992 ABA opinion. Because the parties had settled the case, the Court limited its sanction to this opinion.

When William Aramony sued the United Way of America for wrongful discharge, four UWA lawyers and three paralegals spent 769.5 hours culling 630,000 pages to remove privileged material, which its senior

---

[901] Lois Sportswear v. Levi Strauss & Co., 104 F.R.D. 103 (S.D.N.Y. 1985).
[902] Resolution Trust Corp. v. First of America Bank, 868 F. Supp. 217 (W.D. Mich. 1994).
[903] American Express v. Accu-Weather, Inc., 1996 WL 346388 (S.D.N.Y. 1996).

attorney then reviewed.[904] Approximately six months after the nonprivileged material was delivered to Aramony's lawyers they informed UWA's lawyers that this included a 51-page memorandum evaluating the strengths and weaknesses of the case. UWA demanded its return the next day. The court found the disclosure inadvertent and the demand for return timely.

After a year-long investigation of alleged securities fraud involving HealthTech International, the U.S. Attorney's Office (USAO) for the Southern District of New York prepared a 69-page prosecution memorandum asking the Organized Crime and Racketeering Section of the Department of Justice to approve the filing of a proposed 75-page indictment.[905] The memo was not marked privileged. The USAO provided both documents to Special FBI Agent McNulty, who combined them into a single file, with the indictment on top, and distributed it to other members of the task force. Special Agent Young graduated from the FBI Academy in July 1996 and was assigned to the Task Force in February 1997. The following November he asked for the indictment and was told to pick up a copy from McNulty's desk. (By then the indictment had been superseded.) He collected the file in McNulty's absence, made two copies, returned the original, and gave one to another agent. Reading it four days later, he did not find it strange that the memo was attached, perhaps because he had never seen an indictment before. The next day he participated in the arrest of Hall, one of the accused, in Arizona and Hall's presentment before a Magistrate Judge by Assistant U.S. Attorney Stooks, an experienced prosecutor and former state court judge. Asked for the indictment, Young told Stooks he had left it in the FBI's Arizona field office and went to fetch it. Stooks gave the Magistrate Judge the file, calling it "a copy of the indictment . . . about a hundred pages," although the indictment was 75. The Court said the indictment contained 97 counts, but this (superseded) version only had 28 counts. Young summarized it for the Court. The clerk provided a copy to HealthTech's in-house counsel, Larson, who made copies for Hall and four other HealthTech employees. When one of these was fired, he gave his lawyer a copy. Agent Young then had five copies filed in a NASDAQ "de-listing" proceeding; portions were read and discussed during the NASDAQ hearing. HealthTech sent a copy to its outside auditors. HealthTech employees distributed 20–40 copies to stockholders, brokers, and potential investors. The document also remained in the U.S.

---

[904] Aramony v. United Way of America, 969 F. Supp. 226 (S.D.N.Y. 1997).
[905] U.S. v. Gangi, 1 F. Supp. 2d 256 (S.D.N.Y. 1998).

District Court file in Phoenix, where at least one outside lawyer obtained a copy. Hall furnished copies to two more of his lawyers, as well as to a codefendant's lawyer. The Phoenix court file was transferred to the Southern District of New York and available to the public there. On December 17, 22 days after the initial disclosure, defense counsel for Hall announced before a Magistrate Judge in New York that he had the memo and had read part of it. Later that day an AUSA finally removed it from the court file and the next day asked defense counsel to return his copy. At the government's request, the District Judge asked prosecution and defense counsel to return all copies, which they did; but he soon learned that distribution had been much more extensive. He found that the government had failed to take reasonable precautions. Here there was only a single document, not the thousands in other inadvertent disclosure cases. Given the widespread distribution, the judge could not undo the damage. Furthermore, it would be unfair if only one of the multiple defendants had access to the memo.

In response to an SEC prosecution, Cassano and other defendants obtained discovery of 50 to 52 cartons of material located in the agency's Boston Regional Office.[906] After an experienced SEC attorney spent days determining that they contained no privileged documents, the boxes were sent to the New York Regional Office, where they were available for inspection for 30 days, after which documents could be copied. Defense counsel soon found a 100-page memorandum reviewing the strengths and weaknesses of the SEC case. They read it with interest, took extensive notes, and then asked that it alone be copied, immediately. The paralegal called the lead counsel in Boston, who approved the request. After defense counsel confirmed that the memorandum was not in the privilege log it was circulated to at least four clients, four other counsel, and a Congressman and his staff. When the SEC learned the contents of the memorandum 12 days later they sought its return. The court found that the SEC had been careless in including the memorandum in the first place, even more in ignoring the red flag request to copy a *single* document at the *beginning* of the inspection, and taking 12 days to discover its error.

Kuehne & Nagel Air Freight mistakenly substituted an allegedly privileged letter addressed to its president for another with the same date addressed to opposing counsel and attached the former to a motion.[907]

---

[906] SEC v. Cassano, 189 F.R.D. 83 (1999).
[907] Local 851 v. Kuehne & Nagel Air Freight, Inc., 36 F. Supp. 2d 127 (E.D.N.Y. 1999).

PART THREE

The court found that counsel "did not take reasonable precautions to avoid disclosure." They failed to label the letter confidential, adequately instruct subordinates about confidentiality, or perform a reasonable review of papers before they left the office. Indeed, counsel admitted, "We all did a very foolish thing. We saw an April 27th date and a letterhead, and said oh, that's the letter." Rather than having to screen thousands of pages, "the purportedly privileged letter was merely one of seven exhibits to a motion. . . ." Fairness also argued for waiver, since the letter spoke to an essential issue in the litigation: whether defendants were acting in good faith.

In response to a discovery request, the defendant's lawyers reviewed over 200,000 pages, selected 70,000 for production, and segregated 3,821 as privileged.[908] A paralegal inadvertently added an archive box containing the latter to the other 22 archive boxes for copying. Five days later the plaintiff's lawyers informed defense counsel. The court found waiver because "easily-accomplished additional precautions were obviously needed." If "the Court does not hold that a waiver has occurred under the egregious circumstances here presented, it might as well adopt the 'never waived' rule. . . ."

During the five years 1999–2003, the First Department punished a few lawyers for excessive zeal or conduct prejudicial to the administration of justice. Learning that the action he had brought on behalf of a landlord had been dismissed before he arrived in court that day, Jaime V. Delio approached the bench and asked why.[909]

> Court: Counselor, I don't have to explain why I have defaults.
>
> Delio: This . . . other than your own self-interest—
>
> Court: I've had enough, Counselor, step back. Counselor—
>
> Delio: You're so pompous on the bench. It's ridiculous. You should remember what your jobs are.
>
> Court: Counselor.
>
> Delio: I don't have to respect you if you're not—
>
> Court: Have a seat, Counselor, have a seat.
>
> Delio: You're wrong.

---

[908] Amgen Inc. v. Hoechst Marion Roussel, Inc., 190 F.R.D. 287 (D. Mass. 2000).
[909] Matter of Delio, 731 N.Y.S.2d 171 (1st Dept. 2001).

> Court: Counselor, have a seat. I'm going to have a contempt hearing.
>
> Delio: It's wrong. She can't hold a contempt hearing. You have to call for one.
>
> Court: Well, I will call for one.

Delio moved to the restore the case three days later, saying in his affidavit:

> [T]here is not one reason I can think of that the Court was restrained [sic] to dismiss the proceedings at 10:30 a.m. other then [sic] its own self interest in keeping the docket clear. . . . However if the resolution part [sic] only concern is the following of arbitrary rules they impose and then the court defends these rules with pomposity and arrogance rather than logic or substantive meaning then there is no way to actually resolve anything. Bulling [sic] litigants with treats [sic] of irrational behavior is not justice or jurisprudence. The Court, when it suits its political temperament is quick to create standards that are unsupported in the law and are thereafter defended with it costs to [sic] much to appeal.

He added a footnote:

> The reason why someone is not where he should be is not the issue. . . . The point is how the Court will deal with these events. Like an ostrich sticking its head in the sand the option is always available to punt and dismiss the case. . . . Being so focused on the time of day the Court does not seem to have the time to provide any type of justice other than dismissal.

Delio only apologized two months later, a month after being served with charges. He was publicly censured.

Westchester County Supreme Court Judge Anthony A. Scarpino wrote the DDC that Agostinho D. Reis had "exhibited an explosive temper and total lack of civility and self control" in a divorce case, engaging in "loud and incoherent tirades, cursing, reckless allegations of criminal conduct, name calling."[910] Reis also had written the judge, insinuating he was part of a conspiracy to steal the property and violate the civil and constitutional rights of his client. In response to the DDC inquiry, Reis wrote the committee twice. First he said: "I can fairly well discern what it is that bothers Judge Scarpino, especially since this is not the first charge of civil rights and constitutional violations lodged against him, as an attorney, as a candidate for judge, and as an FBI agent." In the second, Reis denied having engaged in an outburst when the "court officer ordered me out of the courtroom at gun point." "The only aspect of my behavior which reflects on my *ability to practice law in Westchester* was my refusal to offer the Court a bribe, as a condition for representing my client on a *pro bono* basis." Reis also refused to pay his bar registration fee, claiming he lived in Newark and had retired from practice. In fact, he continued to practice, prompting three complaints of converting client funds, two of neglecting cases dismissed for failure to proceed, and one of disappearing after filing a case without consulting the client. He also failed to respond to DDC letters, including an order to repay the Client Protection Fund $3,172 misappropriated from a client. He was disbarred.

Philip J. Dinhofer told U.S. District Judge Loretta Preska: "This is rampant corruption. I don't know what else to say. This is a sham." "This is blatantly corrupt. You are sticking it to me every way you can." "I'm not rude to [the staff], I'm rude to you, because I think you deserve it. You are corrupt and you stink. That's my honest opinion, and I will tell you to your face." The Southern District of New York publicly censured him and required him to withdraw as counsel. The Appellate Division suspended him for three months.[911]

Steven L. Holley improperly disclosed a sealed court document to the legal affairs editor of *Business Week* and then denied in both a federal court hearing and a DDC deposition that the journalist told him the document had been sealed. The Referee recommended dismissal on the ground that Holley had merely been negligent in failing to ascertain that the complaint, given him by an associate with no warning signs, had been filed under seal. The Hearing Panel affirmed (4–1). Holley had been a member of the ABCNY Committee on Professional and Judicial Ethics from 1988 to 1993. Sullivan & Cromwell had reprimanded him and cut his partnership share 40 percent (several hundred thousand dollars); and he

---

[910] Matter of Reis, 728 N.Y.S.2d 23 (1st Dept. 2001), 739 N.Y.S.2d 148 (1st Dept. 2002).
[911] Matter of Dinhofer, 690 N.Y.S.2d 245 (1st Dept. 1999).

had suffered negative publicity and hostility. But the Appellate Division publicly censured him.[912]

Stockbroker Daniel Kalb had worked for Irene Toth de Escandon. After her death, the estate was probated in Arizona. Her nephew challenged the will. The decedent and Kalb had a joint Citibank account. On July 13, 1990, the Arizona court restricted withdrawals from it. But on December 10, 1992, Kalb withdrew $198,424, as well as funds from another joint account in California. The Arizona probate court held him in contempt and, on July 29, 1993, entered judgment against him in favor of the estate for $468,202. In 1994 Kalb retained Harry Issler to seek a New York declaratory judgment against Citibank that he owned the funds in the joint account. Citibank did not contest, and judgment entered on July 18, 1994. Issler failed to inform the New York court that he knew of the Arizona order, Kalb's withdrawal, and the contempt finding. Knowing that the declaratory judgment was intended as a defense against the nephew, now executor, who was seeking those funds, Issler did not give notice of the judgment to the estate. The nephew sued Issler's firm for fraud and obtained a partial summary judgment, which was settled for $375,000.[913] The Appellate Division publicly censured Issler.[914]

Jeffrey M. Cohn represented Christian Del Rosario, incarcerated for murder. Seeking to obtain a sentence reduction, and knowing that the U.S. Attorney's Office would negotiate for third-party information only if it had not been purchased, Cohn hired a private investigator to obtain the information and gave it to Christian's brother, Humberto. Cohn attended a proffer session and remained silent while Humberto lied to the government that he had not purchased the information but obtained it from his cousin in the Dominican Republic. The Southern District of New York suspended Cohn for five years, and the Appellate Division imposed reciprocal discipline.[915]

Robert J. Forrest represented a husband and wife injured in an automobile accident. After learning that the husband had died from unrelated causes, Forrest served unsigned answers to interrogatories without informing his adversary of the death. He told the wife not to mention the death at the mandatory arbitration. In response to the arbitrator's inquiry about

---

[912] Matter of Holley, 729 N.Y.S.2d 128 (1st Dept. 2001).
[913] Schindler v. Issler & Schrage, 262 A.D.2d 226 (1st Dept.), appeal dismissed, 94 N.Y.2d 791 (1999).
[914] Matter of Issler, 725 N.Y.S.2d 335 (1st Dept. 2001).
[915] Matter of Cohn, 761 N.Y.S.2d 177 (1st Dept. 2003).

PART THREE

the husband's absence, Forrest said he was "unavailable." After the arbitrator entered awards for both parties, Forrest contacted opposing counsel to discuss settlement, still concealing the death. When he ignored several requests by the defendant to produce the husband for medical examination and failed to reply to counsel's motion to do so, the court ordered the examination. Forrest continued to negotiate settlement, only informing the defendant of the death after the husband failed to appear at the examination. In the disciplinary proceeding in New Jersey (where Forrest principally practiced), he admitted being imprudent but justified his deceit as a means of enhancing recovery. He had not made any misrepresentations but merely withheld information, which he called "bluffing" and "puffing." New Jersey suspended him for six months; New York did the same, successively.[916]

The following case raises difficult questions about what a lawyer must do when he inadvertently obtains a "smoking gun" document from opposing counsel in the course of bitterly contested civil litigation and what the lawyer may say in motions to recuse the judge who subsequently made adverse rulings in the case.

---

[916] Matter of Forrest, 706 N.Y.S.2d 15 (1st Dept. 2000).

Chapter 7

The Purloined Papers

I. Championing a Sexual Harassment Victim

Joan C. Lipin grew up in Scarsdale, graduated from NYU in 1969, and earned an MBA at Boston University in health administration. She worked at Massachusetts General Hospital and MIT and then at New York Hospital, where she managed a $10 million budget. After three years she became executive vice president of a startup and then president of a sole proprietorship. In January 1986 Robert Bender Jr., general manager of the American Red Cross of Greater New York (ARCGNY), hired her as assistant manager for marketing. "On the sixth, in the sixth week of my employment I was told by Mr. Bender, it's so easy" to succeed—just sleep with him.[917] "My professional career was destroyed. My personal life was attempted to be destroyed because I refused to go to bed with Mr. Bender." In November 1987, Lipin "said to Mary Stanton, who was a subordinate of mine, the human resource administrator, I put the Red Cross on formal

---

[917] Unless otherwise noted, all testimony comes from the disciplinary hearing. This problem may not have been restricted to Bender. In 2007 the American Red Cross fired Mark Everson as president six months after he took the job, finding that he had "engaged in a personal relationship with a subordinate employee." "Red Cross Ousts President over Relationship," Los Angeles Times (11.28.07).

notice that if Mr. Bender didn't stop sexually harassing me and discriminating against me, I would in all likelihood have to sue." He fired her on February 5, 1988. Over the next year and a half she warned various Red Cross trustees she would sue if Bender did not stop defaming her.

Edmund S. "Ned" Purves, a friend, referred her to his Larchmont neighbor, Arthur M. Wisehart, in 1989. Purves was of counsel to Wisehart & Koch, a Manhattan partnership, and also practiced with his own Larchmont firm. On June 29 Lipin sued Bender, the ARCGNY, and the American National Red Cross (ANRC) for sexual harassment and sexual discrimination under New York human rights law and 42 USC §§1985(3) and 1983. The ARCGNY retained Weil Gotshal & Manges (WGM). Lipin found their December 12 deposition of her "extremely abusive . . . asking very sensitive questions with respect to my family," such as when her mother first attempted suicide. The next day Wisehart sought court supervision of discovery, which Justice Karla Moskowitz granted,[918] assigning Special Referee Birnbaum. On February 13, 1990, Wisehart requested production of documents. WGM sought a protective order on February 23 on the ground of attorney-client or work-product privilege. Wisehart responded on March 5 that WGM had not met its burden of proof and repeated his discovery request on May 11. ANRC attorney Barbara Cummins (from Morgan Lewis & Bockius—MLB) also asserted privilege on May 21. After oral argument, Judge Moskowitz ruled on October 30 that "defendants have not met their burden of demonstrating entitlement to a protective order."

Wisehart sought to depose Barbara Fletcher, a Red Cross employee who was having an affair with Bender. Lipin claimed Fletcher's "salary increase for minimal qualifications was 40 percent in one year." At a preliminary conference on February 13, 1990, Justice Moskowitz ordered the deposition.[919] Ten days later the defendants moved to strike the interrogatories, sought a protective order with respect to document requests, and

---

[918] Judge Moskowitz graduated from Columbia Law School in 1966 (a year after I did) and then worked in state and local government before becoming a Civil Court judge in 1982, Acting Supreme Court Justice in 1987 and Justice in 1991. She was a member of the State Supreme Court Anti-Bias Committee and has been President of both the New York State and the National Associations of Women Judges. The Women's Medical Association of New York City gave her its Women of Valor Award in 1995; the Women's Bar Association of the State of New York gave her its Founder's Award in 1999.

[919] Respondent's Ex. I: plaintiff's supplemental amended interrogatories.

requested oral argument.[920] Wisehart answered this on March 5, complaining about "the utter lack of good faith on the part of defendants' counsel" and asserting that WGM lawyer Lawrence J. Baer's actions were "prejudicial in the extreme."[921] On May 21 the defendants responded to the plaintiff's notice for discovery and inspection, objecting to every request and producing nothing.[922] ARCGNY rescheduled Fletcher's deposition from May 24 to June 7. But on June 5 Fletcher flew to California. Lipin complained that the "court ordered deposition had been scheduled for a long period of time and we were suddenly told, I think a few days before, that she was leaving the Red Cross, that she would no longer be in New York, and that she would not be made available for her deposition." On October 30 Justice Moskowitz denied defendants' motion to strike plaintiff's interrogatories and for a protective order and ordered an Open Commission for Fletcher's deposition in California on November 19. Plaintiff's questions were "neither overbroad, onerous or an undue burden."[923] But Moskowitz denied both plaintiff's request for sanctions and defendants' cross motion for costs and sanctions. "This is a bitterly contested matter. The parties' conduct, however, does not warrant imposition of sanctions at this juncture." The deposition ultimately occurred on April 5, 1991.[924] Asked about documents favorable to Lipin, Fletcher said "she had shredded them the first business day after Ms. Lipin was terminated, in the office formally [sic] occupied by Ms. Lipin." Wisehart again sought sanctions against WGM, but Justice Moskowitz did not rule.

Lipin started working for Wisehart as a paralegal in March 1990 because she had no income and could not get a job.[925] "Many times I would have the third interview, such as an administrative dean of a medical college, they would say, let us call the Red Cross. And then they wouldn't want to hear from me." "Mr. Wisehart hired me out of compassion, and I started in an administrative capacity and eventually, in order to help me overcome the trauma, he said, how about if you begin to do some paralegal

---

[920] Respondent's Ex. J.
[921] Respondent's Ex. K.
[922] Respondent's Ex. L.
[923] Respondent's Ex. M.
[924] Memorandum of law and affidavit in opposition to Barbara Fletcher's motion in San Diego Superior Court to quash a subpoena for her deposition, Respondent's Ex. G.
[925] The National Federation of Paralegal Associations website believes Lipin was acting as a paralegal, not a client, in the events described below. http://www.paralegals.org. Last visited June 7, 2007.

work and think about going into a new area of education." Wisehart explained that Lipin

> was unable to find any position whatsoever, other than as a receptionist on weekends for the Roadrunners Club for $6.50 an hour. She was heavily into debt. And I just thought this was outrageous. So I thought I would see what she could do to help around the office. She didn't have any qualifications as a paralegal in 1989 or '90, when I employed her ... although she had done some work for other lawyers in patent matters, but I just employed her to provide clerical assistance ... and give her some income. ... I told her that if things developed in the office, she could develop as a paralegal. ...

During preparation of the case "she did an analysis of the factual basis ... which was really extraordinary. ..." Wisehart "felt vindicated ... about taking her on when I saw how well she organized the material in that case." She attended subsequent depositions in her case. (In 1992 Martindale-Hubbell listed her as legal support personnel in the firm.)

The parties were before Justice Moskowitz on May 13, 1991, to hear Baer's motions for supervision of disclosure with respect to documents produced by the plaintiff, which the defendants wanted tested by a forensic expert, claiming plaintiff had whited out parts and added parts later.[926] They also alleged that plaintiff had destroyed documents during litigation. Moskowitz wanted to know why Baer had not just asked Wisehart.

> Baer: Your honor, in all due candor, my dealings with Plaintiff's Counsel over the last two years have been marked by nothing but frustration. We have reached the point where we could not reach—
>
> Court: Excuse me. Do you have any objection to supplying this material for a test; the originals?
>
> Wisehart: I would want to retain control of the documents but I think the whole dispute is a manufactured dispute.

---

[926] This quotation from the transcript was reproduced in Lipin's affidavit in support of her November 30, 1994 motion to reargue the Court of Appeals' affirmation of Moskowitz's dismissal of her complaint, Staff Ex. 13.

> Court: I don't understand what we are doing here, either. . . .
> I think this is a tempest in a tea pot. . .I don't know what this
> has to do with anything.

After they discussed logistics, Moskowitz continued:

> Court: I don't know why you couldn't do this without a flood
> of paper. You have destroyed more trees with these motion
> papers than—it is just uncalled for . . . this was totally unneces-
> sary, this motion. If you want to engage in this kind of motion
> practice, I am going to start imposing costs. You get paid if
> you make these motions, right, you bill your client, and I don't
> think the plaintiff's counsel can do that. So I don't think it is
> fair to motion somebody to death so that the person can't con-
> tinue a case.
>
> Wisehart: . . .these motion papers were served on me . . . within
> two hours after he made his call to me so he clearly had a pre-
> disposition to make this motion regardless of what I said.
>
> Baer: May I respectfully say that if the Court were to examine
> the docket in this case, the number of motions made by
> Plaintiff in this case far outnumber the number of motions
> made by the Defendants. . . .
>
> Court: I don't know who has been making motions, but this
> motion was totally unnecessary. . . .

They then turned to defendants' objection to "four document requests contained in what is a 27 page document request," which "are so overbroad, so blunderbuss that even in reply the Plaintiff could not put forth the reasons. . . ." Moskowitz replied that they had had a "very lengthy discussion on the record" in which she had ruled that "anything that I didn't say limit, I said produce." If defendants could not find the documents, Wisehart had suggested, they should explain their filing system and he would frame his request accordingly. Defendants had described the filing system on April 10 but still sought a protective order on April 19.

> Court: Here is the problem. These were asked for how many
> times?

Wisehart: Starting May 11, 1990.

Court: [to Baer] You are too late. Too late. You are out of order on this one. This was May 11, 1990 . . . demanded again. Too late. Comply.

Wisehart: I have a cross motion to strike the answer of the defendants and/or for sanctions. . . . and also for discovery abuse in connection with the deposition of Barbara Fletcher . . . there were 591 objections and 31 directions not to answer in a deposition of 300 pages. . . . what is called the "Rambo litigator approach". . . to make it impossible to use the deposition in litigation. . . . We are going to have to go back to California, we are going to have to make a motion to compel. We are going to have to bring the witness back. And all of this is absolutely unnecessary. . .when I asked Ms. Fletcher whether she had been told about when her deposition in New York had been scheduled, she was instructed not to answer. . . . I respectfully submit that the sorry history of this case in terms of discovery is such that it ought to be confronted by the court. . . . the claim of attorney-client privilege has never been . . . permitted to be used as a shield for illegal conduct. . . .

Baer: Your Honor, if I may.

Court: Stop it. [to Wisehart] You are asking me to strike the answers based on what happened in this EBT [examination before trial]? . . .

Wisehart: . . . also based on . . . the Dubinsky affidavit, an attorney for the National Red Cross says, "We cannot produce certain information about Red Cross employees . . . because we do not have the social security numbers."[927]

Cummins: May I be heard in reply?

Court: Wait until he finishes. . . .

Wisehart: . . . there was a deliberate alteration of the documents. . . . the Red Cross is in fact paying the attorneys who appear for [Fletcher] . . . she was in continuing touch, both

---

[927] They had redacted the numbers in the documents they produced!

with Mr. Bender . . . and with Mr. Baer. . . . we have to go back. We have to make a motion to compel. We will have to get a ruling from the California Court, all of which is expensive and I undoubtedly will have to go back. . . . I would say it would cost us $3,000. . . .

Baer: . . . at every turn we attempted to cooperate with Mr. Wisehart . . . this is the first time I have ever heard that this deposition has not been completed . . . Mr. Wisehart did not seek to have the deposition continued into the following day in California.

Court: You had to leave, didn't you?

Baer: Of course. . . .

Wisehart: . . . he told me on the record that they would not permit him to go forward the following day. . . .

Baer: I indicated to Mr. Wisehart that the notice for the deposition was only for that day and that he was wasting precious time . . . engaging in obstreperous conduct. . . . 99 times out of 100 the objection was mere "objection, relevance" period. . . .

Court: I really don't say, Mr. Wisehart, that whatever has gone on here is sufficient to strike the defendants' answers. . . . The document requests were made a long time ago and they still haven't been answered. . . . We have been through this ad nauseam. I want these things answered.

She ordered the documents produced by June 17.

Wisehart had also requested WGM's time records since June 1990. "I believe the defendants' law firm was directly involved in that Fletcher left New York on the brink of her deposition and that they have been continuously involved following a period when she was no longer a Red Cross employee." He based his request on "obstruction of justice." Bender sent a memo to staff dated May 8, 1990: "Fletcher is planning to move to San Diego, California area for both career and personal reasons." She left June 5. Wisehart said Fletcher "admitted that there were no career reasons. She hasn't had a job in California since she has been there." Moskowitz allowed Wisehart to question Fletcher and Bender about her move but found the time records irrelevant. She also rejected Wisehart's sanctions motion

Chapter 7

because Fletcher had been directed not to answer by a California attorney. Baer said he had motion papers objecting to further notices to produce, but Moskowitz replied: "I don't want to have any more motion papers. I have been motioned to death in this case." When Baer argued that "Fletcher's pay is not relevant in any way, shape or form to this case," Moskowitz cut him off: "Come on. I know what this case is about. That is ridiculous. Answer the question." Baer objected to Wisehart's demand for documents about ARCGNY's alleged multi-million dollar losses after Lipin's firing. Wisehart also sought documents about ARCGNY's toleration of employee drug abuse in order to show discrimination in its firing of Lipin. Moskowitz ordered production to Wisehart of any records of Bender's drug abuse and to Lipin of any records of other employee drug abuse. "I don't want to have more motions. What I want to do is have a date so that if you have more motions, just make application to me on the record." She refused Baer's request to reschedule the deposition of Delbert Staley, the ARCGNY board chair (and semi-retired chairman of NYNEX). "You picked those dates. You were supposed to check with everybody."

The parties were before Justice Moskowitz again on May 21. Baer said there were no records of drug abuse; Moskowitz ordered him to produce an affidavit attesting to that. When Wisehart objected that documents had not been produced to him the previous Friday, as Moskowitz had directed on May 13, Baer responded that 3,830 out of approximately 4,000 documents had been delivered to Wisehart a few minutes ago. Moskowitz was "not about to sanction anybody" for the three-day delay. Wisehart requested another conference before the May 28 EBT "to see if there has been complete production of the documents."

> Wisehart: I know it is a burden, Your Honor, but we had exactly the same situation happen a year ago with Mr. Baer. It must be in their firm's operating manual.
>
> Court: Cut it out. It probably is a good idea to see if there is something blatantly missing because I really can't take any more of these voluminous motions. . . . I don't want any more motion papers in this case.

Two days later they were back in front of Moskowitz, who had received a letter from Wisehart the previous day with a 36-page attachment listing questions the defendants had not answered.[928] Dean M. Dreiblatt, standing in for Wisehart, had gotten another letter at 1:30 P.M. that day, which was still not responsive. Baer objected that this was "a bald allegation . . . [with] absolutely no specification." Because Moskowitz had suggested a telephone conference with the court, Baer wondered "why we are wasting our time."

> Moskowitz: I am not going to sit here and go through this question by question. I don't have the energy to do it and I don't think that's what a judge is supposed to do. . . . if they are not palpably unresponsive or improper, then that's it.

Dreiblatt insisted that the "defendants were specifically admonished to produce documents" and had been "palpably unresponsive." Baer retorted they had answered all but four questions "that were objected to and ruled upon immediately before we served our responses." They would answer the rest "as soon as our clients get back from their convention in San Diego." Moskowitz was impatient: "why do you have to wait until the end of next week?" She again demanded an affidavit declaring there were no relevant documents. "I want to make sure that . . . all documents . . . that are in your possession are produced so that the EBTs can take place."

On June 14 Wisehart conducted an EBT of Bender before Birnbaum.[929] Wisehart asked if Bender had spent time alone with Barbara Fletcher during a 1987 retreat. WGM lawyer Mark A. Jacoby objected, but Birnbaum allowed the question, and Bender conceded "my presumption is I may have" and it was "conceivable" it happened more than once. Wisehart asked: "Did you and Barbara Fletcher stay together overnight?" Jacoby again objected, invoking the privacy interests of Fletcher and Bender.

> Jacoby: Mr. Wisehart has made an application to the court in California with respect to this matter that is presently pending for hearing I understand on June 21st.
>
> Birnbaum: Oh, there is something going on in California, Mr. Wisehart?

---

[928] Respondent's Ex. R.
[929] Respondent's Ex. U.

Chapter 7

> Wisehart: There has been a deposition of Barbara Fletcher on April 15, 1991. Before that deposition occurred, Justice Moskowitz issued rulings. Can we not have—
>
> Birnbaum: Come on. Come on, Mr. Wisehart.
>
> Wisehart: I am coming on, but I don't think I should be distracted by the levity on the other side of the table. I don't think it's a laughing matter.
>
> Birnbaum. It's not a laughing matter. I am not laughing.
>
> Wisehart: The other side is when I mentioned Justice Moskowitz.

The California judge had conferred with Moskowitz and allowed Wisehart to ask Fletcher about an intimate relationship with Bender; but Fletcher's California counsel told her not to answer. Birnbaum said only a witness could invoke privacy and then refused to let Jacoby object on grounds of relevance because the defendants had questioned Lipin about the retreat during an EBT Birnbaum had supervised in May 1990. But when Birnbaum finally put the question to Bender, he naturally refused to answer on grounds of privacy. Birnbaum asked both sides to brief that issue.

II. Crossing the Line

On June 28 there was a hearing in Birnbaum's conference room on the second mezzanine, concerning WGM's direction to former Red Cross trustee Carl Desch not to answer a deposition, as well as what questions could be asked of ANRC treasurer Barnet Deutch at the deposition to follow that afternoon.[930] Lipin testified that when she arrived about 9:35 A.M., Birnbaum was at the head of the table, Lawrence Baer, Christopher Parlo (MLB) and Hope Kerstman (a WGM summer associate) were on his left (in that order), and Wisehart and she were on his right (in that order).[931] Early in the argument Baer repeated his previous objections to Wisehart's deposition of Delbert Staley concerning the board of trustees' knowledge

---

[930] Respondent's Ex. S.
[931] Elsewhere Lipin testified that when Wisehart and she first entered the room, the defense lawyers were on Birnbaum's *right*; this would explain how their papers were left on that side of the table.

of an allegedly missing $600,000 and Lipin's firing. Lipin must have said something, because Birnbaum interjected:

> Birnbaum: Ms. Lipin, please. . . .
>
> Baer: Mr. Birnbaum, I cannot be distracted by this woman's remarks here. I ask you to direct her not to make remarks here. I ask you to direct her not to make remarks.
>
> Birnbaum: I have made a remark to the plaintiff. That is what I am going to do. She heard what I said and that was it. That is where the matter rests at this time.

They returned to the substantive question.

> Birnbaum: Did the rules provide for the plaintiff or any other fired executive to protest the actions of being terminated to the board of trustees? . . .
>
> Wisehart: No, it is not. . . .
>
> Birnbaum: What do you mean no? Did you hear my question?
>
> Wisehart: Yes.
>
> Birnbaum: Read it back. I am surprised you say no to that question. Read that back. It's self-evident.
>
> Wisehart: Well, if it's self-evident, I say you ought to disqualify yourself.

Wisehart then invoked a March 1990 EEOC guideline requiring employers to have a procedure for hearing sexual harassment complaints. After an interruption, he reiterated that point and then addressed Baer.

> Wisehart: Now, you have complained about my conduct. Will you desist?
>
> Baer: I have a right to consult.
>
> Wisehart: You're not consulting with anybody. You're just sitting over there laughing and making light of the serious matter.

Chapter 7

> Birnbaum: Let's go.
>
> Baer: Mr. Wisehart, I am just amused at your argument and about missing funds and it has to do—

Birnbaum let Wisehart ask about Red Cross rules for such complaints and disciplinary action against executives at Lipin's level. Baer took an exception "to being denied the ability to state the defendants' position on the record." They turned to ANRC procedures for investigating "suspicious" expense vouchers.

> Birnbaum: Does he have to do it if he is traveling with an executive of the same sex or only if he is traveling with an executive of a different sex?
>
> Wisehart: Well, I don't know if this has application to the gay/lesbian situation or not.
>
> Birnbaum: I didn't mean it that way.
>
> Wisehart: . . . I don't know if you were being sarcastic or not.

Wisehart noted that Bender traveled to Washington with Fletcher, who was on personal business, just days before Lipin was fired. Wisehart and Baer argued about whether Birnbaum had previously allowed questions about this expense voucher, in the course of which Birnbaum noted this was his last day before going on vacation until July 15. He sent them up to the fifth floor for the EBT. Noting that he had "a couple of other things, scheduling things," Wisehart asked: "will we see you later in the day?" Birnbaum answered yes and sent him away. Before they left, Wisehart asked defense counsel to identify "the other person" on the record.

> Wisehart: Are you refusing to?
>
> Baer: I identified her as a law clerk with our firm several times if you would bother to listen.
>
> Wisehart: No, you did not.
>
> Baer: If you bother to listen. Your obnoxiousness is beyond all understanding that I will ever have.

Lipin later testified that "within minutes" after the above argument began, "I noticed that there was a pile of papers neatly stacked right in front of the seat in which I usually sat" directly across from Parlo (five feet away). It was four inches thick and two inches from the table edge. The top page (which faced her) read:[932]

> Weil, Gotshal & Manges
>
> MEMORANDUM
>
> December 8, 1989
>
> > To: File
> >
> > From: Lawrence J. Baer
> >
> > Re: *Joan Lipin v. American Red Cross*
> >
> > Meeting with Mary Stanton 9/15/89

After ascertaining the contents, she slipped the papers onto her lap and read them for more than an hour. Opposing counsel "watched me the entire time that I was reading the documents on the table and when I put them on my lap, and they not at one time said anything." When the hearing ended she put them in a Redweld file. Wisehart testified that after the defense lawyers went upstairs Lipin "pulled me aside...she said I've got to talk with you. I've got these documents that were in front of me . . . she said that she had read them . . . she told me that they contained statements about herself, her family and about Bender and female employees."

> [M]y understanding was that she had the right to do that. That they were right in front of her. And if . . . those documents involved her personally, as they did, any responsibility for the lack of due care was on Weil Gotshal. . . . this was a big law firm and they had in that room three lawyers or persons from that firm, and they certainly knew how to handle documents, and those documents directly involved her and her family and were definitely defamatory. . . . I thought she was justified in taking the documents and seeking an opinion.

---

[932] Staff Ex. 3.

Chapter 7

She was acting "as the client, absolutely," not his paralegal, which she did not become until "some time after that."

Baer remembered the scene differently.[933]

> The deposition [of Deutch] was conducted in an "EBT" room located on the fifth floor. . . .
>
> When I entered the examination room prior to the start of the deposition, I unpacked the contents of my briefcase, which include [sic], among other things, typewritten WGM memoranda prepared by me . . . of defendant Bender and other individuals associated with defendant ARCGNY. . . .
>
> I placed the contents of my briefcase on the bench that was positioned along the wall behind me. . . .
>
> At the start of the deposition, I sat in a chair next to the witness. We sat together on one side of the table and in front of the bench upon which I had placed the contents of my briefcase. Plaintiff Lipin and her attorney, Arthur M. Wisehart, sat on the opposite side of the table. . . .
>
> I left my remaining papers on the bench behind me. . . .
>
> During our luncheon break and at the conclusion of the deposition, I repacked my briefcase and took all my papers with me. . . .
>
> From time to time during the course of several brief recesses in the deposition, I left my papers unguarded, in the EBT room on the bench behind my chair.
>
> At no time during the course of the deposition, or at any other time, did I ever voluntarily or knowingly show or give to plaintiff or plaintiff's counsel any of the WGM memoranda. . . .

Lipin testified she told Wisehart "I had taken the papers temporarily for my own protection and to seek legal advice." He responded that "he

---

[933] Baer's affidavit, reproduced in Lipin's affidavit in support of her November 30, 1994, motion to reargue the Court of Appeals affirmation of Moskowitz's dismissal of her complaint, Staff Ex. 13.

had had a federal case by which his client had been going through documents that had been produced and they found a smoking gun document and by the nature of that the privilege had been waived and it had been ruled accordingly by the magistrate in that case."[934] During that litigation he learned the relevant federal law of evidence, which he believed applied here because the ANRC was federally chartered and he was invoking a federal statute, albeit in state court. Asked by his counsel if he had thought then "that it might not be necessary to make a copy of the documents, the documents could be returned to the law firm, your adversaries, and that the issue could be raised before the court as to those documents," Wisehart replied that Lipin "told me specifically that she did not trust the law firm or what might happen to those documents in view of the experience that had happened to her other documents that were destroyed. . . . and I felt that she had a reasonable concern." Wisehart advised Lipin that if the WGM lawyers noticed the papers were missing she should say she "picked them up by mistake." She demurred: "I had taken them for my own, my own reconnaissance [sic], for my own protection, and that it was not a mistake."

They "decided that it would be best to go back to the law office where I would make the copies." After she did so "I brought them back. . . they were approximately 200 pages, 35 or so, 39 of interviews and deposition digest and a resume of mine—and [Wisehart] said, let us see if Mr. Baer asks about his documents. And I would have gladly handed them over. But [none of the three] at any time during that day asked or even indicated—." They resumed the Deutch deposition at 2 P.M. When it ended at 4 P.M. Wisehart and Lipin returned to Birnbaum's conference room, but he had left for vacation.[935] On the subway platform "Ms Lipin asked me if I thought we should take the documents back and put them on that table in Mr. Birnbaum's room. . . . I said I thought it would be irresponsible. We didn't know who would see these documents. The nature of the documents was defamatory. We knew he wasn't going to be around."

They returned to Wisehart's office, where Lipin made three more copies and Bates stamped all four. "I put them in a sealed envelope per Mr. Wisehart's instructions, because he did not want to review the documents prior to getting a second opinion." She took a copy home and read

---

[934] Donohue Perez and Thornton v. Pendleton Woolen Mills (unreported).
[935] At the end of the morning argument, in response to Wisehart's question, Birnbaum had said he would be available later that day to discuss scheduling, so Wisehart's expectation was reasonable.

Chapter 7

it over the weekend. "Based upon her description to me of the documents," Wisehart thought they might be those "the defendants had been ordered to produce." That Friday he did some research in the ABCNY library near his 43rd Street office on the legal status of the documents. He did not remember whether he took the documents home that night, but he returned to the office the next day, Saturday, to do more research. He memorialized all this in a memorandum that day.[936]

> Memorandum re Lipin
>
> During the continuation of the Deutch deposition yesterday, JCL came into possession of certain papers carelessly left in the Courthouse by counsel for defendants Bender and ARCGNY (Mr. Baer).
>
> By the time that I was aware that JCL had discovered the papers, she was familiar with their contents.
>
> Although I did not (and have not) read the papers, JCL told me enough about the contents to indicate that they contained substantial evidence confirming B[ender]'s activities with two former assistants, Nan Clingman and Barbara Fletcher, corroborating the allegations in paragraphs 17 and 71 of the complaint, namely that male executives at the ARCGNY have used female executives as "playthings", and that progress within the organization by such female executives is influenced by the granting or withholding of sexual favors. The existence of such a situation relating to B's predecessor, Mr. Shea, is confirmed as well.
>
> The papers also contain evidence supporting the claim of JCL that in furtherance of the conspiracy to retaliate against her, false statements were made with the purpose and effect of defaming her and ruining her career professionally, as well as her personal reputation.
>
> JCL agreed to return the documents subject to them retaining a copy for herself.

---

[936] Respondent's Ex. A. Every page has been stamped CONFIDENTIAL; the first page is different from the other five. Wisehart had added in handwriting: "used as basis of discussion 2.VII.91."

My preliminary conclusions are as follows:

1. To seek a second opinion about the situation from another attorney. John Whittlesey was called several times.
2. To return the papers so that there can be no claim of theft, but to make it clear that JCL intends to utilize them as evidence in support of her case.
3. During the discussion yesterday, I told JCL that I wanted to obtain a second opinion about what to do about the papers. JCL inquired whether I thought she should leave the papers where she found them in the Courthouse. I advised against doing that since no one was there; my conclusion was that it would be irresponsible to do so in view of the defamatory and scandalous nature of the material they contain, and our inability to predict into whose hands they might fall.
4. Subject to any suggestions from John Whittlesey, or Ned Purves, what I propose to do is to take the following action:

    a. To send a letter to Mr. Jacoby requesting him to attend a settlement conference at 2 p.m. on Tuesday, July 2, 1991 (with a copy to Ms. Cummins).
    b. To state at the conference that it is being held on a confidential basis in order to attempt to arrive at a settlement.
    c. To return the papers to Mr. Jacoby and to state that copies are being produced by my client in accordance with her discovery obligations.
    d. Details concerning how JCL came into possession of the papers will be treated as privileged information other than to state that she came into possession of them legitimately after finding them carelessly left openly available and was familiar with their contents before I knew of their existence.
    e. To state that my client is extremely upset about the evidence in the papers that concerning the malicious use of libelous statements about her by Red Cross personnel. For her own protection, should anything happen to her, plaintiff is retaining a copy of the papers.
    f. To state that the papers also indicate probable perjury on the part of the defendants in taken depositions in this case.

CHAPTER 7

    g. To make a settlement demand based upon the following terms:

        (1) The immediate termination of Bender
        (2) the taking of suitable action by defendants to withdraw with apologies the false info maliciously disseminated about JCL, and to rehabilitate her professional and personal reputation.
        (3) Further disciplinary action to be taken as appropriate against other Red Cross personnel who participated in the cover-up and the communication of false info about plaintiff.
        (4) A settlement in an amount substantial enough to reflect not only upon the personal injury to ["to" crossed out; "suffered by" written in] my client but also upon the benefit to the Red Cross in exposing and eliminating the existence of a condition that is highly detrimental to the welfare of the organization, as well as to make an example of those who victimize professional employees by vicious defamation when their true motive is to destroy their civil rights as alleged in para 71 of the complaint.

    h. The withdrawal of Weil, Gotshal & Manges as counsel for ARCGNY on grounds (i) that it was a knowing participant in the conspiracy and that appropriate disciplinary and corrective action therefore should have been recommended by Weil, Gotshal & Manges and taken by ARCGNY, and (ii) that it demonstrably had a conflict of interest in placing the interests of defendant Bender in opposition to the interests of the ARCGNY based upon the evidence in its possession showing that Bender had violated Red Cross rules involving his treatment of female executives.

[signed] AMW A.M.W.

    Wisehart consulted Purves the next day (Sunday) at Wisehart's Larchmont home. Purves "said he thought [the documents] had been put there deliberately." Together they opened the envelope for the first time and read all the documents, concluding that they had no relevance to either of the June 28th proceedings. Wisehart already knew of the relationship between Bender and Fletcher (evidenced in the documents) from ten other sources. Carol Cohen, a former Red Cross employee, had called it "open and notorious."

That Monday (July 1) Wisehart wrote Jacoby and Cummins.[937]

> I request that you come to a meeting at 2 p.m. on July 2, 1991, in my office, to discuss, on a confidential basis, the advisability of settling the above action.
>
> If 2 p.m. is not convenient, the conference can be scheduled for any time later in the day.
>
> However, a recent development cause my [sic] to suggest that immediate attention should be given to the subject of settlement from all points of view.

He did not tell the court or opposing counsel about the documents because "I didn't feel that I could do something to discredit my own client. And she had told me that she took those under a claim of right for her own protection. And as far as I could tell, there was a reasonable basis for her belief. And I was not able to take action that would be adverse to her interest."

> I felt that based upon my examination of the documents, a claim of privilege or confidentiality could not be maintained based upon their content. And that she needed that information to...be able to support that position.... I felt that there was a possibility that the documents could be lost or destroyed, or altered.... I concluded that those documents were required to have been turned over by the Red Cross or its attorneys, pursuant to discovery orders that Justice Moskowitz had previously issued in the case.

Before the July 2 meeting he prepared a second memo.[938]

July 2, 1991

---

[937] Staff Ex. 4.
[938] Respondent's Ex. B.

Chapter 7

Memo to File: Lipin

Mr. Purves and I discussed in some detail the situation under which JCL found herself in possession of the Weil, Gotshal papers.

I confirmed to him that, before the hearing before the Special Referee started;

1. I had observed that there was a stack of papers on the table in front of where she was sitting.[939]
2. I paid no further attention to them. Obviously, however, those were the Weil, Gotshal papers, although I did not know it at the time.
3. Mr. Purves had a further extended discussion with the plaintiff concerning the circumstances, during which she described in great detail how the papers were in front of her, and that she was glancing through them while I had my back turned to her and was addressing arguments to the special referee in connection with the rulings that he was in the process of making.
4. The plaintiff confirmed to Mr. Purves that I was unaware that she had the papers or knew of their contents until the hearing before the special referee had concluded, and we were going through the hall for the purpose of going to the fifth floor of the Courthouse for the continuation of the deposition of Mr. Deutch. The hearing before the Special Referee lasted over an hour (from 9:30 a.m. to 11:00 a.m.).
5. The plaintiff also confirmed to Mr. Purves that she was familiar with the contents of the papers at that point and particularly about the matters involving the Bender/Fletcher and the Bender/Clingman as well as personal comments about herself.
6. The plaintiff also confirmed that she intended to retain a copy of the papers for her own protection, and referred to the admission by Bender/ARCGNY that approximately half of the papers relating to plaintiff has [sic] been "discarded" shortly after her termination, as stated in the Bender/ARCGNY Supplemental Interrogatory Responses sworn to by Bender March 7, 1990

---

[939] This is inconsistent with his earlier account that *Lipin* alone saw the papers and slipped them off the table and into a folder while Wisehart was preoccupied with arguing to Birnbaum.

(p.19). Fletcher, in her deposition, corroborated that she had been the person who destroyed the documents by shredding them (Tr. pp. 121–125).

7. The significance of this is shown by the statements in Mr. Baer's memo of December 8, 1989, indicating that Mr. Jacoby of Weil, Gotshal had been consulted by Bender at or before the termination of plaintiff (pp. 1, 7). Thus it is clear that Weil, Gotshal, knowing that litigation might ensue, was in all probability involved in the destruction of evidence by Fletcher/Bender.

8. Plaintiff also confirmed to Mr Purves that when she asked for advice as to what to do, I immediately said that I would want to get a second opinion before arriving at any decision. She also confirmed that prior to yesterday evening, the papers had been kept under seal, and that I had not read the papers.

[signed AMW] A.M.W.

At the July 2 meeting Wisehart gave the original to Jacoby and a copy to Cummins. "I said...that [Lipin] had gotten them but was claiming privilege as to the circumstances, but that I was satisfied that she had received them properly, and she was asserting a claim of right." He also told Jacoby that Lipin, "for her own protection," kept a copy over which he had no control and which she might release to the press. After the meeting he prepared a memorandum describing it.[940]

July 2, 1991

Memo to File: Lipin

At 2 p.m. today a settlement conference was held with Mr. Jacoby and Ms. Cummins in this office. Mr. Purves was introduced as of counsel in the case and the attorney who referred the plaintiff to the undersign[ed added in script]

I began the meeting by saying that we had a mutual problem that I hoped that we would be able to solve in a responsible way. I stated that I did not know if it would be possible but I felt that at least we should try to solve the problem, stating

---

[940] Respondent's Ex. C.

Chapter 7

that my client was very upset about information that had recently come into her possession.

I stated that the docs had come into her possession while we were the Courthouse [sic] in connection with the deposition of Mr. Deutch on June 28, 1991. I produced the original documents to Mr. Jacoby in an envelope and produced as discovery documents copies of them to Mr. Jacoby and Ms. Cummins. The copies were all Bates stamped.

I stated that I was satisfied that the docs had come into the possession of JCL on a legitimate basis, and that she was familiar with the contents before I knew that she had possession of them.

I think I referred to excerpts from the interviews with Messrs. Bender, Cinti and Wood as reflected in the documents. The portions referred to are noted on attachment A.

I then stated that this showed that the position that Bender had a right of privacy was not tenable in view of the fact that both his employer ARCGNY and National were aware of the Bender/Fletcher affair and also Bender's involvement with Fletcher's predecessor, Nan Clingman. I stated that the evidence in the documents corroborate the allegations in paras 17 and 71 of the complaint.

I also stated that JCL is very upset about what the documents show, and that she takes strong exception to the statements made about her personally, referring to some of those statements.

I stated that in view of the contents of the docs, it appeared that perjury had probably occurred on the part of one or more Red Cross witnesses who had denied any knowledge about Bender/Fletcher affair or the complaints of JCL about Bender.

I then stated that it seemed to me that it would be in the best interest of everyone if this litigation could be settled, and I outlined the terms of a proposed settlement as found on pages 4–6 of the attached memorandum.

After I concluded, Mr. Jacoby said that the settlement discussion was over and he demanded to know how JCL got possession of the papers.

I again stated that I was satisfied that she had received them in a legitimate way, and stated that the information was ["not" handwritten in] privileged.

While I did not so state at the time, another consideration was that I did not want to expose his associate, Mr. Baer, to unnecessary criticism by referring to his carelessness.

Mr. Jacoby demanded return of all copies of the papers. I reiterated that I had concluded that the plaintiff had obtained possession of the papers in a legitimate way and that a copy was being retained by her for her own protection in view of their contents. I also stated that the basis upon [which] I was permitted to obtain original docs was upon the agreement that she could retain a copy.

Mr. Jacoby inquired when I first read the papers.

I said that I had determined that I would obtain a second opinion about this matter, that I did so, and that I read the papers for the first time last night.

I stated that JCL was outraged by what she saw in the papers and that if defendants chose to escalate this matter the consequences could be unpredictable, but that I had hoped that we would be able to resolve things in a responsible way since it was clear that Bender's behavior was know [sic] to have violated established rules of the Red Cross.

They left after Mr. Jacoby said that they would not be going forward with the deposition of Dr. Rothschild tomorrow as they had this matter to take under advisement.

I objected to the cancellation of the Rothschild deposition.

A.M.W. [no signature]

Jacoby immediately sought an order to show cause. His affidavit stated that he received Wisehart's hand-delivered letter before 10 a.m. on July 1.[941] The parties had not discussed settlement since fall 1990. Wisehart told them "he was 'convinced' that his client had obtained the documents

---

[941] Staff Ex. 4.

Chapter 7

'legitimately'" because "counsel had left the documents carelessly about the courthouse." Wisehart gave Jacoby and Cummins copies and excerpts and proposed a settlement. "I stated that the settlement discussions for the day were over, and that I now wished to know precisely how plaintiff Lipin had obtained our firm's privilege/work product documents." Wisehart refused to answer, invoking attorney-client privilege, and said Lipin and he retained copies. Jacoby told Wisehart "he had a legal duty as an officer of the court to return all copies" or secure them. Wisehart "refused to do so. He added that he could not control his client and that she conceivably could give the documents to the press." Cummins immediately gave hers to Jacoby.

Wisehart also hand-delivered a letter to Cummins on July 3.[942]

> Plaintiff hereby requests that the information discussed yesterday be brought to the attention of the President of the ARC for the purpose of instituting proceedings to terminate or suspend the General Manager of the ARC in GNY. . . .
>
> The information shows that, virtually from his inception in that office, the current GM has violated the ARC Code of Conduct Guidelines para 6 by operating in a manner contrary to best interests in the ARC in his dealings with female executives.
>
> . . .
>
> Further, the conduct of the GM. . . is the same type that National is believed previously to have found to be inappropriate on the part of his predecessor. . . . [Wisehart described Fletcher shredding the files.]
>
> The assistant is a person with whom Mr. Bender had been having intimate relations at the time to the knowledge of the staff of ARCGNY. . . .
>
> The information referred to yesterday shows that Mr. Bender at or about the time plaintiff was terminated consulted Mr. Jacoby of the firm of WGM.
>
> Thus it appears probable that destruction of such records relating to plaintiff was known to and approved by counsel for ARCGNY and Mr. Bender.

---

[942] Respondent's Ex. F.

> The conduct of the litigation in this case on a cover-up basis involving the intentional destruction of relevant evidence surely can not be considered to be in the best interests of the ARC....
>
> Plaintiff therefore demands that the President take immediate action pursuant to her powers in the Code of Procedure so that the pending litigation will be conducted in the true interest of the ARC rather than an adjunct of a cover-up scheme orchestrated by a misbehaving Red Cross officer and his counsel.
>
> cc: Mark A Jacoby, esq.

III. The Best Defense Is an Offense?

Judge Moskowitz heard the defendants' show cause motion on Wednesday, July 3. Jacoby testified that Lipin[943]

> obtained these documents through means that we do not know, but certainly without our knowledge and consent. And proceeded to read them herself in their entirety.... [Wisehart] has told us that he made a deal with [Lipin] ... that she could keep a set of these documents...even though he was aware that they were defendants' privileged and work product documents. Third, [Wisehart] ... has read the documents.... Fourth, he made excerpts of the documents.... Fifth, he attempted to deliver copies of these documents to counsel for the co-defendant without our consent.... Sixthly, he attempted to misuse the documents in a crude and bad faith attempt yesterday to bludgeon defendants into a settlement, one which would include a quote, substantial, closed quote, monetary payment.... Seventh, [he] refused to explain to defendants' counsel yesterday how plaintiff had obtained these documents from us during the course of the deposition on Friday claiming attorney-client privilege.... Eighth, plaintiff's counsel refused our request for return of all copies.... Ninth, [he] refused our request to place all the copies ... under seal until this matter could be addressed by the court. And, tenth, he

---

[943] The transcript was Staff Ex. 5.

Chapter 7

> attempted to misuse the documents again a second time today in a letter that he sent to co-counsel.... [Wisehart] had a duty... to make disclosure to us, to return the documents, not to read them, and not to make any use of those documents....

Wisehart claimed that both he and the defendants wanted a court-supervised deposition to determine "how these items got into our possession," but Moskowitz objected: "The problem I see is that however they got into your possession, if these are privileged work product... I don't know if you can do whatever it is that you have been accused of doing...." She offered to hear argument after completing a matrimonial hearing;

> otherwise I will put the TRO on...because I haven't heard from you at all Mr. Wisehart, which means that you can't use any of these documents. In fact, you probably should give me the originals and copies and let me keep them here in court over the holiday....
>
> Jacoby:... our request for interim relief was as limited as possible, simply to have plaintiff be directed to turn them over to her lawyer and for him to secure all copies in his vault.
>
> Wisehart: We have no objection to that.
>
> Court: All right. You will comply with that?
>
> Wisehart: Yes.... I will be responsible for them.
>
> Court: And you will do nothing with them....
>
> Wisehart: Correct.
>
> Court: And your client understands that she cannot disseminate any information?
>
> Wisehart: She will be so instructed.
>
> Jacoby: The record should note that she is in the courtroom....
>
> Court: I hope she hears me.
>
> Wisehart: She certainly does.
>
> Court: Yes?
>
> Lipin: Yes.

Court: That should be sufficient.

Moskowitz agreed to hear evidence the following Monday (July 8).

Court: You understand what you have to do, Mr. Wisehart, I don't have to issue an order, do I?

Wisehart: No.

Court: Satisfactory, counsel?

Jacoby: On counsel's representation and with the acknowledgement of plaintiff in the room.

The judge denied defendants' motion to stay all discovery.

Wisehart reiterated in the disciplinary proceeding: "I was asked to secure the documents and I said I would." Because the next day, Thursday, was July 4, he told Lipin to bring the documents to his office on July 5. In the interim, he said: "do nothing with them. I think I suggested that she memorize them. She asked if she could make notes. I said no." Lipin testified in the disciplinary proceeding: "I think I basically said that it was too late to go all the way up to 89th Street [where she lived] and come all the way back down to the office. The next day was July 4th. That I would bring them first thing on July 5th, which I did do." Wisehart had told her: "do not make any notes from the documents. Just commit to memory what is contained in those documents." But between the evening of July 3 and the morning of July 5, she "started to write a letter to my father who is a neurologist/psychoanalyst, M.D., who lives in Sweden." "I started to put some of the defamatory statements that are contained in those documents about myself, my family, my mother is a lawyer as well as my father being a professional." But she stopped "because I said Justice Moskowitz ordered that no information be dispensed." On July 5 she took the documents to Wisehart's office and put them in a locked cabinet (to which she had the key); she did not look at them again before the July 8 hearing. Wisehart prepared a legal memorandum for the July 8 hearing and supplemented it on July 9 and July 11.

On July 8 Wisehart gave Justice Moskowitz the document in a sealed envelope.[944] Baer immediately objected that Lipin's affidavit and

---

[944] Transcript of the hearing, Respondent's Ex. H.

CHAPTER 7

Wisehart's memorandum of law "breached the directive that you gave" by quoting or paraphrasing material from the documents, and he asked that they be sealed. Jacoby added: "the inclusion of . . . all of the confidential documents is, in our view, a gratuitous attempt to prejudice the proceeding. . . . " Lipin testified that when she arrived in Birnbaum's conference room on June 28, Baer, Parlo and Kerstman were standing on Birnbaum's right, where Wisehart and she normally sat, because three other men were on Birnbaum's left to discuss a hearing he would conduct after theirs. When Wisehart and she entered, the others walked around the table (counter-clockwise) to their usual places at Birnbaum's left: first Baer, then Parlo, and finally Kerstman. The court reporter sat immediately to Birnbaum's right, then Wisehart and she. When Lipin sat down, she did not immediately notice the papers. For the argument, Wisehart and Baer turned their chairs perpendicular to the table to face Birnbaum.

> Within minutes I noticed that there was a stack of documents squarely in front of the place that I regularly sit. . . . What I noticed immediately was that they had the caption of my case. . . . I started to glance through the papers and there was such derogatory statements initially on the first page, as well as the involvement of Mr. Mark Jacoby. . . . I immediately became outraged. And I got very upset. And I continued to go through the papers.

They contained Baer's interviews of Bender, Mary Stanton, Angelo Cinti, Irving Wood and Marion Foster, conducted shortly after Lipin's termination and then in March–April 1990.

When the argument ended, defense counsel and the court reporter left.

> [A]s Mr. Wisehart and I were walking across the room I said I have to speak to you before we go up to the EBT room on the fifth floor to continue Mr. Desch's [sic; she meant Barnet Deutch's] deposition. . . . I informed you in the corridor. . . . I told you that I was going to hold on to those papers for my own protection. And you told me that before you did anything you wanted to make sure that you had a second opinion. . . .

Under cross-examination, Lipin said she had worked for Wisehart since March 1990, receiving a weekly paycheck for office management and paralegal work. Baer kept trying to get Lipin to testify about her knowledge of the attorney-client privilege, but Moskowitz sustained repeated objections, even prompting Wisehart to make them when he neglected to do so and suggesting the grounds (making an assumption). Lipin repeated:

> I was riveted and very upset and outraged at the involvement of [Baer] in my case in these papers pre and post termination and all of the defamatory statements made about me in these papers. As well as Mr. Bender's admission in September of 1989 when he was interviewed by Mr. Baer that his affair with Miss Fletcher began in August of 1987 and that he slept with his prior assistant.
>
> Jacoby: I will object. . . . Miss Lipin, isn't it a fact that Mr. Baer made objection to Referee Birnbaum about the fact that you are whispering out loud to Mr. Wisehart and required an admonishment because it was distracting him from the proceeding?
>
> Lipin: No, Mr. Jacoby, once again that is a mischaracterization. It's very difficult—
>
> Court. Wait. Next question.
>
> Jacoby: Did Referee Birnbaum ask you to be quiet during that proceeding?
>
> Lipin: I responded to Mr. Jacoby.
>
> Court: Answer the question
>
> Lipin: Mr. Birnbaum admonished me for speaking out to him, Mr. Jacoby. . . . This was after [I started reading the papers] because I was so engrossed in what these papers said about me that I was not paying very much attention to anything other than the horror that I was reading, Mr. Jacoby.
>
> Jacoby: So, were you speaking to Referee Birnbaum out loud about what was in the papers?

Chapter 7

> Lipin: Mr. Jacoby, you know that is a falsehood and not true. No, I was not. . . . .I said something in response to one of the rulings. It may have been with regard to Mr. Bender's expense reports, Mr. Jacoby.
>
> Jacoby: Miss Lipin, haven't you had to be admonished repeatedly in the proceedings before Referee Birnbaum?

Moskowitz sustained an objection. Lipin testified there had been three to five minutes of heated colloquy that morning before they went on the record. Jacoby asked about the papers she found.

> Lipin: Mr. Jacoby, I have testified already that they were a stack of papers. And I might add that if Mr. Parlo thought that anything was amiss he could have at any point in time between ten to ten and 11 o'clock either said something to me, Mr. Wisehart and/or Mr. Baer or Special Referee Birnbaum.

When Jacoby introduced part of the first page of the documents Wisehart objected: "Justice will be denied unless the entire first page is put in which, among other things, states that according to this witness the plaintiff was quote, dangerously crazy, closed quote. And also refers to Mr. Jacoby." Asked if she had read subsequent pages before taking the pile off the table, Lipin replied: "Yes, Mr. Jacoby. When I read about your involvement in pre and post termination of my case I glanced quickly on through the pages and made on [sic—them?] my own." Jacoby kept asking which pages she read on the table and which on her lap, but she could only say "I was too horrified at what I was read [sic] . . . I was just too upset." Moskowitz asked if Lipin wanted a break. She said yes, and Wisehart added that she had had a fever the previous day. When they resumed, Moskowitz asked if she was all right.

Lipin continued: after they left Birnbaum's conference room she told Wisehart the documents included notes of Baer's interviews. Wisehart replied: "I am not going to read the documents and I want to get a second opinion." "I told Mr. Wisehart that I was going to hold possession of these papers. He concurred with that. . . ." She told him the documents described Bender's relationship with someone other than Fletcher. Jacoby inquired at length about what happened during Deutch's deposition, apparently still convinced Lipin had taken the papers there. She testified there had been a break within minutes of beginning the morning hearing. "I believe Mr. Baer got up in a huff and yanked the witness out. Mr. Parlo may have left the room." They resumed after a minute but recessed at 11:45 A.M. because Wisehart had another hearing.

> Lipin: I told Mr. Wisehart I was going to make a copy of the set of these documents and I was going to lock them up in the filing cabinet because I, for my own protection, didn't want to take any chance that these documents as a material evidence would be destroyed, Mr. Jacoby, as Mr. Bender has admitted that he destroyed with Fletcher having shred [sic] my documents and you being involved in the discussions most likely.
>
> Jacoby: And you have evidence of that, Miss Lipin?
>
> Lipin: Read the papers, Mr. Jacoby.
>
> Court: Excuse me, can we just have questions relating to this witness's testimony and not get into anything else.

Lipin made a copy, locked it up, and returned to the courthouse with the original by 1:20 P.M.

> Jacoby: Did Mr. Wisehart say what would be done if Mr. Baer made inquiry about the documents?
>
> Lipin: He said if Mr. Baer says he has documents missing and asks you, you can't lie so you have to say, yes, you by mistake picked up his documents that were on the table. And I said it wasn't by mistake, it was my own recognizance and my own protection and I would give those documents back to Mr. Baer . . . if he had asked. But Mr. Baer did not call our office nor did you, Mr. Jacoby, from June 28 to July 2nd.
>
> Court: Look, I am going to stop you. Either answer yes or no or don't answer.
>
> Lipin: OK.
>
> Court: Just ask questions with a yes or no.
>
> Jacoby: I have tried to, Your Honor, I have asked the questions, I don't control the answers.

CHAPTER 7

> Court: Just a yes or no otherwise I am going to walk out of the courtroom, all right.

Lipin had talked to Wisehart by telephone while he was meeting Purves the previous Sunday. Jacoby asked about the June 28 afternoon deposition, apparently still convinced she took the documents there. "I remember that Mr. Baer couldn't control himself and that Mr. Wisehart continuously said, 'Until you are able to control yourself we will get up and take a recess.'" "Mr Baer abruptly concluded [the deposition] at 4." When Jacoby questioned her about subsequent events, she replied, "I almost collapsed a week ago Saturday [the day after these events]. And I am warning you, you better be careful with me." She refused to surrender the originals to Wisehart without keeping a copy. At home on the evening of July 3 she took handwritten notes on the documents. "Justice Moskowitz ordered that all of the sets of copies had to be produced to Wisehart & Koch. And I had a set of copies at home and I brought them to the office on Friday, July 5th, the next working day." At Jacoby's insistence Lipin now agreed to bring her notes into the office and Wisehart agreed to put them and the remaining copy of the documents in a place to which only he had access. Moskowitz told Lipin to surrender her key to the cabinet in which the documents were locked, which she did in open court.

In his reply affidavit, Wisehart said Lipin told him enough about the papers on June 28 "to indicate that they contained substantial evidence concerning Bender's intimate relationships with two former female [sic]."[945] On the evening of June 30, in consultation with Purves, Wisehart decided that "in order to determine the proper course of action to advise the plaintiff to take . . . it would be necessary and desirable to examine the documents. . . ." One category was "factual memoranda of an investigatory nature. . .prepared by counsel on the basis of information provided by defendant Bender and other witnesses." They confirmed that "male executives at the ARCGNY have used female executives as 'playthings,' and that progress within the organization by such female executives is influenced by the granting or withholding of sexual favors." That also had been true of Bender's predecessor, Shea. The other documents were deposition indices. Purves and he believed "there was a substantial basis for concluding that any claim of attorney-client privilege had been waived" by careless handling of the documents. Furthermore, "a clear-cut conflict of interest

---

[945] Staff Ex. 6.

[between ARCGNY and ANRC] on the part of WGM also precluded the maintenance of a claim of confidentiality." For that reason "it was concluded that an attempt should be made to give the Red Cross an opportunity to both take appropriate remedial steps and to relieve the Court of the burden of this litigation." "The conflict between Bender's behavior and the ethics criteria of the ANRC . . . makes it clear that such evidence as possessed by WGM could not be considered to be 'confidential.'" There was also evidence that Bender had consulted WGM for the purpose of committing illegal acts, such as wrongful termination and shredding evidence. Wisehart alleged that "any mis-use of said information has been by counsel and its clients in failing to take corrective action on the basis of the ethic [sic] precepts that are mandated by the ARC, and in proceeding to litigate a case on the basis of fictitious and untrue assumptions about the behavior of its chief executive officer in the New York area." He concluded:

> Sexual harassment cases are recognized to be extremely difficult from a plaintiff's point of view because of the heavy reliance upon the circumstantial evidence required to overcome the pretextual reasons typically manufactured by the employer (assisted by eminent counsel, as in the case at bar) as a basis for terminating the employee, aided by numerous sycophants (as here).

The parties were before Moskowitz again on July 11 because Cummins sought a protective order against Wisehart's discovery requests.[946] Wisehart had answered the previous night at 9:40 P.M. A deposition was scheduled for the next day. Cummins offered to hold the motion in abeyance so they could reach an agreement "despite the overwhelming request, size, burdensome, etc." Wisehart balked. "I tried to work with Miss Cummins all last summer and it resulted in correspondence back and forth, quibbling about document production, and I want to have this resolved." Her motion was out of time; and she should have delivered the documents she admitted were relevant.

> Court: I looked at this notice, Mr. Wisehart, a lot of these items are overbroad and I just don't have the energy to cull

---

[946] This transcript was appended to Respondent's Ex. R.

> through this. . . . I am not even going to address this any more, if you are not willing to compromise on this.
>
> Wisehart: I am willing to compromise.

Moskowitz insisted they work it out.

> Wisehart: We are not trying to cause your honor problems.
>
> Court: Yes, you are. You all are.

Wisehart also moved for separate counsel, arguing conflicts of interest between Bender, ARCGNY, and ANRC. He cited a case[947] "that curiously also involves the firm of Miss Cummins . . . and concludes that that firm was involved in unethical conduct because of its representation of clients with conflicting interests. . . . " Jacoby retorted that "none of the cases [Wisehart] cited thus far involved a situation [in] which a plaintiff who is a client in the employ of the attorney stole documents off the counsel table."

The court then returned to how Lipin got the documents.[948]

> Jacoby: Frankly, I don't believe plaintiff's story. . . . I think she stole them at a different time. . . . [but] her admission . . . coupled with the continuous actions. . .that followed within the next 100 hours between her and her counsel that involved the most serious and gross abuse of judicial process that I have encountered in my career as an attorney.
>
> Your Honor, what is involved in this motion is . . . the question of whether or not the rule of law is going to govern in this proceeding. . .or the rule of the jungle is going to prevail. Are we going to have to have private security guards accompany us to the courthouse to keep an eye on the counsel table. . . .
>
> Court: Counselor . . . her testimony isn't that she stole papers, but that she sat down and the papers were in front of her, right?
>
> Jacoby: . . . I don't believe for one minute that this pile of papers was sitting directly in front of her in a neat pile facing her four inches off the table.

---

[947] Fund of Funds v. Arthur Andersen & Co., 567 F.2d 225.
[948] Transcript reproduced in Lipin's affidavit in support of her November 30, 1994 motion to reargue the Court of Appeals' affirmation of Moskowitz's dismissal of her complaint, Staff Ex. 13.

Court: That is the testimony... You didn't bring anybody in to say that the papers were scattered, or the papers were on the other side of the table, or the papers were at the foot of the table, or the papers were in any other location. If I choose to believe the plaintiff, than [sic] her testimony, and I was just looking for it, is that she sat down before argument started and when she sat down, right in front of her, four inches from the edge of the table, was a neat stack of papers.

Jacoby: . . . even if we accept that testimony as true she read the top document, immediately saw it was a document that belonged to defendants' counsel. . . . What did she do? She then proceeded to read. . .a series of interviews of. . .some of the most important witnesses in the case. . . . Then she moved them into her lap. . . . then she took it and put it in a file folder of her attorney. . . .

Court: I don't think she put it in the file folder of her attorney. She put it in the file folder that she had. . . .

Jacoby: . . . it doesn't matter whether it is her folder or his folder, she is a paralegal. . . . She told her lawyer what happened as they walked out of the. . .hearing room. . . . What is a lawyer supposed to do when it happens? He takes the documents back, he goes to the lawyer on the other side and says, "These are your documents." . . . And then face the consequences. . . . What happened, they conspired. . .for her then to bring them up to his office, photocopy them, leave a copy there and then return them so that if Mr. Baer realized . . . they weren't there, he might ask and they would have the originals to give him. . . . How can a lawyer possibly make that copy of documents that he has been told involved privileged communication and which his client has told him . . . she took them at counsel table?. . . If this court doesn't take control of this matter here and now then there are no rules. And certainly we will be before the Appellate Division on this matter if control isn't taken of this proceeding, Your Honor, and I don't mean that as a threat of course.

Court: It certainly sounds like it. Counsel, I'm not going to listen to you if that is the way you insist on speaking.

Chapter 7

Jacoby: Your Honor, I mean it as an indication of the seriousness of . . . what happened here and the fact that the Appellate Division has already made it clear in the Beiny case . . . where Sullivan & Cromwell were disqualified for surreptitiously taking and using the privileged documents belonging to another. . . . I don't think there is a question whatsoever that he should be disqualified. The question really is . . . what plaintiff herself has done . . . as to whether or not the case gets dismissed. In the matter of Beiny, the case was dismissed. . . . We can't have proceedings, your honor, where people steal documents off the counsel table and take them and put them away, and then photocopy them, and then use them to extort or blackmail a settlement. . . . I hope you will . . . measure Mr. Wisehart's behavior with Sullivan and Cromwell's behavior. The rules that apply to big firms apply to small firms as well. . . .

Look what happened, your honor, even after we were before you on July 3rd. . . . Between July 3rd and July 5th she digested them by hand and retained the notes at home. She then brought the copies in on July 5th and put them in a cabinet that she had the keys to. I mean, this is Kafka like. . . . after you elicited a specific representation and agreement from them . . . that's why I can say, your honor, this case is . . . so aggravated it is very clear that this is a case where plaintiff's claim has to be dismissed. . . .

Your honor, in this case I have suffered a lot of abuse from Mr. Wisehart with false allegations, one after another, and I can take it. . . . What I believe you have to deal with is a situation that is out of control and you have to deal with it by the rule of law. . . .

Wisehart invoked a case he had litigated in Oregon, but Moskowitz saw "a difference in attorneys . . . actively handing over material in a discovery process and inadvertently putting something in there." Wisehart added lack of reasonable precautions and defamation. He accused Jacoby of involvement in Bender's termination of Lipin: "it is well settled that evidence of illegal activities at the time a plan was being developed by counsel is not a privileged communication. . . . " Jacoby "specialized" in "being the architect of developing pretextual reasons for wrongfully terminating employees."

> We think that it's clear that there has been a continuing cover-up in this litigation that applies ... to the original shredding of approximately half of the documents that were relevant to my client three days after her termination, no doubt to the knowledge of Mr. Jacoby. . . . And we also say that the involvement of Mr. Jacoby's firm, and Mr. Baer in particular, was implicated in Fletcher's sudden absconding from New York to California so her deposition could not be taken.

Although Moskowitz had to leave for a doctor's appointment, she gave Jacoby one minute.

> Jacoby: I think Mr. Wisehart's soliloquy is the best example of why it is necessary for this court to take control of this case and take control of it now and prevent this from continuing. That entire statement has absolutely no support in the documents whatsoever.

On July 29 Wisehart moved to recuse Birnbaum, in the course of a motion to compel Bender to produce expense reports and answer questions about them.[949] Birnbaum had sustained the defendants' objections on April 12, 1990, but Moskowitz reversed him on October 30, reaffirming this on March 28 and April 3, 1991, and ruling that Birnbaum "has been too restrictive in his rulings of what has to be turned over." Wisehart now alleged that Birnbaum has "overtly demonstrated bias and prejudice." "There has been disruption and interference on the part of defendants' attorneys, and excessive and irrelevant colloquy on the part of such attorneys, which has not been subject to control by the presence of the supervising referee...." "On May 24, 1990, as President of the New York Lawyer's Union 5226 of B'nai B'rith, Mr. Birnbaum solicited from both plaintiff's and defendants' attorneys contributions to and attendance at a dinner given by that organization on June 21, 1990, at which he was being installed as an officer." He had ex parte contact with Baer. He "has repeatedly sought to take over the questioning in place of counsel for plaintiff.... " He was

---

[949] Staff Ex. 7.

CHAPTER 7

out of his office at the end of the day when Wisehart wanted to schedule further proceedings. He had "directly interfered" with the June 14, 1991, deposition concerning Bender's destruction of documents. He had "shown further bias in tolerating repetitive tactics by counsel for defendants and issuing directions not to answer. . . . " The motion concluded:

> Plaintiff and her attorney have no confidence in Mr. Birnbaum's conduct of the proceedings and firmly believe, based on such conduct, that he will continue to hamper and hinder production of relevant information by defendants; acquiesce in the dilatory, repressive and oppressive tactics of defendants' attorneys; and unless he is replaced, will continue to prejudice plaintiff.

On January 9, 1992, Justice Moskowitz ruled from the bench on Baer's motion (in which Cummins joined) to disqualify Wisehart as Lipin's counsel, suppress and return the defendant's attorney's work product, and (as amended) dismiss the action.[950] Wisehart's argument that the placement of the papers waived confidentiality had "absolutely no merit. The uncontroverted proof is that these documents were clearly on their face attorney's work product." Although Moskowitz referred to "plaintiff and her attorney," she ruled that "Miss Lipin, as a paralegal in her attorney's office, had an obligation to return and turn these over to the lawyer, and he had an obligation to turn them back over to Mr. Baer." Wisehart "utilized these documents to try to extract a settlement." Moskowitz did not "even see anything in these papers in relation to this lawsuit. But that really is not necessary for my decision."

> I have to conclude that the actions of the plaintiff and her attorney were so egregious in taking this material that was clearly the attorney's work product, clearly interviews with the defendant's employees, clearly not for perusal by any other attorney or litigant in this litigation, so heinous that the only remedy, as much as I dislike to do this, is to dismiss the lawsuit. Otherwise, there is no meaning to privilege, there is no meaning to conduct among attorneys, and there is no rule of law. Whatever was in these papers was confidential. That confidentiality

---

[950] The transcript was Staff Ex. 1.

> was broken. It was repeatedly broken by both the litigant and the attorney, and cannot be countenanced by the Court. Therefore, I am dismissing the lawsuit in its entirety. . . . I am also aware that this lawsuit is important to the plaintiff. However, she was the one that read these materials. Whatever she thought was in this material did not justify taking this confidential information. She has to then suffer the consequences. . . . Likewise, Mr. Wisehart did not comply with the requirements imposed upon an attorney in this state in his use of the material and failure to guard it.

She ordered Wisehart to turn over everything within ten days of service of her order. "You are not to do anything with that material, and your client is not to do anything with that material in the interim." He said "All right." Moskowitz sealed what she had and issued the written order January 27.

Apparently in response to Wisehart's motion to use the documents in his appeal, Baer responded on January 22 proposing the following stipulated order: Wisehart could retain his copy of the documents and Lipin's notes "in his office safe or vault, not accessible to plaintiff," pending the outcome of the appeal.[951] He would make no further reference in papers filed with the court to information in the documents except "in a general manner." Two days later Wisehart refused to stipulate. Baer replied that day.

> Unfortunately, your flat rejection of the offer to stipulate, without offering any counter proposal, will require further seemingly needless motion practice before the Appellate Division. . . . Defendants-respondents' position is that any specific reference. . .further violates the orders of the Court below and is contrary to your duties of professional responsibility and the standards of conduct of attorneys in this state. Obviously, your continued reference . . . is at your peril. . . . I must address your misrepresentation of my comments to you while we were present in the Appellate Division Clerk's office on January 17, 1992. You state that I threatened your

---

[951] This and the following were attachments to Respondent's Ex. R, filed with his August 4, 1992 opposition to the order to show cause.

associate, Mr. Prince, that I intended to put your firm out of business and that he would be without a job if you pursued this appeal. Your statement is totally false. First, my remarks were directed at you and not to Mr. Prince. Second, I stated to you that I thought you were taking a great risk with your continued livelihood by bringing this matter to the attention of the Appellate Division, which as you know, supervises the ethical conduct of attorneys in this state, in view of the findings of serious misconduct on your part made by the Court below. Third, I stated to you that, in my opinion, Mr. Prince's continued employment as your associate might be threatened if severe disciplinary action were taken against you by the Court.

At no time did I threaten you or anybody else.

IV. If at First You Don't Succeed

On June 17, 1992, Lipin filed a new action in the U.S. District Court for the Southern District of New York against Bender, ARCGNY and ANRC, now adding the WGM lawyers (Mark A. Jacoby, Lawrence J. Baer, and Jesse D. Wolff) and several other Red Cross employees (Mary Stanton, James T. Byrne, Jr., Carl Desch, and Barbara E. Fletcher) and including "a broader obstruction of justice claim encompassing destruction and obfuscation of evidentiary documents and concealment of a deponent."[952]

On July 10 the defendants obtained from Moskowitz an order that Lipin and Wisehart show cause why they should not be held in contempt of her January 9 order for using the documents in the federal action and why Moskowitz should not restrain further dissemination, sanction Lipin and Wisehart, seal the complaint, disqualify Wisehart and Purves and their firms from representing Lipin in any action, and confirm that she had dismissed the case "with prejudice."[953] Purves submitted an affidavit declaring: "In view of plaintiff's treatment in this Court . . . as well as the Court's arbitrary and capricious action in dismissing plaintiff's Complaint, plaintiff had every reason to prefer the Federal forum, as well as the right

---

[952] Opinion by Leonard B. Sand, USDC, SDNY, January 17, 1996, in Lipin v. Bender, Staff Ex. 15.
[953] Respondent's Ex. O.

THE PURLOINED PAPERS

to proceed in that forum."[954] WGM "are of the view that they can get by making such an overreaching request only because of the undue influence which they feel they or their clients are in a position to exert upon this Court." He invoked Lipin's rights to counsel, free speech, and to petition for redress of grievances. Lipin did "not have the financial resources to invest in other counsel." Because Baer had never asked for the documents back, Purves had "long been of the view that the documents were deliberately placed there by an attorney of the law firm WGM . . . in order to cause intense mental anguish and emotional distress to plaintiff." "I have never been able to understand why the court would impose its wrath upon the plaintiff rather than upon the attorney from WGM." WGM should pay damages to the Red Cross for "breach of fiduciary duty." "If any attorneys are to be disqualified, it should be the attorneys from WGM" because of "placing the papers," the conflict of interest between Bender and the Red Cross, and "because three attorneys of that firm. . .are named defendants in the federal action." "In such circumstances, Mr. Jacoby's involvement in obtaining the order to show cause . . . appears to me to be a dereliction of duty."

On July 21 Wisehart moved to recuse Moskowitz from hearing the contempt motion. He also moved to strike the defendants' answers, disqualify WGM, seek sanctions against the defendants and their counsel, and compel a determination of his October 23, 1991, cross-motion to disqualify WGM.[955] Lipin's affidavit declared that, in contradiction to Baer's "false affidavit" of July 3, 1991, Jacoby's affidavit of July 10, 1992, "has now finally admitted that an attorney from his firm had placed open, unsealed documents about me on the conference table in the location at which I customarily sat." "[I]t is time for Justice Moskowitz to face up [to] the fact that *those documents were deliberately placed there by Mr. Baer* with the deliberate intent of either intimidating me or derailing this litigation (or both)." Moskowitz had failed to deal with "instances of obstruction of justice and heinous discovery abuse" by WGM. She showed "personal bias or prejudice" in dismissing the complaint and "carelessness" and "evident unpreparedness" in that decision, which contained "excessive and abusive language." She "rendered her decision orally from a bench cluttered with books and papers in an obvious state of disarray, with extended pauses in a distraught effort to search through and read what was before her."

---
[954] Respondent's Ex. P: Affirmation of Edmund S. Purves (July 22, 1992).
[955] Staff Ex. 8.

She had read "highly inflammatory, prejudicial and false manufactured statements" by defendants' counsel "without making them a part of the record."

"Only naked political power or influence can account for the fact that a matter for which a simple order of preclusion or suppression would suffice" led to dismissal. "The nexus between the political clout of the Red Cross and my case is very clear." Andrew Cuomo sought to work with the Red Cross, using Jesse D. Wolff of WGM as an intermediary. During 1991 "Karla Moskowitz, then a civil court judge with only 'acting' status in the Supreme Court, was desirous of obtaining official Democratic Party designation as a Supreme Court Justice from the Democratic Party Screening Panel." The September 25 *New York Law Journal* described nine judges seeking the three positions. "Approval of influential persons in Democratic politics such as Mr. Andrew Cuomo, is obviously an important factor taken into account in deciding which Judges to elevate." Moskowitz was appointed in November 1991. "Just a short time later, on January 9, 1992, Karla Moskowitz hurriedly, and obviously with only minimal preparation, announced her decision...."

She showed "bias and prejudice" by permitting "Mr. Jacoby to follow the time-honored technique of using chicanery in a sexual misconduct case to convert the accuser into the accused." She "appears to have harbored a prejudice against me as a novice paralegal." Justice Moskowitz knew "I have had to contend with the entire gambit of every conceivable kind of abusive discovery tactics pervasively perpetrated against me...." She indulged in "punitive excessiveness" and had entertained defendants' application to punish her and Wisehart further "for attempting to obtain protection and a determination of my constitutional rights in Federal Court." "[T]his is a 'Trout in the Milk' case. Justice, the product dispensed through the judicial system, has been watered, tainted, or otherwise adulterated by the political power of the defendants in this case." "[T]he use of 'heinous'... is the trout in the milk...." Moskowitz's "clearly" false statement that there was nothing in the purloined papers related to the lawsuit was "the ultimate in bias and prejudice." She was "clearly" attempting to suppress facts "directly relevant to my claim of sexual harassment." She "'clearly' does not understand the significance of the orchestrated acts under the continuing direction of the 'litigation strategies' experts of a law firm such as WGM to retaliate against me...." She engaged in "punitive intimidation" and "effective deprival of and interference with my counsel."

Justice Moskowitz has despised or abhorred the plea of the afflicted; she has hid her face from me; she has not heard when I cried unto her, but only paid attention only to the evildoers who encircle me . . . in the evident expectation that I would silently depart.

But I am a child of victims of the Holocaust, on both sides of my family. I do not intend to be intimidated or silenced about what has happened to me, or to meekly disappear with my claim for sexual harassment to the legal equivalent of Auschwitz, the obvious purpose of the Order to Show Cause that Justice Moskowitz signed.

Fidelity to my heritage compels me to request that the judge be recused or disqualified. . . .

I request as well that my rights to due process, equal protection of law, and my privileges and immunities as a Citizen of the United States, including the right of access to a Federal Court system, free from the pervasive influence of New York City Democratic Party politics, be respected and honored.

Moskowitz heard the contempt and recusal motions on July 23. Before the case was called Wisehart moved to adjourn the contempt proceeding and argue recusal. "[T]he court, having dismissed the complaint in this case, no longer has jurisdiction." But Moskowitz cut him off: "This is number 28 on the calendar . . . you can't jump ahead." When the case was called Wisehart jumped in.

Wisehart: Your Honor, may it please the court.

Jacoby: Your Honor, I am the moving party.

Wisehart: But this is on our cross-motion

Jacoby: We are the moving party.

Wisehart: This is on our cross-motion. We asked for an adjournment on their order to show cause. . . .

Court: I am going to take the whole thing now.

Wisehart: I am not prepared on the order to show cause. The court has no jurisdiction. The courts' recusal has been requested.

Chapter 7

> The U.S. Supreme Court has held that a state court has no jurisdiction over this matter. And their order to show cause— we've demanded the right of jury trial.

Moskowitz brushed this aside, started with the motion to recuse, and asked Wisehart's reasons. He referred her to Lipin's affidavit. Moskowitz had not gotten his papers until this morning.

> Wisehart: They were delivered to your chambers yesterday.
>
> Court: I was here until 6 o'clock last night, counsel, and I didn't get them.
>
> Wisehart: . . . Your Honor, there is a person out at the door who will not permit people to go further and they were delivered yesterday.
>
> Court: I did not see this until this morning.
>
> Wisehart: Well, that is not our fault, Your Honor. . . . [Nevertheless, he summarized.] Your Honor has personal knowledge of the contents of the disputed documents . . . personal bias, and . . . cannot act impartially
>
> This case involves a situation which the Court will recall was one of extreme confusion and difficulty. Nevertheless, the Court, on the basis of affidavits submitted by the [WGM] firm, [which] we had asked to be disqualified as counsel in the case, rendered a decision that my client's action was heinous and that my action was heinous in a manner that would require an entirely different type of terminology.
>
> My client, as Your Honor knows, was not a trained lawyer. She was a beginning paralegal. She saw these documents. We believe those documents were placed in front of her deliberately by Mr. Baer in order to entrap her. You said that she should not have read the documents.
>
> Your Honor, I would submit that a person in that situation—
>
> Court: You are rearguing the original decision and order. . . . and I am not going to listen to your argument. If you want to talk about recusal, I'm quickly reading the papers. And I don't

> know what is going on about all this political stuff here. I don't know who these people are and I don't think it has anything to do with anything. The question is what I saw happened and what I found after a hearing, and I made a decision. And the question now is whether or not you violated the order of this Court. . . . I don't see that there is any reason I should recuse myself at this stage. And I'm going to deny your motion for recusal.

Wisehart took an exception and raised the jurisdictional question but quickly proceeded to the other relief the defendants requested. Moskowitz said there "is jurisdiction still in the Supreme Court to enforce the orders of this court." When Wisehart retorted "not if that was not an injunction," Moskowitz dismissed that as "argument in opposition to the motion." Jacoby agreed "it is very clear as a matter of law that the Court has jurisdiction."

> Wisehart: That just shows why the Court is prejudiced in this matter. They have not even submitted one case that says that. We have provided a memorandum in which we cited cases which shows [sic] the Court does not have jurisdiction.
>
> Why counsel just has to get up and say the Court doesn't [sic] have jurisdiction. And that's it, Your Honor, the Court should recuse herself in this matter. The firm of WGM, which should have been disqualified by our cross-motion dated October, 1991, which was never decided by this Court, can get away with anything. Let them plant papers in front of my client in a public hearing room. They can come before this Court after having received our memorandum and make contentions like that without citing one case. They can participate in the obstruction of justice, which they did repeatedly in discovery in this case, even to the extent of aiding and abetting a fugitive from justice from testifying in this court. And knowing that documents were destroyed. And not one word is said about that, but—
>
> Jacoby: Your Honor, I object to these scurrilous allegations.
>
> Wisehart: But . . . [that] doesn't raise one issue as far as they are concerned. All they have to do is say abracadabra and that's what happens.

CHAPTER 7

> Jacoby: Your Honor, plaintiff made an application to the Appellate Division for a stay. That application for a stay was denied—
>
> Wisehart: I am not finished.
>
> Jacoby: is in full force and effect.
>
> Court: I am not listening to this anymore. I have jurisdiction to hear this. . . . in terms of specific points that are asked, there may be—
>
> Wisehart: I'm not done with the jurisdiction point.
>
> Court: I am finished listening to you.
>
> Wisehart: There is a Supreme Court case that is controlling.

But Moskowitz moved on. "That's all of the cross-motion I'm going to decide at this time." In response to Wisehart's motion for an adjournment she offered him "as much time as you want." Because she would be on vacation, she scheduled the next hearing for August 6.

Lipin promptly renewed the recusal motion on July 29.[956] Moskowitz "starkly and vividly" showed bias and prejudice at that hearing by denying the earlier motion "peremptorily and without any serious consideration." She "merely scanned my affidavit of 31 pages, plus substantial attachments totaling 36 pages, for no longer than only approximately two to three minutes." She "demonstrated her predisposition to accept arguments brazenly put forward by WGM without consideration, reflection, study of the authorities, or without even the citation of any authority . . . and to make [a] snap judgment in favor of that firm's clients." She "declined even to hear argument from my attorney, obviously because she had already made up her mind in advance to go along with whatever the Juggernaut from WGM might choose to say" and accept it "hook, line and sinker." Wisehart's memorandum of law added that "many other attorneys were present, and the cursory, flippant attitude of Justice Moskowitz in the serious matter . . . constituted an affront to the standard established by the chief administrator of the courts. . . . "[957]

---

[956] Staff Ex. 10.
[957] Staff Ex. 11.

Wisehart also filed an affirmation in opposition to the defendants' order to show cause.[958] Moskowitz's January 1992 order "contemplate[d] that plaintiff and her counsel would be permitted to make use of . . . the documents . . . for the purpose of prosecuting an appeal to the Appellate Division." Use in the federal action, which "plaintiff has been forced to bring in order to protect her rights," was "no different in substance." In his January 24, 1992, letter, Baer "belatedly admits that the documents in question were found by plaintiff." They "were delivered to her . . . by defendants for the purpose of derailing this litigation or intimidating her. . . . " Lipin was "fully justified" in filing the federal lawsuit by reason of "the deliberate deceit of the Court by attorneys from WGM." Baer's letter contains "the threats that Baer has repeatedly made to lawyers in this firm, threatening to put this firm out of business if we continued to seek to enforce plaintiff's rights." Because Baer's January 24 letter established "without a doubt that Mr. Baer is a necessary witness in any further proceedings," his firm must be disqualified. Lipin's federal complaint made only "general references" to the documents "to a very limited extent as necessary to preserve" her legal rights. Wisehart again raised jurisdictional objections.

Moskowitz heard Lipin's second recusal motion on August 6.[959]

Jacoby: There is no additional basis for recusal offered in these papers. It is perfectly, absolutely frivolous, apart from being scurrilous in the allegations against the Court.

Court: I think these are scurrilous allegations.

Wisehart: Can I be heard before you rule?

Court: No, you cannot be heard.

Wisehart: I cannot be heard?

Court: No, because I am going to tell you something right now. I have read all these papers—

Wisehart: Well, I have something further to say, Your Honor.

Court: Could you just keep quiet?

---

[958] Respondent's Ex. R.
[959] Staff Ex. 12.

Chapter 7

Wisehart: Your Honor.

Court: Mr. Wisehart.

Wisehart: I insist on being heard. If you are going to send me to The Tombs because I want to be heard, you go ahead and do it.

It says "In God We Trust" up there. We do not trust in this Court as it is presently constituted.

[Whereupon, the Court stepped down from the bench and exited the courtroom. Whereupon the Court entered the courtroom.]

Court: I am directing the Court Reporter to take what I am saying and what nobody else is saying. And sit down Mr. Wisehart.

The material that Mr Wisehart has provided on the recusal subject is so scurrilous and so baseless and so ridiculous that I cannot even begin to be fair to any parties in this case after reading this.

I am so concerned about this that if it were under his affirmation instead of his client's affidavit, I would feel compelled to turn this over to the grievance committee. Because for an attorney to stand up in court and address the court the way Mr Wisehart did last time, and to supply the Court with such ridiculous—I don't even—such off-the-wall allegations about a sitting judge is so egregious that I really can't even see and I can't even look at this case anymore and dispense justice.

Now, that means Mr Wisehart has accomplished exactly what he had set out to accomplish, which is to obtain my recusal from this case. But I am not doing it for the reasons that his clients [sic] set forth in an affirmation, because I don't even understand them. They are so off the wall, they are so baseless that they would never really cause me to recuse myself in any other circumstances. But Mr. Wisehart's comments last week in open court, and his screaming and his loss of control in open court, and his addressing of the court in the way he did, and his addressing today of this court, have made it so that

I cannot be fair to either side in this case anymore and I am recusing myself. It can go back in the wheel and can go to another judge, as far as I am concerned, and that's it.

Wisehart: Your Honor.

Court: That's it. I don't want to hear anything from anyone in this case anymore. I don't have to stand up in a courtroom and be addressed by an attorney, who is supposedly an officer of the court, in a manner that Mr. Wisehart addressed me last week and the manner he addressed me this week. And I will not listen this week. I recuse myself. That's it.

Wisehart: I demand to be heard. I am an attorney nearing the end of my career.

Court: I am leaving and I direct the court reporter not to take anything else in this case.

[Whereupon, the proceedings were concluded.]

V. Denouement

On July 7 U.S. District Judge Leonard B. Sand stayed the federal action on defendants' motion and sealed the complaint pending resolution of the state court proceedings. Two weeks later Lipin moved to reargue. But when she appealed the stay to the Second Circuit, the District Court determined that the appeal deprived it of jurisdiction to consider the motion to reargue. Lipin asked the Second Circuit for leave to proceed in the District Court with the motion to vacate the July 7 stay, but the Circuit Court dismissed plaintiff's appeal for lack of jurisdiction and denied the motion to proceed as moot.

On October 23 Baer filed an affidavit in opposition to Lipin's motion to reargue,[960] which he said was based in part on her contention that the Second Circuit

> might be biased against her in light of her distant familial relationship with another litigant who has appeared before this court. Plaintiff's counsel asserted that defendants would use

---

[960] Respondent's Ex. V.

> this relationship. . . . Neither defendants nor their counsel were aware of plaintiff's familial relationship.

Baer also complained that "in a variety of fora, including this Court, plaintiff has accused me of submitting a false affidavit to Justice Moskowitz on July 3, 1991. . . . " At the time he believed Lipin had taken the documents in the EBT room, but "she admitted she took the documents" in Birnbaum's conference room.

> My July 3, 1991, affidavit was based on my best belief at the time. . . . It was only during the hearing held before Justice Moskowitz on July 8, 1991, that I learned, for the first time, that plaintiff actually took the Privileged/Work Product documents from me while they were on counsels' table in a judicial hearing room at a time when I was engaged in a hotly contested oral argument before state court special referee Birnbaum. At no time did I ever deceive the State Court or any Court. . . .

Lipin moved again to lift the stay on the ground of Moskowitz's recusal; Judge Sand denied this on October 29. Two weeks later she moved to recuse *him*; he declined. On March 4, 1993, Sand denied another motion to vacate the stay. The next day Lipin filed a *second* federal action. On January 17, 1996, Judge Sand dismissed Lipin's first federal case with prejudice as res judicata.[961] Lipin had started it before perfecting her first state appeal. The Second Circuit affirmed on December 12, 1996.[962] When Lipin petitioned for rehearing, the Second Circuit vacated its previous order and reissued it on the ground of claims preclusion on May 22 1997.[963] Lipin petitioned the U.S. Supreme Court on October 16, 1997, contending that although claims preclusion raised a question of "exquisite difficulty," the Second Circuit had "brushed off the matter in two inconsistent, publication-barred summary orders, in a shocking departure from the standard of judicial review required for proper performance of the appellate function."[964] Denouncing the court's "superficial treatment," Wisehart sought to relitigate everything, claiming that the appeal raised constitutional

---

[961] Lipin v. Bender, 1996 WL 18901 (S.D.N.Y. 1996).
[962] A corrected order was filed on May 22, 1997. Lipin v. Bender, 113 F.3d 1229 (2d Cir. 1997) (Ellsworth A. Van Graafeiland, Dennis Jacobs, and Guido Calabresi).
[963] Staff Ex. 17.
[964] Petition for Certiorari, 1997 WL 33549782 (U.S.).

issues and state court interference with federal jurisdiction. In his reply, he relied heavily on an *ABAJ* article headlined "Courts Behaving Badly - Task forces say some judges impatient with job bias cases."[965] The Supreme Court denied certiorari in January 1998.[966]

Justice Carmen Ciparick heard defendants' state court contempt motion. In November 1992 Lipin filed an affidavit in opposition to the July 10 order to show cause on the ground that Jacoby's supporting affidavit[967] "falsely stated" that Baer's "back was turned to address the special referee" when Lipin saw the document. On the contrary, Baer "looked directly at me *on a number of occasions*." "During the oral argument, because Mr. Baer's left side was turned to me, I was in Mr. Baer's peripheral vision and in full view of Christopher Parlo and Hope Kerstman. . . ." The documents "had been deliberately placed prior to my arrival at the location at which it was *known* by Mr. Baer that I would be sitting . . . the purpose was entrapment." She was there as a client, not a paralegal. "I testified that *I did not know where Mr. Baer's briefcase or papers were* and therefore *did not take anything from Mr. Baer.*" The previous day they had been before Birnbaum for rulings on defendants' objections to questions Red Cross Treasurer Carl Desch was to be asked, the next day about Bender's expense reports, Fletcher's salary increases, and $600,000 in missing funds. That "makes defendants' motives highly suspect in view of their extreme apprehension that Special Referee Birnbaum would rule in favor of my discovery requests and that the cat involving large amounts of missing funds would then be let out of the bag."

In response, defendants accused Lipin and Wisehart of "diversionary tactics," including

> the filing of several, specious motions here and in the USDC . . . the filing of frivolous notices of appeal. . .and engaging in scurrilous accusations. . . . Plaintiff's obvious tactic is to bury the Court in an avalanche of papers containing an endless series of false accusations and meritless legal theories to avoid facing the consequences of her own misconduct and that of her counsel (who is also her employer). . . . Defendants' counsel are not necessary fact witnesses as to any disputed factual

---

[965] Reply to Brief in Opposition to Petition for Certiorari, 1997 WL 3549405 (U.S.).
[966] Lipin v. American Nat'l Red Cross, 522 U.S. 1047 (1998).
[967] Ex. J to Staff Ex. 13.

CHAPTER 7

> issues relevant to the instant Order to Show Cause for Contempt and plaintiff's asserted grounds for disqualification of defendants' counsel are baseless.

Defendants sought "an 'air tight' suppression order that plaintiff and her counsel cannot evade through their imaginative and preposterous interpretations," as well as contempt citations and disqualification of Wisehart. "Plaintiff brazenly argues that. . .the Court's Order *permitted* her to use the information contained in the Privileged/Work Product Documents in any manner she wished *after* they were returned to defendants' counsel."

Lipin's reply affidavit quoted Baer's October 23, 1992, affidavit acknowledging that his July 2, 1991, affidavit "was based on my best belief at the time that *plaintiff had taken the Privileged/Work Product Documents from me* some time during the deposition of Barnett Deutch."[968] "[T]he universal truth . . . is that no person could or would avoid reading defamatory statements about themselves that have been placed in front of them. . . . "

In December, without a hearing, Ciparick denied without prejudice defendants' motions for contempt, to disqualify Wisehart and Purves, and to confirm that dismissal was with prejudice but granted their demand for suppression of the documents. He denied plaintiff's motion to disqualify WGM and her cross-motion to set aside and vacate Moskowitz's January 1992 dismissal because Lipin had appealed it.

In May 1993 the Appellate Division unanimously affirmed Moskowitz's dismissal.[969] Although it did not find the premeditation present in *Beiny*,[970]

> Plaintiff's initial conduct is equally or even more egregious in terms of an appropriate sanction inasmuch as it was plaintiff herself who seized the opportunity presented to obtain an unfair advantage over her adversaries in this litigation. Her improper conduct was then compounded by counsel, who

---

[968] Respondent's Ex. J.
[969] Lipin v. Bender, 193 A.D.2d 424, 597 N.Y.S.2d 340 (1st Dept 1993); Alan Kohn, "Court Declares Suit's Dismissal Proper Sanction," 5/13/93 N.Y.L.J. 1 (col. 3). Wisehart made several motions in the course of appealing to the Court of Appeals, all of which were denied: 197 A.D.2d 942 (1st Dept. 1993); 83 N.Y.2d 993 (1994); 84 N.Y.2d 858 (1994).
[970] In the Matter of Beiny, 129 A.D.2d 126 (1st Dep't 198).

could have readily returned the documents or sought further direction from the court, rather than permitting his client to return to his office and make copies of the disputed documents and then sought [sic] to take advantage of such improper conduct by scheduling a "settlement conference."

Lipin's other arguments were "worthless." Her

> attempt to portray the defendants as having engaged in dilatory and sharp practices appears to have but one purpose—to obscure the issue of her own misconduct. Moreover, there is no support for her claim that defendants waived any attorney-client privilege and, regardless of whether the documents were privileged, the highly improper manner in which they were obtained, combined with their subsequent use by plaintiff's counsel to defendants' detriment, constitutes a sufficient basis for the court's action.

In August 1994 Justice Martin Schoenfeld, who took over the case from Justice Moskowitz, ruled that her January 1992 dismissal had been with prejudice.[971] He found that

> plaintiff, who by then was employed as a paralegal in the office of the attorney representing her in the instant action, surreptitiously secreted a series of internal memoranda that were written by *defendants'* counsel off of a table and into her possession. Plaintiff and her counsel thereafter attempted to use the contents of these documents, copies of which they made, in settlement negotiations.

After Justice Ciparick's December 29, 1992, decision restraining Lipin from disseminating the information in the documents, "plaintiff commenced another action in federal court 'arising', in defendants' words, 'out of the same nucleus of operative facts' as the instant matter."

> Before addressing the specific issues presented here, this Court feels compelled to opine that—whatever the intentions of the

---

[971] Respondent's Ex. Y.

parties and their attorneys—the instant applications embody an unfortunate example of litigation run amok. Lawyering and adjudication *are* not, or at least *should* not be, such arcane, abstruse arts that the practitioners thereof cannot understand one another, or follow simple rules and directions.

Plaintiff commenced a garden-variety lawsuit. During discovery, she and her counsel knowingly obtained documents belonging to her adversaries. A judge rules—rightly, wrongly, or indifferently—that the documents should be returned and the case should be dismissed. An appellate court affirmed. The state's highest court will soon be reviewing the matter.

This simple, straightforward history notwithstanding, a slew of motions, appeals, applications, and even other lawsuits in another court have mushroomed up, inordinately consuming judicial and other resources. This court hopes that in its own small way today's decision will help to put the entire matter to rest. In any event, sanctions are always at hand where an attorney's zealous advocacy crosses the border into obstinate refusal to take "no" for an answer. Litigation, like life itself, must one day come to a close. . . . [Justice Moskowitz clearly intended dismissal to be with prejudice.] In now directing the court clerk to enter a final judgment reflecting the reality of this dismissal, this court is merely ordering the consummation of a previous determination by a judge who subsequently recused herself. Such a direction is purely ministerial and remedial in nature.

Furthermore, Justice Moskowitz made absolutely clear that what plaintiff and her counsel did with defendants' documents was, to the extent possible, to be undone. This determination was unqualified, subject only to plaintiff's right to appeal. Thus in granting the relief now requested by defendants, this court is merely attempting to clarify—assuming any further clarity is necessary—and to effectuate—assuming any further effectuation is necessary—what has already been decided.

The Appellate Division affirmed in June 1995[972] and denied reargument in September.

---
[972] 216 A.D.2d 131, 629 N.Y. Supp. 2d 3 (1st Dep't 1995).

In Lipin's appeal of the May 1993 Appellate Division decision to the Court of Appeal, Pace University law professor Jay Carlisle filed an amicus brief arguing that the trial court lacked jurisdiction to dismiss the complaint.[973] During oral argument in September 1994 the Court of Appeal was quite hostile to Wisehart, who now argued that *no* sanctions were appropriate.[974] When Judge Titone asked if it was not "egregious ... when you steal papers off a table," Wisehart denied Lipin had done so. When Chief Judge Kaye called them "confidential papers," Wisehart replied they were not marked confidential. Titone observed: "they belonged to somebody else ... and she took and put it on her lap. Now you tell me what that is." He was unpersuaded by Wisehart's citation of the Oregon case about inadvertent delivery: "How were they delivered if they were on a table in front of her?" When Wisehart called it "foreseeable that she would be sitting" there, Judge Simons interrupted: "I don't think you are going to prevail in this court by trying to justify what she did." Wisehart invoked a ruling that "the rights under the New York Human Rights Law are ... a constitutionally protected property interest. The decision below takes away a Constitutional right of my client." Although the lower court had found that the documents were attorney work product, Wisehart insisted "there's a question" about this. When Judge Bellacosa asked if a client would be entitled to pick up a judge's notes from the bench, Wisehart wisely answered no. Jacoby was indignant:

> Have we reached the day where counsel sitting here in this room have to worry that their adverse counsel [who] may be sitting right next to them in the setup in this courtroom, will lift those documents off the table?

The "facts" are "just so outrageous." Asked by Kaye if "there was ... a violation of the court's direction?" Jacoby said "absolutely ... they used them in subsequent papers." Wisehart concluded by asking "this court to do justice and have mercy."

But on November 1, 1994, the Court of Appeal agreed with the Appellate Division.[975] It noted that following Moskowitz's dismissal "plaintiff's counsel thereafter simply recommenced the litigation in the U.S.

---

[973] Respondent's Ex. T.
[974] Transcript of videotape of argument on September 22, 1994.
[975] Lipin v. Bender, 84 N.Y.2d 562, 620 N.Y.S.2d 744, 644 N.E.2d 1300 (1994); Gary Spencer, "Dismissal Affirmed for Discovery Abuse," 11/2/1994 N.Y.L.J. 1 (col. 3).

Chapter 7

District Court for the Southern District of New York, on the theory that—despite the tenor and substance of the trial court's opinion—the dismissal was not 'with prejudice.'" That litigation was stayed. Plaintiff's "Counsel also tried, by subpoena, to obtain a copy of the documents for use on appeal, but this Court granted defendant's motion to quash."

> Having deliberately taken the initial misstep of secretly reading what she recognized as attorneys' confidential documents, plaintiff was presented with several opportunities to purge herself and minimize prejudice to defendants. At each juncture, however, she chose the course of action that exacerbated the harm.

Both lower courts found that the documents "plainly fell within the ambit of work product and the attorney-client privilege." There was "no basis" for plaintiff's claim that defendants had waived their privilege by leaving the documents on the table. The plaintiff "knowingly and deliberately intruded herself into plainly private communications between defendants and their attorney, and by retaining and hand-copying the documents preserved the information gleaned for maximum advantage to herself. . . ."

Wisehart called the opinion "disappointing."[976] "We think this is punitive on the part of the court." Lipin filed an affidavit on November 30, 1994, in support of a motion to reargue.[977] The *New York Times* had reported on June 22, 1992, that Justice Moskowitz had been diagnosed with breast cancer in December 1991 and was "completing a course of chemotherapy following a mastectomy"; her father had died two months before the diagnosis.[978] "As a trained health care professional, and the daughter of an eminent neuro-psychiatrist, I know that cancer in general and mastectomies in particular typically involve trauma with profound psychological consequences." Lipin claimed "professional experience and training in the field of health service."

> It is clinically known that women who are diagnosed with breast cancer in general, and those women who must undergo a single or double mastectomy in particular, may experience

---

[976] John Caher, "Court Throws Out Red Cross Sex Discrimination Suit," Times Union (Albany), November 2, 1994, at B2.
[977] Staff Ex. 13.
[978] Nadine Brozan, "Chronicle," New York Times, June 22, 1992.

> profound psychiatric trauma and stress resulting in intense anger directed inwardly and outwardly towards other "normal" women, loss of sexual self-worth and attractiveness as a woman, and severe depression resulting in short and long term psychological consequences.

She quoted many texts purporting to describe the consequences of cancer diagnosis and chemotherapy.

> [T]o my own direct observation, the impairment of Justice Moskowitz fairly to decide the dismissal of my complaint due to her breast cancer condition and mastectomy and its ensuing treatment, distorting her sense of reality and perspective, is demonstrated by the changes in the demeanor and behavior of Justice Moskowitz following the diagnosis. . . . I personally saw Justice Moskowitz reduced to tears in open court as a result of the badgering of Lawrence J. Baer, Esq. of WGM. . . .
>
> I am informed by a Special Master in the Supreme Court that the bizarre behavior exhibit [sic] by Justice Moskowitz during this period resulted in her being referred to by other clerks in the New York County Courthouse as "la Loca" (the crazy one).

Moskowitz's demeanor at the January 9 hearing,

> approximately a day before she entered the hospital for a mastectomy, contrary to her previous behavior, was that of an individual who was disoriented, distracted, and irrational.
>
> She was not, apparently, able to focus on her surroundings. She insisted, for example, after having begun to dictate her ad hoc decision, left the bench and courtroom, entered the robing room, returned and ordered me to remove my person from a seat close to the bench to the back bench in the courtroom and remain there, and ordered the armed bailiff, who was not present prior to her departure to the robing room, to keep me under surveillance. At no time did I give any indication whatsoever of disorderly conduct.

Chapter 7

> Justice Moskowitz had piles of documents and books on her bench to which she had great difficulty making reference and therefore gave up in referring to them. She appeared unaware of what was on her bench. She was agitated, given to jerky and uncertain motions, and seemed clearly hostile, aggressive and disoriented throughout the proceeding.
>
> When I ran up to console my attorney when he was unable to raise [sic] from his chair because of his shock-induced trauma caused by the conclusory draconian dictated decision...Justice Moskowitz seemed to be jolted out of her daze and she herself seemed shocked as to what she had just done.

Three attorneys who entered the courtroom to speak to the clerk "were shocked by Justice Moskowitz's lack of appropriate judicial demeanor."

> Approximately five minutes went by after Justice Moskowitz uncontrollably jumped up from the bench and ran out of the courtroom in front of her law clerk [and] went into the judge's robing room.
>
> When Justice Moskowitz stomped back into the courtroom and onto the bench, she was visibly out of control and hysterical....
>
> Upon leaving the courtroom I heard Justice Moskowitz state to my attorney that if he didn't immediately leave the courtroom she would order the bailiff to throw him out.

The dismissal was "a marked departure from her prior findings and rulings." The "180 degree turn about...can only be explained by her medical condition, which continued at least until her self-recusal on August 6, 1992...." Moskowitz "appeared to have no energy to manage the case" and "failed to enforce her own discovery orders...." She "lapsed into disoriented behavior patterns...." "[F]aced with a severe operation and distracted by the battery of tests and treatment to which she was necessarily subject, she sought to clear her docket despite her capacity [sic] to do so." Her "demeanor on July 23, 1992...amply shows her disorientation at that time also." Her "irrational behavior is shown by her comment...

'I have decided all I needed to decide.'" On August 6 she appeared "agitated and out of control."

Lipin noted that in March 1994 Moskowitz and Chief Judge Kaye were listed among the 26 founders of "Judges and Lawyers Breast Cancer Alert," Kaye as past co-president and Moskowitz as newly elected co-president.[979] "Chief Judge Kaye would have had personal and ex parte knowledge of such circumstances affecting the judicial decision making process, and a partisan, non-judicial interest in the existence of such disability on the part of Justice Moskowitz...."

The motion concluded:

> [T]he timing of the entrapment ploy by respondents' counsel is significant because it occurred ... approximately six weeks after Justice Moskowitz instructed counsel for respondents, on May 13, 1991, to either settle the case or she would send it to trial ... approximately two weeks after the rulings of Special Referee Birnbaum on June 13, 1991 ... that questioning of respondent Bender with respect to the Bender/Fletcher relationship was permissible; that the Bender deposition was to be continued on July 17 and/or 19, 1991....

Wisehart's memorandum of law repeated many of the allegations.[980] "Chief Judge Kaye understandably would have sympathy for Justice Moskowitz with a concomitant but unconscious tendency to overlook deficiencies in the performance of her judicial function." He concluded: "this Court has, albeit unwittingly, aligned itself on the side of a sexual abuser and harasser and its decision will undoubtedly increase the number and extent of the depravity of such miscreants whose actions are sheltered under the panoply of institutional power conferred upon those in control of powerful organizations." The Court of Appeal denied reargument in January 1995.[981]

---

[979] Moskowitz and Kaye had helped found the group in December 1991 in response to the death from breast cancer of Appellate Division Justice Sybil Hart Kooper. This was the month Moskowitz was diagnosed. Broznan, supra.
[980] Staff Ex. 14 (12.1.94).
[981] Lipin v. Bender, 84 N.Y.2d 1027, 647 N.E.2d 454, 623 N.Y.S.2d 182 (1995).

VI. The Disciplinary Proceeding

On April 18, 1996, the DDC charged Wisehart with eight counts: dishonesty, fraud, deceit or misrepresentation; conduct prejudicial to the administration of justice; disregarding a tribunal ruling in the course of proceedings; undignified or discourteous conduct degrading to a tribunal; and knowingly making false accusations against judges; all of which adversely reflected on his fitness to practice law.[982]

Two counts involved an unrelated matter. Wisehart testified that his firm had hired Dawn Levy-Weinstein soon after she graduated from law school. At the time the firm represented April Nell in a slip and fall, which had caused "a very rare debilitating condition that subjected her constantly to intense pain."

> An important part of [Levy-Weinstein's] responsibilities had to do with assisting April Nell in the prosecution of her case which was going to trial momentarily ... Levy-Weinstein was going to accompany her client in an ambulance and look after her in court. And when the case was on the brink of trial, I got a two-week notice that Ms. Levy-Weinstein had accepted employment from another attorney who had been my adversary in a matter. And I thought that was totally unprofessional and contrary to the commitments that had been made.

The firm sued her for breach of fiduciary duty. She moved to dismiss, and Wisehart moved to disqualify her counsel (presumably her new employer and his former adversary). On December 6, 1992, Justice Beverly Cohen granted Levy-Weinstein's motion, denied Wisehart's, dismissed the action, and assessed $1,000 in sanctions against his firm for

> commencing an action which, on its face lacks merit ... maintaining an unsustainable position on this motion by using irrelevant and contradicting argument; asserting a gratuitous, totally wanton claim in his reply to defendant's counter-claim ... and, by cross-moving, attempting to oppose defendant further by depriving her of counsel.

---

[982] DR 1-102(A)(4) and (5), 7-106(A) and (C)(6), 8-102(B), and 1-101-2(A)(7).

In the disciplinary hearing Wisehart insisted that, although he specialized in employment law, "I didn't know that she was an atwell [at will] employee. I never thought that that applied to her situation in view of a Court of Appeal decision on her higher professional responsibility of lawyers who undertake to pursue the interest of a client."

The disciplinary case was heard by Arthur W. Greig (chair), Fordham law professor Bruce A. Green and Telesforo DelValle, Jr. (all lawyers) and Rachel Child (lay member) on November 12 and December 10 and 17, 1997. Andral N. Bratton represented the DDC and John W. Whittlesey and Patrick M. Wall the respondent.

Wisehart was born in 1928 and grew up on a Midwestern farm. He worked his way through college and law school at the University of Michigan, where he made law review and Order of the Coif and earned an M.P.A. He was an associate at Chadbourne Parke Whiteside Wolf and Brophy from 1954 to 1959, when "one of the partners wanted me to go with him to set up the legal department for American Airlines." Wisehart stayed until 1969, becoming corporate secretary and assistant general counsel. "I specialized in a number of matters including labor relations. And I wrote a number of law review articles on the subject." Then he was recruited to REA Express and "tried for five years to keep it going" as senior vice-president, general counsel, corporate secretary, and director. On June 1, 1974, he established a partnership with Koch (who had since died), specializing in age discrimination.

DelValle asked if "you would have done something different—if you could revisit that day?"

> I have gone over that a million times in my mind. . . . subsequent events have reinforced . . . the view that we did the things the right way. And I felt that I was prudent to get a second opinion and I felt that bringing the matter up first to the adversary law firm was the correct thing to do . . . but I certainly regret the, the fact that the Disciplinary committee feels that I may have not behaved properly.

Although his own file memoranda (reproduced above) were privileged work product, the WGM memos were not "because they contained statements by third persons about Ms. Lipin and her family that were directly called for by prior discovery orders." They memorialized WGM interviews with clients and witnesses but "contain statements that by their very nature, were defamatory." Asked if that made them discoverable, he shifted ground: "they were required under prior orders to produce those documents." "[I]f I could tell you what that statement was, I think you would agree with me." The parties were still contesting whether these were privileged. There was a possible distinction between WGM documents and those by the ARCGNY and ANRC.

> Wisehart: I felt the proper procedure in a matter like this, is first to raise it with adversary counsel, and then see if it could be resolved, which I thought it could be, because Judge Moskowitz had emphatically declared in May that we should try to settle this case. . . .
>
> DelValle: I'm trying to understand . . . with a prior favorable ruling from Judge Moskowitz concerning the requested documents, why you just didn't make a motion, attach everything you had, and say, judge, this is what we have, and we're entitled to some of this stuff.
>
> Wisehart: Well I just thought I did it the right way, by raising it first with opposing counsel. And I felt that if they didn't agree, they would take it up with the court and there would be a ruling. That's what happened. . . .
>
> DelValle: Did you ever advise the court that [Lipin] had had that copy at home during that time?
>
> Wisehart: I don't think it came up. We were in court on the third until about five o'clock . . . I said I would secure the documents. I told her to secure the documents. She said . . . can I bring them in on the fifth? . . . And I said, yes. As far as I was concerned, I could rely on her statement. After all, she worked for me.

Wall submitted a 53-page post-hearing memorandum in August 1998. He argued that Wisehart gave ANRC counsel a copy of the document on July 2 because 42 USC §1986 requires anyone who knows that a violation of §1985 is about to be committed do what they can to prevent it. Indeed, the next day Wisehart sent MLB a letter "calling upon the ANRC to suspend Bender because of his misconduct." Even though Wisehart had just testified that Lipin "worked for me," Wall argued that she acted exclusively as a client, attending every appearance in this case and none in any other. The documents were not privileged because they were treated carelessly and subject to a prior discovery order.

In December, Martin C. Seham (Wisehart's new counsel)[983] asked Greig to recuse himself.

> (1) You had no jurisdiction to make statements which were intimidating to Ms. Lipin, in an off-the-record telephonic conference.
> (2) In your function as Hearing Panel Chair, having heard Ms. Lipin's testimony on December 10, 1997 . . . *and in your functional capacity as "Convenor" of the Democratic Judicial Convention for the 1st Judicial District on September 24, 1998,* you have direct knowledge that Ms. Lipin attended as an elected Alternate Delegate. . . .[984]

Seham quoted allegations of political manipulation in judicial elections.

Two days later Seham moved to dismiss the charges "in light of the concessions made by staff counsel at a telephonic conference" that "there is no evidence to support the multiple statements in staff counsel's memorandum . . . that Joan Lipin . . . came into possession of the disputed documents illegitimately, or as a result of 'theft.'" Before this Staff Counsel "always [used] this provocative hysterical characterization to gratuitously degrade the practitioner with over forty years of distinguished experience."

> Of the hundreds of thousands of legal practitioners, there is an almost infinite variety of operation and even conduct. There are firms today with literally hundreds of attorneys, officially graduated paralegals, clerks for files, internal messengers, kitchens, servants, and an atmosphere which would be kindly received in Bermuda. That is not the way all of us practice law.

---

[983] Seham, who came from a working class Jewish family in Brooklyn, worked his way through Amherst College (graduating Phi Beta Kappa) and Harvard Law School (where he was a law review editor). Wisehart and he shared an office as associates at Chadbourne Parke; when Wisehart was in the American Airlines general counsel's office, Seham's small firm represented unions of pilots, flight attendants, and airline mechanics. Seham died in May 2006 after struggling with Parkinson's for 21 years. "Seham, Martin Charles," New York Times, May 14, 2006.

[984] Emphasis in original.

Chapter 7

Many practice law in an atmosphere in which the most slender needs of the practitioners are met. . . . Particularly in the areas of discrimination, whether it be against ethnic or racial groups, age or gender, Mr. Wisehart has typically worked on the side of people who would otherwise have had very rough going. . . . This is not the kind of environment where a waiting servant receives a lawyer's hat when he enters through the front door. The practitioner, like Wisehart, is at the same time doing the bookkeeping, paying taxes, writing invoices, writing briefs and papers without aid or assistance, attending bar association activities, renting space, making phone calls and receiving messages. . . . It is that lawyer whose standard of conduct we must respect and who must be given room within which he can tend to all these matters as they develop. . . . Mr. Wisehart did what any other normal single practitioner would do. He did not call on any staff to go through the papers or to engage in research; he did not set up a billing file or check to see which papers were marked "draft" . . . one has to consider the likelihood that a major law firm would leave four inches of paper out of its control or not knowing its whereabouts . . . most lawyers do not have their own vaults as a repository for the settlements in personal injury cases. . . .

Where does the Viper Lie? . . . The scheme began when someone on the other side of the table withdrew four inches of material from the Weil Gotshal & Manges venue and put it down. . . . The character of that move was deliberate as suggested by the fact that the papers appeared in a neatly compounded file. . . . This deliberate placement of the pile of papers so as to implicate Ms. Lipin and Mr. Wisehart is itself a violation of ethical standards. . . .

By Their Own Petard

We fail to see how there can be any doubt that Mr. Wisehart had nothing to do, either directly or indirectly, with obtaining possession with the disposition of the papers. . . . The large gap in the chronology is the location and possession of the papers on their journey to the "temptation" of Ms. Lipin. . . . the conclusion remains that somehow these papers were deliberately kept from the particularization of this episode's events. . . . the extraction of pages from Weil Gotshal & Manges was the beginning of a nefarious journey [that] destroyed the privilege of any sanctity thereafter.

He denied Lipin ever threatened to go to the press: "no reasonable person would turnover [sic] to the press papers containing defamatory statements about his client and her family." Wisehart's behavior did not fall within the "ten most common ethical violations" (the title of an article by panel member Bruce Green).[985] By contrast, WGM committed three of them: conflict of interest, incompetence, and filing perjured and misleading affidavits. "[B]ut nothing whatsoever was said by staff counsel about the attorneys at Weil, Gotshal & Manges, a mega-firm which assuredly collected munificent fees in connection with every step of the *Lipin* litigation for which Mr. Wisehart was further punished by receiving nothing...." Seham also alleged a failure to prosecute Sullivan and Cromwell for a similar charge.

> It therefore appears that the targets of such self-initiated proceedings by staff counsel are predominantly small firm practitioners such as Mr. Wisehart rather than large firm lawyers who nevertheless are compensated exorbitant amounts and are shown to have skated on thin ice with respect to ethical violations. The result is a denial of equal protection and due process for Mr. Wisehart....

After his motion to dismiss was denied, Seham moved on December 11 that, because Justice Moskowitz declined to sanction Wisehart, "Staff Counsel therefore should be the party collaterally estopped from relitigating the issue." Seham also tried to relitigate Moskowitz's dismissal of the civil case and denial of the recusal motion.

> It may have been unwise for the plaintiff to pursue the *reasons* for the judge's inconsistent, and incorrect statement concerning her change in view. Respondent stretched as far as his reach could go in order to develop some position from which he could argue that a serious error had been made in the dismissal of Ms. Lipin's case.... for the plaintiff, whose life and

---

[985] 24(4) Litigation 48 (Summer 1998).

Chapter 7

livelihood both literally depended on her vindication in this sexual harassment case, it was difficult to deny access to every possible argument particularly when statements about the judge's medical condition were made in the press, and his client herself, was highly knowledgeable about such matters by training and experience as a health services professional.

At a December 21 hearing Greig declined to recuse himself. Seham moved to submit additional exhibits.

> Arthur Wisehart is a member of the Bar without complaint, without ill finding for 40 years. . . . He is lately, a defender of the poor and brings legal services to people and individuals who, because of apparent disabilities, can ill afford to have competent counsel of their own. . . . There was no theft of money here. There was no facelessness to the client. . . . the charge . . . which besmirches this whole hearing is the charge of theft. . . . what is interesting, if not downright spell casting is what happened to the documents from the time they left the briefcase of Weil Gotshal, until the time they arrived at Mr. Wisehart's assistant's desk. . . . Mr. Wisehart is faced with a strange sourceless unidentifiable pile of papers four inches thick. . . . How do you carry four of these? Do you carry them under your arm? . . . it had to pass through the gauntlet of adversary lawyers. . . . What is left open is the creation of those papers. . . . We only have an explosion of faith that these are real and that these implicate Wisehart at all. . . . It's the eve of the Fourth of July and a patently phony set of documents is wending their way through to Mr. Wisehart and he sees four inches of sliced garbage, because no one, particularly the firm of Weil Gotshal. . .would allow four inches of legal documents in this investigation to go careening around the countryside. . . . One of the associates of that firm was asked how they got there. He said, I don't know. They got there somehow. So Wisehart has these "somehow-documents" in his hand on the Fourth of July. . .and there's a question as to what does he do with them? According to the law . . . he can do anything he wants with them. . . . Somebody else—and we have our suspicions, put them down there, put them in front of her, put them

where she would be put in jeopardy of—by entrapment, have it in her possession . . . and she put them down and took them to Mr. Wisehart. . . . So his first thought . . . is, they're abandoned. Certainly there's no rush. . . . These are ordinary—less than ordinary documents.

When Seham offered to "vouch for the accuracy of Ms. Lipin's affidavit," Bratton objected. Greig agreed: "You can't vouch for the testimony of a witness. . . . certainly not that witness." Seham resumed his defense of the sole practitioner.

> The city is swarming with sole practitioners who must be sustained if we're to bring justice to our entire community. . . . The single practitioner does all [the functions performed by large-firm support staff] . . . and he cannot be held to the same comfortable standard that the firm of Weil Gotshal and other firms of its kind practice. . . . I've practiced in those firms myself and been a partner . . . there is a real difference . . . between the response time of an Arthur Wisehart, who may be involved in a dozen tasks, and the firm of Weil Gotshal or for a vast many more, Sullivan Cromwell. . .what reasons the . . . other firms involved in this suit have for their prosecution of Mr. Wisehart, I don't know. But if it's for a compulsion to meet artificial, grandiose standards, then it is a disservice to the community. . . . to decide this case in any way against Mr. Wisehart . . . would infect the judicial system in this state. It would put lawyers in jeopardy in a fashion that's unfair and misleading. There are so many facts in this case that are dubious—the four inches being just one of them. . . . [He resisted the collateral estoppel effect of Moskowitz's dismissal.] The test is whether justice is the same if it is in one dose or in two doses with one of the doses a little bit off color. . . . Forty years ago I was Arthur Wisehart's roommate at the firm of Chadbourne Parke Whiteside and Wolf. . . .

Bratton agreed that "Mr. Wisehart was clearly dedicated to his client," but "that well could be a reason why Mr. Wisehart got into so much trouble." Before reading the documents and talking to Ned Purves "he already has a plan. He's going to use these documents to attempt a settlement

Chapter 7

in terms very, very critical to Ms. Lipin." "Every opportunity Mr. Wisehart had to seek the conservative safe path, he disregarded it."

The Panel filed its report on guilt on December 24. It again rejected the recusal motion: the meeting in which Greig and Lipin had participated included 131 delegates and 50–75 alternates. The panel granted the motion to dismiss counts one (condoning theft of privileged documents) and two (failing to comply with Justice Moskowitz's directive and making false accusations against her and Judge Kaye). It found violations of counts one (dishonesty), four (discourtesy), and six (unfitness) but not three (disregarding judicial ruling), five (accusation against a judge), and seven and eight (the Levy-Weinstein matter).

Wisehart moved for rehearing the next month. Indicating the counts upheld just by rule number

> is simply inadequate notice to an attorney who finds his very livelihood threatened by an obscure ruling. . . . Mr. Wisehart continues to believe that his acts were not wrong and the deletions in the original charges are proof that the accusations are not always right. . . . Staff Counsel are not threatened with disbarment or other punishment because of what have now been found to be grievously prejudicial errors. . . . Mr. Wisehart similarly does not claim infallibility in everything he ever did when actions taken under truly extraordinary circumstances in a hotly contested litigation are measured against 20-20 hindsight. . . . the uncertainty of the nature of the charge not only skews the panel's decision, but also undermines the process by inviting the parties to blindman's bluff game . . . there is material that has been offered but not received for the record which can produce such further findings as will invalidate the panel's report.

Seham sought to subpoena the original purloined documents.

> The respondent has a *right* to know the precise nature of the acts remaining that are considered to have been improper so that he can respond definitively to the actual findings which may lie deep in the general presentation of the record. This difficulty might have been avoided, in whole or in part, if Mr. Wisehart were permitted to submit a demand for a bill of

particulars. . . . If . . . Mr. Wisehart is not guilty of any wrong in the original securing of the documents, how has the panel taken into account that confirmation of integrity with a renewed finding of fault?

VII. Aggravating Mitigation

Because Wisehart had never been disciplined, Bratton presented no evidence in aggravation at the June 14, 1999, sanctions hearing. Seham quoted Gilbert and Sullivan: "let the punishment fit the crime." He concluded from the interim report that there "was no evidence, no indication that there had been any further crime." "[W]hat was done that was wrong?" "[I]f we have no clear evidence and we do not satisfy the requirements of due process, then you must find that no sanction be applied. . . . " The chair reminded Seham that Wisehart had been found guilty of four charges. Seham replied: "Once you exculpate Mr. Wisehart from liability in taking the papers in question, then it necessarily follows that the other events have to be examined." He wanted Patrick Wall to testify about "the propriety of Wisehart's actions after the papers were seen by him."

> Chair: [Y]ou seem to not be hearing me. So I'll say it again. The panel has found liability on four of the charges . . . therefore, we are moving to the sanctions and mitigation section.

Wall could not be an expert witness on sanctions because he was Wisehart's lawyer; if he took the stand, Bratton would cross-examine him without Wisehart being able to invoke the lawyer-client privilege.

> Seham: . . . Mr. Wall will testify. . .on the basis of his membership in the bar and expert background, etc., etc., etc. . . . I think we should not lose sight of the fact that the CPR is a very broad and, if you will, vague proclamation. And what we are trying to do, presumably, is match Wisehart's conduct with those vague requirements of propriety.

The Chair warned against relitigating.

> Seham: . . . what we're asking for is the opportunity to present a case against what is left of the original charges.

Chapter 7

Green: But this panel found that Mr. Wisehart violated. . . .

Seham: No, I don't think that's quite true. . . . if he did not condone any theft, what does that do to the credibility of the accusations that he did something else . . . what we are saying is that the notice we received was in effect a different case. . . . there was no way we could have argued the relationships that we now believe existed at the . . . law firm of Weil Gotshal. . . .

Chair: You mean to tell me, Mr. Seham, that simply because this panel found that Mr. Wisehart did not condone the actual theft of the documents, you believe that gives you carte blanche to make allegations against the law firm?. . .

Seham: The nexus is that in making your findings—and in our favor, you necessarily come to some other conclusions. . .being that Wisehart had no purpose, had no objective, had no utilization of the documents and in fact turned them over as soon as he possibly could.

Chair: That's wrong . . . the record is clear that Ms. Lipin stole the document. And that—

Mr. Seham: Well for instance that, that comment of yours is staggering to me, because I don't find anything in the record . . . that makes that finding.

But after he quoted from the record the chair advised him "to not go down the road."

Seham said Wisehart went to Wall "in mitigation of what he had done thus far, or was planning to do." He did not act "out of pride, out of self-satisfaction or anything else. He thought . . . he was doing the right thing. And in order to verify with an outside source, he went to reputable lawyers and reputable members of the bar, for guidance." But Seham conceded that Wisehart had not consulted Wall while these events were transpiring. Wall would testify about the proper behavior based on "the complete set of facts." When Green asked if that meant the facts found by the panel, Seham demurred.

> Well that again is a problem we have with the due process aspect of this case. Because you proceed with a determination

of the legal requirements on the basis of facts developed with respect to a single practitioner. In other words, in revolutionary times we had a bill of attainder...that was outlawed...and that is why Wall's testimony would be relevant, because it—it provides a steady beacon light as to what was in Wall's mind [sic—he means Wisehart's]...there was a period of time when the papers were disposed of—went someplace else. Certainly Wisehart is not responsible for the disposition of those papers, unless it's proven that he—that he did it.

When Green and DelValle resisted hearing Wall, Seham suggested: "perhaps you are out of step with the regular or the expected imposition of sanction." It turned out Wall told Bratton that similar cases, on which Wall had sat, received private reprimands. When the chair asked for an offer of proof, Seham replied "I don't want to argue the point to the extreme of belittlement." After an adjournment the chair rejected his offer that Wall testify about a case that was confidential because it ended in a private reprimand.

> Chair: Mr. Seham, as I think I ruled pretty clearly before, unless you present and make an offer of proof that Mr. Wall is going to testify to something relevant in this hearing, I am going to rule that Mr. Wall cannot testify as an expert....
>
> Seham: But he says that there is relevance.
>
> Chair: He says? He, who?
>
> Seham: Wall
>
> Chair: Mr. Wall is not a member of the panel.
>
> Seham: But he's proffered as a witness...who alone among the sea of humanity, knows what this case is all about and—

The chair was unmoved.

Bratton then asked an observer to identify himself. This turned out to be Wisehart's son, Winston. Wisehart explained: "I asked him if he would please attend as a member of my family. My family is all involved in this proceeding. It's my reputation that's at stake." Although not a lawyer, Winston had also worked in his father's office for a number of years.

Chapter 7

"He's familiar with my character, what I've done with my time, who I represent."

Finally Wisehart spoke about his childhood on a farm, first legal job at Chadbourne Parke, and subsequent employment by American Airlines and REA. "I did this, of course, for compensation, but I also did it because I thought it was a very important public service." He now represented retirees claiming against pension funds and had just won "a precedent making case" in the Second Circuit.

> I am fighting for the rights of people who have small resources against entrenched interests, in trying to bring some rationality out of this downsizing mania which has, in my view, caused such injury in our society, to the interests of older people, people who, for the most part, are not able to obtain justice. In addition, I represent other employees and former employees who . . . have been subjected to sexual harassment, sex discrimination, age discrimination. . . . in doing this type of work in the latter part of my professional career, I'm motivated by a feeling of making a contribution in an important public service. I mean what I am doing as a lawyer is not motivated by greed or making money. If you want to see my Schedule C for the years 1992 to 1997, it will show a substantial loss every year. And this case. . .has, of course, made a very substantial contribution to that loss. And it does impact upon my family. . . . Now I don't say that I'm a perfect person. But I have a sensitivity to ethics questions. I've been an elder in the Presbyterian Church in Larchmont, New York, a member of the choir for 30 years. I've been head of the education program . . . for a number of years. . . . a sanction that would cripple my ability to represent people of that kind would really not be in the public interest. Nor . . . would . . . a kind of sanction that would cause further injury to my reputation. That's already been done. It's not necessary . . . in fact it's not constitutional . . . to have duplicate punishment. All you have to do is to look on Lexis and you see case after case citing this particular litigation. . . . And that is having a definite effect on my reputation already. . . . That stain is already there. And it causes harm not just to me but to the other clients that I represent.

Justice Ciparick had denied the contempt motion.

> So, if you apply the concept of collateral estoppel to that, you would say, well it's already been decided . . . it's not necessary for the panel to do more . . . a case in which I could recover no fee whatsoever, dismissed. And I've spent hours having the value of, I would estimate, $500,000 . . . the goddess of justice, you know, has a balance. . . . I don't believe that the standards of the disciplinary code are such that you have to be always right. . . . with 20-20 hindsight, you could probably always say, well I would have done something differently. But if you're on the firing line as an active practicing lawyer and those papers suddenly come to your attention and it's Friday afternoon on June 28, 1991, and you're trying to get ready for depositions that are going to be conducted upstairs . . . what do you do? I mean that is a real true life situation, one that may never occur again. Never. So, to impose some kind of precedential sanction on a situation that is so sui generis that it may never occur, seems to me to be going too far. . . . At the end of the day, we went down to see if the special referee was there, to bring this to his attention. And guess what? The lights were out. He was gone . . . and he would be gone for an extended period. I was sweating bullets because the weekend was coming up. . . . So I go to my home in Larchmont. I go to my friend. This is George Barige, who started at Chadbourne with me and was a classmate at Michigan Law School, on law review with me. . . . He said, I can't get involved, he was retired at that time. . . . I called a lawyer who had worked with me somewhat on this case previously, John Widdelsey [Whittlesey], a graduate of Harvard Law School, who had been chief labor counsel for Union Carbide for many years . . . and he told me he wasn't available. . . . I got hold of Ned Purves . . . after the hearing . . . he indicated his view that the documents had been put there deliberately as part of an entrapment scenario. Obviously, since he was the source of the client, I had to give a lot of weight to what he said. But . . . as I also indicated in my testimony, that came to be my own conclusion also. Now I know the panel has made a contrary ruling on this point . . . you haven't really decided on entrapment. But this morning you

made it clear that you still think the documents were stolen. So we have a dispute about that. But I think that if the panel looked at the documents . . . they would come to the opposite conclusion . . . I think that it's not due process for those documents not to be looked at, especially in deciding what I should have done at that particular situation. . . . I didn't think those documents were privileged. I know that the information in those documents had been ordered to be produced. . . . As far as bringing them up in the discussion that I had about the possibility of settlement, Justice Moskowitz . . . had told us just a short time before, settle this case or it's going to come to trial. And don't bother me with any more motions. . . . [I hoped] you would say, certitude in things like this, that you have to decide on the spur of the moment, is impossible. But we do commend somebody who does walk an extra mile, who seeks a second opinion or a third opinion. . . .

In 1951 the U.S. Supreme Court refused to dismiss an employment case on the ground that the employee stole crucial papers.

This case doesn't involve any intentional taking of that sort, by a person who is still an employee. . . . depriving the client of her claim and certainly having the consequences financially on me that I told you about. I think that's more than enough punishment. . . . I have remorse about this—lots of remorse. And I'm sorry you disagree with me in certain respects. . . . the remorse is, you can't be perfect in making decisions like this. You . . . do your best with what you have, to represent the interest of your client. . . . virtually every Sunday, I say a creed that I believe in the communion of the saints and the forgiveness of sins. And if you feel I've sinned, I ask to be forgiven.

Seham added: "I hope the panel does not injure a treasure of the bar."

Bratton was sympathetic. Wisehart had an otherwise unblemished record. The case *was* sui generis. Although respondents often claim to have suffered enough, that argument "has some weight to it" here. Not only was Lipin's claim dismissed, but that news "was on the front page of *The New York Law Journal.*"

The Purloined Papers

> On the other hand, Mr. Wisehart brought this publicity on himself. . . . we've had this case for three years now. And there's been no sense of remorse for what he did, until the very end of his testimony today. Now, a death bed conversion is better than no conversion at all. But what kind of conversion is this? . . . the entire tone of today's presentation, as well as the presentation he's been giving to us for the past three years, is, I've done nothing wrong. . . .if he had come in at any point during these three years and said, I blew it. I made a mistake. I shouldn't have done what I have done. I was zealous in trying . . . to represent my client and I just made a big mistake, that's one thing. But what we've had in the past three years is, I've done nothing wrong. At all times I behaved properly. . . .Mr. DelValle asked Mr. Wisehart, basically, knowing what you know now, would you have done the same thing over again? And I remember Mr. Wisehart's basic conclusion was, yes, I would have done the same thing. I did the right thing. . . .this is just not behavior to be shrugged off. Particularly when that behavior is missing some acknowledgement of wrongdoing. Because if someone doesn't acknowledge the wrongdoing, aren't we just giving him a green light to do these kind of things all over again?

He agreed to search the unpublished private reprimands for comparable cases.

The Hearing Panel reported in March 2000. Some of the documents were privileged no matter how Lipin obtained them. Wisehart should have told opposing counsel "immediately" and had Lipin return them. Instead, he "instructed Lipin to tell defendant's counsel that she had 'mistakenly' picked up the documents. . . ." The two kept the documents without informing opposing counsel or the court "for the entire three day July 4th weekend."[986]

> Despite the Court's clear direction not to use any of the information contained in the documents in litigation, on or about July 29, 1991, respondent submitted a memorandum of law to Special Referee Birnbaum (Staff Exhibit 7) which made specific

---

[986] Actually, it was the previous two-day weekend.

references to the Bender/Fletcher relationship, and Weil
Gotshal's alleged knowledge of that relationship . . . [which]
could only have come from the privileged documents. . . .

The Panel faulted Wisehart for failing to "refute or seek to explain any of the bizarre, convoluted allegations" in Lipin's July 21, 1992, motion to recuse Moskowitz and for seeking "to provide legal support and justification for those statements and allegations." It also criticized the "reckless allegations" about Moskowitz's breast cancer and treatment in his December 1, 1994, motion to reargue in the Court of Appeal. "Once again, respondent's memorandum of law affirmatively seeks to add legal justification to his client/employee's bizarre affidavit, and does not refute or temper any of the spurious conjectures of Ms. Lipin." The Panel quoted a U.S. District Judge:

> Litigation is not a game of hare and hounds, where rules are easily bent, where truth is skirted by lies and evasions and cheap victory is sought at the expense of fairness and candor.[987]

Lipin's case was "a tragedy of epic proportions." It was dismissed although, had the documents been "properly and *fairly* used, he was poised to win."

> But it is even more tragic that in pursuit of victory in litigation, respondent, an attorney for nearly 50 years, apparently lost sight of his moral, ethical and legal obligations to the court, the public, and his opposing counsels, and saw fit to use any and every means and avenue available to him in his efforts to "win." . . . Respondent wanted to "win" his case, and apparently was willing to lie, distort, slander, smear and impugn anybody and everybody who might get in his way, on the barest of substantive proof, even if it meant using improperly obtained, privileged information to "bludgeon" a settlement out of an opponent. Even if it meant violating a court directive to refrain from using information from wrongfully obtained documents. Even if it meant arguing that a judge's adverse

---

[987] Schmidt v. Ford Motor Co., 112 FRD 216 (D. Colo. 1981).

The Purloined Papers

> decision was the result of her alleged "impairment" or "incapacity" due to breast cancer, and breast cancer treatment. Even if it meant asserting that the judge was subject to "mind altering side effects from drugs used for chemotherapy." Even if it meant implying that a decision of the Chief Justice of the Court of Appeal was predicated on "sympathy" for a fellow jurist and her alleged knowledge of that jurist's medical condition.
>
> The recklessness of respondent's actions in this matter has been astounding, particularly in light of respondent's substantial experience as a litigator.

Although he claimed to have sought a second opinion from Ned Purves, "respondent chose **not** to call Purves as a witness." The Court of Appeal judgment that the documents were privileged was collateral estoppel. "Respondent's attempts to characterize his decision to use the documents as a mere 'honest mistake' are belied by his actions, his forty years of experience in practice, and his apparent familiarity on issues involving privilege."

> More significantly, at each juncture in the underlying case and even before this tribunal, respondent has sought to sully and disrupt the record and proceedings with extraneous charges of impropriety against neutral parties based on alleged activities having no nexus with the issues in his case.

It cited Wisehart's charges against Birnbaum, Moskowitz, Kaye, and Greig.

> Thus respondent's pattern and practices are clear—when all else fails, he simply conjures up false, reckless and highly *personal* charges against the "offending" tribunal, and seeks recusal in an effort to delay or otherwise obfuscate the issues.

In a recent disciplinary matter another respondent made reckless statements to the press concerning a judge.[988] But he

> fully cooperated with the Committee in admitting the charges, stipulated to a public censure, and personally apologized to

---

[988] Matter of Golub, 190 A.D.2d 110 (1st Dept 1993).

CHAPTER 7

the judge. Here, respondent has never apologized to any Court, maintains that he may have only made an "honest error" on the privilege issue, and had vigorously contested (as is his right) the charges.

In another recent case the respondent accused a federal judge of corruption. Although the lawyer admitted the offense, apologized, and agreed to public censure, he was suspended for three months.[989] This Panel recommended the same penalty.

VIII. Defeat Is Impossible

Wisehart responded two months later by filing a *third* lawsuit in the SDNY on Lipin's behalf.[990] The 70-page complaint named the ANRC, its insurer, four of its lawyers, and Hearing Panel chair Arthur W. Greig. It accused Greig of "perpetrating the deceit in an unissued report . . . derived from the false and perjured affidavits utilized by defendants Baer and Jacoby . . . and relied upon by . . . Parlo and Wall." Greig lacked jurisdiction because the report "was maliciously prepared to further injure plaintiff . . . and makes false and defamatory statements about plaintiff . . . " Greig's motivation was "retaliation for [Lipin's] political activities seeking to bring about the merit selection of judges" and "end . . . the present system that Greig has used to his profit." Wisehart repeated the charge that Moskowitz, one of six judicial candidates, "was not well known, and a relative newcomer" but received one of two nominations "as a result of the political maneuvering and backing of Denny Farrell." Greig "had personal knowledge with respect thereto, and direct knowledge that plaintiff Lipin has objected to said process. . . ." Greig himself had "received judicial appointments as a Receiver and also performs services as the Counsel to the Democratic County Committee, New York County. . . ."

Lipin was denied equal protection by the DDC's refusal to investigate her October 1992 complaint against Baer and Jacoby that "false affidavits had been used by New York 'big firm' lawyers, whose services are considered to be so valuable as to warrant charges of $300–$500 per hour,

---

[989] Matter of Phillip J. Dinhofer (1st Dept May 20, 1999) (unpublished).
[990] Staff Ex. F to Petition to Confirm.

and more, in furtherance of a scheme to obstruct justice, and to retaliate against and smear, defame and ruin" her reputation and "obtain dismissal of her case, on the basis of a conspiratorial hoax. . . ." The DDC "caused further injury to the plaintiff . . . by commencing disciplinary proceedings against a small law office, plaintiff's employer, seemingly on a *sua sponte* basis. . . ." The Greig report violated "the rights to equal protection of the laws of plaintiff and the class of other impecunious clients represented by the small office representing her" by displaying "bias . . . in favor of big firm lawyers . . . who can and do offer salaries to inexperienced beginners of over $100,000 per year, and profits to partners in the range of $1,000,000 per year or more. . . ." Wisehart noted that Lipin was applying to law school. The "Panel's mandated requirement that a non-lawyer be on the Panel was abrogated when Dr. Child abruptly resigned and withdrew, invalidating the entire proceeding. . . ." "Attorney Prince is believed to have since left the legal profession for a career in journalism as a result of said threats" by Baer.

> Defendant Greig is functus officio and without jurisdiction because his function and the panel that he chaired represented a procedure that had been abandoned, rejected and superseded on the basis that such procedure had been found to be defective and inherently unfair more than a year before Greig's Report. . . .

The complaint sought an "order enjoining Arthur W. Greig from causing further injury to plaintiff" and treble damages and attorney's fees.

On August 1, DDC Chairman Denis McInerney petitioned the Appellate Division to confirm the Panel recommendation, whose findings "have since been proven prophetic" by the "bizarre, convoluted allegations" in the third federal lawsuit. McInerney urged a more severe penalty "given respondent's continued total lack of remorse, his inability to discern his own wrongdoing and his continuing reckless conduct."

On November 30 Wisehart (now represented by Michael A. Gentile) filed a cross-motion to disaffirm the report. Wisehart's lengthy affidavit repeated Seham's earlier claim that the charge of stealing the documents was a "provocative hysterical characterization [used] gratuitously to degrade a practitioner with over forty years of distinguished practice." The "ultimate recognition of the hyperbolic nature of that allegation may have

Chapter 7

even more relevance to the few remaining Charges." "[T]he temperature of this case was lowered dramatically by a reflective Panel after it had the opportunity to hear my testimony and evaluate me both as a person and as a lawyer." He argued against the collateral estoppel effect of the Court of Appeals decision. He had "only hours to deal with a problem, not of my own making, that it took the courts years to resolve." The Hearing Panel could not "have decided the pivotal issues of my state of mind, my intent and my dilemma about those documents **without reviewing them**." He had never claimed "infallibility." "I did my best . . . in a context of my total surprise, a hotly contested litigation and a severely compressed time period. . . ." The Panel refused "to go to the 'scene' and view the logistics that were in place in that conference room." His own lawyer, Patrick Wall, "repeatedly said that had he been confronted by the same situation he would have done exactly as I had done . . . and that had I not acted as I did, I would have been subject to criticism from my client." Wisehart could not be liable for his client's statements.

He described his "**VALUE TO THE CLIENT PUBLIC**." "**Recent recognition of the importance** of the public interest in the services I have performed is shown in . . . my designation as a 'New Century Honoree' in the *2000 Barons Commemorative Edition*." "I am not by any stretch of the imagination a 'loose cannon' or a cantankerous old man. I have much left to offer clients who are desperate for the continuation of my services on my [sic—their] behalf. . . ." "Any suspension of my license, however brief, will not only further injure me and my already wounded reputation, but will surely jeopardize" clients, such as the Retired Employees Protection Association. "At my stage in life the operative time segments are measured in days and months, not in years." (He was 72.) "This proceeding has already been the most upsetting and traumatic experience of my entire career."

> I believe that I have made many more deposits than withdrawals at the bank of life and to the profession that I love. I ask that, while I still possess the physical and mental ability to do so, I be allowed to end my life and career by continuing to help my less fortunate contemporaries without interruption.

The same day Wisehart filed a memorandum of law in the third federal suit. "[R]etaliatory acts of the kind as alleged [sic—ascribed] to defendant Greig were held to be violative of First Amendment rights. . . ."

Greig "also instigated the instant proceedings to interfere directly with this court's jurisdiction." "The injury has resulted in cruel and unusual punishment" of Lipin. Greig "is not only a political opponent of the plaintiff . . . but also is disqualified because his position as Counsel for the Democratic County Committee is foremost among his activities as a lawyer." How Greig "came to Chair the hearing panel is the 'trout in the milk'. . . ." Wisehart denounced "the strategic use of 'soft money' . . . to facilitate what is euphemistically called 'tort reform,' by selecting judges favorable to the use of pretexts to dismiss cases that are unpopular with entrenched interests, which was the fate of Ms. Lipin's case under Justice Moskowitz, a Greig selectee. . . ." "On November 4, 1998, defendant Greig as Chair of the hearing panel, made the threat directly to Ms. Lipin that he would make Ms. Lipin 'suffer for what had happened'. . . ."

> A conspiracy to destroy small firm lawyers who on a pro bono basis represent clients engaged in civil rights litigation against the Goliath law firms, in which the rawest and most inexperienced associates are fobbed off on the judicial system at a salary of $165,000 per year, that seek to crush them and stamp them out by a one-sided application of disciplinary rules facilitated by using lawyers such as defendant Greig who are thirsting to receive lucrative assignments that such large firms can make available to those who trade in dispensing judicial selections as political patronage plums.

Greig had no immunity. "Activities motivated by political patronage concerns are not subject to immunity when they violate . . . First Amendment and free speech rights." He sought discovery "to determine how defendant Greig came to be Chair of the panel."

Bratton's December 5 reply affirmation urging confirmation of the Hearing Panel recommendation attached Lipin's November 3 motion for temporary and preliminary relief in the civil action, which sought to enjoin the disciplinary proceedings and requested costs from Greig and his attorney.[991] Her affidavit repeated many of the factual allegations and added others. She accused the petition to affirm of seeking "to interfere with the jurisdiction of this Court" by attaching her complaint "in support of the request that the penalty against my attorney even more severely"

---

[991] Ex. A.

CHAPTER 7

and "by creating a stigma against me and my credibility." She questioned whether McInerney "had even read the complaint . . . when he signed the Notice of Petition which appears to have been prepared for his signature for [sic—by] some other unspecified person, such as Mr. Greig" and sought discovery to identify "those persons." Greig and three other defendants had moved for sanctions against Wisehart. "The Notice of Petition to the Appellate Division . . . obviously was intended to create an impossible situation in responding to their extensive papers in this litigation," by being "served on the former counsel [Seham] of my attorney, a person who was known to be afflicted with a serious disability." When Wisehart

> sought to request that the Appellate Division hold proceedings in abeyance until this Court has an opportunity to consider the multiple motions to dismiss that had been filed before it previously, the new counsel, who my attorney retained in desperation, made the prediction, apparently as the result of threats that he had received from Staff Counsel for the Disciplinary Committee that even making such a request to the Appellate Division would cause retaliation in the form of the imposition of a greatly enhanced penalty upon my attorney that would in all probability, at his age, as he nears the sunset of his career, would make it permanently impossible for him to continue to practice law or even to continue to prosecute this litigation on my behalf.

Lipin had observed Staff Counsel seeking "to extort the consent of my attorney to the withdrawal of this litigation." "Greig and those aiding or abetting him . . . are clearly motivated by malice." Wisehart's counsel in the Appellate Division "recently filed a motion to withdraw so that no responsive papers can be filed." Greig's "unlawful conduct in connection with the election of state court judges . . . is shown most recently by his action as the Convenor of the Democratic Judicial Convention for the First Judicial Department on September 21, 2000, at which I was present as a delegate alternate." His behavior was "a perversion of the democratic process." The "event was conducted by defendant Greig as a way of purging all of the judicial candidates by forcing them to withdraw their nominations or applications unless they had received the required political endorsement and were approved by Mr. Greig."

> Defendant Greig knew full well that my attorney has a small office and would have difficulty responding to all of the motions to dismiss by October 27, 2000, in accordance with the schedule that has been established by this court. Defendant Greig nevertheless activated the serving and filing of the Notice of Petition in the Appellate Division so that the responsive papers would have been required to be prepared and filed at virtually the same time. . . . Greig is a past master at political manipulation, and was able to secure his designation as Chair of the Panel, as a matter of political intrigue, for the malicious purpose and intent of causing the maximum injury possible to myself and my attorney.
>
> Defendant Jacoby signaled the plan when he wrote to Justice Moskowitz on July 15, 1991, threatening to cause disciplinary proceedings to be instituted.
>
> Within six months after having been alerted to the plan, just after her election as Supreme Court Justice facilitated by defendant Greig and his political allies . . . Justice Moskowitz obediently dismissed my sexual harassment claim . . . a knee-jerk reaction necessitated by the demands of political expediency in a surprise decision dictated extemporaneously.

Lipin criticized the Hearing Panel report's reference to "details of defendant Bender's romantic involvement with one Fletcher and one Clingman."

> Rather than being "romantic," the relationship between Bender and his harem involved gross and disgusting displays of pure raw, unadulterated sex, going far beyond the Monica Lewinsky scandal, conducted by the Chief Executive of the New York Red Cross who, instead of being disciplined or reprimanded, was later promoted to being an adviser to Elizabeth Dole when she was President of Red Cross. . . .

"While he was obsessing about Bender's 'romantic' involvement," Greig "totally ignored . . . the offensively defamatory statements . . . 'dangerously crazy' . . . of the kind used by Hitler and his cronies as a pretext for ridding himself of the Jews as political opponents by sending them away to

CHAPTER 7

concentration camps and gas chambers in Germany during the Nazi period." Similarly Moskowitz sought "to rid herself of me."

> The denial of due process in what occurred therefore is pervasive in the disciplinary process dominated by defendant Greig, as the political puppet of the attorneys from Weil, Gotshal & Manges, and Morgan, Lewis & Bockius, who . . . instigated, planned and orchestrated it from the beginning.

Bratton also attached the June 30, 2000, decision by U.S. District Judge Richard Owen in a wrongful termination and age discrimination lawsuit Wisehart had filed on behalf of Charles Polin in 1993.[992] On October 26, 1994, Judge Owen had dismissed Wisehart's motion to disqualify Morgan, Lewis & Bockius as defense counsel.[993] After "four years of pre-trial litigation and numerous discovery disputes," both sides agreed to arbitration. Wisehart chose Freeman (his recent client) and proposed as independent arbitrator Jonathan Liebowitz, whom the defendant accepted. Wisehart secretly recorded a conference call on defendant's motion to quash his document subpoena. When Liebowitz realized this was happening he called it "totally unauthorized." After three more days of hearing, Wisehart rested. But when the defendant moved to dismiss, Wisehart insisted on calling two more witnesses and sought subpoenas for four rebuttal witnesses. Liebowitz objected:

> You don't even know what the heck it [defendant's rebuttal case] is, and you're already subpoenaing witnesses. . . . You're trying to load this record . . . you're trying to run up a tremendous bill for [the defendant, who was paying for the arbitration,] and not doing anything.

The arbitrators denied the subpoenas. Two days later Wisehart made serious accusations against Liebowitz to the American Arbitration Association. When the other two arbitrators gave Wisehart a chance to substantiate them, he declined "on constitutional grounds as well as jurisdictional grounds." The panel unanimously dismissed the case and sanctioned

---

[992] Polin v. Kellwood Co., No. 93 Civ 7876, 1994 WL 673496 (S.D.N.Y. Dec. 2, 1994) ($500 sanction against Polin for wrongfully delaying discovery); 1996 WL 665639 (Nov. 13, 1996); 103 F. Supp. 2d 238 (S.D.N.Y. 2000).
[993] Polin v. Kellwood Co., 866 F. Supp. 140 (S.D.N.Y. 1994).

Wisehart by requiring that he personally pay half the arbitration costs (more than $150,000). It found that he had misrepresented what a witness would say; falsely accused the defendant and its counsel of interfering with witnesses' testimony, maintaining false financial documents, and destroying evidence; improperly and secretly transcribed the telephone conversation with Liebowitz; unduly prolonged the hearings by repeating questions and raising spurious objections; pursued a frivolous age discrimination claim; and committed contempt of the panel by writing the AAA before the proceedings had terminated, making false and unsubstantiated charges against Liebowitz. Wisehart responded by moving in federal court to vacate this award, appending two memoranda by his arbitrator, Freeman, which he characterized as "dissents." But Freeman repudiated these "dissents," which he said Wisehart had misrepresented, and apologized to the defendant's arbitrator and counsel for giving them to Wisehart.

> I marked myself an idiot for believing he would act ethically. He has deliberately submitted quotes that he knew were not valid in order to give the reader the impression that this was currently my belief. I had refused to do what he asked so he fraudently [sic] submits this, aware that I had repudiated it. . . .

Judge Owen noted the parallels to both *Lipin* and *Lightfoot v. Union Carbide Corp.* (discussed below),[994] where Wisehart "in an apparent effort to evade an undesired conclusion, moved, without basis, to recuse Judge Harold Baer." When the defendant brought this case to Owen's attention, Wisehart responded by accusing the defendant's lawyer of "attempted extortion" for seeking to recover the arbitration costs awarded by the panel; Wisehart also revived his charge that MLB lawyer Christopher Parlo had engaged in an "entrapment conspiracy" in *Lipin*. Wisehart demanded treble damages. He accused Liebowitz of threatening to terminate the arbitration if he were not paid (but offered no evidence). He challenged Liebowitz's $2,000 per diem (which he had earlier accepted). He accused Liebowitz of bias, objecting that the defendant had paid the arbitrator's ongoing costs (but it was Wisehart who had demanded that), and offering as evidence the testimony of his own lawyer, Seham, who called

---

[994] 1997 U.S. Dist LEXIS 13279, No. 98 Civ. 6411, 1997 WL 5430766, at 2 n.2 (S.D.N.Y. Sept. 4, 1997), aff'd, 175 F.3d 1008 (2d Cir.), cert. denied, 145 L.Ed.2d 49, 120 S. Ct. 56 (1999).

Liebowitz "demonic and irrational" and "bizarre." (During this hearing Wisehart told Seham that the defendant's arbitrator, Kleinman, "said you are a joke.")

Owen found "not a scintilla of evidence before me to support any of these claims. . . ." "The argument of 'willful misconduct and misbehavior' by the arbitrators that Polin makes based on an affidavit of John W. Whittlesey, Esq., hardly needs comment. Whittlesey was a part-time law associate of Wisehart." Freeman himself said Liebowitz had been "impartial . . . if anything, initially very much, leaning toward one side, to give the Plaintiff every opportunity." Wisehart accused Kleinman, Liebowitz, and defense counsel of having "collaborated to destroy or incapacitate the law firm of WISEHART & KOCH." Owen concluded that Wisehart attacked Liebowitz in order "to destroy this arbitration which Wisehart saw was going against his client." Noting the parallel to Wisehart's success in provoking Moskowitz to recuse herself, Owen affirmed the sanctions.[995] Wisehart simultaneously moved for reconsideration and appealed but abandoned the latter when told it deprived the trial court of jurisdiction. Having "already found these claims to be utterly without support," Owen considered only the new elements "on the third go-around." He refused Wisehart's offer to prove Liebowitz's threats and deplored that "these continued allegations of foul play in the panel's conduct seem to be the distressing standard of approach here." Wisehart had now filed a "baseless irrelevant smearing attack on a young associate attorney" for the defendant. Owen denied the motion for reconsideration.[996] When Polin sued Wisehart for malpractice, the federal court rejected Wisehart's invocation of work-product immunity to resist Polin's discovery[997] and denied his motions for summary judgment for failure to state a cause of action and "unclean hands," as well as his motion for summary judgment for unpaid fees.[998]

Wisehart tangled with Weil Gotshal & Manges in several other cases, which did not figure in the disciplinary proceeding. When he sued the ARCGNY for discriminating against Henrietta Cooper, WGM had him disqualified.[999] Wisehart represented former Red Cross Personnel Director Edward Talvy in an employment discrimination case against the

---

[995] Polin v. Kellwood Co., 103 F. Supp. 2d 238 (S.D.N.Y. 2000).
[996] Polin v. Kellwood Co., 132 F. Supp. 2d 126 (S.D.N.Y. 2000).
[997] Polin v. Wisehart, 2002 WL 1033807 (S.D.N.Y.).
[998] Polin v. Wisehart, 2004 WL 1944721 (S.D.N.Y.).
[999] Noted in Talvy v. American Red Cross of Greater New York, 205 A.D.2d 143 (1st Dept 1994).

ARCGNY, Bender, and Mary Stanton, alleging that Stanton and Bender "harassed" Talvy for refusing to sign a "false and defamatory" statement about Lipin on July 13, 1989. After Wisehart persuaded the state trial court to disqualify WGM, the Appellate Division reversed.[1000] Wisehart represented six employees seeking $80 million in damages for employment discrimination from Leslie Fay. After a Bankruptcy Court denied his motion to withdraw the claims and decided against him, Wisehart challenged "almost every aspect" of the decision, including the award of nearly $11 million in fees and expenses to WGM as debtors' counsel, in what U.S. District Court Judge Rakoff called "blunderbuss fashion." The court found all his claims meritless.[1001]

Wisehart also refused to accept defeat in other cases, often responding to adverse rulings by attacking the decision makers. In November 1991, after initiating arbitration of an employment discrimination claim, he sued the employer. Although he told the arbitration panel "I intend to abide by the award or lack of award this panel comes up with," he refused to accept their unanimous adverse decision in September 1992. The court dismissed his claim as res judicata in January 1994.[1002]

After Wisehart won a $750,000 jury verdict against Union Carbide for employment discrimination, U.S. District Judge Harold Baer issued a remittitur to $75,000. On appeal the Second Circuit ordered Baer to offer plaintiff the alternative of a new trial.[1003] Following a pre-trial conference before the retrial, Wisehart moved to recuse Baer because the judge insisted the evidence did not support more than $75,000 damages, saying:

> What do you think I am going to do this time around? Don't you believe I still think $750,000 is way too much? Don't you think I thought about it before I reduced the first jury's award to $75,000? You've got to believe what I think. . . . What are you going to do here, just go around and around again?

Wisehart also objected to Baer's characterization of his appellate brief as a lot of "silliness" and "nonsense." Noting that Wisehart had filed a recusal motion before in this case and in at least four others, including Lipin, Baer found that Wisehart "has a peculiar habit of filing recusal

---

[1000] Id.
[1001] Falbaum v. Leslie Fay Companies, 222 B.R. 718 (S.D.N.Y. 1998).
[1002] Siegel v. Daiwa Securities Co. Ltd., 842 F. Supp. 1537 (S.D.N.Y. 1994).
[1003] Lightfoot v. Union Carbide Corp., 110 F.3d 898 (2d Cir. 1997).

motions ... often based on evidentiary or other rulings of the judge in question." This "practice calls into question either his good faith ... or his grasp of the applicable legal issues." Baer denied the recusal motion in September 1997.[1004] The second jury awarded only $20,000. Wisehart appealed again, seeking a new judge for the third trial.[1005] This time the Second Circuit was dismissive: his "principal contention need not detain us long, for it was rejected in *Lightfoot I*," and his "claim that the district judge should have recused himself is meritless." Wisehart petitioned for certiorari, urging the U.S. Supreme Court to use its supervisory power to disqualify Baer.[1006] In his reply brief he reiterated the bias claim, again offering the *ABAJ* article as "proof." He disparaged the Second Circuit's "unpublishable decision" as "apparently" written by Lucille Carr, a clerk. The Court denied certiorari.[1007]

After Wisehart won a $530,000 jury verdict for employment discrimination and rejected remittitur to $232,748, a second trial awarded only $190,000 in July 1996. Wisehart appealed, charging that the trial judge's "inappropriate behavior" conveyed "the impression that the Court held an unfavorable opinion of both plaintiff's case and his counsel." The Second Circuit agreed that "some of the sidebar colloquies plainly do indicate a degree of frustration (understandably, in light of the record) at the refusal of plaintiff's counsel, Wisehart, to comply with the court's prior rulings...." But it found that "all of the [opposing counsel's] objections were prompted by inappropriate arguments by Wisehart," and the court's own interruptions were "in response to plainly improper arguments." It dismissed the appeal in June 1998.[1008]

IX. Finality

On March 8, 2001, the Appellate Division confirmed the Hearing Panel report with respect to the sustained charges, sustained count three as well (that Wisehart had disregarded Moskowitz's order not to disclose the contents of the documents), and suspended him for two years.[1009] "Even as of

---

[1004] Lightfoot v. Union Carbide Corp., 1997 WL 543076 (S.D.N.Y.).
[1005] Brief for Plaintiff-Appellant, 1998 WL 34091879 (2d Cir.).
[1006] 1999 WL 33640697 (U.S.).
[1007] 528 U.S. 817 (1999).
[1008] Kirsch v. Fleet Street, Ltd., 148 F.3d 149 (2d Cir. 1998).
[1009] Matter of Wisehart, 281 A.D.2d. 23, 721 N.Y.S.2d 356 (1st Dept 2001); Cerisse Anderson, "Attorney Suspended for Two Years for 'Bizarre' Claims Against Judges," 3/9/2001 N.Y.L.J. 1 (col. 3).

a decade ago, Respondent had been practicing law for 35 years, and should have known better." The court rejected the Ninth Circuit's requirement of "objective malice."[1010] It quoted from the CPR Preamble: "Attacks such as respondent's 'derogatory, undignified and inexcusable' remarks ... tend to undermine 'the respect and confidence of the members of his profession and of the society which he serves' and will not be countenanced." The order was effective April 9.

But on March 28 Wisehart obtained a 30-day stay because of the still pending federal case. On April 16 he moved for leave to appeal on the grounds that the penalty was arbitrary and capricious, the decision was inconsistent with others, there was an error in applying collateral estoppel, and he was denied his rights to due process, a jury trial, free speech, and to be free of cruel and unusual punishment (citing *BMW v. Gore*[1011]). The suspension would last until he was 74.

> Judicial notice can be taken of the insuperable difficulties to be encountered by a 74-year-old lawyer attempting to make a comeback and resuming the practice of law in the highly competitive fast track that is characteristic of the practice of law in New York County.

The penalty was "much more drastic than such a penalty imposed upon a younger person with a longer career span and more career options available." His clients would suffer. Some "are the victims of terminations that occurred on the eve of a bankruptcy proceeding in which the members of the top management have recently been implicated in criminal financial fraud [presumably Leslie Fay]." Bratton's reply dismissed these arguments. A recent case held that disbarment was not cruel and unusual punishment.[1012] "Respondent was sanctioned for a unique combination of gross discovery abuses and misconduct vis-à-vis two judges, the seriousness of which he apparently continues to be unable or unwilling to grasp." Wisehart responded by accusing Bratton of "mischaracterize [sic] both the state of the record and my own state of mind."

> Mr. Bratton incorrectly asserts that "the seriousness" of the sanction imposed is something that I "apparently continue[]

[1010] Standing Committee on Discipline v. Yagman, 55 F.3d 1430 (9th Cir. 1995).
[1011] BMW of North America, Inc. v. Gore, 517 U.S. 559 (1996).
[1012] In re Smith, 123 F. Supp. 2d 351 (N.D. Tex. 2000).

to be unable or unwilling to grasp," and that in . . . seeking leave to appeal I seek "to groundlessly burden the Court."

The devastating effect of a punitive suspension on the career to which a 72-year-old lawyer has devoted his life can not be accurately or fairly characterized . . . to be a "groundless burden" in the context of a claim of violation of fundamental constitutional rights.

The suspension represented 40 percent of his "remaining worklife expectancy," compared with 5 percent for lawyers in their twenties, who could obtain other employment. "Also important is the stress factor. Stress is frequently identified by experts in cases [in] which I represent older people who have been terminated as the 'silent killer.'" He sought to relitigate whether he had violated Moskowitz's order. But the Appellate Division denied leave to appeal on May 24, 2001, ending a ten-year saga. On September 20 the Court of Appeals, on its own motion, dismissed his further attempts to appeal.[1013] He was suspended on October 10, 2001, and did not apply for readmission.[1014]

Joan Lipin graduated from New York Law School in 2005.[1015] Even before that she had begun contributing to the "Attorney Professionalism Forum" in the *New York State Bar Association Journal*, responding to lawyers' requests for ethical guidance. Both of the cases she chose echoed her own. The first lawyer had filed a civil rights complaint raising "extremely sensitive" issues touching on "a continuing scandal" in which some of the defendants were attorneys.[1016] An attorney for one defendant threatened the writer with disciplinary sanctions. Lipin commended him for "standing firm in order to protect your client's First Amendment rights and interests, and in accordance with your own First Amendment duties." Withdrawing the lawsuit in response to such threats would itself have violated the disciplinary rules. "This is what John Adams refused to do in agreeing to defend the British soldiers in Boston when no one else would take their case." The lawyer was obligated "to represent her [client] zealously."

[1013] 9/24/2001 N.Y.L.J. 18 (col. 1).
[1014] He did respond to the U.S. Supreme Court's notice to show cause why he should not be disbarred from practice before it, but it still did so on February 7, 2002.
[1015] The New York County Lawyer published its congratulations to her as a law school member in its April 2005 issue.
[1016] 76(2) New York State Bar Journal 56 (February 2004).

A grievance against the threatening lawyer "may be in order." "In conclusion, your fitness as a lawyer should be commended." The second inquiry was by a law firm associate whose supervising partner directed him to engage in "file cleansing," electronically deleting material the client's general counsel had failed to produce during discovery on the advice of predecessor outside counsel.[1017] Lipin found the answer "simple." Such "improper" behavior "carries substantial risk for you, your firm, and the client's own legal staff." Any lawyer who engaged in such behavior would be subject to professional discipline and criminal prosecution and personally liable for treble damages and attorneys' fees. When I contacted Lipin, she sent the above comments but said it might not be ethical to discuss her own case "since the litigation remains pending."[1018]

X. The Pitfalls of Partisanship

The Hearing Panel called this case "a tragedy of epic proportions." The purloined papers showed that Lipin had strong claims of sexual harassment, sexual discrimination, and wrongful discharge. Justice Moskowitz initially seemed sympathetic, agreeing to court supervision of discovery in response to WGM's intransigence, ordering Fletcher's deposition, and appointing a commission after she fled to California.[1019] The judge appeared to blame WGM for much of the procedural bickering, accusing it of running up the meter against an adversary who could not bill *his* client. She berated WGM for violating her document production orders, dismissing their objections as "too late. Too late." She agreed with Wisehart that Baer had obstructed Fletcher's deposition in California and called Baer's objection to Wisehart's motion to produce "ridiculous." She ordered the Red Cross to produce employee drug abuse records, required Baer to submit an affidavit that there were none, and refused to reschedule a Red Cross employee's deposition. Birnbaum, by contrast, was openly hostile to Wisehart. At the crucial hearing (at Baer's instance) he rebuked Lipin for commenting and brushed off Wisehart's question as "self-evident," provoking Wisehart to tell Birnbaum "to disqualify yourself."

[1017] 78(6) New York State Bar Journal 48 (July/August 2006).
[1018] The defendants made repeated motions to dismiss the third federal action and also sought sanctions. The case was dismissed on March 29, 2002. Lipin appealed; the last docket entry on Pacer is dated May 17, 2004.
[1019] In the Columbia Law School class of 1966, Moskowitz would have been one of less than a dozen women. Throughout her career she has championed women lawyers and judges.

CHAPTER 7

But Moskowitz also was losing patience with Wisehart: "I don't want to have any more motion papers. I have been motioned to death in this case. . . . I am not going to sit here and go through this question by question. I don't have the energy to do it, and I don't think that's what a judge is supposed to do." Yet in the hearing about the purloined papers she expressed solicitude when Lipin became upset, sided with her against Jacoby about how she got the papers, and took umbrage at Jacoby's threat to go to the Appellate Division.

Wisehart's behavior typifies what David Shapiro calls the "paranoid style."[1020] The paranoid "looks at the world with fixed and preoccupying expectation, and he searches repetitively, and only, for confirmation of it." His attention is "not only unusually acute and intense, but also unusually active" and "continuous" in the search for a "clue." The "suspicious person can be at the same time absolutely right in his perception and absolutely wrong in his judgment." He "loses a sense of proportion." Because "it is necessary to maintain rigid self-directedness . . . 'giving in' to external pressure or authority can [not] be tolerated." The paranoid are "extremely aware of power and rank, relative position, superior and inferior, who is boss and who is obliged to take orders, or who is in a position to humiliate whom." They "are acutely concerned with the evaluation these people will make of them and are acutely sensitive to rebuff." Some "seem to live a constant round of battles with a series of bosses. . . ."

This case illustrates many of these traits. Relations between opposing counsel quickly deteriorated. Wisehart and his colleagues (Purves, Whittlesey, and Seham) seem to have shared the resentment common among small firm practitioners toward the resources, pretensions, and condescension of the Wall Street giants (WGM and MLB). Wisehart and Seham had shared an office as associates at Chadbourne Parke; they may have resented not making partner at a firm that today has more than 400 lawyers in 12 locations. Seham argued the need to preserve solo practitioners, who had a different "response time" and should not be judged by "artificial, grandiose standards." Wisehart raised equal protection objections to the Hearing Panel report because the DDC had rejected Lipin's grievance against the WGM lawyers. He portrayed himself as one of those "small firm lawyers who on a pro bono basis represent clients engaged in civil rights litigation against the Goliath law firms." (But of course he worked on a contingency basis, not pro bono.) He tangled with WGM and

---

[1020] Shapiro (1999: chap. 3).

MLB in other cases. Wisehart believed WGM had instructed Fletcher to destroy files implicating Bender the day after he fired Lipin and had engineered Fletcher's flight to California to evade being deposed; Wisehart sought the firm's time records to prove this. Both sides moved for sanctions as early as October 1990. They did so again in May 1991, accusing each other of obstruction, intransigence and argumentativeness. The defendants accused Lipin of tampering with and destroying documents. Wisehart sought sanctions against WGM for a *three-day* delay in producing documents, sneering that "it must be in their firm's operating manual."

By June 1991 WGM lawyers were openly laughing at Wisehart and mocking him for not listening. At the crucial hearing Baer declared: "Your obnoxiousness is beyond all understanding. . . ." That afternoon Wisehart provoked Baer to leave the EBT room with his witness and ultimately to terminate the deposition prematurely. At the July 8 hearing on the purloined papers Wisehart gratuitously attacked both the defendants and their lawyers. Three days later Jacoby called Wisehart's behavior the "most serious and gross abuse of judicial process that I have encountered in my career as an attorney" and accused him (twice) of replacing the "rule of law" with "the rule of the jungle," the equivalent of no rules, no control. (Moskowitz later employed similar language in dismissing the case.) Jacoby urged that Wisehart be disqualified from representing Lipin and the case dismissed. At the time, defense counsel believed Lipin had stolen the papers from their counsel table after Wisehart deliberately provoked Baer to storm out of the EBT room. Wisehart denounced this accusation as a lie. After Moskowitz dismissed the case, Wisehart claimed that Baer had threatened his associate, Prince. Baer admitted warning Prince he might be out of a job if Wisehart were disciplined. Engaging in tit-for-tat, Wisehart sought to disqualify WGM in the federal action on the ground that its lawyers had deliberately misplaced the papers and had a conflict of interest; he also named them as defendants so he could call them as witnesses, forcing disqualification.

As these examples suggest, Wisehart had difficulty maintaining appropriate boundaries with people. His heart was anything but wise. He transformed opposing counsel into personal enemies. He identified very strongly with Lipin, hiring her as a paralegal, whose principal (perhaps sole) responsibility was her own case. Although he insisted that she had attended the crucial hearing as a party (making her alone responsible for appropriating and retaining the papers), she had already completed the factual analysis of her case for him and was listed as a paralegal in

Chapter 7

Martindale-Hubbell. Lipin had been referred by Ned Purves, a mutual friend, who was of counsel to Wisehart. Wisehart relied on Purves—hardly a disinterested spectator—for advice on what to do with the purloined papers. (Purves may even have expected a cut of Wisehart's contingent fee for the referral.) Wisehart had Purves represent him in the contempt proceeding and later write an affidavit for him. Wisehart sought to have his own lawyer, Wall, testify for him in the penalty phase. He had Seham, one of his oldest friends, represent him in the disciplinary hearing.

Wisehart adduced elaborate rationalizations for using the papers. The defendants and their lawyers had been obligated to produce them on discovery. Wisehart already knew their contents. The papers were not marked "confidential." They undermined Bender's and Fletcher's claims of privilege by showing that the ARCGNY knew of their affair. The contents showed that Bender had committed perjury and WGM had counseled Bender and Fletcher to destroy Lipin's papers. They upset Lipin, who had acted independently. It was a "universal truth" that "no person could or would avoid reading defamatory statements about themselves that have been placed in front of them...." The decisions to take and keep the papers were made by Lipin as a client, not by Wisehart or his paralegal. (But explaining why he let Lipin bring the papers into his office on July 5 rather than July 3, he said: "As far as I was concerned, I could rely on her statement. After all, she worked for me." And Seham referred to Lipin as Wisehart's "assistant.") How Lipin obtained the papers was privileged information. Wisehart refused to reveal it in order to conceal Baer's negligence from his firm. The defendants had left the papers on the table either negligently[1021] or intending to entrap the plaintiff. Lipin took the papers in plain view of opposing counsel, who could have stopped her or later sought their return. (In fact, she read them surreptitiously, slipping them into a folder on her lap; defense counsel did not know they were missing until Wisehart surprised them four days later.) Wisehart could not give the papers to Birnbaum, who had left for vacation (but he could have lodged them with the court clerk). Wisehart was obligated to bring evidence of WGM's conflict of interest to the attention of the American National Red Cross (but he actually sought to turn the ANRC against Bender and the ARCGNY). He claimed WGM should pay damages to the

---

[1021] That Wisehart could draw a highly strained analogy to cases where a party negligently includes privileged information in response to discovery suggests how badly he wanted to believe he was entitled to the papers.

ANRC (but of course had no standing to make that claim). He had made diligent efforts to get independent advice on what to do with the papers, resorting to Purves only when two other lawyers (wisely) turned him down. Wisehart portrayed his use of the papers and Lipin's threat to publicize them in order to extract damages from the defendants as a good faith effort to follow Moskowitz's direction to the parties to try to settle the case. He claimed he had brought the papers to Moskowitz's attention by using them to blackmail WGM, who promptly complained to Moskowitz. Wisehart quoted from the documents in his motion papers for the July 8 hearing, thereby exposing Moskowitz to them. He claimed that her permission to use the contents of the purloined papers in appealing her dismissal also authorized him to use them in filing a federal case (before the appeal was heard). He sought to distract attention from his own behavior by arguing that the ARCGNY had violated ANRC rules and that defense counsel based their case on "fictitious" facts. He justified filing the federal lawsuit on the ground that WGM had been mistaken about where and when Lipin had taken the papers. Dismissal "takes away a Constitutional right of my client."

These rationalizations were not only incoherent, incorrect, and inconsistent but also stumbled over inconvenient facts. Wisehart directed Lipin to lie to Baer that she had taken the documents by accident—which she rightly refused to do. Although Wisehart had promised in court (with Lipin's acquiescence) to sequester the documents over the July 4 holiday, he allowed Lipin to keep her set and instructed her to memorize them. When he did "sequester" them, Lipin had a key to the cabinet.

As several participants observed, Wisehart's typical response when cornered was to attack and seek to disqualify the decision maker on extraneous but scandalous grounds, in order to try again in another forum. In *Polin* he moved to disqualify the independent arbitrator on the basis of serious unfounded accusations and misrepresentations of his own arbitrator's views. In *Lightfoot* he *twice* moved to recuse the judge and then sought a different judge in a third trial. A month after taking the WGM papers he moved to recuse Birnbaum. He objected to the Special Referee's rulings on discovery as "too restrictive" and criticized his failure to control "disruption and interference" and "irrelevant colloquy" by the defendants' attorneys, as well as his ex parte contacts, usurpation of Wisehart's role in questioning deponents and "bias in tolerating repetitive tactics by counsel for defendants." Wisehart even raised a 16-month-old incident in which Birnbaum had "solicited" contributions from and attendance by both

Chapter 7

counsel at a dinner honoring him. Wisehart's motion to recuse Moskowitz from hearing the contempt proceeding was replete with reckless accusations: she failed to deal with the defendants' lawyers' misconduct and had ex parte contact with them; her dismissal of the complaint demonstrated bias; she displayed a "distraught manner," "carelessness," "evident unpreparedness," and "excessive and abusive language." She made "clearly" false statements, "clearly" attempted to suppress facts, "clearly" misunderstood the defendants' strategy, and was guilty of "punitive intimidation." He had the chutzpah to complain that she knew the contents of the purloined papers, when it was *he* who had revealed them to her in violation of *her* order. He advanced the first of several conspiracy theories, claiming that politics was the "trout in the milk." Moskowitz had been seeking a regular appointment as Supreme Court Justice; Andrew Cuomo was a Democratic heavy who wanted ANRC support for his gubernatorial aspirations; WGM's Wolff was the intermediary between them. Moskowitz's dismissal of his action was "a knee-jerk reaction necessitated by the demands of political expediency." Lipin's affidavit went further, in language Wisehart condoned and probably helped craft. (Inverting the conventional lawyer-client relationship, Wisehart consistently made Lipin his mouthpiece in order to evade responsibility—and both judicial sanctions and bar discipline—for her words.)

> Justice Moskowitz has despised or abhorred the plea of the afflicted; she has hid her face from me; she has not heard when I cried unto her, but only paid attention only [sic] to the evil-doers who encircle me . . . in the evident expectation that I would silently depart.

Lipin invoked her status as the child of Holocaust survivors against a Jewish judge and analogized Jacoby calling her "dangerously crazy" to Hitler's "pretext for ridding himself of the Jews as political opponents by sending them away to concentration camps and gas chambers in Germany during the Nazi period."

When Moskowitz rejected Wisehart's allegations of political bias he just renewed the motion, accusing her of mental imbalance caused by the cancer diagnosis and imminent treatment. Perhaps because this had the desired effect, Wisehart raised Moskowitz's cancer again when he appealed to the Court of Appeals 30 months later—knowing Chief Judge Kaye had campaigned with her against breast cancer. Indeed, he argued that this made it impossible for Kaye to participate. This time Lipin went even further. Claiming to be a "trained health care professional" (when her degree was in *management*), she called Moskowitz "disoriented, distracted, and irrational." The judge was "agitated, given to jerky and uncertain motions, and seemed clearly hostile, aggressive." A special master had called her "La Loca." Moskowitz "was visibly out of control and hysterical."[1022] Wisehart moved to recuse DDC Hearing Panel chair Greig, because as convenor of the Democratic Judicial Convention at which Lipin was an alternate delegate, Greig was guilty of "political manipulation," "political intrigue," and "malice." When Judge Sand stayed the federal court proceedings, Wisehart moved to recuse him. When Wisehart lost that motion he simply filed the suit again. Wisehart moved to reargue the federal court's stay (pending resolution of the state court proceedings) on the ground that the Second Circuit "might be biased against [Lipin] in light of her distant familial relationship with another litigant who has appeared before his court."

Wisehart seemed unable to separate feelings from lawyering. Just as he overidentified with Lipin and could not distinguish his adversarial stance toward opposing counsel from personal enmity, so he picked unnecessary and counterproductive fights with judges. (Rather than being merely expressive, some of these may have been calculated attempts to provoke overreactions he could use strategically.) When Moskowitz denied receiving Wisehart's papers, he complained that the guard at the door prevented him from delivering them and then disbelieved the judge's denial. When she refused to listen to further argument about her jurisdiction to hear the contempt motion he simply continued to cite cases and accused her of not reading his papers. In his second recusal motion he called her "cursory, flippant attitude" an "affront" to judicial standards. When she cut him off he insulted her:

> I insist on being heard. If you are going to send me to The Tombs because I want to be heard, you go ahead and do it.
>
> It says "In God We Trust" up there. We do not trust in this Court as it is presently constituted.

[1022] I, too, observed the striking contrast between Moskowitz's very neat, legible handwriting in her October 30, 1990, order concerning discovery and the almost illegible scrawl of her January 9, 1992, bench order dismissing the case.

Chapter 7

That did the trick. Moskowitz retired to chambers to collect herself. When she returned she denounced his accusations as "so scurrilous and so baseless and so ridiculous that I cannot even begin to be fair to any parties in this case after reading this." His "off-the-wall allegations" were "so egregious that I really can't even see. . . . " His "screaming and his loss of control in open court, and his addressing of the court in the way he did" made it impossible for her to be "fair to either side." Wisehart repeated the tactic 30 months later when he said the Court of Appeals had "aligned itself on the side of a sexual abuser and harasser and its decision will undoubtedly increase the number and extent of the depravity of such miscreants. . . . " Seham (Wisehart's lawyer and friend) moved to dismiss the disciplinary proceeding on the ground that staff counsel "always" used a "provocative hysterical characterization to gratuitously degrade the practitioner with over forty years of distinguished experience." He offered to vouch for the truthfulness of Lipin's affidavit. He offered Wisehart's original lawyer, Patrick Wall, as an expert witness about "the propriety of Wisehart's actions." Asked to explain the relevance of such testimony, Seham said *Wall* would demonstrate its relevance. He "alone among the sea of humanity knows what this case is all about." Wisehart offered as evidence of arbitrator misconduct the affidavit of Whittlesey, who was of counsel to his own firm.

Wisehart refused to admit defeat. To the very end he denied there had ever been a final judgment about his right to the purloined papers: "we have a dispute." In Justice Schoenfeld's words, he could not "take 'no' for an answer" or accept that "litigation, like life itself, must one day come to a close." Instead, Wisehart simply started over. The result was "an unfortunate example of litigation run amok." Cited for contempt, he relitigated Lipin's case against the ARCGNY. He did the same in the recusal motion. He contended that Moskowitz's dismissal of the case stripped her of jurisdiction to hear a contempt motion for his violation of the dismissal order. He sought a jury trial of the contempt. When Moskowitz refused to recuse herself he simply refiled the motion, reargued the underlying case, and called her denial of the first motion evidence of bias and thus grounds for his second. When the federal court stayed its proceedings pending resolution of the state court case, Wisehart moved to reargue but then appealed without waiting for the outcome. He moved to lift the stay on the (irrelevant) ground of Moskowitz's recusal. When Judge Sand refused, he moved to recuse the judge. When that was denied, he again moved to lift the stay. When that was denied he started a second federal action, now adding the defense lawyers as defendants. When Judge Sand dismissed his action with prejudice on the ground of res judicata because it was filed even before Wisehart perfected his state appeal, Wisehart appealed to the Second Circuit and moved to reargue its affirmation.

In Wisehart's disciplinary hearing his counsel, Seham, sought to relitigate both the dismissal of Lipin's civil claim and Moskowitz's initial refusal to recuse herself. In his motion to submit additional exhibits, Seham denied that Wisehart had stolen the papers and even that they belonged to WGM. He referred to them as a "sourceless unidentifiable pile of papers," "four inches of sliced garbage," "somehow-documents," "ordinary—less than ordinary documents." "We only have an explosion of faith that these are real and that these implicate Wisehart at all." Making the inevitable motion for a rehearing on liability, Seham, for the first time, claimed lack of notice of the charges. "Mr. Wisehart continues to believe that his acts were not wrong and the deletions in the original charges are proof that the accusations are not always right." Seham sought to introduce the purloined papers, as though their contents affected the ethical violation. He started all over again in the penalty phase: "what was done that was wrong?" The chair reminded him that Wisehart had been found guilty of four charges. But Seham blithely persisted: "Once you exculpate Mr. Wisehart from liability in taking the papers in question, then it necessarily follows that the other events have to be examined." The Hearing Panel responded.

> Green: But this panel found that Mr. Wisehart violated. . . .
>
> Seham: No, I don't think that's quite true . . . in making your findings—and in our favor, you necessarily come to some other conclusions . . . that Wisehart had no purpose, no objective, had no utilization of the documents and in fact turned them over as soon as he possibly could.
>
> Chair: That's wrong . . . the record is clear that Ms. Lipin stole the documents. And that—
>
> Seham: Well for instance that, that comment of your [sic] is staggering to me, because I don't find anything in the record . . . that makes that finding.

He agreed with the Panel that he sought to relitigate Wisehart's mens rea, denouncing the proceeding as a bill of attainder. Justice Ciparick's

CHAPTER 7

decision not to hold Wisehart in contempt was collateral estoppel with respect to disciplinary proceedings.

In response to the Hearing Panel report, Wisehart filed a *third* federal lawsuit, this time adding Greig as a defendant and reiterating two rejected arguments: Greig's bias (raised in the recusal motion) and the DDC's lack of jurisdiction. He accused Greig of violating Lipin's First Amendment rights, threatening her, and subjecting her to cruel and unusual punishment (presumably by denying her Wisehart's continued representation). He baselessly blamed Greig for filing the grievance, attributing it to the panel chair's alleged personal animus against Lipin. Accusing Greig of being a "political puppet" of WGM and MLB (which allegedly retained him), Wisehart sought discovery about how he had been chosen. Declaring that the disciplinary proceeding interfered with federal court jurisdiction (because the DDC sought to enhance Wisehart's penalty for filing a third federal action), he sought to enjoin it. Like many lawyers charged in disciplinary proceedings, Wisehart argued denial of equal protection, here on the ground that the DDC had rejected Lipin's October 1992 grievance against Baer and Jacoby based on their (erroneous but understandable and hardly unethical) belief that she had taken the documents from the EBT room rather than Birnbaum's conference room. Wisehart persisted in what Judge Rakoff called his "blunderbuss" approach to discrediting adverse decisions: the lay member had resigned from the panel, and the procedure had changed after his case. In his motion to disaffirm the Hearing Panel decision, Wisehart called the theft charge a "hyperbolic" and "provocative hysterical characterization." He sought to relitigate the collateral estoppel effect of the state court judgment, accused the Hearing Panel of not having read the documents, and criticized it for not viewing the conference room where Lipin took the papers. He argued that Wall (his own lawyer) thought he had acted properly (testimony the Hearing Panel refused to admit). He accused McInerney of not reading the petition to affirm before signing it and sought discovery about who had prepared it. He claimed that the motion to affirm interfered with his ability to respond to the four defendants (including Greig), who had moved for sanctions in the third federal action. His office was too small to deal with Greig's simultaneous motions to affirm the Hearing Panel report and to dismiss the federal claims against him (but it was *Wisehart* who had filed the civil action—for the fourth time). Wisehart used the third federal action to obtain a stay of the Appellate Division judgment.

Most people find it hard to admit error; for some lawyers it is almost impossible. As late as 1997 Wisehart was utterly unrepentant: he had done the right thing; gotten "a second opinion or a third opinion" about his actions, to which he "had to give a lot of weight" because it was from Purves, who had referred Lipin; discussed those actions with opposing counsel (by trying to blackmail them into settling in order to avoid exposure of Bender's sexual misconduct and the ARCGNY's condonation); and did so in response to Moskowitz's pressure to work out disagreements. He constantly devised new justifications: he was using the documents to prevent a violation of 42 U.S.C. §1985. He had "lots of remorse" but only that "you disagree with me in certain respects." "[Y]ou can't be perfect in making decisions like this." After expressing that limited remorse he filed the third federal lawsuit, making accusations against Greig totally inconsistent with accepting his own wrongdoing. In the penalty phase he continued to maintain that the Panel "haven't really decided on entrapment" and "we have a dispute" about the facts. Its refusal to examine the documents was a "denial of due process." He advanced multiple reasons why he should receive special treatment: his sole practice and his age (which made stress more dangerous and loss of the remaining years of practice more costly). When Bratton rightly observed that Wisehart still could not acknowledge the seriousness of his wrongdoing and groundlessly burdened courts with pointless appeals, Wisehart reenacted his solipsism: he recognized the seriousness of the *penalty*; *he* did not experience the appeal as a groundless burden. He rewrote history in pursuit of mitigation. His work as house counsel for American Airlines and Railway Express Agency was "public service." He took employee discrimination cases at a loss (in fact, he earned a contingent fee on the often large verdicts). His only interest was in his clients and the fact that *they* would suffer, not he. But then he argued that dismissal of Lipin's claim and with it his contingent fee was "more than enough punishment." He had suffered enough in defending himself against the grievance, devoting $500,000 of his own time to the case. That professional colleagues learned of the disciplinary proceedings through Lexis publication of the cases *he had brought* rendered anything else "duplicate punishment" and "not constitutional." Lawyers did not have to be "always right" in "spur of the moment" decisions; "certitude" was "impossible." "[Y]ou can't be perfect in making decisions like this." Given its unique circumstances, the case could have no precedential value. He was a church elder who weekly asked "forgiveness of sins." But forgiveness requires confession, the one thing Wisehart could not do.

Chapter 8

Restoring Trust

Reading the disciplinary cases presented above could easily breed cynicism about the possibility of changing such behavior. All but one of the lawyers were convinced they had done nothing wrong. Few could have been identified as potential rule violators in advance; indeed, all but one had practiced law successfully, some for many decades. The disciplinary process not only failed to reform them, it actually made them more self-righteous. I do not see these stories, however, as grounds for despair, for resigned acceptance that any barrel will contain a few bad apples. The costs of lawyer betrayal are too high for clients, the legal profession, the legal system, society, and even the lawyers themselves. I wrote these case studies in the belief that only by understanding the social, structural, and psychological conditions of lawyer deviance can we take effective steps to rebuild the trust that is the essential foundation of our legal system. The responses to all forms of deviance (street and white-collar crime, terrorism) too often fall into two common traps: more regulation ("there oughta be a law") and harsher penalties ("lock 'em up and throw away the key"). This final chapter looks for alternatives. I begin with an overview of the troubling behaviors, seeking commonalities across the cases. Then I consider conventional modes of social control: tinkering with the norms,

CHAPTER 8

inculcating them more effectively, identifying potential deviants, and deterring violations. On the basis of these case studies, as well as the literature on lawyer discipline (and deviance generally), I have become convinced that the potential gains from ex post social control are severely limited. Therefore, I conclude by exploring a variety of structural changes that might reduce the opportunities and incentives for lawyers to betray trust.

I. What Went Wrong

I have borrowed this heading from Lawrence Dubin's 1985 video profiling four disciplined lawyers, which was one inspiration for this book.[1023] Like his, my cases are very diverse, in both the actions committed and the underlying character traits. That insight, of course, is the starting point of modern criminology. Ethical rules, like criminal laws (indeed, all laws), are socially constructed categories, which sweep into their nets a wide variety of highly disparate behaviors. For each crime, there is no typical perpetrator, no phrenological or sociopathic marker. Yet there are some revealing similarities among actors and actions (in both how they practiced law and how they responded to the disciplinary process).

Occam told us to keep it simple. *Cherchez l'argent* is at least as good a rule of thumb as its racier original. Look for greed or need (which often are indistinguishable).[1024] Almost all lawyers practice in order to make money.[1025] (I provoke embarrassed laughter when I kid my first-year students that most are in law school because they want a secure place in the middle class and can't add or stand the sight of blood.) All of the lawyers I studied were upwardly mobile (except perhaps Cardozo). Despite an undistinguished academic record, Kreitzer had constructed a money-making machine that used inexperienced associates and lay employees to settle large numbers of tort claims at minimal cost. When cash flow became a problem, he paid insurance claims adjusters kickbacks to expedite payment. The recurrence of his cancer and the burden of his children's college tuition may have increased his need. Drawn to the Big Apple's bright lights, Muto found he could make more as a "per diem" lawyer than he had ever earned upstate and quickly saw he could double or triple that income by working for "travel agencies." Furtzaig was motivated to generate

---

[1023] Dubin (1985).
[1024] This is a less jargon-ridden, but perhaps more faithful, way to capture the behavior Donald Cressey (1953) called "non-shareable financial problems."
[1025] Chusmir (1984) (lawyers have high "need achievement"); Houston (1992).

money for his firm, not himself. Indeed, to forestall the wrath of his demanding father figure, Warren Estis, he spent $60,000 of his own money to resolve mistakes he had made by taking on too much responsibility. Cardozo and Brashich chose to settle Babette Hecht Rose's trust dispute in a way they believed would entitle them to a contingent fee: a third of her $1.75 million. Yet Cardozo conceded he would have claimed in quantum meruit even if his client had lost. "I don't work for nothing. Not with this kind of money involved." Brashich could not (or would not) comply with a court order to repay Ljubica Callahan $263,000. Byler urgently needed Morgan's $53,000 IRS refund to pay work and household expenses. Byler and Brashich were constantly trying to raise their hourly rates. Wisehart took Lipin's case on a contingent fee (as he must have done for most of his employment discrimination clients). Stonewalling by the Red Cross and its lawyers forced him to invest thousands of hours in discovery. He had to win in order to collect; by establishing both liability and perhaps punitive damages, the smoking gun in the purloined papers promised he would win big.

The lawyers' motives, however, were by no means purely mercenary. Law is a helping profession (despite what critics say). Lawyers offer unconditional loyalty to clients, just as doctors and therapists do to patients, soldiers to their country, and priests to penitents. Lord Brougham famously wrote that the advocate "knows but one person in all the world, and that person is his client." David Melinkoff depicted lawyers responding to "the saddest of all human cries: 'Who will help me?'" Charles Fried defined the lawyer as "friend."[1026] Most lawyers come to believe in most of their clients (if not in everything those clients say).[1027] Law practice would be intolerable otherwise. Lawyers derive psychic benefits from client dependence. They come to want, and expect, gratitude. A divorce client said of a letter that her lawyer had written to her estranged husband's lawyer, "It kind of let me feel that finally . . . I'd found a knight in shining armor."[1028] Babette Hecht told her son Toby that she "loved Ben [Cardozo] to death." Toby agreed that his mother saw Brashich and Cardozo as "knights on white horses." Deborah mocked them as her mother's "latest sympaticos." During my own year practicing family law, I was struck by the transference of my (female) clients both to me and to the (male) judges who granted their divorces.

[1026] All these are discussed critically in Luban (1984).
[1027] Robert Nelson (1985) found that large-firm lawyers rarely perceive fundamental moral conflicts with their clients.
[1028] Sarat & Felstiner (1986).

Chapter 8

Muto expressed the lawyer's need most poignantly:

> Virtually every one of my clients is overjoyed and happy with my services. There's no greater feeling than seeing a man's case being granted and having him shake my hand and saying she-she, thank you in Chinese—bowing to me and just grabbing my hand. It's heartening to take a walk through Chinatown as I did with my daughter a couple of weeks ago on a Sunday afternoon, and going into a store and having someone come up to me and shake my hand and saying thank you, Muto. Thank you, thank you, lawyer.

Kreitzer's personal injury victims depended on him to secure their often desperately needed compensation. Byler derived enormous satisfaction from helping his good friend Morgan, displaying both his technical expertise and dedication. He expected gratitude in return, not defiance, threats from Morgan's brother, a disciplinary complaint, and a lawsuit. Babette and three of her children unquestioningly paid Cardozo and Brashich the $375,000 they demanded. Ljubica was so grateful to Brashich that she compromised his $263,000 debt for a conditional $75,000 and never even sought to recover that. Lawyers threatened with discipline generalize the dependence of clients to argue that they are performing an essential service to society, which will suffer most if they are suspended or disbarred.

Some lawyers take identification with clients to an extreme. Wisehart and Lipin became a *folie à deux*. Wisehart hired Lipin as a paralegal in her own lawsuit. He passionately championed her cause, expressing his strong emotional investment through repeated attacks on opposing counsel, Referee, and judges. At the same time, Wisehart hid behind Lipin: *she* took the papers; *she* should tell opposing counsel it had been a mistake; *she* made the copies; *she* kept one for herself, which *she* might release to the press. He put the most scurrilous accusations against Moskowitz into *Lipin's* mouth in order to evade responsibility.

Once these lawyers committed themselves to an action, they found it difficult to change course. Instead, they constructed an alternative reality, which made their conduct acceptable, laudable, even imperative. This often required profound self-deception. Kreitzer insisted that he diligently pursued his clients' interests. Muto maintained that he did quality work for grateful clients and was praised by judges—even that he could get on a plane. Both denied that their cases required any more work than they invested.

Byler convinced himself that Morgan had assigned him the entire refund. He was so self-righteous he could not even acknowledge Morgan's disagreement. Byler offered his representation of Moor-Jankowski as evidence of a client grateful for high quality work—even though Moor-Jankowski challenged his fee! Even after being disciplined for his representation of Babette Hecht, Brashich invoked it as justification for the fee he charged Ljubica. Wisehart's rationalizations for retaining and using the papers did not pass the laugh test.

Many of these lawyers blamed others. Kreitzer and Muto sought to shift responsibility to uncooperative clients for their own failure to pursue cases vigorously, file papers in a timely manner, and appear at hearings. Muto even claimed that clients sent impersonators, although he could not explain why. Byler sought to discredit Morgan as a chronic tax evader—precisely the problem for which Morgan had hired Byler. Kreitzer blamed subordinates for neglect and mistakes, even employees he instructed to engage in unauthorized practice of law. Several lawyers accused judges of misconduct. Muto cited immigration judges' different rates in granting asylum and insisted that some disliked him personally (true) and treated him unfairly (false). Brashich assailed Emanuelli and had a character witness testify that all upstate surrogate judges were biased against New York City lawyers. And Wisehart systematically moved to recuse *every* judge who had ruled against him or might do so, concocting bizarre conspiracy theories about their alleged biases.

The most striking trait shared by these otherwise diverse lawyers—and the most surprising, given their professional identity—was their conviction that they were above the law. Kreitzer felt entitled to pay kickbacks for settlements because other lawyers did so. Muto felt no obligation to appear at hearings if he would have to drive long distances. He expected judges to give special consideration for his fear of flying, even though he did not disclose it. He felt no obligation to file papers on time or even to seek an extension. He claimed special treatment because his mother was dying but told no one. Furtzaig forged legal documents he knew would be discovered, perhaps in order to be caught—a form of professional suicide, fortunately less catastrophic than his contemplated leap from an office window. Brashich and Byler defied orders to repay disputed fees. Wisehart was the most colorful:

> I insist on being heard. If you are going to send me to The Tombs because I want to be heard, you go ahead and do it.

CHAPTER 8

> It says "In God We Trust" up there. We do not trust in this Court as it is presently constituted.

This had its calculated effect of so infuriating Moskowitz that she recused herself. Many of these lawyers remained convinced of their righteousness throughout the disciplinary hearing. The ethical mandate to advocate vigorously creates a *déformation professionelle*, making it impossible for lawyers, like bulldogs, to let go. The very traits and technical skills that made Byler, Brashich, and Wisehart effective lawyers also made them tragically self-destructive before the DDC.

II. Character Is Destiny

Ever since Heraclitus, writers have commented on the persistence of personality.[1029] Lawyers typically become embroiled in disciplinary proceedings in the middle of their careers, not at the beginning. Habit is their tragic flaw, not inexperience.[1030] None of the lawyers in this book was a novice; all had practiced more than 10 years, some more than 40. The acts for which they were disciplined were not aberrational. Muto repeatedly promised to reform—beginning with his application for readmission following suspension—but could not do so. Only a bureaucratic structure could correct his fatal disorganization. Kreitzer's lawyer protested that many clients were *not* complaining—but that hardly proved they had been well served. The inevitable errors Furtzaig made as a result of overwork forced him to engage in ever more compromising cover-ups. He so feared displeasing his father figure that he seriously contemplated suicide. Brashich's treatment of Ljubica bore troubling similarities to the way he had just treated Babette. He bragged to me that because he was a Serb he always fought. Byler's fee dispute with Morgan resembled his earlier dispute with Moor-Jankowski. In both of those, and throughout the disciplinary proceeding, he was compulsively self-righteous. And Wisehart constantly attacked the integrity of judges, before, during, and after his representation of Lipin.

The legal profession and the legal academy have a limited repertoire of solutions to these problems. First, they tweak the rules (an unsurprising

---

[1029] Daicoff (1997–1998); Regan (2007). A recent study of medical malpractice claims concluded that "physician characteristics can be used to distinguish between more and less malpractice-claims-prone physicians": Rolph et al. (2007: 149).

[1030] For a phenomenological study of the contrasting habitus of two lawyers, see Scheffer (2007).

RESTORING TRUST

choice for lawyers). The ABA and state and specialist bars devote an extraordinary amount of energy to revising the official norms.[1031] Almost all the voluminous academic writing on the subject addresses the content of those norms. As a common law lawyer, I acknowledge, of course, that there are cases at the margins, which clarify and modify the rules. But the rules and their application are clear in the vast majority of breaches, including those in this book. Second, reformers argue that the problem is ignorance. In response to Watergate—whose perpetrators were lawyers from the president on down—the ABA required accredited law schools to mandate instruction in professional responsibility.[1032] The compulsory course tends to be unpopular (as I know, having taught it for most of the last 34 years). State bars also require the Multistate Professional Responsibility Examination—which most law students pass after cramming for one weekend. And state continuing education requirements often include refresher courses in ethics.[1033] Although many commentators retain an unsubstantiated and unwarranted faith in the power of exhortation and instruction,[1034] the limited empirical data suggest that compulsory instruction only increases cynicism.[1035] Indeed, the exercise seems about as productive as Article 3 of the Chinese education law: "In developing the socialist educational undertakings, the state shall uphold Marxism-Leninism, Mao Tse-tung Thought and the theories of constructing socialism with Chinese characteristics as directives and comply with the basic principles of the Constitution."[1036]

Ignorance does *not* seem to be the problem.[1037] As Ado Annie sings in *Oklahoma*, "It ain't so much a question of not knowin' hut to do/I knowed what's right an' wrong since I've been teen." Studies of decision making have found that those with more experience encounter greater difficulty in learning from their mistakes.[1038] Larger firms are professionalizing the ethical guidance they offer members.[1039] Surveys find that even

---

[1031] Abel (1981; 1989: 142); Schneyer (1989).
[1032] "A law school shall require that each student receive substantial instruction in: . . . (5) the history, goals, structure, values, rules, and responsibilities of the legal profession and its members." ABA Standard 302(a)(5).
[1033] N.Y. Comp. Code R. & Regs. Tit. 22, § 1500.22(a) (2003).
[1034] E.g., Powell (1994: 288); Re (1994: 124–30).
[1035] Carlin (1966); Patton (1968); Pipkin (1979); Goldberg (1979); Zemans & Rosenblum (1981); ABA Center for Professional Responsibility (1986).
[1036] Mitchell Landsberg, "Marx Loses Currency in New China," Los Angeles Times A1 (6.26.07).
[1037] Daicoff (1997) (responses to hypotheticals).
[1038] Schoemaker (2006).
[1039] Compare Lazega (2001) with Chambliss (2006).

solo and small firm practitioners are conscious of encountering ethical dilemmas with some frequency. Few consult the rules, which they find divorced from reality (suggesting that the law school courses that teach the rules can have little effect). But lawyers do seek ethical guidance.[1040] Both Byler and Wisehart turned to colleagues. The advice they received, however, merely confirmed their own bad instincts.[1041] Muto learned to work for travel agencies from David Rodkin, his first New York City employer. Among the solo and small firm lawyers Leslie Levin interviewed, one "recounted stories about an earlier employer, a sole principal, from whom he 'learned how to break every rule in the universe.'" Another learned billing abuse in a large firm. When a third encountered the first client who wanted to pay cash under the table in a real estate transaction, she consulted three lawyer relatives, all of whom told her, "That's just how it works sometimes. Just make sure that you're not in the room where the cash is happening, you know? Go get a cup of coffee."[1042] Indeed, Jerome Carlin found that "office climate" tended to produce less, rather than more, ethical behavior.[1043] For years, lawyers have paid and received fees for referring cases, in blatant disregard of ethical rules.[1044] Lawyers consistently disregard the conflict of interest with their clients inherent in the contingent fee.[1045] The problem seems to be that lawyers develop schemas for routine action and then rationalize an ethical justification.[1046] As lawyers, not surprisingly, they are very good at doing so.

III. Discipline as Social Control

Self-regulation lies at the core of every profession. Everett Hughes, a pioneering sociologist of the professions, observed that the "colleague group . . . will stubbornly defend its own right to define mistakes, and to say in the given case whether one has been made." The layperson looks to the profession for pure technique, but "to the people who practise it, every occupation tends to become an art." Artistry can be judged only by the adept,

---

[1040] Levin (2004–2005: 335, 362–68); Schiltz (1998: 713).
[1041] But see Economides & O'Leary (2007).
[1042] Levin (1998: 890–93).
[1043] Carlin (1966: tables 73–78).
[1044] 71 ABAJ 48–49 (February 1985).
[1045] Levin (2004–2005: 336).
[1046] Levin (2004–2005: 376), citing Scott Plous, The Psychology of Judgment and Decisionmaking 30, 219 (1993).

who possess an esoteric knowledge of ritual.[1047] Police form a silent blue wall when charged with abuse.[1048] Doctors refuse to report or testify against those accused of malpractice.[1049] Hospitals ignore whistleblowers.[1050] The military tries combat-related offenses in courts martial staffed by combat veterans. When outsiders condemn such self-dealing, back-scratching, taking care of their own, asking *"quis custodet ipsos custodes?"* occupational groups reluctantly establish regulatory bodies with nominal independence, just as the British Medical Association (the doctors' trade union) separated from the General Medical Council.[1051] But even independent agencies must be staffed by professionals who have acquired the same knowledge and experienced much the same socialization process as those they judge.

Lawyer self-regulation has been severely criticized for decades.[1052] One fatal flaw is that, even more than most forms of social control, it is almost entirely reactive. There are no cops on the beat, CCTVs photographing license plates, random drug checks, or financial audits. As a result, the "dark figure" of uncorrected misconduct totally overshadows the few who are caught. Control depends almost entirely on clients complaining. But few do: only 2 percent of the dissatisfied clients of English solicitors complained, in the only empirical study yet conducted on the subject.[1053] Clients do not know the ethical rules. Much lawyer conduct is (deliberately) hidden from them. Lacking the expertise to evaluate

---

[1047] Hughes (1951: 322, 324–25).

[1048] After the California Supreme Court ruled that disciplinary records were confidential, the California legislature failed to pass bills backed by the Los Angeles Chief of Police, which could have overturned the decision, swayed by lobbying by the Professional Peace Officers Association, Police Officers Research Assn of California, the Orange County Sheriff, and the Los Angeles Police Protective League, as well as dozens of police officers from around the state. Patrick McGreevy, "Effort to Open Files on Police Thwarted," Los Angeles Times B1 (6.27.07).

[1049] Medical Economics (8.28.61); Bernstein v. Alameda-Contra Cost Medical Ass'n, 293 P.2d 862 (Cal. App. 1956) (local medical society expelled complaining doctor). Not much has changed in the last half century. Christopher Lee, "Study Finds Gaps Between Doctors' Standards and Actions," Washington Post A8 (12.4.07); "Falling Short of Professional Standards," New York Times A20 (12.24.07) (editorial); Campbell et al. (2007b).

[1050] Tracy Weber and Charles Orenstein, "'No One Would Listen,'" Los Angeles Times (10.16.07); "Report Criticizes Kaiser for Lack of Action," Los Angeles Times B1 (1.26.08).

[1051] See also Powell (1986).

[1052] E.g., ABA Special Committee (1970); Nader & Green (1976);Gilb (1956); Marks & Cathcart (1974); Shuchman (1968); Steele & Nimmer (1976); Tisher et al. (1977); Guttenberg (1994); Rhode (2000: 158–65); Zacharias (2002); Barton (2003).

[1053] Abel (1988: 252). On the passivity of clients, see Hunting & Neuwirth (1962: 107–08); Rosenthal (1974: 31, 43–44, 47–48); Felstiner (1997: 125–26); Hosticka (1979); Steele & Nimmer (1976: 955–57).

competence, they rely on imperfect signals of quality: firm size, office location and décor, formal credentials, the lawyer's dress and personality. Some clients—like Ljubica Callahan and all the Hechts except Deborah—are so grateful to and dependent on their lawyers that they refuse to complain even when shown the harm. Others, like Lipin, actively seek to benefit from the violation. There is a systematic mismatch between the harms clients most commonly suffer (primarily neglect) and the willingness of disciplinary authorities to impose significant penalties.[1054] Such bodies typically act only when neglect becomes chronic.[1055] Commentators are rightly skeptical about the capacity of discipline to address the problem of incompetence.[1056]

Only 13 percent of a survey of American clients and just 17 percent of English knew where to complain.[1057] But why should the few who did bother to take the trouble? As in all criminal prosecutions, victims lose control once they file a complaint. They usually hear nothing about what is happening (often the very grievance they had against their lawyer). The outcome takes years, especially because lawyers are highly motivated to fight (given the stakes and their personalities) and are able to do so (having acquired the skills and resources). Rarely does the process produce compensation for the victim. Muto's clients were the exception because immigration judges had made disciplinary complaints a prerequisite to reopening asylum petitions. Any attempt to lower these obstacles to client complaints would provoke fierce opposition from lawyers, who fear (with some justification) that the grievance process already is abused by cranks and deadbeats trying to evade paying their bills (Byler's allegation against Morgan). The English Law Society requires all solicitors to create an infirm grievance mechanism and tell clients about it, but compliance has been grudging and spotty.[1058] The Law Society also has made "inadequate

---

[1054] Royal Commission on Legal Services (1979: vol. 1: 312–14; vol. 2: 233, 244, 254).
[1055] Compare Friday v. State Bar, 144 P.2d 564, 569 (Cal. 1943) (en banc) (suspending a disrespectful, incompetent lawyer for six months), and Fla. Bar v. Neale, 384 So.2d 1264, 1265 (Fla. 1980) (per curiam) (refusing to discipline malpractice), with In re Albert, 212 N.W.2d 17, 21 (Mich. 1973) (per curiam) (years suspension for a lawyer who neglected five clients), and Comm. on Legal Ethics v. Mullins, 226 S.E.2d 427, 432 (W.Va. 1976) (suspending negligent attorney indefinitely). See also ABA Comm. on Ethics and Prof'l Responsibility, Formal Op. 335 n.1 (1974) (requiring "consistent failure to carry out the obligations" or "a conscious disregard for the responsibility owed to the client"); ABA Comm. on Ethics and Prof'l Responsibility, Informal Op. 1273 (1973) (requiring "more than a single act or omission").
[1056] Frankel (1977); Martyn (1981); Spaeth (1988).
[1057] Steele & Nimmer (1976: 962–63); Royal Commission (1979: vol. 1: 292; vol. 2: 263).
[1058] Abel (2003: 359); Christensen et al. (1999).

professional services" a disciplinary offense: solicitors may have their costs disallowed and be directed to rectify the error and pay up to £30,000 compensation.[1059] But in 1999 the Office for the Supervision of Solicitors was so underfunded and understaffed that it told new complainants their files would not even be opened for 12 months.[1060] And a decade earlier, the California disciplinary procedure completely shut down for lack of money.[1061]

Clients may be more motivated to sue for malpractice, which offers the possibility of significant compensation. Like disciplinary complaints, these claims disproportionately target small firms (though not solo practitioners, perhaps because they have no partners to share liability), personal injury and real estate practitioners, more rather than less experienced lawyers, and litigation rather than transactional work, and they occur mostly because of missed deadlines.[1062] The deterrent effect of malpractice liability is mediated by insurers, who seek to hold down rates by monitoring the insured.[1063] However, the market for lawyer malpractice insurance seems even more imperfect than insurance markets generally.[1064] Only Oregon requires insurance; estimates of the proportion of lawyers uninsured in other jurisdictions range from 25 to 50 percent.[1065] The legal profession's failure to mandate insurance is inexcusable. The English Law Society required solicitors to insure more than 40 years ago. Because the Society operated its own monopolistic mutual insurer, attempts to experience-rate premiums have fomented sharp conflicts based on firm size and substantive area.[1066]

If it is difficult to encourage clients to file more complaints, then who else might bring them? Unlike clients, lawyers know the rules and observe much of each others' conduct. But they are both too reticent and too ready to complain. Some remain silent by reason of collegiality. In Missouri, 34 percent of rural lawyers and 71 percent of urban lawyers said they would report misconduct, but only 11 and 27 percent had ever

---

[1059] Abel (2003: 355, 357); Moorhead et al. (2000b).
[1060] Abel (2003: 378); Moorhead et al. (2000a).
[1061] Fellmeth (1987a; 1987b; 1987c).
[1062] Gates (1984; 1985-1986).
[1063] Wycoff (1962) (doctors); Galante (1986: 8); Baker & Simon (2002).
[1064] Pfennigstorf (1980: 237 n.8); Galante (1985a; 1985b; 1985c); Winchurch (1987).
[1065] Snider (1986); Fellmeth (1987b: 9, 26). With the encouragement of the ABA, which adopted a Model Court Rule on Insurance Disclosure in 2004, at least 23 states now require some form: www.abanet.org/cpr/clientpro/malprac_disc_chart.pdf.
[1066] Abel (1988: 258-60; 2003: 381-93).

CHAPTER 8

done so.[1067] Professionals (including judges) file less than a tenth of all grievances in the United States[1068] and just 14 percent in Britain.[1069] We saw Ann Hsiung's reluctance to complain against Muto, whom she barely knew. Lawyers are no more eager to wash dirty linen in public than are members of other collectivities. Warren Estis was unusual in complaining against Furtzaig, his protégé; but the misconduct was blatant, and the firm potentially liable to clients. The ABA has urged states to mandate a duty to disclose.[1070] But subordinates understandably are afraid to complain against superiors in their firms because many jurisdictions treat employment as "at will" and offer no protection against retaliation.[1071] Lawyers also may file too many complaints, or unfounded ones, in order to gain tactical advantage over an adversary.[1072] We saw that Wisehart and WGM moved to disqualify each other, and Wisehart made similar motions in other cases. Muto objected (wrongly) that the complaints against him came from the Lord and Taylors of practice, trying to put his Filene's Basement operation out of business.

Judges are less likely to be either overprotective or vindictive. Immigration judges complained against Muto for multiple reasons: solicitude toward his clients, who risked losing legitimate asylum petitions; anger at him for wasting their time; and frustration at their own lack of disciplinary procedures. When Deborah Hecht's refusal to pay their fees forced Cardozo and Brashich to petition the Surrogate, Judge Emanuelli criticized them for failing to present Babette with alternative settlements that would have produced a lower fee. Judge Moskowitz dismissed Lipin's case because of her and Wisehart's misconduct. In the aftermath of Hurricane Katrina, Judge Arthur L. Hunter, Jr., of the Orleans Parish

---

[1067] Landon (1982: 482).
[1068] Steele & Nimmer (1976: 973). An unusual example is a federal judge who complained about an Assistant U.S. Attorney to both the state bar and the U.S. Attorney General. Adam Liptak, Federal Judge Files Complaint against Prosecutor in Boston, N.Y. Times (7.3.07).
[1069] Royal Commission (1979, vol. 1: 315) (1973–1978).
[1070] ABA Commission on Professionalism (1986); ABA Commission on Evaluation of Disciplinary Enforcement (1991).
[1071] Wieder v. Skala, 609 N.E.2d 752 (N.Y. 1992); Bohatch v. Butler & Binion, 977 S.W.2d 543 (Tex. 1998); Balla v. Gambro, Inc., 145 Ill.2d 492 (1991); Jacobson v. Knepper & Moga, P.C. 195 Ill.2d 371 (1998); Kelley v. Hunton & Williams, 1999 U.S. Dist. Lexis 9139 (E.D.N.Y.); Griffin (2006).
[1072] Victor (1986) (Cadwalader, Wickersham & Taft against Skadden); Frank J. Prial, "A Year After Settling the Johnson Estate, Lawyers Still Battling over Ethics," New York Times § 1 p. 18 (5.7.87) (Milbank, Tweed against Sullivan & Cromwell); E. R. Shipp, "Court Faults New York Law Firm for Unethical Behavior in a Suit," New York Times § 1 p. 20 (6.28.87) (Patterson, Belknap, Webb & Taylor against Sullivan & Cromwell).

Criminal District Court, criticized both prosecution and defense for inadequate representation.[1073] But many ethical violations are invisible to judges: Kreitzer's neglect of clients and participation in the ten percenter scheme, Byler's appropriation of Morgan's IRS refund, even Furtzaig's forgery of court documents. And some judges are prone to forgive lawyers. District of Columbia Superior Court Judges protected the lawyers they appointed as guardians and conservators of incompetents.[1074] Judge Hamilton explained, "You have to be careful about barring someone from cases. It may be the person's only source of practice." Judge Lopez preferred to let attorneys withdraw because removal could hurt their reputations. And when a lawyer sought to excuse years of failing to submit mandatory reports on the ground that her computer had crashed and she needed surgery, Presiding Judge Long responded, "I understand." Lawyers and judges are no more likely than clients to expose the "dark figure."

Even were complaints to increase significantly, however, other problems would remain. Much of the discontent with lawyer discipline stems from its leniency.[1075] Like most regulatory processes, it exhibits radical attrition between filing and punishment. New York City offers better historical data than most jurisdictions.[1076] Between 1905 and 1920, the Association of the Bar of the City of New York (ABCNY) investigated 8,500 complaints but sanctioned only 260 lawyers (3 percent), just 16 lawyers a year in a bar with more than 15,000. Between 1925 and 1935, the ABCNY received 22,800 complaints, held 900 hearings (3.9 percent), found 314 guilty (1.4 percent), suspended 39 (0.2 percent) and disbarred 108 (0.5 percent). In 1958–1959 it received 1,429 complaints, heard 85 (5.6 percent), suspended 4 (0.3 percent) and disbarred 4 (0.3 percent). Between 1958–1959 and 1972–1973 it received 30,810 complaints, heard 663 (2 percent), suspended 200 (0.6 percent) and disbarred 178 (0.6 percent). In 1983 it received 8,766 complaints, prosecuted 491 (5.6 percent), suspended 86 (1 percent), and disbarred 65 (0.7 percent). Data from Kansas,[1077] California,[1078]

[1073] Ann M. Simmons, "New Orleans Judge Fights Poor Defense," Los Angeles Times A12 (6.27.07).
[1074] Leonnig et al. (2003).
[1075] Goode (1967).
[1076] Blaustein (1951: 265–66); Martin (1970: 184, 201, 213); Brown (1938: 213–14); Sam Roberts, "When Secrecy Seems More like Professional Courtesy," New York Times § 4 p. 8 (12.1.85); Abel (1988: tables 36a, b).
[1077] Mills (1949: 81).
[1078] State Bar of California (1939: 5); Phillips & McCoy (1952: 97-98); Blaustein & Porter (1954: 256); Myrna Oliver, "Bar's Disciplinary Policies at Root of Dispute over Dues," Los Angeles Times § 1 p. 3 (12.16.85); Abel (1988: table 34a).

CHAPTER 8

Chicago,[1079] England,[1080] Scotland,[1081] Northern Ireland,[1082] and Australia[1083] display similar patterns. Factors that would aggravate punishment for ordinary crime—such as substance abuse and marital and financial difficulties—mitigate sanctions for professional misconduct.[1084] Even disbarment—the capital punishment of lawyer discipline—is far from final. Many of those disbarred continue to practice in other jurisdictions or successfully apply for readmission.[1085] Both specific and general deterrence are diminished by secrecy. Oregon is the only American jurisdiction to make all complaints public.[1086] Others publicize only those complaints that eventuate in a public reprimand, suspension, or disbarment. Social control agencies independent from the profession are more stringent. Between 1892 and 1913, the English Supreme Court (which then regulated solicitors) imposed punishment in 83 percent of the matters it heard; among those whose punishment was specified, it suspended 15 percent and struck 56 percent off the Roll. But in a 20-year period (1919–1939), soon after the Law Society obtained the power to discipline, it punished only 36 percent of those tried.[1087] When disciplinary authority was transferred from the Chicago Bar Association (1969–1970) to the independent Attorney Registration and Disciplinary Commission (1974–1975), the proportion of complaints investigated increased from 17 to 43 percent, and the proportion heard from 3.5 to 13.5 percent.[1088] When the Law Society transferred discipline to the independent Solicitors Complaints Bureau, complaints doubled, the new adjudication committee heard four to six times as many as its predecessor, and the Solicitors Disciplinary Tribunal punished twice as many.[1089]

[1079] Phillips & McCoy (1952: 115); Blaustein & Porter (1954: 261).
[1080] Abel (1988: 252–54).
[1081] Royal Commission (1980).
[1082] Royal Commission (1979).
[1083] New South Wales Law Reform Comm'n (1980).
[1084] Tisher et al. (1977: 97–98); Cook (1986).
[1085] Mills (1949: 81) (half of those disbarred in Kansas; a quarter of those admitted were disbarred again); ABA Special Committee (1970); Phillips & McCoy (1952: 120, 122, 124).
[1086] Jeannine Guttman and Brad Bumsted, "Public Access to Disciplinary Hearings Varies," Cincinnati Enquirer E6 (10.21.86). The Solicitors Disciplinary Tribunal opened all hearings in England, but most complaints never get that far. Abel (2003: 358).
[1087] Abel (1988: 250).
[1088] Powell (1976: 46–47).
[1089] Abel (2003: 357).

Similar effects have been observed in Queensland[1090] and Western Australia.[1091]

The criticisms advanced above—that too little unethical behavior is named, blamed, claimed,[1092] and punished—assume that more social control would be better.[1093] If that is the view of most outsiders, however, many lawyers believe just the opposite—that discipline is unfair, oppressive, and counterproductive. In the 1950s, solo practitioners complained that the Chicago Bar Association

> represent[s] the layman against the lawyer, rather than the lawyer's view. . . . We feel they're dominated by a small group of blue-blood lawyers . . . [who] represent the railroads and insurance companies. . . . The big difference between the large firm lawyer and the average practitioner is that the big firms give out more bullshit, superfluity, and unnecessary research.[1094]

Criminal defense lawyers rightly believe that they are disciplined frequently, whereas prosecutors routinely condone police perjury and withhold exculpatory evidence with impunity.[1095] Several of the lawyers I studied were convinced they had been singled out because they charged too little, were sole practitioners, refused to back down, or were neither female nor Jewish. Aside from Furtzaig (whose misbehavior was also aberrational—trying to do too much for his firm, at great personal cost), all the others effectively practiced alone: Muto managed by "travel agencies"; Kreitzer running his own personal injury practice independent of his criminal defense partner; Byler "of counsel" to a small firm (but billing separately and paying overhead); and Cardozo, Brashich, and Wisehart as sole practitioners. Given their ethnoreligious and class backgrounds and the status of the law schools they attended, Kreitzer, Muto, and Furtzaig could never

---

[1090] Levin (2006).
[1091] Shinnick et al. (2003).
[1092] Felstiner et al. (1981).
[1093] Fisse & Braithwaite (1985); Groves & Newman (1986); Green (1990).
[1094] Carlin (1962: 178, 180, 183).
[1095] In 381 murder cases where the defendant received a new trial for prosecutorial misconduct, none was disbarred; in 120 death row exonerations, none was disciplined. Adam Liptak, "Prosecutor Becomes Prosecuted," New York Times § 4 p. 4 (6.24.07); Gershman (1999). The disbarment of Durham District Attorney Mike Nifong for his rape prosecution of the three Duke University lacrosse players was exceptional. Duff Wilson, "Prosecutor in Duke Case Disbarred by Ethics Panel," New York Times § 1 p. 16 (6.17.07).

CHAPTER 8

have joined large firms. Cardozo and Brashich graduated from NYU when it was much lower ranked than it is today; their generations also would have encountered high ethnoreligious barriers. Wisehart and Byler were white Anglo-Saxon Protestants, had attended prestigious law schools (Michigan and Harvard), and had been large firm associates, but neither had made partner.

Observers have repeatedly confirmed that solo and small firm practitioners are overrepresented among disciplined lawyers.[1096] Sometimes this is deliberate: both the ABCNY and the Chicago Bar Association targeted plaintiffs' personal injury lawyers and ambulance chasing.[1097] But closer scrutiny has shown that the disproportion is attributable to *complaints*, not to their treatment by bar associations.[1098] Solo and small firm lawyers "often find themselves so overworked that they miss deadlines or fail to communicate with clients" and "do not have enough support staff to manage correspondence or back them up when they are involved in a trial, become ill, or take a vacation."[1099] Large firms suffer neither problem, and their clients can mobilize market pressures to ensure quality. Yet even if the complaints of solo and small firm practitioners are unjustified, their sense of persecution is one of the classic neutralization devices, which facilitates deviance and undermines the deterrent effect of discipline.[1100] In the course of this research, some have criticized me for reproducing the ethnoreligious and class biases built into the grievance process. I would echo the response of criminologists criticized for focusing on street crime committed disproportionately by racial minorities: the harms of both street criminals and solo and small firm practitioners are real—and the victims are even more disadvantaged and vulnerable than the perpetrators.

[1096] Carlin (1966: 57, 178, 180, 183, and tables 42, 44, 45, 48, 74, 76, 117, 133); Auerbach (1976: 48–49); Rhode (1985a: 548; 1985b: 641 n.168); Curran (1986: 30); Shuchman (1968); New South Wales Law Reform Commission (1980: 16); Arnold & Kay (1995: 227–38); Levin (1998: 62 n. 275); State Bar of New Mexico (2000: 46); Hal R. Lieberman, "How to Avoid Common Ethics Problems: Small Firms and Solos Are Often Subject to Disciplinary Complaints and Malpractice Claims," N.Y.L.J. S4 (10.28.02); William McIntyre, "Whose Interests Does Texas' Disciplinary Process Protect?" Tex. Law. 27 (8.5.02); Mark Hansen, "Picking on the Little Guy: Perception Lingers that Discipline Falls Hardest on Solos, Small Firms," ABAJ 30 (March 2003).
[1097] Cappell & Halliday (1983: 329); Powell (1988: 20, 23–24); see also Baxter (1974).
[1098] State Bar of California (2001).
[1099] Id. 1–2.
[1100] A "sense of injustice" is one of the classic neutralization techniques. Matza (1964: chapter 4).

Sanctions also may be ineffective for reasons other than perceived bias. Lawyer discipline satisfies many of what Harold Garfinkel called the "conditions of successful degradation ceremonies."[1101] Because discipline is based on lawyers' ultimate "grounds" or "reasons" for their behavior, it affects their "total identities." It expresses public moral indignation, reinforces professional group solidarity, and inverts ceremonies of investiture and elevation (swearing in new members of the bar). The denunciation is impersonal. And both behavior and perpetrator are made to look "strange," "out of the ordinary," by contrast with rule-abiding lawyers. The legal profession presents discipline as proof that it takes its responsibilities seriously. By purging the worst malefactors, it proclaims the integrity of all other lawyers. But what is the actual effect of discipline on its subjects?

The explicit goal of the penalty phase is to elicit expressions of remorse. In practice, however, it seems to intensify self-righteousness. True, it has to work with difficult material. Lawyers are self-selected and trained to be fighters and are rewarded for their ferocity and intransigence. Like all professionals, lawyers achieve their privileged status and material rewards by working hard and following rules. Uniquely among professionals, they spend their lives telling others what they have done wrong. Not surprisingly, lawyers are legalistic.[1102] All of us find it hard to admit and learn from mistakes.[1103] But for all these reasons lawyers find it especially difficult to admit they have screwed up, to acknowledge that others may be right and they are wrong.[1104] Byler is a vivid illustration: he rejected a private admonition; he insisted that escrowing the disputed funds would admit wrongdoing; and he failed to gain readmission at the end of his suspension because he could not feign contrition. He could make promises about the future but not admissions about the past. He and Wisehart both stressed years of active participation in church as evidence of good character. This inability to confess error led some (like Furtzaig) into cover-ups that aggravated their misconduct. Yet the problem is not just lawyer character. The structure of the disciplinary process is profoundly unconducive to repentance. The penalty phase follows the guilt phase, sometimes immediately. During the former, the accused defend themselves vigorously, raising every possible procedural objection, drowning

---

[1101] Garfinkel (1956).
[1102] Tapp & Levine (1974); Willging & Dunn (1981); Landwehr (1982).
[1103] Dweck (2006).
[1104] Bohn (1971) (law students are higher than normal in self-confidence, dominance, exhibitionism); Solkoff & Markowitz (1967).

CHAPTER 8

the tribunal in paper, endlessly seeking review. Lawyers often appear pro se because they cannot afford representation and are (overly) confident in their legal abilities; some may even find that role cathartic. But even represented accused actively participate in litigation strategy, sometimes upstaging their lawyers. After such displays of defiance, contrition could hardly be credible.

Rather than accept responsibility, the accused advanced a variety of what Scott and Lyman call "accounts."[1105] As I discussed above, they claimed to have been scapegoated for behavior that many others committed with impunity. Muto offered numerous excuses, including the deaths of his mother and cousin and his inability to fly. (A District of Columbia lawyer who neglected the incompetent for whom she had been appointed guardian said "My priority was my family, and it will be. And I don't care."[1106]) Muto pled to incompetence and "disorganization" but denied moral failings. Several accused said they had been motivated not by selfishness but by concern or responsibility for others (usually their families). The accused denied causing harm; these were victimless crimes, malum prohibitum, not malum in se. Any injuries were deserved: Morgan *was* a tax evader; he owed Byler most of the $53,000 in quantum meruit. The accused emphasized what they had *not* done, such as stealing from client trust accounts. They invoked their *satisfied* clients (some of whom turned out to be less satisfied). They appealed to higher loyalties: Byler to the rule of law, Wisehart to justice for his client. They attacked both their accusers (clients and prosecutors) and their judges (those before whom they had appeared and those adjudicating discipline). Remember the light bulb joke? How many psychiatrists does it take to change a light bulb? Just one, but the light bulb really has to want to change. Lawyers aren't light bulbs.

Lawyer discipline shares some of these problems with the prosecution of white-collar crime. In ordinary crime, someone is clearly guilty; the question is "Who Done It?" In white-collar crime there is rarely doubt about the perpetrators' identity; the question is whether the conduct was criminal. Ordinary criminals often acknowledge their guilt (at least to themselves), unless there are strategic reasons to deny it. White-collar criminals often remain adamantly convinced of their innocence. Ordinary criminals—at least the professionals—experience no loss of reputation from conviction and punishment; jail time can even enhance their reputation

---

[1105] Scott & Lyman (1968).
[1106] Leonnig et al. (2003).

with some audiences. White-collar criminals suffer enormous reputational harm just from being accused.[1107] Like drivers stopped for speeding or audited taxpayers, such lawyers tend to be more careful, at least for a while. Therefore, many white-collar accused (including some lawyers) contend they have suffered enough from being prosecuted and found guilty and should be spared further sanctions—the process is the punishment.[1108] Muto could not see why his apologies were insufficient. A lawyer whose client had complained about a $500 fee objected, "You don't understand how stressful that is. . . . You can't even do any work, it's so stressful."[1109]

In light of these problems, how could discipline be made more effective? One mechanism is clear: publicity is the greatest deterrent.[1110] There is *no* justification for private reprimands, the most common punishment in some jurisdictions. Some of the lawyers I studied had received many such reprimands and blithely continued to disregard ethical rules. Prospective clients should have easy access to disciplinary records (i.e., online). Publicity also affects intra-professional reputation. Many lawyers acknowledge (sometimes shamefacedly) that the first thing they read in professional journals is the disciplinary cases.[1111] The media construct a contemporary urban analogy to the informal sanctions that used to operate in smaller urban bars and still do in rural communities. The more difficult question is whether to publicize accusations as well as convictions.[1112] On one hand, that would give notice of all client complaints, not just the few that culminate in sanctions, and do so years before a final judgment. On the other, it would publicize false positives, harming innocent lawyers in ways that cannot easily be undone by ultimate vindication.

Charles Bosk's classic study of social control among surgeons offers valuable insights for lawyer discipline.[1113] He distinguishes between two

---

[1107] But see Schwartz & Skolnick (1962) (unskilled workers merely charged with assault found it much more difficult to get employment; doctors sued for negligence suffered no loss of referrals). See Zacharias (2008).
[1108] Feeley (1979).
[1109] There is some evidence that any exposure to the disciplinary system renders lawyers more wary. Levin (2004–2005: 371).
[1110] Haller (2003).
[1111] Levin (2004–2005: 373).
[1112] BrokerCheck does this for investors. Lynnley Browning, "Site That Tracks Brokers Questioned on Erased Cases," New York Times C10 (12.4.07) (information on more than 670,000 securities professionals, including client accusations of wrongdoing).
[1113] Bosk (1979). For a precursor, see Stelling & Bucher (1973). See also Jerome Groopman, "Mental Malpractice," New York Times A25 (7.7.07).

kinds of errors: technical and normative.[1114] Attending physicians "can forgive even the most serious lapses in technique" by residents (also called houseofficers) if they are "speedily noticed, reported, and treated" and not repeated. Nevertheless, all residents "report that their errors are etched indelibly in their memory."[1115] (Both features echo Bosk's title, *Forgive and Remember*.) Forgiveness "obligates the subordinate who is forgiven" to become "more vigilant in the immediate future."[1116] Control of technical performance "is built into the fabric of everyday life as minidiscussions of surgical problems, as anecdotes or horror stories, as hypothetical questions or future considerations, or as mild rebukes."[1117] Normative errors are role violations. The attending's single most important rule is that the resident should present "no surprises." Failure to keep the attending informed of the patient's condition implies that the resident "was lazy, negligent, or dishonest." Residents are responsible for getting along with nurses and managing patients and their families. Residents' normative errors "destroy their credibility as responsible workers." An attending commented,

> Covering up is never really excusable. . . . A certain amount [of mistakes] are inevitable. But it is the obligation of everyone involved in patient care to minimize mistakes. The way to do that is by full and total disclosure.[1118]

Residents cannot blame others. As in the Army "there were only three answers you could give: 'yes sir'; 'no sir'; and 'no excuse, sir.'" The attending is the sole authority on correct clinical practice.[1119] Attendings collectively determine residents' futures. The technically competent and normatively proper will be offered permanent positions; the technically incompetent but normatively proper will be advised to move into another specialty in the same hospital; the normatively improper will have to leave medicine.[1120] Because a "moral error breaches a professional's contract with his client" it is "treated more seriously than [a] technical one." Although there is no

---

[1114] Residents also commit quasi-normative errors by deviating from their attending's clinical style. Bosk (1979: 186–87).
[1115] Id. 37–40.
[1116] Id. 178.
[1117] Id. 173.
[1118] Id. 51–60.
[1119] Id. 76.
[1120] Id. 153–56.

clear limit to the tolerable number of technical errors, "the minimum number of moral breaches needed to dismiss a professional from practice is clear-cut: one will do."[1121]

If control of residents is intensely hierarchical, control of attendings is extremely egalitarian. Grand rounds "provide attendings an arena to display their virtuosity." Successfully treated patients are brought in and shown off, with or without clinical or scientific justification.[1122] Failure is analyzed in the Mortality and Morbidity Conference (MMC), which no physician misses. Because attendings are subordinate to no one, their errors are always defined as technical, not normative. For the same reason, attendings take full responsibility, because the subordinate residents lack authority to make judgment errors. As "part of a chivalrous code of behavior," attendings "put on the hair shirt." This ritual has multiple purposes. It is a cautionary tale for all those present. It "instill[s] professional 'super-egos' in junior staff." And it "mitigate[s] the rigid hierarchical authority system of a surgical service." "The major punishment of the practice is the embarrassment of a public confessional and the pain the outcome itself actually causes the surgeon's conscience."[1123]

The two forms of social control share a central element, despite their differences:

> The houseofficer confesses to his attending. The attending confesses to the entire collegium, which is his superordinate. Both humble themselves and in turn are forgiven and embraced. . . . Confession is ipso facto proof that an individual adheres to group standards . . . [and] is punishing himself for his faults.[1124]

Both processes seek to correct technical mistakes and warn against normative errors, whose commission leads to banishment. Forgiveness of technical errors (and its counterpart, moral condemnation of those who cover up) strongly encourages transparency. Residents are subjected to a much milder degradation ritual than the one evident in lawyer discipline, and attendings are actually rewarded for self-abasement in the MMC, rather than humiliated. Both residents and attendings are powerfully

---

[1121] Id. 171–72.
[1122] Id. 123–25.
[1123] Id. 128, 138, 142–45.
[1124] Id. 179.

motivated to change what they can—technique—without being penalized for the constancy of what they cannot change—character. The intense, personal scrutiny of residents and the winnowing of a few have suggestive parallels in large law firms. But the solo and small firm practitioners who dominate the disciplinary docket (and the cases considered here) undergo no comparable institutional socialization and selection.[1125]

IV. Alternatives to Punishment

My case studies confirm what criminology has known for centuries. Deviance has powerful motivations, both material and psychological. Character is difficult to change. People have an extraordinary determination, and capacity, to rationalize misconduct. Education is ineffectual. Punishment can be counterproductive. If tweaking norms, intensifying regulation, and strengthening sanctions are unlikely to make much difference, what could we do to reduce the real harms lawyers inflict on clients, the legal system, and society? Once again, I think lawyers can learn from doctors. There are many reasons why we tolerate more errors (both malpractice and misconduct) by lawyers than doctors: lives rarely are at stake (though liberty is, and lots of money); the consequences often take years, rather than hours, to manifest; and there is less consensus about the goal (both complainants and lawyers feel morally worthy; justice is far more ambiguous than health). But medicine teaches that we do not have to resign ourselves to what all agree is an unacceptable status quo.[1126]

In his recent book, Atul Gawande offers several ways doctors have discovered to ensure they do "*Better.*"[1127] As a surgeon, he realized that "our usual approach of punishing people for failures wasn't going to eliminate the problem" of objects left inside the body, so he "soon found [himself] working with some colleagues to come up with a device that could automate the tracking of sponges and instruments."[1128] We already have similar solutions to some common forms of lawyer misconduct. English solicitors, for instance, must make mandatory contributions to a Compensation Fund, which has an incentive to police abuse of client trust

---

[1125] On mentoring of lawyers generally, including its effect on moral reasoning, see Hamilton & Brabbit (2007); Kay et al. (2009); Kay & Wallace (2007a; 2007b).

[1126] Danny Hakim, "State Watch for 2 Percent of Doctors," New York Times C15 (5.7.08) (New York supervises more than 2% of doctors); Rolph et al. (2007).

[1127] Gawande (2007). See also Wachter & Shojania (2004: chapters 18–22).

[1128] Id. 255. A recent study made similar observations about needlestick injuries among trainee surgeons. Makary et al. (2007).

accounts (especially by solo practitioners, who have no liable partners with an incentive to look over their shoulders). And solicitors must regularly submit financial accounts to the Law Society.[1129] Many American states require banks to inform disciplinary bodies of overdrafts on client trust accounts. Recognizing that temporary financial difficulties tempt American lawyers to dip into client trust accounts (a close analogy to the "non-shareable financial problems" that made Cressey's subject embezzle), Leslie Levin proposes that bar associations make short-term low-interest loans to financially distressed members (giving those bodies an incentive to help borrowers extricate themselves from debt).[1130] I agree with her that we ought to consider requiring all lawyers to have partners, for whom they would be financially responsible. And it is unconscionable that we require car owners to insure but not lawyers. The remainder of this conclusion will look for similar ways to anticipate and forestall the problems identified by the case studies: vulnerable clients, conflicts of interest, inappropriate fees, overzealous lawyering, and inadequate quality. Unlike conventional generic ex post remedies—increasing apprehension rates or penalty severity—ex ante solutions are individualized to the problems they address.

The clients of most of the accused lawyers were highly vulnerable: elderly, immigrant, financially needy, jobless, injured, facing financial penalties (or worse) and deportation, confronting powerful adversaries. Unlike the repeat-player corporate clients served by large firms, they were one-shot customers, not even capable of warning others against the lawyers who failed them. (Injured workers, by contrast, can confidently use the lawyers unions recommend for compensation claims because those lawyers derive significant ongoing business from the unions.) As a result, the accused lawyers risked little reputational capital by betraying client trust. In all these respects, the clients were typical of individuals who retain lawyers. Most do so reactively rather than proactively, to litigate rather than structure transactions. But because lawyers are expensive, few people have legal expenses insurance, and legal aid is drastically underfunded. Non-wealthy individuals can hire lawyers only in limited circumstances: after death (and a lifetime of wealth accumulation); following injury, including employment loss (because tort damages capitalize lost earnings and commodify both bodies and feelings); in real property transactions

---

[1129] Abel (1988: 257–58).
[1130] Levin (2004–2005: 387)

(because mortgages spread buyers' costs over decades); in bankruptcy (which can eliminate years of accumulated debts); and when confronting serious threats (eviction, firing, fines, liability, prison, deportation). Most people retain lawyers just a few times in the course of their lives, so they have little experience of lawyers in general, much less an ongoing relationship with a particular lawyer.[1131] Those who receive sudden, often unexpected, windfalls may express gratitude toward their lawyers by uncritically paying the lawyer's fee (Babette Hecht and her three children, Ljubica Callahan, perhaps Kreitzer's personal injury clients). Byler expected Morgan to do so. Those in extremis (like Muto's immigration clients) have no alternative but to trust the lawyer.

Gawande offers an imperfect but suggestive analogy. Many doctors must perform intimate examinations of their patients. (The definition of intimacy naturally varies greatly across cultures.) Gawande recognizes that "no one seems to have discovered the ideal approach." Shame and prudery can obstruct accurate diagnosis; but disregarding patients' feelings can violate their trust. He describes Britain's "stringent" standards:

> A chaperone of the appropriate gender must be offered to all patients who undergo an "intimate examination" ... irrespective of the gender of the patient or of the doctor. A chaperone must be present when a male physician performs an intimate examination of a female patient.

Deploring the absence of any guidelines in the United States, he argues that "the most important reason to consider tightening standards of medical protocol is simply to improve trust and understanding between patients and doctors."[1132] I believe the same is true for law practice. Clients should be told what they can expect from lawyers, perhaps in the form of a client bill of rights, drafted by the profession and presented to the prospective client at the first encounter.[1133] Clients should be able to obtain a confidential second opinion from an independent lawyer about what their prospective lawyer is proposing to do and about his/her fee arrangements. Similar advice should remain available throughout the lawyer-client relationship. Such protections will not be cheap. But a legal profession that

---

[1131] Curran (1977: 190) (mean of 2.15 lawyer consultations/lifetime).
[1132] Gawande (2007: 74, 77–78, 80).
[1133] See Rhode (2000: 210).

wants to restore trust would do much better to invest in them than in public relations spin doctoring.

Conflicts of interest attract more attention than any other ethical problem. Casebooks devote more space to them.[1134] Large law firms expend substantial resources monitoring and avoiding conflicts, which limit both the cases and clients they can accept and firm expansion. Business clients demanding unconditional loyalty raise conflicts issues with their lawyers. Lawyers assert conflicts strategically in order to disqualify adversaries. Fortunately, scholars have begun to conduct empirical research on conflicts through case studies[1135] and interviews with lawyers.[1136] But because the lawyers I studied (and those disciplined more generally) tend to represent one-shot clients with discrete problems, they rarely encounter the typical conflict *between* clients. Most of Levin's small firm lawyers conducted no formal conflicts check, relying on an "in your head" method. None consulted "of counsel" or suitemates. Most were conscious of encountering the problem less than once a year. Some represented both sides in business deals and divorces. When conflicts were nonwaivable, lawyers referred the matter to others, who made reciprocal referrals to them.[1137] The one conflict that did arise frequently pitted lawyer against client over fees, my next topic.

All fee arrangements create conflicts of interest between lawyers and clients. Contingent fees motivate lawyers to minimize effort; even without that perverse incentive such fees can produce an unearned windfall.[1138] In Babette Hecht's case, they led Cardozo and Brashich to favor the settlement that produced a contingent fee far greater than they would have earned in quantum meruit. Fixed fees have the same effect. Hourly fees motivate lawyers to maximize effort, running up the meter with diminishing returns to clients (or none).[1139] Additional problems arise when fee agreements are ambiguous or non-existent. Babette Hecht signed a confused, contradictory retainer because she was so grateful to and dependent on Benjamin Cardozo. She was destitute, living with friends, doing badly paid, humiliating work—and she had been rejected by four other lawyers.

[1134] I did not systematically examine every casebook because I think the proposition is obviously true. See, e.g., Rhode & Luban (2004) (131 pages); Noonan & Painter (2001) (158 pages); Lerman & Schrag (2005) (194 pages); Hazard et al. (2005) (127 pages).
[1135] Kelley (2001: chapter 4); Regan (2004).
[1136] Shapiro (2002).
[1137] Levin (2004–2005: 349–54).
[1138] E.g., Beam (2006) (tobacco settlements).
[1139] Lerman (1999); Fortney (2000); Kelley (2001: chapter 5).

Chapter 8

Cardozo offered to work on contingency for a retainer of just $7,500, most of which Babette's friends advanced. Ljubica Callahan, an immigrant with limited English and earning capacity, faced a will contest with her dead husband's hostile relatives. She was so grateful to Deyan Brashich, a fellow Serb, that she accepted a (contingent) $75,000 in satisfaction of the $264,000 repayment the court ordered and never even sought to recover that from Brashich. Facing a $200,000 IRS deficiency at a moment of financial embarrassment, James Morgan turned to his good friend, Philip Byler. Morgan expressed his gratitude by assigning the returned security deposit to Byler and, later, casually saying *something* about the anticipated refund. All three instances exemplify the danger of mixing business with friendship. When courts rejected the contingent fees, the lawyers had to substantiate the effort they had exerted. Byler's claims about both hours and rates seemed arbitrary and result driven (the $10,000 "non-bill bill" he thought Morgan would accept, a second bill with greatly increased hours that produced exactly the amount of the IRS refund). Neither Cardozo nor Brashich could prove or justify the hours they claimed.

These problems (which are common, despite the unusual facts in the cases cited here) suggest several responses. Lawyers might be required to offer written fee quotations in advance, as they must in Britain.[1140] Just as lawyers proposing business deals to clients must advise them to obtain independent advice, so clients might be offered an independent review of their retainers. Bar associations might create panels of lawyers trained to do this and willing to serve at little or no cost. (Retired lawyers are a possible pool.) Lawyers who fail to comply with these requirements might be limited to quantum meruit claims, governed by rigorous criteria for proof of hours and judicial determination of rates. In most of the common law world, where losers pay both their own lawyers and their adversary's, there are elaborate procedures for independent calculation of fees.

The problems discussed above arose because lawyers favored the interests of others (including themselves) over those of their clients. Social scientists have described a variety of situations in which lawyers compromise the ethical obligation of vigorous advocacy by seeking to appear "reasonable" to judges and opposing counsel,[1141] cooling out personal

---

[1140] Abel (2003: 363).
[1141] Katz (1982); Landon (1990).

injury victims,[1142] criminal defendants,[1143] and divorcing spouses[1144] in order to encourage their clients to accept less than optimum settlements. But the opposite can happen as well. Just as combatants jettison the laws of war out of fanaticism, or because their opponents are not complying, so lawyers can advocate for clients too vigorously. Some shamelessly corrupt the legal system.[1145] For clients interested in preserving the status quo (e.g., tenants resisting eviction), delay may be the best tactic.[1146] Discovery, intended to shorten and improve trials by giving both sides all the information to which they are entitled, has become a battleground where lawyers withhold essential unprivileged information, drown adversaries in a sea of irrelevant paper, and bully them into surrender by driving up the cost of litigation.[1147] Prosecutors conceal exculpatory evidence[1148]—most recently Mike Nifong in prosecuting the Duke lacrosse team.[1149] Sometimes the initiative comes from the client, who makes the lawyer complicit in illegal conduct: perjury,[1150] forged documents,[1151] tax evasion,[1152] concealment of income or assets, or phony injuries.[1153]

Arthur Wisehart was an extreme example of a lawyer who flouted procedural rules in a ruthless effort to vindicate his client, Joan Lipin. True, it was she who took the first illegal step by reading, hiding, and keeping defense counsel's file on her. But Wisehart immediately took command, instructing her to make copies and even to lie about how she had obtained the papers. And he quickly devised rationalizations for reading the papers himself and using them (and the threat that Lipin would publicize the contents) to try to extract a $1 million settlement. His motivations seem to have included intense identification with his client (a younger woman, whom he had hired as a paralegal after ARCGNY had made her unemployable) and fury at opposing counsel (both for their conduct—alleged complicity in Lipin's retaliatory firing, defamation, and abusive discovery—and their patronizing attitude toward him, which may have

---

[1142] Rosenthal (1974).
[1143] Blumberg (1967); McIntyre (1987); Mello (2006) (persuading the Unabomber to plead guilty).
[1144] Sarat & Felstiner (1995); Mather et al. (2001).
[1145] Rovere (1947).
[1146] Yale Law Journal (1973); Lazerson (1982).
[1147] Brazil (1980a; 1980b); Nelson (1998).
[1148] Gillers (2006).
[1149] David Zucchino, "Nifong Loses Law License in Duke case," Los Angeles Times A16 (6.17.07).
[1150] Abel (1988: 143).
[1151] Kelley (2001: chapter 1).
[1152] Rostain (2006a).
[1153] Levin (2004–2005: 337–38).

Chapter 8

occurred elsewhere). But there is also evidence that his behavior—never accepting defeat or finality, moving to recuse every judge who ruled or threaten to rule against him—extended to other cases and clients.

Despite the substantial differences, doctors who practice "heroic medicine" offer an interesting analogy. Gawande observes that "the seemingly easiest and most sensible rule for a doctor to follow is: Always Fight. Always look for what more you could do." As a surgeon, he was personally sympathetic to that algorithm, especially because of the temptation to surrender too soon. "In the face of uncertainty, wisdom is to err on the side of pushing, to not give up." But he also recalled being upbraided by an angry ICU nurse: "What is it with you doctors? Don't you ever know when to stop?" He acknowledged that "you have to be ready to recognize when pushing is only ego, only weakness... when the pushing can turn to harm." "Good doctors should understand 'This is not about them. It's about the patient.'"

Because it is an interpersonal contest, the adversary system breeds even stronger loyalties, which can extend over years. Lawyers sometimes risk hurting clients by fighting too hard.[1154] But unrestrained partisanship poses a graver danger to the integrity of the legal system. As WGM correctly observed, the rule of law depends on lawyers being able to leave confidential documents on hearing room tables without having to fear their adversary will appropriate and read them. Moskowitz's dismissal of the lawsuit (eliminating Wisehart's contingent fee) was harsh but appropriate. I can think of two imperfect prophylactics for overzealousness. Partnership might inhibit excessive partisanship. Partners might be exposed to liability for disciplinary sanctions; in any case, the firm would suffer from the notoriety. It is noteworthy that the first two friends Wisehart approached for advice about the purloined papers rebuffed him. But partners' and colleagues' loyalty and ideological commitment might also intensify adversary zeal, as shown in Seham's embarrassing representation of Wisehart and the testimony that Purves gave and Wall offered. The "cab rank rule," which obligates British barristers to represent any client who can pay their fees and seeks services they are competent to perform, purports to moderate excessive partisanship. Before the creation of the Crown Prosecution Service it was not uncommon for a barrister to

---

[1154] In one of the vignettes in Lawrence Dubin's 1985 video *What Went Wrong*, a caring lawyer decided not to seek damages for a sexually abused mentally ill client he felt could not withstand the stress of litigation.

appear for the Crown in one case in the morning and for the accused in another that afternoon. But barristers have argued that the rule requires solo practice, one reason why solicitors have refused to adopt it.

Surveys of clients, quantitative analyses of disciplinary complaints and outcomes, and my own case studies all confirm that the legal profession's most pervasive, and intractable, problem is the inadequate quality of legal services. Solo practitioners—still more than a third of all lawyers and almost half of private practitioners in 2000[1155]—confront unique problems. More than 40 years ago, a solo matrimonial practitioner observed, "You can't be in the office and circulating at the same time. And you have to circulate to get known. But then office work takes a lot of time, a great deal of clerical work."[1156] Because the only facet of the lawyers' monopoly that is visible, and therefore is policed, is court hearings, many solo practitioners must spend a great deal of time in court. Muto bragged that he "practically live[d] at 26 Federal Plaza." He was not unique: a study of that Immigration Court found another eight lawyers appearing in 23 to 76 cases a month.[1157] Solo practitioners who cannot attend a hearing (because they are in another court or have personal obligations—or, as in Muto's case, cannot fly) hire "per diem" lawyers, who are likely to be unfamiliar with the case, unprepared for the hearing, and even totally inexperienced (the New Orleans lawyer Muto retained). Because they spend so much time in court, solo practitioners have difficulty completing out-of-court work. Some, like Kreitzer, delegate legal tasks, such as drafting complaints, to non-lawyers.[1158] Some lawyers just neglect these tasks. A few high-volume lawyers use large support staffs.[1159] But many solo practitioners have only a part-time secretary, and some not even that.[1160] A 1999 survey found that 41 percent of solo practitioners did all their own word processing.[1161]

[1155] Carson (2004: 7, table 7).
[1156] O'Gormon (1963); Seron (1996: 115, 118).
[1157] Mottino (2000).
[1158] In re Sledge, 859 So. 2d 671 (La. 2003) (solo practitioner disbarred for giving his signature stamp to law clerks and non-lawyers who drafted and filed pleadings, discovery responses, and correspondence); Spencer v. Steinman, 179 F.R.D. 484 (E.D. Pa. 1998) (lawyer sanctioned for failing to supervise paralegal who issued subpoena to nonparty without notice to parties); Mays v. Neal, 938 S.W.2d 830 (Ark. 1997) (lawyer disciplined for improper delegation to non-lawyers); Richmond (2003).
[1159] Levin (2004–2005: 343); Seron (1996: 99–100).
[1160] Levin (2004–2005: 343).
[1161] ABA (2000: 159).

CHAPTER 8

Muto may have been an outlier, but he was not unique.[1162] Levin's informants conceded,

> We're all over the place, the files are constantly pulled out and left around because I don't have time in the day to tend to housekeeping, and it's a problem because if a file is missing or misplaced, it's gone for all purposes....
>
> I can't tell you how much time I lose to files that you can't find....
>
> You can't always prosecute your cases as diligently as you should... a lot of things really do lie fallow... you have to say that something's done before it's done.[1163]

A Manhattan solo practitioner who relied on court appointments to represent indigent criminal defendants told a reporter, tossing an imaginary folder across the room, "I use the same filing the judges do." "They just throw it in the basket and someone else files it." But he did not have anyone else. "Sometimes I come back here and I throw it down and then when the deadline comes for the motions, I miss them." He was comfortable being a .250 hitter. But the three out of four clients whose cases he lost were not.[1164] A California criminal defense attorney was jailed by a judge for repeatedly missing hearings.[1165]

Solo and small firm lawyers have difficulty achieving profitability and can only be awed by, and envious of, the extraordinary incomes of their large firm colleagues. Most of their clients are poor, the amounts in controversy low, and opponents often intransigent. One lawyer said that for "most clients, it's a toss-up [between] whether it's fast and cheap or cheap and fast."[1166] Lawyers, like all service providers, have only one commodity to sell: their time. In order to maximize the return on time, they want a queue of consumers waiting for their services.[1167] Like doctors or

---

[1162] Adam Liptak, "The Verge of Expulsion, the Fringe of Justice," New York Times (4.15.08) (Frank R. Liu referred to 2nd Circuit disciplinary panel for "seriously deficient" work; he agreed: "Some attorneys, including myself, do not spend enough time.... I was probably not qualified to do the job.).
[1163] Levin (2004–2005: 344–45).
[1164] David Rohde, "Caseloads Push System to Breaking Point," New York Times A1 (4.9.01).
[1165] Jack Leonard, "Tardy lawyer thrown in jail," Los Angeles Times B1 (6.6.08).
[1166] Seron (1996: 108).
[1167] Casper (1972: 102); Hensler et al. (1985: 90–91); Mather (1979: 24) (public defender); Dingwall & Durkin (1995: 375–76); Felstiner (1997: 121, 140–41).

building contractors, they overbook, in part because they suffer no penalty for doing so. In the 1960s, a divorce lawyer complained,

> A lawyer to live must have volume. I have volume, but it is killing me. . . . One week you're as busy as you can be, and then you sit around for weeks or months until another busy spell sets in. . . . To tell you the truth, I'm in no position to refuse any kind of client.[1168]

Thirty years later, an Oregon State Bar survey found that 27 percent of lawyers had more work than they could handle and another 42 percent were at the limit of their workloads.[1169] Under that pressure, lawyers will accept clients they are not competent to represent (as Muto took on divorce clients in Syracuse when threatened with mortgage foreclosure and then abandoned them because he did not know how to do divorces). Lawyers compensate for low profit margins by increasing volume.[1170] The court-appointed criminal defense lawyer quoted above (who lost his files and three-quarters of his cases) earned $125,041 in 2000 by handling 1,600 clients.[1171] A court-appointed guardian for incompetents explained, "I was overwhelmed by a tremendous amount of work. I only had sporadic and temporary clerical help. I had enough work for several lawyers."[1172] The "franchise law firms" pioneered by Jacoby & Meyers and Hyatt Legal Services emulate managed health care and compete in price by truncating client interviews. One lawyer employee said "I'm not interested in their life stories. When you have people scheduled only 15 minutes apart, I don't have time for it and it's not necessary."[1173] Lawyers tend to be workaholics. Solo practitioners, like other small businesses, often drive themselves brutally hard.[1174] Some feel that because they punish themselves, clients have no right to complain. But of course there is no connection.

[1168] O'Gorman (1963: 47, 63–64).
[1169] Ramos (1994: 1715 n.358) (almost all worked alone or in small firms).
[1170] Until 2003 New York paid $40 an hour in court and $25 an hour outside—with the result that lawyers did no work out of court. Susan Saulny, "Lawyers' Fees to Defend Poor Will Increase," New York Times B1 (11.13.03).
[1171] David Rohde, "Caseloads Push System to Breaking Point," New York Times A1 (4.9.01).
[1172] Leonnig et al. (2003).
[1173] Van Hoy (1997: 57).
[1174] Levin (2004–2005: 342) (more than 70 hours a week).

CHAPTER 8

Again I found insights in medicine's quality controls.[1175] Many iatrogenic injuries are not the outcomes of complex judgments about which reasonable doctors could disagree. Each year American hospitals infect 2 million patients, 90,000 of whom die as a result. Health care providers have known since 1847 that a principal cause of infection is their failure to wash their hands adequately: only a third to a half do so today. The main obstacle is time, especially as cost-cutting forces speed-ups. Alcohol gel, which has been used in Europe for two decades, is faster than soap and water. By substituting it, one American hospital increased compliance from 40 to 70 percent. But the infection rate did not drop because even 70 percent was not good enough. The hospital then hired an industrial engineer, who systematically eliminated wasted time. As compliance rose, infection rates from the most common bacteria fell almost 90 percent. But the innovations did not spread to other units and were abandoned when the engineer left. A 2006 study by Johns Hopkins University researchers found that a five-step checklist reduced the rate of bloodstream infections from intravenous lines by two-thirds in three months.[1176] Unfortunately, the federal Office for Human Research Protections ruled that the intervention constituted human experimentation and therefore required prior consent of each of the thousands of patients.[1177] (Coincidentally, another study found low levels of compliance with standard procedures for urinary catheters, which correlated with high levels of urinary tract infection.[1178])

A 1933 study found that although two-thirds of maternal deaths in childbirth and an even higher proportion of neonatal deaths were preventable, rates had not improved for two decades.[1179]

> Many physicians simply didn't know what they were doing: they missed clear signs of hemorrhagic shock and other treatable conditions, violated basic antiseptic standards, tore and infected women with misapplied forceps.

[1175] Gawande (2007: 14–24); Anemona Hartocollis, "In Hospitals, Simple Reminders Reduce Deadly Infections," New York Times A22 (5.19.08).

[1176] Pronovost et al. (2006); Atul Gawande, "The Checklist," The New Yorker 86 (12.10.07); Jane E. Brody, "A Basic Hospital To-Do List Saves Lives," New York Times D7 (1.22.08).

[1177] Atul Gawande, "A Lifesaving Checklist," New York Times § 4 p. 8 (12.30.07). The New York Times editorialized against this: "Pointy-Headed Regulation," New York Times § 4 p. 15 (1.27.08).

[1178] Saint et al. (2008).

[1179] Gawande (2007: 179–92).

Midwives had better outcomes. By the 1950s—after hospitals instituted training, regulated who could perform deliveries and what steps to follow, limited the use of forceps, and investigated all maternal deaths—they declined from 0.7 percent to 0.01 percent. But more than 3 percent of neonates were still dying, a rate that had not changed for a century. In 1953 Dr. Virginia Apgar published her scheme for scoring the condition of neonates, turning "an intangible and impressionistic clinical concept ... into numbers that people could collect and compare." Hospitals created neonatal ICUs for the most vulnerable. Doctors competing for better scores found that spinal and epidural anesthesia produced them. In difficult births, a few highly skilled obstetricians could produce as good a result for the infant with forceps as with C-sections, which were much more traumatic for mothers. But because most doctors were not adept with forceps, they were replaced by C-sections. As a result, neonatal deaths have declined from more than 3 percent to 0.02 percent, and maternal deaths have fallen to 0.001 percent.

Data on the quality of the 117 specialist-certified treatment centers for cystic fibrosis found that patients had a 30-year life expectancy at the average center but enjoyed 46 years at the best.[1180] The director of the latter "insists on a degree of uniformity that clinicians usually find intolerable." The same Bell curve is found in many other procedures. The likelihood of a recurrence following a hernia operation varies from 10 percent at the bottom to 0.2 percent at the top. Risk adjusted death rates in neonatal ICUs vary from 6 to 16 percent. The success of in vitro fertilization ranges from 15 to over 65 percent.

Gawande believes that publicizing such differences can motivate improvement among those at the bottom. The comparative information a private service sold through the Internet was virtually useless. In 1986, in response to *The New York Times*, the federal government produced an index ranking all hospitals by death rates for elderly and disabled Medicare patients.[1181] Because this "Death List" did not control for entry condition and exhibited high annual volatility, it was withdrawn under pressure from the hospitals in 1992. In June 2007, the Department of Health and Human Services released a report on some 5,000 hospitals, identifying 42 where heart patients were most likely to die and 55 where they were least

---

[1180] Id. 205–28.
[1181] Gardiner Harris, "Report Rates Hospitals on Their Heart Treatment," New York Times A11 (6.22.07); "(Sort of) Rating Hospitals," New York Times A24 (6.26.07). The list is available at www.hospitalcompare.hhs.gov.

CHAPTER 8

likely (controlling for patient health and medical history).[1182] The American Hospital Association had cooperated with the study "because we believe that patients should have the information they need to make choices." (In fact, patients got only the information above; information about the other 99.8 percent of hospitals in the middle went only to those hospitals.) One low-ranked hospital called it "a statistical anomaly related to hospice-type patients" and concluded, after a review, that it had provided appropriate care to each patient who had died. But another low-ranked hospital said "we take the data very seriously." Veterans' hospitals and some teaching hospitals record and compare surgeons' complications and death rates; and four of the most populous states publicize such data on every cardiac surgeon. Consumers' Checkbook recently persuaded a federal judge to force the Department of Health and Human Services to release data on the 700,000 doctors who treat 40 million Medicare patients.[1183] Medicare is also paying doctors a 1.5 percent bonus for reporting quality measures.[1184] Under pressure from Mayor Bloomberg, the New York City Health and Hospitals Corporation (the largest public health system in the country) will release data on infection and death rates at its 11 hospitals.[1185] Gawande concludes that

> the scientific effort to improve performance in medicine—an effort that at present gets only a miniscule portion of scientific budgets—can arguably save more lives in the next decade than bench science . . . research on the genome, stem cell therapy, cancer vaccines.[1186]

Geisinger Health System in Pennsylvania charges a flat fee for elective heart bypass surgery, including 90 days of follow-up treatment.[1187] This creates a strong incentive to avoid errors (which result in additional hospitalization, typically costing $12,000–$15,000). Studies have found

---

[1182] See the full-page advertisement "Compare the Quality of Your Local Hospitals," New York Times A11 (5.21.08) (www.hospitalcompare.hhs.gov).
[1183] Ricardo Alonso-Zaldivar, "Ruling May Unlock Key Data on Doctors," Los Angeles Times (8.30.07). See www.hospitalcompare.hhs.gov.
[1184] Manoj Jain, "Putting Pay on the Line to Improve Health Care," New York Times F5 (9.4.07).
[1185] Sarah Kershaw, "New York City Puts Hospital Error Data Online," New York Times B1 (9.7.07).
[1186] Gawande (2007: 232).
[1187] Reed Abelson, "In Bid for Better Care, Surgery with a Warranty," New York Times A1 (5.17.07).

that large proportions of patients are denied the most basic treatments: the right kind of antibiotics for pneumonia at the right time, aspirin after heart attacks, antibiotics before hip surgery. Noting that heart surgery mortality varied from zero to nearly 10 percent within Pennsylvania, Geisinger standardized its heart bypass procedure, which its seven surgeons each had done differently. It identified 40 essential steps, increasing compliance with all of them from 59 to 100 percent. It boasts that its mortality rate for coronary artery bypass grafts is 0.7 percent, compared with a national benchmark of 2.1 percent.[1188] Regenstrief Institute in Indianapolis has created a patient medical record database covering five hospital chains, 20 public primary care clinics, 30 public school clinics, and 3,000 medical specialists, which has achieved major gains in health care quality.[1189]

Lawyers could draw many useful lessons from doctors. Almost no doctor practices alone today; it is not clear that any lawyer should do so. Litigators need others to make appearances and mind the office. (Although English barristers must be sole practitioners, they work in chambers whose clerks keep their calendars and find substitutes when there are time conflicts.) Multi-lawyer firms would have a reputational interest in preventing misconduct and a financial incentive in ensuring minimum quality (malpractice liability and insurance premium levels). Missed deadlines are the iatrogenic infections of law. Rapid advances in information technology make electronic tickler systems foolproof (except for data entry). There is no more excuse for litigators to operate without them than for car drivers not to buckle up. Legal clinics (also known as franchise law firms) have demonstrated that standardizing practice can reduce both errors and cost.[1190] The quality of a nation's justice is determined less by how it handles the rare high profile case than by how it routinely processes garden variety claims. Compulsory partnership would disproportionately burden minority lawyers, who are overrepresented among sole practitioners, but it also would disproportionately benefit their clients, who are also more likely to be minorities.

Lawyers should be allowed to compete freely. In the 30 years since the U.S. Supreme Court recognized lawyers' First Amendment rights in

---

[1188] www.geisinger.org.
[1189] Shekelle (2006), cited in Simon Head, "They're Micromanaging Your Every Move," 54 (13) New York Review of Books 43 (8.16.07).
[1190] Van Hoy (1997).

CHAPTER 8

commercial speech, state bars have persisted in restraining advertising.[1191] Clients are as needy and deserving of information about the cost and quality of legal services as patients are about medical care. The variance in quality between Joseph Muto and Jan Reiner or Ann Hsiung was at least as great as that between the worst and best doctors. Clients need an Apgar score for successful lawyering. The largest private physicians' practice in California, serving more than 500,000 patients, has posted the price of 58 common procedures on its website;[1192] lawyers could do the same. Malpractice claims and disciplinary complaints and their outcomes (including settlements) should be available online.[1193]

Medicine began certifying specialists decades ago. Law has been slow to follow suit, often grandfathering in practitioners on the basis of experience without assessing expertise. In Britain, patients first must consult general medical practitioners, who alone can refer them to specialist consultants. Until recently, British clients first had to consult solicitors, who alone could refer them to barrister advocates. Specialization would force lawyers to develop measures of quality. (There is a danger, of course, that it could become yet another restrictive practice, allowing specialists to extract higher monopoly rents.)

Given the difficulty laypeople encounter in evaluating quality, referral sources could play an invaluable role.[1194] Merely aggregating client reactions—the equivalent of Zagat's for restaurants, online ratings for hotels, and Angie's List for many other services—risks letting superficial judgments of style eclipse substantive measures of lawyer performance.[1195] Controversy has raged over publicizing consumer complaints and evaluations of children's toys, child-care providers, police, and judges.[1196] But for-profit

---

[1191] Compare Bates v. State Bar of Arizona, 433 U.S. 350 (1977), with Florida Bar v. Went For It., Inc., 115 S. Ct. 1792 (1993); see Maria Aspan, "Getting Law Firms to Like Commercials," New York Times C5 (6.19.07) (in February 2007, New York prohibited lawyers from using actors in television advertisements without identification, client endorsements, or images or slogans). See Rhode (2000: 211).
[1192] Lisa Girion, "Doctors' List Puts a Price on Care," Los Angeles Times A1 (5.28.07).
[1193] See Rhode (2000: 211).
[1194] Zacharias (2007: 631–40). But the referral sources would have to be regulated. Kirk Johnson, "Vast Legal-Aid Fraud Laid to Two Brothers," New York Times A14 (2.16.08) (Legal Aid National Services and Legal Aid Divorce Services took money and did nothing).
[1195] Shari Roan, "The rating room," Los Angeles Times F1 (5.19.08) (www.RateMDs.com; www.Dr.Score.com; www.Healthgrades.com; www.vitals.com; www.nursesrecommenddoctors.com; www.angieslist.com. Zagat has even collaborated with Wellpoint Inc.).
[1196] Noam N. Levey, "Fight looms over consumer database," Los Angeles Times (3.6.08); Donna St. George, "Parents Weigh Day-Care Options Online," Washington Post A1 (4.14.08); Rebecca Cathcart, "Irked by a Ticket? Now Drivers Can Rate the Officer Who Issued It,"

referral sources (perhaps using legally trained evaluators) could assess and monitor the lawyers to whom they make referrals, transforming one-shot clients into repeat players, who would have the market power to demand quality (as unions allow members to do).[1197] One online service uses "years in practice, disciplinary history, professional achievements and industry recognition."[1198] Referral sources would have to be transparent about financial relationships with the lawyers to whom they refer and liable in negligence for the information they sell. They would rightly be concerned about liability, given lawyers' litigiousness.[1199] Third-party payers (Medicare, Medicaid, private insurance, and the employers who pay most of the insurance premiums) have long monitored the price and quality of medical services.[1200] But there is no realistic prospect of replicating this for legal services. Legal aid is drastically underfunded, serves a tiny segment of the population, and is severely limited in the functions it may perform; no constituency promotes its expansion. Legal expenses insurance is virtually universal in Germany and has become much more widespread in Britain since the government replaced legal aid for money claims with conditional fees. But few Americans have legal expenses insurance, which covers only a narrow range of services.

The boundaries of the legal monopoly (which includes advice) are broader in the United States than anywhere else and should be drastically contracted.[1201] Much of what solo and small firm lawyers do badly laypersons could do better and more cheaply. Indeed, much of it *is* done by laypersons but billed by lawyers, who pocket the surplus value. In Britain,

---

New York Times A11 (4.22.08); "More Information on Judges," New York Times A18 (3.12.08).

[1197] The enormous influence of the U.S. News and World Report ranking of colleges and universities has prompted them to produce their own websites with comparative information. Alan Finder, "Colleges Join Forces on a Web Presence to Let Prospective Students Research and Compare," New York Times B8 (7.4.07).

[1198] http://www.avvo.com.

[1199] Adam Liptak, "On Second Thought, Let's Just Rate All the Lawyers," New York Times (7.2.07) (Avvo.com sued by criminal defense lawyer whose rating was low because of admonition over fee dispute); "National Briefing: Northwest: Washington: Lawyers Can Take a Number," New York Times A24 (12.20.07) (U.S. District Court in Seattle dismissed lawsuit by John Henry Browne and Alan J. Wenokur).

[1200] Ellen Nakashima, "Doctors Rated but Can't Get a Second Opinion," Washington Post A1 (7.25.07); Ricardo Alonso-Zaldivar, "Medicare data should stay private, government says in appeal," Los Angeles Times A21 (4.19.08).

[1201] For an example of abusive enforcement of unauthorized practice rules, see Vladeck (2006). The U.S. Supreme Court recently recognized the rights of parents to represent themselves in seeking relief under the Individuals with Disabilities Education Act. Winkelman v. Parma City School District, 2007 WL 1461151 (U.S.). See Rhode (2000: 209).

Chapter 8

immigration consultants do much of the work for which travel agencies had to hire Muto, and claims agents do much of the personal injury settlement negotiation that Kreitzer delegated to his subordinates.[1202] But the American Immigration Lawyers Association wants the federal government to criminalize lay advice.[1203] And other bar associations continue to police their indefensible rules against unauthorized practice of law. If laypeople were allowed to perform functions currently restricted to lawyers, states would need to regulate quality and ensure that service providers were financially responsible for errors.

For more than a decade, American lawyers have bewailed the crisis in their profession, wringing their hands about its bad image. But their response has been limited to wasting money on public relations, mandating education of no demonstrated value, tinkering with ethical rules, and cracking down in a tiny number of high visibility cases. These measures will do nothing to solve the problems exposed by my six disciplinary case examples. The structural changes described above are first steps in restoring the public trust in lawyers. Can the profession muster the political will to reform?

[1202] Abel (2003: 230–33, 314–15).
[1203] "Consumer Protection and the Unauthorized Practice of Law," AILA Dispatch 7 (7/8 2003).

References

ABA (American Bar Association). 1995. Non-lawyer Activity in Law-Related Situations: A Report with Recommendations. Chicago: ABA.

———. 1998. The Legal Assistant's Practice Guide to Professional Responsibility. Chicago: ABA.

———. 2000. 1999 Legal Technology Survey Report. Chicago: ABA Legal Technology Resource Center.

ABA Center for Professional Responsibility. 1986. A Survey on the Teaching of Professional Responsibility. Chicago: ABA.

ABA Commission on Billable Hours. 2002. Report 2001–2002. Chicago: ABA.

ABA Commission on Evaluation of Disciplinary Enforcement. 1991. Report to the House of Delegates: Lawyer Regulation for a New Century. Chicago: ABA.

ABA Commission on Nonlawyer Practice. 1994. Nonlawyer Practice in the United States: Summary of the Factual Record. Chicago: ABA.

ABA Commission on Professionalism. 1986. "In the Spirit of Public Service," A Blueprint for the Rekindling of Lawyer Professionalism. Chicago: ABA.

ABA House of Delegates. 1998. Guidelines for Litigation Conduct. Chicago: ABA.

ABA Section of Litigation, Modest Means Task Force. 2003. Handbook on Limited Scope Legal Assistance. Chicago: ABA.

ABA Special Committee on Evaluation of Disciplinary Enforcement. 1970. Problems and Recommendations in Disciplinary Enforcement (Clark Report). Chicago: ABA.

ABA Standing Committee on Lawyers' Professional Liability. 1986. Profile of Legal Malpractice: A Statistical Study of Determinative Characteristics of Claims Asserted Against Attorneys. Chicago: ABA.

———. 1989. Characteristics of Legal Malpractice: Report of the National Legal Malpractice Data Center. Chicago: ABA.

———. 1996. Legal Malpractice Claims in the 1990s. Chicago: ABA.

———. 2001. Profile of Legal Malpractice Claims 1996–1999. Chicago: ABA.

References

ABA Standing Committee on Paralegals. 1991. Model Guidelines for the Utilization of Paralegals. Chicago: ABA.

ABCNY (Association of the Bar of the City of New York) Ethics Committee. 1996. "The Evolving Lawyer-Client Relationship and Its Effect on the Lawyer's Professional Obligations," 51 The Record 441.

Abel, Richard L. 1981. "Why Does the ABA Promulgate Ethical Rules?" 59 Texas L. Rev. 639.

_____. 1987. "The Real Tort Crisis: Too Few Claims," 48 Ohio State L. J. 443.

_____. 1988. The Legal Profession in England and Wales. Oxford: Basil Blackwell.

_____. 1989. American Lawyers. New York: Oxford University Press.

_____. 1998. Speaking Respect, Respecting Speech. Chicago: University of Chicago Press.

_____. 2003. English Lawyers between Market and State: The Politics of Professionalism. Oxford: Oxford University Press.

_____. 2006. "Practicing Immigration Law in Filene's Basement," 84 North Carolina L. Rev. 1449.

_____. 2007. Review of Galanter (2006), 57 J. Legal Educ. 130.

Acker, J. Alex. 1995. "Alex's Story," chapter 5 in Gonsiorek.

Akerlof, G. 1970. "The Market for 'Lemons': Qualitative Uncertainty and the Market Mechanism," 84 Q. J. Econ. 488.

Anabtawi, Iman. 2004. "Secret Compensation," 82 North Carolina L. Rev. 835.

Angell, Marcia. 2005. The Truth about Drug Companies: How They Deceive Us and What to Do about It. New York: Random House.

Apfel, Roberta J. and Susan M. Fisher. 1984. To Do No Harm: DES and the Dilemmas of Modern Medicine. New Haven: Yale Univ. P.

Arnold, Bruce L. and John Hagan. 1992. "Careers of Misconduct: The Structure of Prosecuted Professional Deviance among Lawyers," 57 American Sociol. Rev. 771.

_____. 1995. "Self-regulatory Responses to Professional Misconduct within the Legal Profession," 32 Canadian Rev. Sociol. and Anthrop. 168.

Arnold, Bruce L. and Fiona Kay. 1995. "Social Capital, Violations of Trust and the Vulnerability of Isolates: The Social Organization of Law Practice and Professional Self-Regulation," 23 Int'l J. Sociol. of Law 321.

Arrow, Kenneth. 1974. The Limits of Organization. New York: Norton.

Arthurs, S. 1970. "Discipline in the Legal Profession in Ontario," 7 Osgoode Hall L. J. 235.

Aubert, Vilhelm. 1952. "White-Collar Crime and Social Structure," 58 American J. Sociol. 263, reprinted as chapter 10 in Geis & Meier (1977a).

Auerbach, Jerold J. 1976. Unequal Justice: Lawyers and Social Change in Modern America. New York: Oxford University Press.

Axelrod, Robert. 1984. The Evolution of Cooperation. New York: Basic Books.

Bachrach, Michael and Diego Gambetta. 2001. "Trust in Signs," chapter 5 in Cook (2001).

Baker, Tom and Jonathan Simon, eds. 2002. Embracing Risk: The Changing Culture of Insurance and Responsibility. Chicago: University of Chicago Press.

Ball, Harry. 1977. "Social Structure and Rent-Control Violations," chapter 11 in Geis & Meier (1977a) (first published 1960).

Ball, Howard. 1986. Downwind: America's Atomic Testing Program in the 1950s. New York: Oxford University Press.

Barber, Bernard. 1978. "Control and Responsibility in the Powerful Professions," 93 Pol. Sci. Q. 599.

_____. 1983. The Logic and Limits of Trust. New Brunswick, N.J.: Rutgers University Press.

Barlow, Hugh D. 1993. "From Fiddle Factors to Networks of Collusion," 20 Crime, Law and Social Change 319, reprinted pp. 127–36 in Shover & Wright (2001a).

Barnes, Jennifer. 2003. "The Lawyer-Client Relationship in Immigration Law," 52 Emory L. J. 1215.

Barton, Benjamin H. 2003. "An Institutional Analysis of Lawyer Regulation—Who Should Control Lawyer Regulation, Courts, Legislatures, or the Market?" 37 Georgia L. Rev. 1167.

Baumhart, Raymond C. 1961. "How Ethical Are Businessmen?" 39 Harvard Bus. J. 6, 156.

Baxter, Ward. 1974. Illegal Attorney Referral Activity in Los Angeles County. Los Angeles: Los Angeles County Board of Supervisors.

Beam, Alex. 2006. "Greed on Trial," chapter 10 in Rhode & Luban (2006).

Bebchuck, Lucian A., Yaniv Grinkstein and Urs Peyer. 2006a. Lucky CEOs. Cambridge, Mass: Harvard Law School (Discussion Paper 566).

_____. 2006b. Lucky Directors. Cambridge, Mass.: Harvard Law School (Discussion Paper 573).

Becker, Howard S. 1973. Outsiders: Studies in the Sociology of Deviance. Glencoe, Ill.: Free Press.

Bekelman, Justin E., Yan Li and Cary P. Gross. 2003. "Scope and Impact of Financial Conflicts of Interest in Biomedical Research," 289 JAMA 454 (Jan. 22).

Benedectis, Don J. 1991. "California Bar Drops Technician Plan," 77 ABAJ 36 (Nov.).

Bennett, Alan. 2006. Untold Stories. New York: Farrar, Straus & Giroux.

Benowitz, Mindy. 1995. "Comparing the Experiences of Women Clients Sexually Exploited by Female Versus Male Psychotherapists," chapter 18 in Gonsiorek.

Benson, Michael L. 1985. "Denying the Guilty Mind: Accounting for Involvement in a White-Collar Crime," 23 Criminol. 583.

Bera, Walter H. 1995. "Betrayal: Clergy Sexual Abuse and Male Survivors," chapter 10 in Gonsiorek.

Berle, Adolf A., Jr. and Gardner C. Means. 1932. The Modern Corporation and Private Property. New York: Commerce Clearing House, Inc.

References

Berman, Harold J. 1963. Justice in the U.S.S.R.: An Interpretation of Soviet Law. Cambridge, Mass.: Harvard University Press.

Bero, Lisa A., A. Galbraith and D. Rennie. 1992. "The Publication of Sponsored Symposiums in Medical Journals," 327 NEJM 1135 (Oct. 15).

Bianco, W. T. 1994. Trust: Representatives and Constituents. Ann Arbor: University of Michigan Press.

Bissell, Leclair and Robert W. Jones. 1976. "The Alcoholic Physician: A Survey," 133 Am. J. Psychiatry 1142–46.

Blair, Jayson. 2004. Burning Down My Masters' House: My Life at the *New York Times*. Beverly Hills, CA: New Millennium Press.

Blau, Peter M. 1964. Exchange and Power in Social Life. New York: Wiley.

Blaustein, Albert P. 1951. "The Association of the Bar of the City of New York, 1870–1951," 6 The Record 261.

Blaustein, Albert P. and Charles O. Porter. 1954. The American Lawyer: A Summary of the Survey of the Legal Profession. Chicago: University of Chicago Press.

Blomquist, Helle. 2000. Lawyers' Ethics. Copenhagen: DJØF Publishers.

Blum, Richard. 1972. Deceivers and Deceived. Springfield, Ill.: Charles Thomas.

Blumberg, Abraham S. 1967. "The Practice of Law as a Confidence Game: Organizational Cooptation of a Profession," 1 Law & Soc'y Rev. 15.

Blumberg, Paul. 1989. The Predatory Society: Deception in the American Marketplace. New York: Oxford University Press.

Bohn, Martin J. 1971. "Psychological Needs of Engineering, Pre-Law, Pre-Medical, and Undecided College Freshmen," 12 J. C. Student Personnel 359.

Bok, Derek. 2003. Universities in the Marketplace. Princeton, N.J.: Princeton University Press.

Bosk, Charles L. 1979. Forgive and Remember: Managing Medical Failure. Chicago: University of Chicago Press.

Boston Globe Investigative Staff. 2002. Betrayal: The Crisis in the Catholic Church. Boston: Little Brown.

Bovbjerg, Randall R. and Kenneth R. Petronis. 1994. "The Relationship between Physicians' Malpractice Claims History and Later Claims. Does the Past Predict the Future?" 272 JAMA 1421.

Box, Steven. 1983. Power, Crime and Mystification. London: Tavistock.

Braithwaite, John. 1984. Corporate Crime in the Pharmaceutical Industry. London: Routledge & Kegan Paul.

_____. 1985. "White Collar Crime," 11 Annual Review of Sociology 1.

_____. 1989. "Criminological Theory and Organizational Crime," 6 Justice Q. 333.

Braithwaite, John and Gilbert Geis. 1982. "On Theory and Action for Corporate Crime Control," 28 Crime and Delinquency 292, reprinted in Shover & Wright (2001a).

Braithwaite, Valerie and Margaret Levi, eds. 1998. Trust and Governance. New York: Russell Sage.

Braithwaite, John and Toni Makkai. 1991. "Testing an Expected Utility Model of Corporate Deterrence," 25 Law & Soc'y Rev. 7.

Brann, P. and M. Foddy. 1988. "Trust and the Consumption of a Deteriorating Resource," 31 J. Conflict Resolution 615.

Brazil, Wayne D. 1980a. "Views from the Front Lines: Observations by Chicago Lawyers About the System of Civil Discovery," 1980 Am. Bar Fndn Res. J. 217.

_____. 1980b. "Civil Discovery: Lawyers' Views of Its Effectiveness, Its Principal Problems and Abuses," 1980 Am. Bar Fndn Res. J. 787.

_____. 1981. "Improving Judicial Controls over the Pretrial Development of Civil Actions: Model Rules for Case Management and Sanctions," 1981 Am. Bar Fndn Res. J. 875.

Brennan, Troyen A. et al. 2006. "Healthy Industry Practices That Create Conflicts of Interest: A Policy Proposal for Academic Medical Centers," 295 JAMA 429 (Jan. 25).

Brewster, Mike. 2003. Unaccountable: How the Accounting Profession Forfeited a Public Trust. New York: John Wiley.

Brickman, Lester. 1995. "Contingent Fees without Contingencies: Hamlet without the Prince of Denmark?" 37 UCLA L. Rev. 29 (1989).

_____. 1996. "ABA Regulation of Contingency Fees: Money Talks, Ethics Walks," 65 Fordham L. Rev. 247.

Bridger, Harold. 1971. "A viewpoint on organizational behavior," in G. Wolstenholme and M. O'Connor, eds., pp. 187–90 Proceedings of CIBA Foundation Symposium on Teamwork for World Health. London: J. and A. Churchill.

British Medical Association. 2003. BMA Survey of Waiting Times. London: BMA.

Brockman, Joan and Colin McEwen. 1990. "Self-regulation in the Legal Profession: Funnel In, Funnel Out, or Funnel Away?" 5 Canadian J. Law & Soc'y 1.

Brody, Howard. 2007. Hooked: Ethics, the Medical Profession and the Pharmaceutical Industry. Lanham, Md.: Rowman & Littlefield.

Bromberg, Walter. 1965. Crime and the Mind: A Psychiatric Analysis of Crime and Punishment. New York: Macmillan.

Brown, Esther Lucille. 1938. Lawyers and the Promotion of Justice. New York: Russell Sage Foundation.

Burgess, Ann Wolbert. 1981. "Physician Sexual Misconduct and Patients' Responses," 138 Am. J. Psychiatry 1335–42.

Burt, Ronald S. and Marc Knez. 1996. "Trust and Third-Party Gossip," chapter 5 in Kramer & Tyler (1996).

Butler, Sharon and Seymour L. Zelan. 1977. "Sexual intimacies between therapists and patients," 14 Psychotherapy 139–45.

Cahn, Edmond. 1955. "Cheating on Taxes," in The Moral Decision. Bloomington: Indiana University Press.

Callahan, David. 2004. The Cheating Culture: Why More Americans Are Doing Wrong to Get Ahead. Orlando, Fla.: Harcourt, Inc.

References

Campbell, Eric G., Russell L. Gruen, James Mountford, Lawrence G. Miller, Paul D. Cleary and David Blumenthal. 2007a. "A National Survey of Physician-Industry Relationships," 356 NEJM 1742.

Campbell, Eric G., Susan Regan, Russell L. Gruen, Timothy G. Ferris, Sowmya R. Rao, Paul D. Cleary, and David Blumenthal. 2007b. "Professionalism in Medicine: Results of a National Survey of Physicians," 147 Annals of Internal Medicine 795.

Caplovitz, David. 1963. The Poor Pay More: Consumer Practices of Low-Income Families. Glencoe, Ill.: Free Press.

Cappell, Charles L. and Terence C. Halliday. 1983. "Professional Projects of Elite Chicago Lawyers, 1950–1974," 1983 Am. Bar Fndn Res. J. 291.

Carey, James T. 1978. Introduction to Criminology. Englewood Cliffs, N.J.: Prentice-Hall.

———. 1987. "Benton Harlow: Distributor of Unsafe Drugs," chapter 13 in Hills.

Carlin, Jerome E. 1962. Lawyers on Their Own: A Study of Individual Practitioners in Chicago. New Brunswick, N.J.: Rutgers University Press.

———. 1966. Lawyers' Ethics: A Survey of the New York City Bar. New York: Russell Sage Foundation.

Carroll, Lewis (Charles Dodgson). 1940. Alice in Wonderland. Mount Vernon, NY: Peter Pauper Press (first published 1865).

Carson, Clara N. 2004. The Lawyer Statistical Report: The U.S. Legal Profession in 2000. Chicago: American Bar Foundation.

Casper, Jonathan D. American Criminal Justice: The Defendant's Perspective. Englewood Cliffs, N.J.: Prentice Hall.

Caudill, Harry M. 1987. "Manslaughter in a Coal Mine," chapter 7 in Hills.

Centrella, Michael. 1994. "Physician Addiction and Impairment—Current Thinking: A Review," 13 J. Addict Diseases 91.

Chambliss, Elizabeth. 2006. "The Professionalization of Law Firm In-House Counsel," 84 North Carolina L. Rev. 1515.

Chambliss, William J. 1967. "Types of Deviance and the Effectiveness of Legal Sanctions," 1967 Wisconsin L. Rev. 703.

Charles, Sara C., Jeffrey R. Wilbert and Kevin. J. Franke. 1985. "Sued and Nonsued Physicians' Self-Reported Reactions to Malpractice Litigation," 142 Am. J. Psychiatry 437–40.

Chesler, Phyllis. 1972. Women and Madness. Garden City, N.Y.: Doubleday.

Chibnall, Steven and Peter Saunders. 1977. "Worlds Apart: Notes on the Social Relativity of Corruption," 28 Brit. J. Sociol. 138.

Chin, Gabriel J. and Scott C. Wells. 1999. "Can a Reasonable Doubt Have an Unreasonable Price? Limitations on Attorneys' Fees in Criminal Cases," 41 Boston Coll. L. Rev. 1.

Christensen, Christa, Suzanne Day and Jane Worthington. 1999. "'Learned Profession?—the Stuff of Sherry Talk': the Response to Practice Rule 15?" 6 Int'l J. Legal Prof. 27.

Chusmir, Leonard H. 1984. "Law and Jurisprudence Occupations: A Look at Motivational Need Patterns," Com. L. J. 231 (May).

Clarke, Michael. 1990. Business Crime: Its Nature and Control. Oxford: Polity Press.

Clinard, Marshall B. 1952. The Black Market. New York: Rinehart.

_____. 1977. "Criminological Theories of Violations of Wartime Regulations," chapter 5 in Geis & Meier (1977a) (first published 1946).

Clinard, Marshall B. and Robert F. Meier. 1979. Sociology of Deviant Behavior (5th ed.). New York: Holt, Rinehart and Winston.

Clinard, Marshall B. and Peter C. Yeager. 1980. Corporate Crime. New York: Free Press.

Cohen, Albert, Albert Lindesmith and Karl Schuesller, eds. 1956. The Sutherland Papers. Bloomington: Indiana University Press.

Coleman, James S. 1990. The Foundations of Social Theory. Cambridge, Mass.: Harvard University Press.

Coleman, James W. 1985. The Criminal Elite: The Sociology of White Collar Crime. New York: St. Martin's Press.

_____. 1987. "Toward an Integrated Theory of White-Collar Crime," 93 Am. J. Sociol. 406.

_____. 2001. "Competition and Motivation to White-Collar Crime," in Shover & Wright (2001a) (adaptation of 1987).

Coney, S. 1994. "Medical Manslaughter in New Zealand," 343 Lancet 1091.

Conklin, John E. 1972. Robbery and the Criminal Justice System. New York: Lippincott.

_____. 1977. "Illegal But Not Criminal": Business Crime in America. Englewood Cliffs, N.J.: Prentice-Hall.

Connolly, Paul R. J., Edith A. Holleman and Michael J. Kuhlman. 1978. Judicial Controls and the Civil Litigative Process: Discovery. Washington, D.C.: Federal Judicial Center.

Cook, Alberta I. 1986. "Complaints Rise Against Lawyers," 9(7) Nat'l L. J. 1 (Oct. 27).

Cook, D. 1989. Rich Law, Poor Law: Different Responses to Tax and Supplementary Benefits Fraud. Milton Keynes: Open University Press.

Cook, Karen S., ed. 2001. Trust in Society. New York: Russell Sage.

Cooper, J. B. et al. 1978. "Preventable Anesthesia Mishaps: A Study of Human Factors," 49 Anesthesiology 965–75.

Cooper, Jeffrey B., Ronald S. Newbower and Richard J. Kitz. 1984. "An Analysis of Major Errors and Equipment Failures in Anesthesia Management: Considerations for Prevention and Detection," 60 Anesthesiology 34–42.

References

Cressey, Donald R. 1953. Other People's Money: A Study in the Social Psychology of Embezzlement. Glencoe, Ill.: Free Press.

Croall, Hazel. 1988. "Mistakes, Accidents or Someone Else's Fault: The Trading Offender in Court," 15 J. Law and Soc'y 293.

———. 1989. "Who Is the White-Collar Criminal," 29 Brit. J. Criminol. 1571–1574, reprinted in Shover & Wright (2001a).

———. 2001. Understanding White Collar Crime. Buckingham: Open University Press.

Crystal, Nathan M. 2001. "Core Values: False and True," 70 Fordham L. Rev. 747.

Cullen, R. M. 1995. "Medical Discipline and Sexual Activity between Doctors and Patients," 108 N. Z. Med. J. 481–483.

Curran, Barbara A. 1977. The Legal Needs of the Public: The Final Report of a National Survey. Chicago: American Bar Foundation.

———. 1986. "The Legal Profession in the 1980s: Selected Statistics from the 1984 Lawyer Statistical Report," 20 Law & Soc'y Rev. 19.

Dacey, Norman F. 1965. How to Avoid Probate. New York: Crown.

Daicoff, Susan. 1997. "Oxymoron? Ethical Decision-Making by Attorneys: An Empirical Study," 48 Florida L. Rev. 197.

———. 1997–1998. "Asking Leopards to Change Their Spots: Should Lawyers Change? A Critique of Solutions to Problems with Professionalism by Reference to Empirically-Derived Attorney Personality Attributes," 11 Geo. J. Legal Ethics 547.

Daly, Kathleen. 1989. "Gender and Varieties of White-Collar Crime," 27 Criminol. 769–93.

Dana, Jason and George Loewenstein. 2003. "A Social Science Perspective on Gifts to Physicians from Industry," 289 JAMA 252–55 (July 9).

Dasgupta, Partha. 1988. "Trust as a Commodity," chapter 4 in Gambetta (1988a).

Davies, Mark R. 1998. "The Regulation of Solicitors and the Role of the Solicitors Disciplinary Tribunal," 14 Prof. Negl. 143–71.

Deckard, Gloria, Mark Meterko and Diane Field. 1994. "Physician Burnout: An Examination of Personal, Professional and Organizational Relationships," 32 Medical Care 745–54.

Degi, Keith J., G. Douglass Talbott and David G. Warren. 1997. "The Chemically Impaired Physician," chapter 3 in Lens & van der Wal (1997a).

De Haan, Willem and Ian Loader. 2002. "On the Emotions of Crime, Punishment and Social Control," 6 Theoretical Criminology 243–53.

Denckla, Derek A. 1999. "Nonlawyers and the Unauthorized Practice of Law: An Overview of the Legal and Ethical Parameters," 67 Fordham L. Rev. 2581.

Denzin, Norman K. 1977. "Notes on the Criminogenic Hypothesis: A Case Study of the American Liquor Industry," 42 Am. Sociol. Rev. 905.

Dickens, Charles. 1991. David Copperfield. New York: Alfred A. Knopf (first published 1849–50).

Dingwall, Robert and Tom Durkin. 1995. "Time Management and Procedural Reform," in A. A. S. Zuckerman and Ross Cranston (eds.), Reform of Civil Procedure: Essays on "Access to Justice." Oxford: Clarendon Press.

Ditton, Jason. 1977. Part-Time Crime: An Ethnography of Fiddling and Pilferage. London: Macmillan.

Dix, Andrew. 2002. "Crime and Misconduct in the Medical Profession," pp. 67–78 in Smith (2004).

Doig, Alan. 2000. "Investigating Fraud," chapter 4 in David Canter and Laurence Alison, eds., The Social Psychology of Crime: Groups, Teams and Networks. Dartmouth: Ashgate.

Douglas, Mary. 1970. Natural Symbols. London: Crescent Press.

Downes, David and Paul Rock. 1995. Understanding Deviance: A Guide to the Sociology of Crime and Rule Breaking (2d ed.). Oxford: Clarendon Press.

Draper, Robert. 2003. "The Toxic Pharmacist," New York Times Magazine 83 (June 8).

Dubin, Lawrence. 1985. What Went Wrong? Conversations with Disciplined Lawyers (video). Birmingham, MI: Weil Productions.

Dubois, Olivier and Pierre Haehnel. 1997. "When the Doctor Is Ill," chapter 12 in Lens & van der Wal (1997).

Durkheim, Emile. 1947. The Division of Labor in Society (George Simpson trans.). Glencoe, Ill.: Free Press.

_____. 1951. Suicide: A Study in Sociology (John A. Spaulding & George Simpson trans.). Glencoe, Ill.: Free Press (first published 1897).

Dweck, Carol S. 2006. Mindset: The New Psychology of Success. New York: Random House.

Economides, Kim and Majella O'Leary. 2007. "The Moral of the Story: Toward an Understanding of Ethics in Organisations and Legal Practice," 10 Legal Ethics 5.

Edelhertz, Herbert. 1970. The Nature, Impact and Prosecution of White Collar Crime. Washington, D.C.: U.S. Department of Justice, Law Enforcement Assistance Administration, National Institute of Law Enforcement and Criminal Justice.

Ely, John W., Wendy Levinson, Nancy C. Edler, Arch G. Mainous III and Daniel C. Vinson. 1995. "Perceived Causes of Family Physicians' Errors," 40 J. Fam. Pract. 337–344.

Ensminger, Jean. 2001. "Reputations, Trust, and the Principal Agent Problem," chapter 6 in Cook (2001).

Entman, Stephen S., Cheryl A. Glass, Gerald B. Hickson, Penny B. Githens, Kathryn Whetten-Goldstein and Frank A. Sloan. 1994. "The Relationship between Malpractice Claims History and Subsequent Obstetric Care," 272 JAMA 1588.

Erikson, Erik H. 1959. Identity and the Life Cycle. New York: International Universities Press.

_____. 1963. Childhood and Society (2d ed.). New York: Norton.

References

Erikson, Kai T. 1976. Everything in Its Path. New York: Simon and Schuster.

Fairer, J. G. 1983. "Murderous Doctors," 53(3) Medico-Legal Journal 150–165.

Fallberg, Lars H. and Edgar Borgenhammar. 1997. "Problem Doctors and No Fault Liability Insurance: A Swedish Approach to Quality of Care," chapter 9 in Lens & van der Wal (1997).

Fama, Eugene. 1980. "Agency Problems and the Theory of the Firm," 88 J. Pol. Econ. 288.

Feeley, Malcolm. 1979. The Process Is the Punishment: Handling Cases in a Lower Criminal Court. New York: Russell Sage Foundation.

Fellmeth, Robert C. 1987a. Initial Report to the Assembly and Senate Judiciary Committees and Chief Justice of the Supreme Court: A Report on the Performance of the Disciplinary System of the California State Bar (unpublished).

_____. 1987b. The Discipline System of the California State Bar: An Initial Report. 7(3) California Regulatory Law Reporter 1.

_____. 1987c. First Progress Report of the State Bar Discipline Monitor (unpublished).

Felstiner, W. L. F. 1997. "Professional Inattention: Origins and Consequences," in Keith Hawkins, ed., The Human Face of Law: Essays in Honor of Donald Harris. Oxford: Clarendon Press.

Felstiner, William L. F., Richard L. Abel and Austin Sarat. 1981. "The Emergence and Transformation of Disputes: Naming, Blaming, Claiming . . . ," 14 Law & Soc'y Rev. 631.

Fine, Gary and Lewis Holyfield. 1996. "Secrecy, Trust, and Dangerous Leisure: Generating Group Cohesion in Voluntary Organizations," 59 Soc. Psych. Q. 22.

Finkel, Michael. 2005. True Story: Murder, Memoir, Mea Culpa. New York: HarperCollins.

Fischman, Wendy, Becca Solomon, Deborah Greenspan and Howard Gardner. 2004. Making Good: How Young People Cope with Moral Dilemmas at Work. Cambridge, Mass.: Harvard University Press.

Fisse, Brent and John Braithwaite. 1985. The Impact of Publicity on Corporate Offenders. Albany: State University of New York Press.

Flager, Elizabeth A. and Sheila M. Malm. 1997. "The Problem Doctor: A Canadian Perspective," chapter 10 in Lens & van der Wal (1997).

Fortney, Susan Saab. 2000. "Soul for Sale: An Empirical Study of Associate Satisfaction, Law Firm Culture, and the Effects of the Billable Hour Requirements," 69 UMKC L. Rev. 239.

_____. 2003. "I Don't Have Time to Be Ethical: Addressing the Effects of Billable Hour Pressure," 39 Idaho L. Rev. 305.

_____. 2005. "The Billable Hours Derby: Empirical Data on the Problems and Pressure Points," 33 Fordham Urban L. J. 171.

Fortune, Marie M. 1995. "Is Nothing Sacred? When Sex Invades the Pastoral Relationship," chapter 3 in Gonsiorek.

Fox, Richard Wightman. 1999. Trials of Intimacy: Love and Loss in the Beecher-Tilton Scandal. Chicago: University of Chicago Press.

France, David. 2004. Our Fathers: The Secret Life of the Catholic Church in an Age of Scandal. New York: Broadway Books.

Frank, Jerome. 1930. Law and the Modern Mind. New York: Brentano's.

Frank, Nancy. 1987. "Murder in the Workplace," chapter 8 in Hills.

Frank, Robert. 1988. Passions Within Reason: The Strategic Role of the Emotions. New York: Norton.

Frankel, Marvin E. 1977. "Curing Lawyers' Incompetence: Primum Non Nocere," 10 Creighton L. Rev. 613.

Frankel, Tamar. 2006. Trust and Honesty: America's Business Culture at a Crossroad. New York: Oxford University Press.

Frankel, Tamar and Mark Fagan. 2007. Trust and Honesty in the Real World: A Joint Course for Lawyers, Business People and Regulators. Anchorage, Alaska: Fathom Publishing Co.

Frawley-O'Dea, Mary Dale. 2007. Perversion of Power: Sexual Abuse in the Catholic Church. Nashville, Tenn.: Vanderbilt Univ. P.

Freedman, Monroe H. 1966. "Professional Responsibility of the Criminal Defense Lawyer: The Three Hardest Questions," 64 Mich. L. Rev. 1469.

_____. 1975. "Perjury: The Lawyer's Trilemma," 1 Litigation 26 (Winter).

Frenkel, Douglas N. Robert L. Nelson and Austin Sarat. 1998. "Bringing Legal Realism to the Study of Ethics and Professionalism," 67 Fordham L. Rev. 697.

Fried, Charles. 1976. "The Lawyer as Friend: The Moral Foundations of the Lawyer-Client Relation," 85 Yale L. J. 1060.

Friedrichs, David O. 1996. Trusted Criminals: White Collar Crime in Contemporary Society. Belmont, Calif.: Wadsworth Publ. Co.

Gabbard, Glen O. (ed.). 1989. Sexual Exploitation in Professional Relationships. Washington, D.C.: American Psychiatric Press.

_____. 1994. "Sexual Misconduct," in J. M. Oldham and M. B. Reba (eds.), 13 American Psychiatric Press Review of Psychiatry 433–456. Washington, D.C.: American Psychiatric Press.

Gale, Edwin. 2003. "Between Two Cultures: The Expert-Clinician and the Pharmaceutical Industry," 3 Clinical Medicine 538–41 (Nov./Dec.).

Gallagher, William T. 1993. Controlling professions: The "Crisis" of Professional Self-regulation in the California State Bar. Ph.D. dissertation, U. C. Berkeley, Jurisprudence and Social Policy.

_____. 1995. "Ideologies of Professionalism and the Politics of Self-Regulation in the California State Bar," 22 Pepperdine L. Rev. 485.

References

Galante, Mary Ann. 1985a. "Malpractice Rates Zoom," 7(38) Nat'l L. J. 1 (June 3).

———. 1985b. "Insurance: Lawyers Face New Fights on Malpractice Coverage," 7(51) Nat'l L. J. 3 (Sept. 2).

———. 1985c. "$26M Legal Malpractice Judgment Upheld," 7(50) Nat'l L. J. 11 (Aug. 26).

———. 1986. "Insurance Costs Soar; Is There Any Way Out?" 8(26) Nat'l L. J. 1 (March 10).

Galanter, Marc. 1974. "Why the 'Haves' Come Out Ahead: Speculations on the Limits of Legal Change," 9 Law & Society Review 95.

———. 2005. Lowering the Bar: Lawyer Jokes and Legal Culture. Madison: University of Wisconsin Press.

Gambetta, Diego (ed.). 1988a. Trust: Making and Breaking Cooperative Relations. Oxford: Blackwell.

———. 1988b. "Mafia: The Price of Distrust," chapter 10 in Gambetta (1988a).

Gandossy, Robert P. 1985. Bad Business: The OPM Scandal and the Seduction of the Establishment. New York: Basic Books.

Ganzini, Linda, Bentson McFarland and Joseph Bloom. 1990. "Victims of Fraud," 18 Bull. Am. Acad. Psychiatry & Law 55, reprinted in Shover & Wright (2001a).

Garfinkel, Harold. 1956. "Conditions of Successful Degradation Ceremonies," 61 Am. J. Sociol. 420.

———. 1967. Studies in Ethnomethodology. Englewood Cliffs, N.J.: Prentice-Hall.

Garment, S. 1991. Scandal: The Culture of Mistrust in American Politics. New York: Random House.

Garth, Bryant G. 1998. "Two Worlds of Civil Discovery: From Studies of Cost and Delay to the Markets in Legal Services and Legal Reform," 39 Boston College L. Rev. 597.

Gartrell, Nanette, Judith Herman, Silvia Olarte, Michael Feldstein, and Russell Localio. 1986. "Psychiatrist-Patient Sexual Contact: Results of a National Survey, I: Prevalence," 143 Am. J. Psychiatry 1125–1131.

Gartrell, Nanette K., Nancy Milliken, William H. Goodson III, Sue Thiemann and Bernard Lo. 1992. "Physician-Patient Sexual Contact: Prevalence and Problems," 157 West J. Med. 139, reprinted as chapter 2 in Gonsiorek (1995).

Gates, William H. 1984. "The Newest Data on Lawyers' Malpractice Claims," 70 ABAJ 78 (April).

———. 1985–1986. "Lawyers' Malpractice: Some Recent Data about a Growing Problem," 37 Mercer L. Rev. 559.

Gawande, Atul. 2002. Complications: A Surgeon's Notes on an Imperfect Science. New York: Metropolitan Books.

———. 2007. Better: A Surgeon's Notes on Performance. New York: Metropolitan Books.

Gehring, Verna V. 2003. "Phonies, Fakes, and Frauds—and the Social Harms They Cause," 23(1/2) Philosophy & Public Policy Quarterly 14 (Winter/Spring).

Geis, Gilbert. 1977. "The Heavy Electrical Equipment Antitrust Cases of 1961," chapter 7 in Geis & Meier (1977a) (first published 1967).

Geis, Gilbert and Colin Goff. 1983. "Introduction," in Sutherland (1977).

Geis, Gilbert and Robert F. Meier (eds.). 1977a. White-Collar Crime: Offenses in Business, Politics, and the Professions (rev. ed.). New York: Free Press.

_____. 1977b. "Introduction," in Geis & Meier (1977a).

Geis, Gilbert, Henry Pontell and Mary Jane O'Brien. 1985. "Fraud and Abuse by Psychiatrists against Government Medical Benefits Programs," 142 Am. J. Psychiatry 231.

Georgetown Law Journal. 1988. "Note, How To Thread the Needle: Toward a Checklist-Based Standard for Evaluating Ineffective Assistance of Counsel Claims," 77 Geo. L. J. 413.

Gershman, Bennett L. 1999. Prosecutorial Misconduct. St. Paul: West Publ. Co.

Gilb, Corinne L. 1956. "Self-Regulating Professions and the Public Welfare: A Case Study of the California Bar," Ph.D. dissertation, history, Radcliffe College.

Gilligan, Carol. 1982. In a Different Voice: Psychological Theory and Women's Development. Cambridge, Mass.: Harvard University Press.

Gillers, Stephen. 2006. "In the Pink Room," chapter 4 in Rhode & Luban (2006).

Girard, Donald E. and David H. Hickam. 1991. "Predictors of Clinical Performance among Internal Medicine Residents," 6 J. Gen. Int. Med. 150.

Glass, Stephen. 2003. The Fabulist. New York: Simon and Schuster.

Glendon, Mary Ann. 1994. A Nation Under Lawyers: How the Crisis in the Legal Profession Is Transforming American Society. New York: Farrar, Straus and Giroux.

_____. 1952. On Cooling the Mark Out," 15 Psychiatry 451.

Goffman, Erving. 1959. The Presentation of Self in Everyday Life. Harmondsworth: Penguin.

_____. 1961. "Role Distance," in Encounters. Harmondsworth: Penguin.

_____. 1963. Stigma: Notes on the Management of Spoiled Identity. Harmondsworth: Penguin.

_____. 1971. Relations in Public: Microstudies of the Public Order. Harmondsworth: Penguin.

Goldberg, Stuart C. 1979. "1977 National Survey on Current Methods of Teaching Professional Responsibility in Law Schools," in Patrick A. Keenan, Stuart C. Goldberg, and G. Griffith Dick, eds., Teaching Professional Responsibility. Detroit: University of Detroit Law School.

Gonsiorek, John C. (ed.). 1995. Breach of Trust: Sexual Exploitation by Health Care Professionals and Clergy. Thousand Oaks, CA: Sage Publications.

Goode, William J. 1967. "Protection of the Inept," 32 Am. Sociol. Rev. 5.

References

Green, Bruce A. 2003. "Criminal Neglect: Indigent Defense from a Legal Ethics Perspective," 52 Emory L. J. 1169.

Green, Gary S. 1990. Occupational Crime. Chicago: Nelson-Hall Pub.

Griffin, Leslie C. 2006. "Bohatch v. Butler & Binion: The Ethics of Partners," chapter 2 in Rhode & Luban (2006).

Groves, W. Byron and Graeme Newman, eds. 1986. Punishment and Privilege. Albany, NY: Harrow and Heston.

Guarasci, Richard. 1987. "Death by Cotton Dust," chapter 6 in Hills.

Guare, John. 1994. Six Degrees of Separation. New York: Vintage Books.

Guttenberg, Jack A. 1994. "The Ohio Attorney Disciplinary Process—1982 to 1991: An Empirical Study, Critique and Recommendations for Change," 62 U. Cinn. L. Rev 947–1028.

Hake, Bruce A. 2000. "A Great Wind: The New INS/EOIR Attorney Discipline Regime," 5 Bender's Immigration Bulletin 885.

Haller, Linda. 2003. "Dirty Linen: The Public Shaming of Lawyers," 10 Int'l J. Leg. Prof. 281.

Hamilton, Neil and Lisa Montpetit Brabbit. 2007. "Fostering Professionalism through Mentoring," 57 J. Leg. Educ. 102.

Hancock, Linda. 1997. "Addressing the 'Problem Doctor,' Professional Misconduct and Avenues of Complaint in Australia," chapter 11 in Lens & van der Wal (1997).

Hand, Learned. 1926. "Deficiencies of Trial to Reach the Heart of the Matter," in James N. Rosenberg et al. (eds.), 3 Lectures on Legal Topics 89. New York: ABCNY.

Handler, Joel F. 1967. The Lawyer and His Community. Madison: University of Wisconsin Press.

Hanlon, Gerald. 1994. The Commercialisation of Accountancy: Flexible Accumulation and the Transformation of the Service Class. New York: St. Martin's Press.

Hardin, Russell. 2001. "Conceptions and Explanations of Trust," in Cook (2001).

_____. 2002. Trust and Trustworthiness. New York: Russell Sage Foundation.

Harlow, Harry F. 1958. "The Nature of Love," 13 Am. Psychologist 673.

Harr, Jonathan. 1995. A Civil Action. New York: Vintage Books.

Hartung, Frank E. 1950. "White-Collar Offenses in the Wholesale Meat Industry in Detroit," 56 Am. J. Sociol. 25.

Hawthorne, Nathaniel. 2006. The Scarlet Letter. Boston: Bedford/St. Martin's (first published 1850).

Hazard, Geoffrey C., Jr., Susan P. Koniak, Roger C. Cramton and George M. Cohen. 2005. The Law and Ethics of Lawyering (4th ed.). New York: Foundation Press.

Heafey, Richard J. 2005. "Return to Sender?: Inadvertent Disclosure of Privileged Information," 28 Am. J. Trial Advocacy 615.

Heimer, Carol. 2001. "Solving the Problem of Trust," chapter 2 in Cook (2001).

Heinz, John P., Robert L. Nelson, Rebecca L. Sandefur and Edward O. Laumann. 2005. Urban Lawyers: The New Social Structure of the Bar. Chicago: University of Chicago Press.

Henry, Stuart. 1978. The Hidden Economy: The Context and Control of Borderline Crime. Oxford: Martin Robertson.

Hensler, Deborah et al. 1985. Asbestos in the Courts. Santa Monica, Calif.: Rand Corporation.

Herzog, Don. 2006. Cunning. Princeton, N.J.: Princeton University Press.

Hills, Stuart L. (ed.). 1987. Corporate Violence: Injury and Death for Profit. Totowa, N.J.: Rowman & Littlefield.

Hirschman, Albert O. 1984. "Against Parsimony: Three Easy Ways of Complicating Some Categories of Economic Discourse," 74 AER Proceedings 88.

Hobbes, Thomas. 1994. Leviathan. Indianapolis: Hackett Publ. (first published 1676).

Hochschild, Arlie Russell. 1983. The Managed Heart: Commercialization of Human Feeling. Berkeley: University of California Press.

Hoffer, Peter Charles. 2004. Past Imperfect: Facts, Fictions, Fraud. New York: Public Affairs.

Homans, George C. 1958. "Social Behavior as Exchange," 63 Am. J. Sociol. 597.

Hopkins, Kevin. 1999. "Law Firms, Technology, and the Double-Billing Dilemma," 12 Geo. J. Leg. Ethics 93.

Horning, Donald M. 1970. "Blue-Collar Theft: Conceptions of Property, Attitudes Toward Pilfering, and Work Group Norms in a Modern Industrial Plant," in Erwin O. Smigel and H. Laurence Ross, eds., Crimes against Bureaucracy. New York: Van Nostrand Reinhold.

Horton, Richard. 2004. "The Dawn of McScience," New York Review of Books 7 (March 11).

Hosticka, Carl. 1979. "We Don't Care What Happened, We Only Care What Is Going to Happen," 26 Soc. Probs 699.

Horowitz, Michael. 1995. "Making Ethics Real, Making Ethics Work: A Proposal for Contingency Fee Reform," 44 Emory L. J. 173.

Houston, John M. et al. 1992. "Assessing Competitiveness: A Validation Study of the Competitiveness Index," 13 Personality & Individual Differences 1153.

Hughes, Everett C. 1951. "Mistakes at Work," 17 Canadian J. Econ. & Pol. Sci. 320.

Hunting, Robert and Gloria S. Neuwirth. 1962. Who Sues in New York City: A Study of Automobile Accident Claims. New York: Columbia University Press.

Hutter, B. 1988. The Reasonable Arm of the Law? Oxford: Clarendon Press.

Hyman, David A. and Charles Silver. 1998. "And Such Small Portions: Limited Performance Agreements and the Cost/Quality/Access Trade-Off," 11 Geo. J. Leg. Ethics 959.

Irvine, Sir Donald. 1997. "Problem Doctors in the UK: Role of the General Medical Council," chapter 7 in Lens & van der Wal (1997).

References

Jenkins, John and Verity Lewis. 1995: Client Perceptions. London: Law Society.

Jesilow, Paul, Henry N. Pontell and Gilbert Geis. 1993. Prescription for Profit: How Doctors Defraud Medicaid. Berkeley: University of California Press.

Jones, James H. 1993. Bad Blood: The Tuskegee Syphilis Experiment (expanded ed.). New York: Free Press.

Jorgenson, Linda Mabus. 1995. "Sexual Contact in Fiduciary Relationships: Legal Perspectives," chapter 20 in Gonsiorek.

Justice, Kathleen E. 1991. "Note, There Goes the Monopoly: The California Proposal to Allow Nonlawyers to Practice Law," 44 Vanderbilt L. Rev. 179.

Justice. 1970. Complaints Against Lawyers. London: Justice.

Kakalik, James S., Deborah R. Hensler, Daniel F. McCaffrey, Marian Oshiro, Nicholas M. Pace, and Mary E. Vaiana. 1998. "Discovery Management: Further Analysis of the Civil Justice Reform Act Evaluation Data," 39 Boston College L. Rev. 613.

Katona, George. 1946. Price Control and Business. Bloomington: Indiana University Press.

Katz, Jack. 1982. Poor People's Lawyers in Transition. New Brunswick, N.J.: Rutgers Univ. P.

Kay, Fiona M., John Hagan and Patricia Parker. 2009. "Principals in Practice: The Importance of Mentorship in the Early Stages of Career Development," 31 Law & Policy (forthcoming).

Kay, Fiona M. and Jean E. Wallace. 2007a. "Mentors as Social Capital: Gender, Mentor Capitalization, and Career Rewards in Law Practice" (unpublished).

_____. 2007b. "The More the Merrier: Mentoring and the Practice of Law" (unpublished).

Kelley, James L. 2001. Lawyers Crossing Lines: Nine Stories. Durham, N.C.: Carolina Academic Press.

Kelman, Mark and Gillian Lester. 1997. Jumping the Queue: An Inquiry into the Legal Treatment of Students with Learning Disabilities. Cambridge, Mass.: Harvard University Press.

King-Casas, Brooks, Damon Tomlin, Cedric Anen, Colin F. Camerer, Steven R. Quartz, and P. Read Montague. 2005. "Getting to Know You: Reputation and Trust in a Two-Person Economic Exchange," 308 Science 78.

Kohn, Linda T., Janet M. Corrigan and Molla S. Donaldson, eds. 2000. To Err Is Human: Building a Safer Health System. Washington, D.C.: National Academic Press.

Kramer, Roderick M., Marilynn B. Brewer and Benjamin A. Hanna. 1996. "Collective Trust and Collective Action: The Decision to Trust as a Social Decision," chapter 17 in Kramer & Tyler.

Kramer, Roderick M. and Tom R. Tyler, eds. 1996. Trust in Organizations: Frontiers of Theory and Research. Thousand Oaks, Calif.: Sage Publications.

Kramer, Roderick M. and L. Goldman. 1995. "Helping the Group or Helping Yourself? Social Motives and Group Identity in Resource Dilemmas," in D. A. Schroeder, ed., Social Dilemmas. New York: Praeger.

Krimsky, Sheldon. 2004. Science in the Private Interest: Has the Lure of Profits Corrupted Biomedical Research? Lanham, Md.: Rowman & Littlefield.

Kritzer, Herbert M. 2002. "Seven Dogged Myths Concerning Contingency Fees," 80 Wash. U. L. Q. 739.

Kronman, Anthony T. 1993. The Lost Lawyer: Failing Ideals of the Legal Profession. Cambridge, Mass.: Belknap Press.

Kugel, Yerachmiel and Gladys W. Gruenberg. 1977. International Payoffs. Lexington, Mass.: Lexington Books.

Landon, Donald D. 1982. "Lawyers and Localities: The Interaction of Community Context and Professionalism," 1982 Am. Bar Fndn Res. J. 459.

_____. 1990. Country Lawyers: The Impact of Context on Professional Practice. New York: Praeger.

Landwehr, Lawrence J. 1982. "Lawyers as Social Progressives or Reactionaries: The Law and Order Cognitive Orientation of Lawyers," 7 Law & Psychol. Rev. 39.

Lane, Robert E. 1977. "Why Businessmen Violate the Law," chapter 6 in Geis & Meier (1977a) (first published 1953).

Law & Social Inquiry. 1998. "From the Trenches and Towers: The Kaye Scholar Affair" 23 Law & Social Inquiry 243.

Lazega, Emmanuel. 2001. The Collegial Phenomenon: The Social Mechanisms of Cooperation among Peers in a Corporate Law Partnership. Oxford: Oxford University Press.

Lazerson, Mark H. 1982. "In the Halls of Justice, the Only Justice Is in the Halls," chapter 6 in Richard L. Abel, ed., The Politics of Informal Justice, Vol. 1: The American Experience. New York: Academic Press.

Leff, Arthur A. 1976. Swindling and Selling. New York: Free Press.

Lemert, Edwin M. 1964. "The Behavior of the Systematic Check Forger," in Howard S. Becker, ed., The Other Side: Perspective on Deviance 211–24. Glencoe, Ill.: Free Press.

Lens, Peter and Gerrit van der Wal, eds. 1997. Problem Doctors: A Conspiracy of Silence. Netherlands: IOS Press.

Leonard, William N. and Marvin Glenn Weber. 1970. "Automakers and Dealers: A Study of Criminogenic Market Forces," 4 Law & Soc'y Rev. 407.

Leonnig, Carol D., Lena H. Sun and Sarah Cohen. 2003. "Under Court, Vulnerable Became Victims," Washington Post A1 (June 15).

Lerman, Lisa G. 1990. "Lying to Clients," 138 U. Penn. L. Rev. 659.

_____. 1994. "Gross Profits? Questions about Lawyer Billing Practices," 22 Hofstra L. Rev. 645.

References

_____. 1998. "Scenes from a Law Firm," 50 Rutgers L. Rev. 2153 (1998).

_____. 1999. "Blue-Chip Bilking: Regulation of Billing and Expense Fraud by Lawyers," 12 Geo. J. Legal Ethics 205.

Lerman, Lisa G. and Philip G. Schrag. 2005. Ethical Problems in the Practice of Law. New York: Aspen.

Levi, Michael. 1981. The Phantom Capitalists. London: Macmillan.

Levi, Michael, Hans Nelen and Francien Lankhorst, eds. 2004. "Lawyers and Crime Facilitators in Europe," 42(2–3) Crime, Law and Social Change (special issue).

Levin, Leslie C. 1994. "Testing the Radical Experiment: A Study of Lawyer Response to Clients Who Intend to Harm Others," 47 Rutgers L. Rev. 81.

_____. 1998. "The Emperor's Clothes and Other Tales about the Standards for Imposing Lawyer Discipline Sanctions," 48 Am. U. L. Rev. 1.

_____. 2004–2005. "The Ethical World of Solo and Small Law Firm Practitioners," 41 Houston L. Rev. 309.

_____. 2006. "Building a Better Lawyer Discipline System: The Queensland Experience," 9 Legal Ethics 187.

Levine, Dennis B. 1991. Inside Out: An Insider's Account of Wall Street. New York: Putnam.

Lewicki, Roy J. and Barbara Benedict Bunker. 1992. "Developing and Maintaining Trust in Work Relationships," chapter 7 in Kramer & Tyler (1996).

Lewis, Verity. 1996. Complaints Against Solicitors: The Complainants' View. London: Law Society (Research Study No. 19).

Liederbach, John. 2001. "Opportunity and Crime in the Medical Professions," pp. 144–156 in Shover & Wright (2001a).

Lifton, Robert Jay. 1986. The Nazi Doctors: Medical Killing and the Psychology of Genocide. New York: Basic Books.

Limerick, David and Bert Cunnington. 1993. Managing the New Organization. San Francisco: Jossey-Bass.

Linowitz, Sol M. with Martin Mayer. 1994. The Betrayed Profession: Lawyering at the End of the Twentieth Century. New York: C. Scribner's Sons.

Llewellyn, Karl N. and E. Adamson Hoebel. 1941. The Cheyenne Way: Conflict and Case Law in Navajo Jurisprudence. Norman: University of Oklahoma Press.

Lofland, John. 1969. Deviance and Identity. New Jersey: Prentice-Hall.

Lowenstein, Roger. 2004. Origins of the Crash: The Great Bubble and Its Undoing, New York: Penguin.

Luban, David. 1984. "The Adversary System Excuse," in David Luban (ed.), The Good Lawyer. Totowa, N.J.: Rowman & Allanheld.

_____. 1993. "Are Criminal Defendants Different?" 91 Michigan Law Review 1729.

Luhmann, Niklas. 1979. "Trust: A Mechanism for the Reduction of Social Complexity," in Trust and Power. New York: John Wiley.

Lyn, Laura. 1995. "Lesbian, Gay, and Bisexual Therapists' Social and Sexual Interactions with Clients," chapter 17 in Gonsiorek.

MacNeal, Mary Helen. 1997. "Redefining Attorney-Client Roles: Unbundling and Moderate-Income Elderly Clients," 32 Wake Forest L. Rev. 295.

Macaulay, Stewart. 1963. "Non-Contractual Relations in Business: A Preliminary Study," 28 Am. Sociol. Rev. 55.

Machiavelli, Niccolo. 1940. The Prince and The Discourses. New York: Modern Library (first published 1513).

Mackie, Gerry. 2001. "Patterns of Social Trust in Western Europe and Their Genesis," chapter 8 in Cook (2001).

Madden, Carl. 1977. "Forces Which Influence Ethical Behavior," pp. 31–78 in Clarence Walton, ed. The Ethics of Corporate Conduct. Englewood Cliffs, N.J.: Prentice-Hall.

Mahar, Maggie. 2004. Bull! A History of the Boom, 1982–1999. New York: HarperBusiness.

Makary, Martin A., et al. 2007. "Needlestick Injuries among Surgeons in Training," 356 New England J. Med. 2693.

Malinowski, Bronislaw. 1926. Crime and Custom in Savage Society. London: Routledge & Kegan Paul.

_____. 1935. Coral Gardens and Their Magic. London: G. Allen & Unwin.

Marks, F. Raymond and Darlene Cathcart. 1974. "Discipline within the Legal Profession: Is It Self-Regulation?" 1974 Illinois L. Forum 193.

Marquess, John J. 1994. "Legal Audits and Dishonest Legal Bills," 22 Hofstra L. Rev. 637.

Mars, Gerald. 1972. An Anthropological Study of Longshoremen and of Industrial Relations in the Port of St. John's Newfoundland, Canada. Ph.D. dissertation, University of London.

_____. 1973. "Hotel Pilferage: A Case Study in Occupational Theft," pp. 200–10 in M. Warner (ed.), The Sociology of the Work Place. London: Allen & Unwin.

_____. 1974. "Dock Pilferage: A Case Study in Occupational Theft," pp. 109–28 in Paul Rock and M. McIntosh (eds.), Deviance and Social Control. London: Tavistock.

_____. 1982. Cheats at Work: An Anthropology of Workplace Crime. London: Unwin.

_____. 2006. "Changes in Occupational Deviance: Scams, Fiddles and Sabotage in the Twenty-first Century," 45 Crime, Law and Social Change 285.

Mars, Gerald and M. Nicod. 1984. World of Waiters. London: George Allen and Unwin.

Maruna, Shadd. 2000. "Criminology, Desistance and the Psychology of the Stranger," chapter 9 in David Canter and Laurence Alison, eds., The Social Psychology of Crime: Groups, teams and networks. Dartmouth: Ashgate.

References

Martin, George. 1970. Causes and Conflicts: The Centennial History of the Bar Association of the City of New York. Boston: Houghton Mifflin.

Martyn, Susan R. 1981. "Lawyer Competence and Lawyer Discipline: Beyond the Bar?" 69 Geo. L. J. 705.

Mather, Lynn M. 1979. Plea Bargaining or Trial? Lexington, Mass.: Lexington Books.

Mather, Lynn, Craig A. McEwen and Richard J. Maiman. 2001. Divorce Lawyers at Work: Varieties of Professionalism in Practice. New York: Oxford University Press.

Matza, David. 1964. Delinquency and Drift. New York: John Wiley & Sons.

_____. 1969. Becoming Deviant. Englewood Cliffs, N.J.: Prentice-Hall.

Maurer, David W. 1999. The Big Con: The Story of the Confidence Man. New York: Anchor (first published 1940).

McBarnet, Doreen J. 1988. "Law, Policy and Legal Avoidance: Can Law Effectively Implement Egalitarian Strategies?" 15 J. Law & Soc'y 113.

_____. 1991. "Whiter than White-Collar Crime: Tax, Fraud, Insurance and the Management of Stigma," 42 Brit. J. Sociol. 232–244.

McBarnet, Doreen and Chris Whelan. 1999. Creative Accounting and the Crossed-Eyed Javelin Thrower. New York: John Wiley.

McCabe, Donald L. 1992. "The Influence of Situational Ethics on Cheating Among College Students," 62 Sociological Inquiry 365.

_____. 1999. "Academic Dishonesty among High School Students," 34 Adolescence 681.

McCabe, Donald L. and William J. Bowers. 1994. "Academic Dishonesty Among Males in College: A Thirty Year Perspective," 35 J. College Student Development 5.

McCabe, Donald L. and Linda Klebe Treviño. 1996. "What We Know about Cheating in College: Longitudinal Trends and Recent Developments," 28 Change 29 (January/February).

_____. 1997. "Individual and Contextual Influences on Academic Dishonesty," 38 Research in Higher Education 379.

McCabe, Donald L., Linda Klebe Treviño and Kenneth D. Butterfield. 2001. "Cheating in Academic Institutions: A Decade of Research," 11 Ethics & Behavior 219.

McClintick, David. 1982. Indecent Exposure: A True Story of Hollywood and Wall Street. New York: William Morrow.

McConville, Michael and Chester L. Mirsky. 1987. "Criminal Defense of the Poor in New York City," 15 NYU Rev. L. & Soc. Change 581.

McIntyre, Lisa J. 1987. The Public Defender: The Practice of Law in the Shadows of Repute. Chicago: University of Chicago Press.

McKiernan, Terence. 2004. "Confidentially Theirs: Documenting the Sex Abuse Crisis in the Catholic Church," paper presented to Law and Society Association annual meeting (May 27).

McLean, Bethany and Peter Elkind. 2003. The Smartest Guys in the Room: The Amazing Rise and Scandalous Fall of Enron. New York: Portfolio.

Mellinkoff, David. 1973. The Conscience of a Lawyer. St. Paul: West Publ. Co.

Mello, Michael. 2006. "United States v. Kaczynski: Representing the Unabomber," chapter 5 in Rhode & Luban (2006).

Melville, Herman. 1964. The Confidence-Man: His Masquerade. New York: New American Library (first published 1857).

Mendelson, Danuta. 1998. "Euthanasia," pp. 149–166 in Smith (2004).

Merton, Robert. 1930. "Social Structure and Anomie," 3 Am. Sociol. Rev. 672, reprinted in Social Theory and Social Structure 185 (1968).

Messick, David M. and Roderick M. Kramer. 2001. "Trust as a Form of Shallow Morality," chapter 3 in Cook (2001).

Messick, David M., H. Wilke, M. B. Brewer, R. M. Kramer, P. E. Zemke and L. Lui. 1983. "Individual Adaptations and Structural Change as Solutions to Social Dilemmas," 44 J. Personality and Soc. Psych. 294.

Meyerson, Debra, Karl E. Weick and Roderick M. Kramer. 1996. "Swift Trust and Temporary Groups," in Roderick M. Kramer and Tom R. Tyler, eds., Trust in Organizations: Frontiers of Theory and Research. Thousand Oaks, CA: Sage Pubs.

Miller, Gary. 2001. "Why Is Trust Necessary in Organizations? The Moral Hazard of Profit Maximization," chapter 10 in Cook (2001).

Mills, C. Wright. 1956. The Power Elite. New York: Oxford University Press.

Mills, William M., Jr. 1949. "Development of Requirements for Admission to the Bar in Kansas," 18 Bar Examiner 75.

Mintz, M. 1985. At Any Cost: Corporate Greed, Women, and the Dalkon Shield. NY: Pantheon.

Mitford, Jessica. 1954. "The English Aristocracy," in Mitford (1956) (first published 1954).

_____, ed. 1956. Noblesse Oblige: An Inquiry into the Identifiable Characteristics of the English Aristocracy. London: Hamish Hamilton.

Moliterno, James. 2005. "The New Politically Motivated Bar Discipline," 83 Wash. U. L. Q. 725.

Moorhead, Richard, Sarah Rogers and Avrom Sherr. 2000a. Willing Blindness? OSS Complaints Handling Procedures. London: Law Society and Institute of Advanced Legal Studies.

Moorhead, Richard, Avrom Sherr and Sarah Rogers. 2000b. Compensation for Inadequate Professional Services. London: Institute of Advanced Legal Studies.

Mottino, Felinda. 2000. Moving Forward: The Role of Legal Counsel in Immigration Court. New York: Vera Institute of Justice.

Mullenix, Linda S. 1998. "The Pervasive Myth of Pervasive Discovery Abuse: The Sequel," 39 Boston College L. Rev. 683.

Nader, Ralph and Mark Green, eds. 1976. Verdicts on Lawyers. New York: Crowell.

References

Neal, David and Russell G. Smith. 1998. "Criminal Negligence in Health Care," pp. 140–48 in Smith (2004).

Nee, Victor and Jimmy Sanders. 2001. "Trust in Ethnic Ties: Social Capital and Immigrants," chapter 13 in Cook (2001).

Nelken, David. 1983. The Limits of the Legal Process: A Study of Landlords, Law and Crime. London: Academic Press.

_____. 1994. "White-Collar Crime," in Mike Maguire, Rod Morgan and Robert Reiner, eds., Oxford Handbook of Criminology. Oxford: Oxford University Press.

_____. 1997. "White Collar Crime," in Mike Maguire, Rod Morgan and Robert Reiner, eds. The Oxford Handbook of Criminology (2d ed.). Oxford: Clarendon Press.

_____. 2002. "White-Collar Crime," chapter 23 in Mike Maguire, Rod Morgan and Robert Reiner, eds., The Oxford Handbook of Criminology (3rd ed.). Oxford: Oxford University Press.

Nelson, Robert L. 1985. "Ideology, Practice, and Professional Autonomy: Social Values and Client Relationships in the Large Law Firm," 37 Stanford L. Rev. 503.

_____. 1998. "The Discovery Process as a Circle of Blame: Institutional, Professional, and Socio-Economic Factors that Contribute to Unreasonable, Inefficient, and Amoral Behavior in Corporate Litigation," 67 Fordham L. Rev. 773.

New South Wales Law Reform Commission. 1979. Complaints, Discipline and Professional Standards—Part I. Sydney: New South Wales Law Reform Commission.

_____. 1980. The Legal Profession. Sydney: New South Wales Law Reform Commission (Background Paper—III).

Noonan, John T., Jr. and Richard W. Painter. 2001. Professional and Personal Responsibilities of the Lawyer (2d ed.). New York: Foundation Press.

O'Gorman, Hubert J. 1963. Lawyers and Matrimonial Cases: A Study of Informal Pressures in Private Professional Practice. Glencoe, Ill.: Free Press.

O'Neill, Onora. 2002. A Question of Trust. Cambridge: Cambridge University Press.

Overbeke, John A. 1997. "Malfunctioning Doctors in Medical Research and Scientific Publishing," chapter 5 in Lens & van der Wal (1997).

Palmer, Vernon Valentine. 2008. "The Louisiana Supreme Court in Question: An Empirical Study of the Effect of Campaign Money on the Judicial Function," 82 Tulane L. Rev.

Parikh, Sara. 2001. Professionalism and Its Discontents: A Study of Social Networks in the Plaintiffs' Personal Injury Bar. Ph.D. dissertation, sociology, University of Illinois, Chicago.

Passas, Niko and David Nelken. 1993. "The Thin Line between Legitimate and Criminal Enterprises: Subsidy Frauds in the European Community," 19 Crime, Law and Social Change 223–43.

Patton, Michael J. 1968. "The Student, the Situation and Performance during the First Year of Law School," 21 J. Legal Educ. 10.

Perlman, Andrew M. 2005. "Untangling Ethics Theory from Attorney Conduct Rules: The Case of Inadvertent Disclosures," 13 Geo. Mason L. Rev. 767.

Peters, J. G. and S. Welch. 1980. "The Effects of Charges of Corruption on Voting Behavior in Congressional Elections," 74 Am. Pol. Sci. Rev. 697.

Petersen, Melody. 2008. Our Daily Meds. New York: Farrar Straus & Giroux.

Petroski, Henry. 2003. Paperboy: Confessions of a Future Engineer. New York: Vintage.

Pfennigstorf, Werner. 1980. "Types and Causes of Lawyers' Professional Liability Claims: The Search for Facts," 1980 Am. Bar Fndn Res. J. 255.

Phillips, Gerald F. 2002. "Time Bandits: Attempts by Lawyers to Pad Hours Can Often Be Uncovered by a Careful Examination of Billing Statements," 29 W. St. U. L. Rev. 265.

Phillips, Orie L. and Philbrick McCoy. 1952. Conduct of Judges and Lawyers: A Study of Professional Ethics, Discipline and Disbarment. Los Angeles: Parker & Co.

Pinaire, Brian K., Milton J. Heumann, and Jennifer Lerman. 2006. "Barred from the Bar: The Process, Politics, and Policy Implications of Discipline for Attorney Felony Offenders," 13 Virginia J. Soc. Poly' & L. 290.

Pipkin, Ronald M. 1979. "Law School Instruction in Professional Responsibility: A Curricular Paradox," 1979 Am. Bar Fndn Res. J. 247.

Polanyi, Karl. 1944. The Great Transformation: The Political and Economic Origins of Our Time. Boston: Beacon Press.

Porter, Bruce. 2004. "A Long Way Down," New York Times Magazine 50 (June 6).

Powell, Burnelle. 1994. "Lawyer Professionalism as Ordinary Morality," 35 S. Texas L. Rev. 275.

Powell, Michael J. 1976. Professional Self-Regulation: The Transfer of Control from a Professional Association to an Independent Commission. Paper presented to the annual meeting of the American Sociological Association, New York (August).

_____. 1986. "Professional Divestiture: The Cession of Responsibility for Lawyer Discipline," 1986 Am. Bar Fndn Res. J. 31.

_____. 1988. From Patrician to Professional Elite: The Transformation of the New York City Bar. New York: Russell Sage Foundation.

Powell, Walter W. 1996. "Trust-Based Forms of Governance," chapter 4 in Kramer & Tyler.

Pronovost, Paul, Dale Needham, Sean Berenholtz, David Sinopoli, Haitao Chu, Sara Cosgrove, Bryan Sexton, Robert Hyzy, Robert Welsh, Gary Roth, Joseph Bander, John Kepros and Christine Goeschel. 2006. "An Intervention to Decrease Catheter-Related Bloodstream Infections in the ICU," 355 New England Journal of Medicine 2725.

References

Psaty, Bruce M and Richard A. Kronmal. 2008. "Reporting Mortality Findings in Trials of Rofecoxib for Alzheimer Disease or Cognitive Impairment," 299 JAMA 1813.

Punch, M. 1996. Dirty Business: Exploring Corporate Misconduct. London: Sage.

Putnam, Robert D. 1993. Making Democracy Work: Princeton, N.J.: Princeton University Press.

_____. 2000. Bowling Alone: The Collapse and Revival of American Community. New York: Simon & Schuster.

Quinney, Earl R. 1963. "Occupational Structure and Criminal Behavior: Prescription Violation by Retail Pharmacists," 11 Soc. Probs 179.

_____. 1964. "The Study of White Collar Crime: Toward a Reorientation in Theory and Research," 55 J. Crim. Law, Criminol., and Police Science 208.

Quinney, Richard. 1977. "Occupational Structure and Criminal Behavior: Prescription Violations by Retail Pharmacists," chapter 12 in Geis & Meier (1977a), first published in 11 Social Problems 179 (1963).

Ramos, Manuel R. 1994. "Legal Malpractice: The Profession's Dirty Little Secret," 47 Vanderbilt L. Rev. 1657.

_____ 1995. "Legal Malpractice: No Lawyer or Client Is Safe," 47 Florida L. Rev. 1.

Rapoport, Nancy B. and Bala G. Dharan, eds. 2004. Enron: Corporate Fiascos and Their Implications. New York: Foundation Press.

Re, Edward D. 1994. "The Causes of Popular Dissatisfaction with the Legal Profession," 68 St. John's L. Rev. 85.

Regan, Milton C., Jr. 2004. Eat What You Kill: The Fall of a Wall Street Lawyer. Ann Arbor: University of Michigan Press.

_____. 2007. "Moral Intuitions and Organizational Culture," 51 St. Louis University Law Journal 941.

Reichstein, Kenneth J. 1965. "Ambulance Chasing: A Case Study of Deviation and Control within the Legal Profession," 13 Soc. Probs 1.

Reutter, Mark. 1987. "The Invisible Risk . . . ," chapter 5 in Hills.

Rhode, Deborah L. 1976. "Project: The Unauthorized Practice of Law and Pro Se Divorce: An Empirical Analysis," 86 Yale L. J. 104.

_____. 1981. "Policing the Professional Monopoly: A Constitutional and Empirical Analysis of Unauthorized Practice Prohibitions," 34 Stanford L. Rev. 1.

_____. 1985a. "Moral Character as a Professional Credential," 94 Yale L. J. 491.

_____. 1985b. "Ethical Perspectives on Legal Practice," 37 Stanford L. Rev. 589.

_____. 2000. In the Interests of Justice. New York: Oxford University Press.

Rhode, Deborah L. and David Luban. 2004. Legal Ethics (4th ed.). New York: Foundation Press.

_____, eds. 2006. Legal Ethics Stories. New York: Foundation Press.

Richmond, Douglas R. 2003. "Subordinate Lawyers and Insubordinate Duties," 105 W. Va. L. Rev. 449.

Riss, R. W. and J. Patric. 1942. Repairmen Will Get You If You Don't Watch Out. Garden City, N.Y.: Doubleday.

Robb, George. 1992. White-Collar Crime in Modern England: Financial Fraud and Business Morality, 1845–1929. Cambridge: Cambridge University Press.

Robin, Ron. 2004. Scandals and Scoundrels: Seven Cases That Shook the Academy. Berkeley: University of California Press.

Rochon, Paula A. et al. 1994. "Evaluating the Quality of Articles Published in Journal Supplements Compared with the Quality of Those Published in the Parent Journal," 272 JAMA 108.

Rolph, John E., John L. Adams and Kimberly A. McGuigan. 2007. "Identifying Malpractice-Prone Physicians," 4 J. Empirical Leg. Studies 125–53.

Rose, Jonathan. 2002. "Unauthorized Practice of Law in Arizona: A Legal and Political Problem That Won't Go Away," 34 Arizona St. L. J. 585.

Rosenthal, Douglas E. 1974. Lawyer and Client: Who's in Charge? New York: Russell Sage Foundation.

Rosenthal, Marilynn M. 1987. Dealing with Medical Malpractice: The British and Swedish Experience. London: Tavistock.

Ross, Alan S. C. 1956. "Linguistic class-indicators in present-day English," in Mitford (1956).

Ross, Edward Alsworth. 1977. "The Criminaloid," chapter 1 in Geis & Meier (1977a) (originally published 1907).

Ross, William G. 1991. "The Ethics of Hourly Billing by Attorneys," 44 Rutgers L. Rev. 1.

_____. 1997. The Honest Hour: The Ethics of Time-Based Billing by Attorneys. Durham, N.C.: Carolina Academic Press.

Rostain, Tanina. 2006a. "Travails in Tax: KPMG and the Tax Shelter Controversy," chapter 3 in Rhode & Luban (2006).

_____. 2006b. "Sheltering Lawyers: The Organized Tax Bar and Tax Shelter Industry," 23 Yale J. on Regulation 77.

Rovere, Richard H. 1947. Howe & Hummell: Their True and Scandalous History. New York: Farrar Straus & Giroux.

Royal Commission on Legal Services. 1979. Final Report. London: HMSO (Cmnd 7648).

Royal Commission on Legal Services in Scotland. 1980. Report. Edinburgh: HMSO (Cmnd 7846).

Ruggiero, V. 1996. Organized and Corporate Crime in Europe: Offers that Can't Be Refused. Aldershot: Dartmouth.

Rutter, Peter. 1995. "Lot's Wife, Sabina Spielrein, and Anita Hill: A Jungian Meditation on Sexual Boundary Abuse and Recovery of Lost Voices," chapter 9 in Gonsiorek.

Sahl, John P. 1999. "The Public Hazard of Lawyer Self-Regulation: Learning from Ohio's Struggle to Reform Its Disciplinary System," 68 U. Cincinnati L. Rev. 65.

Sahlins, Marshall. 1972. Stone Age Economics. New York: Aldine de Gruyter.

References

Saint, Sanjay, Christine P. Kowalski, Samuel R. Kaufman, Timothy P. Hofer, Carol. A. Kauffman, Russell N. Olmstead, Jane Forman, Jane Banaszak-Holl, Laura Damschroder and Sarah L. Krein. 2008. "Preventing Hospital-Acquired Urinary Tract Infection in the United States: A National Study," 46 Clinical Infectious Diseases 243.

Sante, Luc. 1999. "Introduction," in Maurer (1999).

Sarat, Austin. 1998. "Enactments of Professionalism: A Study of Judges' and Lawyers' Accounts of Ethics and Civility in Litigation," 67 Fordham L. Rev. 809.

Sarat, Austin and William L. F. Felstiner. 1986. "Law and Strategy in the Divorce Lawyer's Office," 20 Law & Soc'y Rev. 93.

_____. 1995. Divorce Lawyers and Their Clients: Power and Meaning in the Legal Process. New York: Oxford University Press.

Scheffer, Thomas. 2007. "File Work, Legal Care, and Professional Habitus—An Ethnographic Reflection on Different styles of Advocacy," 14 Int'l J. Leg. Prof. 57.

Schlegel, Kip. 1993. "Crime in the Pits: The Regulation of Futures Trading," in Gilbert Geis & Paul Jesilow, eds., White-Collar Crime. 525 The Annals 59–70 (Jan.).

Schiltz, Patrick J.1998. "Legal Ethics in Decline: The Elite Law Firm, the Elite Law School, and the Moral Formation of the Novice Attorney," 82 Minn. L. Rev. 705.

_____. 1999. "On Being a Happy, Healthy, and Ethical Member of an Unhappy, Unhealthy, and Unethical Profession," 52 Vanderbilt L. Rev. 871.

Schneyer, Theodore J. 1989. "Professionalism as Bar Politics: The Making of the Model Rules of Professional Conduct," 14 Law & Social Inquiry 677.

Schoemaker, Paul J. H. and Robert E. Gunther. 2006. "The Wisdom of Deliberate Mistakes," 84 Harvard Business Review (June).

Schoener, Gary Richard. 1995. "Historical Overview," chapter 1 in Gonsiorek.

Schoener, G. R., J. H. Milgrom, J. C. Gonziorek et al., eds. 1989. Psychotherapists' Sexual Involvement with Clients: Intervention and Prevention. Minneapolis: Walk-In Counseling Center.

Schrag, Philip G., Andrew I. Schoenholtz and Jaya Ramji-Nogales. 2008. "Refugee Roulette," 60 Stanford Law Review 295.

Schuck, Peter H. 1987. Agent Orange on Trial: Mass Toxic Disasters in the Courts. Cambridge, Mass.: Belknap Press.

Schulman, Kevin A., et al. 2002. "A National Survey of Provisions in Clinical-Trial Agreements Between Medical Schools and Industry Sponsors," 337 NEJM 1335.

Schwartz, Richard D. and Jerome H. Skolnick. 1962. "Two Studies of Legal Stigma," 10 Soc. Probs 133.

Scott, Marvin B. and Stanford M. Lyman. 1968. "Accounts," 33 Am. Sociol. Rev. 46.

Secrest, Merle. 2004. Duveen: A Life in Art. New York: Knopf.
Selinger, Carl M. 1996. "The Retention of Limitations on the Out-of-Court Practice of Law by Independent Paralegals," 9 Geo. J. Leg. Eth. 879.
Selling, Lonell S. 1944. "Specific War Crimes," 34 J. Crim. Law, Criminol. and Police Science 303.
Seron, Carroll. 1996. The Business of Practicing Law: the Work Lives of Solo and Small-Firm Attorneys. Philadelphia: Temple Univ. P.
Seuss, Dr. (Theodor Geisel). 1937. And To Think That I Saw It on Mulberry Street. New York: Vanguard.
Shapin, Steven. 1995. A Social History of Truth. Chicago: University of Chicago Press.
Shapiro, David. 1999. Neurotic Styles. New York: Basic Books.
Shapiro, Susan P. 1990. "Collaring the Crime, Not the Criminal: Reconsidering the Concept of White-Collar Crime," 55 Am. Sociol. Rev. 346, reprinted in Shover & Wright (2001a).
_____. 2002. Tangled Loyalties: Conflict of Interest in Legal Practice. Ann Arbor: University of Michigan Press.
Shekelle, Paul. 2006. Costs and Benefits of Health Information Technology. Santa Monica, Calif.: Rand Corporation.
Shepherd, George B. and Morgan Cloud. 1999. "Time and Money: Discovery Leads to Hourly Billing," 1999 U. Ill. L. Rev. 91.
Shinnick, E., F. Bruinsma and C. Parker. 2003. "Aspects of Regulatory Reform in the Legal Profession: Australia, Ireland and the Netherlands," 10 Int'l J. Legal Prof. 237.
Shover, Neal and John Paul Wright, eds. 2001a. Crimes of Privilege: Readings in White-Collar Crime. New York: Oxford University Press.
_____. 2001b. "Conceptual Issues and Skirmishes," chapter 1 in Shover & Wright (2001a).
Shover, Neal, Greer Litton Fox and Michael Mills. 1994. "Long-term consequences of victimization by white-collar crime," 11 Justice Q. 75–98.
Shuchman, Philip. 1968. "Ethics and Legal Ethics: The Propriety of the Canons as a Group Moral Code," 37 George Washington L. Rev. 244.
Shuckman, Miriam. 2005. The Drug Trial: Nancy Olivieri and the Science Scandal that Rocked the Hospital for Sick Children. Toronto: Random House.
Silk, Howard L. and D. Vogel. 1971. Ethics and Profits: The Crisis of Confidence in American Business. New York: Simon & Schuster.
Simon, David R. and Stanley Eitzen. 1993. Elite Deviance (4th ed.). Boston: Allyn & Bacon.
Simon, William. 1993. "The Ethics of Criminal Defense, 91 Michigan L. Rev. 1703.
_____. 2007. "The Market for Bad Legal Advice: Academic Professional Responsibility Consulting as an Example," Columbia Public Law Research Paper No. 07-158. http://ssrn.com/abstract=1025984.

References

Simpson, Sally. 1986. "The Decomposition of Antitrust: Testing a multi-level, longitudinal model of profit-squeeze," 51 Am. Sociol. Rev. 859.

Slapper, Gary and Steve Tombs. 1999. Corporate Crime. Harlow: Longman.

Smigel, Erwin O. 1956. "Public Attitudes toward Stealing as Related to the Size of the Victim Organization," 21 Am. Sociol. Rev. 320.

Smigel, Erwin O. and H. Laurence Ross, eds. 1970. "Introduction," pp. 1–14 in Crimes Against Bureaucracy. New York: Van Nostrand Reinhold.

Smith, Adam. 1976. An Inquiry into the Nature and Causes of the Wealth of Nations (Edwin Cannan, ed.). Chicago: University of Chicago Press (originally published 1776).

Smith, Dame Janet. 2004. The Shipman Inquiry. London: Stationary Office.

Smith, Rebecca and John R. Emshwiller. 2003. 21 Days. New York: HarperBusiness.

Smith, Reginald Heber. 1961. "Disbarments and Disciplinary Actions," 47 ABAJ 363.

Smith, Russell G. (ed.). 2002. Crime in the Professsions. Burlington, Vt.: Ashgate.

Snider, Robert M. 1986. "Legal Malpractice Insurance," Los Angeles Lawyer 18 (Feb.).

Solkoff, Norman and Joan Markowitz. 1967. "Personality Characteristics of First-Year Medical and Law Students," 42 J. Med. Educ. 195.

Sonnenfeld, Jeffrey and Paul R. Lawrence. 1978. "Why Do Companies Succumb to Price Fixing?" 56 Harv. Bus. Rev. 145.

Sorensen, James E., Hugh D. Grove and Thomas L. Sorensen. 1980. "Detecting Management Fraud: The Role of the Independent Auditor," chapter 10 in Gilbert Geis & Ezra Stotland, eds. White-Collar Crime: Theory and Research. Beverly Hills, Calif.: Sage Publications.

Spaeth, Jr., Edmund B. 1988. "To What Extent Can a Disciplinary Code Assure the Competence of Lawyers?" 61 Temple L. Rev. 2122.

Spencer, John C. 1965. "White Collar Crime," pp. 233–66 in E. Glover, H. Mannheim and E. Miller, eds., Criminology in Transition. London: Tavistock.

State Bar of California. 1939. Proceedings of the Twelfth Annual Meeting. San Francisco: State Bar of California.

———. 2001. Investigation and Prosecution of Disciplinary Complaints Against Attorneys in Solo Practice, Small Size Law Firms and Large Size Law Firms. San Francisco: State Bar of California.

State Bar of New Mexico. 2000. Task Force on Minorities in the Legal Profession II, The Status of Minority Lawyers in New Mexico: An Update 1990–1999. Albuquerque: State Bar of New Mexico.

Staw, Barry M. and Eugene Szwajkowski. 1975. "The Scarcity-Munificence Component of Organizational Environments and the Commission of Illegal Acts," 20 Admin. Sci Q. 345.

Steele, Eric H. and Raymond T. Nimmer. 1976. "Lawyers, Clients and Professional Regulation," 1976 Am. Bar Fndn Res. J. 917.

Stelfox, Henry Thomas, Grace Chua, Keith O'Rourke and Allan S. Detsky. 1998. "Conflict of Interest in the Debate Over Calcium-Channel Antagonists," 338 New England J. Med. 101.

Stelling, Joan and Rue Bucher. 1973. "Vocabularies of Realism in Professional Socialization," 7 Soc. Sci. & Med. 661.

Stolle, Dietlind. 2001. "Clubs and Congregations: The Benefits of Joining an Association," chapter 7 in Cook (2001).

Stone, D. G. 1990. April Fools: An Insiders' Account of the Rise and Fall of Drexel-Burnham. New York: Donald Fine Co.

Strauss, Anselm. 1959. Mirrors and Masks: The Search for Identity. New York: Free Press.

Strodtbeck, Frederick L. and Marvin B. Sussman. 1955–1956. "Of Time, the City and the 'One-Year Guarantee': The Relations between Watch Owners and Repairers," 61 Am. J. Sociol. 602.

Suchman, Mark C. 1998. "Working Without a Net: The Sociology of Legal Ethics in Corporate Litigation," 67 Fordham L. Rev. 837.

Sutherland, Edwin H. 1977. "White-Collar Criminality," chapter 2 in Geis & Meier (1977a), originally published in 5 Am. Sociol. Rev. 1 (1940).

———. 1983. White Collar Crime: The Uncut Version. New Haven, Conn.: Yale Univ. P.

Sutton, Adam and Ronald Wild. 1985. "Small Business: White-Collar Villains or Victims?" 13 Int'l J. Sociol. L. 247.

Swartz, Mimi with Sherron Watkins. 2003. Power Failure: The Inside Story of the Collapse of Enron. New York: Doubleday.

Sykes, Gresham M. and David Matza. 1957. "Techniques of Neutralization: A Theory of Delinquency," 22 Am. Sociol. Rev. 664.

Talamante, Ryan J. 1992. "Note, We Can't All Be Lawyers . . . Or Can We?" Regulating the Unauthorized Practice of Law in Arizona," 34 Arizona L. Rev. 873.

Tapp, June Louin and Felice J. Levine. 1974. "Legal Socialization: Strategies for an Ethical Legality," 27 Stanford L. Rev. 1.

Taylor, Laurie and Paul Walton. 1971. "Industrial sabotage: motives and meanings," pp. 219–45 in Stanley Cohen, ed. Images of Deviance. Harmondsworth: Penguin.

Tempelaar, André F. 1997. "The Problem Doctor as an Iatrogenic Factor: Risks, Errors, Malfunctioning and Outcomes," chapter 2 in Lens & van der Wal (1997).

Thompson, E. P. 1970. Warwick University Ltd. Harmondsworth: Penguin.

Thompson, Jon, Patricia Baird and Jocelyn Downie. 2001. The Olivieri Report. Halifax, N. S.: James Lorimer.

Tillman, R. and Henry N. Pontell. 1992. "Is Justice 'Collar-Blind'?: Punishing Medicaid Provider Fraud," 30 Criminol. 547.

Tisher, Sharon, Lynn Bernabei and Mark Green. 1977. Bringing the Bar to Justice: A Comparative Study of Six Bar Associations. Washington, D.C.: Public Citizen.

References

Titus, Richard M. 2001. "Personal Fraud and Its Victims," in Shover & Wright (2001a).

Toffler, Barbara Ley with Jennifer Reingold. 2003. Final Accounting: Ambition, Greed and the Fall of Arthur Andersen. New York: Broadway Books.

Topol, Eric J. and David Blumenthal. 2005. "Physicians and the Investment Industry," 293 JAMA 2654.

Tucker, J. 1989. "Employee Theft as Social Control," 10 Deviant Behavior 319.

Turnbull, Colin. 1972. The Mountain People. New York: Simon & Schuster.

Turner, Erick H., A. M. Matthews, E. Linardatos, R. A. Tell and R. Rosenthal. 2008. "Selective Publication of Antidepressant Trials and Its Influence on Apparent Efficacy," 358 New England Journal of Medicine 252.

Twain, Mark (Samuel Clemens). 1993. The Adventures of Huckleberry Finn. New York: Modern Library (first published 1884).

Tyler, Tom R. 2001. "Why Do People Rely on Others? Social Identity and the Social Aspects of Trust," chapter 9 in Cook (2001).

Tyler, Tom R. and Peter Degoey. 1996. "Trust in Organizational Authorities: The Influence of Motive Attributions on Willingness to Accept Decisions," chapter 16 in Kramer & Tyler (1996).

Tyler, Tom R. and Roderick M. Kramer. 1996. "Whither Trust?" chapter 1 in Kramer & Tyler (1996).

U.S. Department of Justice, Executive Office for Immigration Review. 2001. Statistical Year Book 2000. Washington, D.C. EOIR.

Uslaner, Eric M. 2002. The Moral Foundations of Trust. Cambridge: Cambridge University Press.

Uzzi, Brian. 1997. "Social Structure and Competition in Interfirm Networks: The Paradox of Embeddedness," 42 Admin. Sci. Q. 35

Van Hoorebeeck, Bart. 1997. "Prospects for Reconstructing Aetiology," 1 Theoretical Criminology 501.

Van Hoy, Jerry. 1997. Franchise Law Firms and the Transformation of Personal Legal Services. Westport, Ct.: Quorum Books.

Vaughan, Diane. 1982. "Transaction Systems and Unlawful Organizational Behavior," 29 Social Problems 373, reprinted in Shover & Wright (2001a).

_____. 1996. The Challenger Launch Decision: Risky Technology, Culture, and Deviance at NASA. Chicago: University of Chicago Press.

_____. 1998. "Rational Choice, Situated Action, and the Social Control of Organizations," 32 Law & Soc'y Rev. 23, reprinted in Shover & Wright (2001a).

Veblen, Thorstein. 1912. The Theory of the Leisure Class. New York: Macmillan.

Victor, Kirk. 1986. "Firms Facing More Ethical Challenges," 9(12) Nat'l L. J. 1 (Dec. 1).

Vladeck, David C. 2006. "In Re Arons: "The Plight of the 'Unrich' in Obtaining Legal Services," chapter 9 in Rhode & Luban (2006).

Wachter, Robert M. and Kaveh G. Shojania. 2004. Internal Bleeding: The Truth Behind America's Terrifying Epidemic of Medical Mistakes. New York: Rugged Land.

Wallace, Anthony F. C. 1988. St. Clair: A Nineteenth-Century Coal Town's Experience with a Disaster-Prone Industry. Ithaca, N.Y.: Cornell University Press.

Walsh, M. E. and D. D. Schram. 1980., "The Victim of White-Collar Crime: Accuser or Accused?" in G. Geis & E. Stotland, eds., White-Collar Crime: Theory and Research. Beverly Hills, Calif.: Sage.

Ward, Stephanie Francis. 2007. "Top 10 Ethics Traps," 29(11) Am. Bar Association J. 30 (November).

Weir, David. 1987. The Bhopal Syndrome: Pesticides, Environment, and Health. San Francisco: Sierra Club Books.

Weisburd, David, Stanton Wheeler, Elin Waring and Nancy Bode. 1991. Crimes of the Middle Classes: White Collar Offenders in the Federal Courts. New Haven, Conn.: Yale University Press.

Wheeler, Stanton. 1992. "The Problem of White-Collar Crime Motivation," chapter 4 in Kip Schlegel and David Weisburd (eds.), White-Collar Crime Reconsidered. Boston: Northeastern Univ. P.

Whelan, Christopher J. 2007. "Some Realism About Professionalism: Core Values, Legality, and Corporate Law Practice," 54 Buffalo L. Rev. 1067.

Whiteside, Thomas. 1997. The Pendulum and the Toxic Cloud: The Course of Dioxin Contamination. New Haven: Yale University Press.

Wilbers, D., G. Veenstra, H. B. M. van de Wiel, and W. C. M. Weijmar Schultz. 1992. "Sexual Contact in the Doctor-Patient Relationship in the Netherlands," 304 Brit. J. Med. 1531.

Willging, Thomas E. and Thomas G. Dunn. 1981. "The Moral Development of the Law Student: Theory and Data on Legal Education," 31 J. Legal Educ. 306.

Willging, Thomas E. et al. 1998. "An Empirical Study of Discovery and Disclosure Practice under the 1993 Federal Rule Amendments," 39 Boston College L. Rev. 525.

Williams, Andrew. 2002. "Crime and Misconduct in the Accounting Profession," pp. 55–65 in Smith (2002).

Williamson, Oliver. 1993. "Calculativeness, Trust, and Economic Organization," 36 J. Law and Econ. 453.

Willott, Sara and Chris Griffin. 1999. "Building Your Own Lifeboat: Working-class Male Offenders Talk about Economic Crime," 38 Brit. J. Soc. Psych. 445.

Willott, Sara, Christine Griffin and Mark Torrance. 2001. "Snakes and Ladders: Upper-Middle Class Male Offenders Talk About Economic Crime," 39 Criminol. 441.

Winchurch, Susan. 1987. "New Funds for Lawyers Emerge," 10(3) Nat'l L. J. 3 (Sept. 28).

References

Wolfe, Thomas. 1987. The Bonfire of the Vanities. New York: Farrar, Straus Giroux.
Woodley, Richard. 1982. "The Importance of Being Number One," pp. 117–125 in Leonard D. Savitz and Norman Johnston, eds., Contemporary Criminology. New York: Wiley.
Wooley, Alice. 2005. "Evaluating Value: A Historical Case Study of the Capacity of Alternative Billing Methods to Reform Unethical Hourly Billing," 12 Int'l J. Leg. Prof. 339.
Wycoff, Robert. 1962. "The Effects of a Malpractice Suit upon Physicians in Connecticut," in Albert Averbach and Melvin Belli, eds. 2 Tort and Medical Handbook. Indianapolis, In.: Bobbs-Merrill.
Wydick, Richard C. 1995. "The Ethics of Witness Coaching," 17 Cardozo L. Rev. 1.
Yale Law Journal. 1973. "Note: Legal Services and Landlord-Tenant Litigation: A Critical Analysis," 82 Yale L. J. 1495.
Yamagishi, Toshio. 2001. "Trust as a Form of Social Intelligence," chapter 4 in Cook (2001).
Zacharias, Fred. 2002. "The Future Structure and Regulation of Law Practice: Confronting Lies, Fictions, and False Paradigms in Legal Ethics Regulation," 44 Arizona L. Rev. 829.
_____. 2007. "The Preemployment Ethical Role of Lawyers: Are Lawyers Really Fiduciaries?" 49 William and Mary L. Rev. 569.
_____. 2008. "Effects of Reputation on the Legal Profession," 64 Washington & Lee L. Rev.
Zemans, Frances K. and Victor G. Rosenblum. 1981. The Making of a Public Profession. Chicago: American Bar Foundation.
Zeitlin, Lawrence R. 1971. "A Little Larceny Can Do a Lot for Company Morale," 14 Psychology Today 22.
Zeitz, Dorothy. 1981. Women Who Embezzle or Defraud: A Study of Convicted Felons. New York: Praeger.
Zuckoff, Mitchell. 2005. Ponzi's Scheme: The True Story of a Financial Legend. New York: Random House.

Index

A
accountants, trust in/betrayal by, 20
Accu-Weather, 381
advertising
    fraud in, 30
    by lawyer, 111, 526
    by service agency, 170, 178, 180
age discrimination, 472
American Bar Association (ABA), 380, 497, 502
American Express, 381
American Immigration Lawyers Association, 528
American Red Cross of Greater New York (ARCGNY). See documents, privileged
Anker, Laurie, 195
anomie theory, 40
anti-solicitation rules, 69–70
antitrust violation, 29, 31
apartment fire case, and lawyer neglect, 88
Association of the Bar of New York City (ABCNY), 380, 503, 506
asylum granting, 145 n.658
Australia, 55, 57, 58, 504, 505
authors, trust in/betrayal by, 18–19
auto accident, possible harm to unborn child case
    personal injury, and lawyer neglect, 84–87
auto accident case, and lawyer neglect, 76, 88–89
auto accident with Transit Authority bus case
    personal injury, and lawyer neglect, 82–84
auto repair company, betrayal by, 10–11

B
Baer, Lawrence J., 392, 393, 394, 395, 396, 415–416, 417, 425, 435, 437–438, 439, 467, 475–476
bakery roundsmen, fiddling by, 46–52
    blame for, 46–47
    as commercial *vs.* legal, 51–52
    employee fiddling employer, 47–48
    guilt reduction devices, 49–50
    motives for, 48–49
    response to accusations, 49
Barber, Bernard, 3
Bartels, John R. Jr., 238, 241, 268–269
Bashian, Gary, 219, 222, 255
Becker, H., 29, 31, 37–38
betrayal
    difference from mistake, 7–8
    difference from ordinary crime, 8
    as illuminating indispensability of trust, 25. See also trust
betraying trust, case studies
    American embezzlement, 39–43
    English fiddles, 43–52
        bakery roundsmen, 46–52
        donkey job fiddles, 44
        hawk job fiddles, 43–44
        vulture job fiddles, 44–45
        wolfpack job fiddles, 44–45
bias, research, 54–55

INDEX

bill padding, 45, 47, 209–210
Birnbaum (Referee), 390, 397–400, 400, 403, 416, 417–418, 419, 425–426, 438, 439, 463–464, 466, 479, 483–484
Bosk, C., Bosk, Charles, 7, 509–512
Bottger, Walter F., 241, 242, 254
Brashich, Deyan, 219–220, 225, 230, 231, 232, 237–238, 243, 244, 245–247, 248
Bratton, Andral N., 346–349, 358, 449, 455–456, 457, 459–460, 462, 469, 477–478
breach of fiduciary duty, 448
Brewster, Evans V., 219, 222, 224, 233, 253, 256–257, 266, 269
Bridger, Harold, 44
Brigandi, John, 229–230
broker-agents, trust in/betrayal by, 15
Bukszpan, Joanna M., 147–151, 181
Byler, Philip. *See* fee dispute case

C

cab rank rule, 518–519
Cahill, Thomas J., 122, 333
Callahan, Ljubica, 270–275, 276–277, 278, 279, 281
Carlin, Jerome, 54–55
Carlisle, Jay, 443
case overload, 33, 194, 204, 521
Chang Kui Lin case, and lawyer neglect, 109–125
charities, trust in/betrayal by, 14–15
Chen, Cathy, 106, 127, 128, 130, 132–133, 134, 135, 174, 180, 185
Chen, Howard, 120, 171
Child, Rachel, 449, 467
Ciparick, Carmen, 439, 441, 461, 487–488
civil judgments, nonpayment of, 56
clergy, trust in/betrayal by, 14
client neglect, by lawyer
Client Protection Fund, 385–386
client trust accounts, 56. *See also* trust income dispute
Clinard, Marshall B., 30, 35
Cohen, Beverly, 448
Cohen, Neil, 200–202, 203
Cohen, Sherry K., 106, 120, 129–130, 132, 133–136, 142–143, 158–159, 165, 167–168, 169–170

Cohn, Jeffrey M., 387
Coleman, James W., 37
collateral estoppel
in privileged documents case, 455, 461, 465, 468, 477, 488
in trust income dispute, 259, 269, 270, 274, 278–279, 285
Cometa, Angelo, 316, 318–319, 320, 358
confidence games, 25–28
conflict of interest, in privileged documents case, 420–421, 422, 453
conflict-of-interest rules, 25
Conforti, Michael, 72, 74–75, 81, 82, 83, 85, 86, 90
conventionalization, 49
Cooper, Nicholas C., 72, 74, 82–83, 85–86, 87, 88–90, 97, 100, 102
Cressey, D., 35, 39, 40–41, 46, 52
Criminal Justice Act (CJA), 213
Croall, Hazel, 37
Crown Prosecution Service, 518–519
Cummins, Barbara, 390, 394, 407, 408, 410, 412, 421, 422

D

Daly, Mary C., 72
DeFonzo, Paul A., 145, 181
de Haan, Willem, 37
de la Hoz, Hector, 84, 90
delinquent subculture, 32–34
Delio, Jaime V., 384–385
Del Valle, Margarita, 75–76, 90
DelValle, Telesforo Jr., 449, 450, 459
Denmark, fee disputes in, 58
Desch, Carl, 398, 415, 428, 439
differential association theory, 31, 32
Dinhofer, Philip J., 386
disbarment, 504
after felony conviction, 56
and Muto, 165–166, 167–168, 169, 170–171, 172
disciplinary records, as research source, 53–54
Ditton, J., 46–52
diversionary tactics, 439–440
documents, privileged, 413–415
American Arbitration Association sanctions Wisehart, 472–473

Appellate Division affirms Moscowitz
  dismissal, 440–441
attack and seek disqualification strategy,
  483–485
attorney-client privilege, 420, 444
background to case, 389–392
Bender EBT, 397–398
bizarre behavior by judge, 445–447
championing sexual harassment victim,
  389–398
collateral estoppel, 455, 461, 465, 468,
  477, 488
conflict of interest, 420–421, 422, 453
contempt motions, 429, 431, 440, 486
court supervision of discovery
  granted, 390
denouement, 437–447
deposition, 393, 394
deposition of Deutch, 398–413
deposition of Red Cross employee
  requested by plaintiff, 390–391
deposition of Staley objected to by
  defendant, 398–399
disciplinary proceeding, 448–457
  charges, 448
  continuing defense of Wisehart,
    454–455
  Hearing Panel report, 456, 487–488
  motion to dismiss, 451–453
  motion to dismiss denied, 453
  move for rehearing, 456, 487–488
  original documents subpoenaed,
    456–457
  request for recusal, 451, 453–454, 456
diversionary tactics allegations,
  439–440
document requests by plaintiff,
  393–396
documents alteration allegation by
  plaintiff, 394–395
documents read by Lipin during Deutch
  deposition, 401–413
  deliberate placement of documents,
    alleged, 401, 416, 422–423, 426,
    429, 432, 439, 443, 452–453
  documents ordered turned over,
    414–415, 427
  Lipin culpability, 426–427, 444
  Lipin reaction to, 401, 416, 417

entrapment allegations, 432, 439, 447,
  455, 461, 473, 482, 489
lawyer-client privilege, 457
Lipin files new action, 428–437
missing funds allegations, 439–440
Moskowitz recuses self, 436–437
motion to reargue, 437–439, 444
motion to reargue denied, 442
motion to stay all discovery denied, 415
motion to vacate, 437
move for rehearing, 456
paranoid style behavior of Wisehart,
  480–482
protective order against discovery
  requested by defendant, 421–421
rationalizations by Wisehart, 482–483
reckless statements
  by Lipin, 444–445, 464–465, 484–485
  by Wisehart, 429–431, 456, 464,
    465–466, 484
recusal motions, 430–437, 438, 451
Red Cross sexual harassment guidelines,
  399–400
Red Cross suspicious expense voucher
  guidelines, 400
request for documents, 390
sanctions motion by plaintiff rejected,
  395–396
sanctions hearing, 457–466
  contempt motion denied, 461
  evidence in aggravation, 457
  Hearing Panel report, 463–465
  lack of remorse, 463
  relitigation warning, 457–458
  Wisehart testifies on own behalf,
    460–462
show cause motion of defendant heard,
  413–415
supervision of documents requested by
  defendant, 392–393
suspension of Wisehart, 476–479
third lawsuit filed, 466–474, 488
  complaint, 466–467, 469–472
  memorandum of law filed, 468–469
  movement for reconsideration
    denied, 474
  move to recuse, 473
Wisehart as unrepentant, 489
Wisehart refusal to stipulate, 427–428

LEARNING FROM ATTORNEY DISCIPLINARY PROCEEDINGS   563

INDEX

dog bite case, and lawyer neglect, 87
Dong (Dung), Tiffany, 109, 110
donkey job fiddles, 43–44
drift theory, 32
Durkheim, Émile, 3, 40

E
Edelstein, Mady J.
   and Byler case, 279, 301–302, 311–312,
      316, 322, 324, 326–327, 332, 335,
      336, 340–341, 343
   and Furtzaig case, 199–200, 240, 243,
      259, 268, 270, 279
Ellenbogen, Joan, 296, 298, 316–317, 322,
   323–324, 327, 328, 354, 358, 359
Emanuelli, Albert J., 224, 227, 229–230,
   240, 241–242, 246–247
employment discrimination. *See* wrongful
   discharge
England
   cab rank rule in, 518–519
   fee disputes in, 58
   neglect complaints in, 58
   solo practitioners in, 525
English Law Society, 500–501
entrapment, 51, 432, 439, 447, 455, 461,
   473, 482, 489
environmental polluters, trust in/betrayal
   by, 9–10
Erikson, E., 2
escrow obligations, 329–330, 332, 334–334,
   338–339, 340–341, 346–347, 364–365
Estis, Warren, 193, 194, 199, 203, 204
ethical rules
   and lawyer motives, 53
   lawyer surprise/outrage when caught, 53
   reasons lawyer violates, 52–53
excessive zeal, 56–57, 58–59, 377–388
   and administration of justice, 384–386,
      387–388
   court sanction examples, 378–379
   disciplinary body sanction examples,
      379–380
   privileged documents, 380–385,
      386–387. *See also* documents,
      privileged; overachiever
Executive Office for Immigration Review
   (EOIR), 123, 131–132
expert witnesses, trust in/betrayal by, 17

F
Fales, Haliburton II, 314–315
fatalism, 33
Federal Rules of Civil Procedure 26,
   380–381
fee arbitration boards, 210
fee dispute case
   behavior persistence, 333–348
      Byler files affidavit of compliance,
         338–339
      Byler files memorandum of
         law, 335–336
      Byler seeks leave, 336–337
      Byler seeks reinstatement, 339,
         341–349, 361–362
      reinstatement denied, 342–343
      reinstatement opposed, 340–341
   bill padding, 45, 47, 209–210
   bragging by Byler, 352–353, 360,
      365–366
   Byler refuses private admonition, 356
   Byler sends Morgan non-bill bill for
      services, 292
   character of Byler, 353–361
   Client Benefit Chart, 335, 363
   cost of contrition, 349–366
      justifications for not escrowing
         refund, 352
      justifications for pocketing refunds,
         351
      non-bill bill, 349
      refund check disposition, 349–351
      rhetorical overkill and lawyerly
         detail, 351, 359
      written retainer never executed, 349
   Court of Appeals denies motions for
      reconsideration, 337–338
   disciplinary actions, 211–212
   disciplinary complaint, 314–321
      Byler admonished by DDC, 314
      Byler demands formal hearing, 315
      Byler response to admonishment,
         314–315
      Byler response to complaint, 314
      Byler served with charges, 315–316
      nature of complaint, 314–315
   disciplinary hearing
      Byler reason for not having retainer
         letter, 316

Byler reason for not sending bill to
Morgan, 317–318
Byler reinstated, 348
Byler requests dismissal of case, 321
Cometa withdrawal, 320–321
Lauer testifies, 318
non-bill bill, 317–318
obligation to put refund in escrow,
316–317
post-hearing brief, 319
post-hearing brief, reply to, 319–320
escrow obligation, 329–330, 332,
334–334, 338–339, 340–341,
346–347, 364–365
fee discussion from viewpoints of
Morgan and Byler, 290–291,
295–296
fee dispute, 296–314
brother of Morgan intervenes,
304–305, 308–310, 312–313
Byler denies fee dispute, 307–309
Byler letter delay to avoid stop
payment on check, 298
Byler letter explaining IRS refund
check disposition, 296–298
Byler new "bill," 298
Byler on original agreement, 305–306
Byler on whether Morgan disputing
fee, 299–300
Byler reason to consult third
party, 301–302
Byler response to questions,
300–301
Byler settlement offer, 313
Morgan faxes questions about refund
to Byler, 299
Morgan on original agreement,
302–304
Morgan revokes power of attorney,
313–314
non-bill bill, 310–312, 313
friendship destroyed, 353
IRS disallows tax shelter, 289–290
IRS reduces tax deficiency, 293
mitigation hearing, 321–333
Byler client releases him, 326–327
Byler on returning money, 324–325
Byler personal finance problems,
325–326

Byler proclaims innocence,
323–324
Byler reason for resisting admonition,
322–323
Byler seeks admonition, 332
escrow obligation, 329–330, 332,
334–334
Panel questions Byler, 328–331
suspension proposed, 332, 334
Morgan civil suit against Byler,
318–319, 339
Morgan gives Byler checks for future
payment, 294–295
Morgan tells Byler to keep possible IRS
tax refund, 293–294, 295
New York state tax claim, 293, 294
quantum meruit fee, 324, 331, 339, 363,
368, 369, 370, 371–372
remorse, Byler inability to express, 359,
361–365
reply to Abel by Byler, 367–373
fees
for class action suits, 211
and client funds, 213–214
and conflict of interest, 212
contingent fee caps, 211
disputes, 58 (*see also* fee dispute case)
minimum schedules as antitrust
violations, 209
and restoring trust, 515–516, 526
See also quantum meruit fee
Feldman, Justin, 221, 232, 263
felony conviction, disbarment after, 56
Ferris, Noel A., 110, 113–119, 114n,
120–121, 123, 124, 177, 181, 184
fiduciary duties, 3
financial managers, trust in/betrayal
by, 20–21
Finnell, John F., 145, 146, 180
First Amendment, 468, 469, 478, 488,
525–526
Fletcher, Barbara, 390–391, 396, 397–398,
407, 425, 439, 471
forgery
by Furtzaig, 202, 203, 495
by Muto, 127, 141, 174
Forlenza, Philip R., 296–297, 299,
307–308, 322–324, 326, 330, 331,
336–337, 354, 358

Index

Forrest, Robert J., 387–388
franchise law firm, 521, 525
fraud, 56
   in advertising, 30
   securities fraud, 382–383
Friedman, Louis F., 197
Furtzaig, Lawrence M. *See* overachiever

G

game theory, on trust imperative, 2–3
Gawande, Atul, 7, 512, 514, 518, 523–524
Geist, Jerry, 255–256
gender difference, in embezzlers, 41–42
Germany, 527
Gibson, Shirley E., 82–84, 90
Gilman, Allen, 195
Gilman, Jeffrey, 195
Godcons, 14
Goffman, Erving, 46, 48
Green, Bruce A., 449, 458–459, 487
Greig, Arthur W., 449, 455, 466, 467, 468–469, 470–472
guardians ad litem, 241
gunshot wound hospital treatment, and lawyer neglect, 77–78
Guo Ping Lin case, and lawyer neglect, 125–127

H

Haig, Robert L., 316, 328
Hamilton, Sarah J., 72, 86–87
Hand, Learned, 280
Handler, J., 55
Haneef, Mohamed, 377
Hardin, Russell, 5
hawk fiddles, 43–44
health care systems, patient complaints about delay, 56, 56 n.501–57 n.501
Hellerstein, David, 200–201
HighTech International, 382–383
Hobbes, T., 2
Holley, Steven L., 386–387
Homans, George C., 2
Horan, John, 318–319, 320–321, 335, 344
Hsiung, Ann, 120–122, 177, 183
Hua Ye case, and lawyer neglect, 140–145
Hughes, Everett, 498
humanism, 33

I

immigration law, and lawyer neglect
   Abdul Karim case, 153–158
      client hires another lawyer, 156
      court date issues, 154–156
   admonishment for neglect, 182
   Chang Kui Lin case, 109–125
      agency role in, 119–120, 177
      asylum granted, 125
      ayslum application denied, 117
      change-of-venue motion denied, 113–114
      complaint filed, 122–123
      deportation ordered, 117
      failure to file motion on law office failures, 115–116
      July 14 hearing, 123–124
      July 27 hearing, 124–125
      missing documents, 116–117
      motion for extension of time, 120
      Muto blames others during disciplinary hearing, 120
      Muto withdraws from case, 118–119
      referral to another lawyer, 119, 120–122
      translation fee, 124
      voluntary departure, 124–125
   charges against Muto, 105–106, 169
   client referrals denied, 135, 144
   confidentiality breaches, 175, 184
   culpability, 158–160
   disciplinary hearing testimony, 107–108
      Cohen seeks disbarment, 165, 167–168
      disbarment of Muto, 172
      Hearing Panel agrees to disbarment, 169
      Muto response to possible disbarment, 165–166, 170–171
      Referee recommends disbarment, 169
   disciplinary hearing testimony, by Muto, 163–164
      on education/professional background, 159–160, 161
      on fees, 164
      on how clients find him, 163
      on suspension in 1994, 162
      on taking out-of-town cases, 163–164
      on volume of practice, 163, 164
   disposition, 168–172

employee pay, 135
evidence submitted late, 147–148
excuses of Muto, summary, 174, 175
failings admitted by Muto, 175–176
flying phobia of Muto, 139–140, 163
forged signatures on documents, 127, 141, 174
Guo Ping Lin case, 125–127
Hong Ren Lin case, 145–147
Hua Ye case, 140–145
   complaint filed, 141–142
   forgery by Muto, 141
   Muto testimony at disciplinary hearing, 142–145
immigration specialist witness on nature of practice, 108–109
incompetence of Muto, summary, 172–176
Ju Jin Jing case, 147–153
   evidence submitted late, 147–148
   Muto appears, 149–150
   Muto fails to appear, 148–149, 150–151
   Muto testimony at disciplinary hearing, 151–153
   other lawyer sits in for Muto, 149, 150, 151–152
lawyer fees, 135–136, 143, 153, 159–160
malpractice insurance lack, 133–134
office address issues, 106, 114, 117, 157, 158, 180, 184
out-of-town clients, 130–140, 179
   Ming Yuan Lu case, 136–138
   Xue Jie Chen case, 130–134
per diem substitutes, 179
recordkeeping, lack of, 145, 158
reinstatement in Syracuse, 162, 182
resignation in Syracuse, 162, 182
response by Muto, 188–191
service agencies, 119–120, 168, 169, 171, 177–180
success rate of asylum cases, 166–167, 177
suspension for misappropriation, 182
telephonic appearances by Muto, 130–131, 133, 136, 139
third-party, 136–137, 139
third-party involvement, 127

threats to clients, 69–70
trust account rule violations, 158
understanding neglect by Muto, 172–187
   admits to most charges, 182
   apology strategy by Muto, 186–187
   blame for problems of Muto, 183–185
   delusions of grandeur displayed by Muto, 176–177, 182–183
   incompetence of Muto, 172–176
   lies by Muto, 185–186
   Muto relationship to agencies, 177–180
   reasons misconduct scrutinized, 180–181
workload, 135, 136
Yi Chin case, 127–130
   disciplinary complaint filed, 128
   disciplinary hearing testimony by Muto, 128–130
   missed hearing, 127–128
income disparity, among lawyers, 40
inconsistency, 33
infant compromise order, 88, 89, 100, 101
insider trading, 21, 28
institutionalized envy, 44
Insull, Samuel, 29
inter vivos trust, 239, 253
investment firms, trust in/betrayal by, 19–20

J

Jacoby, Mark A., 407, 409, 410–412, 413–415, 417–419, 422–425, 433, 435, 471
Jaffe, Karen G., 105, 111–112, 113, 161, 179, 180, 184
Johnson, Henry, 88–89, 90
Ju Jin Jing case, and lawyer neglect, 147–153

K

Kahn, Irwin, 72, 81–82
Kalb, Daniel, 387
Karim case, and lawyer neglect, 153–158
Keim, Stephen, 377
Kreitzer, David. *See* personal injury, and lawyer neglect
Kuehne & Nagel Air Freight, 383–384
Kuntashian, Gregory, 110, 111, 123, 171, 179, 180, 184, 188–189

Index

L
Lauer, Louis, 301, 318, 322, 330, 344, 345, 355
Lawrence, Mark, 196
lawyer-client privilege, 457, 514–515
laypersons, allowable limited functions of, 68
Lee, Michael, 105, 106, 119–120, 127–128, 134, 135, 168, 179, 180, 184
Leff, A., 14, 45, 50
legal aid, 58, 68 n.574, 513, 527
Lehner, Edward, 339
level playing field, 22–25
Levi Strauss, 381
Levit, Leonard, 78–82
Levi-Weinstein, Dawn, 448
Lewis, Frank, 339
Lieberman, Hal, 141–142, 314, 315, 320
Liebowitz, Jonathan, 472–473
Lightfoot v. Union Carbide Corp., 473, 475–476
Lin Li Li, 141
Lipin, Joan C.
 graduates law school, 478–479 *See also* documents, privileged
Lipman, Frederick, 220, 221, 222, 255
Loader, Ian, 37
Lofland, John, 49
Luhmann, Niklas, 3

M
Machiavelli, Niccolo, 2
Malinowski, Bronislaw, 2
malpractice, neglect as cause in claims of, 58, 63
malpractice insurance, 63–64, 91–92, 501–502
manufacturers, trust in/betrayal by, 10–12
Maratea, Claude, 119–120, 123, 171, 177, 179, 180, 184
marginal professions, 34
Mars, Gerald, 43, 46
Matter of Lozada, 121, 122
Matza, David, 32, 33, 34, 49, 51
Maurer, David W., 42, 45
McGrath, Lawrence, 136–137, 139, 175, 181
McInerney, Dennis, 333, 467, 470
McShea, Sarah D., 220–221, 239, 261, 263–264, 268, 270

medical analogies to law, 509–512, 512, 514, 518, 522–525
medical experts, and personal injury, 85–86, 88–89, 97, 99, 100
medical malpractice, 213
medical services, trust in/betrayal by, 11–17
Meltzer, Curt, 69–70
Merton, R., 29, 40
micro-loan program, 5
Midonick, Millard L., 262–263
Milligan, James, 72
Mills, C. W., 37–38
Ming Yuan Lu case, and lawyer neglect, 136–138
misrepresentation, 36, 90, 377
 in immigration law case, 183
 in overachiever case, 196, 198–199, 202
 in privileged documents case, 427–428, 448, 483
 in trust income dispute case, 246, 254, 259, 270
Model Rules, 63–64, 209, 380
Moor-Jankowski, Jan, 325, 326–327, 334, 354, 355, 361
Morgan, James. *See* fee dispute case
Morgan, Thomas, 301, 304
Moskowitz, Karla, 390, 393, 396–397, 413, 418, 421–422, 429–431, 432–437, 440–441, 444–445
Muto, Joseph F. *See* immigration law, and lawyer neglect

N
neglect
 case studies (*see* immigration law, and lawyer neglect; personal injury, and lawyer neglect)
 lawyer excuses for, 48, 65–67
 as most common complaint, 57–58
Nelken, David, 37
neutralization techniques, 33, 49
New York cases, choosing, 56–57
Northern Ireland, neglect complaints in, 58

O
Office for the Supervision of Solicitors, 501
Office of Court Administrator (OCA), 106, 158, 173, 184

Ohebshalom, David, 196
Oregon, malpractice insurance requirements, 63
Orrico, Angelina, 213–214
Orrico, Nathan, 213–214
overachiever, 193–205
　admits to charges, 199
　background of Furtzaig, 193–194
　blame for problems, 200
　clinical psychologist testifies on behalf of, 200–202
　difficulty admitting mistakes, 205
　failure to appear excuses, 197–198
　false reports to client by Furtzaig, 195–196
　fired by firm, 199
　lies to clients by Furtzaig, 196–197, 205
　lies to firm by Furtzaig, 199
　misrepresentation, 196, 198–199, 202
　mitigating factors, 203, 205
　suspension of Furtzaig, 202
　workload, 194, 204
Owen, Richard, 472, 473, 474

P

paralegals, 69, 86
parents and surrogates, trust in/betrayal by, 8–9
Parlo, Christopher, 473
per diem lawyers, 519
Perez, Anna, 89, 90
personal injury, and lawyer neglect
　admonishments, prior, 91, 97
　apartment fire case, 88
　appeal denied, 96
　auto accident, possible harm to unborn child case, 84–87
　auto accident case, 76, 88–89
　auto accident with Transit Authority bus case, 82–84
　background to law practice of Kreitzer, 71–72
　bill of particulars request delay, 77–78, 79, 82, 87, 88, 101
　case dismissal, 79–82
　case never callendared, 74–75
　chronology of neglect cases, 98–99
　client consults other firm, 73–74, 75, 86
　criminal charges for commercial bribery and fraud, 92–96
　critical defendant omitted from case, 97
　dates of hearings, 72, 76
　deposition, 73, 74
　depositions not taken, 84
　discontinuance without client knowledge, 84–85, 86–87
　discovery demands disregarded, 88, 97, 100
　divorce case, 86
　dog bite case, 87
　excuses for delays by Kreitzer
　　case load, 100
　　employees, 83–84, 86, 89, 101–102
　　exercise of professional judgment, 87
　　ignorance, 101
　　personal illness, 76, 78, 87, 93–95, 100
　　strategy, 100–101
　　ten percenter scheme, 102
　expansion of law practice of Kreitzer, 72, 91
　failure to answer motion to dismiss, 97
　failure to move for default judgment, 97, 100
　failure to prepare infant compromise order, 88, 89, 100, 101
　failure to seek default judgment, 87
　failure to supervise employees, 89–90
　gunshot wound hospital treatment, 77–78
　hearing findings, 90
　hearing length, 72
　HOZ, 84
　inexperienced associates, 83–84, 91, 97–97
　Kreitzer response to charges, 76
　lack of/postponement of EBT, 74, 97
　lost files, 86, 100
　malpractice policy, 91–92
　medical expert issues, 85–86, 88–89, 97, 99, 100
　method of operation by lawyer, 96–97
　motion to vacate denied, 76
　move to dismiss case, 82
　panel members, 72
　paralegal, 86
　penalty, 90–92
　police officer fall from window, 76–77

INDEX

personal injury, and lawyer neglect (*cont.*)
  railway accident case, 72–75
  referral cases, 97
  settlement dissatisfaction, client, 100
  slip-and-fall cases, 75–76, 89
  statute of limitations missed, 82–83, 84, 100
  suspension recommendation, 91–92, 94
  wrong defendant served, 97
  wrongful death, 78–82
personal injury clients, solicitation of, 56, 67
pharmacist, trust in/betrayal by, 36
pharmaceutical company, trust in/betrayal by, 11–12, 13–14, 16–17, 30
police officer fall from window, and lawyer neglect, 76–77
Polin, Charles, 472, 474
positive misconduct, 64
Preska, Loretta, 386
price fixing, 30, 35
professionalism, decline of, 36
Purves, Edmund S., 390, 406–407, 408–409, 420–421, 428–429, 465

Q
quantum meruit fee
  in fee dispute case study, 324, 331, 339, 363, 368, 369, 370, 371–372
  in trust income dispute case study, 219, 230, 241, 244, 250, 254, 269, 281–282, 284

R
railway accident case, and lawyer neglect, 72–75
Raphael, Jason, 150
recusal motions, 451, 453–454, 456, 473, 475–476
Reiner, Jan A., 108, 177–178
Reis, Agostinho D., 385–386
restitution, 34, 49, 53, 275, 277, 332
Richardson, Donna, 88, 90
Rivera, Carmen, 75, 90
Rodd, Alice O., 241, 250, 254
Rodgers, Charles, 271
Rodkin, David J., 105, 113, 147, 162, 166, 171, 175, 177, 178, 180, 184, 190
Rohan, Patrick J., 322

Ronnell, Donna, 140
Rose, Babette Hecht. *See* trust income dispute
Rosenberg, Gary, 194
Ross, Edward A., 29, 31
Ross, Michael, 199, 201

S
Sahid, Joseph R., 321–322, 324, 327, 331
Sand, Leonard B., 437, 438, 486–487
Scarpino, Anthony A., 385–386
Schmidt, Laura, 83–84
Schneider, Saul, 149, 151, 152–153, 174, 185
Schoenfeld, Martin, 441
scientists, trust in/betrayal by, 17
Scotland, neglect complaints in, 58
securities fraud, 382–383
Seger, Bruce, 86
Seham, Martin C., 373–474, 451–454, 456–459
selling *vs.* swindling, 26
service economy, trust in/betrayal by, 12–22
  accountants, 20
  authors, 18–19
  broker-agents, 15
  charities, 14–15
  clergy, 14
  expert witnesses, 17
  financial managers, 20–21
  investment firms, 19–20
  journalists, 17–18
  medical services, 11–17
  scientists, 17
Severa, Carolyn, 84–87
Shapiro, David, 480
Shapiro, Susan, 38, 55
Six Degrees of Separation scam, 5
Sixth Amendment, 64
slip-and-fall cases, and lawyer neglect, 75–76, 89
small-firm practitioners
  difficulties of, 519–521
  percentage of all practitioners, 56
Smith, A., 3
solo practitioners
  difficulties of, 519–521
  overrepresentation in disciplinary cases, 54, 55, 506
  percentage of all practitioners, 56

Stanton, Mary, 389
Stanton, Michael K., 322
statute of limitations, and lawyer neglect, 82–83, 84, 100
Stern, Edward. *See* trust income dispute
Stith, Gene, 156
Strohman, Charle, 89, 90
subterranean convergence, 34
Sutherland, Edwin, 28, 31, 34, 38
swindling *vs.* selling, 26

T

Talvey, Edward, 474–475
Tartaglia, John, 87, 90
telephonic appearances, by lawyer, 130–131, 133, 136, 139
transference, 14
trust, 1–7
  game theory on, 2–3
  and level playing field, 22–25
  and power, 6
  as public good, 3–4
  and reciprocity, 2–3, 8
  in traditional society, 4. *See also* betrayal; service economy, trust in/betrayal by; trust violations
trust, restoring
  alternatives to punishment, 512–528
  analogies to medicine, 509–512, 512, 514, 518, 522–525
  commonalties across cases, 496–498
  conflicts-of-interest, 515
  fees/fee arrangements, 515–516, 526
  flouting of procedural rules, 517–518
  ineffectiveness of sanctions, 507–509
  laypersons, 527–528
  lenience with lawyer discipline, 503–504
  overbooking, 521
  overview of troubling behaviors, 492–496
  partisanship, 518–519
  publicity as deterrent, 509
  publicizing consumer complaints, 526–527
  punishment as social control, 504–505
  reluctance to bring charges, 501–503
  self-regulation as problematic, 498–502
  small firm/solo lawyer difficulties, 519–521

trust income dispute
  alternate split trust-no distribution proposal, 254, 269, 285
  ambiguous fee agreements, 283–285
  Babette personal background, 215–217
  Babette relation with brother Edward, 216, 218–219
  Babette retains Cardozo, 217
  Cardozo hires Brashich as trial counsel, 217–218
  children of Babette, 220, 221–222
  client difficulty in recognizing/complaining about misconduct, 281–282
  collateral estoppel, 259, 269, 270, 274, 278–279, 285
  contingent fee agreement, 246, 253, 285
  Deborah agrees to settlement, 249
  Deborah blocks settlement, 233–239
  Deborah objects to fees, 241–242, 247–248
  Deborah relationship with husband, 225–227
  explanation for actions of Cardozo and Brashich, possible, 285–288
  failure to disclose monies received, 241
  family tensions among clients, 282–283
  first disciplinary proceeding, 259–270
    Babette letter to Deborah, 260–261
    Babette testimony on Cardozo and Brashich, 261
    Babette testimony on fees, 262
    Babette testimony on Surrogate, 261–262
    Brashich background, 265–266
    Brashich character witnesses, 267–268
    Brashich on justified admonitions, 266–267
    Brashich previous neglect admonitions, 264–265
    Cardozo character witnesses, 263–264
    charges, 259
    Hearing Panel Report findings, 269–270
    Midonick on not disciplining, 263
    public censure recommendation for Cardozo, 268
    suspension recommendation for Brashich, 268

INDEX

trust income dispute (*cont.*)
    Toby testimony on Surrogate disinterest, 261
    guardians ad litem for grandchildren, 241
    health of Cardozo, 262
    increase in worth of trust, 219
    initial mistake by lawyer, 218
    inter vivos trust, 239, 253
    lawyer communication with client, 220
    lawyer fees paid, 239–248
    meeting with Surrogate Emanuelli, 232, 256–257
    original worth of trust, 216
    proposed removal of Stern as trustee, 219, 221
    quantum meruit, 219, 230, 241, 244, 250, 254, 269, 281–282, 284
    removal of Stern as trustee, 234
    resistance of Toby to stock distribution proposal, 227–233
    second disciplinary proceeding, for Brashich, 270–280
        Brashich on noncompliance with Surrogate order, 274–275
        Brashich seeks admonition/censure, 276–277
        Brashich testifies on fees, 272
        charges, 270–271, 274
        DDC seeks suspension, 275–276
        disallowed fees, 272–273
        Hearing Panel recommends public censure, 277–279
        order to repay Ljubica, 273
        prior admonition against Brashich introduced, 274
        readmission by Brashich, 279–280
        Referee on Brashich liability, 277
        suspension of Brashich, 279
    settlement approved, 239
    settling trust dispute
        children of Babette involvement, 220, 221–222, 223–225
        first settlement offer from Cardozo refused, 219
        first settlement offer from Lipman refused, 220, 221
        problems among siblings, 224–226, 234–235, 237, 247–248
        proposal for two trusts rejected, 222
        reciprocal indemnification proposal rejected, 222
        stock distribution proposal, 222–224, 251–252
    Surrogate award ruling, 254, 256
    Surrogate award ruling appealed, 255
    Surrogate award ruling for guardian, 258–259
    Surrogate hearing
        Brashich on Deborah and settlement, 237–238, 248
        Brashich on fees, 245–247
        Brashich on Surrogate approval for legal fees, 241
        Cardozo on legal fees, 229–230, 243
        Cardozo on Surrogate approval for legal fees, 240–241
        Cardozo reasons for refusing first settlement, 220–221
        Cardozo testifies about meeting with Surrogate Emanuelli, 232
        stock settlement agreement not tied to retainer, 224
        Toby on lawyer fees, 243–245
        Toby on Surrogate fees, 240
        Toby testifies about meeting with Surrogate Emanuelli, 232–233
    Surrogate justification for fee claim, 249–254
    Surrogate meetings, 231–232
    Surrogate review, attempted evasion of, 285–286
    time and task basis for fees, 250–251
    Toby as trustee, 231, 239
    trust-termination proposal, 257–258
    vulnerability of individual clients, 280–281
trust violations
    confidence games, 25–28
    white-collar crime, 28–38. *See also* trust; trust, restoring

U

unauthorized practice of law
    by agencies, 109, 169
    examples of, 67–68
    by non-lawyers, 168
unbundling, 69

United Way of America (UWA), 381–382
U.S. Attorney's Office (USAO), 382

V
Van Hoorebeck, Bart, 37
Veguilla, Evans, 76–78, 90
Virginia, allowable limited functions of laypersons in, 68

W
Wall, Patrick M., 449, 457, 459, 468
Warren, Irwin H., 322
Webber, Robert, 73–75, 90, 96
Weil Gotshal & Manges (WGM). *See* documents, privileged
white-collar crime
    confidence games, 25–28
    embezzlement, 39–43
    English fiddles, 43–52
    repercussions for accused, 508–509
Whittlesey, John W., 449
Wilkinson, Frederick D., 296, 316
Willot, Sarah, 31
Wilson, Andrew, 150, 185
Wisehart, Arthur M.
    employment discrimination cases of, 474–475
    recusal motions filed by, 475–476
    sanctioning of, 448. *See also* documents, privileged
wrongful death, and lawyer neglect, 78–82
wrongful discharge, 381–382, 472. *See also* documents, privileged

X
Xue Jie Chen case, and lawyer neglect, 130–134

Y
Ye, Eddie, 110, 111, 112–113, 123–124, 179
Yeager, Peter C., 35
Yi Chin case, and lawyer neglect, 127–130

Z
Zeitz, Dorothy, 41–43
Zlatow, Jeffrey, 130–131, 136, 137–139, 181, 184